INTERNAL COMBUSTION

Also by Edwin Black

BANKING ON BAGHDAD
Inside Iraq's 7,000-Year History of War, Profit, and Conflict
2004

WAR AGAINST THE WEAK
Eugenics and America's Campaign to Create a Master Race
2003

IBM AND THE HOLOCAUST
The Strategic Alliance Between Nazi Germany and America's
Most Powerful Corporation
2001

THE TRANSFER AGREEMENT
The Dramatic Story of the Pact Between the Third Reich
and Jewish Palestine
1984 and 2001

FORMAT C
A Novel
1999

INTERNAL COMBUSTION

HOW CORPORATIONS AND GOVERNMENTS

ADDICTED THE WORLD TO OIL

AND DERAILED

THE ALTERNATIVES

EDWIN BLACK

ST. MARTIN'S PRESS 　　 NEW YORK

INTERNAL COMBUSTION. Copyright © 2006 by Edwin Black. All rights reserved. Printed in the United States of America. No part of this book may be used or reproduced in any manner whatsoever without written permission except in the case of brief quotations embodied in critical articles or reviews. For information, address St. Martin's Press, 175 Fifth Avenue, New York, N.Y. 10010.

www.stmartins.com

Design by William Ruoto

LIBRARY OF CONGRESS CATALOGING-IN-PUBLICATION DATA

Black, Edwin.
    Internal combustion : how corporations and governments addicted the world to oil and derailed the alternatives / Edwin Black.
        p.   cm.
    Includes bibliographical references.
    ISBN-13: 978-0-312-35907-2
    ISBN-10: 0-312-35907-1
    1. Internal combustion engines—History.   2. Petroleum as fuel.   3. Automobiles—History.   4. Power resources.   5. Fossil fuels—Environmental aspects.   I. Title.

TJ753.B53 2006
333.8'232—dc22   2006040627

First Edition: September 2006

10 9 8 7 6 5 4 3 2 1

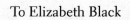

To Elizabeth Black

CONTENTS

ACKNOWLEDGMENTS

Reaching back to the beginning of recorded history and forward to civilization's resulting industrial denouement required a sophisticated, aggressive, and dedicated team of researchers and experts willing to help me eke out the smallest particles of fact to establish the big picture.

My question was simple: How did we get here, to the crumbling apex of mankind's century-plus addiction to petroleum—an addiction that threatens to destroy us and our planet? I found the answers, but I could not have done it alone. I had help—a lot of it.

Once again, as with my five previous books, I assembled a stellar team of several dozen extraordinary minds working at more than one hundred repositories in four countries to help me exhume the documentation and excavate history. The challenge was great and required constructing a knowledge base stretching from ancient times to the near future. Many on my team were veterans of my previous research efforts, *IBM and the Holocaust*, *The Transfer Agreement*, *War Against the Weak*, and *Banking on Baghdad*. After working with several hundred researchers and interns over the years, I can honestly declare my team to be among the best researchers in the nation. More than that, they bonded with the subject matter because this time the history becomes the road map for our future existence.

More than just research, all of my books require an elaborate factual infrastructure. Every document—and in this case there were more than fifty thousand—must be reviewed with the mentioned dates highlighted so they can then be filed in chronological order, one folder for each month of the twentieth century, and more encompassing folders for the prior decades of the Industrial Age. Then the relevant documents were placed into thematic folders, for such topics as "coal," or "electric vehicles," or "GM and the Nazis." Then documents were further organized into archival files that mirror the unique filing systems of the original repositories. This meant that many documents were reviewed, copied, and cross-referenced a dozen or more times. Just processing documents was a massive undertaking.

Leading the team in my Washington office was my chief documentarian, Paul Dwyer. Dwyer has worked as a team member on two prior books, *War Against the Weak* and *Banking on Baghdad*. But this time, Dwyer sat in the number-one chair, coordinating several dozen other researchers, overseeing the mass copying of some fifty thousand documents and the building of triple cross-referenced archive and reference files, which now consume twelve legal-size filing drawers. Plus, he managed the review of scores of books and periodicals. He also oversaw the footnoting and fact-checking operation that required the hair-splitting cross-examination of thousands of findings with thousands of footnote entries, which were then yellow-lined and placed in folders organized by footnote number for instant recall. Dwyer is a monumental intellect.

Also in my Washington office: Barb Jewell, who spent months organizing documents, assembling facts, and footnoting the early chapters; Anna Snodgrass, who helped footnote the later chapters; and John Corrado, a star footnoter who worked the night shift on some of the last chapters. In addition, David and Melissa Keleti worked overnight to organize records. Sarah Collins, Patricia Montesinos, Rachel Black, Eric Moore, Rebecca Corrado, and several others also assisted. I cannot mention all who labored long hours in Washington, but they created an ideal team, and I was blessed with their help.

Detroit was a major center of research, and there our team was headed by Estelle Davidson, who worked with me during my visits to the Benson Ford Research Center, several branches of the Detroit Public Library holding archival collections, Wayne State University Library manuscript collections, and other facilities. Estelle, who hails from the Wayne State University Law School, undertook voluminous archival searches — from the original papers of Henry Ford to those of the United Auto Workers. She also headed up our fact-checking operation, working for months to trace back the sources of other secondary materials. This required examining documents and publications often more than a century old. Frequently, she found the errors other researchers had made, allowing us to correct the record and history. Estelle was on occasion assisted by Sandra Maurer and others. I cannot mention them all, but everyone worked diligently, achieving important results.

In California, Adam Chapman, Allyson Rowen Taylor, and others worked beside me tirelessly in the Huntington Library; and energy experts Mark Abramowitz and Hank Wedaa provided extraordinary technical materials regarding hydrogen and alternative fuels. Dr. Paula Vastine headed up our Texas research, working with me at the DeGolyer Archives of Southern Methodist University, as well as at the libraries of Tarrant County College, University of Texas, Texas Christian University, and the University of North Texas, among other locations. In Boston, Jennifer Mazzucca and others researched at Harvard University's several libraries.

Elizabeth Black performed invaluable research on National City Lines at the Georgia State University archives, studied obscure taxi and vehicle industry records at the New York Public Library's Science, Industry, and Business Library, devoted many long days to scrutinizing century-old automotive editions at Washington's Smithsonian Museum of American History, and reviewed the highly restrictive manuscript collection at Yale's Sterling Library detailing GM's protracted collaboration with Nazi Germany. She also helped in the close editing of my chapters, as she has done so effectively on my five prior books. Liz's support during this project, as always, was indispensable and irreplaceable.

Eve Jones in New York, who has worked on several of my books, rendered invaluable research at Columbia University's libraries and archive collections, working with eye-straining oral-history transcripts; she also pored over hundreds of folders in the unprocessed holdings of the Edison National Historic Site in West Orange, New Jersey. In addition, Eve periodically traveled to Washington to join the footnoting team. Eve's exacting intellect shows in all her work. Eve was assisted in New York and in New Jersey by Adam Dokoupil, Dorothy McMahon, and others.

A major months-long investigation of the unprocessed Milwaukee Road files at the Milwaukee Public Library was undertaken by Suzanne Davidson, who also assisted with line-by-line proofing of the text. Suzanne was a powerhouse of editorial assistance and generally the last stop before the manuscript was submitted to the publisher. Frequently, Suzanne worked while I and others on the team slept.

Carol Disalvo worked long and hard at Nova Southeastern University in Fort Lauderdale, and at other repositories. Nancyrae Kjelgaard provided many hours at the Tampa Historical Society and other local facilities. Derek Hansell worked in several archives in Minneapolis. Phyllis Bailey headed up efforts in Canada and assisted with French-language translation. Nick Charles, a brilliant London researcher, provided excellent research at the British Library, the Public Record Office, and other British repositories; Nick has worked with me on several projects, and his keen knowledge of history makes his work invaluable.

In a special category are our many virtual researchers who mined the databases, sometimes while we slept, and not infrequently on a moment's notice during daylight hours. This large group included Lorraine Ramsey and Jamie Awamleh in California, David Arnold in St. Louis, and Paula Vastine in Fort Worth. But our superstar of database and electronic research was Adam Finkel, who began the project reluctantly and knowing little about the exacting and punishing demands of my deadline-driven brand of research. Within a year Adam evolved into a fearsome and skilled data warrior to whom we turned day and night to substantiate facts miniscule and major; Adam's fingerprints can be seen at the bottom of many pages. There were other virtual researchers, too numerous to mention.

Having worked in hundreds of archives around the world—the best and the worst—I have learned to respect the contribution made by archives and archivists, those who hold our history both in the palm of their hands and in the back of their minds. First among the many archival heroes of this project are Maryanne Gerbauckas, Leonard DeGraaf, and others of the National Park Service who bent over backward to open not-yet-public or not fully processed files of Thomas Edison's and make them available within the original Edison buildings, which were closed for more than a year for much needed renovation. Imagine reviewing unprocessed, original, handwritten early-twentieth-century letters and company records of Edison's in Edison's mansion. Over several days, the scene replayed: a long table loaded with boxes of antique documents in the mansion's large but bare garden room, beneath the ghost of Edison, my laptop plugged into the updated remnants of his original electrical system. I have turned fragile pages in the palatial archives of Berlin's Bundesarchiv, Paris's Bibliothèque Français, and California's Huntington Library, but I will never forget those electric moments in West Orange, New Jersey, where the electric age actually came into being.

Just as important were the continuous, diligent efforts of the magnificent staff at the Benson Ford Research Center and the Henry Ford Museum in Dearborn, Michigan. Here I mean Terry Hoover, Linda Skolarus, and John Bowen. They mobilized staff archivists and reference librarians for my project, and these included Judy Kirsch, Kathy Steiner, Peter Kalinski, Melissa Janz Barbey, and Carol Whittaker, who were assisted by Chela Weber, Ryan Moitozo, and others. Not only were my team and I graciously hosted on short notice, but the Henry Ford staff continued for months providing bits and pieces for follow-up research. The Henry Ford is a first-class operation headed up by first-class colleagues who stand at the tip of the spear of American automotive and Americana research.

Pivotal access was also afforded by the staff of the National Archives–Great Lakes in Chicago. Donald Jackanicz, Martin Tuohy, Scott Forsythe, Peter Bunce, and others performed miracles, providing numerous boxes and mass-copying documents during my whirlwind visit there. After discovering they held crucial forgotten court records, I called one day at noon and raced to the airport; the next morning more than a dozen boxes were waiting on trolleys, with the staff doing all in their power to process my mushrooming document requests. I also worked with staff at the main National Archives in Washington, and there was aided by Marie Carpenti and David Pfeiffer, who dug for long-buried Interstate Commerce Commission records plus the details of American highway history.

Another fast-acting archivist was Lauren Kata of the Southern Labor Archives at Georgia State University, who responded on overnight notice as we flew to Atlanta to delve into her institution's files. American Automobile Association historian Matthew Roth in California helped us with his rare collection.

In England, I thank the archival staff at the Public Record Office, the New Forest Museum, and the National Motor Museum. I also thank the BP Archives in Coventry, whose oil company files were accessed earlier, with all records graciously opened to me and employed in the present project. In France, various local libraries dug through their holdings to provide obscure local coverage of nineteenth-century electric-vehicle races.

In a special category is Southern California's famed Huntington Library and Museum, graced by opulent gardens and majestic statuary. The Huntington holds a unique position in transportation research. First, the institution is blessed with some of the most talented and insightful curators, archivists, and transportation experts in the field. This list includes such dedicated and gracious individuals as Dan Lewis, Bill Frank, and Peter Blodgett. They were a pleasure to work with during my days spent onsite and afterward. These men are a valuable asset to any who have the good fortune to work with them. That said, the Huntington is part of the problem, not part of the solution. Having accessed hundreds of archival repositories in seven countries, I can easily declare the Huntington the most restrictive and obstructive institution I have ever encountered.

When I first contacted the Huntington, I was told entry is blocked to nearly all journalists, local, state, and federal government officials, and also all serious researchers except certain "qualified" PhD's who can produce multiple references acceptable to the institution. I was admitted under a special exemption for academic authors, but only after producing multiple written references. Even though I was granted access, I protested, as did the scholars who provided my recommendations. Since my protests, the institution has slightly liberalized its access policies to allow more exemptions. The problem is that the Huntington holds key corporate railway records, Los Angeles mayoral files regarding congestion, and other governmental records vital to understanding how Southern California's transit nightmare evolved. Ironically, the institution derives its fortune from the families and corporate entities directly involved in California's scandalous transportation history. These important records must be made broadly available to all reporters, policymakers, elected officials, administrators, and others. Certainly, textual records just as precious, if not vastly more so, are made available to all by the leading public, private, and academic repositories of the world.

The Huntington, which enjoys federal tax-exempt status, should immediately be required by lawmakers to transfer its key transportation holdings to any public, private, or academic archive willing to superintend the papers for the better understanding of society—not restrict them from the overwhelming majority of those who need to access them. Until the Huntington transfers these holdings, lawmakers, policymakers, journalists, university students, and ordinary citizens will not be able to grasp the historical precedents that propelled our automotive society to its present condition.

Archival records are called "manuscript collections" when held by libraries. These collections are key. Special thanks are due to the many underpaid and overworked librarians who assisted my efforts. Chief among them would be the librarians of the Detroit Public Library and its several branches, including the Burton Historical Collection and the Skillman branch's National Automotive History Collection. Detroit librarians Mark Patrick, David Poremba, and Margaret Bruni struggled to make their vast collections available on my schedule in spite of profound budgetary cuts that have eviscerated many of their most important library services. Detroit's library is a special case and requires outside assistance if its precious holdings are to be preserved and made accessible to the country. Detroit's collection does not belong to Detroit alone—it belongs to the entire nation because Detroit molded the nation. These people need and deserve assistance. Corporate and philanthropic givers should pay attention.

Next, I thank Chris Cotrill at the Smithsonian's Museum of American History Library. Cotrill hosted me and my researchers for many days and for months thereafter answered follow-up queries, faxing key documents. Other Smithsonian staffers assisted, including Roger White and Dave Burgevin. Additional thanks are due to Bill LeFevre and staff at the Archives of Labor and Urban Affairs at Wayne State University's Walter P. Reuther Library. The Milwaukee Public Library genuinely pulled out all the stops to make available unprocessed and partially processed records of the Milwaukee Road; in that vein, special thanks are in order for the staff of the Humanities Room, as well as its coordinator, Virginia Schwartz, and the library's communications director, Lorelei Starck. Great assistance was also rendered by the staff at the Science, Industry, and Business Library of the New York Public Library; more than a half dozen reference librarians and copy-service staffers worked to find and copy uncataloged materials. I also thank Russell Martin, Kathy Rome, and the staff of the DeGolyer Library at Southern Methodist University in Dallas, and Dave White at Kettering University Archives in Flint.

Special acknowledgment is made to Richard Szary, director of Yale University's Sterling Library special collections. Szary oversees thousands of pages of General Motors documents chronicling that company's protracted collaboration with the Third Reich. This bizarre collection of vital documents is available only by accessing a CD-based database at a terminal screen at the library. Actual paper versions are not permitted. Hence, a researcher studying a fifty-page report, for instance, would not have the usual ability to compare page content. No photocopies by researchers are permitted without the specific authorization of General Motors, which is not expected, meaning all scrutiny of these voluminous files must be done at the terminal. Other than notes and personal transcription, researchers cannot bring away the evidence—just notes. I know of no other collection of Nazi-era documents anywhere in the world, public or private, arranged in this fashion. I can only conclude that it is calculated to obstruct, not facilitate, research regarding its collaboration in Nazi war crimes. Most archives would have refused so restrictive an accession.

Yale should never have agreed to host the papers, thereby giving political cover to General Motors for its involvement in Nazi crimes. This arrangement allows GM to pretend it has made the papers public, while doing all in its power to frustrate normal access. Indeed, the papers should be returned to GM, laying bare the situation, until the company is willing to abide by universal norms of archival access of Nazi-era documents. That said, Szary did his utmost to make key documents available to me and my researchers at the specified terminal. He deserves thanks and recognition for making the best of an intolerable situation.

Numerous libraries throughout the United States and in Europe granted me special borrowing privileges or otherwise facilitated my work. At the top of the list is Nora Quinlan of the Alvin Sherman Library, Research, and Information Technology Center of Nova Southeastern University in Fort Lauderdale. Quinlan extended me and my team user cards, made her stacks available, and even offered to ship books to my Washington office. Nova opens it doors to all in the community and really stands as a paragon of resource and knowledge sharing. Similarly, we thank many in Harvard University's several libraries who made obscure books available, as well as various units of Columbia University and Temple University libraries who greatly expedited requests for dissertation and thesis copies. Elizabeth Rogers of Tarrant County College likewise did all in her power to advance the project. As usual, the Montgomery County Library in Maryland performed miracles with a mass interlibrary loan effort that brought dozens of books in and out. Many other libraries assisted, and I thank them all.

Only one library did not cooperate, the library of American University in Washington, D.C. AU's librarian Pat Wand would not extend the privileges I requested. Fortunately, however, several professors and students stepped in and obtained numerous indispensable volumes for me from AU shelves. I obtained every needed book. I thank all who helped in that regard. That said, AU should be encouraged to follow the shining example of numerous other university libraries, such as Nova, that see their holdings, and knowledge itself, as too precious to horde. Any institution of higher learning that enjoys a massive tax exemption on large tracts of land that would otherwise return money to the community's tax base must also consider sharing with the neighboring community and the larger scholarly world. Tear down that academic wall.

Nearly all car companies cooperated with my inquiry, providing both historical and vehicle-development information and arranging for test-drives of their future alternative-fuel cars. Brightly heading the list is American Honda, which granted me continuous, unfettered access to strategic management insights and extended real-world test-drives of their compressed-natural-gas, hybrid-electric, and hydrogen vehicles. During most of the time, Honda did not know the exact nature of my inquiry, but nevertheless cooperated in a spirit of openness and respect for journalistic tradition. I thank Stephen Ellis, Timothy Cunningham, and Adell O'Bryant.

Special kudos also go to the Ford Motor Company, which previously knew me only for investigating Henry Ford and the company's pivotal role in American anti-Semitism and fervent links to the Hitler regime. That did not stop Ford company representatives from unstintingly cooperating completely in my inquiry, providing information, management insights, and test-drives of some of their most advanced experimental vehicles. Ford people never knew the nature of my project and just cooperated for the sake of openness. I thank Tom Hoyt and Linda Bairsley. Naturally, unlimited company documents were also made available at the Henry Ford Museum.

Toyota and BMW personnel also deserve thanks for providing incisive insights into their future development strategies. The names of those who helped must remain confidential.

Only one automaker did not cooperate: General Motors. The most telling conversation with the company was my brief initial exchange with corporate spokeswoman Geri Lama. It began, "Can you give me the address of the corporate archive?" She answered in a monotone, "No." I followed, "Do you wish to amend that response?" Lama again replied, "No," then hung up. GM has maintained a special combative niche in the annals of American corporate history, achieving a reputation for suppressing books, destroying or obscuring archival records, and frustrating critics such as Ralph Nader. GM president Alfred Sloan and the company's automotive engineer Charles Kettering are the same men who gave their name to the Sloan-Kettering Foundation, which has created a worldwide reputation for combating disease. But what was their involvement in American health and the killing qualities of internal combustion before that foundation came to pass? This information is still coming to light in spite of GM.

Other companies obstructed my efforts. IBM refused me access to its archives to check on its involvement with GM's Nazi activities. Big Blue serviced the major Nazi industries, the government, and the Nazi party throughout the twelve-year Reich. Since the revelations of my 2001 book, *IBM and the Holocaust*, the company has feared further disclosures.

In addition, Exide Technologies, successor to the Electric Vehicle Company, refused all information about its all-important and controversial role in American transportation and battery power. When I asked a company official if it maintained corporate archives, he responded, "I don't know if that is information I am prepared to share with you. Why on earth would you or anyone care about our company? There are so many publicly traded companies." When asked if the company even maintains a corporate library, he replied, "That is not something I am prepared to share with you."

VeraSun, a major ethanol producer, refused to accept questions. Likewise, Archer Daniels Midland, prosecuted and fined $100 million for massive price-fixing, would not answer questions. Cargill, the subject of many investigations for misconduct worldwide and once dubbed a member of "the Toxic Ten" by *Mother Jones* magazine, was reluctant to answer questions about its record. Nor would the Coal Utilization Research Council, involved in the controversial Clean Coal Initiative, return a phone call. ExxonMobil refused to discuss its unprecedented profits.

Although GM was resistant, many of that company's corporate traveling partners tried hard to help. This includes Hertz Corporation and Greyhound. Media contacts at those companies were themselves astonished to discover that virtually no information existed on their rich, albeit scandalous, antecedents. Indeed Hertz Corporation had not even developed a bio on its founder, John Hertz, and instead relied on a few innocuous sentences drawn from an Internet tidbit. Concerned Hertz company officials conceded that this strange information vacuum "cannot be explained." Likewise, a Greyhound spokesman worked diligently for many days to dig up its records, but could not. I thank both Hertz and Greyhound for trying.

Other extremely helpful companies among a large gallery of helpful firms include Calpine, General Electric, Konarka, and Solar Integrated Products.

Numerous public interest and health advocacy organizations also assisted, often on little notice. The long list includes the Alliance to Save Energy, the American Lung Association, the Center for Public Integrity, the Environmental Literacy Council, the Natural Resources Defense Council, and the Union of Concerned Scientists. An equally long list of professional and industry associations also made great efforts to assist me, here again on a pressing-deadline basis. The list is headed by the California Hydrogen Business Council, which worked tirelessly to provide insights, facts, and contacts. Also energetically assisting were the American Public Transit Association, the Geothermal Energy Association, and the National Hydrogen Association. Other cooperative organizations include the American Wind Association, various societies within the Institute of Electrical and Electronics Engineers, a source at the National Ethanol Vehicle Coalition, key sources at the Renewable Fuels Association (the ethanol lobby), the Solar Energy Industries Association, and many others.

Federal agencies cooperating included various branches of the Departments of Energy, Transportation, and Justice, the Pentagon, the Environmental Protection Agency, the National Energy Research Laboratory, the Energy Information Agency, the Government Accountability Office, the U.S. Forest Service, the Bureau of Land Management, the Federal Highway Administration, the Federal Energy Regulatory Commission, and many other agencies that I admit overlap on Washington's organization chart. A few sources did not want their names used for fear their forthrightness might cause them a problem. Numerous state agencies also assisted, especially in California, which leads the nation in environmental action.

Several dozen historians, experts, and scientists took their valuable time to assist me in the area of general or niche expertise. Some only spoke to me on the phone, some via e-mail, some just helped me delve into the issues, and several scrutinized my manuscript or parts of it. These include Martin Gilbert on the subject of civilization, David Israel on Thomas Edison, Bruce Epperson on bicycles and Albert Pope, Max Wallace on Ford's anti-Semitism, Melvin Oken on electricity, George Muncaster on the Hostmen, Jude Janes on medieval forest law, and Jeff Schramm on dieselization. On the subject of horse manure, smoke, and the nineteenth-century urban condition, I thank Clay McShane, Joel Tarr, and others. On the GM Conspiracy, trolleys, and the Roger Rabbit controversy, I thank Al Mankoff first and foremost, but also Sy Adler, Martha Bianco, John Diers, Bradford Snell, Van Wilkins, and many others too numerous to list. On electric vehicles, I thank David Kirsch.

On the subject of hydrogen, I gratefully thank Hank Wedaa, a national treasure on the subject; also Mark Abramowitz, Alan Lloyd, hydrogen pioneer Karl Kordesch, and Patrick Serfass. On the topic of geothermal, I thank Karl Gawell. In addition, I thank the many government energy experts and bureaucrats who spoke to me on condition of anonymity, pointing me toward places to independently document the vagaries of energy policy.

I received inspiration from J. S. Bach, John Barry, BT, Sean Callery, Danny Elfman, James Newton Howard, KIVA, Moby, Thomas Newman, Paul van Dyke, Hans Zimmer, and the music of Rachel Black at www.rachelblack.com. Special assistance was also rendered by attorneys William Davis, Esq., and Mark Lerner, Esq.

Finally, I thank my agent, Lynne Rabinoff, for her continuing faith in me and her unflagging enthusiasm for this project. Lynne persevered when the going got tough. No one ever had a better agent. I am making this declaration for the sixth time and will do so again. In addition, I thank my St. Martin's Press editor, Phil Revzin; it was a pleasure working with an experienced professional who understood my compulsion to get it right.

I also pay homage to a world careening toward a destiny with internal combustion. I hope this work helps steer mankind back to the correct path before it is too late. If it does, then all the people who have helped and hindered me will know what role they played.

Edwin Black
www.edwinblack.com
Washington, D.C.
April 18, 2006

INTRODUCTION

When I conceived *Internal Combustion*, I focused on one concept. It was not our dwindling energy supply and the oil crisis that intensifies each day. Look around. We all know this. It was not the need to rescue our rivers and bloodstreams, as well as our planet, from the toxic fruits of our industrial addiction to petroleum. Listen to the nightly news or pick up the morning newspaper. We all know this. It was not to futurize and fascinate with distant alternatives. The Internet and pop media are filled with enticing promises of a future technology that will be clean and renewable.

My purpose was to connect the dots of greed and deception that have governed energy from ancient times to the present. I stated it in words of one syllable, "This book is not about *green*, it is about *greed*." My endeavor was not just another lament on the widening shelf of "oil shortage" books. No one had connected the historical dots to discover the protracted continuity of avarice, fallacy, and manipulation that has now ensnared the world.

This enabled me to expose a century of lies about internal combustion that arose from a millennium of monopolistic misconduct in energy. This legacy has deeply wounded the world's collective health, fractured a fragile environment, and ignited a deadly petropolitical war that has escalated into nothing less than a cataclysmic clash of cultures.

Oil is the root of all this tribulation. In energy as in politics, power corrupts. Through the ages, power has indeed corrupted those who produce it, those who control it, and those who need it. Today our high-energy world teeters at the brink. The gauge is edging toward empty, and as it does, the political, environmental, medical, and economic costs continue to squeeze humanity. The crisis is not new, but now it has become more urgent. This time it is not money at stake—it is mankind.

It has been impossible for the general public to wipe its collective windshield clear enough to actually see the truth. But once the haze is rubbed away—even a little—the world will peer into the past and discover that to achieve clean energy independence and petropolitical security we do not need to reinvent the wheel. We need to exhume that wheel from whence it was deliberately buried by those who have diligently worked to keep us focused on petroleum.

The first energy monopolies were controlled by pharaohs and kings—they controlled who could and could not use common trees to burn as fuel to heat their homes and ultimately stoke furnaces to forge wealth and weapons. The presence of timber helped determine who would invade and who would be invaded. Timber was the prerequisite to power.

Eventually, medieval England was able to create a woodless world of peasants so that its kings could build great halls, long swords, and swift warships and could harbor the best venison to make wealthy men fatter—this while the common people starved and shivered, making do with smelly peat and pilfered branches to create flame.

When wood became scarce, the world turned to poisonous coal. It choked all who came close to it, but it burned. Coal required more than gathering. It required industry, capital, and technology. Coal required businessmen. A corrupt, extortionist fourteenth-century cartel soon emerged. Their secretive order, known as the Hostmen of Newcastle, established dominion over the black rock, feigning shortages and forcing compliance with their economic ultimatums. In the process, London's skies turned black, as did the skies above other cities. Lost to history, but bequeathing their manipulative ways to succeeding generations of energy moguls, the Hostmen ruled in one way or another until about the eighteenth century.

All technology eventually subsumes itself. Eventually, King Coal gave birth to the steam engine, which gave rise to the Industrial Revolution. As part of that technological coup, the steam-powered railroads, born of coal and powered by coal, opened the territories of all modern nations. Railroads became national power no matter whose land they traversed. At their helm were robber barons who would have made the Hostmen envious.

The fast-industrializing outposts of civilization scattered across great distances were made possible by trains. This growth gave rise to the need for commercial electricity. But those who used electricity craved wireless

power—ability to store electricity and use it far from the center of generation. Behold: The world needed a storage battery—the most revolutionary
power concept since fire. Today, the idea is simple and small enough to
balance on a fingertip. But in the decades after the American Civil War,
the "box of electricity" was the sensational stuff of legendary false advertising, great stock manipulation, calculated corporate deceit, commercial
looting, technology fraud, and epic, destructive patent litigation that sup-
pressed the real scientific advances in favor of instant profits. In the process, the corruption subdued society's desire to energize simply, cleanly,
and inexpensively.

At the same time, the simple bicycle revolution allowed men to move
about without a horse. Here too a rapacious monopoly ruled—the bicycle
cartel of Hartford, Connecticut. As bicycles were fading, automobiles were
rising. Most cars were propelled by storage batteries, but a few operated off
a controversial controlled explosion called *internal combustion.* Internal
combustion was the nemesis of societal betterment. Petroleum exhaust
spewed sickness, fire, and pollution everywhere in its wake. Gasoline cars
spread their soot everywhere they found a path or a road. The spread of
these noisy machines was called "progress." It was misportrayed as desirable by those who opposed electric.

At the turn of the twentieth century, automobile makers formed their
own emerging cartel and then joined forces with the receding bicycle cartel to form a new supercartel of gasoline-burning cars. The enemy was anyone or any company that did not pay tribute.

A century before I began typing this page, battery-powered electric
automobiles were abundant. They were planned to recharge and refill
quickly and cleanly at the electrical equivalent of "gas stations" and also at
curbside charging poles. Eventually, Thomas Edison and Henry Ford
planned to make them universal in a forgotten project that briefly took the
country by storm but then faded. That effort, swallowed by history, was undermined in favor of internal combustion machines.

What's more, modern, gadget-filled, energy-self-sufficient homes
were constructed almost a century before I began typing this page. The
idea, also crafted by Edison, would have eliminated central utilities operated by Wall Street connivers and manipulators in favor of compact generators in basements or backyards, eventually connected to small windmills.
These tiny units were to power the smallest and most remote residence, as
well as great urban factories. That effort too was swept away in the forgotten struggle over Edison's war against internal combustion.

The evolved dependence on oil hinged on a supply always known to be diminishing. In 1919, America and its allies concluded that their countries would soon run out of petroleum—unless they drilled for it in Mesopotamia, the Middle Eastern country reshaped, reformed, and renamed by Western oil imperialism as the oil state Iraq.

The lies about energy have now found their second century, this amid the turmoil of natural catastrophes, Mideast terrorism, petropolitical and nuclear blackmail, and national strife over the next tanks of gas. Now the world is being fed half-truths, quarter-truths, and outright lies about ethanol, about coal, and about the real alternatives and energy salvations that are too simple, too easy to achieve to be harnessed by a giant corporation or a foreign capital. They are as endless and free as the howling wind, the frothing waves, and the magic of molecules.

This is a sorry saga that will surely anger all. You will discover how many good ideas were sabotaged, how many bad ones triumphed—at the expense of all society—for the transient benefit of a few, and how we are operating under those same heartless distortions today. But this saga can also infuse hope to many who will discover the simple truth: clean, renewable energy independence is not a distant dream. It is available right now. This triumph will never be achieved by public policy, an inert gas that has failed so consistently over so many centuries to ignite the needed change. But it is achievable with the concerted action of individuals, energizing themselves.

As I have implored in all of my earlier books, I fervently ask all readers, do not skip around, do not read out of order. If you cannot read this entire book in order, don't buy it, don't read it at all. Put it down and ask someone else. That said, this is arguably the first trade book to be published in partnership with a Web site. Vast additional layers of information submitted to the publisher simply could not be included. Instead of being lost to a desk drawer, the longer version of certain chapters and other augmenting material has been placed at www.internalcombustionbook.com

Please ignite your understanding. Only history can power the piston of the people to change the future. This is *Internal Combustion*.

CHAPTER ONE

THE PLAN AGAINST OIL

Explosions and flames suddenly shattered the quiet afternoon at Thomas Edison's West Orange, New Jersey, laboratory complex. Time and date: 5:20 P.M., Wednesday, December 9, 1914. Upon hearing the blast, a stunned Edison ran from his laboratory and into the courtyard. There the famous inventor watched with astonishment as his film repository suddenly erupted in flames. A moment later, Edison's fire-alarm gongs began clanging violently, echoing distress throughout the eighteen-structure complex. Scores of employees scrambled down the stairs of their offices, across the compound, and toward the street as intense flames raced through the "fireproof" buildings. Blast after blast, fiery outbreak after fiery outbreak, like a flaming barrage from within, spreading from the rear and then left and right, closing in from the front, and everywhere in between, most of Edison's grounds soon became an inferno. As though on an incendiary rampage, the fires systematically devoured the contents of Edison's headquarters and facilities.[1]

Quickly, carefully, intrepidly, Edison and his wife pulled his most important papers from their offices and raced out to safety. Everything seemed to burst into blaze in just moments. The phonograph recordings and motion-picture materials burned out of control. Wait. Not the batteries. Save the batteries. Edison dashed across the street to the storage-battery building and ordered his private fire brigade to protect that first. With bravado, Edison himself directed much of the firefighting.[2]

Not until midnight was most of the fire put down. Some buildings continued burning until 2:00 P.M. the next day. The flames were so intensely hot that one employee who tried to deploy a fire extinguisher was "burned to a crisp with a fire extinguisher alongside of him."[3]

Few understood the voracious fire's extraordinary speed and broad destruction. Ten buildings completely burned to the ground. All but Edison's lab and the storage-battery building were reduced to fire-ravaged rubble. It was hypothesized that a random spark from a switch in the film department suddenly ignited the surroundings. Yet it was as though the fire erupted all at once from everywhere across the fireproofed compound in building after building, and even across the walkways. Certainly Edison's complex was filled with every form of flammable chemical and material. But no one could explain certain "funny capers," as they were termed.[4]

Reports soon documented that for some reason "in one of the little low red buildings, they found 2,000 gallons of very high proof alcohol that wasn't damaged." What's more, investigators "also found on some of the floors cans of gasoline that didn't even ignite. The flames swept right over the top of them. Corners in the concrete building weren't even touched with fire." Some rooms emerged without any fire damage at all.[5]

How did the fire spread from one fireproof concrete building to another fireproof concrete building? Everyone assumed it was the wooden window frames and their heat-broken panes. But no one could explain the massive blaze that destroyed much of Edison's life work. The majority of the $5 million property loss was not insured, precisely because the concrete buildings were considered so impervious to fire and because a private on-premises fire brigade was always on duty.[6]

Edison's dreams—past, present, and future—were now reduced to char and ash. A lifetime of invention had succumbed in the twinkling of an eye. Standing amidst the scorched ruins and smoldering memories, a smoke-battered yet still strong and undefeated Edison emerged to bravely and boldly announce to gathered reporters, "Although I am over 67 years old, I'll start over again tomorrow."[7]

But in truth the disaster was not only the final blow to Edison the man, but also to a bold venture by two titans of American invention and entrepreneurship—Thomas Edison and Henry Ford. Their plan was to blunt the world's irrepressible and growing appetite for oil and the internal combustion machine. If successful, Edison and Ford—in 1914—would move society away from the ever more expensive and then universally known killing hazards of gasoline cars: air and water pollution, noise and noxiousness, constant coughing and the undeniable rise in cancers caused by smoke exhaust particulates.[8]

Thus in 1914, the two great men of American innovation joined forces to give the world the gift of a cleanly powered and wirelessly energized world where every home and factory generated, and every city block transmitted, its own on-site electricity. Eventually they envisioned that all power would come from clean, renewable sources, such as wind, that would quietly churn independent of great energy companies.[9]

Their goal was nothing less than the death of the internal combustion machine and the birth of a clean, empowered, and independent civilization.

Why not? At the beginning of the twentieth century, thousands of clean, quiet, and easy-to-operate electric taxicabs, passenger cars, and delivery trucks coursed through city streets across America—from Boston to San Francisco. But electric vehicles and the batteries that made them run became ensnared in corporate scandals, fraud, and monopolistic corruption that shook the confidence of the nation and inspired automotive upstarts. This corruption infected all who came close after the nineteenth-century bicycle monopoly teamed up with the emerging twentieth-century electric-battery monopoly in league with Wall Street's most rapacious stock manipulators. Called the Lead Trust, this cartel tried to control all transportation in America and eventually the world—not for the good of mankind, but for the betterment of their private bank accounts.[10]

Adventurous advocates of the rumbling, smoking, gasoline-burning internal combustion machine rebelled and claimed they could go farther and faster than most electric vehicles. They falsely argued that the noise and rattle, as well as the smoke and sensation of oil-burning cars, were proof of the innate superiority of internal combustion. The noisier, the smellier, the smokier, the better, they insisted. What's more, gasoline and gasoline cars in the first years of the twentieth century were far cheaper than the heavy, price-fixed lead batteries and expensive, elitist electric cars produced by the Lead Trust. In some cases, gasoline was as cheap as water. A willing public impressed with the muscular nature of internal combustion in tandem with an aphasic public policy chose the smoking, choking automotive populism of gasoline cars.[11]

But then the upstart internal combustion industry joined its own nemesis, the affluent battery combine, to jointly kill electric vehicles and create a new monopoly of oil-burning cars that smoked like dragons to rule the roads to the exclusion of any other automobile save the ones that bore their license. Indeed, they conspired that no man, small or great, rich or poor, could buy or sell or transact in automotive commerce without their mark.[12]

From 1907 to 1911, Henry Ford had fought a public war of litigation against the new high-priced internal-combustion carmaking supercartel.

He was determined to create his own simple and affordable version of an internal combustion automobile. Ford won. His wrenching victory allowed Ford to place a cheap, mass-produced $600 Model T in barns and garages across the country, making his rendition of the gasoline car the everyman vehicle of choice. This too helped accelerate the demise of electric cars.[13]

But by 1912, Ford had changed his mind about internal combustion. He saw the whole concept as a device of monopolist manufacturers dependent upon a deadly and massively polluting energy source subject to constant financial and supply manipulations.

Edison agreed. He was always fascinated by motive power and always knew electricity could prevail over internal combustion. Edison believed that only electricity—independently generated and wireless—could ensure American independence. He wanted to literally convey all power to the people—whether they were stationary or moving.

A system of charging electric vehicles at home, right from the socket, along with public battery-fueling stations, was devised, this to be supplemented everywhere with curbside electrical recharging hydrants as common as parking meters. Discharged batteries would be swapped out for fresh ones at service stations in less than seventy-five seconds, enabling long-distance travel.[14]

The country was more than ready. True, the sound and fury of internal combustion had long been hypnotic. But the trance was rudely being interrupted by an upwardly spiraling cost of oil. By fall 1912, a shortage of refined supply had boosted gas prices some 75 percent over the previous year. Oil was no longer a "negligible" expense. The September 18, 1912, edition of *Horseless Age* published a three-page article exploring fuel alternatives in view of the shortage. The opening sentence set forth the problem: "The recent sudden rise in the price of gasoline, following gradual increases during the past several years, all over the world, together with the enormous number of automobiles, commercial cars and other users of this fuel, has called attention again to the fuel question in a marked manner. Whereas the previous retail price of 16 cents a gallon seemed high enough, it now retails all over New York City at from 18 to 22 cents. . . . A year ago, it could be had at 14 retail, and as low as 10 cents wholesale. This represents a rise of about 75 per cent within a year." A gallon of gasoline that cost twenty-two cents was equal to a twenty-first-century gallon costing $5. One 1912 tank of gasoline could easily exceed two days' wages of the average factory worker who assembled such cars.[15]

Vehicular growth was vastly outstripping gasoline production. The number of autos had increased from three hundred thousand in 1910 to seven hundred thousand in 1912. In the year before 1912 alone, some two hundred thousand cars had been purchased; that represented a one-year vehicle increase of some 66 percent. During the same time, crude oil supplies increased by less than 4 percent, from 209.5 million barrels to 217 million barrels. Prices continued to skyrocket even as automobiles became more popular.[16]

In many cities, a "gasoline war" was declared, that is, a battle to keep prices down. New York was particularly hard hit by increases because of its monumental auto growth and rocketing consumption. Whereas gas sold for 15 to 18 cents per gallon in Connecticut and Massachusetts, in metropolitan New York the cost was 20 to 25 cents.

The *New York Times* reported the problem this way: "In spite of plans and undoubted intentions to build more automobiles in the present year than ever before, it is not denied that the motor industry, as well as the motorcar owner, faces a most serious problem and possible setback in the soaring price of gasoline. It is predicted that gas will reach 40 cents or more a gallon in the coming summer." Forty cents would equal $8 in twenty-first-century money.[17]

What's more, the environmental damage was beginning to accrue in palpable ways. Billows of smoke from tailpipe exhaust combined with clouds from railroad engines and industrial smokestacks to darken the air and burn the lungs. Oil and grease effluent from garages swirled into rivers, poisoning the water. Hydrologists were concerned that groundwater was becoming irreparably toxic.[18]

Petroliferous runoff into the sewer systems of major cities was causing urban explosions. New York's Explosives or Combustible Commission declared "an absolute need to prevent the flowing of waste gasoline and oils from garages into the city sewers." Periodically, such sewers would simply ignite. The *New York Times* reported one such incident under the banner SEWER EXPLOSION TERRIFIES A BLOCK. The explosive force was so great that one manhole cover was hurtled "over the roof of a five-story building."[19]

Electrics suddenly became popular again. After years of stagnation, the electric vehicle industry was experiencing resurgence. In 1910, the Electric Vehicle Association of America formed to bring car manufacturers and utilities together to promote their common interest in battery-run automobiles. As the price of gasoline escalated 75 percent in the prior year, membership in the association experienced a concomitant rise, from 197 manufacturing companies in 1911 to 317 by the third annual convention on October 8, 1912. The steep increase in electric vehicle adoption was becoming obvious to many, especially in trucking. In New Jersey, the Public Service Corporation would soon announce it had seen a 1,000 percent increase in electric vehicles since 1911. In 1911, only 30 electric trucks were in use; two years later that number soared to 304, plus 206 battery-powered pleasure cars. In Massachusetts, registrations of electric trucks went from 227 to 389 the next year, a 71 percent jump. In fact, in 1913, Ford and other leading Ford Motor Company executives purchased for their wives the popular and sporty Detroit Electric. Ford bought a second Detroit Electric and presented it to Edison as a Christmas gift.[20]

Momentum for electric vehicles continued in 1913 as Ford and Edison posed for an advertisement in the *Saturday Evening Post*. HENRY FORD AND THOS A. EDISON BUY THE DETROIT ELECTRIC read the banner headline ensconced above bookended pictures of each man proudly standing beside his dapper new electric car. The subhead beckoned, "How would you like to have these Master Minds Help you Choose Your Electric Car?" Three columns of copy testified to the world that both Ford and Edison believed that the electric was the best automotive choice.[21]

By 1913, Edison had announced the result of some fifty thousand experiments conducted during seven painstaking years—a radical new energy-self-sufficient home. He called it the Twentieth Century Suburban Residence. Ostentatiously overstuffed with every modern gadget and appliance from a coffee percolator to a washing machine, from room heaters and coolers to phonographs and tiny movie projectors, the mansion was an electric marvel. Every device and system, basement to roof, was powered by batteries replenished continuously by a small-scale on-site household electrical generator.

The *New York Times*, September 15, 1912: "The Powers of Darkness have suffered another rout . . . for Mr. Edison has perfected a combination of gasoline engine, generator, and storage batteries by which, for a modest expense, every man can make his own electricity in his own cellar, utterly and for all time independent of the nearness or farness of the big electrical companies. He can buy a farm in the Middle West or New England. . . . He can erect a tent in the desert, if he is so minded, and still read himself to sleep at night under a convenient electrical chandelier, and shave himself the next morning with water heated on an electrical stove."[22]

The first fully operational self-sufficient home was Edison's own grand mansion at Llewellyn Park, New Jersey. The pocket generating plant was a narrow and compact machine, designed to be situated either in the yard, in a shed, or in the basement. Its cost: as little as $500, although it came in larger and more expensive sizes capable of supplying greater-scale housing and could one day be networked to power factories. Initially, the generators would operate off a small tank of gasoline that periodically needed to be refilled. Clearly, this temporarily retained the tether to petroleum. But Edison planned to switch from dependence on a modicum of weekly gasoline to small residential windmills. Self-sufficiency would no longer be a vision for tomorrow, but a reality.[23]

Finally, in 1914, it was happening. The automobile revolution, which had begun as an electrical phenomenon, would return to the concept advanced nearly a generation earlier. The world could become a cleaner, quieter, more efficient place, drawing its strength from electricity. The American spirit of independence would be achieved not only by permitting mobility but by enabling stunning individual self-sufficiency.

How perfect would be the vindication if Ford and Edison now collaborated to mass-produce an automobile that would be better than internal combustion, better than lead-battery power—better than both.

Edison considered the replacement of both the reviled lead battery in electric vehicles and the gasoline motorcar to be his own nickel-iron Type A battery. Newspapers coast to coast hailed the achievement of nickel and iron. The *Detroit Free Press* typically bannered EDISON PERFECTS STORAGE BATTERY, NEW BATTERY WILL REVOLUTIONIZE CAR SYSTEMS.[24] But would Edison batteries be mass-produced cheaply enough to replace the internal combustion machine?

Ford's plan was nothing less than astounding. He committed to building some 12,500 such vehicles monthly in just the first year. Moreover, to avoid any suggestion of a combine, Edison would be allowed to sell his dynamic new batteries to any electric vehicle manufacturer.[25]

Ford, a man of great wealth and almost no outside investments, bankrolled the ramp-up of Edison's production lines. The pioneer automaker provided Edison an immense order fortified with the certainty of cash payment. This would in essence finance the project, an undertaking so gigantic that it dwarfed all other prior electric vehicle output combined. Edison prepared a stockholder letter. His scribbled notes confirmed, "We have an order from the Ford Auto Co for about 4 million dollars worth of battery per year. They build next year 150,000 autos." Between Edison's money and Ford's infusion, an estimated $1.75 million was funneled into the new enterprise—an amount that equals about $350 million in twenty-first-century money—just as a start-up.[26]

On January 9, 1914, speaking from New York's Hotel Belmont, the mercurial Ford told swarms of reporters about his plan to mass-produce Edison-powered electric vehicles selling as cheaply as $500 to $700. Beaming his admiration for the inventor, Ford declared, "I think Edison is the biggest man in the world today. I even live on Edison Avenue in Detroit."[27]

At the same time, Ford, a man considered one of the wealthiest in America, made clear he intended to die poor. "It is a disgrace to die rich," he told reporters. "I do not expect to leave any vast fortune to my relatives because I do not believe they would know how to use it." Ford believed the new electric vehicle enterprise might not be profitable at first, but he did not care.[28] He and Edison just wanted to change the world.

Ford went on to reveal that he and Edison had actually been "working for some years" on the vehicle to ensure it would be "cheap and practical." He added some specifics: "The car we propose to build will contain battery equipment weighing 406 pounds, and the entire car will weigh but 1,100 pounds. It will run for 100 miles [without recharge]. The cost will be about $600 to the public," he said, quipping, "How does that compare with the great, heavy and expensive electric cars?"[29]

News about the cheap Ford-Edison electric automobile streaked across America like a meteor shower. Dozens of newspapers' headlines lit up brightly with the bold promise, as did every auto showroom, carmaker office, and American family household that had craved an automobile but was precluded because of high oil or battery prices or reliability problems.

Would Ford and Edison be allowed to succeed? If they did, it would overturn everything the two men had previously stood for—big internal combustion machines and big utility companies—and replace it with everything they now stood for—clean, self-generated independent electricity.

The answer was seeded long before 1914, centuries earlier when timber was the greatest power in the world and therefore the protected realm of monarchs who controlled it to govern their realms and conquer the realms of others. Timber was worth killing for because it was the secret behind the earliest making of metal, the stuff of wealth and weaponry. When the trees became too scarce, the monarchs turned to monopolists and corporate scoundrels for a new burning substance, this one not green but black. It was coal.

Thus, the first private international energy cartel began in England centuries ago with a secretive Newcastle order called the Hostmen. The Hostmen powered the Industrial Revolution but poisoned the air and water as part of their bargain. The coal cartel gave rise to later generations of energy monopolists who built great steam railroads that further poisoned the environment and spread cancer to those who lived near. Anyone who stood in their way to find cleaner alternatives was ruthlessly defeated by the men of wealth and power who defended their brand of energy and transportation.

When the electric vehicle took hold at the end of the nineteenth century, circumstances—both popular and predatory—combined to replace battery cars with internal combustion, and in the process replaced clean technology with burning oil. This oil was brought from faraway places at great risk so men could travel noisily down the street. Then the forces of internal combustion conspired against electric rail transportation within the cities and between the cities, leaving only petroleum engines and exhaust in their triumphant wake.

Now all the polluted clouds have gathered and created the petropolitical and ecocidal thunderstorms that overshadow the twenty-first century.

In their constant war with electricity, the forces of internal combustion have always won. How did it happen? How did the world choose the other way, and who chose that way for the world? How did corporations and governments addict the world to oil and subvert the alternatives? How can the multimillennial ravages of bad energy be undone today before more war, terrorism, petropolitical blackmail, and climate change collapse our way of life around us? Why has it not been done already? What can be done today to stop our high-velocity advance toward the brink?

The answer lies first in understanding the chain of explosions that constitute the past, the present, and the future of mankind's own grandly self-inflicted, never-healing wound: internal combustion.

CHAPTER TWO

POWER STRUGGLE

Man's ascent throughout the ages has always been calibrated as a coefficient of power. From the earliest precivilized societies, man's ability to lift, move, propel, and ignite endowed him with the decisive advantage over every competitor, human or not. True, the use of tools separates man from beast. But the ability to dynamically utilize those tools separates one man from another. Hence, the concepts of *better*, *faster*, and *farther* have always been the measure of any society's capacity to flourish, manufacture, defend, and conquer—and thereby succeed, however transiently until outdone by another.

From the first waterborne boats and wheels of ancient Mesopotamia fifty-five hundred years ago, to the Industrial Revolution and our twenty-first-century world, competitive man has been in a power struggle, that is, a struggle to discover and harness the energy needed to achieve or maintain supremacy. He who controls energy controls the key to any society's prosperity or demise. In consequence, the quest to master nature's second-greatest mystery—after life itself—compels society to eagerly reach for the power, if necessary walk into the flame, even when it burns.

Energy cannot be created. It can only be captured or released by technology or an act of nature. As far back as prehistoric times, even the omnipresent elements of wind, sun, fire, and water, as well as the readily available brute force of man and yoked beast, all required technology to make them work. Rudimentary wheels, simple riverboats, pulleys, torches, bows, crude waterwheels and grindstones, all constituted the cutting-edge technological advances of their day. They enabled survival for many and wealth for a few. Throughout history, energy has been used to decisively advance society—but always at a high price that enriched the few who controlled it. The history of society's dependence on energy is a chronicle

of monopoly, manipulation, and merciless profiteering from time imme-
morial.

The masters of energy and its technology always became the masters
of men, and likewise, the masters of men regularly acquired the newest se-
crets of technology in a pattern of dominion and resource exploitation. He
who dominated also exploited. Whether in the spotlight or the shadows,
the struggle to marshal energy throughout the ages became mankind's
truest power struggle.

Beginning with civilization's earliest chapters, the supply of energy
sources to be tapped became as pivotal as the technology itself. From the
Stone Age to medieval times, humanity thrived on a single depletable energy source, a precious fuel that heated dwellings, cooked food, yielded all
manner of comfort, and eventually propelled armies and navies into battle.
Controlling its supply motivated endless invasions and conquests and
brought great wealth to the masters of that supply.

That fuel was *wood*.

More than a mere source of Promethean sustenance to thwart the
cold and cook one's meat, wood was quite simply mankind's first industrial
and manufacturing fuel. Over ten thousand years ago early people used
campfires to create hardened pottery and ceramics and concomitantly
learned that certain rock metals melted into molten slag that could end-
lessly be shaped by hammering and casting. Now all sorts of hardened
tools, weapons, and ornaments were possible. From the prized ashes of
simple society arose the smelting industry.[1]

Pyrotechnic production required higher temperatures than the heat
of a campfire, which typically burns at a temperature of about 600–650°.
Hearths, kilns, and furnaces that intensified fire to above 800° followed,
and then superheated forges, capable of 1,300° flames. This technology
catapulted the manufacture of sophisticated tools, weapons, jewelry, and
ornaments. It enabled the creation of coins—metal money—which was
the prerequisite for expansive trade.[2]

Smelting became the industrial dynamo of conquerors and the exalted. Its manufactured product permitted trade. It facilitated agriculture.
Smelting enabled civilization itself. It was the technological font from
which everything else flowed.

But it all required massive supplies of trees and brush. Only seven
metals were known to ancient smelters: gold, going back eight thousand
years; copper, going back some sixty-two hundred years; and subsequently,
silver, lead, tin, iron, and mercury. The craving for jewelry and the fruits of

metalworking swept through the ancient world. In industrialized regions where smelting flourished, forests were depleted faster than they could be restored. A felled tree for tomorrow's smelter could be replaced only after a generation of growth.[3]

In the ancient world, palace doors were festooned with regal insignia. Metallic temple gods were arrayed in statuary grandeur. Knives cut deep. Swords cleft swift and sure. Tiny awls and needles dug into minuscule places. Crafted bracelets and amulets graced the perfumed bodies of both men and women. Before all those products were created, a tree furnished the energy to make them. Trees burned for fuel beneath black, sooty smelters made the world more beautiful, more efficient, and, of course, more deadly. Supplying these trees gave rise to an ancient lumber trade as lucrative as the one for gold and diamonds.

Cyprus bears witness. The island of Cyprus itself became synonymous with copper smelting. The metal copper itself is actually named for Cyprus. In Latin, copper was known as *cyprium* or "metal of Cyprus." Romans and other ancients imported virtually all their copper from the Mediterranean isle. In the desert kingdoms of the Nile and Mesopotamia, the timber needed to stoke the smelters was scarce. Cyprus emerged as the leading copper supplier not because of its many craftsmen—who could be found elsewhere, or the presence of copper deposits—which could be found in mines throughout the greater Middle East region, but because the island possessed the vast forests needed to fuel the smelters. Cyprus had the power.[4]

The island's supply was bountiful. A typical Cypriot copper ingot weighed about sixty-five pounds. These mass-produced ingots became a veritable unit of trade throughout the Mediterranean. More than twenty-thousand pieces of copper slag were unearthed near the furnace fragments of just a single copper-smelter on Cyprus. One shipwrecked vessel alone, sailing either to or from Cyprus, was sent to the bottom hauling more than eleven tons of pure copper.[5]

Copper smelting was not merely the concern of craftsmen who toiled at the smelter's scorching flames. The topic infused the conversations of kings, who marveled at the awesome products that emerged from the pyre.

"Now I have sent five hundred talents of copper to you," wrote the Cypriot king of Alasiya to the Egyptian pharaoh in Amarna in the mid-1300s BCE. The king of Alasiya added, "I have sent it to you as a gift for my [regal] brother [the pharaoh]. Do not . . . be concerned that the amount of copper is too little, for in my land the hand of [the god] Nergal, my lord, has killed all the men of my land [with a plague], and so there is not a single copper-worker. Therefore, do not let my brother be concerned. Send your messenger along with my messenger quickly, and all the copper that you desire I will send you."[6]

During the subsequent Bronze Age, Cyprus quickly became an exporter of not only smelted goods, but also of the timbers needed to fuel smelters elsewhere in the arid and often treeless Near East. That same mid-1300s BCE letter to the pharaoh in Amarna reminded the Egyptian, "Furthermore, my brother, the people of my land speak to me about the lumber that the king of Egypt receives from me. So, my brother, make the payment to me."[7]

In all lands, wood as a fuel to smelt copper, bronze, and iron, and also to fire pottery, always competed with its requirement as a construction material for ships, furnishings, weapons, and other basic uses. Therefore, in the ancient Mediterranean basin, Cyprus became a pivotal supplier to the warring kingdoms, many of which lacked the abundant forests needed to power their sieges and conquests.[8]

One of the mightiest of the contending kingdoms was Egypt. The pharaoh would not permit his Cypriot timber supplies to dwindle. To forestall an Egyptian invasion to seize the woodlands, the Cypriots regularly paid massive amounts of lumber tribute to the pharaoh. Eventually, in the early 1500s BCE, Thutmose III would not settle for tribute. He annexed the island outright and plundered long tracts of trees, completely denuding many areas of the island. But long before the takeover, the smelters, woodcutters, builders, and plunderers had almost totally deforested Cyprus. Many centuries later, the island is still treeless along much of its terrain. Arid conditions set in.[9]

Without wood fuel there was no food, no warmth, and, even more important to ancient monarchs, no capacity for war. The raging appetite of the warring nations was insatiable and reflected little regard for the replenishment of their precious power source. After Cyprus became depleted, ancient rulers looked to other lush coastal areas to secure wood fuel. The lands that became Greece, Spain, and Italy all fed the wood-fuel machine. One typical Grecian lime kiln engorged one thousand muleloads of juniper wood in a single burn. Fifty such kilns would devour six thousand metric tons of trees and brush annually. Buried within the Mediterranean littoral are some seventy to ninety million tons of slag from ancient smelting, about a third of it concentrated in Iberia. This ceaseless industrial fueling caused the deforestation of an estimated fifty to seventy million acres of woodlands.[10]

Agricultural settlement also cleared broad tracts of trees throughout Central Europe and especially in England.[11] Controlling the forests for fuel as well as game animals, construction purposes, and agrarian enterprise continued throughout the centuries as a raison d'être for invasion and became fundamental in the definition of wealth. Timberland not only furnished valuable fuel, it also represented strategic territory.

Hence, throughout the Common Era, monarchs understood that even if wood was not the world's most precious commodity, such as dazzling gems and fine spice, it was certainly the most important. Without wood, industrial fueling and building were impossible. In England, for example, the Norman kings coveted the vast forestlands for fuel as well as for game and building material. Quickly, it became the trees that really separated the peasant people from their ruling monarchs. Trees, in many ways, defined the class struggle itself.

It began with William the Conqueror of Normandy in the years after he was crowned king of England in 1066. William was a sometimes compassionate but often ruthless ruler. He banned most capital punishment in favor of gouging out the eyes and cutting off the testicles, which he claimed was a compassionate and humanitarian substitute. The hard-battling monarch was also profoundly consumed with the details of every natural and economic asset extant in his realm. Everything of value was enumerated. Everything was taxed. William received the tax revenues, aggrandizing his war-making and personal coffers. This in mind, William commissioned the fabled Domesday Book, an exhaustive inventory and census of every person, every asset, and every natural resource in all of England's 13,418 settlements. The survey itemized seventy-eight hundred wooded areas with an average tree cover of 15 percent.[12]

As part of this all-encompassing approach to national asset management, William ordained the repressive Forest Law. Prior to William I, the Anglo-Saxon kings had maintained large swaths of land to protect game animals, but the peasants were free to cut trees to use as firewood and to use in the assembling of rough-hewn furniture. Once enthroned, William I revised the Anglo-Saxon traditions, annexing land from the barons to create what he termed the New Forest. The New Forest was a massive and enlarged protected realm where deer and trees became sacrosanct and humans could be executed for seeking nature's meat and warmth. Only the king and his favored parties and designates could hunt venison and boar, and only they could cut wood for any use, personal or industrial. Hunting and woodcutting by peasants and even barons was prohibited under penalty of fine, mutilation, or death. In practice, money was always preferred to mutilation by both the defendant and the king.[13]

Some believe that William I's New Forest, along with a collection of other protected forests, comprised as much as 25 percent of England's total landmass. The process called *afforestation,* that is, adding lands to the New Forest, engulfed more than just obvious woodlands. The New Forest extended over purely residential villages and church sites, establishing a unique regal definition of "forest" that included not just dense wooded acreage, but also small clusters of trees along the side of the roads, hedgerows, and waterways and even those sparsely located amidst the grasslands.[14]

While William's main motive in establishing the New Forest, often fenced in by impalers, was to protect the habitat of the venison and boar he loved to hunt, he wanted to lock in more than just a personal food supply. Controlling all the trees of the New Forest enriched the king with the wealth of timber, not only for building, but also for fuel.[15]

The barons and mercantile class became obliged to curry favor to secure wood. William I created hunting and woodcutting "exemptions" for his noble friends and important personages — but at a price. Being well-to-do only increased the king's vexatious levy.[16]

What became costly for the comfortable man was oppressive for the common man. New Forest policies deprived the subsistence population of the very trees they needed for everyday living. To cook their meals and fight the cold English nights, the peasantry resorted to traveling on foot beyond the closest forest border to find wood fuel. If they were in or near the New Forest, they nervously felled protected trees at night or engaged in clandestine *coppicing* and *pollarding,* methods of cutting live trees for rapid regrowth.[17]

Further brutalizing the common man, special "forest courts" were established to try both poachers of game and gleaners of royal limbs and branches. These ruthless courts were insulated from all other legal processes, capriciously administered, often viciously punitive, and it forged an hour-to-hour source of hatred and resentment toward the Crown. He who dared saw off a tree limb or even a branch in the king's forest to heat his home would be fined a ruinous amount, which if he could not pay, meant jailing; or the offender could have his hand hacked off, and sometimes his eyes ripped from their sockets or his testicles cut away. No one could predict how harsh or lenient any judgment would be because Forest Law was by definition arbitrary justice.[18]

Meanwhile, the new technology of *charcoal* made the king's forest and all other woodlands even more valuable as a fuel source. Charcoal, oven-dried wood devoid of moisture, generated more energy per measure than wood, but more important it weighed far less than cut firewood. The price of every bundle of medieval wood fuel incorporated a transportation cost of about 20 percent, often more. The lighter the load, the cheaper the shipping cost, so wood fuel became more affordable when converted to charcoal. Hence, much of London's industrial wood fuel entered the city as charcoal. Lightweight and delivered in handy sacks, charcoal quickly became the choice of iron smelters.[19]

In 1189, Richard I elected to raise money by *disafforesting*, that is, by detaching lands from the New Forest and selling them back to the barons and others who needed wood for industrial fuels, heating, and ordinary building. Wood and charcoal distribution flourished under a small group of favored woodmongers and dealers located around London's Wood-wharf.[20] Although the power source had shifted from the king's near monopoly into an elite oligopoly, the masses were still afflicted when they sought wood fuel.

But through the oligopoly, charcoal fuel proliferated throughout London's trades and industries. By the 1200s, brewers and bakers, tile makers, glassblowers, pottery producers, and a range of other craftsmen all became hour-to-hour consumers of charcoal.[21] This only further magnified the indispensable nature of the oligopolists.

In 1215, King John consented to the Magna Carta in response to the seething grievances of "the people," that is, the barons and mercantile class who rebelled against the sting of regal prerogative. Among its many other provisions, the Magna Carta also seemingly dismantled the New Forest and its odious practices. "All forests that have been created in our reign shall at once be disafforested. . . . All evil customs relating to forests and warrens, foresters, warreners, sheriffs and their servants . . . are at once to be investigated in every county . . . and within forty days of their enquiry the evil customs are to be abolished completely and irrevocably."[22]

But in practice, England's forest inequities continued. Shortly after the Magna Carta was promulgated, King John's son and successor, Henry III, announced a supplement, the Charter of the Forest, to appease unaddressed continued mass discontent over the woodlands. The Charter rescinded mutilation and blinding as penalties for wood and game en-croachment.[23]

Yet the Charter of the Forest still did not open wood fuel to the com-mon man. Instead, the reform merely amplified the wood oligopoly's abil-ity to exploit the forests and manipulate the price of this precious but dwindling resource. In cycles that alternated between ample supply, hoarding, and calculated shortages, wood became simultaneously indis-pensable and often impossible to obtain except at a great price.

By 1300, the fast-growing iron industry and the equally fast-depleting timber supply had precipitated a protracted energy crisis. Everyone needed wood. They took it faster than the harvested trees could be replaced. London's bak-ers and brewers alone consumed about 30,000 tons of firewood each year. The whole city, population 80,000 strong, burned about 140,000 tons annu-ally. The Middlesex and Surrey counties by themselves may have consumed 518,000 acres of forest each year, or about 10 percent annually of the wooded acreage in those two counties. By this time, transport, mainly by river, came to constitute some 20 percent of wood charcoal's cost, just as it did with plain wood. In fact, overland costs could double and even quadruple the price of firewood, depending upon the distance traversed and tolls paid. Therefore, proximity and geography were a decisive factor in any supply.[24]

Add the substantial nonfuel uses of wood, such as construction, ship-building, carving, and fence making, as well as broad clearances for agri-culture and settlement, and it was clear to all that the woodlands of England were depleting faster than they could be replenished.[25]

Throughout the 1500s, the populace roiled over a constellation of grievances of which the forest emerged as a key focal point. The popular late Middle Ages fictional character Robin Hood, dressed in green to sym-bolize the forest, dodged fines for forest offenses and stole from the rich to give to the poor. His character was fictional. But his appeal was painfully real and embodied the struggle over wood.[26]

More people in medieval England would have gone hungry, and more forest acres would have been cleared, had it not been for some rank and unlikable alternatives. The first alternative was peat. Peat can best be described as rotted vegetable matter, carbonized over millennia, but cap-tured only midway in the coalification process. Found in dense bogs, peat can be cut into sections and burned as fuel. Peasants had resorted to peat for generations, but it required wading into thick muck to slice off portable squares. In their homes, villagers endured an awful sulfuric stench when incinerating peat for heat or food preparation. Not everywhere abundant, peat was concentrated in certain districts of the British Isles, mainly available to those living near the malodorous bogs in Ireland, Wales, and Scotland. But peat was also transported to city centers, including London, for those residences and businesses that could not afford or could not obtain dependable supplies of ordinary firewood or charcoal.[27] The foul solution of peat drove home to the peasantry that wood fuel was a fulcrum of their class struggle.

In the 1500s, peat fuel was surpassed by an even more distasteful alternative: coal. The same millennial process that produces peat also yields coal after final aeons of geological pressure. Known for its noxious, smelly smoke and grime, coal, in spite of its repulsiveness, trapped more concentrated carbon energy per pound than firewood, charcoal, or peat. True, it was mined from the ground in hazardous operations. True, this dismal fuel alternative transformed England into a sootscape.[28] But by virtue of its immense power yield, coal defined centuries of English industrial life and concomitantly allowed that country to preserve her rapidly dwindling forestlands for more important things, such as building naval warships.

Coal use began not with the well-known ore extracted from subterranean seams, but with a similar substance called sea coal, which washed up along the coast near Durham in England's northeast. Later, the more familiar rock was also discovered inland, exposed in the hillsides and the banks of the nearby river Tyne. The Romans certainly employed it in the early centuries of the Common Era. The combustible nuggets produced the fuel to forge Roman military metal and operate Caesar's war fortifications. By the twelfth and thirteenth centuries, the peasant class, especially those without access to peat, were compelled to rediscover coal as a substitute for wood.[29]

The royal wood monopolies and hoarding regimens had made the repugnant sea coal a necessity for the average man's survival, as well as for industrial and commercial growth. In the last four decades of the thirteenth century, the cost of wood increased about 70 percent, while sea coal only increased 23 percent. Coal became affordable. For most in London, wood was not. Even though the New Forest had been dismantled, cartel hoarding kept the woodlands out of reach of most households and manufacturing concerns. Londoners had no choice but to resort to sea coal, which was rapidly becoming known simply as coal. By 1300, London's total annual wood-fuel demand was seventy thousand acres. By 1400, it was only forty-four thousand, despite prodigious industrial, commercial, and population growth. Why? Because wood and charcoal continued to hover out of reach for the many.[30] That said, the abundant use of cheap coal, toxic and polluting as it was, actuated the city's extraordinary expansion, turning London into an economic powerhouse—a sooty, choking powerhouse, but nonetheless a powerhouse.

Yet almost from its inception, coal became more than just an abundant substitute source of fuel to benefit the advancing Western European civilization. For mankind, coal was both a blessing and a curse. This black combustible was plentiful in the ground. It was also poison in the air. That said, a nugget of coal was power in the palm of one's hand. But whose hand? Quickly, coal became the basis for a rapacious controlling medieval cartel that manipulated its supply, gouged the price, and waged war against competitors. The Lords of Coal achieved great personal wealth, but doing so required continuous deception, price fixing, and other monopolistic tactics to the disadvantage of an entire society that depended upon their commodity.

The glissando of coal cartels began in the Church, which owned the original northeastern coastal lands that contained the ore deposits, especially around Durham. In the late 1100s and throughout the 1200s, the prince bishops of Durham controlled much of northeast England's best coal. The holy men of the Durham diocese were called prince bishops because they enjoyed the independent power to convene their own parliament, raise armies, levy taxes, and control the woods and mines of Durham County.[31]

For many years, the ecclesiastic monopoly was able to manipulate coal prices by restricting its supply. In 1303, the prince bishop of Durham, under increasing pressure from London to reduce his secular activities, leased key coal lands to wealthy speculators. By this time a budding rival cartel was emerging in nearby Newcastle on the Tyne. No matter how much coal was pulled up in baskets from the dugout mines and excavated from the deep pits of Durham, the coal depended upon the river Tyne for transport. Newcastle and its monopolistic guilds controlled the river Tyne. After a bitter feud with the prince bishops, the merchants of Newcastle wrested the monopoly from the Church, and built their own powerful coal cartel.[32]

The successor cartel, not controlled by Church or Crown, was a combine of private merchants known as the Hostmen of Newcastle. The Hostmen—so named because they "hosted" other merchants and traders—were willing to squeeze and starve all of coal-dependent Britain and Western Europe for their financial gain. Their success was guaranteed by the great geographic fortune of a river they controlled and, of course, the dearth of wood, which made coal increasingly indispensable. Certainly, coal deposits existed and were mined elsewhere in England, Wales, and Scotland. But the Tyne River allowed Newcastle to treat their coal not as a local commodity but as an export to the fuel-hungry cities, such as London. Coal was transported by water. Those cities that imported coal became dependent upon the Hostmen and their river-empowered monopoly.[33]

The almost invincible coal monopoly of the Hostmen lasted for centuries. The Hostmen wrote the rulebook and the schoolbook for all fuel monopolies to follow, even into the twenty-first century. They invented the calculated energy shortage.

Coal in the 1200s and 1300s was a relatively newer aspect of commerce, one not covered by Newcastle's powerful guilds. The Hostmen seized upon coal commerce. Being seagoing merchants, the Hostmen owned the boats. Thus, they exercised total control over the restive wage-earning keelmen. That gave them effective control over the coal, regardless of who owned the coal mines. No coal could be carried down the river unless Hostmen keelboats serviced the anchored cargo vessels.[34]

The aggrandizement of the Hostmen continued throughout the 1300s during successive royal reigns with Crown writs of protection directed against the Church and other competitors. In 1404, Henry IV formally recognized the Hostmen as an official company. The Encoppicement Act of 1483 mandated that charcoal-producing woodlands be left protected for seven years at a time. As wood availability dwindled, coal continued to ascend, with the Hostmen at the helm.[35]

By the 1500s, the Hostmen rigidly controlled every keelboat and keelman on the river Tyne. Their river-ferrying consolidation coincided with Henry VIII's dissolution of ecclesiastic powers throughout England beginning in 1536. This permitted the Hostmen to move beyond the river. They acquired and/or leased many of the nearby coal mines themselves. Then they went further and purchased interests in the great coal ships known as colliers. By the 1550s, the Hostmen commanded the coal—from ground excavation to river distribution—that much of England and several Western European nations depended upon for their social and industrial lifeblood. The town of Newcastle grew to some ten thousand inhabitants, many directly or indirectly involved in supplying coal to England and Western Europe. Coal was Newcastle. Newcastle was coal. Newcastle functioned almost like an insulated and autonomous exporting nation, but situated within the kingdom.[36]

With the rise of the Royal Navy and other national fleets in the mid to late 1500s, massive amounts of wood were diverted for war vessels. This too further pinched the availability of wood for charcoal. In 1578, Elizabeth I, who owned the coal lands of the Newcastle region, decided to profit more personally. She issued an advantageous 99-year lease to her favorite moneylender and industrialist, Thomas Sutton. Her so-called Grand Lease gave Sutton control of vast stretches of Newcastle coal holdings.[37] Sutton and Elizabeth could rule the nation's energy supply.

But Sutton was not a Newcastle freeman and was instead considered an outsider. Although he owned the mines through royal lease, Sutton was unable to buy or influence his way into the Hostmen's favor—despite the queen's personal backing. They froze him out of freeman status and prohibited the keelmen from ferrying any of his loads. Within five years, the influential Sutton was forced to sell his leasehold to the Hostmen for a mere £4,750.[38]

But Elizabeth I still owned much of the Newcastle coal lands, whoever exploited them. Moreover, royal counselors advised the cash-strapped queen to quietly lease additional coal tracts in Durham from other owners. That meant the Church. Elizabeth successfully pressured the bishop to approve cut-rate land leases to her. Then, acting as a pure middleman, the queen released the land to genuine mine operators at a profit, thus adding shillings to every coal consumer's fuel cost.[39]

In 1570, when Elizabeth had passed a law against the further cutting of trees for smelting in her own remaining royal forests, this to preserve wood for navy shipbuilding, demand for her coal lands had simultaneously soared. That demand continued to grow exponentially due to the onslaught of better and more charcoal-consuming smelters. With the rise of navies, the need for iron cannons, anchors, and fittings multiplied. The forests literally sprouted blast furnaces and forges, especially since smelting operations were by necessity located within ten miles of a forest and its charcoal supply. A man traversing the forest would discover one blazing smelter every two square miles. Each such ironworks consumed the annual regrowth of 70,000 wooded acres.[40]

Surely, by the end of the sixteenth century, the new forbidden fruit for the masses was not an apple, but a tree branch. Wood was reserved only for the most essential needs or affluent customers. Every preserved tree only increased the power of the Hostmen. In 1590, the lord mayor of London complained to Queen Elizabeth's treasurer, Lord Burghley, "of the monopoly and extortion of the owners of Newcastle coals."[41] Unbeknownst to most, during the prior few decades, Queen Elizabeth had herself become an entrenched albeit unseen member of coal's cabal.

In 1600, Elizabeth went further, incorporating the Hostmen syndicate as a guild with a royal charter, thus cementing their power over the precious black rock. Although the Hostmen ostensibly numbered in the hundreds, their network was controlled by an inner elite of a few dozen influential men, most of them also merchant adventurers, and most doubling as officials of Newcastle's municipal government. What the Hostmen elite, the Lords of Coal, could not accomplish through bruising business tactics, they affected through bureaucratic maneuvers. It was these powerful men that Elizabeth specifically named for the royal charter.[42]

By 1600, coal had essentially replaced wood as the dominant fuel of England. Within a decade more, the Hostmen were annually shipping nearly 240,000 tons of coal down the river Tyne, about 10 percent of it destined for foreign ports. That was more than twenty times the coal shipped by the minuscule surviving coal industry in nearby Durham, which shipped via the river Wear. By 1630, approximately eighty blast furnaces across England and Wales burned day and night, annually disgorging an estimated 25,000 tons of pig iron destined to be fabricated into everything from battle-axes to banisters to belt buckles. Elizabeth's heir, James I, created several greed-driven cartels. But coal was perhaps the most bloated. The people groaned under the weight of those monopolies.[43]

A 1623 parliamentary statute forbade all monopolies. Just one was exempted: the Hostmen of Newcastle. With the ability to halt coal to any city, stop its industry, disrupt naval operations, and throw any population into the dark or winter frigidity, the Hostmen were too powerful to stymie, too influential to cross. A journal in 1637 recorded that of the "many monopolies spoken of," the most awesome provided "that only ten men may sell coal throughout England."[44]

Coal became a national security issue as well. The long supply route from Newcastle to London and other southeast English cities worried military planners. They proposed a squadron of warships devoted to protecting the irreplaceable and indispensable coal convoys. Dependence upon Newcastle extended beyond the English cities to the south. To feed Western Europe's industrial lifeline, French importers would dispatch fleets of forty or fifty cargo vessels at a time to haul Newcastle's black gold to ports in France, Germany, Flanders, and beyond. Clearly, disruption of a single cargo flotilla could shut down the industrial infrastructure of any number of foreign nations.[45]

No power rivaled the power to enable power. The Hostmen possessed that power. They knew it. England knew it. Western Europe knew it.

King Charles could not resist skimming Newcastle's accelerating coal revenues. In about 1637, with a cancellation of the royal charter always looming, Charles sealed a secret deal with the Hostmen to sell their coal to him, as a sub-rosa middleman. He would then resell at a profit to the entire country, creating a surcharge on every chaldron—justified by nothing more than the Crown's desire to accrue more wealth. This payoff was of course incorporated as a cost of doing business, passed on to the coal ship owners, and from them to the struggling consumers. So broad a skimming operation, involving numerous royal sales agents and brokers, could hardly be kept a secret. Word circulated. Fierce protests against the king's avarice arose from both the shipowners and the public at large. Charles was forced to rapidly abort his effort to siphon Hostmen profits.[46] This only proved that the Hostmen could survive efforts to share their power. Their profits remained intact and undiluted.

Indeed, the Hostmen's monopoly was continuously fortified against all comers with well-honed frivolous litigation, shadowy municipal obstruction, and raw intimidation. Each year, their lock became stronger. In 1638, one coal mine operator rigorously compared Hostmen tactics to "other irresistible Oppressions, like the Spanish Inquisition."[47]

Clearly, only force could disrupt the grip of the Hostmen. England's brutal civil war in the 1640s targeted the Hostmen when the Newcastle cartel, which owed its existence to a royal charter, sided with the monarchy against Cromwell's Parliamentary forces. Scots allied with the Parliamentarian insurrection invaded Newcastle, trying to assure supplies to the Cromwell side while denying them to those who remained loyal to the throne. The Parliamentarians themselves decided that high taxes on coal would only help finance mercenaries to fight for the Royalists. In 1643, Cromwell's forces decided to forgo coal from Newcastle and blockaded the river Tyne to prevent the Royalist Hostmen from profiting. Misery walked the streets and alleyways of London as coal supplies dried up. London shivered that winter, using dried dung, straw, and anything else that would burn, just to stay warm and fed.[48]

Finally, by force of arms, Cromwell loosened the Hostmen's ironclad monopoly in Newcastle by revoking the Hostmen leases and opening the coal trade up to nearby rivals, thereby relieving London's suffering.[49]

But the civil war only slightly relaxed the Hostmen's grip. London learned that the entrenched coal supply line could not effectively be replaced. Within a few years of the first stage of the civil war's conclusion in 1646, the Hostmen leases were reconfirmed, thereby ensuring a reliable supply of fuel to all of southeastern England. The Newcastle syndicate's mighty hold was restored, so much so that a swell of new Hostmen members began appearing. These included "fitters," or "agents" for non-Hostmen coal operators desperate to achieve Hostmen sanction so they could also tap the swirling updraft in coal demand. An elite inner cabal of the wealthiest Hostmen reacted to preserve the Hostmen legacy. The most senior Lords of Coal, such as the Lidell family, the Ridells, the Carr clan, and the Claverings, policed the larger fraternity, purging it of those who tried to beat the group by joining it.[50]

After the Great Fire of London of 1666, Parliament began taxing coal for urban reconstruction. There were taxes for Warwicke Lane, Paternoster Row, and Watling Street, to rehabilitate ruined parishes, and to rebuild St. Paul's Cathedral. Eventually, eleven separate taxes were levied over the next several decades, so much so that all increases in the price of coal arose not because of further price hikes, but because taxes were passed through to the public. As much as £40,000 annually was generated by coal taxes. Unfortunately, many of the admirable public works cited never saw the money. Instead, the coal taxes went to reduce national debt and finance a war with Spain and France.[51]

Even as they were taxed, the Lords of Coal found new ways to increase their profits and manipulate the coal supply. One was to secure tiny lengths of roadway called "way leaves" and extort from coal miners huge tolls to pass. It was the same notion as the keelboat exaction, but these blockaded yards were on dry land. Another scheme was to pay miners to keep their coal in the ground. That kept supply tight. Uncooperative competitors would soon find their mines "drowned," that is, flooded. Parliament passed a law against drowning of mines, but that statute was also ineffective. In consequence, tax or not, glut or not, mass poverty or not, the Hostmen secured profits as high as 65 percent.[52]

In 1703, Queen Anne demanded Parliament halt the Hostmen's unique ability to "enrich themselves by a general oppression of others, and particularly the poor." One hapless complainant lamented, "The world is now come to that sad pass that an honest man cannot live; for if he gives to every one his due, he gains nothing; and if he does not . . . he shall have no trade."[53]

As deep as the mines are the tales of Hostmen devices to manipulate coal prices, and these antics, sometimes coercive and sometimes just conspiratorial, continued throughout the eighteenth century. When thwarted by laws and investigations, the Hostmen extracted extra moneys out of their miserable workers, the keelmen and the coal miners themselves. The keelmen commonly organized labor strikes or even rioted. Municipal militias, civil lawsuits, lockouts, and prosecution broke their strikes. Coal miners broke their backs beneath the oppressive weight of the ore they pulled and pickaxed from the pits, so often iconically appearing as two white eyes within a disconsolate face of soot, breathed blackened air through blackened lungs, and from time to time were killed by drowning, suffocation, and gas poisoning, or crushed by cave-ins, or blasted to bits by explosions. For their wretched toil, coal miners earned one or two shillings per day.[54]

What eventually happened to the Hostmen? As part of their efforts to trim expenses and eke out productivity gains, they helped sponsor and promote a new invention: a steam-driven engine that could be made portable to haul loads. Locomotives running on steel rails were able to drag tons of coal more cheaply than any combination of man and horse. Railroads quickly proliferated throughout the 1800s, not only as coal haulers, but also as general cargo trains and passenger conveyances. Mighty and mightier locomotives created a symbiotic engine for growth. Railroads moved coal more cheaply, opened up vast lands, connected coasts and countries, invented new economic systems, created cities, defined national territorial claims everywhere in the world, and changed man's ability to travel and learn, trade and thrive, conquer and dominate. Bloody wars were fought to ensure their ownership and operation. Trains and the evolution of that industry spawned thousands of romantic chronicles by numberless buffs and historians in every country, enough to fill many libraries. That said, every time a train pulled out of the station, its coal cars brimmed. Encapsulated within those blackened heaps was the legacy of the Hostmen.

With trains, coal mines far beyond Newcastle were finally able to free themselves from river transport. That was how the Hostmen cartel was finally broken up. Although the syndicate could not be defeated by labor riots, civil wars, parliamentary investigations, regulatory statutes, and the will of the people, the Hostmen could not resist the unstoppable wave of technological progress. The quiet and gradual atomization of the Hostmen was hardly the end of an era. Rather, it was the beginning of a tradition bequeathed from fuel cartel to cartel as an established robber-baron style of business. From the coal cartel of the Hostmen emerged the trains and the key ingredient needed to fire steam engines.

Steam engines helped cause their own revolution, the Industrial Revolution. Burning coal created the heat needed to boil water into steam, which then updrafted through turbines that turned great machines. These machines, simple and complex, enabled mass factories, mass production, and jetting economic advance. Now the concept of a craftsman laboring with personal skill in a workshop was replaced by multitudes of laborers whose hard, repetitive toil in compressed factories fed the final product of the steam-driven, coal-fired machines. Did the machines make possible the workers? Or did the workers make possible the machines? Who served whom? That unanswerable debate gripped all of society throughout the eighteenth century. But in truth, they served each other and, in so doing, transduced society into another era where lives and nations were even more dependent upon coal energy.

The by-product of the Industrial Revolution was an accursed trade-off: great economic and manufacturing advance in exchange for a deadly pollution of the air and body. From the onset, England knew its growing dependence on coal was slowly killing its citizens. A royal commission in 1258 concluded that sea coal was dangerous to the health of all, asserting, "The air is infected and corrupted to the peril of those frequenting . . . and dwelling in those parts." Similar commissions throughout the thirteenth century concluded the same. So noxious were the fumes that, in 1298, one group of London smiths decided that their artisans "should not work at night on account of the unhealthiness of coal and damage to their neighbors."[55]

Edward I, in 1307, issued a proclamation against using coal in kilns because "an intolerable smell diffuses itself throughout the neighboring places and the air is greatly infected . . . to the injury of their bodily health." His proclamation was ignored. Within two weeks, yet another royal commission tried to "punish offenders by grievance ransoms." But such police actions were mere lip service, as London continued to coalify its air and the lungs of its inhabitants.[56]

In 1661, commentator John Evelyn of the Royal Society of London complained bitterly of the worsening coal pollution. "Men could hardly discern one another for the cloud," he wrote, citing the nearby smoke-stacks, and blaming "that hellish and dismal cloud of sea-coal." Vehemently, Evelyn deplored coal's "impure and thick mist, accompanied by . . . filthy vapor, which renders them obnoxious to a thousand inconveniences corrupting the lungs, and disordering the entire habit of their bodies."[57]

A few years later, another Royal Society fellow, John Graunt, often called "the father of demography," reported that before 1600, the mortality rate in London and the countryside was essentially identical. But with the widespread urban adoption of coal, that had all changed. By 1665, "Little more than one of 50 dies in the country," he reported, "whereas in London it seems manifest that about one in 32 dies." He stressed that these deaths were "over and above what dies of the Plague." Why? Because "sea-coals . . . are now universally used," he wrote.[58]

But in the mid-1700s, another revolutionary answer, a new form of energy, appeared. It was totally clean and nonpolluting. This newly discovered source was mightier than all the wood in the forest and all the coal in the ground. It emulated the power of all the seas and winds. One could only marvel in awe at this magical new energy that did not lie beneath the grounds of Newcastle or within the perimeters of the New Forest, but was in fact *everywhere*. Everyone already knew it. It tore through the heavens, lay quiet in every object, and, in the intellectual lingua franca of the day, dwelled within the soul—waiting to be released or captured.

No one in the eighteenth century pretended to understand this stunning, newly apprehended force, for science and physics during the early modern period were manifestations of a learned kinship of endeavors called natural philosophy. In plain words, it was the proto-scientific study of nature. Natural philosophy sought to explain the movement and makeup of man, his world, and the heavenly bodies, as well as the harmony, clashes, and chaos of existence in philosophical and theistic terms imbued with mathematics and reason. The prodigious discoveries, observations, and explanations of humanity's greatest minds, the sketches of Leonardo da Vinci, the universal laws of gravitation propounded by Isaac Newton, the astronomy of Edmond Halley—these were all encased within the proto-science known as natural philosophy.[59]

Natural philosophy orbited a core belief in *Weltseele*, or the spiritual force of the world that inhabits all things, the force that mystically imbues the extremes of unified existence. Opposites dance. This Godforce was the new energy.

Life and death, destruction and creation, weather, chemical reactions—all of it in the mind of the great intellects of the day devolved from the finger of God. Those who explored the great movements of God's hand chose not to challenge the deity, not to supplant him, but only to better comprehend the universe they traveled in. This new energy was the ultimate juxtaposition of opposites, capable of moving mountains with God's miraculous strength.

But this new energy force was not merely the oft-exalted finger of God. This was his very bloodstream, the all-powerful animating dynamo of existence some thought too terrible to embrace. They knew from their Bibles that their Lord dwelt in a special place between the metallic surfaces of the gold cherubim atop the Ark of the Covenant. Exodus 25:22: *There above the cover between, between the two cherubim that are over the ark . . . I will meet with you and give all my commands.*

Leviticus 16:2: *The LORD said to Moses: "Tell your brother Aaron not to come whenever he chooses into the most holy place behind the curtain in front of the atonement cover on the ark, or else he will die, because I appear in the cloud over the atonement cover.*

Within the eighteenth century mind-set of those who discovered this new force, it was also too frightful to handle. Those who even touched it would be shocked or could be killed. Yet this energy could uplift the world. Awesome in every way, utterly incomprehensible, impeccable in its purity, miraculous in its might, the world changed when it discovered the new omnipresent, inexhaustible, completely clean power source.

In 1752, Benjamin Franklin discovered modern electricity.

To read the expanded story of the Hostmen coal monopoly and cruel medieval forest laws in England, see the excerpt at www.internalcombustionbook.com.

CHAPTER THREE

METALS AND MONOPOLIES

Tiny iron nails secured Luigi Galvani's metal scalpel to a polished bone handle. Little did Galvani know that his assistant's incision with this simple device would open not just a sheath of frog muscle but also a world of power and industry. His momentous discovery in 1780 was one of the most important errors ever made.

Galvani, a deeply religious mid-eighteenth-century Italian scientist, a paragon of theistic natural philosophy, almost began his scientific life by joining a monastery. Like many who became monastic scientists, Galvani believed in "eternal Providence, which develops, conserves, and circulates life among so many diverse beings." For Galvani, the quest for knowledge was integral to the struggle to comprehend God's mystic way. But the teenaged Galvani was convinced by family to bypass the monastery and instead pursue medical studies at the University of Bologna. Shortly after graduation in 1762, he was appointed to the university's chair of anatomy, where the dapper, wig-adorned Galvani excelled at comparative anatomy and surgery, both human and animal.[1]

Galvani, like many leading scientists of his day, was fascinated by all forms of electricity: *static electricity* or what he called *"artificial" electricity* caused by friction, *atmospheric electricity* conveyed by lightning, and *"animal" electricity* thought to be innate within all living things and conveyed by some "electric fluid." Finally Galvani sought the elusive *generated* and *stored* form that so fascinated the chief exponents of natural philosophy.[2]

True, the modern concept of electricity had been discovered by the great colonial inventor Ben Franklin in Philadelphia in 1752. But, in fact, nature's omnipresent shocking force had always been bright in man's consciousness. The first cavemen trembled with amazement as electrical storms and lightning bolts crackled in the skies. The ancient Greeks in 600

BCE discovered that rubbing amber and other substances could produce a static electrical charge. In 1600, while writing on magnetism in his treatise *De Magnete,* Sir William Gilbert dubbed these well-known precepts "electricity." Gilbert named the force *electrica* from the Greek word *electron,* which means "amber," referring to that resinous substance. The quest to store and transmit static electricity from friction was finally achieved in 1745 by Dutch physicist and mathematician Pieter van Musschenbroek. Musschenbroek developed a glass water-filled jar with a protruding wire that could store and transmit electricity after being brought into contact with a static electrical charge, generally produced by simple friction. His rudimentary device was called a Leyden jar, named for Musschenbroek's hometown of Leyden.[3]

In the mid-eighteenth century, Leyden jars became the rage among scientists as they continually improved the device's ability to store and discharge electricity. Scientists studying electricity called themselves electricians. Sparking gadgets, electroshock units, and other "electricity machines" based on discharging Leyden jars were popular. One Leyden jar demonstration in Paris in 1746 shot an electric shock through a chain of 180 Royal Guards as an astounded King Louis XV looked on. Another French spectacle dispatched a shocking current through a kilometer-long line of monks, causing them to leap into the air like so many syncopated clavier hammers.[4]

Franklin brought electricity into the modern age in 1752 when he tapped into the mighty power of lightning with his famous key-and-kite experiment. He demonstrated in a scientific fashion how electrical forces exist naturally in the world, not just as a result of man's rubbing. He documented that electricity travels from positive to negative through conducting materials; he was to store his electricity in a Leyden jar that could later be discharged. In a way, Franklin began it all, creating his own lexicon of electricity with such terms as "positive charge" and "negative charge," "plus" and "minus," and "conductors" and "nonconductors." It was Franklin who assigned the word "electricians" to those who studied this phenomenon.[5]

For years, the natural philosophy movement believed in "animal electricity," a term that replaced the sacred concept of animal spirits. Natural philosophers knew that animals, even when decapitated, could be stimulated by an electric shock generated by a Leyden jar. Scientists certainly did not understand this physiological process—only that it happened. In 1780, as part of this investigation, Galvani was routinely dissecting yet another frog in his Bologna laboratory when something extraordinary happened.[6]

"I dissected a frog and . . . placed it on the same table as an electrical machine," wrote Galvani. "The animal was completely separated from and removed at a considerable distance from the machine's conductor. When one of my assistants by chance lightly applied the point of a scalpel to the inner crural nerves . . . suddenly all the muscles of the [frog's] limbs . . . appeared to have fallen into violent tonic convulsions."[7]

Excited, Galvani repeated the process personally and recorded more "violent contractions," which in some cases seemed to create sparks, even though the nearby electrical machine was not connected. Galvani repeated the experiment numerous times, careful to utilize the identical bone and metal scalpel with iron nails. Sometimes muscle contractions were seen and sometimes not, but these always seemed to coincide with sparks, again without involvement from the nearby electrical machine.[8]

Galvani concluded that the innate electricity within the frog and the human hand were conducted and connected by the metal scalpel, that is, as he wrote, "when the fingers touched the metal blade or the iron nails that secured the blade." In Galvani's mind, he had observed nothing less than a miracle of God's creation in the form of innate electricity. Thus the laws of physics and God's powers completed a wondrous circuit allowing the frog's electricity to flow.[9]

Nonetheless, Galvani was reluctant to widely publicize his findings. For a decade, he continued to experiment on endless frogs with numberless permutations of metal hooks and plates, and different incisions, keeping the details confined to local lectures and some brief essays. Finally in 1791, he published his famous treatise, *The Effects of Electricity on Muscular Motion*, documenting in exacting detail the character of positive and negative human and animal electricity.[10]

But Galvani was wrong. The nature of his error was the real turningpoint discovery that changed humanity.

Galvani's close friend Alessandro Volta was a rival virtuoso electrician of international fame. Volta, in 1775, had perfected the "electrophorus." This device consisted of two metal plates separated by insulation that, when rubbed, produced static electricity that was not only stored but continuously renewable. Some called it a perpetual electrical machine.[11]

Volta immediately recognized that his friend Galvani's conclusion about innate electricity was flawed wishful thinking. In a key section of *The Effects of Electricity on Muscular Motion*, Galvani noted that he was able to trigger the frog's violent electrical reaction when he placed the animal on an iron plate and suspended the carcass from a brass hook. "I immediately repeated the experiment in different metals," wrote Galvani. "The results were the same, except that the contractions varied with the metals used."[12]

Metals? Contact? *Electricity?*

Volta understood that it was not the innate quality of life that produced the frog's violence but physical contact between two dissimilar and completely inanimate metals separated by a moist and chemically resisting conducting medium—the frog—that created the electricity. In truth, it was the scalpel briefly touching the metal plate beneath the frog that generated the spark. This principle was the same employed by Volta in his electrophorus. In other words, it was not life that breathed electricity into the inanimate world, but the inanimate world that breathed electricity into life. Volta spent the remainder of the 1790s writing and lecturing on Galvani's error, igniting a worldwide scientific firestorm. Eventually, the acrimonious debate debunked Galvani and elevated Volta to the pinnacle of electrical science.[13]

In 1800, Volta applied his understanding of Galvani's error along with the concept of the disparate metals in his electrophorus and created something new and stunning. Volta's so-called pile, a long series of copper and zinc disks separated by moistened cardboard sections, could absorb a significant amount of generated current that could be stored and then released in a measured fashion at will. This rudimentary contraption was the world's first genuine battery.[14]

For the next few decades, the battery existed as a scientific curiosity devoid of any real industrial application. As a matter of pure research, electrical engineers laboriously modified such piles to last incrementally longer. In 1839, William Grove invented the hydrogen fuel cell, combining hydrogen and oxygen in the presence of an electrolyte to generate electricity. Grove called his creation "a beautiful instance of the correlation of natural forces." A century later, Grove's invention was seen as a great energy solution to save coming generations from energy starvation. But at the time, in the early 1830s, Grove's gas batteries and variations of Volta's metal batteries stored and generated current so weak that the devices were considered mere exercises in electrochemistry.[15]

Everything changed for batteries in the late 1830s with the development of a new communications device, the telegraph, which sent battery-supplied electric current over a long-distance wire. First the wire extended one mile, and then many miles. Samuel Morse developed a language of interrupted current to convey the electronic equivalent of language over such wires—the so-called dots and dashes of Morse code. The first formal test message on a completed working line, financed by Congress, was keyed by Morse himself on May 24, 1844. Standing in the U.S. Capitol, Morse sent a message to his colleague in Baltimore, presaging a new era. His eighteen-character message in forty-two pulses recited the ancient lament from Numbers 23:23: "What hath God wrought?"[16]

None could have even imagined.

Quickly, telegraph poles raced across the continents, often before the railroads. Suddenly, there was a pressing need to situate stored electrical energy in remote locations of the North American continent and Europe, to transmit telegraphic messages and bring the world closer together.[17] Batteries were no longer mere electrochemistry and the subject of metaphysical debate. That was long over. Batteries were now needed for a fast-accelerating world racing frenetically toward an undefined future.

In 1859, commercial oil was discovered in Titusville, Pennsylvania. Pennsylvania briefly became the oil capital of the world, engendering massive regional industrialization. Railroads, with government assistance, exported that industrialization every place they could lay track on level ground. Lands belonging to Indian tribes were seized by superior military force, allowing American settlers to act out America's dream of manifest destiny. Half of Mexico had already become American territory after Mexico lost its war with the United States. When not enough settlers were available, millions were imported from Russia and Western Europe to make the wheels work and ride the wheels west. The wheels of expansion, conquest, urbanized growth, and industrial strength spun fast across America.[18]

Around 1860, the French electrician Gaston Plante finally brought batteries into the modern industrial era. He had experimented over and over with various polarized metals and alloys: tin, aluminum, copper, gold, and silver, measuring their conductivity and formation practicality. Finally, Plante found the heavy metal lead to be the most efficient.[19] Lead was crucial to all that followed. Lead was heavy, very heavy.

During the next two decades, Plante evolved his clumsy lead battery into one practicable enough to manufacture and useful enough to service the growing telegraphic industry. But there was much more than telegraphy. The 1870s launched two decades of the fastest urban and commercial growth in American history. The budding telephone, railroad-braking, illumination, as well as electromagnetic- and electrical-device businesses were among the many work savers, muscle multipliers, distance shrinkers, and magical boxes that spilled forth from the fertile mind of the inventive and eager America. This was the electrifying era of pioneers such as George Westinghouse, Thomas Edison, Nikola Tesla, and Alexander Graham Bell.[20]

Dynamos now generated electricity at steady rates. At the 1876 Philadelphia Centennial Exposition, electrified arc lights thrilled the throngs. In 1878, the Paris Exhibition unveiled its Gallery of Machines, with all manner of modern work-saving devices from doorbells to motorized conveyances, all running on electricity. Electricity promised to bring the day into night, the warmth into cold, and the force of nature to the common task. That same year, on September 16, 1878, the *New York Sun* bannered this headline: EDISON'S NEWEST MARVEL, SENDING CHEAP LIGHT, HEAT, AND POWER BY ELECTRICITY.[21]

There was no stopping civilization now. Behold, by the end of the 1870s, electricity had become a commercial necessity, commercially viable, and commercially within reach of those who could afford it, and indeed many who could not. The fissionlike, infecting, and seductive proliferation of electricity powered what became known as the Second Industrial Revolution.[22] Stand away King Coal and King Steam. The inextinguishable power source had arrived.

Commerce changed everything about electricity—the way it was generated, stored, distributed, and owned. Batteries were seen as a magical method of storing the awesome power of electricity. But as the United States and the world entered the magical age of electricity and batteries, it did so just as America and the world experienced a pandemic of corporate fraud, collusion, and unfair competition. Monopolies and pernicious trusts, operated by rapacious robber barons and their white-collar squires, seized almost every commodity and useful device in fast-industrializing America. Supplies and prices were fixed, shortages rigged, competition stifled, and the average family as well as society at large became the ultimate loser.

From the 1870s, the future was forged by the few. Modern technology shaped humankind, its prosperity, progress, and way of life. But too often these Promethean advances were not developed for the benefit of the society so enormously affected. Instead, technological change was shaped and molded on a corporate potter's wheel for the personal gain of the manipulating men who controlled it. Hence, society's true access to the most needed technology was not determined by the best idea and best product, but by the financial rewards and ramifications that would accrue to and flow from the combines—even when that technology worked to the detriment of society at large. The key to this abuse of technology was constructing a monopoly, that is, the close and manipulative control of supply, quality, and price.[23]

For centuries before the electricity industry developed, monopolies had thrived as a fact of life. Since ancient times, state or monarchial monopolies defined the very outlines of wealth and power. The ancient pharaohs of Egypt controlled its mines and minerals. The kings of England established monopolistic reins over a natural resource as basic as wood. The private guilds of medieval England were granted monopolies over any number of simple commodities from grappling hooks to bread to beer. The Hostmen of Newcastle's coal extended the concept of energy monopoly from regal control to private merchants, placing a nation at their mercy.[24]

But in 1870 the nature and scope of monopoly and trust were reinvented by John D. Rockefeller. His maze of Standard Oil enterprises controlled nearly all the refineries, pipelines, and other channels of distribution in the United States, as well as in several foreign lands. His well-known tactics: deceit, extortion, surreptitious combines, market manipulation, price fixing, and artificial shortages. So immense was this one man's power that Congress took action to craft antitrust legislation. The courts would later dismantle Rockefeller's empire into twenty-two smaller companies, although each was a giant commercial presence in its own right.[25]

The collusive actions of the railroad robber barons and Rockefeller inspired an entire community of conspiratorial trusts manipulating and controlling almost every aspect of commercial life. The American people quickly learned to hate the monopolists. In 1873, crusading attorney David C. Cloud wrote in *Monopolies and the People*, "There is a power in the land, possessing elements destructive not only of the industrial and producing public, but of the very form and spirit of republican government." One union protester reflected popular sentiment when he marched through Manhattan with a placard broadcasting WE MUST CRUSH MONOPOLIES LEST THEY CRUSH US.[26]

In 1875, when Franklin Gowen, president of the Reading Railroad, a man reviled by many as the country's largest and most scurrilous owner of anthracite coal mines, testified before Pennsylvania legislators about his collusive corporate control of coal companies, he defended himself by stating that he was hardly alone. Such conduct was a feature of all major business in America.[27]

"Every pound of rope we buy for our vessels or for our mines," Gowen protested to the Pennsylvania legislators, "is bought at a price fixed by a committee of the rope manufacturers of the United States. Every keg of nails, every paper of tacks, all our screws and wrenches and hinges, the boiler flues for our locomotives, are never bought except at the price fixed by the representatives of the mills that manufacture them. Iron beams for your houses or your bridges can be had only at the prices agreed upon by a combination of those who produce them. Fire brick, gas pipe, terra-cotta pipe for drainage, every keg of powder we buy to blast coal, are [all] purchased under the same arrangement. Every pane of window glass in this house was bought at a scale of prices established exactly in the same manner. White lead, galvanized sheet iron, hose and belting and files, are bought and sold at a rate determined in the same way."[28]

Enter the battery cartel. Lead as the battery's chosen metal and monopolistic misconduct as its chosen style of business were two determining factors that, by their crushing weight, governed the future of stored electricity. Those two factors—one electrochemical and the second moral—ultimately affected the future of all automobiles and transportation in America, and indeed the world. What happened next invented the future.

CHAPTER FOUR

STENCH AND SCANDAL

Horse manure was everywhere. Manure piles towered high in late-nineteenth-century America. People now saw horse dung and smelled its stench at every urban turn. They gingerly stepped around it and often through it. They breathed it. In essence, all of society coexisted with horse dung as a partner in progress.

In dry, windy weather the excrement flew through the air in pulverized form. During rainstorms, thick gobs of it mixed with rivers of urine and sloshed down the streets. Swarms of flies spread typhoid fever and all manner of disease. In 1898, during the Spanish-American War, while only hundreds died of battlefield injuries, thousands of soldiers died of typhoid spread by flies. In the cities, horses died every hour of every day. Carcasses by the thousands needed to be promptly removed. The ever-present reek of horses and their muck was an undeniable fact of urban American life.[1]

Progress, both urban and industrial, had its price: horses and horse dung crowded the scene everywhere humans engaged in useful work. Shakespeare's Richard III cried, "A horse! A horse! My kingdom for a horse!" But in post–Civil War hyperindustrializing America, the horse *was* the kingdom. Without millions of such beasts pulling burdens, treading mills, and clopping down cobblestones, without the sheer power that this massive equine population generated, all commerce and industry would collapse with a reverberating thud.

The 1870 Census counted 8,690,219 horses throughout the country, of which more than 1.5 million worked in cities. By 1900, the nation's horse count increased to more than 21.2 million animals, and the stabled urban horse population had almost doubled to nearly 3 million. New York: 130,000; Chicago: 74,000; Philadelphia: 51,000. Horses provided a power source for mills. They also served as the main source of land transportation, pulling omnibuses. Introduced in New York in 1829, omnibuses were group passenger vehicles like modern buses, but pulled by horse teams. By the late 1850s, Philadelphia operated 322 such horse-drawn omnibuses. New York boasted more than 683 omnibuses carrying more than 120,000 passengers daily.[2]

More efficient than omnibuses were horsecars, similar to omnibuses but pulled along rails. These horse-drawn railroads helped increase commuting range and enabled cities to spread out. By 1890, 32.5 million passengers annually used 5,783 miles of rail-borne streetcar lines operated by 789 companies. Little of it was cable driven or electrified. Most of this traffic was pulled by 84,000 horses and mules.[3]

Horses delivered the goods and made America's wheels turn. They reliably pulled bread, beer, and milk wagons as well as every other form of delivery vehicle, day in, day out, hour to hour, city block to city block. Equine brute force also pulled the construction winches, pulleys, and elevators that erected the great construction projects, from wide dams to tall buildings. They also mindlessly walked treadmills to turn gears, thereby transducing muscle strength into driveshaft power. In 1850, horses generated more than half the power of all work performed in American cities. That 50 percent ratio of horse muscle to total power stayed constant in the urban centers until the end of the century.[4] Indeed, the very measure of a motor was expressed in horsepower.

Nineteenth-century America rode to its great industrial destiny on horseback.

Without horses, the nation would come to a standstill. This frightening truth was easily proved. In the first week of November 1872, virtually every horse in Boston was struck with a debilitating or fatal equine flu. The epizootic—the animal version of an epidemic—began in Toronto, spread to Rochester and New York, and from there to Boston. With almost every horse in Boston coughing, wheezing, and dropping dead in the street, deliveries virtually ceased, commuting stopped, and industrial power dwindled to nil levels. On November 9, 1872, a fire broke out in downtown Boston, blazing for thirty-five hours, burning down some 776 buildings, and costing $73.5 million. Boston's economy was charred along with the ruins. Why? That week, with the epizootic in full virulence, no horses were available to pull fire-department pump trucks to the fires. *Nation* magazine was among those that stood in awe of American dependence on the horse, warning in an editorial, "The present epidemic has brought us face to face with the startling fact that the sudden loss of horse labor would totally disorganize our industry and commerce."[5]

Millions of horses pulling, transporting, treading, and delivering throughout the streets of American cities created a titanic mess of horse dung and urine. Each horse dropped between fifteen and thirty-five pounds of manure daily, as well as upward of two gallons of urine. Generally, the feces dropped and urine gushed where and when the horse chose; more often than not within the urban environment. In New York, that amounted to as much as 3.25 million pounds of horse dung daily. Small armies of muck handlers were employed to collect, remove, and recycle as much as possible into fertilizer. But the malodor was pervasive. In Manhattan, the Citizen's Association "Report upon the Sanitary Conditions of the City" lamented, "The stench arising from these accumulations of filth is intolerable."[6]

Roiling fly populations accompanied the dung heaps, creating veritable engines of disease, including typhoid, cholera, infantile diarrhea, and tuberculosis. When it rained, the urine and manure formed torrents that swept through the city and over the feet of all who walked the streets. In dry heat, the dung became pulverized into an aerosol dust, coating windows and forming a noxious inhalant. Paved streets, a function of urban progress, only worsened the coproscape. Cobblestone and pavement helped pool and canalize the excreta in wet times. On baked summer days, hard paved surfaces caused the hooves to grind up the droppings and beat them into the air.[7]

The annoyances went beyond the stench. The clippity-clop of thousands of horse hooves on cobblestones and pavements created an urban cacophony that leading publications of the day decried as making sidewalk conversation impossible. One transportation journal admitted that horses had brought with them the "Age of Noise."[8]

An unloaded horse could travel almost 15 mph for a single hour but less than 5 mph when driven for ten hours. The average urban horse lived only four years or so. It generally pulled its burden until it simply dropped from exhaustion. In such a case it was killed. If the beast slipped or broke a leg on cobblestones or a slick pavement, it became useless; once again it was killed. Dead horses were ever present in urban America. Some 15,000 horse carcasses were removed from the streets of New York in 1880. Each horse weighed some 1,300 pounds, creating daily tonnage. Carcasses were shoved into the river so they could float away or were stacked into massive collection centers for reprocessing. The endless supply of re-cyclable horsehair, bones, rendered fat, and leather created industries in their own right.[9]

Accompanying the horse stench was the stinging, eye-burning haze of coal and cinders wafting in heated public buildings, billowing into the air from numberless chimneys, kilns, and smokestacks, and settling as par-ticulate on surfaces within and without.[10] America's gateway to modern convenience unleashed unending filth.

As the United States entered the last decade of the nineteenth cen-tury, the country was ready—more than ready—for relief from its frenetic pursuit of progress and expansion. People had stepped in it and smelled it until life itself was imbued with horse reek and coal fumes. No wonder modern late-nineteenth-century society reacted with wonderment and ex-citement at a new invention. This machine was noiseless and odorless, could do the work of a team of horses, never slept, and required no feeding. This invention promised to propel humankind into a dazzling new era of possibilities. Enter the electric vehicle, also known as a horseless carriage. This newfangled contraption would usher in the new century, a new age, and a new lifestyle.

Unfortunately, the brave new device depended upon a marvelous but controversial invention: the battery.

Electricity flowed from the very quintessence of nature. However, it was not submolecular particles, but rather sub-rosa corporate manipulations that determined how this potent force would serve humankind. Like all the other great energy sources and inventions throughout the centuries, like the English kings' wood, like the Hostmen's coal, like the robber barons' railroads, like all the monopolistic enterprises of the post–Civil War era, the fast-gathering electrical industry, as well as batteries, became a tool of rapacious businessmen who used the technology to positively charge their pockets first, regardless of how society was impacted.

Quickly during the post–Civil War era the battery, that is, the "box of stored electricity" that had evolved from the Galvani's blade and arose from the subsequent marriage of metals chemically separated, emerged from its utility as a mere telegraphic support. The battery loomed as a po-tential power source for all things motive and dependent upon energy. This industrial imperative meant that the world of batteries would be marked by corporate facades, spurious patent litigation, financial ploys and playbooks, strategic bankruptcies, stock swindles, and other forms of commercial manipulation.

In other words, batteries were business as usual.

As such, while the public hoped for a battery revolution, they reviled the companies leading that revolution. People wanted to believe, but they believed little of what they heard. This distrust was pivotal because public bitterness and distaste over monopolies and conglomerates helped shape the course of this desperately needed technology. As the electricity drama played out, it struck the public as endless episodes of thieves battling thieves for the right to defraud society and average investors. Here was an exciting new technology, but one that was constantly exaggerated by companies whose promises were as vaporous as their motives were avaricious.

For most nineteenth-century decades, Plante-style batteries were devices tediously handcrafted one at a time in wizardly workshops. When battery electrodes received a current of external electricity, the surfaces of the embedded lead strips were electrochemically altered, with the positive electrode slowly *accumulating* a thin coating of peroxide of lead. The coating in turn helped those lead strips store the electricity. This slow process could take from three to twenty-four months just to create a single battery with a usable charge. Hence, batteries were often called accumulators. The very name suggested a slow, gradual process.[11]

But if rechargeable batteries were to proliferate, batteries would need to ascend from quaint workshops to large-scale manufacturing. The intoxicating new incandescent-lightbulb industry and a growing patchwork of "central stations" that supplied electricity to the homes and businesses that could afford the luxury created the first lucrative posttelegraphic market stimulus. Batteries could store electricity generated at the central stations during peak time and dispense it during off hours, or when mechanical difficulties arose.

In the fall of 1880, French chemical engineer Camille Faure, familiar with both telegraphy and electroplating, became the first to devise an efficient formation and manufacturing process for Plante-style lead-acid batteries. Faure had become entranced with electricity two years earlier during his visit to the 1878 Paris Exhibition, which thrilled so many with its magnificent illumination display. By 1879, with the advent of more practical lightbulbs from inventors on both sides of the Atlantic—Thomas Edison, Joseph Wilson Swan, and others—the world became mesmerized with the bright new possibilities of incandescence.[12]

Faure's new methods of juxtaposing and perforating battery metals, and then causing their rapid electrochemical coating, reduced the charging and production time needed to create a single Plante-style battery from months to hours. His new design was hardly a whole new species of electrical storage, but it was certainly a major practical advance over Plante's device. Genuine commercial manufacturing was now possible. Home lighting, machine power, and locomotion could be enabled in a spectrum of dynamic new ways. In October 1880, Faure rushed to the patent office.[13]

With arcane workshops left behind, big business stepped in. A Paris company immediately incorporated to exploit Faure's battery patent. Faure's new stockholder-seeking company, La Force et La Lumière (Force et Lumière), launched sweeping promotions for its device, promising the newspapers and the public dazzling applications and society-changing energy-distribution methods. Batteries would be delivered daily at the average man's door right along with milk bottles and ice. An array of 40,000 batteries would be installed at Niagara Falls to generate 80,000 volts to the city of Buffalo, New York. All the ideas were good and alluring. Prestigious scientists were recruited to lend their authority to the schemes. The promise to society was profound. Batteries were no longer an obscure telegraphic power source; they were now broadly anticipated by the general public.[14]

But who was behind Force et Lumière? It was not Faure, but rather Belgian financier Simon Philippart along with members of his family. Who was financier Simon Philippart?

Simply put, Simon Philippart was one of Europe's most notorious stock swindlers and corporate con men. His was an iconic name to financiers, speculators, and the media, as well as to men of importance throughout the economic world. Philippart was nothing less than a fiscal Siren, always promising great riches but too often delivering economic ruin. His elastic ability to bounce from ill repute to high demand, and back again to infamy, was nothing less than a testament to society's irrepressible quest for quick riches.

"Philippart burst like a meteor on the financial horizon of Paris in late 1874," a wire story appearing in major American newspapers reported. Within months, Philippart became known as the King of the Bourse, the Paris stock exchange. There he acquired an infamous reputation for manipulating French speculators, capable of creating artificial riches overnight for everyone from an assistant editor of a local paper to the most powerful banker. "All that he touches turns to gold," wrote one newspaper correspondent. "If Philippart says that a certain stock, languishing at eighty, shall go up to one thousand, it goes up with the greatest rapidity, and when Philippart invests, everybody is crazy to get the same kind of stock. The power wielded by this one man is something astonishing."[15]

Yet few in mid-1870 financial circles knew anything about the mysterious millionaire. "There is great inquiry here," wrote one Paris newspaper in 1875, "as to whom this man is who is occupying so large a share of public attention. All that is known of him [Philippart] is that he was a Belgian woolen manufacturer, who began to build railroads . . . connecting the central roads of Belgium with those of France."[16]

By mid-1875, Philippart was compelled to resign as chairman of the scandal-ridden European railroad construction bank Crédit Mobilier. Under his baton, the bank's stock had dropped by 50 percent within just a few months, inflicting a loss of ten million francs upon the angry stockholders. They sued Philippart, who settled without a cash payout by convincing his partners that their troubles were not his fault. Disillusioned investors decided to simply let Philippart quietly disappear.[17]

But within a few years, the disgraced Philippart had bounced back. In 1879, he organized yet another bank, Banque Europienne, authorized to raise one hundred million francs. Once capital began flowing in, Philippart fled with much of the proceeds, leaving his bank partners to cover his expropriation. Again, he was compelled to resign as chairman after stockholder suits and thousands of claims.[18]

At the time, few knew that the shadowy tycoon flitted from one investment scandal to another. Finally, the major newspapers exposed him: "[Philippart] became President of the Crédit Mobilier and attached himself to many other companies. He came to grief and was declared a bankrupt, both at Paris and Brussels, his liabilities amounting to 28,000,000 francs." A French magazine declared, "The market has been affected for a long time by the achievements of this great and tireless profiteer." One headline called Philippart nothing less than A BOLD BANK WRECKER.[19]

Philippart was eventually prosecuted for financial swindles, but then acquitted. The slippery Philippart was always either acquitted or successful on appeal. Even when courts sentenced him to prison for stealing stockholder funds, the sentences were vacated. For example, in 1878, a French court convicted him on stock-fraud charges, sentencing him to six months. But by August 1880, he was allowed to dissolve his holdings, keep his creditors at bay, and overturn the prison sentence.[20]

Within two months of Philippart's voided prison sentence, that is, in October 1880, Faure had applied for his battery patent. A truly commercial concern was needed to make it a success. Philippart was ready with his latest concoction, the Faure Electric Accumulator Company.

Public excitement over batteries swelled in mid-1881 during the run-up to Paris's International Electrical Exhibition, scheduled for that summer and fall. The exhibition was so anticipated and well received, one electricity expert declared that "electrical engineering was born" at the convention. In June 1881, during a peak of media enthusiasm over Faure's batteries, Charles Brush, the American inventor of arc lightning, suddenly filed his own similar patent application. Indeed, Brush had filed as many as twenty patents for batteries and other electrical devices.[21]

Who was Brush? Charles Brush was the Ohio electrical guru and entrepreneur famous for inventing fast-whirring dynamos to generate electricity, and arc lamps that radiated illumination from carbon tips made white-hot by electricity. Like many giant electrical pioneers, Brush quickly became wealthy. He diverted significant moneys from his personal fortune to fund eugenic research into genocidal programs designed to reinvent the human race and subtract racial "undesirables" by forcibly halting their reproduction. Brush also invested heavily in batteries. Moreover, he was an expert at patent litigation. In fact, Brush regularly used patent litigation to block other good ideas in electricity that he could not control.[22] Brush arose as the perfect duelist to confront Philippart.

Thieves and manipulators now battled thieves and manipulators during the scorching London summer of 1881, months when the heat blazed above 90° Fahrenheit and opportunities appeared as heat-rippled enticements.[23] The rush was on—by hook or crook—by Faure, Brush, or any of the lesser-known but equally knowledgeable experts, to capture a commanding position in the promising new battery market.

Among the players was the French inventor Ernest Volckmar, a manager in Faure's Paris workshop. When Philippart sailed to London to organize a British branch of his Parisian battery business, Force et Lumière, Volckmar was left in charge. While the elder Philippart was occupied in London, Volckmar schemed with Philippart's minor son, Gustav, described by family members as "inexperienced." Volckmar and young Gustav transferred some of Faure's precious patents out of the company. The British Patent Office refused to recognize them under Volckmar's name, but that did not stop him. By October 1881, Volckmar wielded his own array of patents. Once Philippart learned of the betrayal in Paris, he became furious, and the two culprits—young Gustav and Volckmar—escaped across the Channel to London.[24]

Gustav returned to the family, leaving Volckmar to continue alone. By the end of that year, 1881, Volckmar had discovered a new accomplice, John Sellon, a British electrical engineer who enjoyed his own portfolio of battery patents. Many of Sellon's patents were similar to those that Volckmar had acquired after the debacle with Philippart's young son. Even still, for some reason, Sellon became enamored of Volckmar as "a gentleman of great power of work and perfection in every detail." Soon thereafter, Sellon used his connections with other prominent British electricians to license their patents along with his own. This allowed Sellon and Volckmar to join forces to create a formidable venture to manufacture batteries.[25] A battle now loomed as Philippart's battery combine readied an international launch of Faure batteries threatened by Volckmar.

On March 4, 1882, Philippart deftly incorporated what appeared to all as a British enterprise, the Faure Electric Accumulator Company (FEA). To that end, the FEA board of directors listed only English gentlemen. Internationally respected British physicist William Ayrton was prominently advertised as a consulting engineer. Ayrton, a pioneer in telegraphy and electricity, was the scientist who helped England establish a telegraph network in India. Of course Faure's famous name dominated the company's moniker, and he was listed as a consultant along with Ayrton. But Philippart's name was hidden from view, and in all ways this new corporation appeared to be British to the core.[26]

However, the new British firm was in fact a front for Philippart's own French company, Force et Lumière. Unbeknownst to the British, Philippart would quietly control the new London entity by virtue of a self-dealing agreement to license Force et Lumière's patents in exchange for half of Faure Electric Accumulator Company's stock.[27] Therefore, all those British investors, from the average hopeful to the well-to-do, would see their money surreptitiously exported to Philippart's coffers in Paris.

Three weeks later, at the end of March 1882, the American electrical entrepreneur Brush, who had bided his time since 1880, joined the fray. That previous summer, Brush had copied Faure's technology, filing his own duplicative patents. Now, at the end of March 1882, the recently incorporated Anglo-American Brush Company created a spin-off, the Electric Power Supply Company. Who was a pivotal EPS board member? It was Sellon, the man in league with Volckmar. Their battery was named the Sellon-Volckmar. Going further, Volckmar began convincing FEA employees to defect to Brush's new company.[28]

Now the stage was set for a clash between the two would-be battery titans, Brush's EPS and Philippart's FEA, both claiming similar technology, each seeking to erect a monopoly.

Understandably, batteries and electricity in general became known as a scandalous technology, rife with scientific deception, get-rich-quick schemes, and stock manipulation. In the first five months of 1882, a cavalcade of companies burst upon the British financial scene, seeking a total of £9 million, of which £7 million had already been subscribed. Sixteen new electricity entities appeared in the first half of May 1882 alone, even as Brush's EPS and Philippart's FEA did legal battle. Stock manipulations, rumors, and wild trading wracked the financial markets, with all of them directly or indirectly tied to the big player, Brush's EPS. Indeed, that May EPS itself saw its own stock devalued by £600,000 within three days. This ruinous speculation was dubbed the Brush Bubble.[29]

Faure and Philippart, of course, had every reason to believe that Brush's EPS had absconded with their battery patents. Threats of legal action against Brush's EPS from Philippart led to public name-calling in the technical press as Faure, Sellon, Volckmar, and members of the Philippart family all traded insults. Faure finally charged Volckmar in a Paris court, protesting, "It was not long before he [Volckmar] grievously abused the confidence which had been placed in him, [and] that, in fact, he [Volckmar] used his influence to lead astray from his duties Mr. Gustav Philippart, another son, who was at that time a minor, and succeeded in inducing this inexperienced young man to cheat his father and the company in whose service he was . . . and that since then the two have used all their endeavors to corrupt the workmen of La Force et La Lumière Co., and to compete treacherously against their former masters."[30]

Volckmar promptly sued in a British court for libel and slander once Philippart commented to the electrical trade press and openly labeled Volckmar a scoundrel.[31]

By early May 1882, Philippart's FEA joined in corporately, suing Brush's EPS for infringement. The lawsuits did not last long. Key shareholders of FEA, over the protest of Philippart, declined to spend the time and money to litigate. Within weeks, the two adversaries agreed not to fight on for years, but rather to simply divide the industrialized world between them. A complex and serpentine out-of-court settlement called for

Brush's EPS to monopolize much of the battery business in the United Kingdom, while Force et Lumière retained the European continent. The emerging United States market, one that lagged behind Europe, would be split between the two companies. The Sellon-Volckmar batteries were re-named for the three main characters and became Faure-Sellon-Volckmar batteries.[32]

Ironically, the latest victim in Philippart's machinations was the London-based Faure Electric Accumulator Company, established by Philippart himself. The supposedly British subsidiary at the heart of the row now found itself squeezed out of the global battery deal between the American-owned EPS and the French-owned Force et Lumière. FEA's in-vestors would be left with nothing.[33]

That is exactly what happened. By November 1882, hapless FEA investors were told their company would no longer be a battery-manufacturing concern but a holding company to license the patents to two other Philippart captives across the Channel in France. The two new captives would be French Electric Storage Company, to produce batteries, and the Metropolitan General Electric Company, to use those batteries in self-propelled omnibuses that would function as "electric streetcars." When any of the 357 individual shareholders protested, Philippart, who held a 75 percent controlling vote, informed the others that his family— and only his family—would decide how the assets of FEA were spent. FEA's British board resigned in protest. That mattered not.[34]

Within a year, the house of cards began collapsing. During 1883, Force et Lumière, French Electric Storage Company, and the Metropoli-tan General Electric Company invested considerable resources in creat-ing electric streetcars to travel across Paris. But while the streetcars were shiny and showy, designed to attract investors and stimulate much hub-bub, they were dynamically unsound. The system required an electric streetcar weighing 7,700 pounds, outfitted with heavy lead batteries weigh-ing 7,000 pounds, to move a group of passengers weighing some 2,400 pounds. These motive monstrosities just never worked. But for stock pro-motion, they were excellent.[35]

While the new investors bemoaned their losses, and while many hopes were again dashed, the profiteers found the experience rewarding. Philippart continued his extravagant lifestyle and international business antics. Predictably, he returned to dubious railway construction schemes. On April 12, 1883, the Parisian authorities arrested Philippart on warrants from Belgian prosecutors citing forged financial records. A few weeks later, he agreed to extradition, which landed him in a Brussels prison cell. Bail was denied.[36]

At the end of May 1883, FEA auditors discovered that their books had also been forged. Whereas at the beginning of the year, Philippart was registered for twenty thousand shares, those same books now showed him as owning only fifty. Simultaneously, Philippart's Parisian holding company, Force et Lumière, was suddenly registered for thirty thousand shares.[37] The fraud was more than obvious.

Miraculously, Philippart finally made bail and on June 26, 1883, convened an FEA shareholders' meeting where he passionately encouraged support for the company's great Faure-Sellon-Volckmar batteries.[38] It was all a stall tactic.

Force et Lumière, French Electric Storage Company, and the Metropolitan General Electric Company simultaneously went bankrupt in April 1884. On April 16, Philippart told disillusioned stockholders that it was their original decision almost two years earlier to settle with Brush's EPS that started the downfall—not his personal financial manipulations.[39] Not unexpectedly, while the company and battery business in general languished, Philippart continued to escape justice and accrue fortune.

As for Volckmar, whose name was on every battery, he flitted back and forth through the streets of London and Paris "in a manner indicating a person of great wealth," as an 1884 meeting of eminent battery engineers in Philadelphia sneeringly described him. Indeed, Volckmar had siphoned a reported $500,000 from the enterprise. It was clear to virtually the entire electrical community on both sides of the Atlantic that their former colleague had left the ranks of science and joined the financial predators. "Mr. Volckmar," a speaker castigated at that 1884 battery engineering conference in Philadelphia, "succeeded in playing his part of a plunderer."[40]

Volckmar's professional colleagues may have been merely scornful, but in the wake of the stock scandal, as well as the shredded hopes and abused confidences of investors, many bitter victims were nursing ruined lives. Undoubtedly, they were unnerved as Volckmar flaunted his pilferage with his pomp and ostentation.

On July 22, 1884, Paris police were summoned to a bank of the Seine River. There, they fished out a fresh, floating corpse. They checked the dead man's pockets. Empty. They checked the waterlogged body. A bullet hole had pierced the forehead. An examination positively identified the victim. It was Volckmar.[41]

The upheaval of the battery business did not end with the disgrace of

Philippart, the brutal murder of Volckmar, or the ravaging of the British and French battery companies. Within a few years, the legacy of their rapacious escapades would be transplanted to the streets of America's cities. There it would create a technological fork in the road for the industrialized world. Would America and all of modern society adopt a transportation system based on clean battery-powered electric vehicles? Just as important, could anyone trust anything with a battery?

CHAPTER FIVE

BATTERIES AND BICYCLES

Speed changed man's field of vision, cantankerously combining blur with clear focus, creating two realities: one beckoning, one unfathomable. Man's first exposure to true sustained speed—face against wind, nose against window—was bestowed by the railroad. Except for short bursts from racehorses, most ordinary horse-borne distance transportation moseyed along at just 4 to 6 mph. Bicycles could go faster, but only briefly. Hence, it was the huffing and puffing steam-driven railroads, beginning in the 1830s and extending to century's end, that propelled man over long distances at previously unheard-of speeds: 50, 60, even 100 mph.[1]

What did velocity do to the human psyche?

When a passenger in a railroad car gazed out the window, left or right, everything in the speeding foreground flashed by as an indistinct blur. Only the distance remained sharply in focus. Therefore, as society beheld the prospect of propulsion, it could always see the alluring horizon, but often not the speeding terrain in front of its nose. That is exactly how man envisioned and pursued his dreams and fears of automobiles, and that is how he bartered his world in exchange for the elusive elixir of speed. And what an addicting elixir it was.

In 1884, even as Volckmar's cold body was being fished from the flotsam of the Seine, even as the ashes of Faure and Philippart's international battery combine were being swept into oblivion, the industrialized world was still hopeful that dishonest businessmen could be separated from the promise of battery power. The world needed to move. Faster, farther, freer. Batteries could transduce the electricity to power man's rewritten reality.

Faure's batteries first arrived in America in May 1882 aboard the French steamer *Labrador*, the same month the litigation between Brush and Philippart commenced. Days later, in June 1882, a group of Philadelphia entrepreneurs formed the United Gas Improvement Company (UGIC) to work with Philadelphia gas utilities. Shortly thereafter, at 3:00 P.M. on September 4, Edison opened his Pearl Street Station, a central generating station to provide electricity to the city of New York. With the lift of a switch, Edison lit up a third of lower Manhattan's financial district and, to the marvel of reporters, stopped the 7:00 P.M. dark from entering the newsroom of the *New York Times*. In doing so, he helped society escape what he called the "evil" of reeking, explosive gaslight, a "vile poison" that would "vitiate the atmosphere."[2]

Instantly, America radiated excitement over electricity. Everyone wanted it. Everyone wanted to produce it. Everyone wanted to provide it by every inventive means. Thousands of patent applications suddenly rained down upon Washington's undermanned Patent Office. The unending torrent of applications continued for years, testifying to the breadth of electrical innovation, real and supposed.[3]

United Gas Improvement Company executives were always concerned about their emerging competitor, electricity. They saw the future changing as dozens of electricity companies suddenly leaped into existence, vying for the chance to illuminate and power America's households and industries. The executives saw nothing less than what they termed a "mad scramble for electrical lighting franchises." Nearly all the companies desired reliable, working batteries to keep the generated loads constant when their dynamos went down, or to store power during nonpeak hours, and of course to purvey that power to locations and machines not connected to the still-embryonic grid.[4]

Batteries could make it all sensible, make it all possible. Battery power was, in fact, wireless power. By 1885, the many newborn electrical companies formed the National Electrical Light Association. Within a year, UGIC saw so much promise in electricity that it began buying up small electrical companies that were financially battered by an 1885 economic slump and therefore ripe for acquisition.[5]

But as much as everyone craved batteries to usher the world into the next century, batteries were synonymous with lying and deception, fraud and speculation, exaggeration and misrepresentation. Who could trust a battery—or any company that offered one?

Comments made throughout 1883 were typical of the era. In January, for example, Edison declared, "The storage battery is, in my opinion . . . a mechanism for swindling the public by stock companies. The storage battery is one of those peculiar things which appeal to the imagination, and no more perfect thing could be desired by stock swindlers. . . . Just as soon as a man gets working on the secondary battery, it brings out his latent capacity for lying."[6] Even though Edison's derogatory characterization was undoubtedly intensified because of his competition with Brush's electrical enterprises, the famous inventor's contempt summed up popular feeling and deeply resonated with both the public and the profession.

Edison's rebuke stuck. A full year later, in 1884, at a decisive electrical engineering convention in Philadelphia dedicated to the battery and attended by the top electricians in the world, the keynote speaker opened with this jab: "Mr. Edison himself has declared that this question of storage batteries has developed the most remarkable power of man's latent capacity for lying." The crowd laughed approvingly, prompting the speaker to add, "I very much agree with Mr. Edison's definition, for I think there has been more lying and rascality done over this question of storage batteries than over any other department of electrical science."[7]

In fact, the condemnatory mind-set held fast for more than a decade. Three years later, in 1887, a National Electric Light Association meeting still enjoyed repeating the familiar denigrations, stating, "Storage batteries are chiefly remarkable for their power of stimulating the propensity for lying."[8] Notably, this scorn was ingrained within the very electrical industry association considered a pivotal channel for any wide-scale battery adoption.

In fact, years into the next century, electricity experts were still maligning batteries. Typical were remarks made at the American Electrochemical Society in 1903, where members lamented, "The amount of money which has been lost in the endeavor to force upon the market secondary batteries having little or no intrinsic value, to say nothing of the heartaches to honest investors from unqualified dreams, makes the history of the storage battery's development almost tragic."[9]

Worse yet, most of the decision makers who urgently needed batteries genuinely believed they simply were too primitive to work. Industry leaders believed that the corporate scoundrels who trafficked in storage batteries had unpardonably overlooked the opportunity to make the devices reliable. Certainly, electricity proponents in the 1880s had confidence in the future of the battery, if enough solid, unrushed science could be applied. But a decisive majority was convinced that the battery was a scientific achievement whose practical days had not yet arrived.

In February 1883, the *Boston Herald* reported the opinion that "various persons have from time to time announced the invention of storage batteries . . . but none of these have had . . . [more] than mere scientific value." A few months later, the *New York Evening* reported, "The storage battery is still considered an expensive toy . . . as yet unfit for practical work." In January 1884, the British journal *The Electrician* belittled Brush's EPS by declaring, "The batteries that were so full of promise twelve months since (when EPS began manufacture) have disappointed their best friends. [As for] the Faure-Sellon-Volckmar battery . . . [the] defects are insurmountable." In 1886, a prominent electrician predictably berated the entire battery field, declaring, "The man who comes out with a kind word for the secondary battery is set down either as a knave or a fool."[10]

The reason for all the scientific pessimism: basic materials and construction. The type of metals and how they were juxtaposed and electrochemically treated in the battery box dictated the quality and sureness of the charge. But the electrochemistry of it all was still tenuous and unpredictable. An 1882 *New York Times* report explained to average readers that the peroxide of lead accumulating on the plates was often "not of sufficient thickness to insure [electrical] current of proper duration for valuable results. . . . More than this . . . the layer of peroxide would often peel off from the plates, rendering the battery useless."[11]

Moreover, electricians knew that despite abundant hype and advertising, the plates themselves tended to disintegrate after they left the lab. An 1884 battery conference complained, "The force generated in these plates, tending to buckle them, is enormous." As for the newly developed bichromate battery, one scientist energetically argued, "The carbons do not last more than twelve months," adding that in some cases a molded battery carbon "would not last more than two or three months." Reinforcing the rejection, he assured his colleagues, "They do disintegrate: they tumble to pieces, they become quite soft and spongy."[12]

The prospective buyers of batteries as well as the scientists who promoted them were largely confident all the confounding problems would rapidly disappear with uncorrupted research and development. For example, electricians knew that the July 1885 EPS battery was 2.7 times more powerful than Faure's 1881 version. They knew that efforts to deploy batteries to operate machinery were increasingly successful and efficient.[13]

In other words, despite their nefarious reputation, batteries were becoming progressively more durable and more powerful. Hence, the promise of great untethered power, a promise oft-broken and oft-distorted, still allured the believers. The late-nineteenth-century world remained filled with such believers.

Among those who believed most were the automobile men. No corporate failure could deflate them; no mechanical disappointment could deter them. These men ate wind and road bumps the way ordinary men ate bread and salt. Constructed of the same rugged stuff that made such indefatigable American explorers as Lewis and Clark, the impetuous men who constructed and drove those first automotive vehicles irrepressibly created their envelope just to push it. How fast, how far, and how intrepidly could their hand-built contraptions propel a willing human? For these men, batteries were the future, and the future was too tempting to wait.

Of course, automotive vehicles were nothing new to the men of the late nineteenth century. The dream had always churned. Primitive self-propelled vehicles, driven by steam, gasoline, and electrical engines, had rolled down European and American city streets and country lanes for many decades.

The earliest proponents of steam vehicles well remembered that Hero of Alexandria in 100 BC had designed a spinning ball-shaped proto-rocket called the aeolipile, powered by steam pressure. A modern reconstruction of Hero's device could rotate at 3,500 revolutions per minute. Hero also sought to deliver man to the gods by devising a rudimentary steam-powered contrivance of counterweights that could open heavy temple doors to any man.[14]

Throughout the 1700s, steam engines were used in the coal mines of England to pump out flooded pit holes and haul heavy cargo. The stationary machines were soon made portable to create railroads, then further adapted for automotive travel. The first steam truck was built in 1769 by French military engineer Nicolas-Joseph Cugnot. Cugnot's three-wheeled, elongated freight wagon, outfitted with a large steam boiler, hauled artillery loads weighing up to four tons at speeds of 4 kph. But when the truck crashed into a brick wall, Cugnot was pensioned off and the project discontinued. Still, during subsequent decades personal steam-driven carriages arose again and became commonplace. Within a century, by the 1860s, Connecticut became a center of steam-automobile activity. For example, during the 1860s, a Hartford man named Christopher Spencer enjoyed roaring up and down the rural byways in his steam-powered vehicle, and the House brothers ferried small groups between Bridgeport and Stratford in their newfangled steam automobile.[15]

In the early to mid 1830s, Thomas Davenport in America and Robert Davidson in Scotland were among the first to construct working self-propelled vehicles, powered by nonrechargeable electric batteries—what became known as horseless carriages. Their pioneer electric vehicles were humming decades before Plante created his rechargeable battery in 1865. The advent of rechargeable batteries only accelerated the drive to create reliable electric transport. In 1881, one of Paris's most established coach makers, Charles Jeantaud, using Faure's new lead battery, engineered a significant advance over prior electric-vehicle efforts. More than just better locomotive contraptions, Jeantaud's well-crafted vehicles reflected his luxury-carriage approach to personal conveyance. A succession of exquisite Jeantaud electrical vehicles, featuring the finest leathers and interior detail work, were designed to appeal to a genteel, affluent patron, accustomed to a coachman. The coachman remained to steer and control the vehicle. But the horse was gone. It was this crop of vehicles that truly launched the nascent electric-vehicle industry.[16]

As steam and electric vehicles were taking hold, so were internal combustion machines, that is, machines that caused forward propulsion by virtue of an explosion captured within a cylinder connected to a drive wheel and gears. The whole idea of riding atop a series of contained explosions was abhorrent to many. Yet internal combustion remained a muscular aspiration to those who believed it was possible, a belief born of man's macho fascination with cannon fire, black powder, and flammable pitch. In 1807, Swiss inventor François Isaac de Rivaz constructed an early internal combustion vehicle that burned a mixture of hydrogen and oxygen fuel. A half century later, Belgian automotive engineer Jean Lenoir drove a kerosene-burning, spark-plug-ignited three-wheeler. Following the 1859 discovery of commercial oil in Titusville, Pennsylvania, Lenoir in 1863 switched to petroleum, an improvement that powered his vehicle some fifty miles. Petroleum offered dense energy and gave the driver range while adding little weight. A decade later, the American inventor George Brayton constructed a two-stroke kerosene engine that was considered practical, followed by Nikolaus August Otto's four-stroke.[17]

Early internal combustion vehicles literally defined the rise of German automotive engineering. They stressed gasoline as a lightweight, speed-enabling, range-endowing power source. First came Gottlieb Daimler's true fuel-injected gasoline vehicle in 1885, which led to Karl Benz's improved version in 1886 and Wilhelm Maybach's 1890 four-cylinder, four-stroke petroleum automobile.[18]

By the early 1890s, new automobile types were appearing fast and furious in all the power varieties: steam, electric, and the daring, new explosive variety, that is, the gasoline-based internal combustion machine. They rolled out of barns, toolsheds, bicycle shops, stables, and sometimes even a factory. But it was the battery that appealed to so many because it was a visionary solution to the eye-burning, nose-stinging world of horse and steam-generated transportation. Batteries would replace the ever-present wafting haze and the surface-coating ash resulting from coal- and wood-powered steam engines. Stored electricity would also do away with ever-swirling horse urine and omnipresent fly-infested fecal piles. The vision was that the miasmas and blight would be succeeded by a modern marvel: the clean and noiseless propulsion of electricity.

"Electricity is the natural medium for the application of motive power," wrote one trade journal. "Its supply is unlimited. It is everywhere. It is to movement what the sun is to growth."[19]

The men of United Gas Improvement Company were ready for batteries to come of age. More than ready, they, like the automobile men, were unwilling to wait for the battery to be perfected. But batteries were still out of the question because anyone who tried to join the fray was forcibly immersed in a floodwater of patent litigation. In August 1887, the National Electrical Light Association reiterated the settled wisdom that "storage batteries are chiefly remarkable for their power of stimulating the propensity for lying." But at that very time, French battery designer Clement Payen came to America. True, UGIC executives believed that French batteries were part and parcel of what they later called a "wild orgy of financial speculation." But Payen's new battery design seemed radically different. It employed pellets of lead chloride and zinc to be converted into a charged crystalline structure, thus vastly increasing the battery's working surface areas, shortening its manufacture cycle and increasing its power yield.[20]

Payen's revolutionary design appealed to UGIC general manager William Gibbs. Gibbs was known as a dynamic huckster, smooth talker, and showman. One Philadelphia newspaper columnist described the bearded Gibbs as second only to P. T. Barnum in salesmanship, and as a slick operator who could have made a fortune selling water wings to Saharan desert tribes. Gibbs himself was a paragon of caution. An associate who worked with him on batteries described him as "fierce" on the subject. Only after putting Payen's design through a series of validated laboratory tests did Gibbs conclude that, yes, this new French battery did work—and work better.[21]

On June 5, 1888, several UGIC officials gathered before a New Jersey official to incorporate a new company, the Electric Storage Battery Company (ESB). This new company, ESB, issued 100,000 shares at $100 each, declaring its capitalization to be $10 million. In truth, the ESB only possessed $2,500 cash. The rest of the $10 million bubbled from Gibbs's imaginary valuation of its battery patents. But within six months, at least two dozen outside investors had purchased shares based on the inflated prospectus. Despite the outside investment, almost 90 percent of those 100,000 shares were closely held by UGIC. Gibbs himself controlled 44,000 shares, Payen held 29,000, and three trusted UGIC managers shared 15,000. The remaining 12,000 shares were dispersed among the twenty-four minority investors, people who poured in cash but enjoyed no control.[22]

During those first corporate months, that is, the second half of 1888, ESB did little more than prepare to build batteries and spend money to fight patent suits. The market for batteries was nil. The president of the New York's Consolidated Electric Storage Company assessed the lackluster market, stating, "The aggregate demand for storage batteries throughout the whole country is small at best; and it would require all the customers for storage batteries in the United States to keep a [single] factory of moderate size in full operation if indeed that would be sufficient to do so."[23]

Moreover, patent litigation by Brush, and by and between a gaggle of other pretenders to the battery throne, was killing the newly established ESB, draining it of resources and targeting customers. Under prevailing patent infringement laws, customers were equally liable. Who would buy a battery if the device included a guaranteed lawsuit by Brush?

A senior ESB official, Samuel Wyman Rolph, eventually admitted, "Things looked pretty bad," especially since the company lacked "the money needed to ride out the storm of patent litigation let loose when a Federal Court Judge decreed that two United States patents had been issued to Brush and Faure for one and the same type of battery." Rolph continued, "The legal action which followed dissipated capital which the industry should have spent for development. Prospective customers were afraid to buy *any* American battery for fear of being entangled in suits for infringement—so they imported batteries of either English or German manufacture."[24]

By the end of the first six months of its existence, that is, by December 31, 1888, ESB, the $10 million company that had begun its corporate life with only $2,500 in cash, was forced to operate off bank loans. By year's end, its cash on hand was exactly $2.01.[25]

To stave off the end, Gibbs sold ESB's British patent rights to Payen's battery, raising just enough money to devote more fees to patent litigation in America.[26] The ceaseless suits, countersuits, requests for injunctions, and demands for damages emanated from the far-flung corners of the American electrical community ipso facto of being in the battery world. With the tumble of mergers and acquisitions, partial buy-ins and buyouts, reorganizations and new organizations, start-ups, spin-offs, and wind-downs, it took studious attention to keep track of just who was suing whom. The shifting shares of illumination and battery companies made it all a confusing jumble at best, decipherable mainly by the battalions of attorneys who earned fees off the frivolous filings designed less to protect rights than to block competition and stymie development.

What a maze of ownership and commercial conflict. For example, in 1889 and 1890, Eastern Electric Light and Storage Battery purchased a minority interest in Brush's Anglo-American Storage Battery Company, and shortly thereafter Consolidated Electric Storage Battery Company swallowed Julien Storage Battery Company, and Crosby Electrical grabbed the assets of the troubled Federal Electrical, even as Southern States Electrical Storage reassigned its Faure rights to the Electrical Accumulator Company.[27] The long list of corporate name changes and realignments continued on and on.

The lawsuits attached to the companies were too numerous to casually catalog. For example, Electrical Accumulator Company and Brush both launched infringement suits against Julien Storage Battery. Then Electrical Accumulator Company and Brush both sued each other. Then Brush sued Milford and Hopedale Street Railroad Company. Eventually Brush sued ESB as well.[28] The roll call of litigants enlarged as time progressed.

By 1893, ESB's deficit had swelled to $128,000, its once-stellar credit line had faded to red, and all this bad news was offset by total battery sales of just $20,000. Under these conditions, all battery companies would fail. No one could afford the cost of victory or survive the rigors. Throughout 1894, hard-fought negotiations poppled between the litigants and investors. An all-conquering plan with a single victor finally ascended from the intractable contention. ESB would win, and win big, if it could muster the cash. Millions would be needed to simply buy everybody off. ESB stockholders donated half their 100,000 inflated shares back to the company to resell to attract new investment. The 50,000 shares retained by the founders were designated preferred shares with more worth and control. The newly available 50,000 shares were floated in a major common stock issue, attracting $3.5 million in new capital. With that leverage, ESB was able to secure a $450,000 bond issue. ESB's new war chest totaled $3.95 million.[29]

On December 15, 1894, wielding the power of its newly infused $3.95 million, ESB, in one massive prearranged maneuver, purchased approximately five hundred patents from a spectrum of battery companies, litigants, patent holders, estates, and heirs to estates as well as portfolio trustees all across the American electrical and battery landscape. By the end of that year, 1894, ESB owned it all and would soon control some 95 percent of the U.S. battery market. For the near road ahead, patent litigation was ended and progress was finally possible.[30]

Now the historic threads would come together in one tumultuous series of events that would set the future motive course for the industrialized world. The awesome potential of electrical power, the desire of mankind to burst through the doors of the twentieth century behind the wheel of an automobile, the centuries-long legacy of energy monopoly, the bold and the banked, those who drove and those who steered, the wrenching choice between clean speed and oily velocity—all these volatile threads tortuously wended into a Gordian knot that more than a century later is still waiting to be halved by Alexander's sword.

During the summer of 1894, Philadelphia's cobblestone streets echoed not only with the usual syncopation of clippity-clop horseshoes, but also with the unexpected rhythmic thudding of automobile tires. That dull beat of auto wheels was generated by the new Electrobat, an electric vehicle built by electrochemical engineer and battery specialist Pedro G. Salom and mechanical engineer Henry Morris. Since June 1894, the two men had been experimenting with a three-horsepower General Electric boat motor connected to chloride batteries. When the prototype was ready in August 1894, the first test drive down Broad Street required a special permit from City Hall as well as a mounted policeman riding ahead shooing easily spooked horses to the side. Curious passersby looked on with amazement. The horseless carriage that rolled down Broad Street weighed a hefty 4,200 pounds, due in no small part to the 1,600 pounds of lead batteries—a total of sixty heavy chloride accumulators—needed to propel the machine.[31] But this first cumbersome model merely presaged a new blossoming for electric vehicles.

Just as the men of United Gas Improvement Company had realized the future of electricity and foreseen the mass production of storage batteries at the close of the 1880s when they'd formed Electric Storage Battery Company, they also envisioned a future in which transit and travel would be battery-powered. Therefore, they were ready to give birth to yet another venture: this time, organizing the mass production of electric vehicles to bring America to motorized transportation.

A few years earlier, ESB had provided batteries to the Holtzer-Cabot electrical company, which had been commissioned by an affluent Bostonian to design an electrical vehicle. The resulting machine, dubbed the Electrobat, resembled a multibenched open stagecoach powered by ESB batteries connected to a motor that turned a chain that moved the wheels. This initial effort proved to ESB that the time for the mass production of battery-powered vehicles had finally come. The Electrobat was designed to be more compact and personal. In 1893, in anticipation of creating a major new market for its batteries and a major change for American society, ESB organized the Electric Vehicle Company.[32]

That next year, 1894, during extensive test drives down the streets of Philadelphia and through the boulevards of that city's gracious Fairmount Park, the Electrobat proved impressive for its mobility and reliability. The accrued distance of those test drives spanned several hundred miles. As usual, Gibbs wanted proof. Yes, the machine worked. But the forty-two-hundred-pound buggy was too heavy to be realistic. Just as battery-powered omnibuses and trolleys in Paris, London, New York, and Chicago were too laden with heavy lead batteries to be operated economically, the Electrobat would have to become sleeker and lighter to make popular sense.[33]

Weight was the bane of locomotion. Lead was heavy. Since the days of Plante's first lead battery in 1860, everyone understood that the inherent dead weight of the crucial metal—lead—proffered a challenge of physics, finance, and logistics.

At a convention of battery engineers in Philadelphia, one electrician candidly expounded to his colleagues, "Lead has some weight, as is well-known, and when you make a battery of sufficient size to last any length of time, you will have . . . enormous weight. For any other purposes than putting it down in the cellar, the weight is a great factor." He continued by rattling off some realistic numbers: a lead plate twelve inches square would weigh about six pounds, and therefore an array of eleven or so of these plates creating a single cell could weigh between sixty and seventy pounds. "If you want to use electromotive force," the electrical engineer concluded, "it would be fifty of those cells . . . about three thousand pounds."[34]

The sheer weight of a set of auto batteries in turn required heavier axles and heavier tires, both of which precipitated an attendant upward spiral of poundage that only required more batteries to power the load. Automotive engineers quickly discovered that as one weight problem was solved, others surged to the fore. Only persistent science and engineering could begin to solve the never-ending cavalcade of weight and materials problems facing automobile designers. But, importantly, the problems *were* solvable, as they were for any emerging technology.

Salom and Morris could be proud of their first contraption, but to make the car mass-producible they needed to solve the weight and bulk problems. That is exactly what they did—and quickly. In a real-world, nuts-and-bolts testament to how far battery-powered electric transportation could advance in a short time with some genuine science-based research and development, Salom and Morris within a single year constructed Electrobat II. They shrank everything. Then a coach maker reshaped and recast the entire assembly, creating not just a compact, working self-propelled device but an appealing and debonair horseless carriage. All the mechanisms were hidden and trimmed out, and the design lines were made sleek. The impressive new electric vehicle weighed just 1,650 pounds as compared to the original 4,200 pounds. Most importantly, Electrobat II carried only 160 pounds of batteries, one-tenth the burden of the first machine.[35] That was fast progress.

Electrobat II was immediately entered into the horseless-carriage race being staged that Thanksgiving 1895 along Chicago's lakefront by the *Chicago Times-Herald*. Publishers in America and Europe were among the main promoters of motoring. Racing events staged as publicity stunts became enormously successful forums to advertise the sponsoring newspapers and magazines.[36] These races of man-machine speed and endurance created wellsprings of motorcar advance and excitement, where the best and brightest, the great new successes as well as the dismal duds, all contended for the vehicular limelight, this to the echoing hurrah of an eager public and validating press coverage.

But that Thanksgiving, a sudden storm blanketed all of Chicagoland with a thick, wet snow cover. Of the numerous snowbound entrants in the

Chicago Times-Herald race—steam, gasoline, and electric—only six vehicles actually pulled up to the Jackson Park starting line. Many hard rubber tires, common for most cars of the day, sank right into the moist Chicago drifts. However, Salom and Morris's vehicle rode on thicker pneumatic tires capable of wheeling atop the snow rather than digging into it. Their design could actually move. The two men had prepositioned battery refills along the fifty-mile route and were hoping for a long-range triumph.[37]

But in fact, the Electrobat II ran out of power before it could get to one of the prepositioned batteries. Salom and Morris never finished the race. However, their spiffy vehicle did receive a gold medal for best design.[38] That in itself was a major vote of confidence. The industry was now abuzz over the Electrobat II. Big things were in store.

Over the next several months, Salom and Morris in tandem with ESB executives created a new enterprise, the Electric Carriage and Wagon Company. The firm was incorporated with a modest $300,000 in capitalization, headed by a board of directors dominated by ESB officials, led of course by Gibbs. By spring 1896, their revolutionary ideas went public. Electric Carriage and Wagon would mass-produce electric vehicles and offer them to New Yorkers as rentals, thus launching the general consumer automobile age. Initial plans called for a centralized "charging station," functioning as a garage where the batteries for these horseless carriages would be recharged and the overall vehicle maintained. The garage was patterned after the livery stable, but the facility would service vehicles instead of animals. Rental costs would be $1 per day, or $300 for the year, for either personal cars (the term "car" was short for "carriage") or commercial delivery wagons. After drivers became more acquainted with the operation and upkeep of these machines, and in the long run, after "the first one hundred machines" were produced, Electric Carriage and Wagon Company would sell them outright to individuals, launching a broad car-owning class. As electric vehicles and delivery wagons were adopted by the public, more charging stations and general recharging infrastructure would naturally follow, just as it had for the fast proliferation of electricity and illumination. Salom and Morris eventually intended to put electric cars and charging stations in every city of America.[39]

But Salom and Morris were hardly alone in the sudden new electric-vehicle race. The movement for electric vehicles had been building throughout the nineteenth century, and 1895 was a watershed year, culminating in that *Chicago Times-Herald* race. Several dozen electric-vehicle inventors had long been readying their engines along the emerging automotive roadway. Holtzer-Cabot of Boston, Sturges of Chicago, Barrows of Connecticut, Riker of New York, Dey of Rhode Island, Arnold of Chicago, Perry of St. Louis, Baker and Elberg of Kansas City, Thomson-Houston of Massachusetts, Columbia of Chicago—these were some of the designers, schemers, hardworking devotees, and irrepressible tinkerers hoping to lead the automotive vanguard into the world of tomorrow. Even Thomas Edison built himself an electric vehicle that year and concomitantly began trying to perfect a lightweight alternative to the lead battery.[40]

Indeed, more than thirty books on the subject of automobiles had been published before 1850, with dozens more seeing print in the subsequent half century. Numerous automotive periodicals on both sides of the Atlantic regularly covered the ins and outs and ups and downs of electric cars right alongside their reportage of steam and gasoline vehicle progress. One of these periodicals, *Horseless Age*, issued monthly and then twice monthly, was among the most active, bringing together inventors, enthusiasts, and suppliers, helping to drive a fast-growing industry. In this self-battling industry three main types of propulsion were constantly fighting for supremacy—steam, gasoline, and electric.[41]

Motoring excitement was international. Germany, France, and Belgium led the Continent in constructing automobiles of all three types. In 1895, England joined the movement in earnest. That next year, 1896, Britain finally repealed its infamous "red flag" laws that required a man on foot to race ahead of any motor vehicle, waving a red flag and blowing a horn warning all in its path. To horse and human both: Get out of the way—a dangerous vehicle approaches! The demise of these profoundly stunting laws was called Emancipation Day by the British motoring community and celebrated with cross-Atlantic jubilation and auto parades.[42]

Within the panoply of automobiles, the electric vehicles proffered the greatest promise for society, promising to undo a modern era of stink and soot, of noise and nuisance, and bestow the magical gift of clean, virtually soundless personal locomotion. The electric-vehicle vision for America and the world was almost utopian, especially when compared to the leading automotive alternative: petroleum-burning internal combustion.

Salom summarized it best in a much circulated essay originally provided to the *Journal of the Franklin Institute*. "The electrical vehicle is almost noiseless," he wrote. "It does not begin to make the noise that even a horse makes on a dirt road, while a gasoline vehicle must, perforce, make a continuous puffing noise, due to the exhaust from the motor, and this is not only disagreeable, but to some people alarming."[43] Indeed, gasoline cars, with their explosive backfires, had already caused numerous highly publicized accidents, many fatal, by spooking horses and cattle and igniting not a few fires when their sparking engines cruised past.

Naturally, the foul smell of gasoline cars compared to the odorless electric vehicle was another prime factor in considering propulsion systems. Salom wrote in his essay, "Of course, there is absolutely no odor connected with an electrical vehicle, while all the gasoline motors we have seen belch forth from their exhaust pipe a continuous stream of partially unconsumed hydrocarbon in the form of a thin smoke with a highly noxious odor. Imagine thousands of such vehicles on the streets, each offering up its column of smell as a sacrifice for having displaced the superannuated horse, and consider whether such a system has general utility or adaptability."[44]

Gasoline proponents argued back that their dirty, noisy, smoky machines were simply the latest obnoxious manifestation of progress. Indeed, in many ways, internal combustion devotees virtually defined "progress" as a progression of modern machines that were progressively more intrusive, noisome, filthy, and fouling. Petroleum advocates guessed that one day their machines would be more powerful and faster and offer more range than any electric competitor because of sheer weight, that is, the lead battery versus the gallon of gasoline. Quite simply, the tank of gasoline needed to propel an internal combustion machine was far lighter than the array of several dozen batteries needed to power an electric vehicle. The grimy bargain of range and speed in exchange for noise and filth, gasoline devotees insisted, was worth it—plain and simple.

Internal combustion pioneer Charles Duryea was typical of the "worse is better" mind-set when he argued against clean, silent-running electrical machines and in favor of noisy, polluting automobiles. Employing equal amounts of scorn and defensiveness, Duryea passionately defended his choice against all objections. "The history of almost every invention of importance," he wrote in an August 1896 column in *Horseless Age*, "is that in its earlier stages it is met with some of the most unreasonable objections, and the objectors lived long enough to see their objections forced down their throats."[45]

Duryea ticked off a few of the chief complaints, beginning with noise pollution. "Perhaps the most important objection is that of noise," he confirmed, but then parried, "Humanity is accustomed to noise and that noise is a requisite rather than an objection in the perfect vehicle. . . . If the article [an automobile] does the work, the people will accept it regardless of noise, danger or manageability. The railroad train is not a silent affair, it is a pandemonium of noise compared with the old stage coach on the dirt road, but where will you find stage coaches today running in opposition to a railroad? The steamship is not so quiet as the sailing vessel, and yet few passengers take passage for Europe except on a steam vessel. . . . If the [gas-propelled] motor wagon will accomplish its purpose of carrying its load where the load is to go, the public will accept it, regardless of whether it is noisier than the horse or not."[46]

Duryea moved to air pollution. "Time and again, the motor vehicle has been condemned," he conceded, "because it gives out a different odor than is given out by other things now in use, and being different it impresses the observer as very vile, and therefore certain to prevent the public use of the motor vehicle." He mockingly quoted a critic: " 'Imagine a street full of such vehicles! Why, you could not live in the same town!' observed one. . . . [But] it is also true," he answered, "that everybody rides behind locomotives which give out not only the products of combustion of coal, but sulphuric gases arising from impurities in the fuel, cinders, and specks of soot and coal blown out by the forced draft. They [passengers] do not revel in these objectionable features . . . but they patronize that method of travel and do not usually complain."[47]

Duryea's main point was "if Americans were to refuse to ride until better accommodations were afforded, the accommodations would be forthcoming in short order." Duryea continued his examples, insisting that from black-billowing industrial smokestacks to rumbling emissions of internal combustion, noise and filth were the hallmarks of progress.[48]

Petroleum engine advocates believed the great new society ahead would measure its greatness not in ergs that were clean and quiet but in muscular lifting achieved by increased decibels and ever more choking air. One front-page article in *Horseless Age* insisted, "Noise is inseparable from locomotion, and the higher the speed, as a rule, the greater the noise."[49] In other words, the rumble was a selling factor.

The proponents of electric vehicles believed the opposite. In their minds, the real mark of progress was an automotive future that subtracted the cacophonous environment, the mucky streets, and the poisoned air while bestowing upon humanity a new tradition of clean and silent running.

Mechanized electricity loomed over the century's horizon, restive and waiting to be unleashed as soon as the world was truly ready. Advocates understood that electric vehicles would improve. Batteries would become lighter, drive farther and faster, and the coming infrastructure of charging stations would yield great range. Thus, the electric vehicle would be able to outperform any internal combustion competitor. But few in the public had confidence that big business could be trusted to devote the science required. Gas-driven internal combustion vehicles, on the other hand, were handcrafted by dashing, grease-smeared mavericks, rugged individualists, all devoted to making cars perform better for the sole sake of betterment, exuding and exemplifying the American spirit of independence. It was them against the elements in their flamboyant, rackety machines. Internal combustion advocates were counting on the charisma of their craft and the corruption of their competitors to win the automotive sweepstakes.

Beyond the noisome aspects of the internal combustion machine, the recurring question of oil shortages bedeviled automobile enthusiasts and the general public. Since commercial oil was discovered in Titusville, Pennsylvania, in 1859, America had reigned as the world's leading oil producer. Oil—drilling, refining, and distribution—was in the hands of dishonest, monopolistic businessmen such as John D. Rockefeller and his combine of Standard Oil companies. Highly publicized oil shortages and gluts, real and manipulated, calculated to scare and to scam, were regular occurrences. In some cases, oil boomtowns, such as the famous Pithole, Pennsylvania, gusher region, suddenly went dry, creating an oil scarcity. Just as often, a fuel drought was created for the sole purpose of inflating the price of kerosene or petroleum. Thus, even as electric vehicles were agitating for primacy over petroleum-propelled cars, a front-page article in *Horseless Age* tried to reassure motoring devotees not to fear the latest "oil famine." The publication acknowledged the belief by some "that if this fuel [petroleum] comes into general use for vehicle propulsion, we shall sooner or later be brought face to face with an oil famine" because eight million tons of the substance were drilled that year with the number ever increasing. No one knew for sure whether any oil shortage was real or connived.[50]

The whole idea was dismissed by *Horseless Age* with the following words: "If in the distant future, the natural sources of the hydrocarbon should become exhausted, artificial means may very likely be resorted to to meet the wants of civilization. . . . As to future generations, we can safely trust them to settle their own difficulties and satisfy their own wants."[51]

Now society, in 1896, would travel toward one of many forks in the road. Which would it choose: electric or petroleum? Clean or clang? Big-business transportation moguls or fearless, homegrown auto challengers?

The tortuous answer started to come together late in 1896. In September of that year, Electric Carriage and Wagon promised the public that within about sixty days the first electric vehicles for hire would hit the streets of New York and Philadelphia. They would possess a range of twenty-five miles per charge, which was perfect for city driving. The first two advertised models were a stylish coupe and a hansom resembling the finest carriages of Boston or London, boasting a classy enclosed cab made of fine woods and leathers. The driver's perch was positioned up high where the horse-reining coachman normally sat—except there was no coachman holding reins, merely a chauffeur steering a tiller.[52]

By January 1897, Electric Carriage and Wagon's much vaunted central recharging station opened on Thirty-ninth Street in Manhattan, to service the first of fourteen electric cabs. By late March, the full complement was rolling through the streets of Manhattan, mainly responding to calls from partygoers, theater patrons, and the usual taxied crowd. These fine gentlemen and their ladies, even while dressed in chic finery, were accustomed to the piercing smell of the horse's hind end as they elegantly rode just a few feet back in the carriage. But these new vehicles provided odorless, smooth-running rides that quickly became de rigueur. The idea, whose time had come, was catching on. Similar operations, run by calculating financiers and industrialists, and not a few swindlers, began sprouting in Chicago, London, Paris, Madrid, Berlin, and other cities.[53]

But none of the also-rans projected the science-based vision of Salom and Morris and their Electric Carriage and Wagon Company. The company worked to laminate economies of scale and sense to good electromotive mechanics. A central garage crew of only six, and that included a washer, was all the staff needed to keep the dozen or so cabs humming seven days each week. Using specially constructed garage cranes, slightly elevated auto rails, and removable vehicle trays, batteries could be swapped out by a single mechanic in just seventy-five seconds. Spent batteries were then mechanically shuttled to the recharging room for the overnight refresh. Cruising at speeds of 10 to 20 mph, each taxicab covered some eleven city miles per day. In constant use, the small fleet transported approximately a thousand passengers monthly over a rough average of about one thousand miles per week. Accidents and mishaps occurred only once every 360 miles, but this number diminished as drivers gained more experience with the new machines.[54]

On August 3, 1897, Electric Carriage and Wagon Company advertised that it would add an additional hundred electric vehicles within the next month. Sales to private individuals had been promised after that first one-hundred-vehicle threshold. Additional central generating stations and battery replacement sites were planned for "every large city in the Union where a private individual who desires a carriage can have it properly charged and cared for." Moreover, thought had also been given to the installation of "electrical hydrants" throughout the city, to recharge parked vehicles. Intended to be as common as a policeman's call box or a horse hitching post, these "electrical hydrants" were to be positioned curbside to recharge batteries while vehicles were parked. Hence an urban infrastructure of electric recharging was planned to accompany the growing network of lampposts, fire hydrants, telephone lines, and other utilities. After New York and Philadelphia, other cities were slated for an electrified auto infrastructure.[55]

What's more, research and field experience on the streets of New York were continuously driving the evolution of both the battery and electric vehicle into lighter, more agile, more economically feasible propositions. The public and the profession were taking notice. As men of science and engineering first and businesspeople second, Salom and Morris studiously labored at improving their base before expanding. The public loved the whole idea and kept every taxi busy every day.

Even trade publications that had previously excoriated storage batteries and their scandalous promotion bestowed kudos upon Electric Carriage and Wagon Company. "It is very evident to the average observer," editorialized the New York edition of *Electrical World* in August 1897, "that the so-called horseless carriage is looming up as an important factor in the urban transportation problem. Animal power for the propulsion of street cars has been almost entirely superseded, in this country at least, by electromechanical power and the horse seems to be threatened with further degradation by the substitution of like power for the propulsion of wagons and other vehicles in city streets. In this city, a company [Electric Carriage and Wagon Company] has taken the matter up in earnest and is giving the public an electric cab and carriage service which for its reliability and comparative perfection is justly entitled to the support and admiration of all lovers of progress and enterprise."[56]

Electrical World continued its praise, "[It] is indeed remarkable and reflects great credit upon the promoters for their foresight; upon the engineers for their skill in solving all the problems involved in the development of this industry; and upon the managers for the excellence of the service rendered to the public. There is every reason to believe that the electric vehicle industry is well established on a sure foundation and that it will grow rapidly, especially in the estimation of the public, without which support no enterprise of a semi-public nature could long exist."[57]

Imitators loomed across the country—from Boston to Los Angeles—as engineers and craftsmen polished their plans. The electrical automotive revolution was about to leap onto the American scene.

But within days of those starry-eyed August 1897 announcements, Electric Carriage and Wagon Company suddenly ceased to exist. Salom and Morris simply faded into the background, absorbed into the white haze of history. Their partner, Electric Storage Battery Company, whose key officials sat on Salom and Morris's board, decided it was time to simply swallow Electric Carriage and Wagon Company. The firm was folded into ESB's Electric Vehicle Company, the entity that had been incorporated by ESB three years earlier. Electric Carriage and Wagon Company's fourteen taxicabs, its central station, the plans, the goodwill, and everything else were either purchased outright or seized.[58] After all, ESB was the leading creditor. The parent company had provided the batteries and key financing. Indeed, ESB officials controlled the all-important batteries that made any electric-vehicle enterprise viable. ESB executives held the power over their power.

With little delay, ESB began the swift selling of Electric Vehicle Company stock to a bevy of eager investors. By September 8, the company's stock rolls were oversubscribed.[59] But more stock money was to be made.

On September 27, 1897, ESB officials reincorporated their Electric Vehicle Company, this time in New Jersey with a capitalization of $10 million, half of it preferred stock, half of it common. By this time, ESB's Gibbs had been forced out of the company presidency and replaced by German-born financier Isaac Rice. Rice had given up the academic life at Columbia University to become a railroad attorney. His legal maneuvers on behalf of monopolistic railroad trusts had made him a wealthy man. Now, he had elevated himself to president of the target Electric Carriage and Wagon in time to ensure that the young taxi company was "taken over," as Rice termed it.[60]

As Electric Vehicle Company's new president, Rice displaced Gibbs. However, Gibbs was retained on EVC's board, thus ensuring passage of any vote Rice needed. Rice then began issuing grandiose promises about new taxi service and battery sales. He promised to expand the New York fleet by as many as two hundred new electric taxis. This immediately boosted the company's stock value, stock he personally owned. Self-trading between ESB and EVC meant that the Electric Storage Battery Company could inflate its sales accounts at will. As the left arm of the company ordered batteries as an expense, the right arm theoretically provided them at a profit. Without any batteries actually being produced, the self-generated orders continued to boost the company's stock. Yet despite the hype and promises, EVC continued to field the same twelve to fourteen taxis throughout the fall and winter of 1897.[61] Indeed, who would even manufacture those two hundred vehicles? At the time, mass production of vehicles was nonexistent.

Then came the snows. That winter was an icy nightmare. In city after city across America, all the appurtenances of progress froze, mired amidst the white drifts of blizzards, ice storms, and deep freezes. Neither beasts of burden, nor the trolleys and trains that were rapidly replacing them, could move through the devastating weather of January and February 1898. For some cities, the snowstorms were the worst in a decade. For many, the worst in half a century. For some, the worst on record.[62]

Pittsburgh, January 1: Ten inches fell in ten hours. Recently erected phone and electric lines came crashing down, electrocuting both horses and the humans who rode them. Syracuse, January 1: The New York Central and West Shore railroads were stalled in massive drifts. Gangs of workmen shoveling all night were unable to free the trains. Boston, January 2: Nor'easters gripped the city. Nothing moved. Chicago, January 23: 40 mph winds blasted the city and suburbs, dropping dense snow, halting foot traffic, and strangling all electric trains and trolleys. Horse after horse, pulling wagons, trudged right into downed live wires, electrical nooses that killed them instantly and jolted their drivers into trauma. Most pedestrians could barely walk through the whiteout. The *Chicago Tribune* bemoaned "the demoralization" felt by a paralyzed city. Boston, January 24: With no letup, blizzards continued to sock the city, crippling all surface transportation. *The Boston Globe*, like newspapers in other cities, called the weather assault "demoralizing." Milwaukee, January 24: Railroad engines huffed to a halt amid a monster storm with punishing 50 mph winds. More than 120 passengers were trapped in one frigid railway coach for twelve hours.[63]

East to west, railroad trains collided and derailed, snowfalls of more than twenty inches were recorded, and downed wires electrocuted horses and set fiery blazes that firemen were powerless to extinguish. The term "demoralizing" became the headline buzzword of the moment for a society proud of its recent technological advances, but now faced with the grim reality of man's vulnerability.[64]

From gadgets they hoped for greatness. But nature foiled the gadgets and brought them low—this time with wrathful snow.

February 1, 1898, 3:00 A.M. Merciless snowstorms raged into Manhattan from the north, where the sky had already dumped more than three feet of snow. For twenty-four hours the blizzard continued relentlessly. This new snowfall only added to January's heavy accumulations. With the dense shroud of snow came the stunning quiet of a great clanging city eerily placed on pause. High-powered snowplows could not penetrate New York's clogged streets. Most buses and trains were completely incapacitated. One train from Boston finally crept into Grand Central Station fifteen hours late. Hotels filled up at once, so stranded women and children were ushered against the white winds to the nearest hospitals. By morning, business had come to a standstill. An army of 4,000 groaning laborers struggling with 2,500 pushcarts made little or no progress digging out. Every shovelful of clearance was quickly nullified by the incessant snowfall.[65]

But then Manhattan witnessed what could only have been perceived as a miracle of motion. Even as horse-drawn vehicles proved worthless, even as the trains and trolleys squatted stolid and snow-locked, even as thousands of shoveling men found themselves frustrated by the power of nature, the city watched with wide-eyed amazement as EVC's fourteen electric vehicles energetically, almost arrogantly, glided back and forth across the cityscape—not along the streets but atop the sidewalks. Rice had received police permission to run his electric taxis on the sidewalks, which were the first surfaces to be cleared.[66]

The city could move again, and it was electric vehicles that could move it.

Newspapers and word of mouth marveled at EVC's cars. Those thick tires, which had proved their mettle in Chicago's massive snowfall during the 1895 Thanksgiving Day race, worked again. EVC's feat was not just a stunt; it proved to the nation that once the snows receded, a brilliant new age of electric transportation would be revealed.[67]

Seizing the frigid moment, Rice repeated—and many now heard it for the first time—that two hundred additional taxis would immediately be added to the thoroughfares of Manhattan.[68] The nation was watching.

But so was Whitney.

Who was Whitney? Scion of a powerful and wealthy family, William C. Whitney made the obligatory trek through Yale, where he entered the secret Skull and Bones Society, known for its kings and kingmakers, and then enrolled in Harvard Law School. Whitney first came to prominence as New York's pugilistic corporation counsel from 1875 to 1882, when he successfully fought millions of dollars in fraudulent claims by the political gangster William Marcy "Boss" Tweed. Later, as a major backer of Grover Cleveland's presidency, Whitney was appointed secretary of the navy. In that position, the slim, clean-shaven, and studious-looking Whitney applied his business acumen to help create the modern U.S. navy. Talk of a presidential run by Whitney was silenced when he abruptly left public life. In the private sector, he devoted his energies to financing transportation systems, especially in and around New York. Whitney's Metropolitan Traction Company (MTC) was actually organized in February 1886 as a holding company while he was still secretary of the navy. As soon as Whitney left government, MTC went into action, launching a sequence of pyramid schemes and stock manipulations, as well as quiet and public takeovers of urban railroads. Eventually a local transit dynasty arose.[69]

Beginning in June 1886, Whitney began devouring: the Broadway and Seventh Avenue Railroad, valued at $2.1 million; the Houston Street, West Street & Pavonia Ferry Railroad; the Chambers & Grand Ferry Railroad; the South Ferry Railroad; the 23rd Street Railway Company; the Metropolitan Crosstown Railway Company; and after that many more. If Whitney wanted the line, he took it. Assaulting openly at times, or sometimes through nominees, trusts, and surrogates, the street lines, traction companies, and cable systems fell like dominoes to his merger and acquisition crusade. His takeover maneuvers and syndicates brought him in and out of a circle of elite financiers that included the Carnegies, the Vanderbilts, the Fricks, the Astors, and the Morgans. Whitney was a man-about-town. His philanthropic mark was made on the Metropolitan Opera, the American Museum of Natural History, the Metropolitan Museum of Art, and the other redeeming cultural diversions available to robber barons, the rich, and the powerful.[70]

Unbeknownst to many, among MTC's first flexions was a takeover of the Electric Storage Battery Company. That was natural since many transportation lines depended, or might one day depend upon onboard storage batteries for electromotive power. Nineteenth-century monopolists always preferred to control anything that touched their industry. Whitney quietly purchased $1,092,747 in Electric Storage Battery Company stock, thus seizing a controlling interest in the firm that also owned EVC. Now it was time to conquer Rice. The battle for the command of EVC had been under way for some months before the Great Blizzard of 1898. But with the stellar snow performance of those peppy electric vehicles, Whitney's syndicate was willing to wait no more. The next century was waiting to be controlled, and everyone wanted an early start.[71]

Rice, however, was not eager to relinquish the helm. EVC's stock was trading at $20 per share when Whitney began the takeover. But stubborn Rice refused to sell his substantial shares. Whitney increased the offer. Rice refused. As Whitney's stock raiding and interest in EVC became apparent, the market followed suit, and the price of EVC shares doubled to $40. Whitney increased the offer. Rice refused. The stock doubled again to $80. Whitney increased the offer. Rice refused. The stock pushed past $120. John Jacob Astor and his family were among those that joined the bidding. Rice still refused.[72]

Whitney was determined. Finally, Rice was swayed enough to make Whitney an offer: $141. But the price had been $20! Even now after the frenzied bidding up of shares, the price was topping off at between $100 and $120. "Take it or leave it," Rice told Whitney.[73]

Whitney took it.[74]

He now controlled EVC, and a launchpad of the future. Whitney's scheme called for the creation of a national network of giant transportation monopolies: Chicago, Boston, Philadelphia, and eventually worldwide. Whitney would control it all: the electric vehicles, the batteries, the routes—and of course they would all interconnect with his growing network of urban and regional railways. Electric delivery trucks and sales to individuals were also planned. The new behemoth combine was to be capitalized at $200 million.[75]

Soon, Whitney's associates, including John Jacob Astor, had supplanted Rice's associates on the board, and Rice was ousted as president. By this time the stock had tumbled from $120 back to $20, so small shareholders who'd bought during the updraft began to feel the sting. Nonetheless, the public and the profession were becoming excited about the whole idea of electric transportation.[76]

By February 1899, EVC opened a second garage, thus extending the range of EVC's cab fleet. Whereas EVC had only employed 7,500 battery plates in 1897, by now the company was using 46,000 per year. Lead processing increased from 5.1 million pounds in 1898 to 16.2 million pounds in 1899. Boldly bettering the prior promise of 200 vehicles as the next step for New York, Whitney now promised 1,500 taxis for Manhattan. He promised 15,000 vehicles nationwide. Edison Electric Illuminating Company engineer John Van Vleck created the much anticipated electrical hydrants to be installed curbside right along with fire hydrants. These would recharge vehicles while they were parked on city streets. General Electric produced a commercial version, dubbed the Electrant, to cheaply dispense charges of 2.5 kilowatt hours of electricity for a mere twenty-five cents. Resembling a parking meter, a chest-high box contained wires and a connection to the same electrical grid that powered the rest of the city. GE was merely waiting to install them in every city.[77]

In April 1899, the famous auto racer Camille Jenatzy set a new land-speed record at heroic speed trials staged on the outskirts of Paris.* Jenatzy, known as the Red Devil, and his shiny bullet-shaped speedster, nicknamed *La Jamais Contente*, became the first to break the mile-per-minute record. Challenging the wind and notions of human endurance, he accelerated to 65.8 mph in a vehicle with no windshield. In so doing, he captured the imagination of the entire motoring world, proving that clean electric vehicles were a silent and powerful solution to man's automotive quest.[78]

Just one problem remained: Who was going to produce thousands of electric vehicles? Up to that point, all cars were handcrafted one at a time. Where would 15,000 electric vehicles come from? Where would 1,500 come from? Where would even the first 200 come from? Only one industry could make the mass production of electric vehicles a reality. It would not be the carriage makers, trolley mechanics, or the automotive geniuses. Whitney sought out Colonel Albert Augustus Pope, the man who controlled the manufacture of nearly all the bicycles in America, the man who had created a vast monopoly out of the two-wheel bicycle.

Who was Albert Pope? In the era of trusts, where even the simplest products and commodities were suctioned into iron-fisted cartels and monopolies, Albert Pope of Hartford, Connecticut, and his Columbia Manufacturing Company applied conquest business principles to the simple bicycle. For his success, he was despised by bicycle enthusiasts everywhere. At the turn of the century, *Bicycling World* summarized his vicious grip on the industry this way: "In the position of a Czar . . . Pope was largely hated and the Columbia bicycle was called the 'monopoly machine.'"[79]

Bicycles had appeared on the American scene in approximately 1868 as an exciting new technology that propelled man against the wind

---

*To read the expanded version of Camille Jenatzy's race into the speed history books, see the excerpt at www.internalcombustionbook.com.

in ways that horses could not. Although primitive two-wheeled contraptions had existed for decades, it was the French velocipede, justly nicknamed the boneshaker, that first caught popular fire. A successor version featured a profoundly large front wheel and a tiny rear wheel. It was considered too dangerous to operate in civilized horse-drawn society; cities around the nation, including New York, passed ordinances restricting or banning two-wheelers.[80]

Pope was a Civil War captain turned ruthless tycoon who enjoyed being called Colonel. No one was certain why Pope insisted on being addressed with the higher rank. The promotion may have been an honorary brevet, or it may have been self-awarded. In 1876, the feisty Pope founded a small production and assembly enterprise called Columbia Manufacturing Company in Hartford. Shortly thereafter, he rolled out an improved and more intelligently designed two-wheeler that would come to be recognized as the modern bicycle. By 1890, Columbia had sold sixty thousand bicycles across the country and dominated as the prevailing standard in the immensely popular bicycle business.[81]

Pope's specialty was unifying the entire manufacturing process, from raw materials to assembly. Interchangeability of parts, not custom crafting, was the key. Pope owned his own metallurgy lab and fabricated his own frame tubes, drop forgings, axles, and sprocket chains. He acquired a rubber company to make the tires and contracted with the Weed Sewing Machine Company to use its excess capacity to manufacture the bicycles. Eventually, Weed Sewing Machine was also acquired, completing the circle of expansion. By 1895, Columbia, through its many Hartford-based subsidiaries and controlled entities, employed as many as thirty-five hundred workers in a complex of riverside factories. Columbia produced a good product, built economically. Their well-crafted bicycles cost about $25 to manufacture, yet retailed for $125. Vast profits streamed in.[82]

But beyond mass production techniques and a sharp eye for technological advance, Pope's greatest business asset was a battalion of mean-spirited lawyers who sued and sued and sued to intimidate competitors, shop owners, and even average Americans who might want to purchase any bicycle other than a Columbia without obtaining its license. In 1895, some eight hundred thousand American bicycles were produced, and within two years the volume rose to about a million units. Although Columbia's models were the leading bicycles, the grassroots bicycle business had spawned some five hundred minor producers.[83]

Building a better bicycle became a great American avocation. Better pedals, more comfortable seats, stronger frames, and an easier drive—the endless tweaks and improvements were only natural. But being the leading bicycle manufacturer was not enough for Pope. He wanted it all.

He began in the late 1870s by buying up key underlying French and American patents. With those patents in hand, Pope was able to create a litigation machine against all comers. In June 1879, he threatened virtually every bicycle maker in the nation, demanding a royalty, or he would force them out of business. Within weeks, the first two bicycle makers fell into line. While the royalties paid might seem minimal, one to two dollars depending upon model, the restrictive covenants were calculated to stifle competition and silence any critics. These included strict limitations on bicycle design, wheel size, mandatory tributes, a seemingly never-ending renewal obligation, and an onerous forfeiture of license in the event the agreement was even disputed. Soon other bicycle makers agreed that it was better to comply with Pope's extortionate royalty demand than wade into a costly court battle.[84]

Those who dared to stand up to Pope soon learned the quality of his vengeance, a fire that could angrily burn for years. For example, McKee & Harrington brought out a new design without paying Columbia because they viewed his patent demands as outrageous. In September 1880, he secured a court injunction against them, and that was only the beginning. Two years later, in the midst of an appeal, Pope's attorneys convinced the judge to hold McKee & Harrington in contempt for violating the original order. Finally, McKee & Harrington contacted Pope's lawyers to surrender. After paying back royalties, the owners agreed to quit bicycle making altogether. Shortly thereafter, in an embittered moment, McKee & Harrington publicly denounced Pope's patents as worthless and admitted they gave up the business merely to avoid endless litigation—for that reason and none other.[85]

Nonetheless, more lawsuits were launched. But in October 1881, the U.S. Supreme Court rejected Pope's patents as valueless and unenforceable. No matter, that did not stop Pope from even more patent acquisitions to shore up his assaults, and a wave of fresh lawsuits. In one case, he sued the Overman Company for $50,000 on the mere rumor the firm might bring out a bicycle six months later. Columbia attorneys later added Overman's suppliers as defendants and even filed papers against the suppliers' real estate. One recipient of several threatening letters from Columbia protested that Pope was trying to "bulldoze me" and "leave me crippled."

Pope's attorney wrote back superciliously that it is better to settle and therefore "not be so much afraid of our wishing or trying to cripple you."[86]

One licensee, R. Phillip Gormully, refused to make a cash contribution demanded by Pope to support a so-called industry fund. Gormully had already paid $27,000. Fed up, he declared in plain words, "They wish to extort money from me." In short order, he was sued in federal court. But in 1892, the U.S. Supreme Court threw out that entire license agreement as being unconscionable and unenforceable, denigrating it as "an artfully constructed snare to bind the defendant in a manner which he did not contemplate." The court added, "This contract seems to be so oppressive, and so unjust and inequitable in its terms, and so contrary to public policy that it ought not to be enforced."[87]

The bicycle patent warring did not stop with manufacturers. Shopkeepers who dared sell competitor's bicycles were threatened or their retail franchise canceled. Ordinary consumers who merely wanted to personally purchase a bicycle not licensed by Pope were widely warned that the penalty was a bitter lawsuit. To bolster his grip, Pope took a financial stake in various bicycle publications and established his own cycling organizations, this to control the very mind-set of those who wanted to pedal down the street on a two-wheeler. By Pope's thinking, Columbia-built or -licensed bicycles were the only permissible bicycles.[88]

Whitney and Pope were a perfect match.

But it was more than a genius for monopoly and manufacturing that made Pope the only man capable of bringing EVC's grand schemes to fruition. Foreseeing the end of the wildfire bicycle craze and the coming era of automobiling, Columbia had jump-started into the field of motorized vehicles. Pope's point man for the automobile was Hiram Percy Maxim. Maxim was the son of Hiram Stevens Maxim, inventor of the machine gun. The senior Maxim was visiting the 1881 Paris Electrical Exhibition when someone told him, "If you wanted to make a lot of money, invent something that will enable these Europeans to cut each other's throats with greater facility." Maxim did. His machine gun fired 666 rounds per minute and forever changed warfare. When the senior Maxim met with the czar to sell him the killing machines, a Russian police officer asked, "What is your religion?" The senior Maxim retorted, "I never had need of one." It was said that half the Japanese killed in the Russo-Japanese conflicts were cut down with Maxim's invention.[89]

As an inventor and engineer, the young Hiram Percy Maxim could not help but bring his father's credentials and coattails to Pope when he was hired as chief engineer of the new Columbia Motor Carriage Department. In fact, Maxim later invented the pistol silencer to continue the family legacy. By the time Maxim was hired, he had already dabbled with a gasoline-powered tricycle. In 1895, Maxim officiated at Chicago's Thanksgiving Day auto race and was responsible for granting an award to Salom and Morris for the Electrobat II. As soon as he returned to Hartford, he began the design of an electric vehicle for Columbia, journeying to Philadelphia to purchase specially designed batteries from Gibbs at ESB. Maxim's Mark I prototype was first test-driven in late 1896. On May 13, 1897, Pope's first ten horseless carriages were unveiled to an excited gathering of social and engineering luminaries.[90]

Columbia began producing additional units in assembly-line fashion, averaging about a dozen cars per month. Hence, Columbia now stood out as the largest, most industrialized and streamlined of the many automakers hoping to succeed. But still there existed no real market for the vehicles. Good roads for motoring did not exist. Cars were compelled to drive along the muddy, wagon-wheel-rutted, dung-mucked trails and thoroughfares maintained almost exclusively for horses. Axles and frames commonly broke, and not infrequently a horse would be needed to tow the vehicle to the nearest stable. Indeed, many of Columbia's cars were sent overseas to Europe's aristocratic market. The mere purchase of any car—electric, steam, or gas driven—was cause for a society headline as a special accomplishment. That was not a mass market.[91]

Whitney's late-1898 offer to purchase two hundred vehicles was the first real spark igniting the mass production of cars. Frankly, Pope needed the EVC. Bicycles had more than peaked by 1899.[92] Pope knew that it was only a matter of time until the behemoth bicycle cartel would completely be supplanted by modern technological advances, including urban transit systems, trains, automobiles, and the other modes of group and individual transportation.

But even two hundred vehicles were vastly more than the capacity of Pope to quickly fulfill. Columbia would need to tool up, acquire components, and create a mass-production operation. Negotiations between Whitney's syndicate and Pope's people began in late 1898 during the height of the battle for command of EVC. Ideas of expanding the purchase order to more than a thousand were already floating. A conference was set for April 17, 1899, in Hartford. Whitney and four others, including attorneys, traveled up to Hartford by train and were met at the station, where they were driven to the Columbia plant by traditional horse-drawn carriage. Waiting for them was a magnificent lunch on the top floor of an office building next to the factory on Capitol Avenue. In attendance were Pope, Maxim, and key members of the Columbia production and engineering team.[93]

Whitney laid out his vision of a national interlocking group of monopolies on automobiles—all electric, all manufactured by Pope, all over the nation. This initial order for 1,600 vehicles would only be the beginning. Maxim later recalled Whitney's presentation: "The scheme was a very broad one," wrote Maxim, "promising all manner of possibilities in the way of stock manipulation. Whether it was intended to develop profits out of the earned dividends, or by unloading the stock on the public, I will not venture to guess. In those days of wild finance, unloading upon the public was very fashionable."[94]

It was never about the triumph of technology, it was never about the treasure of transportation; it was always about the money.

The gentlemen talked brass tacks. Pope required a million dollars to expand plant facilities, tool up, and hire the engineers and factory workers needed to efficiently mass-produce thousands of vehicles. Where would that money come from? After a thorough exchange, a proposal was made. The great conglomerates—the battery cartel, the transportation cartel, and the bicycle cartel—would combine to create a new megatrust to be capitalized at the envisioned $200 million.[95]

In truth, the new entity would pull together only $3 million: $1 million in physical assets, trademarks, and patents from Columbia's Motor Vehicle Division. The second million would be contributed by the physical assets, trademarks, and patents of the Electric Vehicle Company. The third million would be cold cash to tool up Pope's factories and drive the enterprise.[96]

But where would the pivotal million in cash come from?

Whitney agreed to provide it. Moments later, one of Pope's lieutenants, Harold Hayden Eames, burst into an adjacent office where anxious executives awaited the outcome of the momentous discussion. Ecstatic, Eames shouted, "We get the million dollars"—the office erupted in jubilation. Then Eames finished his sentence—"and must contact that man Selden."[97] Nothing could be done without a hitherto unheard-of man from Rochester named Selden.

Selden? Who on earth was Selden?

CHAPTER SIX

THE SELDEN STRATEGY

Trusts are like viruses. They mutate and sometimes jump species.

In April 1899, the ESB battery trust and the Pope bicycle trust combined and mutated into a voracious new cartel, the electric vehicle trust. The brash new electric vehicle trust was prepared to stop or impede all in its path, including the independent makers of gasoline automobiles—at a time when they occupied a mere minority niche in automobiling. Then, abruptly, the electric vehicle trust jumped species; that is, it joined its own sworn gasoline-based opposition to create a pernicious new monopoly that would fan the flames of internal combustion until they set an entire nation enthusiastically ablaze.

True, that April 17, 1899, in Hartford, the massive new electric vehicle trust created the monopolistic means for an expanded EVC to develop, distribute, and dominate electric vehicles, and concomitantly to build an electrified infrastructure to conveniently recharge vehicles curbside and in central stations. True, the EVC's hope was to extend that same clean motive power—electricity—to other forms of commercial, passenger, and military transportation. True, this automotive path would change the nation and the world. True, all Whitney, Pope, and their cohorts demanded in return was to become more fabulously wealthy than they already were.

But the grittier truth revealed that Whitney, Pope, and the other financiers were not genuinely interested in dominating and proliferating clean, electric transportation per se. They wanted to dominate *all* transportation and delivery—whether accomplished by electric, steam, or gasoline vehicles. Money, profit, and opportunism—not good technology—would determine the trust's allegiance. As such, the soaring potential of electric vehicles that beckoned at the great door of the twentieth century was a technological marvel that became subordinated to the avaricious winds of the EVC's financial manipulation. All too quickly, those winds became unfavorable for electric.

History thus records that the electric vehicle was sabotaged not by its competitors but by its custodians, that is, the Electric Vehicle Company and its recombinant corporate alter egos. Through a maze of subsidiaries, allied corporations, and stock offerings, the trust contorted and shape-shifted in pursuit of instant profits and corrupt pyramid schemes. Abandoned was the imperative of developing clean technology for the benefit of mankind. These businessmen had the power in the palm of their hands and allowed it to seep into oblivion not for lack of grip, but because they washed their hands of the better idea in favor of the types of financial tricks that had plagued batteries since their inception.

However, all schemes—electric or combustible—depended upon a virtually unknown and hardly innovative Rochester man, a man whose shadowy abuse of the system would suddenly emerge as the blinding and controlling beacon of the motoring industry. Whitney and Pope needed George B. Selden.

Twentieth-century automotive history was cast that day, April 17, 1899, at the Hartford conclave that gave birth to the new electric vehicle trust. Within forty-eight hours, the corporate prestidigitation began. On April 19, 1899, Whitney and Pope incorporated the Columbia Automobile Company, owned fifty-fifty by Pope's Columbia combine and Whitney's Electric Vehicle Company. On May 3, that new company merged into its 50 percent parent company, EVC, and was renamed the Columbia and Electric Vehicle Company. To boost the sales figures of EVC's parent company, Electric Storage Battery Company, the renamed electric vehicle division purchased its batteries at a highly discounted 20 percent above normal cost, thus inflating the stock value of Electric Storage Battery Company. In truth, however, behind the growth lay substandard intracompany revenues that only weakened the entire enterprise even as the stock soared.[1]

Quickly, additional subsidiaries and allied companies were created where they did not exist and absorbed where they did already exist. For example, the New York Electric Vehicle Transportation was newly incorporated to operate Manhattan's electric taxis, making sure they fed passengers into Whitney's rail systems. The Illinois Electric Vehicle Transportation was newly incorporated to deploy Chicago's fleet. The Pennsylvania Electric Vehicle Transportation was newly incorporated to run Philadelphia's cabs. The New England Electric Vehicle Transportation was newly incorporated to run the electric cabs in Boston. Several existing independent firms were consumed to complete the package. The well-established Siemens & Halske Electric Company in Chicago was purchased for local automobile assembly. The up-and-coming Riker Motor Vehicle Company of Elizabethtown, New Jersey, was purchased to eliminate competition; after its acquisition, Riker's patents were absorbed and the company was put asunder.[2] More companies were created, bought up, or dismantled as needed.

Even as the electric vehicle empire was being constructed, Whitney and Pope understood all too well that their new conglomerate would eventually produce internal combustion machines. Pope, who had seen the bicycle craze shrivel before his very eyes, would not bet on a single technology, including electric. His firm was already producing gasoline vehicles for a small, elite clientele, mainly overseas. But during the near term, as electric vehicle stocks were being promoted and hyperinflated, the EVC combine wanted to thwart the expansion of promising internal combustion machines, which would only distract from investor confidence in the electric vehicle.[3] Before committing to their new multimillion-dollar venture, both Whitney and Pope wanted to certify their ability to overcome any challenge to the auto monopoly they envisioned.

Therefore, that April 17, 1899, in Hartford, the subject of troublesome patents came up. Both Whitney and Pope extensively employed patent combat as a weapon in their wealth wars. Thus, the topic was always under consideration. Pope's chief patent engineer, Hermann Cuntz, was aware of a little-known and highly questionable patent that could threaten, or control, the entire automobile industry. The patent, which began life as a near worthless application in 1879, wound its way through the cavernous Patent Office for sixteen years before finally being granted to George B. Selden in November 1895. At the time, few if any took notice, especially the pioneers of internal combustion, who were so busily building their marvelous contraptions one at a time with little economic consequence.[4]

However, Cuntz, a patent aficionado, had feared the Selden patent for years. Although his superiors ignored his warnings, Cuntz dutifully investigated the Selden patent almost as soon as it was granted in 1895. Realizing that while his own company was then manufacturing just a few gasoline cars, he also knew his employer could be sued if production were ramped up and the stakes were raised.[5]

The stakes were now raised. Cuntz was ready.

During the crucial luncheon with Pope, Whitney conditioned his million-dollar cash infusion on a secure patent position for all forms of the automobile. Hearing that, one of Pope's chief managers ran from the dining room to Cuntz's office across the hall. Nervously he blurted, "What can we tell him?"

Cuntz quickly reached into the recesses of his desk file and pulled out three sheets of paper: The first listed all controlling steam patents, the second listed all controlling electric patents, and the third focused on internal combustion. His research showed that only one dominant patent governed internal combustion—Selden's. The three explanatory sheets were brought back into the dining room for examination.[6]

Ten minutes later, the Pope manager emerged again with the exciting news: "We get the million!" But, he added, the cash was completely contingent upon coming to terms with Selden.[7]

On the off chance that his company would need private details on Selden, Cuntz had already hired two attorneys to discreetly investigate "intimate data" regarding Selden's life, work, and character. Armed with that personal information, Cuntz dispatched an unexpected albeit straightforward invitation to Selden's office in Rochester, inviting him to Hartford to discuss his patent.[8]

Who was Selden?

George Baldwin Selden, born in 1846, always wanted to be an inventor but never was. His father, a patent attorney, one of many jurists in the family, insisted Selden take up the expected career in law. Even as a teenager, young George Selden was certain he would rather invent than litigate. During the 1850s and 1860s, he intensely studied locomotion inventions and their patents. After the Civil War, the need for self-propelled machines was widely understood, and Selden was among those who pored over the subject, acquainting himself with the latest steam engines. But in 1871 Selden acceded to family pressure and obtained a law degree. By 1876, he had joined his father's patent law firm in Rochester and within two years began his own patent litigation practice. Although he devoted his days to patent law matters, his spare time was spent cloistered in a basement workshop where he tinkered with a local toolmaker in pursuit of his dream: an internal combustion machine.[9]

Igniting various petroleum distillates and flammables in a stationary chamber was a frustrating and dangerous business that yielded what Selden called enough explosive power to "blow your damned head off if necessary." But the explosions could not effectively be harnessed. Trial and error in containing explosions was time-consuming. "Can't carry on about a dozen lawsuits and do much experimenting at the same time," Selden wrote in frustration.[10]

But he continued on and had by spring moved his tests to a small Rochester machine shop on Platt Street overlooking the Genesee River. Obstructive boards were positioned to keep prying eyes from observing. Kerosene spilled on a plate and ignited by match did not burn well. Benzine, when lit, flamed but generated too much smoke. However, when gasoline was poured onto the plate and ignited, it "went off like a flash," as Selden wrote. By May 1878, a three-cylinder engine mounted on sawhorses was ready for its first test. Selden used gasoline, which represented a more potent fuel, but other than that did little to advance automotive engineering. Indeed, his contraption mainly imitated the two-stroke and four-stroke piston technology of such automotive pioneers as Nicholas Otto in Germany, Alphonse Beau de Rochas in France, Jean Joseph Étienne Lenoir of Belgium, and George Brayton in America, all of whom during the previous decade had designed working internal combustion cars. Most of these were real operating vehicles that had been test-driven dozens of miles or raced between cities.[11]

Selden's sputtering device failed to operate for more than five convulsive minutes, and even then only with a single piston. But Selden was encouraged. After several more tests throughout the year, most of which started and then fizzled within a minute or two, Selden concluded that he had not just ignited gasoline in a stationary chamber, but had on that sawhorse invented the automotive internal combustion engine that would one day rule the roads. If carried through and perfected, the device might have led to true automotive progress. But short on time, Selden felt he had done enough to accomplish his true goal, which was not to invent a workable engine, but rather to stake a technical patent claim that could one day be used to exact tribute from others. This was the custom in patent warfare. As an attorney, Selden was a skillful practitioner of the art. He knew every trick in the book.[12]

First, Selden commissioned a nonworking model and drawings of his machine, disregarding the obligation to build and make available for inspection a true working model. Next he commenced the most protracted and artful manipulation of the patent system on record.[13]

Filing his application on May 8, 1879, was only the beginning. Now ensued an interminably long procession of amendments, resubmissions, revisions, and requests for extensions. This numbing delay lasted sixteen and a half years, designed not to obtain a patent for anything he had innovated but to systematically incorporate all new automotive progress into his own ever-evolving patent and thereby emerge with grandfathered primacy based on the original date of the application. Patent laws enacted in 1870 required that all questions be answered within two years, but a loophole provided for unlimited two-year renewals. Each amendment or renewal was filed by Selden at almost the last day permissible by the rules.[14]

Selden's insufficient application was first rejected on May 31, 1879. His first amendment was filed one year and 360 days later on May 26, 1881, just four days shy of the deadline. With unusual speed, the Patent Office on June 17, 1881, rejected the amended application as well; Selden waited until May 15, 1883—one year and 335 days—to file his second amendment. Within ten days, the Patent Office rejected Selden again, and once more he waited until almost too late, this time until May 18, 1885, to file a third amendment. This tenacious deadline dance repeated itself year after year. In one case, he waited a year and 353 days to amend, and in another year he edged right to the brink, amending one year and 363 days after rejection.[15]

By the time Selden's calculated delays had run their course, he had withdrawn his original nineteen bases for a patent and replaced them with some one hundred modifications and amendments based on the year-to-year progress of other inventors.[16] Hence, he was able to absorb the latest technological advances into his original worthless patent.

Selden was hardly the sole practitioner of the well-known tactic of patent abuse. In 1887, Washington's patent commissioner complained in his annual report, "There are applications now in the Office which have been kept alive nine or ten years and the Office is powerless to compel speedier or earlier action on the part of the applicants." No other patent in American history was marked by so protracted a process, not the years-long conflict over Morse's telegraph, Edison's lamp, or Bell's telephone. Selden's sixteen-and-one-half-year procrastination bested them all.[17]

The Patent Office clearly understood the strategy. Patent protection ran for seventeen years. By manipulating the process, the petitioner could commence the seventeen-year period of protection many years after the original application. Rule 68 prohibited deliberate delaying tactics, but the overworked and undermanned Patent Office was powerless to police the thousands of pending applications, especially when the applicant was himself a skilled patent attorney who understood the intricate letters of the law. The Patent Office commissioner himself conceded to Congress that his office was so poorly organized, with dusty books and filings stacked so chaotically in cramped corridors and alcoves, that searching prior art and making intelligent classifications was virtually "impossible." The commissioner lamented, "There have crept in errors and there remain deficiencies, almost entirely preventable, but inevitable from the vast avalanche of records."[18]

Certainly, some Patent Office examiners remained steadfast in their opposition to granting Selden a patent. For example, in 1893, one reviewer rejected the application because, as he noted, "no [new] invention is believed to lie in substituting a Brayton [internal combustion] engine [developed earlier by American engineer George Brayton] for a steam engine in the manner expressed in said claims." Selden reworded his claim and broadened it to include any and all compression gasoline engines.[19]

In plain words, over some sixteen years, Selden outlasted the besieged Patent Office. On November 5, 1895, patent number 549,160 was finally granted to Selden for a working "road engine" or compression gasoline car, reflecting not the sputtering stationary gadget he had hammered together in 1879, but the latest road-tested improvements of others who had followed him up through 1895.[20]

Because most of America's several dozen auto wizards worked in isolation, not combination, many were unaware of their competitors' work and felt that internal combustion itself was not patentable, just as fire could not be patented. Most in the field adopted the philosophy eschewing patent primacy that was expressed in *Horseless Age*. "Many have contended and still contend," wrote the editor, "that no basic patents can be held in the application of the hydrocarbon engine to the propulsion of road vehicles."[21]

They were wrong.

Cuntz's May 1899 effort to recruit Selden was successful. EVC's preliminary option was quickly signed. Later, it was broadened to a formal three-month option that gave Cuntz time to further investigate all locomotive patent rights. His search was exhaustive. Cuntz dispatched researchers to plumb key technical libraries in Boston, New York, and Washington for engineering records, to scrutinize patent files in London and Paris, and eventually even to examine experiment notes in Austria and Hungary. His team deftly sifted through every available record on propulsion reaching back generations.[22]

On November 2, 1899, Pope's investigators were confident enough to finalize their acquisition of Selden's patent. That day, after long negotiations, Selden signed over his rights for $10,000—a $1,000 down payment already received and $9,000 more to be paid on the first day of the new year, plus a minimum $5,000 annual royalty. Ironically, Pope's own diligent patent lawyers submitted private written objections to the company asserting that Selden's so-called patent could never be sustained in a real courtroom test case. But a satisfied Pope felt legal might would make the patent right. From the view of Whitney and Pope, they now owned all aspects of internal combustion for the dozen years remaining in the seventeen-year patent granted Selden in 1895.[23]

The timing was exquisite. Throughout the late 1890s, hundreds of so-called automobile manufacturers had announced themselves. But most of them were paper creations devoid of factories, designed to sell tens of millions of dollars in worthless stock while producing no vehicles. In 1898, despite the hundreds of entities in the field, only 239 automobiles were actually manufactured throughout the entire country, and these by just seventeen makers. Indeed, that year, all the new cars combined were valued at just $219,000.[24]

But by 1899, a veritable explosion of genuine and legitimate manufacturing occurred, with the number of vehicles constructed that year soaring to almost 3,500. Although steam and electric composed the overwhelming majority—some two-thirds—internal combustion was gaining because of its lighter weight, greater range, and faster speed. Moreover, rumble and sputter were all seen by consumers as the hallmarks of superiority. Gasoline-car inventors and manufacturers began transitioning out of workshops and into factories. Some of them were rolling out as many as fifteen cars per week. The brains and brawn of automobiling were only waiting for investment capital to launch a true mass-production automobile industry. However, Whitney and Pope did not want any industry to rival the one they had created.[25] The Selden patent would stop all comers.

Horseless Age expressed the automobile movement's revulsion at the Electric Vehicle Company's plans, which were now openly being touted. The publication derisively dubbed EVC the Lead Cab Trust, named for the heavy metal that weighed down every battery-powered car. The editor castigated the new Whitney-Pope trust, stating, "They have become grotesque, and if they have any saving sense of humor they will retire and leave the field to the mechanics and manufacturers to whom it rightfully belongs."[26]

While the original value of the Selden patent might have been to restrain gasoline cars from competing with electric vehicles, that outlook
quickly and radically changed even before the Selden patent deal was finalized. In late 1899, EVC's financial house of cards began rapidly collapsing.

During those first financially intoxicating months after Whitney and
Pope formed their giant electric vehicle trust in April 1899, EVC was able
to pay an 8 percent stock dividend based not upon true worth and value
but the combine's clever stock inflation and manipulation. Executives
hoped that later income would justify the attractive payments up front. But
the income was not there, and the cash-strained EVC halted dividends by
late 1899. Its stock price began to tumble from $97 to a third that level.[27]

Financial desperation and insider manipulation by officials at the
EVC forced the firm to secure a $2 million mortgage from the State Trust
Company, a bank Whitney owned and used for his Metropolitan railway
deposits. In a masterpiece of interlocking collateral, cash diversion, self-
dealing, and side-dealing, the loan was made—but not to EVC. This
would have violated state banking loans that forbade bank loans to officers
and directors, which of course included Whitney. Instead, the loan was
made to Daniel H. Shea. Shea was no independent financier with the
money to back up a seven-digit loan. He was a lowly clerk in the office of
one of Whitney's codirectors. Other state officials were implicated as well
for receiving funds in the serpentine loan.[28]

On January 11, 1900, a disgruntled EVC stockholder complained to
New York governor Theodore Roosevelt, who ordered an official investigation. Eventually, Whitney and State Trust were somehow exonerated by
the state examiners, except for technical infractions of making too large a
loan under the fiscal circumstances in contravention of banking rules. But
the press, including the *New York Herald*, inked up spectacular headlines,
which zeroed in on a $2 million loan to "an office boy." The *Herald*'s Jan-
uary 20, 1900, headline blared HOW AN OFFICE BOY GOT $2,000,000. The
whole scandal reinforced the public and investor perception that EVC was
just another rapacious trust.[29]

Horseless Age verbalized the feelings of many when in its January 24,
1900, edition, it sneered, "Since the Lead Cab Trust has got into 'hot water' . . . the backers of this scheme would do well to get out of it before they
are burnt. The long comedy of the promoters is concluding with a roaring
farce." The publication mercilessly attacked the EVC as a "company of
special artists in prevarication, bombast and intimidation. The funniest
part of it is that these late interlopers do not realize that they are playing a

farce. They actually take themselves seriously and are not aware that the American investor understands them and is tired of their shallow tricks. . . . The financiering methods of the Lead Cab Promoters are beginning to leak out at last."[30]

Shaken hard by the bad publicity of the $2 million bank scandal, EVC's precarious financial cards immediately accelerated their downward fall. The stock that had once proudly soared to $97 dipped to just a fraction.[31]

As 1900 opened for business, EVC was wounded as the custodian of electric transportation. The company was trying to recover from a mid-December 1899 factory fire that had destroyed eighteen new taxis and nine others being repaired, reducing the fleet just at a time when visible service and revenue was most needed. The Chicago Siemens & Halske plant was abruptly sold to General Electric at a million-dollar loss. Taxis delivered to the Boston, Philadelphia, and Chicago divisions were shipped prematurely and could not correctly function. The factory workforce in Hartford was severely diminished, and that first heady order for eight thousand taxicabs was quietly slashed to just two thousand. But even those two thousand were not built, and the ones that were constructed were neglected and often inoperable. Eventually, *Horseless Age* bemoaned, "Where thousands of Lead Cabs were to be in service, we find but fifties, groaning around with every sign of wear and tear, half the time in the hospital [garage]."[32]

A few weeks after the $2 million scandal erupted, sensing a teetering EVC cartel, *Horseless Age* in a February issue tried to reassure the independent automobile maker. Its stinging editorial espoused the common belief that the oft-ridiculed Selden patent could never be enforced against a sea of small inventors. "It is true," wrote the editor, "that capitalists of large means have been purchasing motor vehicle patent . . . probably with the intention of some day exacting tribute through their ownership, but of motor vehicle patents there will be no end. They will multiply like dragon's teeth of old—too fast to be successfully monopolized."[33]

The independent automobile companies had forgotten the recent experience of the homegrown bicycle makers, nearly all of whom were beaten into submission by Pope. That record would soon be repeated. But now EVC's motives mutated. No longer was the Whitney-Pope cartel seeking to restrain internal combustion automobiles, but rather to use them to supply royalties to the cash-starved combine. The destiny of electric transportation was now secondary to the need to promote up-and-coming internal combustion so long as it could force cash tribute in the form of Selden licensing fees.

As Cuntz himself later recalled, the Selden court case would "tell us if we had a real monopoly, or just insurance for our investment in the development of the gas cars."[34]

By June 1900, the Electric Vehicle Company had served infringement notices on gasoline carmakers en masse. "Our clients inform us," EVC attorneys warned, "that you are manufacturing and advertising for sale vehicles which embody the invention of the Selden patent. . . . We notify you of this infringement, and request that you desist from the same and make suitable compensation to the owner of the patent therefore." Lawsuits were promised in a follow-up notice.[35]

Motor Age voiced the mood of the carmaking community when the publication declared, "The first gun has been fired in the first great legal battle in the automobile industry." The publication warned, "With practically unlimited means at its disposal, it [EVC] will select for its first attack, some company that is none too strong financially, and, with the best attorneys and the brute force of money, push the suit to a conclusion, without the proper defense having been made. Such a result would be disastrous to all makers of gasoline vehicles and would work incalculable harm to the industry."[36]

Since few among the carmakers understood the previously obscure Selden patent, the Patent Office was suddenly swamped with calls to send copies and soon depleted its supply. What was known to the gasoline automobile community was laughable. One leading patent consultant said the whole idea was "absurd and untenable," adding that the Selden patent was "too preposterous to merit serious consideration."[37]

On July 12 and 13, 1900, EVC launched its test lawsuit in three jurisdictions against the Winton Motor Carriage Company of Cleveland, its Buffalo-based engine supplier the Buffalo Gasolene Company, a young company incorporated the previous year, as well as two sales agents in Manhattan. Winton, one of the nation's most reputable car manufacturers, had already commenced factory-style production. Plans were afoot to construct a huge plant, dramatically increasing output.[38] Bringing Winton down would herd the others into line.

Winton reacted with anger, declaring, "The Selden Patent is preposterous, and should never have been granted by the patent office. It will not have a leg to stand upon when it gets into the courts." But no one genuinely believed merit would decide the case. As *Horseless Age* warned,

"What the [EVC] trust lacks in validity of claims it will not be slow to make up in legal talent and financial strength."[39]

Barely more than two weeks after EVC had launched the suits, twenty automobile makers convened at the Iroquois Hotel in Buffalo to form the Hydrocarbon Motor Vehicle Manufacturers Association, promising to pool their resources and create a common defense fund to fight the Selden claim. Wasting no time in attacking the EVC suit, attorneys for both Winton and Buffalo Gasolene filed preliminary motions called writs of demurrer, to throw the case out. In those days, such pretrial motions were rarely successful, and in this case the writ was rejected by two different courts in two of the three related cases. EVC blared the decision on this one preliminary motion as though it were a trial verdict. Newspaper reporters who did not understand any better treated the motion decisions as final judgments, causing further confusion among both the public and industry.[40]

Winton pressed on. Its first answer in the lawsuit excoriated the Selden patent as a deliberate and fraudulent attempt to abuse the patent system to perpetrate extortion. The legal brief itemized fifty-six earlier American patents from 1844 to 1880, seventeen earlier French patents spanning the years 1807 to 1879, and fifty-three earlier British patents stretching back to 1794. Two years, two thousand pages of testimony, and many months of scouring engineering files later, Winton had spent thousands of dollars in defense costs. In the meantime, the Hydrocarbon group's pledges of support vaporized. Winton's treasury sustained almost all the legal expense.[41]

On December 27, 1900, EVC filed another suit, this one against a New York supplier, Automobile Forecarriage. Three weeks later, on January 19, 1901, EVC served yet another suit, this one against the puny Ranlet Automobile Company, a homespun effort by two rural Vermont boys to construct a single working automobile. The purpose of these suits was not to thwart any real competition but, as expected, to secure judgments against the weakest defendants, judgments that could then frighten the strongest ones. On May 21, 1901, Ranlet agreed to a permanent court injunction, and one week later Automobile Forecarriage failed to properly answer their suit, resulting in a decree against them. These two developments only strengthened EVC's exaggerated claim that it was being vindicated in the courts.[42] In truth, the courts had never tried the Selden claim on its merits. All EVC's victories came from motions and maneuvers.

But the message was beginning to sink in among the gasoline manufacturers. Litigation would be expensive and draining and would probably never resolve the merits of the Selden patent. They began to understand that EVC could outspend them and tie them up for years. Indeed, until the Selden cloud was taken away, suppliers were afraid to furnish parts, dealers were afraid to sell cars, and many customers were afraid to purchase for fear of being sued by EVC. By the fall of 1902, some seven gasoline manufacturers had approached EVC about acceding to demands to purchase a Selden license.[43] Paying EVC royalties and license fees was cheaper than an expensive patent fight.

The so-called Hydrocarbon Association disappeared altogether. Winton discovered it was waging a lonely battle for the entire industry, an industry that was already surrendering. On November 17, 1902, by mutual agreement, discovery in the Winton case ceased.[44] A deal was to be forged.

From EVC's point of view, more money was to be made licensing the mushrooming internal combustion field than proliferating electric vehicles. Its electric vehicle business was in fact being abandoned, sector by sector. A drivers' strike in Chicago in March 1901 prompted the company to immediately close the Illinois company, which was losing money rapidly.[45]

Within sixty days, the Boston-based corporation, which was spending twice its income, began terminating its largest commercial-delivery customers because it could no longer afford to service them. The company was soon dissolved. Although inquiring investors were promised a Boston taxi fleet of hundreds, only twenty-five cabs were found. *Horseless Age* announced the company's demise with front-page rancor, asserting, "After two years of studied deception on the part of the promoters of this colossal speculation the public is finally getting an insight into its rottenness. In spite of the assistance of a purchasable crew of henchmen and a servile press the truth has prevailed. The outraged stockholders have demanded investigation and the figures are public property. Subterfuge will avail no longer."[46]

A subsequent issue of *Horseless Age* used its front page to quote a Boston publication's condemnation of the entire enterprise. "Those concerns were not organized to build motor carriages," the editorial stated. "They were organized to sell stock. . . . The wolves in sheep's clothing who promoted this monstrous scheme . . . will find no vindication from those who are conversant with the facts."[47]

Then the New York company's stock dropped from $30 per share to just seventy-five cents. To continue operating, EVC was compelled to issue

$2.25 million in industrial bonds, made possible only because Morton Trust, another Whitney bank, collateralized the bonds with a sweeping mortgage. Morton's mortgage encompassed EVC's Hartford factory and other real estate and the company's allied share holdings, as well as its thick sheaf of patents, including the precious Selden rights.[48]

To aggravate a terrible situation, a stockholder suit in the fall of 1901 charged company officials with looting the corporation by secretly siphoning off EVC shares for a pittance to its parent company, the Electric Storage Battery Company. What's more, EVC was accused of paying preferential dividends to Whitney's inner circle of financiers.[49]

At the same time, the leading automakers themselves had their own industry problems. Too many newcomers were flooding into the automotive scene. These newcomers were derisively labeled "assemblers." A culture of automotive independence was springing up across America, emulating the bicycle craze. It was now possible for barnyard and backyard mechanics and machine shops to purchase parts helter-skelter, purloin designs, and assemble a small number of cars. Naturally, these low-run vehicles were priced far below the established brands. These assemblers were often backed by little if any capital. In fact, many of the assemblers were honest and talented upstarts beginning in the business just as the more established manufacturers had done some years earlier. But the established carmakers felt threatened by these diverse rivulets of competition, which could undersell them and shift the main auto clientele from the moneyed elite to the average man. At the same time, the establishment wanted to protect their emerging industry against so-called fly-by-nights.[50]

An old boys' club arose among the dominant car companies. While coming together to fight off EVC, they also came together to fight off encroachments from newcomers. The newcomers were invariably branded fly-by-nights, whether ensconced in drafty barns or spanking new manufacturing facilities. Ultimately, it became a contest of "them" versus "us." This contest would become all the more imperative as the gasoline car business exploded into a collective output of thousands of units per month.[51]

By late summer 1902, the monopolistic mating had begun. EVC needed the leading automakers to thrive so it could collect Selden royalties. The leading automakers needed to restrain competition. Cuntz was instructed to begin discreet licensing negotiations with the willing carmakers, thus far between seven and ten companies. They would be encouraged to "step up to the captain's desk and settle." The EVC and carmakers would then come together to create a new joint cartel, using the Selden weapon against others. Winton could join them and settle his suit as well.[52]

On January 3, 1903, representatives of ten gasoline-vehicle makers gathered in Detroit to discuss creating a "protective association" to do "offensive and defensive work," as one of the participants remembers, this under the aegis of the Selden patent. Winton, still technically in litigation, was excluded from the conference. A royalty to EVC equal to 5 percent of the catalog price was rejected by the protective group in favor of 0.5 percent. This money would be paid not to EVC directly but to the new protective association for their joint and several benefits. EVC would be allowed to join the group.[53]

In late February 1903, a number of the manufacturers traveled to New York for the Automobile Show at Madison Square Garden. While there, they unexpectedly received an invitation to finalize their ideas in a private meeting with Whitney himself at his Fifth Avenue mansion. The men agreed to dispatch a small delegation. They harbored two fears: First, could they muster the combined economic muscle to threaten EVC with a protracted, coordinated legal battle? Second, could "the arrogant disposition of the Electric Vehicle Company," as one delegate phrased it, find a way to compromise?[54]

If successful, the melded intimidation of EVC and the manufacturers could incarnate a system for excluding all but a select group of carmakers, maintaining standards and keeping prices high. Word leaked out, and *Automobile Age* called the attempt a "supremely ingenious scheme for beating the law of competition, of supply and of demand."[55]

While traveling to Whitney's mansion in an EVC electric cab, one of the delegation, Elihu Cutler, was appointed spokesman. He pulled a blue envelope from his pocket and scribbled three demands Whitney had to meet before they would create a joint trust. First, the carmakers would divide the royalties between EVC and the association, thus creating a litigation war chest against the "fly-by-nights"; second, the association and only the association would decide who was to be sued; third, the association and only the association would decide which newcomer companies should be admitted to the cartel.[56]

After tendentious bickering, which one manufacturer recalled resembled "rams, mules, lions . . . [and] charging bulls," a deal was struck with Whitney. EVC and ten gasoline car firms then and there invented a monopolistic combine called the Association of Licensed Automobile

Manufacturers (ALAM). Board members included four manufacturers and one of Pope's lieutenants, Milton Budlong, now functioning as a vice president of EVC. Budlong was quickly promoted to EVC president.[57]

The association was unincorporated and therefore claimed jurisdiction in no state. Royalties were fixed at 1.25 percent of the retail price, with payments being divided, two-fifths to the ALAM and three-fifths to EVC. EVC remitted a third of its share to Selden as a royalty. Half of Selden's payment was privately split again with George Day, the outgoing EVC president, who helped broker the entire deal. ALAM moneys not spent on operations or litigation would be rebated to its member manufacturers. By March 5, 1903, the paperwork was signed.[58]

Henceforth, EVC would allow clean electric to flounder in favor of rumbling, smoking, faster-driving gasoline cars. The promise of electric was over before it even began. The trust virus had jumped species, from electric to internal combustion.

Winton joined the ALAM a few days after the group formed. In doing so, he settled his lawsuit. A condition of settlement was that all damning testimony and exhibits amassed by Winton to prove the worthlessness of the Selden patent be withdrawn from the court record and handed over to EVC's attorney, thus preserving the power of Selden. No new defendant would ever see those debunking documents.[59]

Moreover, the ALAM created a "patent pool" composed of the four hundred patents owned by individual manufacturers. In case the threat of Selden litigation did not cow any adversary, there were four hundred more where that came from. ALAM members could employ the patents, but no one else could.[60]

Indisputably, the ALAM was now empowered to permit or deny any it chose the right to manufacture petroleum-based autos. Whom it would admit and whom it would refuse was unknown. Certainly, the quality of automotive technology was important, but so was the simple fact of competitive pricing, something the ALAM wanted to thwart. No attempt was made by ALAM to regulate its own initial eleven members, just everyone else. Fearing the new cartel and the litigation it could rain upon any independent, dozens of vehicle makers asked for membership details. In May 1903, Cuntz began a six-state factory inspection tour of some forty-three companies. Two-thirds were denied.[61]

Instantly, the ALAM was seen as an oppressive trust bent on keeping the supply of vehicles down and prices high. The group spent much time denying the obvious. Typically, their defensive remarks only advertised the very problem. Periodically, the group purchased advertisements and circulated statements assuring that they were not a "trust" or "illegal combination to freeze out competition," using the incriminating words it sought to obviate. Often their self-serving statements only buttressed fears that the onetime underdogs had really become pit bulls. For example, an ALAM official defended their refusal to admit most companies, asserting, "There must be profit in our industry to ensure its development." He added, "We have no desire to oppress anyone, but we propose to protect the business for our agents as well as ourselves."[62]

Indeed, the group felt their expanding production was approaching oversupply. For example, in 1902 the Olds Motor Works rolled out and sold 2,500 vehicles; the firm reached the 4,000-car level in 1903. Output across the ALAM's membership was increasing by thousands per month. Within two years, it would reach more than 21,600 cars annually, 85 percent of which employed gasoline internal combustion. Manufacturers were regularly convinced that their supply was exceeding demand. By fixing manufacturing levels, conceded an ALAM executive, the field avoided the "imminent danger of overproduction" for the next year, 1904.[63] This kept prices high.

Most cars in 1903 cost $1,000 to $2,000. A few vehicles with less horsepower sold for less, but some 85 percent of all vehicles were beyond the reach of the average man and still just playthings of the rich. *Motor Age* articulated the dilemma: "The people all want automobiles and the people have fixed a common price upon the machine they desire. That price is $500 and the car need not be a racer or a luxuriously appointed touring car. It need only be a safe, stout, practicable vehicle for ordinary conveyance. Will the demands of the people be answered?"[64]

To a degree, it was a regional difference. While the urbanized East was content with its fancy, well-appointed horseless carriages, Midwesterners wanted basic transportation and workaday vehicles to bring them into the twentieth century. After a 1903 automobile show, *Motor Age* reminded the industry, "Out in the west are great masses of professional men, merchants, farmers and delegates at large of the so-called great middle class, who wish reliable, moderate price cars of all-around utility, which shall have touring endurance and ability for hard work at fair speed, but with simple construction, easy control and cheap maintenance."[65]

Cheap cars were not in the interest of the EVC or the ALAM, since profit margins and royalty payments were pegged to retail price. By fall

1903, the ALAM, which had swelled to twenty-seven members, began threatening dealers with lawsuits. Then it threatened customers. For example, in conspicuous four-column advertisements in the *Detroit News* and *Detroit Free Press*, the ALAM brashly served notice to "Manufacturers, Dealers, Importers, Agents and Users of Gasoline Automobiles." It warned that anyone even driving an unlicensed machine "would be liable to prosecution for infringement."[66]

One motoring publication warned the public against purchasing any gasoline car other than an ALAM-approved one. "It is an old truism," wrote the journal, "that no sensible man wants to buy into a lawsuit. That holds true with automobiles. The sensible automobilist, therefore, will think twice about buying a machine manufactured by a firm outside the association."[67]

Naturally, any manufacturer outside the ALAM membership was accused of being a threat to automotive sense and safety. We are "discouraging the bringing out of half developed machines," insisted the ALAM, "that are a positive danger to life and limb and a detriment to the whole industry."[68]

One Detroit manufacturer particularly irked and threatened the ALAM. The man behind this upstart manufacturing concern refused to acknowledge the power and the primacy of the Selden trust. His vision was to create through mass-production techniques the inexpensive $500–$600 vehicle for the common man that the ALAM wished to forbid. Therefore, he was the ALAM's and EVC's greatest threat. The ALAM tried to denigrate him as a mere "assembler" of parts, a danger to the field, a financial charlatan, and a risky proposition for all. They were determined to make an example of him, wage war to the finish, and force him into destitution and submission. The war would indeed drag on for eight years. That conflict would change the face of automobiling in America and set the population against clean electric as a monopolistic fraud to be rejected. It would elevate the concept of internal combustion for the average man as a populist cause célèbre.

Who was the man the ALAM was determined to destroy? His name later became synonymous with the American automobile, a man who stood his ground as a popular hair-tousled hero against the coattailed men of the trusts and monopolies. His name was Henry Ford.

CHAPTER SEVEN

DEFIANCE

Few epitomized the American spirit of rugged individualism and stick-to-itiveness more than the disheveled-haired, small-town-legend Henry Ford. The man whose last name became a logotype for the American automobile, and indeed American innovation itself, lived a tempestuous life. Ford bucked the system, and bucked it with gusto, as much as any one man could while still attaining great success within the establishment.

During the opening years of the twentieth century, Ford fought a cascade of well-publicized battles with financiers, banks, and other domineering and often corrupt institutions. He became a folk hero to millions of ordinary Americans who took strength from his tenacious rebellion against undue authority and control by big-city powerbrokers and manipulators. Every attempt from on high to conquer him only reinforced his image as an emblem of American independence and innovation.

After World War I, an egotistic Ford and his company descended into a misguided mania, becoming the leading exponents of anti-Semitism in the United States. He became an iconic hero and inspiration to Adolf Hitler and the entire Nazi movement. In Germany, Nazis endearingly called Ford "Heinrich" and adorned their offices and parlors with his photograph and publications. Hitler openly called Ford his "idol." For his part, Ford and his company materially supported the Third Reich even during the war years. In Berlin, Hitler bestowed upon Ford *der Führer*'s highest medal for a foreigner.[1]

But in 1903, in an earlier life and more than a decade before he went astray as a Nazi ideologue and stalwart, Ford fearlessly personified gumption and bravado during his years-long battle with the powerful moneyed interests of the Selden trust, the Electric Vehicle Company, and the Asso-

ciation of Licensed Automobile Manufacturers (ALAM). The contest ultimately defined not only his future but that of the automobile in America.

How did Henry Ford set a collision course with the ALAM?

The story began during the late 1890s on the Ford farm outside Detroit. Ford was one of many mechanically inclined automobile enthusiasts
who tinkered with internal combustion engines, making them more efficient, more powerful, and more useful. In particular, he experimented
with the Otto engine developed years earlier in Germany. After a stint as
an engineer with the Edison Illuminating Company, Ford in 1899 formed
his own car firm, the Detroit Automobile Company. Ford infuriated his investors by insisting on perfecting his automobiles first, at great cost, before
beginning aggressive consumer sales. Ford parted ways with his backers
rather than compromise, and the Detroit Automobile Company collapsed
into financial ruin.[2]

In 1901, Ford created his second corporation, the Henry Ford Motor
Company. He hoped to advance the art first with racing cars, as was the
fashion of the day, then perfect cars for the public. Once again, Ford had a
falling out with investors who wanted less performance and more sales.
Eventually he was forced from the company that bore his very name.
Henry Ford Motor Company later became Cadillac Automobile Company, a bitter rival.[3]

After failing twice to create a car for the elite, Ford declared, "I will
build a car for the great multitude." He became determined to make a simple, inexpensive, and utilitarian gasoline-powered vehicle that would literally place all America in the driver's seat. The maverick's better idea was to
assemble cars in a streamlined fashion from inexpensive components, that
is, to bring mass-production techniques to automobiles. Ford expressed it
this way to his investors: "The way to make automobiles is to make one automobile like another automobile, to make them all alike, to make them
come through the factory just like one pin is like another pin when it
comes to a pin factory, or one match is like another match when it comes
to a match factory."[4]

At the time, the market for a popular low-cost vehicle simply did not
exist. When Ford's stockholders wondered where the market would come
from, he reassured them, saying, "You need not fear about the market. The
people will buy them all right, because when you get to making them in
quantities, you can make them cheaper, and when you make them
cheaper you can get more people with money, sufficient money, to buy
them. The market will take care of itself."[5]

Ford's populist car would have overturned the entire system. In 1903, most cars were propelled by either electric batteries or steam, and all were produced by several dozen independent manufacturers, or the EVC combine itself. These vehicles were necessarily expensive, being heavy, handcrafted coachlike gems affordable only to the moneyed class, who were mostly East Coast urbanites. That said, steam vehicles were proving more and more impractical because of their intricate internal mechanisms, propensity to explode, general performance, and cost. Electric vehicles were winning the day because of practicality, but they too were inherently expensive due to the high cost of batteries. Moreover, electric vehicles still suffered from range restrictions—about 25 to 40 miles per charge. This also made them city cars.[6]

Tethered to their recharging stations, electric vehicles could not tour the countryside, function as intercity transport, or satisfy the needs of rural and small-town Americans. In contrast, lightweight petroleum cars could extract far greater distance and speed from a gallon of gasoline, and that gallon can—weighing a bit more than six pounds—was lightweight and extremely portable. Making petroleum cars cheaply—$600 or so—for the common man would launch nothing less than America's road revolution, and it would be not electric, but combustible.[7]

Ford predicted he would produce at least 650 of his cheap cars before the end of that year, 1903, and thousands more per year once production ramped up. Thus, Ford threatened the entire automotive establishment even as he struck a chord with the American public. This threat was clearly understood by all. A senior Ford official recalled, "With such a price appeal we believed that we could sell a great many more cars and we therefore upset all of the traditions of the business by planning to sell in volume at a low margin of profit instead of selling a few at a high margin of profit. . . . The cheap, serviceable motor car quickly took the automobile out of the luxury class and put it into the necessity class. . . . Most necessities start as luxuries. Price is the fertilizer that stimulates the growth of a necessity."[8]

On June 16, 1903, with only $28,000 in private investment—none of it from Wall Street—Ford started his third and lasting corporation, the Ford Motor Company.[9]

Ford did not set out to confront the ALAM. Like all other auto manufacturers who had witnessed the EVC's punishing lawsuit against Winton, Ford was aware of the Selden patent's ruinous potential. While he was associated with the Detroit Automobile Company, his attorneys had alerted him to Winton's inability to avoid the EVC action and what the attorneys called the Selden patent's "sweeping character."[10]

At first, Ford tried to be a joiner. As early as the February 1903 Chicago auto show, Ford had asked EVC's Cuntz if he could join the manufacturers' association rumored to be organizing. Indeed, at about that time, the establishment internal-combustion companies were preparing to finalize negotiations with the EVC. But Cuntz did not take Ford up on his offer, especially since Ford's new company did not yet exist. Moreover, Ford was exactly the type of operator the ALAM organizers feared and resented, a so-called assembler. True, all the major companies purchased parts from outside vendors for assembly in their centralized plants. But in the ALAM's mind-set, established assemblers among their ranks were part of the quality circle exercising good production techniques, while newcomer assemblers represented mere "fly-by-nights" to be eliminated.[11]

Just days after Ford's June 16 incorporation, a major Ford stockholder, John Wendell Anderson, approached the ALAM in Detroit seeking peace. Anderson, who had injected a needed $5,000 into the new company, thereby earning himself fifty shares, met with ALAM president Frederic L. Smith. Anderson and Smith had been school chums, and Anderson entertained every expectation of achieving rapport during the meeting. Anderson could not see why Ford's company could not be admitted to the newly created ALAM. Smith shocked Anderson by unleashing a stunning rebuke to Ford and his hopes to build cars.[12]

Hearing the ALAM's determination to forbid "assemblers," Anderson protested, "Fred, we are an assembly plant." Smith answered, "Yes, I know."[13]

"Well, what do you do with companies that are merely assembly companies?" Anderson asked. Combining equal parts of diktat, arrogance, and condescension, Smith was clear: "We will take an inventory of their stocks, machinery, and equipment, whatever they may have, give them a fair value for it, and then they quit business." In other words, there was only one choice: dismantle, disband, and depart Detroit. Anderson's stomach wrenched and tightened.[14] It sounded like a battle to the finish was on the horizon, a battle for survival, a battle for the right to exist.

Anderson was correct.

Smith himself typified the ALAM's fear and loathing of Ford's idea. He was a founder of the Olds Motor Works, which sold one inexpensive model at about the price point Ford was quoting. Therefore, Ford's cheap car might well make Smith's low-end model obsolete. Smith urged the ALAM to create a special subcommittee to review the question of Ford's admissibility to the group. That special subcommittee was created, composed of just one man: Smith.[15]

Despite the derogations and refusals, Ford tried again, this time personally. That summer, he went to Smith's Detroit office to ask once more if his company would be allowed to apply. Naturally, Ford was unwilling to apply unless admission was assured. Smith recalled that he answered Ford bluntly, "not as the exalted president of the ALAM, but as one man to another." Deriding Ford's new factory as "really nothing but an assemblage plant," Smith castigated Ford's mass-production plans as pure "poison to the ALAM." In summary, Ford was told to "abandon all hope of becoming an automobile manufacturer."[16]

That summer of 1903, one final effort was undertaken to convince the ALAM to permit Ford to produce cars. Anderson invited Smith for a business lunch at the Russell House, Detroit's grand old hotel. This time, Ford and several of his feistiest stockholders and officers came with him. Ford's delegates congenially told Smith that the company was prepared to pay the ALAM's $2,500 initiation fee. But Smith was unreceptive and proposed an onerous, insulting, unaffordable, and unpalatable back-royalty payment as well. Moreover, in a bid at price-fixing, Smith suggested the ALAM would consider a Selden license if Ford limited his output to ten thousand vehicles per year and boosted the retail price of his car to $1,000. Smith later remembered that even as he uttered the words he felt "impertinent" and like a "guilty kid" in the presence of true innovators. Back royalties and attempts at collusion prompted indignation by the Ford people. The meeting, which began cordially, quickly turned combative.[17]

Finally, James Couzens, Ford's treasurer and general manager, erupted, bellowing, "Selden can take his patent and go to hell with it!" Ford, balancing casually in a chair slanted against the wall, chimed in, "Couzens has answered you."[18]

Smith shot back, "You men are foolish. The Selden crowd can put you out of business—and will." Couzens reacted with sneering laughter. At that, a provoked Ford scrambled out of his tipping chair, pointed a finger at Smith, and cried, "Let them try it!" Ford's people walked out.[19] The war was about to begin.

Quickly, the rumors of a conflagration between Ford and the ALAM swirled around Detroit, and indeed in auto circles everywhere. On July 16, ALAM agents arranged for a printed insert called "Trade Talk" to be dropped into the auto enthusiast and trade publication *Automobile Topics*.

This opening volley tried to assure the public that the ALAM was trying to protect both consumers and legitimate manufacturers. In its awkward, stilted, and self-incriminating style, the ALAM reminded all, "The association is not a TRUST."[20]

Self-serving position papers did little to deter general excitement about Ford's plans. So ten days later, on July 26, 1903, the EVC and the ALAM launched a scare campaign designed to intimidate anyone who would have anything to do with a Ford car. That Sunday, prominent ALAM "Notice" advertisements appeared in both the *Detroit News* and *Detroit Free Press*, sternly cautioning suppliers, dealers, and even prospective customers that only Selden-licensed vehicles could be purchased without prompting a retaliatory lawsuit. "No other manufacturers or importers are authorized to make or sell gasoline automobiles," warned the ALAM, "and any person making, selling or using such machines made or sold by unlicensed manufacturers or importers will be liable to prosecution for infringement."[21]

Ford responded at once, rushing rebuttal advertisements into the Tuesday newspaper editions. In an act of utter defiance, Ford's advertisement loudly promised all suppliers, dealers, and potential buyers, "We will protect you against any prosecution for alleged infringement of patents." Ford's ad then mocked the Selden patent as worthless, trumpeting, "The Selden patent . . . does not cover a practicable machine, no practicable machine can be made from it and never was as far as we can ascertain." What's more, Ford unmistakably threw down a glove to the EVC's legal marauders, assuring that contrary to the cartel's misrepresentation, the patent had never been tested in court on its merits. "No court in the United States," the advertisement asserted, "has ever decided in favor of the patent on the merits of the case, all it has ever done was to record a prior agreement between the parties."[22]

Tempting the EVC's predilection for lawsuits was itself more than spunk. ALAM agents had already passed the word to trade publications that defending such a suit would cost Ford at least $25,000. Ford's own attorney estimated the expense would exceed $40,000. Yet the newborn company, which on June 16, 1903, had begun life with only $28,000, found itself in late July 1903 with a meager $223 in the bank.[23]

Staggering legal expenses were enough to chill the ardor of even the most eager investor and convince even the most enthusiastic inventor to exit the field while a safe exit was still possible. Indeed, an ALAM internal report documented that as many as eighty-seven independents withdrew from the industry in the first months after the ALAM ordained itself. Several of them were extended temporary Selden licenses to finish the cars in progress. But then they were compelled to shutter their doors.[24] Who could outlast the trust?

But Ford needed only to last long enough to start production, which he did. Every vehicle that rolled off the assembly line was snapped up by a ready market. Ford's lean management style and volume-based profit allowed Ford Motor Company to earn profit every hour, to continuously hover in the black, to operate and expand assembly facilities and devote the hard-won cash necessary to fight any assault from the ALAM. During that first season, beginning in summer 1903, Ford sold 1,700 automobiles—more than any manufacturer before him.[25]

The automobile revolution was beginning. The company's tiny war chest was growing. The battle was approaching.

The ALAM assault was more than just another blood-splattered patent fight. It demarcated a turning point in the public's perception of electric vehicles versus internal combustion cars. Just as importantly, the fight finally reshaped the electric vehicle combine's perception of itself as carrying the torch of electric propulsion and instead revealed its determination to abandon that technology in favor of the coming wave of internal combustion. The EVC could make money on every gasoline car not by manufacturing them but by taxing them and keeping prices high. Capping decades of public distrust of electric batteries and all things associated with them, the EVC-ALAM chose to enter this fight as a self-proclaimed Goliath hell-bent on squashing Ford and any other challengers.

At the same time, the public adopted the view that the best automobile was not the safest, cleanest, or most quiet, but the very opposite. Average Americans beheld the petroleum car's rumble and sooty exhaust as the mark of a better product. The noisier the better. The smokier the better. The shakier the better. Indeed, the frequent mechanical breakdowns that required most gasoline-vehicle motorists to drive only while toting a substantial tool kit appealed to a sense of manliness. Electric vehicles started at the push of a button, but internal combustion required strong arms and a sturdy grasp just to crank up the car, hence it played to the man's muscularity. In that vein, it was commonly said that electric vehicles appealed to women drivers for their ease of operation, clean, fumeless running, and ladylike starts. That sealed it for America's male market. To the man with a car, driving through the countryside was cherished less for its smooth efficiency than for its jouncing, bracing challenge.

No service stations stood ready to assist; they did not exist. Nor were many roads friendly; most were deeply rutted and often little more than muddy trails for horse-drawn wagons. Broken axles, overheated engines, fractured wheels, empty gas tanks, cracked pistons—it was all an adventure, and men craved it the way they craved canoeing, camping, hunting, and exploring.

Gas cars came to symbolize fun, virility, independence, and an invitation to a man to roam where he wanted when he wanted—a modality of unshackled mobility. But the desire to buy a Ford was about more than America's urge to travel freely. It was about the average American's freedom to stand up to monopolistic power and purchase whichever machine was desired, the right to join the automotive age and motor alongside the rich and powerful, the ability to experience the wind on one's face without permission and to be free from consumer fear. For those who were tired of being pushed around, here was a chance to push back. The coming battle would be nothing less than fighting back, nothing less than an expression of the American will to be free.

Henry Ford was asked point-blank to describe his greatest ambition. Without hesitation he replied, "To be free—a free man."[26]

Had the EVC invested its capital in a recharging infrastructure, and a distribution network of batteries to hardware stores to be available on shelves right along with the ever-present kerosene and gasoline canisters, had the EVC continued to improve the durability and range of its batteries, had the company fulfilled its promises and mandate to proliferate its technology, then the American spirit of freedom, wanderlust, and independence could have been achieved as a safer, quieter one, one that did not foul the air, penetrate the lungs, and dim the sky at noon.

Had the EVC not tried to coerce so many small businessmen, had it not declared war on the consumer, had it not tried to threaten its way to the bank, everything might have been different.

Ford actually dared the ALAM to sue. Defiance. He dared the cartel to catapult him, his company, and his cheap, stripped-down car to the forefront of the common man's yearning for justice for the little guy. No wonder Ford bragged that not only would he refuse to pay tribute royalties to the ALAM, he "would give the 'trust' $1,000 if they would advertise his business by commencing suit against him."[27]

Tension mounted that summer of 1903 in Detroit, New York, Chicago, and indeed everywhere automobiles were designed, driven, or desired.

On August 1, just a few days after the ALAM and Ford traded threats and umbrage on the pages of Detroit newspapers, the EVC resumed its intimidation campaign against the average man interested in purchasing a Ford automobile. "The basic principle on which all gasoline cars are constructed," the EVC again warned in *Automobile Topics*, "is known and legally recognized in this country as the Selden patent." The admonition continued, "This fact is of the first importance to a purchaser of an automobile . . . the law allows the owner of a patent to follow up any infringements, even to an innocent third party . . . in the case of automobiles purchased from manufacturers not members of the association. While it is true that no steps have yet been taken to restrain purchasers of such vehicles from using them, it is equally certain that should such litigation once begin, it can have but one ending, as all litigation over the Selden patent has ended, namely, in vindicating the absolute ownership of the principle and patent by the Electric Vehicle Company."[28]

Horseless Age, on August 26, warned, with little question of who was involved, that "a decision was arrived at tending to limit the [ALAM] membership. . . . One manufacturer from the Middle West now has the impression that the association [the ALAM] does not want to admit him, but says that he will continue in business just the same." Shortly thereafter, the publication called a lawsuit against Ford "inevitable" and predicted "it was only a question of time."[29]

The next day, August 27, *Motor World* restated the prevailing fear and trembling among the independents: "Happy the man who makes or sells only steamers or the parts thereof! There is no Selden patent to cause him to shudder by day or see bugaboos by night."[30]

Four days later, August 31, Selden himself ratcheted up the pressure with comments made to the *Hartford Courant*. Speaking directly to Ford and any supplier or dealer who might assist him, Selden emphasized, "No guarantee can be given by any individual firm or corporation against an injunction of a federal court." Selden added a false reading of the patent's legal status, going so far as to claim that no legal defense would even be permitted by a court of law. "All parties," Selden added, "have agreed that it is impossible to build a gasoline automobile without infringing . . . the courts will not waste their time by permitting the discussion of matters already thoroughly settled by their decisions." The ALAM widely distributed Selden's clear exaggeration of the patent's juridical record.[31]

But the threats were not working. People were buying Ford automobiles from dealerships as fast as Ford's volume production could roll them out. Indeed, after just a few months of production, that is, by the end of September, Ford had already sold 195 cars, and 215 more were being readied for shipment—more than many well-established manufacturers with Selden licenses could produce in a year. The first sixty days brought the company $142,481 or $2,374 daily. A Ford dealer's full-page advertising beckoned, "Get a Ford car and enjoy it. We'll take care of the tom-toms [war drums]. Don't give $600 [a license tax] to the Bogey man."[32]

Ford had to be stopped. The ALAM carmakers resorted to brass tags. The association began affixing to doorjambs, dashboards, and other visible car surfaces the Selden-patent insignia embossed on brass tags.[33] The tag—its presence and its absence—was a vociferous reminder. Daring to purchase a car without such a tag was a risk for any citizen.

On September 10, the *New York World* underscored the fear, writing, "If a machine runs without one of these tags, a lawsuit will ensue as quick as the association hears of it." The newspaper added that the Selden trust had deployed its own "corps of men on the watch" for violators. Presumably, these men would troll the streets of big cities on the lookout for cars without the ALAM tag.[34]

Automobile further reflected the anxiety of average potential Ford-vehicle buyers that their cars, once bought, could be seized and demolished. The publication urged its readers to understand that the Selden trust "could have every unlicensed gasoline automobile in the land battered to pieces by officers of the law and utterly destroyed, whether found in the possession of manufacturers or innocent purchasers."[35]

On September 24, Ford Motor Company published yet another defiant rejoinder in the motoring publications. This latest testy letter, drafted and signed by the company's leading officials and attorneys, trumpeted a sweeping defense of the company's right to manufacture and the public's right to purchase Fords. That letter also bitterly condemned the ALAM and its intimidation tactics.[36]

"So far as our plan of action is concerned for the future," Ford's published letter asserted, "it is extremely simple. We intend to manufacture and sell all of the gasoline automobiles . . . we can. We regard the claims made under the Selden patent . . . as entirely unwarranted and without foundation in fact. We do not, therefore, propose to respect any such claims, and, if the issue is forced upon us, shall defend not only ourselves, but our agents and customers to the fullest extent and this, too, without regard to whether or not we join any combination for the purpose of defending against said patent."[37]

Belittling Selden himself, the published letter continued, "In taking this stand we cannot conscientiously feel that Mr. Selden ever added anything to the [automotive] art in which we are engaged. We believe that the art would have been just as far advanced today if Mr. Selden had never been born. That he made no discovery and gave none to the world. If he did, it was a narrow and impracticable one having no value, and that he and his assignees cannot monopolize the entire trade by forcing upon it an unwarrantable construction of his claims by those interested in sustaining them."[38]

Castigating the ALAM, Ford's published letter contended, "It is evident from the foregoing that the Association is not a philanthropic institution. It is in the business to make money at the expense of five or six times as many competitors, and that its members have joined together because of some expected pecuniary benefit in monopolizing the market under cover of the Selden patent, and not because they believe the patent to be impregnable. This is undoubtedly the truth, as is evident, because up to this date, although repeatedly challenged by outsiders and by ourselves, they have brought no action since the Association was formed, that we can learn of, against an alleged infringer."[39]

Daring the ALAM to file a suit, Ford's published letter sneered, "They are no nearer to establishing the Selden patent as a monopoly than they were last April. . . . [This] conclusively shows that the advertisements which they are putting out are intended to influence the public and are a substitute for the proper tribunal—the Courts. In stating our attitude with regard to these mendacious statements and the position of the Selden Association before the automobile public we are confident that we are not only voicing the opinion of ourselves, but of all the outside concerns, in saying that they do not inspire us, nor the outside concerns, with any degree of confidence in the equity of the Association or the bona fides of their claims."[40]

Finally, the letter went so far as to enumerate the company attorney's answers and defenses should any lawsuit be filed.[41]

Stressing the David and Goliath nature of the battle, Ford's published letter made plain, "We are fighting this matter single handed and have not joined any association whatsoever, nor do we anticipate doing so."[42]

Shortly after Ford's stinging public rebuke, twenty-five of the ALAM's twenty-seven members gathered for a two-day, closed-door meeting in Manhattan to decide what to do about Ford. After the conclave, a spokesman ominously predicted, "There will be a piece of news, big news, in a few days." Despite being pressed, no details were forthcoming.[43]

On October 22, 1903, the suspense was broken. The Electric Vehicle Company and Selden jointly launched lawsuits against Ford Motor Company and one of its suppliers, Duerr & Company; shortly thereafter served the Gude Company, a New York advertising agency that had purchased a Ford motorcar some weeks before, and finally the Wanamaker automobile dealership in New York.[44]

Now would ensue eight years of withering depositions, forty-two cross-examinations of experts and witnesses from Hiram Maxim to Henry Ford to George Selden himself, five million written words, and fourteen thousand pages of exhibits, testimony, and motions. The litigation so painstakingly excavated the complete history of locomotion going back generations that the court record in and of itself became a landmark treatise on the history of internal combustion.[45] However, the purpose of the thousands of man-hours and millions of words generated by the EVC's attorneys was not to illuminate anyone, or even determine the facts, but rather to wear down both Ford the man and Ford the company.

The plan did not work.

Question 1. What is your name, age, residence, and occupation?
Answer. Henry Ford is my name; age thirty-nine; residence, Detroit; occupation, automobile manufacturing.

Question 2. Are you connected with defendant, Ford Motor Company, and if so, in what capacity?
Answer. Vice president and general manager.

Question 3. You may state generally how long you have been so connected with them.
Answer. One year.

Question 4. About when was it organized?
Answer. The sixteenth of June, 1903.

Question 5. What has been your general experience as a mechanic and especially with reference to engines, or prime movers?
Answer. In 1880, I was with the Detroit Dry Dock Company.

Question 6. What did you do with the Detroit Dry Dock Works?
Answer. I served my time as a machinist.

Question 7. About when did you leave?
Answer. About 1883.

Question 8. What was your next experience?
Answer. With the Westinghouse Engine Company, of Schenectady, New York, as an expert. Yes, I was on the road, setting up traction engines.

Question 9. How long were you engaged with that company?
Answer. About a year.

Question 10. What was the nature of the engines that you were setting up?
Answer. They were portable steam engines.

Question 11. What year would that be in, did I understand you?
Answer. I think it was in 1884.

Question 12. You speak of these engines as being "portable" and "traction." Please explain what you mean by those terms?
Answer. "Portable" and "traction" mean self-propelled on the road.

Question 13. In those engines that were thus self-propelled, how was the motor connected to the driving axle?
Answer. By a belt with a tightener.

Question 14. Were those self-propelled engines used for any other purpose besides self-propulsion on the road?
Answer. Yes, they [had] done threshing, and all kinds of work.

Question 15. That is, by doing threshing, I understand you to mean, they drove threshing machines for threshing?
Answer. Yes, and doing sawing work.

Question 16. While they were driving threshing machines and doing sawing work, what was the fact about their being self-propelling or not?
Answer. I don't quite understand you.

Question 17. While they were doing threshing, did they drive themselves along the road too?
Answer. No, they didn't drive themselves along the road when they were threshing.

During depositions, both defense and plaintiff attorneys directed rapid-fire questions at Ford for hours on every aspect of his work history, automotive experience, and technological insights. There were hundreds of questions. If a question could be parsed into three or four parts, it was, thereby elongating the process. Nor was the protracted interrogation limited to the key players such as Henry Ford and George Selden. Nor did the witness list end even after a procession of aging auto pioneers had been called. Attorneys also subpoenaed for detailed depositions and affidavits the custodian at the Electric Vehicle Company office, a battery-room superintendent, the first electric-taxi driver in Manhattan, and any number of incidental employees.[46]

From the plaintiff's point of view, the idea was to grow the witness list, bulk up the record, incrementally add extra days, weeks, months, and years to the pretrial discovery, lengthen every proceeding, and drag out to its tensile limit the smallest detail and procedure. No matter how trivial the witness, Ford's attorneys were compelled to attend depositions, often making the expensive and time-consuming journey from Detroit to New York for the occasion. As part of the wearing-down tactic, plaintiff depositions were sometimes postponed at the last minute, just as defense counsel was entering the office, meaning a wasted train trip from Detroit to New York. It was all calculated to drive up Ford's already punishing cost of litigation. Indeed, the total legal bill for both sides was estimated to be in excess of a half million dollars.[47]

Debilitating legal expenses could not be measured in dollars alone, but more properly in ergs of distraction. Ford, however, was not the only party impacted. The EVC found itself more and more consumed by litigation against Ford and indeed other internal combustion carmakers. By the time the EVC had launched its 1903 suit against Ford, the combine had completely lost its way as the leading purveyor and developer of electric vehicles. Indeed, by 1903, the company abandonment of electric in favor of internal combustion was at full throttle. This abandonment was pivotal.

True, in the first years of the twentieth century, the electric-vehicle field was crowded with more than a dozen leading manufacturers, and as many minor firms, producing relatively expensive cars. These vehicles generally cost more than $1,000, and sometimes upward of $10,000, intended for an upscale urban market that not infrequently included American millionaires and European royalty. Hundreds of finely crafted vehicles were produced annually by such independent companies as Baker Motor Vehicle Company, Buffalo Electric Carriage Company, General Electric, National Motor Vehicle Company, Studebaker Brothers Manufacturing, and Woods Motor Company. These firms skirted legal problems either by using battery technology that was old enough to have passed out of patent, or by properly licensing it from the Electric Storage Battery Company. Licensing fees themselves drove up the cost of every car.[48]

Certainly, test-drivers in specially engineered electric cars could set impressive distance and speed records, as far as 192 miles on a single charge at high speed. One ordinary but well-prepared aficionado recorded a 75-mile trip at 25 miles per hour on one battery charge. But these were the stellar exceptions. The average electric vehicle traveled at a steady and sedate 10 to 15 mph and was generally restricted to a round-trip range of about 10 to 25 miles, depending upon model. This virtually tethered the vehicles to urban charging stations, which were few and far between, usually congregated in larger East Coast cities. Thus the ability to drive greater distances, as well as out of town or between cities, was almost nonexistent except for staged marathons and in some cases in the popular New York to Boston corridor. Even then, a battery recharge was a long, carefully planned, and overnight event.[49]

But internal combustion machines could race against the wind in any direction at breakneck speed, and not infrequently did break a few necks. These venturesome vehicles could carry their own spare cans of gas in the boot, or motorists could purchase a container in the nearest hardware or general store. More important, while a battery required an overnight recharge, turning a short intercity trip into a several-day junket, refilling a gas tank took but a brief moment, long enough to pour a gallon of fluid. Moreover, while a replacement battery array could cost $400, and battery recharges could cost a motorist two pennies or more per mile, depending upon the model and the location, gasoline was so dirt cheap — a half penny or less per mile — the price was commonly called "negligible."[50]

Why was oil so cheap? At the turn of the century, America was arguably the greatest oil producer in the world, mainly from the fabulous oil fields of Pennsylvania and Ohio, the black gold that made Rockefeller a competition-killing monopolist and billionaire. Commercial oil in the

Mideast countries, such as Persia, was almost a decade away. American oil supplies, manipulated masterfully by trusts, created an unending pattern of domestic gluts and shortages that artificially drove prices up and down at the whim of the oil barons.[51]

At 10:30 A.M., January 10, 1901, everything changed. Wildcatters at Beaumont, Texas, at a hill called Spindletop, brought in a monster gusher that reached two hundred feet toward the sky and was not capped for nine days. Before Spindletop, American annual production was about 64 million barrels. By 1902, more than six hundred oil companies toiling over some two hundred petroleum-spewing derricks in and around Beaumont began boosting America's annual output by some 1,600 percent. Within twelve months, Spindletop alone had yielded 3.64 million barrels. By 1903, its annual yield was 17.4 million barrels. Rockefeller's Standard Oil monopoly had finally been shattered. Petroleum became so cheap that oil struggled to sell for twenty-five cents per barrel. Gasoline, that final vaporous distillate of petroleum, became so abundant that it could be found in most places that sold the omnipresent lantern illuminant kerosene. No wonder it was common to declare, as *Horseless Age* did in May 1902, "Gasoline cost is so small . . . we may neglect it without harm."[52]

A typical reader's letter to *Horseless Age* tellingly explained an electric vehicle owner's sentimental, even die-hard stance: "My faith is pinned to it [the electric vehicle] and its ultimate success, as evidenced by the fact that so far as I know, I am the only owner of an electric car in my city. I use it every day, enjoy it very much and find it suits the needs of my profession better than a horse and carriage. As a matter of fact, 10 miles is about the best I can average on a level. I am waiting patiently for a car which will cover 50 miles up hill and down and capable of 20 miles an hour on a level, one that will average this for a year, not simply when battery and vehicle are new. I ask nothing better and think thousands in this country are waiting to buy just such a carriage."[53]

But comparing internal combustion machines with battery-driven vehicles was vastly more complex than juxtaposing the obvious negligible cost of gas fuel versus an expensive kilowatt hour, and the clear convenience of instant gas refills versus an overnight charge.

Quickly, gas-burning vehicles became the rage, or rather the norm. The realities of automobile technology seemed overlooked in the excitement of speed and range. The electric vehicle's superiority was submerged by the shake, rattle, and roll of the gasoline car. The harm to the environment and the threat to public health from the fumes, complaints constantly emphasized by electric advocates for years, were costs that the public and public policy never considered.

Of course, producing fuel in the early 1900s was not a clean process for either vehicle type. Generating electricity for batteries was usually accomplished by dirty coal-fired generating plants that fouled the sky of a localized area. Petroleum-drilling operations, refineries, and distilleries were equally if not vastly more noxious to a localized environment. But batteries were charged as a by-product of electrical illumination. The unused electrical power would be wasted if not diverted to batteries. Electricity plants were running anyway, day and night. So the idea of charging batteries during off-peak generating times was ideal. Once charged, the cars drove away with a clean wake and never transferred pollution elsewhere. Gasoline refining, on the other hand, was undertaken explicitly to run engines, and oil-burning cars ipso facto transported toxic exhaust everywhere the car was driven, from the congested cities to the small towns to the countryside. Cars became rolling air polluters.

While batteries were expensive to replace, so were the oily engine innards of gasoline cars. Pistons cracked. Spark plugs wore out.

Internal combustion machines could certainly roar at a higher velocity. But where? The cities were congested with throngs of horses, mules, trains, trolleys, and teeming pedestrians. Any effort to speed down a country or exurban road, or even a cobblestoned city street, could punish the motorcar with a broken axle, burst tire, or fatally jarred mechanism—that is, if the motorcar did not spook a horse into spilling his rider or wagonload. Hence while a few gravel-topped, composite macadam, or other specially leveled thoroughfares did exist, in most cases the gasoline motorist simply could not enjoy the power beneath his seat.[54]

Range always hovered as a pivotal issue. But most urban vehicles, especially fleet vehicles, did not require the long-distance capability of a touring car. Hence, the twenty-five-mile range of an electric vehicle more than sufficed for most users.

Most important, in 1903 no gas stations existed. The same hardware store that carried kerosene and gasoline could carry swap-out batteries that could slide into position within two minutes, as had been done in New York taxi garages, had the EVC developed replacement-battery distribution, or had the EVC created the infrastructure it promised by promoting the proliferation of more charging stations. Handy recharging throughout the city would have been commonplace had the EVC moved forward with the curbside recharging electrant stands readied by General Electric since

1899. Electric performance would have zoomed had EVC research and development continued to make the batteries lighter, more durable, less expensive, and longer lasting as had been promised by battery companies for decades.[55]

Indeed, battery technology never leapt forward as the electrical world knew it could and should. In 1897, heralding the onset of the electric vehicles of Salom and Morris, *Electrical World* expressed its optimism in these words: "There is not the least reason . . . to assume that the accumulator will not undergo great and marked changes and improvements. In general, whenever there is a demand for a specific improvement or invention, it soon makes its appearance." Shortly thereafter, the publication underscored its belief that "the success of electric automobiles will unquestionably cause a desire on the part of their users for a longer radius of travel, which only means an accumulator of greater capacity for a given size and weight. This is almost certain to be produced when the demand for it is sufficiently urgent."[56]

But during the coming two years, the progress the electrical community hoped for never appeared. The research and development effort and dollars needed to improve the power source were simply not forthcoming from the EVC, which was instead focused on building a better conglomerate, not a better battery. Understandably, in June 1899, *Electrical Review* reiterated the amazement and disappointment, asserting, "It has been said that no great invention waits long to appear when the demand for it becomes sufficiently strong. If this is true, it will not be long before a lighter accumulator is produced. There is hardly any improvement in electrical apparatus so greatly needed. Given a light, mechanically strong accumulator that will stand heavy charging and discharging, the electromobile problem becomes comparatively simple. . . . The market . . . will be enormous."[57]

After a year, in September 1900, the same publication, *Electrical Review,* simply could not explain the absence of significant progress: "It has been claimed over and over again, that whenever the conditions absolutely require a new invention, the invention is forthcoming. Never before in the history of the electric arts has there been a more insistent demand for anything than there is now for a storage battery of higher capacity per unit of weight . . . the light storage battery is urgently needed."[58]

In May 1901, *Electrical Review* called the need for a better battery "crying." But by that time, the EVC had already realized that its profits lay not in the electric vehicle but in monopolizing internal combustion. On June 21, 1901, EVC sales manager Arthur Huey wrote a senior EVC official about the problem of selling battery cars in Cincinnati, which featured hilly terrain. "The situation at Cincinnati as far as electric vehicles goes seems to be against the electric vehicle and in favor of gasoline," he wrote, adding that a prospective dealer "questioned very much if the electric vehicle can ever be made a success at that place."[59]

Indeed, early on the EVC began to invest in gasoline cars, and not only those made by Pope's company. By August 1901, the conglomerate had transformed the Riker Vehicle Company, which it had acquired during its massive inauguration, into an internal combustion carmaker. Quickly, Riker began producing eight- and sixteen-horsepower touring gasoline cars with a 150-mile range, not the electrical vehicles for which it had become famous.[60]

An oddity soon became commonplace. Advertisements and promotional literature for oil-burning cars that outperformed battery cars appeared incongruously under the banner of the Electric Vehicle Company, as though the first word in its name were no longer relevant. That fact itself spoke volumes.

Electric vehicles never had a chance. Virtually stillborn, these machines were subverted not by their competitors but by their custodians. It was never about batteries, it was never about breakthroughs, it was always about business.

Therefore, in 1903, as Ford and the EVC stood at the threshold of a years-long war, both electric vehicles and internal combustion machines stood as profoundly imperfect, waiting for greater technology and enabling infrastructure. All engines could be revved, all batteries could be recharged, all motor speed could be increased, all creature comforts could be enhanced, but every manufacturer and owner of every description was confronted by one towering reality: There were virtually no roads in America.

Ironically, the same Albert Pope who popularized the bicycle and became the fulcrum of the electric vehicle, then approved its abandonment, and thereafter became a powerhouse behind the Selden trust, this same man was also the prime mover in the creation of drivable roads in the United States.

America in the 1800s offered virtually no out-of-town roads conducive to motoring. By the 1850s, federal and state governments had constructed several horse-friendly turnpikes connecting parts of New York, Pennsylvania, and Maryland. But when the railroads sprouted in the latter half of the century, government focused on railroads and spurned any involvement with town-connecting roads. The bicycle craze in the 1880s inspired Pope to organize the Good Roads movement to create road surfaces where bicyclists could ride. Pope personally controlled this so-called grassroots movement through the League of American Wheelmen, an organization he financed. The League published its own magazine, *Good Roads*, paid for by Pope's company. By 1885, even the Populist Party joined the movement.[61]

Pope's people even convinced the railroads to push for roads as a means of improving farmer transport to railheads. Little did the railroads understand that these roads would become the enabling infrastructure for the internal combustion machine and become the interurban modality for commercial trucking and personal travel. The road network, needed as it was, undercut the railroads and reinforced the need for automobiles.[62] But which automobiles?

In 1893, the Good Roads movement successfully lobbied for a federal government bureau called the Office of Road Inquiry. The ORI mainly distributed pamphlets and propagandized for the concept of publicly financed roads. The bureau's leadership and corps of experts were all interchangeably bicycle enthusiasts in Pope's movement and not infrequently funded by Pope fronts. In other words, the ORI functioned as a federal extension of Pope's commercial combine.[63]

When the bicycle fad vanished, the Good Roads movement was inherited by internal combustion enthusiasts, again sponsored by Pope, and now in tandem with the EVC. Yet at the turn of the century, the nation was still far from hospitable to the automobile. The ORI's first countrywide survey revealed that less than 9 percent of the roads were surfaced at all, and those surfaces were merely gravel or crushed macadam.[64] Most of those were in the Northeast.

By the time Henry Ford's cheap utilitarian car began spreading across the American heartland in 1903, roads were needed not just for adventurous motoring, but also as basic transportation for the common man, and for truck deliveries. Within the next several years, the agitation of the Good Roads movement merged into the lobbying efforts of newly created American automobile clubs. These automobile clubs, singly and in amalgamation, succeeded in prompting county governments to build exurban roadways. For example, Los Angeles County floated a $3.5 million bond issue to build paved roads, and the State of California followed up with $1.8 million for state roads. Eventually, in 1916, Congress passed the first of numerous federal highway funding acts, beginning with $75 million to connect rural areas. Thus a national network of publicly financed roads was inaugurated. The expenditure, prodigious for its day, was ahead of the justifying volume of vehicles. Its sheer existence made rapid automobile expansion possible. Most important, this embryonic asphalt network was equally capable of empowering electric and petroleum-burning vehicles. But those roads connected towns and cities virtually bereft of battery distribution and recharging facilities. Instead, they featured special installations to pump gasoline and repair vehicles. These were called gas stations. They pumped gas but did not replace battery trays. They had none to replace.[65]

During the years after 1903, as the Selden litigation dragged on, Ford became an icon of American independence, standing up for the little guy against the trusts. While electric vehicle sales plummeted to just a few percent of the overall automobile market, continuing their dramatic slide into nonacceptance, Ford's everyman car was rolling with vim across the nation. In the 1903–4 season, upstart Ford sold seventeen hundred units, holding that level or slightly less through the 1906 season. In the 1906–7 season, as Pope's Good Roads movement showed the first tangible miles of concerted road building, Ford sales quintupled to eighty-five hundred. Neither the litigation nor the intimidation did anything but spur widespread adoption. His chief lieutenant, Couzens, later admitted, "The Selden suit was probably better advertising than anything we could put out."[66]

Then hell opened up for two minutes.

At 5:13 A.M., April 18, 1906, as the dawn readied its appearance and as most of San Francisco slept, the earth groaned and convulsed in an unforgettable, cataclysmic upheaval. A behemoth earthquake, about 8.3 on the Richter scale, shook the city and its environs like a rag doll for two minutes, followed by a series of wrenching aftershocks. As though on cue, ornate but often flimsy wooden, brick, and masonry buildings began collapsing en masse. As panicked citizens dressed in nightclothes scattered into the streets, they were bombarded and crushed by their own crumbling homes. First the chimneys broke apart, then the cornices toppled, then the walls themselves tumbled down, killing, cracking, and maiming until the once elegant city was converted to vast dunes of urban rubble and human carnage. It was said that hundreds died in those first awful moments. Thousands more were mutilated by flying debris. Instants later, San Francisco burst into a blazing inferno. Flames shot up everywhere as gas lines and flammables ignited and set the surroundings burning. The city now resembled the hell of Dante and Tyndale, with fires all around.[67]

As the buildings burned around them, as syncopated explosions continued to define the day, the city's fifty thousand dazed citizens tried to comprehend the monumental disaster that had swept over their city, and the horrible situation that had gripped their families.[68] Where was food? Where was water? Where would they sleep? Where were their lives? What now?

A demoralized reporter from *The Los Angeles Times* filed this report: "I was one of the hungry who robbed grocery stores for their food; one of the parched thousands who eagerly drank water out of the gutter leakage of fire engines." His disconsolate account continued, "I managed at last to join the long caravan of homeless families carrying all the property left to them in the world in sheets. . . . Looking back over all that day of horrors the most piteous and touching sights were women, driven from their homes, trying to make new homes in the parks out of a bit of torn blanket and a few stolen boxes of patent breakfast food. . . . Scores of dead were lying stretched on the lawns and others were walking about hideously wounded. Amid this scene an insane woman was wandering, blithely singing little songs of her own improvisation about the earthquake and the killing."[69]

San Francisco's deadly shudder was felt across the continent. Nineteen minutes later, it slapped seismic needles three thousand miles away in Albany and Washington, D.C.[70] But the reverberations from the Great San Francisco Earthquake did not stop after nineteen minutes, nor did the shock waves cease at the eastern shore of the United States. Before it was over, the drama and the destruction of this earthquake would be felt around the world for years to come. Eventually, the cascade of events now set in motion would topple the Electric Vehicle Company. Why?

The loss of so profound an economic center as San Francisco sent the stock markets careening. Within seven days of the earthquake, thirty-three of the leading stocks collectively lost $200 million in value. Railroads and other transportation stocks were hit hardest. Great Northern Railroad was down $20.8 million; Union Pacific, down $18.7 million; and New York Central, down $10.4 million—these headed a list of transportation losses totaling $140 million. Industrial giants, especially in metals, suffered almost as badly. Amalgamated Copper, down $10.7 million; U.S. Steel, down $9.5 million; American Smelting, down $3.9 million. The average loss among the thirty-three most-traded corporations was $5.9 million.[71]

Devastating stock losses immediately hit the trust banks. Trust banks were largely unregulated. Because they did not maintain the same cash reserves and therefore enjoyed more money to profitably lend, trust banks could pay higher interest to attract deposits. These deposits were then loaned out to big corporate customers, often unscrupulous speculators who commonly collateralized with worthless shares. But when the stock market caved days after the Great San Francisco Earthquake, and stock collateral vaporized, the trust companies were compelled to call in their paper-thin loans. When cash-starved companies could not repay, a chain reaction of defaults and failures ensued.[72]

Adding to the destruction of San Francisco and the Pacific economy, and the intense pressure on banks and trusts, was the pivotal impact of insurance. Before the sun set on the inflamed and shattered San Francisco and its fifty thousand terrified displaced residents, it was clear that the metropolis had suffered millions of dollars in damage—$200 million was the number immediately reported and generally accepted. That was a staggering sum. However, the insurance companies in America and England that had happily been collecting surplus-producing premiums for years from San Franciscans were now reluctant to pay.[73] This outraged the victims, who could only see the big corporations as greedy, heartless, and willing to aggravate their plight.

Even paying minimal claims sent millions in gold from British insurers pouring into California. So much British gold flowed into the United States that the Bank of England took defensive measures to protect its own monetary system, discriminating against the American dollar and raising interest on American sources. Then, overextended British insurers, which mainly indemnified fire claims, flatly announced that they would not pay San Francisco earthquake losses where fire was not the primary cause of destruction. The bewildering decision forced the homeless and ravaged of San Francisco to divine whether their homes were vanquished by the earthquake before they burned, or burned and were then further wrecked in one of the many aftershocks.[74]

"San Francisco's $200 million 'ash heap' involves complications which will be felt on all financial markets for many months to come," wrote London's *Financial Times* on July 6, 1906. The paper warned the fiscal community that "the payment of losses sustained . . . represents a financial undertaking of far-reaching magnitude."[75]

In early May 1906, American insurers met in secret to draw up their own plans to preserve their assets. Their idea was to "tax" every insurance policy in the United States. Newspapers of the day reported, "Insurance managers in secret session in this city [New York] are planning to increase rates to the whole country, thus making the people pay the losses for which the people had [previously] provided a surplus."[76]

America's mushrooming credit crunch and financial squeeze caused a mass run on banks and trust companies—a panic. Many regular banks and trust companies across America began closing their doors the very day the earthquake hit. People could not withdraw their funds. Panic increased. Guards were posted to prevent currency from being looted, from without and from within. Suddenly, cash itself disappeared from the nation's coffers. Treasury Secretary Leslie Shaw rushed $15 million in currency to San Francisco banks to relieve the pressure. But Shaw's fiscal injection could not stop banks and trust companies from failing, not only in America but also in Japan, Germany, and Italy.[77]

Panic continued. Throughout late 1906 and the first nine months of 1907, America's eviscerated economy teetered on a razor's edge. On October 18, 1907, Montana magnate F. Augustus Heinze tried to take advantage of the disarray to corner the copper market. Heinze invested scores of millions in United Copper Company stock, then tried to fix the price to sustain his takeover. But United finally collapsed under the weight of Heinze's wangling. The company's stock fell 76 percent overnight. Heinze lost $50 million in a day. Because Heinze either owned or sat on the board of so many New York banks and trust companies, such as the Mercantile Bank and the Knickerbocker Trust, depositors flocked in panic to withdraw their money. Knickerbocker president Charles Barney was himself a confederate of Heinze's, and his institution was besieged by angry customers. Within hours, Knickerbocker itself was made $8 million lighter. Soon, other banks declined to accept Knickerbocker checks, which in turn only escalated depositor demands to extricate their funds. A few weeks later, a morose Barney stared into a gun barrel and killed himself. More bank dominoes began falling and the stock of distrusted speculator companies dived as well.[78]

The awesome culmination of financial chaos and collapse became known as the Panic of 1907. Many average investors were ruined, and in the smolder of their ruination, a rogue's gallery of speculator companies crashed and burned. Among the corporate casualties was the Electric Vehicle Company, which for many came to symbolize archetypal stock manipulation. Although the conglomerate's New York taxi operation continued for some years as a spin-off entity that was slowly run into the ground, the EVC's ability—or even its pretense of an ability—to do anything to further the cause of electric mobility came to a screeching halt.

Bankrupt and in receivership, nothing viable remained except the company's prize possession: the Selden patent.[79]

That meant that even in receivership the EVC was chiefly interested in continuing the campaign of intimidation against nonmember internal combustion automobile makers, this through its still-functioning alliance with the ALAM. The attacks on Ford were a good investment as they pushed other less defiant companies into compliance. When these companies paid up, they paid not only on future sales, but so-called back damages on all prior cars sold.[80]

But Ford was unfazed. He pushed ahead to new frontiers of cheap cars and in 1906 introduced the Model N, enhanced in 1907, as the vehicle not only mass-assembled from parts, but truly created on an assembly line. Racks were constructed in the factories enabling three motors to be assembled simultaneously, and soon after this technique was expanded to allow seventy-five motors to be finished from five such racks in a single day. The Model N, a four-cylinder, 15 hp car promised a 200-mile range on ten gallons of gas and sustained speeds of 45 mph, all for $500. That magical $500 price point could not be honored long, and the cost soon rose to $600 and more. But even at $600 or more, the farmer, small-town resident, and middle-class urbanite had all found a reliable, bargain-priced car they could call their own. Only about 6,400 cars were purchased in the 1907–8 season. More would have been sold except for the general economic conditions arising from the Panic of 1907.[81]

However, the Model N begat the Model T, which enjoyed the benefits of even more advanced, almost maniacal, assembly-line efficiencies. Every bit of tooling and physical exertion was designed to maximize economic productivity. Virtually nothing was wasted. Even the residue of wood crates was gathered up to create a popular charcoal to help the company's bottom line, called Ford charcoal, later renamed Kingsford charcoal after a family member, E. G. Kingsford, the man who helped Ford build the charcoal plant. Priced at $850 to $950, depending upon the model, Model Ts flew off the dealer floors, and eventually the company stopped taking orders until it could expand its factories. Ford sold 10,607 new cars during the 1908–9 season. By now, the American heartland saw Ford and the automobile as one and the same.[82]

On September 15, 1909, after six years of grinding litigation, Judge Charles Hough finally ruled on the Selden suit. Unschooled in automotive technology and persuaded by the voluminous expert testimony arrayed by EVC's attorneys, Hough decided that technically Selden had in fact made history with his patent. Ford was guilty of infringement. Rather than cowing Ford and intimidating the public that wanted his vehicles, this stunning legal victory for big business seemed only to further energize the public behind the Model T and of course intensify Ford's determination to beat the Selden trust.[83]

Ford telegraphed dealers that he would appeal and "fight to the finish." He promised to battle on, to the Supreme Court if necessary, and continue the war until every penny of the company's $6 million assets and its bonding company was depleted. In the coming three months, newly armed and dangerous, the ALAM was able to wring "back damages" from any number of independent carmakers, all previously staunch allies of Ford, and all now bowed in submission. Maxwell Briscoe Motor Company, $44,440, Reo Motor Company, $43,486, and Dayton Motor Company, $25,714, headed an account sheet of manufacturer submissions that totaled $197,264. Add to that more than $873,000 in new royalties from a sudden expansion of begrudging membership, and ALAM coffers in 1909 were enriched by more than a million dollars. Ironically, with the EVC in shambles and in receivership, the ALAM was able to turn on its prior nemesis-cum-benefactor. Of the million ALAM collected by the last days of 1909, EVC receivers were forwarded only a meager share of $2,143.[84]

Throughout 1910, Ford continued his legal struggle. The appellate process itself seemed to be a rallying cry for the media and the public. In March 1910, the *Detroit Free Press* published an editorial bannered FORD, THE FIGHTER. Its first words reflected the public mood: "Ford the fighter, salute!" Calling Ford "equal to his weight in wildcats," the *Free Press* continued, "As a human figure he presents a spectacle to win the applause of all men with red blood; for this world dearly loves the fighting man, and needs him, too, if we are to go forward."[85]

One independent now out of business was typical in his admiration for Ford's spunk. He railed against the ALAM in a letter to the group, insisting, "When I purchase my Ford car, I don't want Mr. Ford or anyone else to give me an indemnifying bond to operate the same, as I feel that the Supreme Court of the United States will quickly see the injustice of your claims, and award to Mr. Ford such a verdict as will forever close the mouths of a lot of jealous minded manufacturers who are unable to compete with him in both price and quality."[86]

On May 16, 1910, the ALAM launched a dozen more suits against independent carmakers. But it was Ford who possessed the publicly endowed resources to marshal the bonds needed to protect customers. So it was his sales that continued to climb amid public enthusiasm for his defiance and the movement for an affordable automobile. In the 1909–10 season, after the adverse Hough decision had been received, Ford sales increased to 13,364, and during the next season zoomed to 34,528. In essence, the litigation only made the purchase of a Ford internal combustion machine a cause célèbre and a popular automotive mandate.[87]

On January 9, 1911, a three-judge appeal panel reviewing the briefs and oral appeals of some forty attorneys stunned the nation by reversing Judge Hough's decision. Ford was exonerated of any infringement. *Automobile* reported it this way: "Coming at a dramatic moment, while the great automobile show conducted under the auspices of the ALAM was unfolding in all its glory at the [Madison Square] Garden . . . the decision came like a clap of thunder and was entirely unexpected by the exhibitors at the big show."[88]

The Selden trust knew that its years-long battle was finally over, as the patent itself was set to expire in 1912. Indeed a year after the appellate reversal on January 11, 1912, the ALAM dissolved, after it had collected some $5.8 million in tribute, diverted the national emphasis away from electric, stymied the free flow of automotive enterprise, and pivotally helped popularize Henry Ford's internal combustion machine. During the 1911–12 season, Ford sales doubled again, now reaching 78,440, or almost six times the level two years earlier during Judge Hough's original adverse judgment.[89]

Now Ford would commit himself to arguably the biggest turnaround in American business. After pioneering the commonly affordable, road-proven reliable, economically sensible, and morally acceptable internal combustion machine, after fighting for years against the EVC and its surrogate the ALAM, after establishing a name that had become a synonym for gas-burning motorcars, Ford decided he would once again launch a better idea.

The two greatest inventive business minds in America would now unite. It would be Henry Ford and none other than Thomas Edison, the man who had brought music to people's ears with the phonograph, illumination to their nights with the lightbulb, and power to their homes and industries with current. The man of electricity and the man of automotive transport would come together to revolutionize America.

Their shocking idea was to bring to fruition the squandered hope of decades—the dream of personal transportation using clean energy from batteries. Edison and Ford pledged to develop and place in every American household a $600 electric vehicle that would be affordable for every family, offer range and speed to every motorist, and enjoy a national infrastructure of retail battery swapping and independent home energy that would make such cars universally operable. This would obsolete internal combustion. This would obsolete oil. This would remake the face of American transportation and industry forever.

The question was, would anyone let them do it?

CHAPTER EIGHT

1914—THE END OF THE BEGINNING

In the oil and bloodstained annals of the twentieth century already written, and those of the twenty-first century waiting to unfold, one year will stand out above all others as the most pivotal in the affairs of mankind, a fulcrum for all that preceded and followed. What did or did not happen in 1914 has dictated to the world how it would move from place to place, how it would cleave the darkness with illumination, how it would breathe the air and see the sky, how it would create and distribute power, who would enjoy and enjoin energy at what expense and at whose expense. That year will never be forgotten. Nor will it be understood.

In 1914, Thomas Edison and Henry Ford, two of the most inventive, most respected, and most entrepreneurial Americans who ever lived, came together in a gigantic, visionary enterprise. Their paths had crisscrossed for years until, now, they tried to change the world forever. But the saga of their partnership started long before.

Edison was always interested in motive power and always knew electricity could prevail. Even though he publicly excoriated the storage battery industry for its international thievery and stock fraud, he personally believed a better battery could be built. He believed he could build it and in so doing impart true American independence; that is, he wanted to literally convey all power to the people.

Edison was already an iconic, bigger-than-life figure in 1891 when young Henry Ford applied for work at the Edison Illuminating Company in Detroit. Ford had risen within two years to become chief engineer of the company. Edison had loomed as Ford's idol for almost a lifetime. At a famed 1896 chance encounter at a company convention, the young Ford, who was constantly tinkering with internal combustion, was granted a brief interview. Learning that Ford was perfecting a gasoline vehicle, Edison approvingly banged on a table and exclaimed, "Young man, that's the thing! You have it! Your car is self-contained and carries its own power plant."[1]

Ford savored the moment for years, which became legendary in the biography of the automobile. Long after, a successful Ford reminisced fondly, telling a newspaper interviewer, "That bang on the table was worth worlds to me. No man up to then had given me any encouragement. I had hoped that I was headed right. Sometimes I knew that I was, sometimes I only wondered, but here, all at once and out of a clear sky, the greatest inventive genius in the world had given me complete approval. The man who knew most about electricity in the world had said that for the purpose, my gas motor was better than any electric motor could be."[2]

But Edison's famous encouragement was somewhat disingenuous and perhaps intended to misguide an inventive young rival. In truth, Edison believed electricity was the superior motive power. In 1895, a year before he met Ford, Edison had already invented and road tested his own rudimentary battery-operated, three-wheeled electric vehicle. During that time, even as Morris and Salom and the Electric Storage Battery Company in Philadelphia began establishing a name for electric vehicles, Edison was certain a lead-battery power source was just too heavy and brittle to be practicable or yield any range. By mid-1899, he began experimenting in earnest with lighter metals to create his own revolutionary automobile battery. In all, he conducted some ten thousand tests. Beginning in late 1900, Edison developed an encouraging prototype. Finally, in early 1901, the inventor had assembled a lightweight array of nickel and iron plates that produced enough amperes per hour per gram to make his battery sensible. Yet his batteries weighed substantially less than the lead variety. Lead batteries, Edison noted, weighed 125 to 180 pounds per horsepower hour, whereas his nickel-iron creation weighed but 55 pounds per horsepower hour. Moreover, his lighter batteries could propel a vehicle some 75 miles, about twice the distance of a typical electric-vehicle battery.[3]

By April 1901, he had announced his invention to the media and set about building factories for mass production. By the fall of 1901, he had improved his new batteries to yield approximately half an ampere per gram of nickel and iron and felt it was time to commence production. Volume manufacturing and cheapness were mandatory in Edison's view. Years earlier, he had espoused his commercial philosophy to a friend, writing, "I am a believer in insuring the permanency of an investment by keeping prices so low that there is no inducement to others to come in and ruin it. There seems to be a law in commercial things as in nature. If one attempts to obtain more profit than average he is immediately punished by competitors."[4]

In May 1901, Edison formed the Edison Storage Battery Company and in August 1903 began churning out the cells composed of nine iron and nickel plates. Twenty such cells were packed under a Baker runabout and other vehicles and road tested for as many as five thousand rough and bumpy miles to demonstrate durability. Edison's batteries could be recharged in about three and a half hours, or about half the overnight duration required for lead competitors. Most exciting, he planned a handy supportive infrastructure to recharge the batteries. He wanted to create a widespread recharging network at trolley lines and central electrical stations, with such a network extending into the countryside. Where such facilities did not exist, he suggested erecting small windmills attached to electrical generators that would light the home at night and recharge the batteries while occupants slept, thereby creating energy independence for the average home and vehicle. Windmills or electrical siphoning from other facilities, he said, would be cheaper than the growing reliance on gasoline.[5]

Edison considered his new battery the crowning achievement of a lifetime of invention. He was now ready to retire to the good life of pure science. In February 1903, filled with satisfaction, he granted an *Atlanta Constitution* reporter an interview at his West Orange, New Jersey, laboratory. Throwing a pencil at a yellow pad, he fell back into a comfortable armchair and exclaimed, "At last, I've finished work on my storage battery and now I'm going to take a rest." He turned to the window, stared out for a moment of reflection, then admitted, "I'm tired—very tired," adding without adornment, "I'm all worn-out."[6]

Promising himself, the reporter, and the world that he would embark on a long vacation to celebrate the end of his career, Edison chimed, "And the best part of it all is that—it will last two years." Rubbing his hands in a wave of new excitement, he said, "I'm going to have a fine time—splendid time—during these two years. Yes, sir, that's what I am going to do."[7]

Returning to the feeling of exhaustion, he repeated, "Now, however, I'm tired—thoroughly tired—and I've made up my mind to drop industrial science for two whole years and rest myself by taking up pure science—by investigating the thousand and one properties of metals and chemicals that I've got notes about in my book. . . . It will be fun and maybe I'll find out something worthwhile—who can tell."[8]

Waxing philosophical, Edison echoed what others had confessed for centuries before him, that the mystic power that he had been tinkering with—electricity—was incomprehensible. "Why, with all my work in electricity," he admitted, "I don't know what electricity is. True. I've thought out several inventions and made my brain and body weary thereby, and I've got my name noised about, but what have I done—what do I know— after all? Why, simply this: very little, hardly anything, when we think of the things still to be done and still to be learned—of the forces all around us that we don't understand in the least—that we scarcely dream of."[9]

But in his excitement to deliver a mystic miracle of motive power, Edison had simply not done enough testing. The trim and cross-braced rectilinear battery was placed on the market prematurely. His nickel-iron beauty was not "the final perfection of the storage battery" as he boasted to *North American Review*. The electrical industry trade press, stung by decades of battery chicanery and exaggeration, was more than a little skeptical. London's *Electrician* in its October 1902 edition sneered at "ridiculous stories of 1,000 mile runs" by electrical vehicles. The *Electrician* insisted on seeing real-world tests "run under working conditions for six months or a year," before exalting Edison's box of energy.[10]

Unfortunately, the neatly soldered seams of Edison's sleek black battery leaked. Moreover, regular recharging wore down the capacity to the point of requiring reconditioning. Fixing those flaws only revealed additional problems with the electrodes. Yes, the batteries worked, but they were far from carefree and therefore no vast improvement over their lead predecessors. By November 1904, Edison had become fed up with his own miracle. His hopes for a recuperative two-year vacation and then a vigorous romp through the meadows of pure science were dismantled. Producing a vastly superior battery meant going back to work day and night until its unquestioned superiority could be attained. Unrivaled excellence was his only option. Edison's own pamphlet explained that he "closed the big factory, scrapped the machinery and started [again] after that perfect storage battery."[11]

By February 1910, after a tedious half decade in the laboratory and field testing up and down the Northeast corridor, as well as an obsessive expenditure of some $3.5 million, Edison had finally conquered the problems that plagued his miracle. He established a newly refurbished and retooled 200,000-square-foot, four-story battery factory in West Orange. Long rows of wooden counters allowed five hundred cells daily to move from table to table until final assembly. The new version was assured to last more than forty thousand miles—almost a lifetime for many cars of the day.[12]

Edison's improved 1910 batteries were powerful enough to reliably run heavy trolleys in New York, push automobiles up and down the hills of San Francisco, and fuel a test vehicle a thousand miles. He paraded that thousand-mile test vehicle in public places with a large placard affixed to its hood trumpeting the accomplishment. The braggadocio of Edison's battery begged to be challenged, and in every instance its metal proved its mettle. So sturdy and so muscular were these new batteries, they were quickly deemed to be a natural power replacement for the horse-drawn delivery vehicle. Beer, bread, milk, department-store goods, and general deliveries could now be moved far more economically and without the clatter, dung droppings, and piercing stench of the omnipresent equine beast of burden. Electric, with its instant on-and-off motor, was vastly better suited than an idling internal combustion engine to the stop-and-go, haul-in and haul-out, of deliverymen.[13] Beyond just automotive vehicles, Edison was determined to convert riverboats, coastal vessels, railroads, and even lawn mowers to his new battery.[14] It was really a world of transportation and devices in motion that Edison intended to revolutionize. The public was eager and willing.

Six years after his first battery was voluntarily withdrawn, as America entered the second decade of the fast-moving twentieth century, the public had evolved into a new consumer constituency. The nation was more urbanized, more sophisticated, and more automotive. By now, the average man—town or country—was immersed in the national fascination over speed and internal combustion. By 1910, hundreds of thousands of families had purchased cars—either Fords or other makes. Some 300,000 vehicles were plying American roads, and that number would more than double to 700,000 during the coming two years.[15] Almost all those vehicles were gasoline burning. Such cars did not exist without exhaust. Soot and clatter became the new dung and clop of America's daily life. Edison's promise of a smoke-free, noise-free nation of cars, trucks, and trains was now a vision for all to entertain in an age of rising mechanical expectations, in an era where the word "modern" was an adjective of endless possibilities.

At the same time, Henry Ford began to realize that his immensely popular Model T suffered from a significant problem: a faulty electrical ignition system to drive the pistons. Equally important, the brutish hand-cranked motor-starting system needed to become a thing of the past.[16]

Ideas and developments in Detroit and West Orange were converging.

A new electric vehicle like the Model T that would be cheap enough and reliable enough for the common man became more than a bright idea for Edison. It became a consuming mission. On January 9, 1911, the Selden patent trust was dethroned, and the patent made inert. Two natural enemies of Edison and Ford were finally slain: the remnant bogeyman of the Electric Vehicle Company and the so-called Lead Trust, and its partner in coercion and restraint, the establishment internal-combustion carmakers of the ALAM.

How perfect would be the vindication if Ford and Edison now collaborated to mass-produce an automobile that would be better than internal combustion, better than a lead-battery-powered vehicle—better than both.

Certainly, in 1911, Edison still faced stiff competition from the entrenched lead-battery monopoly that had dominated the market since the prior century. The EVC's surviving parent company, the Electric Storage Battery Company, remained the principal supplier of batteries to the nation. Since 1900, it had sold auto batteries under the Exide brand, short for "excellent oxide." The company's new heavy-duty version, the Ironclad, powered commercial trucks and more demanding personal-vehicle loads. Despite Edison's marvelous new battery, the rival to defeat was still the widely used and much advertised Exide.[17]

Throughout 1911, Edison tried to crack Exide's market control. His nickel-iron Type A battery had quickly proved a success for trucks. Now Edison wanted to make his battery the driving force in the "pleasure vehicle" market that was waiting to explode. His chief ally was longtime friend W. E. Anderson, president of the Detroit-based Anderson Electric Car Company. Anderson was a small firm, producing just eighty or so autos per month, but one of the most respected and successful electric runabout manufacturers in the business in a community of minor players. Five of Anderson's 1911 models featured Edison batteries, but about half the company's overall sales still contained lead batteries.[18]

Several other companies, such as Waverly Electric, Ohio Electric, and Babcock Electric, produced an Edison-powered model, but these were mere add-on efforts to comply with antitrust provisions. Baker Electric "got cold feet," an Edison manager reported to the inventor, because "a Jew who is their biggest agent, and by the way a hustler, buys cars without batteries and assembles his own lead battery here," using one "much cheaper . . . than the Exide." The Baker agent offered to purchase Edison batteries at a steep discount that would match his existing expense, but Edison's manager decided to fight the agent through Baker's senior management. Therefore, in the electric vehicle field of 1911, small but worthy Anderson stood out as the vanguard for Edison's market entry.[19]

As such, Edison had granted Anderson a contract that was nearly exclusive, except for token additional representation to avoid antitrust implications. Edison had also assured Anderson of advertising support to counteract Exide propaganda and any attendant Exide whisper campaign about Anderson's choice of batteries.[20]

Edison's efforts seemed to be working all around. Public acceptance of the Type A battery and its variants for a range of power needs—from railroad cars to motorcars—was zooming. Early in 1911, 1,600 cells were being produced weekly. By March, that number had increased to 2,200 weekly. By April, manufacturing volume rose to 2,700 weekly. By late spring 1911, Edison wrote a stockholder that he was ramping up to hit the 1,000-cell-per-day level and boasted that Edison Storage Battery Company enjoyed back orders for 13,500 cells. Battery revenues in fiscal 1907 before the new Type A was introduced were an anemic $256,290. In fiscal 1910, they had more than doubled to $572,963. Within the coming two years, sales would increase to $702,628.[21]

Moreover, Type A cells in various sizes and descriptions were being employed in realms other than transportation. Edison was providing them for a range of electrical uses, from power-station switches to telephones to gun sights to doorbells. A handwritten company list produced in late 1911, stretching four pages, enumerated sixty-four separate applications.[22]

But Edison considered the replacement of both the reviled lead battery in electric vehicles and the gasoline motorcar to be Type A's greatest potential value. Newspapers coast to coast hailed the achievement of nickel and iron. The *Detroit Free Press* typically bannered EDISON PERFECTS STORAGE BATTERY, NEW BATTERY WILL REVOLUTIONIZE CAR SYSTEMS.[23] Even though the kudos and orders were streaming in, Edison knew his revolution required still more real-world testing until his product could certifiably withstand the worst abuse of America's ramshackle road system. He was determined not to repeat the debacle attending his earlier attempt.

In November 1911, Anderson shipped Edison a vehicle for yet another spate of rigorous endurance trials. The new regimen through New Jersey's best and worst city streets and country lanes included straightaways, hill climbs, and bumpy routes variously traversed at high and low speed, at low and high voltage, and for many miles up inclines "when the battery is nearly exhausted." Edison's Type A stood up to the most unforgiving road conditions. By November 30, 1911, Edison was able to write Anderson that despite the grueling challenges "I only charge it [the battery] twice a week."[24]

In the latest proving effort, Edison could not help but feel that his technical breakthroughs and new research were only aiding the competition's research. In November 1911, he wrote Anderson, "Even my enemies are [now] making these tests on heavy grades [inclines] and are finding out a lot of things they never knew."[25] But the pure inventor in Edison would not permit himself to desist. By the end of 1911 he was convinced—he had finally gotten it right.

It was time to take the nation by storm with a clean-running electric vehicle for every home. But with which automobile company? The venture was too enormous for the inventor's network of captive companies. Edison realized this even as he toyed with his own car company.

Several years earlier, Edison had acquired control of the financially strapped Lansden Company, an electric vehicle manufacturer specializing in delivery vehicles that employed Edison batteries. In the first week of April 1912, Edison tested Lansden trucks with heavy loads along long routes of between sixty and ninety miles, often under rainy conditions over muddy roads. Lansden trucks stood up to the treatment, even though cobblestone pounding did dislodge some wiring in one case. In May 1912, an Edison manager was able to brag that a Lansden truck operated by the Phonograph Companies "has completed [the equivalent of] one complete trip around the earth—29,902 miles—and is starting its second lap without out a cent's repair to battery other than solution. . . . Now can you beat that?" But later in 1912, Edison preferred to sell the entity to General Motors, which was then seeking a greater share of the electric-truck market. Thus, he abandoned any idea of building and distributing his own car. He told one unsolicited investor that because he wanted to sell batteries to any and all builders of electric cars, he "could not be [personally] interested in any vehicle company."[26]

Nonetheless, to achieve the real prize, a car for the masses, meant an alliance, not with a small-output manufacturer like Anderson, or any collage of such producers, but with the nation's mass-producing giant, Ford Motor Company. By the fall of 1912, Ford and Edison had decided to act both separately and together to revolutionize the industrial and residential world, freeing it from fuel, power, and transportation monopolies, as well as the Wall Street financiers who controlled them. If successful, every home, automobile, and industrial source would operate independently off its own cheap, clean, abundant, and renewable energy source. The technology would soon be revealed. It would be amazing.

The most dramatic of these shared visions was Ford and Edison's decision to team up and create the long-awaited cheap and practical electric car for the masses. By the fall of 1912, this joint effort was under way.

When Anderson detected the end of his strategic relationship with Edison, and that Ford would replace him as the new partner, his heartfelt friendship with the inventor abruptly evaporated. Anderson had staked his company's future on fighting the Exide cartel, and now Edison was walking on to a better partner. The drop in advertising support was probably Anderson's first big signal. Suddenly, the affectionate salutations on letters and enthusiastic commercial camaraderie ended. In a bitter and caustic protest, Anderson let loose. The diatribe began with a supercilious "Dear Sir" and deteriorated from there into confrontational language.[27]

"Dear Sir: Enclosed herewith I hand you letter and advertisements which will explain themselves. Now, we desire to know what your [advertising] intentions are at this time relative to keeping your battery before the buying public. I intended to have taken this matter up in person with you [during a recent visit], but our time was pretty well occupied with Mr. Ford while there, and this [question] was entirely neglected. I recall, and you must remember also, that after entering into our working arrangement . . . you put your arm on my shoulder and said: 'Anderson, you can depend upon one thing, we will not see you licked, we will help you out in any way that is thought best.' "[28]

Anderson continued, "The question now arises, inasmuch as these people [Electric Storage Battery Company] are spending from $15,000 to $20,000 a month, as to what you are going to do." Ridiculing Edison's advertising consultants, Anderson went on, "I have met two or three men who claim to be looking after your advertising down there, and I beg the privilege of saying they are jokes. They may be all right for Manhattan Island, but they certainly won't do in the Middle West where the big demand is. What you must do is to keep your battery before the people and they must be told its qualities."[29]

Anderson ended his lambasting by attacking Edison for his many personality-driven print interviews, which typically extolled the inventor's great record of painstaking innovation. "We don't want a lot of publicity about yourself," protested Anderson. "I find that people are well posted as to who you are, but they are not well posted as to the quality of the battery."[30]

An uncharacteristically defensive Edison scribbled his response, dated August 18, 1912, atop Anderson's letter, rebutting that his personality interviews were worth their weight in ink. "If you were to get all the printed articles about the E Battery [Edison Battery] which come out in interviews with me and otherwise," asserted the famous inventor, "you would soon realize if no publicity was being given the Edison battery, and in fact [that space] was paid for, it would take a bit of money."[31]

On August 31, 1912, Anderson followed up, trying to appear more promising as a growth partner, and yet plaintive in his need for help against the skilled ravages of the Electric Storage Battery Company. "The outlook for business next year on the electric looks good to us," wrote Anderson. "We are going to increase our output considerably, if the Exide don't put us out of business. The talk is now they are going to form a combine to control all electric cars, including the Anderson."[32]

Indeed, the Electric Storage Battery Company (ESB) had reacted to Edison's competitive spur by improving its lead battery and keeping the price lower than the Type A. The new Exide Ironclad was enjoying preliminary good reviews from the trade press. *Horseless Age* called it "perfect and something unique," adding "the improved Ironclad-Exide battery puts the electric vehicle in an advanced position [that provides] . . . a corresponding improvement in the vehicle as a whole." But like many of ESB's earlier efforts, their product suffered under prolonged real-world use, especially in terms of mileage and longevity. What ESB could not achieve in proven performance, it sought by attack tactics, organizing a subversion campaign against Edison's Type A.[33]

Edison went on the counterattack, placing stark, all-type warning ads. Under the banner THE NEW EDISON STORAGE BATTERY, one such ad centered the word WARNING! Beneath that was printed the following alarum: "The Public is hereby warned against certain manufacturers of ELECTRIC VEHICLES, who, solely to obtain a greater profit from their vehicles, use a cheap lead battery, giving but half the mileage and one tenth the life of the above. Use of the lead battery reduces the total cost of a vehicle, but is PRICE the only thing to be considered in making so important an investment? For the above reason no hesitation has been shown in making all kinds of misstatements regarding THE NEW EDISON STORAGE BATTERY. Mr. Edison certainly would not spend seven years obtaining a battery to solve the problem of vehicle traction in cities, were he not thoroughly convinced the results could never be obtained by the use of a lead battery. The great stores of New York City, after using lead batteries for many years and EDISON BATTERIES but for three years, are discarding the lead, and using the higher priced EDISON BATTERY. WHY? BECAUSE IT IS RELIABLE."[34]

In the fall of 1912, the promise of Edison's new battery rose to the next level. His latest wizardry would allow every home, automobile, and industrial source to function as a freestanding generating station.

In mid-September 1912, Edison announced the result of some fifty thousand experiments conducted during seven painstaking years—a radical new energy-self-sufficient home. He called it the Twentieth Century Suburban Residence. Ostentatiously overstuffed with every modern gadget and appliance from a coffee percolator to a washing machine, to room heaters and coolers, to phonographs and tiny movie projectors—the mansion was an electric marvel. Every device and system, basement to roof, was powered by batteries replenished continuously by a small-scale household electrical generator.

The New York Times, September 15, 1912: "The Powers of Darkness have suffered another rout. Thomas A. Edison, their implacable and indefatigable foe, has devised a final scheme for their undoing, which will follow them to their remotest strongholds and drive them forth even from the recesses of a country farmhouse.[35]

"For Mr. Edison has perfected a combination of gasoline engine, generator, and storage batteries by which, for a modest expense, every man can make his own electricity in his own cellar, utterly and for all time independent of the nearness or farness of the big electrical companies. He can buy a farm in the Middle West or New England and be as free of worries over lighting and heating as if he were a householder on Forty-Second Street. He can erect a tent in the desert, if he is so minded, and still read himself to sleep at night under a convenient electrical chandelier, and shave himself the next morning with water heated on an electrical stove.[36]

"He can travel so far from the haunts of men that nothing remains to him of their memory, but he cannot, unless he deliberately wills it, find a darkness that Mr. Edison has not given him means to overcome."[37]

The system's secret was an array of three simple tanks: one for water, a second for oil, and a third for gasoline—all connected to an on-site mini-generator itself regulated by an automatic voltage adjuster and a series of circuit breakers. The resident was to "start his engine and forget it" for days at a time. The system worked this way: Edison's Type A nickel-iron batteries would run the house and all its gizmos. Every two to three days, the batteries would become discharged. The system would detect the drained batteries. When cued by the system, the on-site generator would automatically replenish the nickel-iron batteries in a seven-hour recharging session, often even as the homeowner slept. A staged and redundant array of batteries ensured that energy levels throughout the abode remained constant even as some units were being recharged. The same generator would recharge the new Type A–powered electric vehicle soon to be mass-produced by Ford, thus completing the circle of individual energy independence.[38]

The first fully operational house was Edison's grand mansion at Llewellyn Park, New Jersey. For its coverage, the *New York Times* photographed the home inside and out, toured all the rooms, and verified demonstrations of endless electrically driven devices, from toothbrush sanitizers to foot warmers. The pocket generating plant was a narrow and compact machine, designed to be situated either in the yard, in a shed, or in the basement. Its cost: as little as $500, although it came in larger and more expensive sizes capable of supplying greater-scale housing. Edison's Twentieth Century Suburban Residence would provide cheap, independent power to any suburban abode with a lot or the needed building space as well as the rural home beyond the lines of city power plants.[39] Self-sufficiency was no longer a vision for tomorrow, but a reality.

Initially, the generators would operate off a small tank of gasoline that periodically needed to be refilled. Clearly, this temporarily retained the tether to petroleum. But plans were to switch from dependence on a modicum of weekly gasoline to small residential windmills—that is, as soon as one could be perfected. Like most Americans, Edison was quite familiar with the utility of windmills. In the early twentieth century, the majority of America's population still resided on farms, where windmills supplying mechanical muscle were commonplace. Industrial windmills to power factory work were just as well-known. For years, Edison had entertained the concept of a shared residential windmill that would provide electrical power to a group of houses. Drawings in his office depicted a small central windmill spinning as a hub and supplying kilowatts to between four and six dwellings. Eleven months before the September 15, 1912, *New York Times* announcement, Edison dispatched letters to leading windmill manufacturers seeking a prototype that could provide not just muscular power but also reliably turn a dynamo to generate electricity to recharge storage batteries.[40]

The responses Edison received were mixed. Charles Jager Company of Boston recalled his company's long "struggle with windmills and storage batteries." Jager proudly recounted his most successful installation, which continuously powered a cluster of three Massachusetts homes with 45 lamp-hours per week during the summer and double that during the winter when heating was required. The Leach Wind Mill and Tank Co. in Chicago replied that when customers were polled, "they all seemed to be favorably inclined to use them [windmills]" for recharging of batteries. "With the storage battery," Leach added, "they do not care whether the wind blows all of the time or not. I am confident that most farmers would buy Storage Battery Autos if they had the means of storing power, or charging the batteries at home." But Woods and Co. in Manhattan dismissed the idea due to the expected "excessive cost of storage batteries which require replenishing from time to time." Appleton Manufacturing, located south of Chicago, also rejected the idea outright because the wind feeding its installations was never reliably constant, "so the motion might vary from 10 to 400 revolutions a minute."[41]

The divergent responses from windmill makers, and a review of a dozen technical articles and books on the subject, undoubtedly convinced Edison that a proper windmill would take much time and experimentation. So in their first version, the generators of the first Twentieth Century Suburban Residence were to operate on gasoline.

Turning to the electric car Edison planned to power for Ford, the outlook was nothing less than astounding. Ford had committed to building some 12,500 such vehicles monthly in just the first year. Moreover, to avoid any suggestion of a combine, Edison would be allowed to sell his dynamic new batteries to any electric vehicle manufacturer.[42] Ford's bitter experience with the ALAM, which had only ended the year before in 1911, surely influenced his determination not to follow in Lead Trust's and Selden Trust's monopolistic footsteps.

Soon, Edison realized that Ford's production demands of 1,500 battery units per day required a prodigious investment in new plants and machinery. William Bee, general manager of the Edison Storage Battery Company, favored inviting financial assistance directly from Ford himself, thus avoiding the unhappy experience of seeking outside investment. Edison finally agreed with the notion, and on October 29, 1912, he approached Ford with a short, handwritten message.[43]

"Friend Ford," wrote Edison, with the first *F* of "Friend" swirled in his trademark penmanship. "Billy Bee seems to be obsessed with the idea of having you do a little gambling with me on the future of the storage battery. Nothing would please me more than to have you join in, it looks as if it has a large future. Up to present time I have only increased the plant with profits made in my other things, and this has a limit. Of course I could go to Wall St and get more, but my experience over there is as sad as Chopin's Funeral March, I keep away. Yours, Edison."[44]

Ford, a man of great wealth and almost no outside investments, gladly helped. He provided an immense order fortified with the certainty of cash payment. This would in essence finance the project, an undertaking so gigantic that it dwarfed all other prior electrical-vehicle output combined. Edison prepared a stockholder letter. His scribbled notes confirmed, "We have an order from the Ford Auto Co for about 4 million dollars worth of battery per year. They build next year 150,000 autos, I am [personally] advancing the money for buildings and machinery [based on Ford's promise to pay]. . . . Ford pays cash. The Co is allowed to make 10% net, from these profits. They pay the machinery and buildings. The principal use for battery is trucks, train lighting and Storage Battery Cars." Between Edison's money and Ford's infusion, an estimated $1.75 million was funneled into the new enterprise.[45]

Edison was now producing 700 Type A batteries daily for all uses. Ford's financial injection allowed Edison to dramatically increase production for Detroit. The inventor wrote another stockholder message, specifying, "This information is strictly confidential. . . . We are ½ finished to go to 1000 [batteries] daily, the Ford order is for 1500 per day additional." But many orders beyond Ford's were streaming in as well. Making the situation clear to shareholders, Edison flatly admitted, "Anderson's exclusive is off and everyone can buy."[46]

Long occluded by a sludge of avarice, bad engineering, public policy neglect, and the intoxicating fumes of gasoline, the electric vehicle's promise was about to be fulfilled. Prior endeavors had hoped to place hundreds of electrics on the road to be championed by well-to-do diehards and niche enthusiasts. The Ford-Edison idea would place hundreds of thousands of electric vehicles in the hands of ordinary Americans to create a new automotive reality in the country. Moreover, any carmaker would be granted access to the same technology. Hence, Anderson and the other preexisting small players of the field could create their own cars for Edison's Type A.[47] A new industry standard would be created.

New partners lined up. General Electric through its General Vehicle Co. subsidiary would join the movement by mass-producing a car specifically designed for the Type A, but along a special concept. The driver would never actually purchase the expensive battery. These would be owned by Edison's partners. Instead, the motorist would merely drive into a special facility and periodically exchange units, paying a small charge for a "refill." Edison dubbed this exchange method the Edison Battery Service System. A November 22, 1912, draft agreement for General Vehicle explained that the Edison Battery Service System was devised so "purchasers of the vehicles can be relieved of the necessity of making investments in batteries or providing facilities for charging and maintaining such batteries." The General Vehicle agreement envisioned a long-range change; it called for a minimum term of six years with a one-year continuity period should it terminate at any time.[48]

Where would owners of electric autos manufactured by General Vehicle and other companies receive their refilled or recharged batteries?

In the urbanized areas, public electric utilities would revive the years-old dream of creating charging stations and then go a significant additional step by opening retail battery exchange services with Edison-equipped cars in mind. This would be the equivalent of the developing trend of creating gas stations for internal combustion cars. But instead of gas in the tank, batteries in the tray would be replenished.[49]

Typical was the negotiation with the Hartford Electric Light Company, the city's main electricity provider. A three-way draft agreement between the Hartford utility, Edison Storage Battery Company, and General Vehicle would ensure that motorists could easily drive into various stations operated by the utility and trade a discharged battery for a freshly charged unit. Experience showed such an exchange could be accomplished in as little as seventy-five seconds. A draft of the three-way agreement incorporated this preamble: "Whereas it is believed by all the parties hereto that the general adoption of the electric vehicle for purposes of transportation would be greatly facilitated, (a) if the purchaser's initial investment is reduced to a minimum, and (b) if the purchaser can be relieved of the battery charging and of the care of the battery for such vehicles," new vehicles would be delivered "minus the charge for the battery." Owners would instead rely upon the Hartford utility to provide fresh batteries. Such utilities would in turn recharge the batteries during their off-peak hours when unused electricity was abundant.[50] Everyone would win.

For infrastructure beyond the self-sustaining home and the urban charging center, Edison planned to distribute his batteries to hardware and general stores everywhere as a common household item, just as lightbulbs were.[51]

Finally. It was happening. The automobile revolution, which began as an electrical phenomenon, would return to the concept advanced nearly a generation earlier. The world could become a cleaner, quieter, more efficient place, drawing its strength from nature, from electricity. The American spirit of independence would be achieved not only by permitting mobility but by enabling stunning individual self-sufficiency.

The country was more than ready. True, the sound and fury of internal combustion had long been hypnotic. But the trance was rudely being interrupted by an upwardly spiraling cost of oil. By fall 1912, a shortage of refined supply had boosted gas prices some 75 percent over the previous year. Oil was no longer "negligible." The September 18, 1912, edition of *Horseless Age* published a full-page article exploring fuel alternatives in view of the shortage. Since most motorcars were propelled by internal combustion, the article was headlined THE RISING PRICE OF GASOLINE AND FAILING SUPPLY BRING UP POSSIBILITY OF USING OTHER FUELS, NOTABLY KEROSENE, WHICH IS CHEAP AND PLENTIFUL. The opening sentence set forth the problem. "The recent sudden rise in the price of gasoline, following gradual increases during the past several years, all over the world, together with the enormous number of automobiles, commercial cars and other users of this fuel, has called attention again to the fuel question in a marked manner. Whereas the previous retail price of 16 cents a gallon seemed high enough, it now retails all over New York City at from 18 to 22 cents, the latter figure being in the majority. A year ago, it could be had at 14 retail, and as low as 10 cents wholesale. This represents a rise of about 75 per cent within a year." One tank of gasoline could easily exceed two days' wages of the average factory worker who assembled such cars.[52]

Vehicular growth was vastly outstripping gasoline production. The number of autos had increased from three hundred thousand in 1910 to seven hundred thousand in 1912. In the past year alone, after the Selden threat had been debunked, some two hundred thousand cars had been purchased; that represented a one-year vehicle increase of some 66 percent. During the same time, crude supplies increased by less than 4 percent from 209.5 million barrels to 217 million barrels. Gasoline was the final distillate in the refining process, which also produced kerosene and lubricants. But less than 10 percent of the petroleum total, or about 20 million barrels, was being refined into gasoline or naphtha. Supplies were further strained by the need to export ever greater quantities of American oil to England; the United States was Great Britain's chief source for petroleum. Since actual fuel sales for car engines was almost four times the available supply, fuel was necessarily adulterated with heavier fractions, impurities, and natural gas condensations and liquefaction.[53] Engine performance and maintenance were deteriorating even as prices skyrocketed.

In many cities, a "gasoline war" was declared, that is, a battle to keep prices down. New York was particularly hard hit by increases because of its monumental auto growth and rocketing consumption. Whereas gas sold for fifteen to eighteen cents per gallon in Connecticut and Massachusetts, in metropolitan New York the cost was twenty to twenty-five cents.

Under the headline CLUB JOINS GASOLINE WAR, *Horseless Age* on October 2, 1912, reported, "Following the recent action of the New York Garage Owners' Association, the members of the Long Island Automobile Club of Brooklyn, N.Y., also have literally taken up the cudgels in the battle waged against the discriminatory action of the oil companies in setting the prices for gasoline in the metropolis. The club has protested the methods followed by the oil companies, and is considering an appeal to the Government. . . . The companies explain that this difference is due to the law of supply and demand. . . . It looks to us," the club was quoted, "more like a case of 'charge what the traffic will stand.' "[54]

The *New York Times* reported the problem this way: "In spite of plans and undoubted intentions to build more automobiles in the present year than ever before, it is not denied that the motor industry, as well as the motor car owner, faces a most serious problem and possible setback in the soaring price of gasoline. It is predicted that gas will reach 40 cents or more a gallon in the coming summer. What this means to the pleasure car maker and owner, as well as to those interested from any viewpoint in motor trucks, may readily be appreciated."[55]

What's more, the environmental damage was beginning to accrue in palpable ways. Billows of smoke from tailgate exhaust combined with clouds from railroad engines and industrial smokestacks to darken the air and burn the lungs. Oil and grease effluent from garages was swirling into rivers, poisoning the water. Hydrologists were concerned that groundwater was becoming irreparably toxic.[56]

In addition, petroliferous runoff into the sewer systems of major cities was causing urban explosions. New York's Explosives or Combustible Commission declared, as *Horseless Age* reported, "an absolute need to prevent the flowing of waste gasoline and oils from garages into the city sewers." Periodically, such sewers would simply ignite. The *New York Times* reported one such incident under the banner SEWER EXPLOSION TERRIFIES A BLOCK. The story led, "An explosion of gasoline that had accumulated in the sewer running under Broadway, 55th Street, Sixth Avenue and 54th Street shook that district like an earthquake at 9:30 o'clock yesterday morning, threw sixteen manhole covers high in the air, and damaged thirty buildings. Ten persons in houses in 54th Street were cut by broken glass from the windows, and the flames that shot from the sewer openings caused a panic among persons passing in the streets." The explosive force was so great that one manhole cover was hurtled "over the roof of a five-story building." Residents complained it was hardly the first time that neighborhood had been rocked by gasoline ignited in the sewers.[57]

Electrics suddenly became popular again. After years of stagnation, the electric vehicle industry was experiencing resurgence. In 1910, the Electric Vehicle Association of America formed to bring car manufacturers and utilities together to promote their common interest in battery-run automobiles. As the price of gasoline escalated 75 percent in a year, membership in the association experienced a concomitant rise, from 197 companies in 1911 to 317 by the third annual convention on October 8, 1912. The steep increase in electric vehicle adoption was becoming obvious to many, especially in trucking. In New Jersey, the Public Service Corporation would soon announce it had seen a 1,000 percent increase in electric vehicles since 1911. In 1911, only 30 electric trucks were registered, and two years later that number soared to 304, plus 206 battery-powered pleasure cars. In Massachusetts, registrations of electric trucks went up from 227 to 389 the next year, a 71 percent jump. In fact, in 1913, Ford and other leading Ford Motor Co. executives purchased for their wives the popular Detroit Electric, a sporty vehicle manufactured by Anderson. Ford bought a second Detroit Electric and presented it to Edison as a Christmas gift.[58]

Nonetheless, the steep spike in electric vehicle interest, often confined to one locale or another, would need to go vastly further before it even began to challenge the internal combustion machine as predominant and unrivaled in American life. This was especially the case since the increased popularity of electrics was still the province of people with money. *Horseless Age* reported that at the latest electric vehicle convention "one or two makes of cars were exhibited selling under $2,000, [but] the great majority ranged well above that." The publication added, "The electric vehicle for the man of moderate means can hardly be said to have arrived."[59]

Edison and Ford got busy. Ford's trusted administrative secretary Ernest Liebold supervised the project for Ford. Edison Storage Battery Company general manager William Bee headed up Edison's development in West Orange. Liebold was the funnel for all that Ford was told and understood in the world. In fact it was Liebold who quietly and knowingly gathered fake and falsified information to convince Ford that an international Jewish conspiracy existed. Bee was devoted to his employer and the mission of energy independence. During the months to come, these two individuals—Liebold and Bee—would hold the fate of the electric automotive revolution in their hands.[60]

Perfection was needed before Ford would begin rolling out tens of thousands of battery-powered vehicles per month. The weight and velocity specifications were constantly being adjusted to find the perfect match. Each slight change in the overall configuration wrought its telling impact on power, speed, and durability. For example, on January 3, 1913, Liebold reported to Bee that by reducing the gearing ratio of the rear axle, overall vehicle speed was reduced as well.[61]

In the meantime, ESB continued to agitate the marketplace against Edison. For example, wherever Edison's people tried to gain a foothold in trucks, ESB tried to undercut the effort by spreading false statements about the Type A. On March 17, 1913, an Edison sales agent in the Pacific Northwest typically wrote back from Portland to West Orange complaining, "I am having more or less of a fight with engineers over the battery on account of the work which has been put in here by the rather unscrupulous methods of ESB Co.'s [west] coast representatives." On April 4, the same Edison agent wrote back from Seattle, "One difficulty which I have seriously encountered has been that the ESB Co. have their emissaries in all large central stations [electric utilities] . . . and they have the confidence of the administrations." Edison's man was convinced that if fairly tested the Type A would overcome the misinformation campaign being waged by ESB. "The battery will take care of itself," he assured West Orange, "and put to rout those who have misrepresented its value."[62]

Both Liebold and Bee understood that development of the Ford electric vehicle was time-sensitive, in order to take advantage of the public mood and maintain the pressure against Exide.

Equally important, Ford's nemesis, Cadillac Motor Car Co., formerly known as the Henry Ford Motor Company, had developed its own electric starter, the device that did away with the daunting and dangerous hand crank. The unpredictable kickback of the crank was forceful enough to break jaws and other bones. In one celebrated case, an auto executive died after a head injury sustained from a recalcitrant crank. The long-sought-after electric starter project was headed up by former National Cash Register engineer Charles Kettering, who escaped indictment when NCR executives were prosecuted for conspiracy and fraud. Interestingly, even before the prototype was delivered to Cadillac, one of the first men to see the starter in action in 1911 was Kettering's good friend and colleague, soon-to-be-convicted NCR star salesman Thomas Watson. Watson later went on to become president of IBM. Kettering's partner in developing the Cadillac ignition starter was the Electric Storage Battery Company, based on its Exide lead battery technology. The same battery technology also powered the lights on Cadillac cars. The ESB-Kettering electric starter eliminated a major advantage of the electric vehicle, the ability to start the car without a muscular, often deadly crank of the motor. ESB's first order from Kettering was the largest in history, ten thousand batteries.[63]

Hence, Edison's team labored to perfect not only a battery to power a car, but an electric starter to counteract Cadillac and ESB. On May 15, 1913, an Edison engineer, M. R. Hutchinson, reported excellent progress to Edison: "The starter on the Buick car works out beyond my expecta-tions. . . . The engine cranked for twelve minutes before stalling. . . . After resting battery for ten minutes, it again cranked engine for 6½ minutes constantly before stalling." The cranking and resting was repeated over and over and "we were able to start the engine many times at various inter-vals."[64]

For Edison's part, on May 20, 1913, he wrote an anxious Anderson, who no longer enjoyed an exclusive, "I am working day and night on a number of important matters, including both the motor and rectifier. Good things take time; bad things are easy." By this time, the new build-ings for battery assembly were three-fourths completed and one thousand battery sets were being manufactured daily in preparation for the mam-moth Ford orders, in addition to orders of other partners. Initially, Ford would simply purchase Edison batteries to power accessory lighting on the gas-burning Model T. But by the first of the new year, Ford would add or-ders for starters, then move to the third and final stage: batteries for the electric vehicle itself. The fourth floor of Edison's main battery-storage building was now beginning to swell with stacks and stacks of various types of batteries. Eventually, one hundred thousand would be stored on that floor awaiting shipment to Ford.[65]

Others in the electrical world were readying as well. That May, the Boston electrical utility inaugurated America's largest recharging station, a facility of about 150,000 square feet, with extra land for growth. The utility installed 108 charging plugs affixed to walls, uprights, and columns. Current of 4,000 volts from a station located miles away fed the facility. *Horseless Age* described the move as nothing less than "preparing for the coming of the electric motor car."[66]

In mid-September 1913, Bee traveled to Detroit to meet with Ford personally and continue the plan to bring America to the electric. Bee's report to Edison was more than encouraging. "Mr. Ford and I," wrote Bee, "spent fully two hours on the subject of how is the best way to help Mr. Edison make a lot of money. I stuck to the building of electric pleasure cars." In that regard, Ford explained, his engineers had already built one electric motor and were starting their second attempt. Ford had already signed an order for a new chassis. To keep "the ball rolling," Ford demonstratively and in Bee's presence contacted the auto body maker and readied an order for ten thousand units. Ford revealed to Bee that he preferred the chassis he had patented sixteen years before for his earlier company, which had become rival Cadillac. Bee wrote, "These patents would run out next June, and it will take fully a year to get started to manufacture electric automobiles, and he thinks he can use the [earlier] design which he got patents on."[67]

By fall 1913, Ford had built the first test vehicle on a Model T frame with a low-slung undercarriage. It was propelled by a single reduction worm drive fabricated from extralight materials by Ford engineer Eugene Farkas and powered by a 400-pound tray of Type A batteries lodged under the driver's seat. Devoid of any body, the austere contraption was little more than an upholstered seat atop a frame, resembling a sort of tiller-steered electric buckboard.[68]

At the same time, Ford shipped Edison an internal combustion machine for the starter program. By November 20, 1913, Edison wired Bee: FORD ENGINE DETACHED FROM BODY WITH NEW DRIVE GAS RUN ONE HUNDRED THIRTY HOURS CONTINUOUSLY WITHOUT A STOP AT EIGHT HUNDRED REVOLUTIONS. THE DYNAMO DRIVE WORKS PERFECTLY. HAS GIVEN FIVE AMPERES OVER THE WHOLE RUN AND HAD NOT BEEN TOUCHED. Bee in turn sent a telegram to Liebold to be handed to Ford, quoting Edison's enthusiastic report. Liebold dutifully passed the good news on to Ford immediately.[69]

As 1913 drew to a close, the two giants were ready to inform the world that everything was about to change.

On January 9, 1914, on the same day and at the same time and in the same place that Ford announced his historic $5 per day living wage and an unprecedented $10 million profit sharing for his employees, he also revealed the secret plan to create a Model T–priced electric vehicle that would transform America. Speaking from New York's Hotel Belmont, the mercurial Ford told swarms of reporters about his plan to mass-produce Edison-powered electric vehicles selling as cheaply as $500 to $700. Beaming his admiration for the inventor, Ford declared, "I think Edison is the biggest man in the world today. I even live on Edison Avenue in Detroit."[70]

At the same time, Ford, a man considered one of the wealthiest in America, made clear he intended to die poor. "It is a disgrace to die rich," he told reporters. "I do not expect to leave any vast fortune to my relatives because I do not believe they would know how to use it." Certainly, Ford had his twenty-year-old son, Edsel, in mind, and also spending his fortune on the new electric. Ford explained that he would appoint Edsel, just two years out of high school, to head up the new electric vehicle company, making the young man work to earn any fortune. Ford believed the new enterprise might not be profitable at first, nor did he care, but he knew it would require devoted work by Edsel.[71] But that was the challenge to his family and to history.

News about the cheap Ford-Edison electric automobile streaked across America like a meteor shower. Dozens of newspaper headlines lit up brightly with the bold promise, as did every auto showroom, carmaker office, and American family household that had craved an automobile but was precluded because of high oil or battery prices or reliability problems. Ford waffled on whether that delivered price would be as low as $500 or as high as $850. To the media he would sometimes say $500 to $600. But in a letter to his dealer network and company branches, he specified $750 to $800, undoubtedly so they would envision greater profit. At the same time, his letter to dealers emphasized that Ford's "ability as a manufacturer in connection with his unlimited capital" assured that the final product would be "a car well worth the price." All things considered, including research, development, plant building, and tooling up, the notice predicted that the superlightweight vehicle might take another year or two to roll off the assembly line.[72]

After titillating reporters with the news, Ford, along with his wife and young Edsel, ceremoniously departed across the river for Edison's laboratory in West Orange to further discuss the spectacular project. On January 12, 1914, the day after his return, Ford proudly told New York reporters, "My visit has been profitable," and then suggested, "You probably want to ask me something about my talk with Thomas A. Edison at West Orange yesterday. . . . Within a year, I hope we shall begin the manufacture of an electric automobile."[73]

Ford revealed that he and Edison had actually been "working for some years" on the vehicle to ensure it would be "cheap and practical." He added some specifics: "The car we propose to build will contain battery equipment weighing 406 pounds, and the entire car will weigh but 1,100 pounds. It will run for one hundred miles [without recharge]. The cost will be about six hundred dollars to the public," he said, quipping, "How does that compare with the great, heavy, and expensive electric cars?"[74]

During the coming months, the mailbags lugged in to Ford and Edison brought excited inquiry after inquiry from eager investors, jubilant auto dealerships, and ready customers. Each man would answer variously that the plans were not final, or sometimes that plans were at least a year from fruition, and in many instances the men issued outright denials. Both men now hunkered down into secrecy, caution, and restraint.[75]

Even as Ford and Edison lowered their public profile in the face of the painstaking additional research and development to come, the Electric Vehicle Association of America (EVAA) relished the thought of Edison within their ranks. On January 21, 1914, the organization pleaded with Edison to send them a public statement of support at their forthcoming convention. The EVAA was an often fractious, often indecisive group that spent much time studying, debating, and planning as they differed over whether the carmakers or the central electricity stations or some committee-created combination thereof would take responsibility for proliferating battery cars. One utility executive complained to an Edison manager, "At the present time, for some unknown reason, the progress is very slow indeed, and the results far from what they should be." Later, that same utility manager joked in exasperation, "The whole bunch of the electric vehicle people seem to be laying down like a bunch of starved pups." Edison's great plans certainly were not dependent on the small manufacturers. Understandably, while Edison joined the organization to promote the new project, he preferred to stay on the sidelines.[76]

Edison scribbled a few trite words to be read to the EVAA conclave. "Evidently," he wrote, "the Electric Vehicle Association of America is doing good work. At a recent musical recital of the Woman's Club in Orange my assistant counted forty-two gas cars and seven electric coupes, whereas last year there were no electrics. Keep pounding."[77]

For the electric vehicle industry, it was not the message that counted, but the fact the words were penned by the great Edison. However, in Edison's mind, the EVAA and indeed the rest of the still-struggling industry would dwell at the margins of the great revolution for which he labored. Working with Ford, the new cheap electric would truly sweep the nation, as the lightbulb had, as the phonograph had, as the Model T had just a few years before.

The next day, January 22, 1914, Edison had more important news to report. He happily told Bee that the prototype starter was working. "I have tested it out under every condition," Edison wrote, "and could easily guarantee that it will start any car inside of two minutes." Bee sent Edison's remarks to Liebold to be handed to Ford.[78]

In early February, the media received announcements that the well-known Boston-based electrical engineering firm of Gray & Davis, employing Edison's batteries, had perfected a starting and lighting system for Ford cars. The system was developed by Gray & Davis's chief engineer, Alexander Churchward, holder of many important electrical patents. Gray & Davis cut the ribbon on a giant 140,000-square-foot facility in Boston, covering three acres, to commence manufacturing the combined starter and auxiliary electrical systems. Some 320 systems would be assembled daily by a crew of six hundred workmen.[79]

By February 20, Ford had contracted with the Peninsular Electrical Light Company, part of the local Detroit Edison utility, and purchased electrical lines for an electric vehicle "experimental shop" to be situated in the barn at the Snell Farm property on Woodward Avenue near other Ford facilities. Liebold signed the Peninsular Electrical application in Ford's name and marked at the bottom that the need would be for "two to five horsepower." The cost would be at least $1 per horsepower. The wide, spacious workshop with a vaulted A-frame ceiling, heated by a potbelly stove, was filled with miscellaneous vehicles on blocks so engines, batteries, and components could be tested. Sometimes Ford, chin in hand, personally watched his engineers experimenting with different combinations.[80]

By now, Liebold was sending Edison the monthly production totals on all Ford motorcars. January 1914 production was almost 24,000 vehicles. February was about the same. The next month the number would rise to 28,706, and the month after to 30,470. Such notices continued monthly, giving Edison a view of the six-digit annual road ahead for electric vehicles.[81]

Momentum for electric vehicles continued throughout February. In fact, both Ford and Edison posed for a forthcoming advertisement in *Saturday Evening Post*. HENRY FORD AND THOS A. EDISON BUY THE DETROIT ELECTRIC read the banner headline, ensconced above bookended pictures of each man proudly standing beside his dapper new electric car. The subhead beckoned, "How would you like to have these Master Minds Help you Choose Your Electric Car?" Three columns of copy testified to the world that both Ford and Edison believed that the electric was the best automotive choice.[82]

New hopeful companies began to sprout to preempt the Ford-Edison onslaught. The Columbia Electric Company suddenly organized in Detroit to produce a low-cost vehicle priced at under $1,000. Tiffany Electric Co., which had earlier changed its name to Flanders Manufacturing to broaden its base away from electric vehicles, restored its electric middle name, becoming Flanders Electric Company. Flanders then announced that its new low-cost electric would be released. At the same time, Baker Motor Vehicle Co. put the finishing touches on a snazzy new roadster "capable of unusually high speed" and designed to appeal not just to women, but men as well—"to the automobilist of either sex." An article in the *Automobile* explained that the Baker was calculated to counteract "the air of sedateness about . . . electrics that fails to make any strong appeal to the automobiling man."[83] The revitalized movement was electric.

For so many, it seemed as though if Ford and Edison could achieve their breakthrough, it would be good for everyone—good for average Americans, good for the economy, good for the environment, and good for an industrialized world. But it was not good for everyone. For some, their breakthrough would be terrible.

Things began to change in March.

For years, engineer Ralph Beach had headed up Edison's battery-powered trolley program. Eventually, Beach left Edison's employ and operated through an outside company run by Lisman, a firm that Edison assisted with a quietly exclusive supply arrangement. Beach had invested his own funds and additional years to help Lisman make the new commercial endeavor succeed. However, on March 17, 1914, Beach wrote Edison a flippant letter explaining that he had suddenly quit the outside company: "I have been compelled to leave Lisman. He did not fire me I just quit, but it amounts to the same thing. I tried for four months to get along with him but simply was wasting my time." Beach had worked for years to promote Edison batteries and now felt bitter and out of a paycheck. Bluntly and with an air that approximated a demand, he laid out his plans: "I do not want to have any contract from you. What I do want is to sell cars and equip them with your batteries in places outside of the United States, where they can do the work." More than that, Beach unabashedly asked for a 20 percent commission. To drive home his point, Beach made clear "the lead battery people have been after me," suggesting that if not assuaged, he might run to the other camp.[84]

One week later, Beach became even more strident and bitter. He sent a letter to Edison implying that his battery was quite flawed. "You and I both know that the battery is none too husky even with the lightweight and economical devices that I went broke developing." Pointedly, he then asked Edison to provide him with some means of making a living selling some sort of Edison products, for example, home illumination devices. "Please understand that I do not want any contract. Simply, you give me a price and the house lighting equipment that will allow me to sell and make a profit. This will give me occupation." Beach was subtly trying to circumvent Edison's contract with his former employer Lisman.[85] Because of the prior contract with Lisman, and because Beach had clearly been in touch with ESB, Edison was not forthcoming.

Meanwhile Ford and Edison were traveling cross-country together. Detroit's testing was now in the hands of Gray & Davis, and more specifically, Churchward and his hand-picked mechanic Samuel F. Wilson, a former Cadillac employee who had worked on the Kettering-ESB starter. From March 30 to April 1, important tests were made on the Edison starter components.[86]

Edison's five-cell batteries, dubbed D6, employing six positive plates per cell with twenty tubes per plate, were run through their paces. The results, recorded by engineer R. Hoyt Roses, proved the Edison batteries to be as advertised—tenacious, resilient, and remarkably capable.[87]

Test 1: "Made 103 starts on the magneto in as rapid succession as possible, averaging 1.5 seconds per start and drawing 80 to 100 amperes at an average of 5 volts. Immediately followed this by cranking the engine continuously with the switch off, for seven minutes until the motor stalled. Then recharged the battery."[88] This was tantamount to turning an auto ignition 103 times in a row, and then one long session for seven minutes.

Test 2: "Made 100 starts on the magneto in as rapid succession as possible" in a nearly identical fashion, but with a long 12.5 minute interrupted session.[89]

Test 3: "Made 100 starts in as rapid succession as possible on the magneto," again with nearly identical results, but with a remarkable 36.5 minute unbroken ignition starting session.[90]

The testing on the D6 batteries continued with slight permutations, documenting one hundred starts in rapid succession with continuous bursts as long as 10.5 minutes. Then five-cell B4 batteries were tested four times in a similar manner with similarly impressive results. Finally, the B4 was reduced to a four-cell variant with like testing.[91]

Then something unexpected happened. Churchward and Wilson declared that the Edison batteries were unworkable due to internal resistance, especially in cold weather. Liebold recalled, "Mr. Ford was in Florida or absent from the city on vacation. The boys [Churchward, Wilson, and others on the project], knowing that the Edison batteries, due to the [claimed] high internal resistance, wouldn't successfully operate the car, put some lead batteries in there."[92]

But Edison's batteries had performed admirably.

When Ford returned from his vacation, he learned that his engineers had substituted lead batteries without permission. He was furious. Liebold recounts that Ford "raised the devil all over the place. He made them get rid of them and told them they weren't building a car for lead batteries, they were building it to use Edison batteries."[93]

On Friday, April 3, two days after initial testing was completed, Bee learned that Gray & Davis engineers had switched the batteries, claiming the Edison products had failed. Bee immediately dispatched his own technical adviser, R. C. Mitchell, to Detroit to keep tabs on future measurements. Bee described Mitchell as "the best man we have in the plant." Mitchell was instructed to carefully inspect batteries not only in the lab but also in various boats that were using Edison stored power.[94]

The next day, Saturday, a clearly concerned Bee express-shipped to Detroit six B4 enhanced "extra high, heavy connector and heavy pole" batteries for further experiments. Then he rushed up to Boston to confer with Gray & Davis, towing batteries. On Tuesday, April 7, Bee stood witness as Gray & Davis started a car perfectly, both with a five-cell and with a smaller four-cell. A day later, Wednesday, April 8, a still defensive but now reassured Bee told Liebold that fresh, enhanced batteries were coming by express. "Do me a favor," wrote Bee, "and put one of these batteries on your car in place of the lead and get [chief Ford electrical engineer] Fred [Allison] to put one on his car also." Bee also assured, "I spent yesterday in Boston with Gray & Davis and they had no trouble doing it." Bee was willing to concede that a lead battery "when new will perhaps do the work better," but stressed that as the battery and car wore on, the Edison battery would dramatically outlast any Exide. Bee stressed that the smaller four-cell battery should not be used, but rather the more powerful five-cell. He was perplexed by the desire to use a weaker battery.[95]

Liebold received Bee's letter and now it was he who was defensive. He replied without the usual "My Dear Bee" or "Dear Mr. Bee" and instead dictated to his secretary the formalized "Dear Sir." It proceeded, "I have your letter of April 8th and have carefully noted content." It seems that those express-shipped batteries intended for the Ford factory were diverted to Ford's home, where they remained unattended. Liebold explained, "Through the misinterpretation of some orders given your Shipping Department these batteries were shipped to Mr. Ford and delivered at his house and remained there a few days before we knew about them." Nonetheless, Liebold promised to "give these my personal attention. I have just given instructions to have a set tested and installed on my car, and I assure you that I will give them a thorough trial and report results to you later. I am inclined to believe that the majority of our trouble with the Edison battery up to date has been on account of using four cells instead of five for lighting purposes, especially when six volt lamps and light equipment is used."[96]

Bee on April 14 retorted in a note, almost snidely, "I see by your letter that you really are not familiar with the characteristics of an Edison Battery. The point was that a 5-cell not a 4-cell unit should be installed." Bee attached curves showing how headlamps and other accessories fared in brightness and duration when the car was running, which meant the generator had kicked in, or standing still, when the battery solely provided power.[97]

In the meantime, Liebold asked his engineers to test the express-shipped enhanced five-cell B4 batteries, which had finally made their way from Ford's home to the factory. The batteries would not start the car. It was a complete failure. Liebold reported the disaster to Bee.[98]

A disbelieving, almost accusatory Bee shot back a letter April 16, 1914: "I am very much surprised to hear that five [enhanced] B-4 specials wouldn't start your car. Why five of our regular cells started it when I was up in Detroit. You remember you watched the test out in the yard. It started it, and started it several times."[99]

Four days later, April 20, 1914, at about three thirty in the morning, Edison returned home from a well-deserved vacation in Florida. When he finally strode into the West Orange laboratory that afternoon, Bee was almost emotionally overcome because his beloved, oft-weary employer seemed so genuinely rested and restored. He penned a letter to Henry Ford personally relating, "I could have cried for joy he looked so good. His eyes were bright, face was full and tanned up and he was in great shape."[100]

But quickly the truth of the disconnect with Detroit descended upon Edison. For some reason, the batteries that worked perfectly in Boston and West Orange somehow did not work when affixed to a vehicle in Detroit.

Answers were needed. Why weren't those batteries working in Detroit? Liebold was asked to double-check. The stunning reply came back in a letter from Liebold sent April 23, 1914.

"Dear Mr. Bee:

"I have your letter of April 16th, and do not doubt that you are surprised to hear that five B-5 specials would not start the car. The fact is that they did, but at the time I wired you I depended upon the information as it was given to me. This test was also witnessed by Mr. Gray of the Gray & Davis Company, and he first gave the information to me and I later had it confirmed by Fred. These experiments were conducted under the direct supervision of your man, Mitchell, and we had every reason to believe that the test was regular."[101] So what happened?

Liebold's next sentence explained. "I was not satisfied with the result and went after Fred again and found that Mitchell advised him that the battery had not been worked up [charged] before being shipped by you and it was consequently necessary to do so before a real test could be made."[102] Bee had routinely shipped the fresh, new batteries uncharged. Gray & Davis engineers had installed and tested them without the benefit of an ordinary overnight charge. Of course they could not start a car.

Liebold continued, "My car is in the factory now . . . and I have given instructions that it is to be equipped with Edison batteries. A starter has been put on Sorensen's car and the speed of the gearing increased. This works wonderfully well, and it seems to me that they are on the right track by doing this to overcome all existing troubles. I expect to be in your vicinity sometime next week and will be glad to go over the matter with you."[103]

Three weeks later, May 14, additional tests were made on Edison's personal Detroit Electric, also propelled by his batteries. One of Edison's own engineers, Jerry T. Chesler, tested the vehicle and prepared the report. They showed unusual watts-per-ton-mile results. Three copies were made of the document, one being sent to Edison's manager. When Edison personally reviewed the findings, he was astonished. After placing check marks next to the watts-per-ton-mile entries, Edison scribbled a note to his engineer. "Hutch—There is something wrong with these tests [that the] Anderson [car] get. 75–80 watts per ton mile—on the worm drive—I would not trust Chesler on any test." For emphasis, Edison drew a massive check mark onto the test report.[104]

By this time, the lead battery people had swayed Beach. After laboring for years promoting Edison batteries, but now seeing his future relationship curtailed, Beach suddenly became an enemy. Soliciting an importer in Australia, Beach wrote, "We have learned that the Edison battery when applied to driving cars cannot be relied upon for permanent service, providing the conditions of the service are such as to raise the temperature of the battery above 115 degrees Fahrenheit. In the early stages of the game we did not know this. . . . It might be said as a general statement that cars can be equipped with the Edison Battery providing the service required of them in miles per day would not exceed about sixty. With this mileage, the battery will be as represented and durable, but if the service requirements are much greater than 60 miles per day, then the battery is almost certain to be overheated and consequently destroyed. In view of this fact I think you will appreciate the hopelessness of attempting to do a general business in driving cars with this battery."

Beach continued his derogation: "Our present feeling is that it is better to use the lead battery . . . [it] is so much cheaper and its voltage characteristic better adapted to this class of service than the Edison. . . . I am very sorry indeed that the Edison storage battery car undertaken proved so disastrous for all of us. We all lost money, but I believe that the place to look for it is right in the place where you lost it."[105]

Various lead battery competitors were making inroads with their denigration and whisper campaigns, and co-option of Edison associates. He tried to fight back. First, his staff prepared a list of the heavy commercial trucks coast-to-coast successfully employing Edison batteries for four years without incident or almost completely expense-free. The roster included trucks for a gamut of enterprises delivering everything from pianos to precious jewelry: Abraham and Straus, Adams Express, Anheuser Busch Brewing, Bender Automobile, Buffalo Smelting, Cincinnati Coffin, Grand Rapids Refrigerator, Liebman Sons Brewing, Otis Elevator, Steinway & Sons, Tiffany and Company. None of those batteries had been replaced. All bore testimony to the Type A's longevity and heavy-duty reliability.[106]

Then on May 27, 1914, Edison granted the *Wall Street Journal* an interview, heralding confidently that his new electric vehicle would take over all automotive transportation in the nation that was now accomplished by internal combustion. Headlined EDISON ELECTRIC MOTOR FUTURE FAMILY CARRIAGE, the subhead stated, "All City Trucking and Carriage Shopping Must Come to Electric, Says Wizard—Electric Trucks Carry Double the Load with Twice the Speed and Half the Space." Leaving little room for doubt, Edison declared, "I have perfected the motors so that an electric machine can be run much more economically than a gasoline car. The machinery has been simplified, every non-essential part eliminated. It will be simplicity itself, so that it can be run by a child. The cost of the car will probably be between $500 and $700." When would the car roll into showrooms? "Mr. Ford is working steadily on the details," replied Edison, "and he knows his business, so it will not be long."[107]

Edison continued, "I believe that ultimately the electric motor will be used for trucking in all large cities, and that the electric automobile will be the family carriage of the future." He added, "All trucking must come to electricity."[108]

For his part, Ford in Detroit began finalizing negotiations to purchase property owned by Chevrolet so he could build an elaborate new factory to manufacture the Ford-Edison runabout.[109]

On June 10, 1914, with the starter system seemingly settled, Ford completed a second experimental car, this time to test the propulsion system. This slightly more elaborate vehicle featured two Edison G7 thirty-cell batteries, one under the seat and one where the Model T's internal combustion engine formerly reposed. First-day testing achieved only 7 mph, but the vehicle was able to climb a 19 percent grade. Ford himself drove in the car and was suitably impressed.[110]

The next day, June 11, 1914, testing was more satisfying. The "Report on Ford Electric Car Experiment" opened with this summation: "A total distance of 59.1 miles on one charge of the battery is the latest and best result obtained on the experiment." More than twenty-five level miles were traveled. Speed doubled to 15 mph even as the vehicle carried the weight of the driver plus one hundred pounds of accessories. Ford and Edison knew that both speed and range could dramatically be boosted by modifying the motor. So several different motors were slated for installation and testing to help achieve the hoped-for hundred miles per charge.[111]

A memo about the test stated, "It is interesting to note what has been accomplished in building this car over the first one, but we have already gathered enough bugs to start right in with building another which should be a vast improvement."[112]

Immediately, a three-week regimen of testing was undertaken. Test notes reflected the excellent progress: "The car is now undergoing the severest test that can be given to any Ford car. In all, the car has run 5,000 miles to date. . . . Starter is working very well indeed. Efficiency is 85% average on four B-2 cells. Generator and drive OK. Battery is always fully charged." In addition, a test on blocks was conducted for seven thousand miles yielding good results.[113]

Moving to actual customer experience, twenty such cars were placed on the road. Drivers were limited to key managers of the Ford and Edison companies. The main concern was the belt drive and its ability to hold up under rain and heat, which was a question of fabric and insulation or perhaps switching to a chain. Efforts were undertaken to ensure that ground wires were connected properly to maximize performance.[114] But otherwise the machine was enticing in its performance.

At the same time, Charles Steinmetz, one of the towering and internationally revered electrical experts, delivered a special paper to five thousand delegates at the thirty-seventh annual convention of the National Electric Light Association in Philadelphia. German-born Steinmetz, whose legendary mathematical analysis of power loss revolutionized the world's understanding of electricity, had risen to become the chief consultant at General Electric. Often dubbed "the foremost electrical engineer in the world," Steinmetz had undertaken a thorough study of the automobile industry. First, he enumerated the many disadvantages of gasoline cars and the attractive simplicity of electric vehicles. Then Steinmetz startled the assemblage by predicting that within a decade the nation's roads would see one million extralight battery-propelled vehicles costing less than $500. These cars would cruise at an average 20 mph with a 30-mile range, he prophesied. Between them, cars and trucks would generate $150 million in new business to the many central stations (electric utilities) that would recharge and exchange the batteries. "In my opinion," Steinmetz proclaimed, "the future of the business and pleasure vehicle undoubtedly belongs to the electric."[115]

But even as Edison and Ford were speeding toward their dream, even as the best minds in the country were planning to bring America to the electric, various lead battery competitors were making further plans to co-opt loyal Edison people and others in the field.

In early June, one Edison field salesman sent a letter to West Orange, writing, "There is a rumor that Dodge Bros. Detroit, are going to build a cheap electric pleasure car equipped with lead batteries to sell for five or six hundred dollars. They are getting together an organization and are approaching all men connected with the battery and electric vehicle business and have sent a man out over the country to interview them. I know a number of men who have been approached including myself." Edison instructed Bee to promptly alert Ford. He did, via Liebold. Liebold assured that the information was passed on.[116]

More bad news. By mid-July, Edison's people learned that General Vehicle was now being swayed into the lead camp. General Vehicle was once so well aligned with Edison that it was considered the principal player in the Edison Battery Service System. On July 17, 1914, M. R. Hutchinson, an Edison employee, reported to Edison, "I am under the impression that they will try to push the lead batteries and only sell an Edison battery when they cannot do otherwise." Hutchinson appended that he doubted that General Vehicle could succeed with the heavy, lethargic lead batteries "as other makers in the field have not been able to sell any vehicles with lead batteries."[117] Despite Hutchinson's reassurance, the further encroachment of the lead cartel into the Ford-Edison plans must have been disheartening to all connected to the project.

In spite of Dodge, in spite of General Vehicle, in spite of Beach, in spite of the many erosions in his closest supporters, Edison took comfort that his dream and the dream of so many others could yet come true because Gray & Davis, the indispensable player, the keystone manufacturer of the ignition systems, was committed to the program. True, for some reason Gray & Davis had tested uncharged batteries. But that mistake was in the past. After all, Gray & Davis and their staff included some of the best minds in electrical engineering. For example, the main mechanic, Wilson, had worked closely with Kettering and the Electric Storage Battery Company to create Cadillac's famous lead-based ignition system. But Gray & Davis would remain in the Edison camp. They had just telegraphed a rush order for 125 sets of batteries.

But in mid-July, Gray & Davis suddenly fell silent. Routine communication about the project ceased. Calls went unreturned. Letters unanswered. Silence. Strange silence. A bad feeling came over Bee.

"July 17, 1914. Dear Mr. Liebold: How about the Gray & Davis starting outfit? I can't seem to find out anything here in the East. Have they stopped the test? Are you still testing one? I would appreciate it if you will write me the latest news on the subject. Kind regards, Bee."[118]

Saturday, July 18, no word from Gray & Davis. Sunday, July 19, still no word from Gray & Davis. Monday no word. On Tuesday, Liebold answered.

"July 21, 1914. Dear Mr. Bee: I have your letter of July 17th, and in reference to the Gray & Davis starting outfit I wish to say that they now intend placing their outfit on the market with lead batteries. They feel that they have done all that is possible in the way of motor design to try and get around the Edison battery and they say now after spending thousands of dollars in experimenting that it is impossible. On the other hand they feel that you have done little if anything toward bringing the battery to a point where they could use it for this work. I have one of their outfits on my car, but as you know it would not work with an Edison battery, and I was consequently compelled to use a lead battery and it has given perfect satisfaction since. I have driven it several days now without a generator and it still starts."[119]

Somehow, Gray & Davis had convinced the Ford Motor Company senior establishment—Liebold and then Ford himself—that the Edison battery would not work. The company's president, William Gray, had traveled from Boston to Detroit to aver that Edison batteries could simply not stand up to cold weather. True, the batteries were starting and powering trolleys and trucks across the most frigid stretches of America. But, argued Gray, these batteries would not start a lightweight car. Unless Edison was abandoned, the entire electric vehicle project would collapse and the starter war would be permanently lost to Cadillac, which was using the cumbersome lead-based Kettering device, but at least it did work. Gray & Davis quickly presented a new apparatus that would interface with a lead battery, but not with the nickel-iron version manufactured by Edison.[120]

Convincing Liebold was the decisive step. Ford relied upon Liebold. Liebold handled it.

Liebold continued in his stunning notification and now chastised Bee: "The final outcome of this matter has irritated Mr. Ford considerably, and I dare say he has somewhat of a sore spot somewhere as a recent talk indicates. He tells me that he has heard from two different sources information purporting to have emanated from you which has been intended as strictly confidential. Personally I am not familiar with the details of it, but I think you had better bring the war paint along when you come. With kind regards, I am very truly yours, Liebold."[121]

Bee was devastated as he saw everything rapidly disappear before his eyes. He had suspected something for several days as the lines of communication grew silent, as the unshipped boxes became conspicuous. Now he knew.

On July 23, 1914, Bee wrote Liebold. "This certainly came to me as a thunder bolt," Bee dejectedly admitted. "I never heard any rumor or had an inkling that Gray & Davis were figuring on lead until I got a letter from [electrical subcontractor] Mr. [A. J.] Picard . . . saying [that] he was going to Detroit to take up a certain subject with Mr. Ford, and he wanted me to go with him. Then I suspected that there might be something doing in regard to lead."[122]

Maintaining some element of restraint, he continued, "Offhand I feel as if the Gray & Davis people haven't been exactly square with us on it. It seems to me if I was in their place I would have kept us posted. The last information I got was their order for 125 sets of Edison and for me to get them all ready for shipping instructions. They telegraphed and urged us to hurry them up. When they were all ready and on the floor ready to ship, I wired them and up to date haven't received any shipping instructions, in fact, haven't been able to get them to acknowledge my letters and I have written once or twice on the subject. Of course, this accounts for it as they have been figuring on using lead.[123]

"The latter part of the second paragraph where you say 'on the other hand they feel that you have done little if anything toward bringing the battery to a point where they could use it for this work,' I understand that our people have tried to carry our Mr. Churchward's suggestion in regard to building batteries according to his suggestion but that it wasn't satisfactory. In other words, it did not make any improvement."[124]

Bee continued, "I am well aware of the fact and have always admitted that while the lead battery is new it does the work easier and snappier than with the Edison equipment that they already have out. On the other hand, what stares me in the face is the fact that I have on my little Ford car a starter which we made ourselves with five Edison cells. It has never had a failure, that is, never had a failure when the battery was charged."[125]

Reminding that uncharged batteries were falsely tested and implying that other improprieties took place, Bee concluded his letter with this telling sentence: "Now Mr. Liebold that is absolutely straight facts, and my battery [the one I am using] has not been tampered with."[126]

Bee tried to divert himself with other work that July 23, 1914. But after one other piece of correspondence, an irritated Bee dictated a second letter to Liebold. "Again referring to yours of the 21st," wrote Bee, answering the notion that Ford might personally be angered, especially about the notion of Bee breaching confidentiality. Bee denied any such breach, coming close to labeling the accusation a deliberate smear. "I don't blame Mr. Ford for being out of patience regarding the lighting and starting outfit. On the other hand, the latter part of the last paragraph of your letter I don't quite understand. Of course, there are always a lot of people in this world who would like to get somebody else in trouble, and if they would tell things exactly and repeat them just as they heard them, it wouldn't be so bad. At any rate, I have a clear conscience and that is worth a good deal."[127]

Bee also tried to salvage the situation by suggesting a new combination of battery cells had been fabricated to create an even stronger model called the J5. These worked flawlessly in West Orange, and Bee express-shipped them to Detroit for inspection.[128]

Liebold replied on July 25, 1914, and was not encouraging. His reply revealed that Gray "came to us [in Detroit] and complained that it was absolutely impossible to make any further progress. He said that they had put in a refrigerating plant to test them out and that under the cold temperature the batteries fell absolutely flat and would not start the car." Reflecting the agitation in the marketplace by the lead proponents, Liebold added, "All along the route of prospective dealers, they found opposition to the Edison battery. They claim that if the starter is furnished with Edison battery it would be taken out and lead substituted at additional cost.[129]

"There are many other reasons," Liebold continued, "which they advance claiming that it would not be possible to use the Edison battery and stated that lead batteries could now be procured with a liberal guarantee and that people using these batteries would have absolutely no difficulty with them. Of course you know Mr. Ford's attitude is that he has nothing to do with it, and as others are putting starters on the market of heavy cumbersome design it appears that Gray & Davis could do the same on equipment which is even better than that which is now being supplied by a great many others."[130]

Liebold concluded his letter, "I assure you that I have no axe to grind, nor am I prejudiced in any way."[131]

On July 27, Bee dashed back a reply, assuring that Edison would turn to the matter personally and cure any defects that might be discovered in the battery. Using all capitals, Bee wrote, "HE WILL MAKE A BATTERY WHICH WILL DO THE WORK." Bee was quick to blame the engineers who had overseen the testing, including those of uncharged batteries. "I do not in any way blame Billy Gray. I realized from the very beginning that he was at the mercy of his engineers and his engineers made certain statements as you are well aware. These statements were made hastily and not based on actual experience as time has proven."[132]

With little delay, Liebold telegraphed Gray in Boston, disclosing the latest communication from Bee. Gray wired back and then wrote a letter of thanks, while continuing the anti-Edison agitation. "I was glad to hear," wrote Gray, "that Mr. Edison was going to give this battery matter his personal attention. I am awfully sorry that he did not do this months ago, as it would have saved Gray & Davis a great many dollars. . . . I sincerely trust that it will not be long before we can get a battery from Mr. Edison that will have the snap and the kick that the lead has."[133]

Edison and Bee hung on to the hope that perhaps they could counter the negative agitation from lead forces, and that the Edison could be improved to achieve some indisputable benchmark. On September 29, Edison told Bee, "Billie, I want to go to Detroit. I am going to go to Detroit and nothing is going to prevent me." Speaking cryptically, even in riddles, Edison referred not to batteries but his phonograph business: "Something happens in the manufacturing of these records that I don't understand. One day they are all right and the next day they are off and I am going to find out just what is the trouble. . . . I am going to Detroit as soon as I have a chance. You tell Mr. Ford so." Bee reported the inexplicable remarks to Liebold, adding his own observation: "Now, Mr. Liebold, that is as much as I can find out."[134]

But it was to no avail. Edison could not solve the problem of why his batteries worked in West Orange, but did not work in Detroit. In late October 1914, Edison canceled his much anticipated lecture "Batteries and the Possibilities of the Electric Vehicle Industry" before the Electric Vehicle Association of America convention.[135]

October 1914. Events went black in Europe. Its muddy fields would run red.

For decades, the entire world had been expecting a vast war between Germany and the Western European nations over the expected breakup of the Ottoman Empire and its as yet virtually untapped oil-rich Middle East colonies. The question of who would take over the strategic Middle East was part of a debate known internationally as "the Eastern Question." The mere expectation of war drove England to spend the prior decade converting its coal-fueled navy to a faster, nimbler oil-burning fleet and at the same time to develop faster petroleum-powered vehicles. Yet the British were fond of saying, "Oil don't grow in England." Nor was it available in the Middle East except in small quantities transported by donkeys. Hence, America supplied 80 percent of England's needs.[136]

On June 28, 1914, at approximately 10:00 A.M., a series of hair-trigger alliances across the Continent began to ignite. On that day, while driving in an open car as part of a six-vehicle motorcade, Archduke Ferdinand and his wife, Sophia, were shot to death.[137]

Europe was thrown into chaos. Throughout a tumultuous and nerve-racking July, Vienna charged Serbia with trying to start a war. The many alliances that had been revving darkly for decades began lining up on either side of the conflict. The Eastern Question was about to be answered on a global scale.

One month after the murders, on July 28, Austria-Hungary invaded Serbia. On August 1, as the czar rushed to bolster his ally Serbia, Germany declared war on Russia, and the next day on Russia's ally France. Britain demanded that the kaiser respect Belgium's neutrality, and when he invaded Belgium on August 4, London declared war on Germany. Within days, Japan too declared war on Germany. The Great War was on.

The conflict deployed great new modes of warfare: submarines, airplanes, massive trenches, tanks, long-range cannons, and many more devices and methods of terrible devastation. Indeed, this was the first industrialized war, a war that wove the profound technological gains of the prior several decades into a new and never before seen capacity for killing. Central to the mechanized slaughter that killed millions was internal combustion. The warring nations of Europe needed gas engines to go faster and farther and carry heavier loads, and no one wanted to wait for electric to painstakingly develop.

The electric moment had been lost. Warfare was too important and the demand for internal combustion too great. The idea of a cheap electric was subsumed by the onslaught on Europe and America's own concomitant preparedness as the nation beefed up its own military.

In early October 1914, Edison wrote to a stockholder that the Ford electric project was on hold, especially in view of "many orders for gas trucks from abroad." He added that his battery factory was now running at "about 50% of capacity." At that same time, Edison admitted to *Horseless Age* that if any mass electric vehicle did appear, it would only be for city traffic. In early November 1914, Gray & Davis announced that their lead-based starter and lighting system would be implemented on Ford's internal combustion machines. Ironically, the lead batteries employed would not be the Exide brand, but from Willard, one of the many other lead battery makers in the country. The Gray & Davis announcement did not even mention the electric.[138]

Indeed, the mass-market electric project was quietly forgotten.

Not completely forgotten. Edison hoped to one day prove that his batteries could work to efficiently propel mass-produced lightweight automobiles. Quietly he toiled in his laboratory. He always believed he would achieve yet another electric battery breakthrough.[139]

At 5:20 P.M., Wednesday, December 9, 1914, Edison was hard at work in his West Orange laboratory when a blast shattered the afternoon. A film repository suddenly exploded. A second later, gongs on Edison's fire alarms clanged into the afternoon air, reverberating throughout the eighteen-structure complex. Scores of employees scrambled to the street as flames raced through the many fireproof buildings as though on an incendiary rampage, devouring the contents. Quickly, carefully, intrepidly, Edison and his wife pulled his most important papers from their offices and raced out to safety. Everything seemed to burst into blaze in just moments. However, Edison dashed across the street to the storage battery building and ordered his private fire brigade to protect that first. Edison himself directed much of the firefighting.[140]

Not until midnight was most of the fire put down. Some buildings remained burning until 2:00 P.M. the next day. The flames were so intensely hot that one employee who tried to deploy a fire extinguisher was "burned to a crisp with a fire extinguisher alongside of him." Only two structures were saved, Edison's private laboratory and the storage battery factory.[141]

Few understood the voracious fire's extraordinary speed and broad destruction. Ten buildings completely burned to the ground. All but the lab and storage battery building were reduced to fire-ravaged rubble. It was hypothesized that a random spark from a switch in the film department suddenly ignited the surroundings. But it was as though the fire erupted all at once across the fireproofed compound in building after building, even across the walkways. Certainly Edison's complex was filled with every form of flammable chemical and material. But no one could explain certain "funny capers," as they were termed. Reports soon documented that for some reason "in one of the little low red buildings, they found 2,000 gallons of very high proof alcohol that wasn't damaged." What's more, investigators "also found on some of the floors cans of gasoline that didn't even ignite. The flames swept right over the top of them. Corners in the concrete building weren't even touched with fire." Some rooms emerged without any fire damage at all.[142]

How did the fire spread from fireproof concrete building to fireproof concrete building? Everyone assumed it was the wooden window frames and their heat-broken panes. But no one could explain the massive inferno that destroyed much of Edison's life work. The majority of the $5 million property loss was not insured precisely because the concrete buildings were considered so impervious to fire and a private on-premises fire brigade was always on duty.[143]

Edison's dreams, past, present, and future, were now reduced to char and ash. A lifetime of invention had succumbed in a flash, in the twinkling of an eye. Standing amidst the scorched ruins and smoldering memories, a smoke-battered yet still strong and undefeated Edison emerged to bravely and boldly announce to gathered reporters, "Although I am over sixty-seven years old, I'll start over again tomorrow."[144]

Yes, Edison resumed work. But it was too late to restore his vision of homes that inhaled wind to exhale their own electricity. It was too late to beat the conjunction of wars in the battery industry, and the wars of a world bent on destroying itself on the battlefield with the greatest acceleration possible. As for Bee, he never recovered. His disappointment became too enormous to carry. He suffered a nervous breakdown. Liebold went on to knowingly assemble a collage of forgeries and fraudulent documents that he used to convince Ford that Jews were the great enemies of mankind, causing Ford to publish *The Protocols of the Elders of Zion* and become a towering Nazi idol—to Ford's everlasting shame. In the forties, the FBI was prepared to arrest Liebold as a Nazi spy, causing Ford in 1944 to summarily fire him.[145]

While lead batteries could start automobile ignitions and power their headlamps, they proved unable to efficiently and economically propel electric vehicles. Diehards tried to keep the concept of electric vehicles alive for years, but to no avail.

1914 was the key year. For it was during that year that America did not go electric. It was during that year that internal combustion became an indispensable part of both civilized humanity and uncivilized inhumanity. It became both a weapon and workhorse, and the two modalities were often one and the same. What's more, so much oil was needed for so many gasoline-burning vehicles that were needed for war and peace that oil itself became a pivot point for both war and peace. 1914 was the year America and the world turned decisively to petroleum and internal combustion.

1914 was the end of the beginning.

CHAPTER NINE

DERAILED

Carved across the sky, the majestic mountains of the Montana Rockies at the Continental Divide displayed brute brown orogeny. Windswept blue-green ponderosa pines, mountain alders, and Douglas firs everywhere stretched toward the sun. Boulder-strewn alluvial fans draped around the slopes like gray work aprons. Glittering streams and waterfalls wove the elements together in a breathtaking tapestry, humbling all who gazed upon its beauty.[1]

Few gazed upon the splendor with more wonderment than those comfortably seated in stuffed leather chairs arrayed along the brass-trimmed windows of the observation car of the Milwaukee Road's gleaming Olympian, pride of the World War I era. Without sway, jar, or jolt, the Olympian silently snaked through the awesome river-cut passes and a network of man-blasted tunnels to traverse the high peaks. The effervescent rivers seemed to both beckon and propel.[2] How?

Above the elegant observation car, complete with its fine decor and tempting haute cuisine, twin connective poles saluted a pair of catenary cables that hovered over every mile of track. These cables transmitted powerful electric currents into the great General Electric engines. The motive muscle of those GE engines forced massive forged-steel wheels round and round, thus hurtling the mighty train ever forward through the daunting, rough-hewn landscape. Pushed and pulled by electricity, the Milwaukee Road's Olympian slid through the mountains with almost insolent ease, but always high environmental respect.[3]

No roof-burning cinders, lung-choking soot, or nose-stinging fumes sprayed the air to mark the Olympian's passage. Those catenary cables above connected to a network of hydroelectric plants and twenty-two substations that harnessed the energy of foaming mountain rivers far upstream and downstream. These facilities delivered three thousand volts to cause the train's gigantic motion—all from the mass of simple water. Hence, here at the Continental Divide, man cleanly and evenly met nature, in harmony and luxury, twice daily aboard the Milwaukee Road as it sped from Chicago to Seattle, spanning five mountain ranges. Of that distance, approximately 650 miles were electrified.[4] It was a marvel.

Sometimes electrified railways seemed to defy the laws of perpetual motion. For example, when the brakes were applied or the train traveled down a slope, the engine actually returned electricity to the grid. Regenerative braking and similar power returns helped the engines pay for themselves. In some mountain ranges, if timed correctly, a heavy downhill train could actually regenerate enough electricity to the grid to power another train passing it uphill. Thus both trains would travel in a minuet of seemingly energy-free motion. That might have seemed to violate the laws of physics, but not the rules of General Electric's wondrous workhorses, which were designed to observe this maxim: It is better to give than receive when it comes to electrical power. Those engines lasted not for years but for decades. Their endurance was measured in millions of miles. They were monumental vehicles that created economic prosperity and environmental balance everywhere they rolled.[5]

But the magic of the Milwaukee and a potential coast-to-coast network of similar electrified rail lines were destined to fail. What happened? Was it the clean, limitless power of electricity that failed, or was it something else?

Trains changed the world. The great iron horses that could pull and push against the elements helped create the Industrial Revolution. Such machines were centuries in the making.

Germany, in the 1550s, established the first primitive "wagonways," that is, roadways embedded with parallel wood rails along which horses lugged heavy wagons. For the next few hundred years, horses continued to pull carts and wagons along the expanding network of wagonways and tramways of Europe. In the 1700s, primitive but powerful steam engines appeared in England's coal regions to pump water out of shafts and more efficiently move crushing loads.[6]

In about 1825, inventors in both the United States and England unleashed a revolution by making the mighty steam engine portable. Great locomotives were created by fixing massive energy-wielding steam engines atop chassis that were latched to flanged wheels that in turn gripped a pathway of iron rails. As the locomotive burned coal, it boiled water, which created steam, which moved great pistons, which made forward motion possible. This was the beginning of the modern, efficient railroad. The ability of these lumbering behemoths to haul tons of freight was nothing less than spectacular, universally redefining concepts of work, industry, time, and space. Passenger traffic was quick to follow, bringing individuals, cities, and nations together in new ways.[7] The railroad age was born.

During the second half of the nineteenth century, the railroad industry exploded globally. Robber barons and their allies in government planted track and rail between key points and across the great empty spaces, everywhere creating and often violating national and regional identities. These new mechanized rivers carried commercial lifeblood wherever they flowed. What's more, the very existence of a railway was both a geopolitical stanchion and a military threat. Any country that constructed a railroad could project its national, diplomatic, and economic power anywhere in the world those rails traveled. Germany embarked upon the Berlin to Baghdad railway to secure its stake in the oil-rich Middle East. Great Britain built rail lines across India to colonize the subcontinent. During the latter 1800s, the great capitals of Europe discovered that land could be conquered or occupied most easily when the front lines were two parallel rail lines. Wars and fortunes were predicated on trains. Likewise trains were predicated on wars and fortunes.[8]

Immediately, trains became indispensable to modern society. More than mere industrial machines, trains and their plaintive wail represented the lure of beyond. Trains represented adventure. Trains brought dreams. Trains inspired romance.

But people soon learned that trains also represented grime. Trains spewed ash. Trains belched coal soot. Trains brought disease. Trains provoked coughing seizures. Trains carried the spoilage of the industrial age and did so indiscriminately into the most remote corners of the world and the tidiest city neighborhoods. If trains represented the new economic soul of industrial mankind, society quickly learned that when it sold that soul, a deadly consequence was part of the bargain.

Quickly, the nineteenth century realized that trains were the filthiest machines on earth. Steam locomotives burned bituminous coal. The ever-billowing smoke of passing engines plugged lungs, coated trees, blackened windows, and darkened the day. Frequently, glowing cinders ignited nearby rooftops, causing wooden homes and buildings to burn to the ground. Unlike stationary industrial smokestacks, the airborne menace of steam locomotives was discharged not up high and not in the distance, but at housetop level and up close. There was no escaping it. Progress was literally defined by a train, and progress into everyone's midst, big-city or rural setting, brought a deadly cinder and choke.[9]

In the era of the nineteenth-century reformers, muckrakers, and social improvers, the public's palpable outrage manifested as the pugnacious "smoke abatement" movement. Sworn to wage war against industrial, household, and railroad smoke, along with its associated evils, the intensely popular smoke abatement movement was a force to be reckoned with, especially within the context of antimonopolist and antitrust sentiment. True, the movement targeted more than steam railroads. The reformers' wrath was focused first on local factory smokestacks and even private household hearths. But their greatest ire was arguably reserved for the trains, because they came and went darkly, drenching all along their route. Yet the railroads supralegally seemed to answer to no one.

None in the nineteenth century believed the problem was new. All understood the hazard was centuries old, dating back to the coal-burning days of the Hostmen and English timber shortages. A review of the book *Smoke Prevention* in a March 1881 issue of *American Architect and Building News* opened with the reminder: "It is now two hundred and twenty years since John Evelyn called attention to the evils of the smoke of London. In 1661 he published a tractate with the title: *Fumifugium, or the Inconvenience of the Air and Smoke of London Dissipated.*" The book review pointedly recalled that after a dismal decline in vegetation, London gardens again flourished ever so briefly in 1644. Why? The review explained, "Newcastle was besieged because but a small quantity of coal was brought to London that year." *American Architect and Building News* reiterated that coal smoke, "that hellish and dismal cloud," was "one of the foulest inconveniences and reproaches that can possibly befall so noble and otherwise incomparable a city. . . . What was bad two hundred years ago has become enormously worse in our own times."[10]

American Architect and Building News readers were also given hard data about the oppressive "fogs" that had recently blanketed some British cities. These fogs were defined as "fog plus smoke," a concept that would later be named smog. The publication explained, "The mortality in the seven weeks ending on the 21st of February, 1880, as taken from the Registrar-General's reports, shows an addition of many thousands to the average and normal rate of death. Sufferers from asthma were the chief victims . . . 220 per cent above the average, during the week of the most oppressive fogs. The deaths from bronchitis rose. . . . 331 per cent above the average. The number of fatal cases in pneumonia, pleurisy, and other lung diseases was largely added to; and, as may be easily understood, the mischief did not cease with the disappearance of the fogs . . . ending in early death, or in constitutions permanently enfeebled and deteriorated."[11]

A *Saturday Review* essay in October 1881 made clear that the same smoke that ate away at the lungs literally ate away at everything in sight. The smoke "disfigures our buildings and stunts our vegetation," complained the *Saturday Review*. "It not only disfigures—it destroys. It eats into our textile fabrics, and slowly wears away the masonry of our buildings. Worse than all, it impedes the functions of the organism."[12]

Organized smoke abatement commissions, committees, and societies began to appear and strengthen throughout the 1880s, in London, Montreal, Chicago, Boston, Pittsburgh, and many other cities. An 1882 smoke abatement congress in London attracted no fewer than 116,000 persons seeking both scientific and regulatory answers to the dilemma.[13]

Well into the 1890s, the notion prevailed that mankind's newest affliction was just a more virulent version of a centuries-old suffocation. An August 1890 edition of the *Chicago Tribune* traced "the plague back six centuries to the time when coal was first brought to London from Newcastle." At the same time, the proliferation of railroads helped catapult steam locomotives to the top of the offender list. Soon, local ordinances restricting railway smoke were enacted throughout the country.[14]

Because Chicago was crisscrossed by rail lines, that city was particularly concerned with train smoke. By December 1890, most rail lines had agreed to attempt to comply with local regulations by installing so-called smoke abatement devices. The Lake Shore line installed burners that reduced the size of the cloud wafted into the air by engines. The Erie, the Burlington, and the Baltimore & Ohio railroads were all adding similar devices to their engines, and the Northwestern promised to launch such a program soon. The public's lack of patience with abatement delay was seen when the Illinois Central suggested some bizarre smoke reduction experiments; the Health Department dismissed those ideas as a mere ploy "to baffle the [health] officers" and demanded the Illinois Central take immediate action to reduce emissions or be dragged into court.[15]

But in fact, smoke abatement devices were mainly cosmetic, or the reduction benefits were too marginal to matter. Many were nothing more than grilles and restrictive burning techniques. By 1903, the Pennsylvania

Railroad's superintendent of motor power confessed, "We know of no method by which a locomotive can be fired with bituminous coal without producing smoke." Moreover, as railroads proliferated, the magnitude of the menace only expanded, dwarfing any token amelioration by screens, grilles, or aerators. In Chicago, railroad tracks innervated the entire city. A 1908 *Chicago Record-Herald* article protested, "There is not a section of this city that is free from railroad tracks. They cut in everywhere; the locomotives puff their smoke into thousands of residences and across the public parks." The problem, complained the *Chicago Record-Herald* in another article, was "the thousands of locomotives that enter the very heart of the city."[16]

For example, the Pennsylvania Railroad, by 1910, operated 249 freight and passenger trains along 263 miles of Chicago-area track, burning 670 tons of coal daily. Moreover, the Pennsylvania constituted only 10 percent of Chicago's daily train volume. A few years later, Cleveland recorded 3.5 million tons of coal smoke discharged into its air annually from all sources. Municipal fines incurred by culprits were merely considered a cost of doing business. The railroads became skilled in dragging out court proceedings, lobbying against regulation, and pressuring smoke inspectors. In one case, after an aggressive Chicago smoke inspector was ousted, forty-six cases of smoke pollution in Chicago were quietly settled by the Pennsylvania for court costs—about one dollar each.[17]

Communities understood that the commercial and industrial benefits of rail traffic were killing them. One study documented the increased mortality during two brief periods in 1909 of oppressive citywide smoke-fog in Glasgow, Scotland. During one instance, deaths rose from eighteen per thousand to twenty-five per thousand, and a second fog saw the rate raised to thirty-three per thousand; meanwhile, death rates remained unchanged in surrounding communities located beyond the Glasgow cloud. In 1910, Pittsburgh calculated the damage to its health and infrastructure as $1 per ton burned. A detailed study by the University of Pittsburgh reported that "the smoke nuisance" cost the city of Chicago $50 million annually, while the United States suffered a $500 million annual loss. A 1913 London study widely reported by newspapers on both sides of the Atlantic made clear that coal smoke brought cancer to every area in which it was burned. A typical *New York Times* headline read FINDS CANCER BRED WHERE COAL IS FUEL. The article added that locales that burned only peat fuel experienced almost no cancers.[18]

The answer was to electrify the railroads.

Smoke abatement advocates had been pressing for electrification for decades. Experimental battery-operated trains had been tinkered with throughout the early 1800s. In 1879, at the Berlin Trade Fair, the German firm of Siemens and Halske finally unveiled the first working electric train, a miniature locomotive hauling thirty passengers some six hundred meters at a top speed of 4 mph. The Siemens and Halske train was powered by generated current transmitted through a so-called third rail.[19]

The next year, on May 13, 1880, Edison significantly advanced the idea, constructing a genuine full-sized electric railway in Menlo Park. His narrow-gauge train achieved a top speed of 40 mph before it broke down. But the device was steadily improved, and like all trains it added whistles and bells. Soon, his newfangled train was taken seriously by the railroad industry. In 1881, Edison was commissioned by the Northern Pacific to create a great electric locomotive powerful enough to pull ten tons at 60 mph, thus replacing its dirty coal-fired steam engines. But financial problems and patent litigation prevented Edison from completing the task. In 1883, Edison incorporated the Electric Railway Company of America to develop electric trains. But the next summer he gave up the enterprise because, as he explained to a reporter in 1884, "I had too many other things to attend to, especially in connection with electric lighting."[20]

By the early 1880s, Siemens had already established a fully functional electrified commuter line in Berlin. American railroad companies knew electrification was feasible as early as 1893 when the Baltimore & Ohio was forced by city officials to electrify its approach to Baltimore through the dank 7,000-foot Howard Tunnel; the tunnel trapped so much smoke, it was considered a gas chamber. Shortly thereafter, the electrified portion was expanded to 3.6 miles, thus reducing the line's in-city emissions. In 1895, the Pennsylvania inaugurated a seven-mile New Jersey electric commuter line. By 1901, New York officials were demanding that the approaches to its city be likewise electrified. Within two years, the New York State legislature passed laws requiring the replacement of steam locomotives in urbanized areas.[21]

Electric was certainly superior to steam. Some of the first electrics in 1893 had accelerated to more than 112 mph, albeit without pulling major loads. In 1905, the New York Central staged a proper "race" between its mightiest steam engine and its latest electric, each pulling comparable passenger trains. For its steam contender, the company deployed Engine No. 2799, a proven behemoth capable of placing 140,000 pounds on drivers to yield 28,500 pounds of fast-moving tractive muscle. Engine No.

2799 was poised against General Electric's Engine No. 6000, the New York Central's forcibly acquired electric capable of routinely dashing down the track at speeds of about 80 mph. From a dead start, Engine No. 6000 required only 127 seconds to attain a speed of 50 mph. This was 76 seconds faster than the steam-driven locomotive, which was left far behind.[22]

No longer could a railroad protest that electrics were inferior. In test after test, electrics outperformed steam competitors. By 1906, the New York Central had finished electrifying its section in and out of Grand Central Station and began deploying the trains on express runs—and this accomplishment also testified that electric trains could run fast as well as clean.[23]

By 1909, smoke abatement officials in Chicago and elsewhere followed New York's example, joining the demand for urban electrification. The railroads could no longer argue that the idea was technologically unfeasible. So the upgrade openly became just a matter of money. However, the companies fiercely balked at the expenditure for new infrastructure. Pennsylvania manager Alfred Gibbs was typical when he asserted, "The time has not yet come when the enormous outlay of capital for the purpose of electrification of the railways would be justified by the returns." One estimate projected an annual cost of $14.6 million for two decades to electrify all Chicago railroads within the city.[24] However, reducing the documented loss of life and the $50 million annual erosion of infrastructure and environment did not provide sufficient incentive for the Pennsylvania or other railroads to undertake the fix.

By 1911, many cities pushed beyond mere demands and enacted legislation with teeth. In Chicago, for example, Chief Smoke Inspector Paul S. Bird crusaded for unwavering enforcement of the antismoke ordinance. Pennsylvania Railroad attorneys admitted, "There is no secret made by his [Bird's] office of the fact that he intends to and does use his office to force electrification of the local railroad terminals." In response, Pennsylvania officials called for "retaliation" against the city by tying up even the smallest smoke complaint in protracted legal proceedings. Eventually Bird was replaced with a less insistent chief inspector.[25]

While many of the railroads declined to electrify, some did, especially when finally forced by powerful city establishments, such as in New York and Chicago. But one railroad, the Milwaukee Road, exceeded all other electrified lines in the scope of its achievement. In doing so, the Milwaukee became a mighty railroad that decided to turn the high initial cost of electrification into a moneymaking asset. How? It began by using clean,

renewably generated hydroelectricity to help it conquer the rugged Rockies in a way that no steam locomotive could. It proved that long-distance
electric railroading could be profitable. Once in operation, the Milwaukee's trains quietly and almost effortlessly traversed the indomitable mountains daily, and this was a testament that the same approach could be
replicated by every railroad everywhere. What happened?

The Milwaukee Railroad came into existence in 1847 as the Milwaukee and Waukesha Railroad, but by the time its first train chugged
across Wisconsin in 1851, the name had been altered to the Milwaukee
and Mississippi. Within two decades, following expansion into neighboring states, the company acquired its more recognizable name, the
Chicago, Milwaukee, and St. Paul. Eventually, everyone called it by its
shortened moniker, the Milwaukee Road, or just the Milwaukee.[26]

In 1881, the Milwaukee became a transportation powerhouse as
Standard Oil figure William Rockefeller, brother of John D. Rockefeller,
joined the Milwaukee board. Others from the Rockefeller clan and the
Standard Oil cartel joined as well. Soon the Milwaukee became a lucrative shareholders' engine as it hauled freight across the Midwest. A gallery
of America's top robber barons—oil magnate Henry Flagler, meatpacking
giant Philip D. Armour, and Standard Oil heir Percy Rockefeller among
them—streamed in to partake of the railroad's riches. In large part, their
idea was to grow the Milwaukee to check the expanding rail interests of
J. P. Morgan and James Hill.[27]

Through the first years of the twentieth century, the Milwaukee was
the picture of financial health. The line earned three times the interest on
its monthly debt service and regularly returned 7 percent dividends to its
wealthy stockholders. Even subordinated junior bondholders received returns of at least 4 percent. The Milwaukee's early management functioned
as a trim, experienced, and efficient cadre, often trained from the bottom
up. Rank-and-file employees, in the main, stood out as satisfied and loyal
even as other railroads were embroiled in contentious labor disputes. The
president of the Milwaukee happily informed the Interstate Commerce
Commission that his firm had gained a reputation as a "gilt-edge investment stock." Even the Panic of 1907 was unable to blunt the Milwaukee's
stellar stock, which remained above $100 per share.[28]

Before, during, and after the Panic of 1907, as urbanized areas expanded and the national economy broadened from the bottom up, the
need for more transcontinental railroads could everywhere be heard as a
clarion call to business and industry. Newspapers across the country, espe-

cially along the proposed route, published arpeggios of seductive analyses and reports beckoning ever more rail construction. For example, on November 8, 1905, the *Seattle Post-Intelligencer* declared that other railroads trekking through the Northwest during the prior month recorded "twice as many carloads of freight shipped east" compared to the previous year, adding, "The business has been so heavy . . . it is impossible to furnish cars enough to meet the demand."[29]

A January 1906 *Wall Street Journal* article crammed with statistics on multimillion-dollar shipping increases, concluded, "Seattle foreign exports in 1905 reached $27,856,285, an increase of $19,690,925. Foreign imports were $9,653,377, an increase of $4,227,575. . . . Total bank clearings were $301,600,000, an increase of $79,000,000. Builders spent during the year $6,684,784." The *Wall Street Journal* concluded, "Little additional comment is needed to explain why the earnings of the Union Pacific, Great Northern, Northern Pacific, Canadian Pacific, and Southern Pacific are constantly increasing, nor to explain why the Milwaukee . . . and possibly the Northwestern are anxious to reach the Pacific Coast. . . . The aggregate value of the six leading cities of the Pacific Coast . . . will probably advance more in the next twelve months than any other aggregate of property anywhere under the sun."[30]

Indeed, a rival Union Pacific director acknowledged it was only a matter of time before the Milwaukee "would be forced to build . . . [because] the traffic . . . will be too much for the Union Pacific." Against a background of commercial enthusiasm, salivating civic support, and raw economic opportunity, the directors of the Milwaukee Road in November 1905 decided in principle to challenge the Union Pacific, as well as the Northern Pacific and the Great Northern, the two so-called Northern Lines controlled by competitor railroad millionaires Hill and Morgan.[31]

The challenge was not as unexpected as the method. Plotting a route that would connect the Midwest to the Pacific Northwest, yet steer sufficient miles south of the Northern Lines, took the Milwaukee directly through the Montana Rockies. Steep grades and formidable wilderness required a feat of railroad engineering. But once the tracks were laid, what would economically power the trains? The new route did not pass through coal country. Hence, traditional steam engines would require coal to be transported in at great cost and then lugged up and down the mountains in heavy coal cars, manned by stokers, and all that would add so much weight and cost to the journey that locomotion itself would be just too expensive. This realization intersected with the national demand for electrification.[32]

The Milwaukee then made history by voluntarily opting for an electrical route as a competitive edge that was coincidentally cleaner, more powerful, and driven by renewable hydroelectric facilities. By this time, the Milwaukee had already installed electric lighting in three hundred cars, more than any other railroad. The company was therefore amenable to the notion of electrification. Passing through remote mountainous terrain made intermediate stops at mountain hamlets less economically important, since these sparsely populated map marks would not measurably add freight or passengers. The Milwaukee's strategy would establish it as a long-haul freight and passenger operation—a giant transportation enterprise.[33]

Until the Milwaukee board voted in November 1905 to reach for the West Coast, all railroad electrification had been coerced by government regulation as a smoke abatement mandate. The Milwaukee decision was radically different—voluntary, and based on sound economics. So even though driven by compelling self-interest and stark engineering realities, an electrified Milwaukee Road represented a bright turning point for the entire railroad industry, the environment, and the communities that endured the charred price of progress.[34]

But a better idea was not enough to ensure success. In the wake of the Panic of 1907, the cash-lessened owners and competitors of the Milwaukee found the good fortunes of the company too tempting to resist. Now began a protracted cascade of looting, raiding, and ravaging, from both without and within, that systematically crippled and eventually dismantled the Milwaukee in the midst of its great electrified railroad revolution. It would take an entire volume to catalog the misdeeds and mistakes that killed the Milwaukee. The process was not quick. The vultures feasted for decades before the bones had been picked dry and the plug pulled on its electrification. When the soot settled, the sad case of the Milwaukee doomed transcontinental electrification for all America and propelled the nation more irredeemably toward diesel-driven passenger trains that predictably failed.

The story begins with the Milwaukee's original estimate for its push to the sea. Company engineers who studied the Northern Lines reliably advised Milwaukee president Albert Earling that the mountains could be crossed and the Pacific reached for about $45 million. By September of 1906, with construction under way, Earling's estimate had grown to $60 million. By the time construction was concluded, mainly before 1920, the price tag had been inflated to roughly $260 million, of which only $23 million was devoted to the actual electrification infrastructure. An Interstate Commerce Commission (ICC) investigation concluded that the total cost, more than quadruple the original estimate, could not be justified by any "adequate engineering or traffic surveys [that] were made. On the contrary, everything indicates that the project was the result of rivalry between powerful groups."[35]

Competitor railroads immediately began snatching up land to sell to the Milwaukee at severely inflated levels or started calculated bidding wars to drive up the price. A Milwaukee director told the ICC that the Great Northern, Northern Pacific, and Union Pacific undertook strategic land acquisitions along the Milwaukee route, forcing the line to "pay a great deal more for the property on account of competitive conditions . . . it was a very vicious competition."[36]

Electricity was vastly cheaper than coal or diesel fuel. But the savings never accrued to the Milwaukee. It started with the very copper needed to conduct electricity over wires. Montana's Anaconda Copper Company was the central supplier because of both its proximity and size. Yet the cost of copper purchased from Anaconda mysteriously skyrocketed far above market prices when the Milwaukee tried to buy. Ultimately, copper price-gouging consumed some 18 percent of the total electrification expenditure, when it was originally thought to be a far smaller expense.[37]

Who controlled Anaconda? William Rockefeller and his son Percy were pivotal directors of Anaconda. John D. Ryan was Anaconda's president. Yet the Rockefellers and Ryan were also key directors of the Milwaukee.[38] The price-gouging and self-dealing became a fact of life at the Milwaukee.

At the same time, hydroelectricity from local water projects had also suddenly jumped in price due to questionable supply contracts. An ICC investigation found that those sweetheart power contracts were so burdensome that the Milwaukee spent millions more on electricity than it ever needed to, and indeed for electricity that was never even used. "The railroad practically [is] always in the position of having to pay for power which it does not use," an ICC investigation concluded. During one three-year period, the ICC asserted, when every dollar was being scrimped from employees and operations to survive, the company paid "at least $1.5 million for power which it was unable to use." The local hydroelectric companies involved included Great Falls Power Company and Thompson Falls Power Company, which executed disadvantageous, unbreakable long-term contracts with the Milwaukee. For example, Great Falls somehow negotiated a ninety-nine year agreement with built-in escalator clauses that virtually obviated competitive bidding for a century. In 1912, both Great Falls Power Company and Thompson Falls Power Company were combined with other local firms to create Montana Power Company.[39]

Who controlled the power companies? Ryan, Milwaukee's director, controlled Great Falls Power Company, and through an investment group he also controlled Thompson Falls Power Company. When Montana Power took over Great Falls and Thompson, Ryan simply exchanged his stock in those two merged companies for an equivalent control of Montana Power.[40]

Milwaukee's electrification infrastructure finally began major construction in late 1914, years after the company's basic decision.[41] Delays had given enough time for economic predators and financial highwaymen to stake out the process. Self-dealing, price-gouging sweetheart contracts and inflated costs fueled the fortunes of key directors, but it slowed the railroad's forward motion. But the dream of electrification, cherished by the men and women of the Milwaukee Road, persevered.

The first equipment contracts were finally let on November 24, 1914. A year later, electrified service was inaugurated in Montana and quickly earned kudos. At 9:05 A.M., November 30, 1915, current was switched on between Eustis and Butte. Some ninety minutes later, mighty Engine No. 10200 began the first movement eastward. During the next several days, more trains began operation. On December 3, Milwaukee proved that its regenerative braking system worked wonderfully. A 1,600-ton train climbed a slope beyond Butte and then controlled its descent down the mountain with power braking supplied by the engine that fed current back into the trolley connection—in other words, Engine No. 10200 controlled its descent without drawing extra electricity and actually returned current to the system.[42]

Several days later, near Janney, Montana, the Milwaukee Road staged a test of its electric engines versus its most powerful steam locomotives. The Butte newspaper reported the contest this way: "A 48-car train weighing 3,000 tons [was] pulled by two electric motors . . . quietly and apparently with the utmost ease at a speed of 16 mph. . . . The steam horses [coal-fired locomotives] toiled up the grade and the engines actually groaned under the strain . . . and only managed to go through Janney at a speed of nine miles an hour. There was something almost pathetic in the game fight which steam put up against its new rival in the transportation field, but it was so visibly and completely outclassed that even a child could have picked the easy winner at a glance. Not one of the half hundred spectators could help feeling he had witnessed the overwhelming triumph of a new power over an old and tried friend that had faithfully served mankind for many decades past."[43]

Another test at Erie, Pennsylvania, staged a brute-force sumo-style wrestle between Engine No. 10251, an electric freshly rolled off the production line at the nearby GE factory, and a top-notch steam-powered locomotive. The two beasts were positioned nose-to-nose to determine which could force the other down the track. The shoving match began when the steam engine huffed, puffed, and billowed muscular clouds as it scored a few feet against the electric. But then electric Engine No. 10251 opened its throttle. The coal-burning engine's forward motion was abruptly stopped. Then, despite its maximum effort, the steam engine was nudged into a retreat. The nudge became an unstoppable assault. The humiliating scene worsened as the steam engine's wheels continued lurching forward, even as electric Engine No. 10251 pushed it farther and farther backward. Finally, the steam crew conceded the lopsided bout.[44]

While electrified locomotives could scale steep mountain grades, traverse daunting gorges, almost magically run on some stretches of track "free of charge" on regenerated electricity, and outshove any coal-fired engine, the Milwaukee's electrified service could not overcome the financial drags.

A chief obstruction to the Milwaukee's success was the so-called Gap. The Milwaukee ran traditional steam locomotives from the Midwest to its electrified section, which began at Harlowton, Montana, and extended to Avery, Idaho, a mainly mountainous distance of approximately 440 miles. At Avery, the line resumed regular steam service over mainly flatlands to Othello, Washington, then proceeded west by electric power another 216 miles to Tacoma, Washington, on the West Coast. The approximately two-hundred-mile nonelectrified portion was infamously called the Gap. The most difficult terrain through the Rockies and the Cascades was understandably electrified first to save money, the intention being to extend the system to the flat middle miles later.[45]

But when funds dwindled due to the inflated cost of electrification and general operation, the Milwaukee was simply unable to complete the Gap. As a result, a cumbersome, costly, and incongruous handoff occurred daily as westbound Milwaukee trains switched from steam to electric at Harlowton, Montana, then back to steam at the Gap, and then back again to electric at Othello, Washington, until the ocean. Eastbound trains repeated this process in reverse. Any financial savings electrification could have conveyed were blocked by the operational and economic nuisance of engine switching at either end of the 200-mile Gap.[46]

Transit across the western United States was made even more unprofitable because the competitor Northern Lines, that is, the Northern Pacific and Great Northern, refused to set joint rates where shipments interlined. Hence, shippers that used either of those Northern Lines to start or complete a shipment were not permitted to seamlessly utilize the Milwaukee's tracks anywhere along the way. This anticompetitive measure violated ICC rules. The Milwaukee suffered because it had counted on such cross-continental interline shipments to make its electrified routes profitable. Ironically, the Milwaukee management declined to lodge a protest with the ICC, thus acquiescing to and perpetuating the damage.[47]

When the Milwaukee found its cash position so strapped, it did not issue additional stock. That the Milwaukee could have done, since its directors were expert at floating shares, and its financial officers knew a ready market existed in spite of financial difficulties. Instead, the company, mainly during the electrification planning and construction years—that is, from 1909 to 1917—issued a series of ten- and fifteen-year bonds and other debt measures, totaling more than an astounding quarter billion dollars. Maturity dates, that is, payouts, were bunched up one upon the other in the twenties and thirties, creating an impossible-to-sustain cascade of seven- and eight-digit multimillion-dollar deadlines. Interest itself sapped more than $10 million annually, and unlike stock dividends, interest payments were an unavoidable expense requiring prompt, regular payment. Milwaukee director and finance expert Donald Geddes, when challenged on the unwise financing, admitted, "Unquestionably, you are right. Our financial structure is very much weaker than if we did not have those serial maturities. . . . You are entirely right in saying that if these maturities had been further off, we might have been better off." The real beneficiaries were of course the investment banks and syndicates, such as Kuhn, Loeb and Company and National City Bank, which scooped up the high-yield bonds. Geddes himself was closely associated with both Kuhn, Loeb and National City Bank. Indeed, in some cases, Geddes was selected by the railroad's bankers to head up a "common stock protective committee."[48] It was said that Geddes was the bank's man in the company.

Outside factors helped compound the problems of internal and external pummeling. The Panama Canal opened in 1914, providing a new route for shippers sending freight coast-to-coast, and this hurt all railroads. Automobile and truck ownership exploded, reducing both passenger and freight rail traffic, especially as railroad-encouraged, government-financed roads, once thought to simply connect shipper markets to train depots, began to connect instead to other roads; these roads quickly created a growing automobile highway system, and this too hurt all railroads. America's entry into World War I on April 6, 1917, led to the government's nationalization of all railroads, which battered the finances of many lines. In 1922, the Milwaukee's peaceful labor relations eroded, and a protracted strike cost the line millions. Rate reductions imposed by both the regulatory and competitive environment further hammered at the Milwaukee's financial strength.[49]

Aggravating every other deterrent to the Milwaukee's survival was a series of monumental management errors. The company's once sharp-eyed management ultimately gave way to a coterie of cronies and personal surrogates endowed with the power to commit millions in Milwaukee dollars to questionable pursuits. Not infrequently, conflicts of interest lined insider pockets to the detriment of the Milwaukee.[50]

For example, the company's president Harry E. Byram was appointed as a surrogate for leading Chicago-based stockholder J. Ogden Armour. Beginning in 1920, Byram embarked on a perilous acquisition campaign. For reasons that bewildered government regulators concerned with the railroad's health, Byram insisted on long-term leases for several failing and virtually useless Chicago-area rail lines. These lines were known within the railroad industry as "orphans," and a director even denigrated one of the two small lines as "two tails without a middle." Byram, who had never been involved in such acquisitions, or transactions of such magnitude, was instructed to lease 360 miles of the Chicago, Terre Haute, and Southwestern Railway for an astonishing 999 years, assuming $19.5 million of the failing railway's debt. Only the Terre Haute's bankers benefited from this dubious transaction.[51]

Chicago banker Frank O. Wetmore, the Terre Haute's banker who oversaw the sale and lease to the Milwaukee, openly conceded to government regulators, "We had been struggling with that property . . . for ten or eleven years. . . . We had been sweating blood." Indeed, a prior bank officer running the failed Terre Haute suffered a nervous breakdown trying to make headway. His replacement endured "sweating of six or seven long, weary years."[52]

No other line would bail out the beleaguered Terre Haute orphan. We "tried to get everybody," Wetmore confessed. "The New York Central, the Pennsylvania, the Big Four, the Chicago Grand Trunk. We could not get any of them to even turn around and look at it. They would not pay any attention to it." Wetmore quipped in one court proceeding, "It is difficult to get rid of an old dog." Until the Milwaukee mysteriously came to the rescue, the banker testified later, "We had to squirm along, do the best we could."[53]

The Interstate Commerce Commission arrived at the conclusion that the Terre Haute "was a distressed property controlled by . . . bankers who wanted to liquidate and who had written the securities off the books of their banks as losses." When Byram was asked by ICC commissioners to explain the irrational move, he provided no answers. The ICC noted in a report, "Upon examination in this proceeding, Byram's mind was a blank as to all phases of whatever negotiations he had with the bankers."[54]

The Terre Haute was just one of several inexplicable "orphan" acquisitions engineered by Byram that caused the Milwaukee's debt to tower ever higher. Moreover, such acquisitions were just part of a string of bizarre management moves that favored bankers at the expense of the Milwaukee.[55]

While many railroads were able to weather the ups and downs of external events, such as war, strikes, new technology, and management missteps, the Milwaukee was already mortally weakened from within when the first major adversities began in 1914. One Milwaukee director, calling on his meatpacking background, explained why the line had no chance of survival while competitors did. The Milwaukee, he stated, "did not have the bacon in the cellar that the other roads had."[56]

Insidious self-dealing, manipulated expenses, massive artificial cost overruns, ongoing restraint of trade, looting, raiding, and the imponderables all combined to bring the railroad and its magnificent electrified transcontinental showcase to a slow but screeching halt.

In 1925, $47 million in bonds were set to mature. For years, the Milwaukee had worried about that due date. Now it was upon them. Unable to pay, the once healthy Milwaukee Road was thrown into receivership and then bankruptcy. At the time, the failure of this half-billion-dollar behemoth glowed sadly as the largest bankruptcy in American history. In the run-up to the collapse, the largest shareholders and security holders controlling the largest blocks of stock all sold their well-appreciated holdings at fifty cents on the dollar and therefore escaped financially unscathed. This group included William Rockefeller with 150,000 shares, J. Ogden Armour with 125,000, E. S. Harkness with 100,000 shares, as well as leading insurance companies and investment groups. Consequently, it was the

masses of junior bondholders, smaller creditors, and little investors who
were smitten by the bankruptcy.[57]

ICC commissioners investigating the monster failure focused on
how the Milwaukee's assemblage of powerful millionaire directors systematically ran the line into the ground. There were few answers. Commission
attorney Daniel Grady asked Percy Rockefeller if he could recall a single
beneficial decision taken for the railroad—even one.[58]

> *Mr. Grady:* Now, Mr. Rockefeller, after fifteen years as a director of this
> railroad, what do you now recall as being the most beneficial thing that
> was ever accomplished during your period of service in behalf of the
> stockholders of this company?
> *Mr. Rockefeller: I don't know as I ever thought of it.*
>
> *Mr. Grady:* Can you think of a single thing that was accomplished, that
> was really for the benefit of the stockholders?
> *Mr. Rockefeller: Everything that I did was in my judgment for the benefit
> of the stockholders.*
>
> *Mr. Grady:* But now looking back over fifteen years, can you recall a sin-
> gle achievement of the board of directors that was to the real benefit of
> the stockholders?
> *Mr. Rockefeller: If it were to be done over, I do not know how it would be
> done differently.*
>
> *Mr. Grady:* I am not asking you that. I am asking you a question. Just
> read the question again. (Question repeated by the Reporter.)
> *Mr. Rockefeller: They [directors] always used their best judgment, and I
> think that their judgment, if it had not been as good as it was, the situa-
> tion might have been worse.*
>
> *Mr. Grady:* That is the only answer you would care to make to that ques-
> tion, is it? I will have it read again if you care to answer it. (Question re-
> peated by the Reporter.)
> *Mr. Rockefeller: They always in my judgment acted in the best interests of
> the stockholders.*
>
> *Mr. Grady:* Is that the only answer you care to make to that question?
> *Mr. Rockefeller: That is the answer I think.*

Mr. Grady: But you cannot recall a single thing that has proven to be of benefit to the stockholders, can you?
Mr. Rockefeller: The situation has been unfortunate.[59]

Ironically, a combination of the Milwaukee's bankers seemed to be most eager to trigger the receivership and bankruptcy. Months before the railroad defaulted on its bonds, the company's own attorneys teamed up with its leading bankers to prepare a blank creditor complaint in search of a collaborator. In March 1925, the obscure Binkley Coal Company, due a relatively tiny debt from the Milwaukee, was selected to do the honors, filling in the spaces and functioning as a proxy for the bankers, such as Kuhn, Loeb and National City Bank and leading mortgage holders. Binkley's reluctant president later testified that he had always been paid by the Milwaukee in the past and never wanted to sue. "We did not feel insecure . . . about our claim against the railroad," he admitted. Indeed, he confessed some twenty months after filing that he was unaware of all the legal paperwork and details done in his company's name. Not to worry. A bank attorney functioned as Binkley's lawyer. He handled all the petitions and motions. Bank attorneys also colluded with Chicago bankruptcy judge Charles H. Wilkerson, privately meeting with Wilkerson in advance to discuss receivership appointments and even ensuring that the judge would be ready and available on March 18, 1925, to hear the petition. Binkley's legal bills and all but a token $200 of its overdue debt from the Milwaukee were later paid through the action of the bankers. That $200 was left unpaid precisely to allow Binkley a pretext to file against the Milwaukee and remain a continuing creditor. By this means and the power of a $200 matchstick, the biggest American bankruptcy scandal to that date—a half-billion-dollar failure that threw thousands of ordinary people out of work and swept the bread from their tables, deprived payments to a long roster of small creditors, many of whom were economically vanquished, and evaporated the stake and savings of thousands of small heartbroken investors—by this $200 was the great Milwaukee debacle consciously ignited.[60]

ICC attorneys probed the incongruity of Milwaukee directors being associated as either directors or leading stockholders of the very banks that benefited from the railroad's bankruptcy by gaining control over the remaining assets.

Walter Fisher, a commission attorney, grilled Jerome J. Hanauer, a senior partner of the investment bank Kuhn, Loeb, which functioned as a principal financial firm for the Milwaukee's stocks and bonds.

Mr. Fisher: Was Mr. Percy Rockefeller at that time closely associated with the National City Bank?
Mr. Hanauer: I cannot testify as to that. . . . I don't remember.

Mr. Fisher: Well, was it not your understanding throughout this entire series of transactions that Mr. Percy Rockefeller was largely interested in and closely associated with the National City Bank?
Mr. Hanauer: . . . There was absolutely no reason—no legal restriction on a director of a railroad company also being a director of a banking house or a bank with which that company did business.

Mr. Fisher: Pardon me—
Mr. Hanauer: And whether he was a director at that time—

Mr. Fisher: I have no objection to your anticipating a possible interpretation of your answer and making an argument against it. You may be wrong in your anticipated interpretation, but I would like to get an answer to the question first, because we are off and down the road on some other issue.
Mr. Hanauer: I cannot testify from actual knowledge of the dates on which Mr. Rockefeller was a director of the St. Paul Railroad or of the National City Bank.[61]

In the decade after the Milwaukee was thrown into bankruptcy, its rail service, including its electrification, stagnated. The company's assets were continually eroded, its routes were undermined, its equipment allowed to decay. Ironically, some found splendid profit in the Milwaukee's evisceration. Every time the steed tried to rise, the predators swooped in.

During its painful reorganization, the Milwaukee struggled to restore its financial health. The twenties were an era of growth and increase for most railroads—but not for the Milwaukee. The ICC observed that the Milwaukee "became bankrupt at a time when general railroad conditions had greatly improved."[62]

But improvement became impossible for the Milwaukee when its bankers continuously gnawed at the firm's cash. For example Kuhn, Loeb, which headed up the reorganization, assessed the company $6.5 million in so-called expenses including more than a million for its own fees. A Senate investigation found the charges hard to believe. Senator James Couzens (R-Michigan) asked pointed questions of Kuhn, Loeb senior partner Hanauer.

Senator Couzens: You put in a statement . . . of the expenses . . . $5 million to $6.5 million. I would like to ask if you consider those reasonable charges for the service that has been performed?

Mr. Hanauer: I should consider it, Senator, the minimum — that is, it is very reasonable. . . . It is really unfortunate that in any reorganization the expenses are so high. . . .

The Chairman: How much do Kuhn, Loeb and Company get out of it?
Mr. Hanauer: . . . We get twenty-five cents per bond, and twenty cents per share, which amounts, altogether, for the National City Company and ourselves, to $1,044,000. . . . It is not all profit by a long ways.

Senator Couzens: How do you arrive at this figure $1,044,000 for your services?
Mr. Hanauer: Of course, it is very difficult to say how one arrives at anything.[63]

By 1935, battered again by the Depression, and again weakened underfoot, the Milwaukee collapsed once more. In the summer of 1935, the Milwaukee filed for bankruptcy a second time. Once again, the same bankers and even the same judge — Wilkerson — controlled and oversaw the failure.[64]

In its second reorganization, numerous interests competed for a piece of the Milwaukee's continued existence. Among them was the Electro-Motive Division of General Motors. The same company that finally became a pivotal contender against Ford's vehicles was also a powerhouse in other forms of internal combustion. This included diesel locomotives, that is, electric locomotives that lugged their own petroleum-burning onboard power plants to generate electricity. Rather than receive current from overhead wires and third rails fed by hydroelectricity and existing utilities, diesel electrics compressed air and oil until the oil exploded or expanded in the piston. Those pistons turned the massive generators that sent electricity into the traction motors moving the train forward. In essence, diesel electrics were hybrids, half powered by oil, half by electricity.[65]

General Electric invented the first diesel electric in 1918 for the Jay Street Connecting Railroad in New York. By the 1930s, GE was greatly challenged by General Motors's Electro-Motive Division, which built the sleek, awesome-looking Pioneer Zephyr. The futuristic Pioneer Zephyr, resembling the wind itself, packed twin boxcar-styled engines with dual 900 hp diesel engines that combined to forge 3,600 hp of raw power. On May 26, 1934, the Pioneer Zephyr set a long-distance record from Chicago to Denver, dashing from dawn to dusk at an average 77.7 mph for thirteen hours and five minutes.[66]

In 1939, the Electro-Motive Division unveiled its FT series, which exceeded the speed records of the Milwaukee's aging electric EF2 and EF3 engines. The only difference was that the diesels burned petroleum instead of using renewable hydroelectric or the excess capacity of nearby electric utilities. Quickly, the Milwaukee's Mechanical Division fell in love with the faster FT diesels.[67]

In 1941, the Milwaukee purchased its first FT diesel and, by the end of World War II, became determined to eliminate its electrified network. After the war, oil seemed cheap and abundant. The FTs were fast and powerful. New, more capable electrics were still being manufactured by General Electric, but those were being exported overseas to Europe and Russia where the clean-running locomotives became the stalwarts of rail.[68]

The fight to destroy the Milwaukee's electrification amounted to an internal company war between Kiley and Wylie.

J. P. Kiley was a Milwaukee vice president determined to eliminate all electric lines. The reasons, Kiley presumed, would be cost, technological obsolescence, and lesser capability.[69] This was the assumption.

Laurence Wylie was an electrical engineer devoted to clean, electric trains. Wylie was appointed by Kiley in 1948 to oversee the dismantling of all electric. Having worked with electric rail since 1919, Wylie balked. On his own volition, Wylie ordered comparative studies of electric versus diesel. His findings contradicted Kiley's theories. The old electric could outpull the new diesels and run cheaper, dollar for dollar. In fact, on one typical run to the West Coast, three diesels were shown to annually cost more than $104,000 extra. In mountainous terrain, diesels fared even worse. Newer electrics constructed by GE in the 1950s for the Soviet Union showed still better results. These powerful new GE electrics, nicknamed Little Joes for Joseph Stalin, were almost twice as economical and powerful as GM's diesels, especially on long runs.[70]

For example, six Electro-Motive Division F7 diesels were needed to haul 3,330 tons, and five Electro-Motive Division GP9s were required for about the same chore. But that same tonnage was easily pulled by just four old GE freight electrics. The electrics also beat the gas-burning locomotives on flatter terrain. Kiley dismissed Wylie's findings and instead relied on his own engineering tests, in large measure provided by the Electro-Motive Division. Wylie, who had worked his way up from a Montana trainmaster to a district superintendent, could not understand why the engineering reports did not jibe. In his campaign to replace electrics with General Motors diesels, Kiley was constantly buttressed by GM's glowing engineering reports. Finally, Wylie realized the newest diesels were being compared not with the newest high-speed electrics, but thirty-year-old electrics. Moreover, other data from General Motors Electro-Motive Division was constantly being skewed in favor of diesel.[71]

Who was heading up General Motors Electro-Motive Division efforts in the late 1940s? It was Dana Kettering, the son of Charles Kettering, the same inventive genius who'd helped Gray and Davis Electrical Engineers develop the starter and battery array that mysteriously undercut Thomas Edison's attempt to create an electric vehicle with Henry Ford. In that instance, the testing had also been challenged as disingenuous.[72]

Eventually, Wylie was forced to concede defeat at the hands of Kiley. Kiley had the power. Wylie did not. By the fifties, it was clear that Wylie would be compelled to oversee the abandonment of the nation's only proven electric route, and the system was permitted to continue deteriorating. Repairs were not initiated. Upgrades were compromised. Electric was forced into a slow, painful decline. Wylie retired in 1956, his dream of sustaining a world-class electric railway shattered.[73]

During the fifties and sixties, the Milwaukee continued to teeter on the edge of yet another failure. But the electrified operation, even though weakened, was never a factor in the railroad's crumbling economics. In fact, "The new electrification paid for itself by 1930, returning 9 percent annually . . . in savings over comparable steam operation," according to an independent cost analysis by rail experts. It continued to make money well into the fifties and sixties. No wonder executives from railways across Europe traveled to the Milwaukee line to marvel at the clean and efficient power of its famous western route. In fact, the Milwaukee's electrification was emulated on forty-one thousand route miles across Europe. Eventually, twenty-six nations worldwide copied the system, adopting Milwaukee-style electric as a standard.[74]

During the postwar decades, the truth about diesel versus electric on long distance hauls was obscured. But slowly information began seeping out. For example, electrics were found to be 40 to 60 percent cheaper to maintain and simply lasted longer. The Internal Revenue Service agreed and refused to accept the notion that diesels possessed a twenty-year life. A study by the Chesapeake and Ohio completed in 1955 demonstrated that diesels could not reliably last the advertised twenty years, but rather about a dozen. So the IRS reduced the permissible diesel engine depreciation first for the C&O, and then for the entire rail industry, to just fourteen years.[75]

In the late 1950s, British engineer Harry Farnsworth Brown risked the wrath of General Motors by widely publishing his findings that diesel was no better than coal. One independent engineering study reported Brown's work this way: "In his effort to verify several claimed advantages of diesel locomotives over steam, Brown found all of them spurious, having been based on invalid comparisons, faulty statistical methods, incomplete and biased data, and various forms of misinterpretation. His results and conclusions were presented before the Institution of Mechanical Engineers of London on November 30, 1960, in a paper entitled "Economic Results of Diesel Electric Motive Power on the Railways of the United States of America." Mr. Brown's conclusions were devastating.[76]

Brown's summary explained, "This study simply states that the all-embracing economies claimed for diesel motive power on the Class I railways of the United States, as a whole, do not appear in the statistical record. The diesel locomotive has not 'revolutionized' American railway economics. In road service, diesel motive power has added to the financial burden of the railways. The comparative analysis made in the paper showed the economic performance of diesel motive power to be about on par with that of steam on its overall application on the United States railways—no better, no worse. . . . In line haul, or 'road' service, the paper showed it to be more expensive than equivalent modern steam might have been. . . . The capital costs had just about cancelled the operating savings."[77]

Moreover, electrics required no petroleum, which even during the postwar period was known to be a diminishing resource. Canadian Pacific Railway senior executive officer Keith Campbell spoke bluntly to a 1972 Railway Systems and Management Association seminar. "As diesel locomotive operators," Campbell insisted, "we are the prisoners of a single fuel, a fuel that is fast becoming a pawn on the chessboard of international politics. It is a fuel, too, for which many users—truckers, for example—have no alternative at the present state of technology. One does not need sophisticated techniques for predicting the future to form the view that, whatever else happens, its price is bound to rise."[78]

On February 20, 1973, the Milwaukee Road issued a press release:

"The Chicago, Milwaukee, St. Paul and Pacific Railroad Company will phase out its remaining electrified operations in Montana, Idaho, and Washington in favor of fully-dieselized service throughout the railroad system, according to an announcement by William J. Quinn, chairman of the board, and Worthington L. Smith, president. The decision came after exhaustive studies carried out by the company over the past several years. . . . 'From a dollars and cents point of view, the railroad had no alternative, but for other reasons it was a difficult decision to reach,' they said. 'Even though electrified operation has actually been in an unofficial phase out stage in recent years, the fact remains that it has been an important part of the Milwaukee Road image, and there is a tremendous amount of sentimental interest in it. When first installed, the Milwaukee's electrified system was vastly superior to steam operation, and even to the diesel power of several years ago. It served us extremely well. Given 1973 facts, however, with highly efficient and versatile diesel locomotives available for both main line and branch line service, compared with the aging electric locomotives confined to main line only, the decision was inevitable.' "[79]

The press release went on, "The Milwaukee Road has 656 miles of electrified main line, the longest in the United States. . . . Between the two sections is a 212-mile segment of main line which for a variety of reasons was never electrified. The 'gap,' as it is known, has been operated by conventional power, a fact which severely limited the versatility and efficiency of the over-all electrified system." Milwaukee officials added that company experts "observed that continuing electrified operation indefinitely would mean not only electrifying the gap but also replacing the entire complex with a modern, high-voltage system and purchasing new electric locomotives. 'In effect,' they said, 'it would be like electrifying from scratch and our studies indicated that such an undertaking would be unwise.'[80]

" 'Because of the extent to which electrified operations have already been cut back, the decision to phase out the system completely over a period of time is of negligible significance from the environmental point of view and will have relatively little impact on the company's system-wide diesel fuel requirements,' the officers stated. Employees now working in electric power substations or engaged in the maintenance of electric locomotives and the overhead power supply system have been notified of the phase out decision. A task force will meet with affected employees within the next 30 days to explain the move and the adjustments that will be required. The task force will also make the remaining decisions with respect to maintenance and operation, locomotive requirements, disposal of electric facilities and related matters."[81]

Milwaukee officers were positive their oil supplies would continue. Eight months later, in October 1973, as a consequence of the Yom Kippur War, Arab exporting countries briefly shut off the spigot, creating the first so-called Oil Shock. Lines to fill up at the gas station were long. The Western world was rocked. By that time, it was too late for the Milwaukee to reverse course. Nearly five years later, rising fuel prices and other costs finished the decades-long destruction of the Milwaukee. It took almost a decade to liquidate the railroad. That was finalized in 1986. Most of its skeleton was sold for scrap.[82]

In the twenty-first century, American railroads consume more than four billion gallons of fuel annually. Electrified railways virtually do not exist outside a few select commuter trains coursing along the Northeast corridor. The gift of renewable, sustainable, and clean electrically driven long-distance rail service is vanquished in the United States. But the legacy of the Milwaukee's great electrified steeds can still be seen elsewhere in the world. In Europe, Asia, Latin America, and Australia, the lands are crisscrossed with electric routes. The Eurostar whisks passengers under the Channel from London to Paris. Japan's high-speed bullet trains exceeding 300 mph are the envy of the world. France, Germany, Switzerland, and the other leaders of Europe have all established a future of electrified rail to move people across borders and bring the Continent together. Russia is ordering new electrics from American manufacturers to span the Siberian frozen expanse. The Milwaukee's legacy lives on everywhere in the world.

But the legacy does not live on in America. In the United States, oil is the fuel of choice for the railroads. In America, electric was derailed.

CHAPTER TEN

THE GM CONSPIRACY

On the bitterest winter night in memory, in an alley behind his apartment building in snowy Minneapolis, crusading editor and publisher Walter W. Liggett had parked his Ford near the side door. Liggett's wife, Edith, and ten-year-old daughter, Marda, were in the car with him. They had just returned from grocery shopping. A fearless journalist and muckraker, Liggett was known for a four-page publication called the *Midwest American* and its unrelenting investigation of Minneapolis's growing crowd of racketeers and their ties to Governor Floyd Olson. Chief among Liggett's editorial targets was the state's most notorious mobster, Kid Cann, whose real name was Isadore Blumenfeld.[1]

The most brazen of Minnesota's many dapper, machine-gun-toting gangsters, Blumenfeld had been arrested and indicted more than a dozen times for a gamut of offenses from pickpocketing to procuring prostitution, from bootlegging to running white-slave traffic, from kidnapping to murder. Except for two conceded minor convictions, Blumenfeld aka Cann always seemed to beat the rap. In some cases, key witnesses were found machine-gunned before they could testify. Sometimes, the jury itself was threatened.[2]

Just days earlier, Liggett had published a scathing article about Olson's ties to the mob. Now the editor was preparing to deliver a speech to the legislature calling for the governor's impeachment over his ties to Cann and a gallery of other underworld thugs. Such crusades were dangerous. Just fifteen months earlier, journalist Howard Guilford had announced a new radio series that would expose "the whole story of Governor Floyd Olson's connection to the underworld." Before he could begin broadcasting the most revealing information, Guilford was murdered by a shotgun blast fired from the window of a passing car.[3]

Now, as Liggett unloaded groceries, a dark car appeared at the end of the alley. He looked at his wife and daughter in the backseat. The car slowly rolled closer, crunching snow beneath its tires. Liggett quickly motioned to his wife and daughter to remain in the Ford. As the ominous car advanced, its passenger window rolled down. Suddenly, headlights from a second car in the alley starkly illuminated Liggett, making him a target. In that moment, Liggett smiled at his family waiting in the Ford.[4]

From the passing car, out came a machine gun barrel, dully glinting in the alley light. Decades later, Marda still remembers, "I ducked down so fast." But Liggett's wife stared straight at the gunman, looking him directly in the eye. Five shots from the machine gun crackled into the night. All five bullets found Liggett. A moment later when Marda looked up, the car was speeding away, and her father lay sprawled across the pavement, fast bleeding to death. Marda ran to his prone body screaming, "Don't die, Daddy; don't die!" Over and over again. "Don't die, Daddy; don't die!" But it was too late. Liggett was dead.[5]

Decades later Marda remembers that her father "was in poverty when he died. He was trying to help the afflicted. He was committed to justice. Money was never a motivating factor for him. My mother had a hard life because of it, but some people have to live for their ideals." The next issue of the *Midwest American* was published on time by Liggett's widow, Edith. The great banner headline blared MY HUSBAND WAS SLAIN BUT HIS FIGHT WILL GO ON.[6]

Edith and another witness went on to identify the killer, a snarling yet smiling man. That man was Blumenfeld, aka Kid Cann. He was arrested, indicted, and prosecuted for the crime. But once again, Kid Cann beat the rap. First burglars broke into the prosecutor's office in an abortive attempt to steal the evidence; prosecutors were expecting it and had secreted the evidence where it would not be found. Then a dozen witnesses, including three bankers and a policeman, gave Kid Cann alibis. Ultimately, this jury too would find him not guilty. The jury foreman explained that if Cann were the machine gunner, the mobster would have been smarter than to allow himself to be recognized.[7]

During the first three decades of the twentieth century, thousands of cities and towns throughout the United States inaugurated or enjoyed access to trolley lines. These rail streetcars were powered by electricity transmitted through overhead catenary wires or hot third rails. Wherever electricity and lighting existed, a trolley system was generally found. Virtually every city and major town enjoyed a system.[8] For most cities and towns, the trolley was a virtual badge of admission to the twentieth century.

Smooth riding and quiet, spacious and clean running, trolleys immediately became popular at the turn of the century as a cherished and vastly more economical alternative to the filthy, cinder-spewing, coal-burning railroads. For example, Connecticut, once the home of major railroads, saw trolleys proliferate throughout its many small towns and larger urban centers. By 1900, passenger traffic on Connecticut's trolleys exceeded the state's steam railroad traffic by 20 percent.[9]

Massachusetts track mileage had increased by as much as 18 percent since 1894. In 1901, that state's trolley lines grew by 242.7 miles while its steam railroad miles began to shrink. By 1902, trolley passenger loads throughout Massachusetts rose to four times the volume carried by steam locomotives.[10]

Trolleys were fun and flexible. Commonly, they picked passengers up and dropped them anywhere along their route. Streetcars ran frequently, and at speeds that safely coexisted with pedestrians and horses; people could just hop on and hop off. Only one of every three hundred million passengers suffered a fatality. Requiring little more than the width of two narrow-gauge rails, trolley lines often wended through pastoral areas, minimally disturbing the beauty of the environment and allowing people to enjoy the countryside. One early-century publication observed that travel on a trolley is "pleasanter than on a steam road, for the breezes can be allowed to blow through without fear of smoke or cinders, and the surrounding scenery is infinitely more attractive. A trolley road can penetrate the most exquisite retreats without spoiling their charm—a steam road has the faculty of making everything it touches hopelessly vulgar and hideous."[11]

A 1903 *McClure's* magazine feature subtitled "The Marvelous Development of the Trolley System" sweetly extolled the virtues of electric trolleys. "More passengers by hundreds of millions are traveling than ever before, but the steam railroads are not carrying the increase. . . . Inch by inch, the field is contested . . . the locomotive is giving way before the insistent trolley." *McClure's*, a nationally admired chronicler of contemporary news and culture, added that it was more than city and suburbs. "Swiftly," the magazine declared, "electric lines [have] flung their spider filaments from town to town until now great sections of the country are cobwebbed."[12]

Serving more than just towns and cities, the trolleys extended between cities, thus creating true intercity transit lines. A trolley line humming between Cleveland and Detroit was inaugurated in December 1901. Pittsburgh's system spread fifty miles in all directions, linking that city with most of western Pennsylvania and parts of Ohio. *McClure's* described Detroit's system as "no longer a timid intermediary between house and office," adding "it leaps boldly 300 miles at a spring . . . [with] flying shuttles [that] weave their web . . . to Bay City and to Kalamazoo. . . . Their extensions now underway [will] span the entire State of Michigan and lead straight through to Chicago." In Iowa, virtually the entire state was innervated by electric trolley lines.[13]

McClure's bragged that with twenty thousand miles of track countrywide, "It will soon be possible to travel by electricity without a break half way across the continent, from the coast of Maine to the middle of Nebraska." The 1903 magazine predicted the journey could be made uninterrupted coast-to-coast once hydroelectric was captured and the way west by rail was electrified.[14]

Streetcars moved through crowded city streets at cautious speeds. But when the route was open, as it was on three hundred miles of track between Indiana cities, or the lines coursing up New York's Hudson River, trolleys easily hit 60 mph. It was understood that electric trolleys could always outpace a coal-burning train.[15]

Moreover, compared to steam railroads, trolleys were cheap to ride and cheap to operate. For example, 1903 town-to-town fares from Joplin in southwestern Missouri to nearby Galena, Kansas, cost passengers a penny per track mile, a third the cost of railroads. From Harlem in New York to Yonkers, passengers paid a nickel for the twenty-six-minute direct ride, which beat train fares costing ten times as much and consuming an hour under the best of indirect connections. "The trolley roads can make money at such prices," reported *McClure's*, "for all their expenses are small. It is estimated that a light country electric road can be built for $7,540 per mile, or $10,540 including power station and car-house. A double-track electric line substantially built for fast traffic can be constructed for $31,500 per mile. These are about half the corresponding figures for steam roads."[16]

Trolleys became more than transportation to the public. They inspired songs and movies. Passengers loved them. They defined lifestyles. *McClure's* painted the picture of 1903 streetcar enjoyment this way: "If you take a trolley ride in the suburbs on a summer evening you will see the open seats filled with cool, comfortable people, sociably chattering, with their hats in their laps, while the breeze blows through their hair or whiskers, as the case may be. The car whirls on, and nobody gets off. It reaches the end of the line, and still nobody leaves it. The passengers merely turn over the seats and ride back. They were not going anywhere—they were simply enjoying a spin in the people's automobile. That is a new luxury of modern life. Neither horse-car nor locomotive ever provided it. The need in human nature to which it responds went unsupplied until the trolley car came into existence to fill it."[17]

McClure's sneered that the joy of trolley riding could not be replicated "by a steam railroad if it were left without competition for a thousand years."

Throughout the first two decades of the twentieth century, trolleys continued to flourish. Some wondered if streetcar usage would decline as a result of the explosion of automobile ownership that occurred during Ford's battle with the Selden monopoly and after the cartel's defeat from 1904 to 1911. That did not occur. In 1906, about six billion passenger boardings were logged on streetcars nationally, or about seventy-five rides per year for every man, woman, and child. This amounted to seventeen million persons daily and climbing. By 1910, the nationwide number had zoomed to ten billion passengers annually. The more than twelve hundred electric lines represented by the American Electric Railway Association predicted that number would double within the coming decade. In January 1911 the *Wall Street Journal* ran a front-page article headlined ASTONISHING GROWTH OF ELECTRIC STREET RAILWAY SYSTEM IN THE PAST TWENTY-FIVE YEARS.[18]

In fact, as the automobile proliferated, thus enabling urban centers to push out farther and farther, trolleys and other electrified transit sustained their popularity. Far from destroying public transit, sprawl only boosted suburban commuting and long-distance pleasure riding. In the twenties, electrified public transit substantially expanded into a three-pronged system—subways and elevated trains, traditional trolleys, and by the end of the decade "trackless trolleys." Trackless trolleys were electrified buses that looked like modern buses and rolled on rubber tires, but they were powered by overhead electric trolley lines.[19]

During the twenties, until the Depression in 1929, there were numerous ups and downs in ridership as the peaks and valleys of economic times dictated the ebb and flow of usage. Moreover, in America's largest cities, such as New York and Chicago, subways and elevated trains became more practical for commuters. But for many, trolleys were still the transit vehicle of choice, attracting between twelve and thirteen billion passenger boardings annually, or between 82 and 89 percent of all electrified urban transportation, and indeed of all transit by any means—petroleum-powered or electric.[20]

A typical feature in the September 19, 1937, *Los Angeles Times* described just one way that urban sprawl symbiotically coexisted with the trolley. The article bore the subhead "Cheap Street Car Trips Through City Popular Recreation." It opened, "Going nowhere at thirteen miles an hour, and at a cost of less than a cent a mile—that's what happens when street cars are used for pleasure riding. It's sort of like riding a merry-go-round—you keep on the go but end up right where you started. Thousands of people living in and near Los Angeles, who don't possess automobiles or who dislike driving in traffic, go for a street car pleasure ride every week. . . . They select a long route, load their families aboard the yellow cars, get a transfer slip for each passenger, and ride for an hour and a half for 7 cents each; less than that if they use tokens."[21]

The *Los Angeles Times* article chronicled an almost idyllic weekend lifestyle that any urbanite would covet: "Through a street car window an interesting and, at times, unbelievable picture of the metropolitan area slowly unfolds. Few of the throng of city dwellers that never get out of the shadow of downtown buildings know that near Inglewood there is an Iowa cornfield with ripening yellow ears almost ready for the harvest. . . . Attractive shop windows make it difficult for one to refrain from getting off the car and changing the street car excursion into a shopping excursion."

The article closed with a section subheaded "Peaceful Scene." It captured the almost dreamy experience of trolley riding for pleasure. "Children eating watermelon on the lawn beneath the shade of a willow; dogs panting in a dusty gutter; schoolboys on bicycles pedaling homeward, their faces scarlet; women shopping in corner markets for something for supper, their hair wet and straggly, their stockings twisted and wrinkled around their stout ankles, their cotton dresses hiked up in the rear by the heat; these are the sights which soon become familiar all along the line, and at a cost of less than a cent a mile. A cheap panorama, to say the least!"[22]

By 1919, Henry Ford was wondering if he should quit auto manufacturing to start a trolley business.[23]

In 1925, electrified systems enjoyed more than sixteen billion annual boardings, whether by traditional rail trolleys, subways and elevated trains, or so-called trackless trolleys. Passenger volume continued to climb until the Depression, when all business suffered a steep decline. By the end of the Roaring Twenties, some of the oldest trolley lines began deteriorating and then disappearing. During the thirties and forties, the pace quickened as small towns and bigger cities everywhere lost their trolleys en masse. By the postwar fifties, virtually all electrified streetcars had vanished in the United States. Even the rails were pulled from the streets, which were then paved over to erase any vestige of their flourishing function.[24]

One by one, the public transit companies of America were either bankrupted out of existence or had converted to expensive diesel-burning, rubber-wheeled bus fleets. Then in many cases those bus fleets also disappeared, leaving urban populations without public transit and reliant on the gas-guzzling automobile. Why?

Scores of these cities interacted with one conglomerate: National City Lines.

What was National City Lines? The Enronesque conglomerate was little more than a front for General Motors at a time when the giant Detroit automaker headed up what all three branches of the federal government— teams of Department of Justice prosecutors, the courts from the lowest district venue to the Supreme Court, and the Senate—called a vast criminal "conspiracy" that insidiously operated across the whole of America. This conspiracy—which also included such petroleum and automotive interests as Mack Truck, Phillips Petroleum, Standard Oil of California, and Firestone Tires—stretched from the nation's largest metropolises such as Los Angeles and St. Louis to the country's smallest cities such as Decatur, Illinois, and Beaumont, Texas. That criminal conspiracy changed urban transportation forever.

What happened and why have the facts been obscured and forgotten?

Most people have never heard of the nationwide mass transit conspiracy set in motion by GM and its coterie of petroleum and automotive confederates. But to a small corps of argumentative urban historians and Internet activists, the entire story has become a virtual urban legend that has continuously and vituperatively been debated for years. No one can properly delve into what GM and its partners actually did without first comprehending how this arcane debate among experts—real and self-appointed— has obscured and prevented the extraordinary details about GM and mass transit from coming to the fore.

In brief, GM's conspiracy had its roots in the twenties when the automobile market became so saturated that auto sales slowed significantly and GM lost $65 million. GM targeted trolley systems across the country for monopolistic takeovers and systematic irreversible conversion from electric streetcars to gasoline- and diesel-burning buses. A series of stealthy mergers and acquisitions began in the midthirties and continued unabated until GM and its corporate cohorts achieved a monopolistic market presence in dozens of cities from St. Petersburg, Florida, to Los Angeles. The conspirators—GM, Mack Truck, Phillips Petroleum, Standard Oil of California, and Firestone Tires—acted through a front company called National City Lines, which they secretly financed. Once National City Lines purchased a transit company, electric trolley service was immediately discontinued, the tracks quickly pulled up, the wires dismantled, and the company switched to GM-made petroleum-burning motor buses.[25]

In 1947, in a landmark case, the federal government prosecuted GM and its corporate partners for a criminal conspiracy to monopolize bus sales and foreclose competition across the United States in the many cities where National City Lines operated. The entire group of oil and automotive companies, as well as their executives, were convicted on one of two similar counts of conspiracy. Despite vigorous appeals by the best defense attorneys in the nation, the Supreme Court allowed the convictions to stand. Eventually, even though GM and National City Lines continued their monopolistic entrenchment in urban mass transit, the scandal faded off the nation's headlines.[26]

A generation later, in 1974, in the immediate aftermath of the Arab-imposed 1973 oil shock, the GM Conspiracy was resurrected by the U.S. Senate Judiciary Committee's subcommittee on Antitrust and Monopoly. In an exhaustively documented study entitled "American Ground Transport," Judiciary Committee staff attorney Bradford Snell accused GM of contributing to the nation's petroleum woes by a deliberate conspiracy against scores of local mass transit systems.[27]

Snell's work was largely, but not exclusively, based upon thousands of pages of documents arising from the Department of Justice's 1947 prosecution of GM and the consortium that had created National City Lines. But going beyond the prosecution, Snell asserted that GM's true motives were not just to convert electric trolley systems into bus lines so it could sell more diesel buses and eliminate competitive electric systems, but also to then cause the abandonment of those very bus companies, thus killing mass transit altogether.[28]

Snell's logic was that with those newly transformed bus companies defunct, America would be converted within a span of several years from a

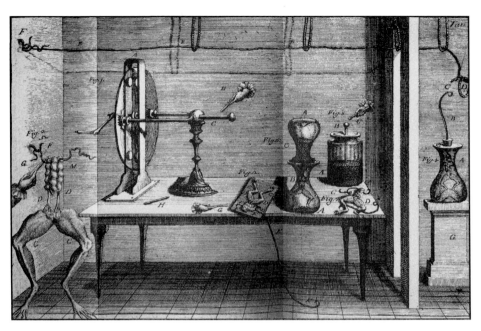

This is a sketch of Galvani's laboratory with frog legs and electrical apparatus, 1791.

An electric taxi in Manhattan circa 1898. *(Courtesy of the Smithsonian Institution, National Museum of American History)*

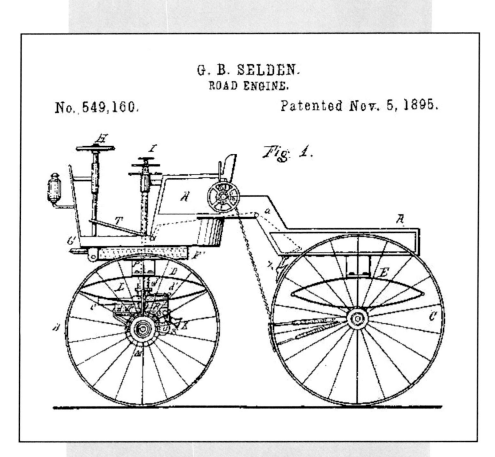

This is George Selden's primitive patent sketch, November, 1895, which controlled internal combustion machines well into the twentieth century.

NOTICE

To Dealers, Importers, Agents and Users of
GASOLINE AUTOMOBILES

We will protect you against any prosecution for alleged infringements of patents. Regarding alleged infringement of the Selden patent we beg to quote the well-known Patent Attorneys, Messrs. Parker & Burton. "The Selden patent is not a broad one, and if it was it is anticipated. It does not cover a practicable machine, no practicable machine can be made from it and never was so far as we can ascertain. It relates to that form of carriage called a FORE CARRIAGE. None of that type have ever been in use, all have been failures." "No court in the United States has ever decided in favor of the patent on the merits of the case, all it has ever done was to record a prior agreement between the parties."

We are the pioneers of the GASOLINE AUTOMOBILE. Our Mr. Ford made the first Gasoline Automobile in Detroit and the third in the United States. His machine made in 1893 is still in use. Our Mr. Ford also built the famous "999" Gasoline Automobile, which was driven by Barney Oldfield in New York on Saturday a mile in 55 4-5 seconds on a circular track, which is the world's record.

Mr. Ford, driving his own machine, beat Mr. Winton at Grosse Pointe track in 1901. We have always been winners.

FORD MOTOR COMPANY,
688-692 Mack Ave., Detroit, Mich.

Henry Ford fights back with a defiant advertisement.

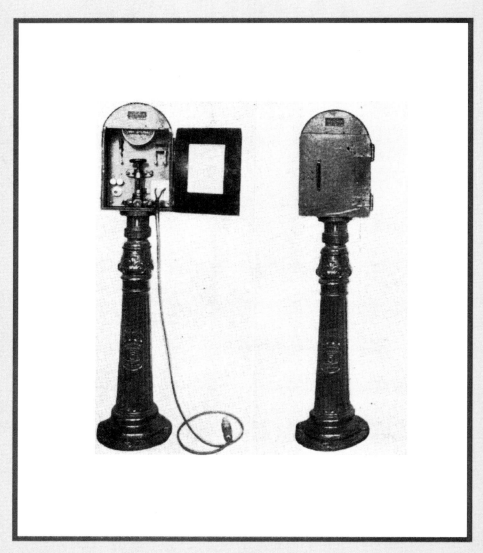

The Electrant, General Electric's public vehicle recharger, invented in 1899 (1914 model shown). *(IEEE* Power and Energy *magazine's reprint of* Electrical World *magazine 1915)*

Henry Ford and Thomas Edison promote electric cars in a 1914 *Saturday Evening Post* advertisement.

Second experimental Ford-Edison electric car, driven by Ford engineer Fred Allison at Ford's Highland Park barn (summer 1914). *(Courtesy of the Henry Ford Collection, Benson Ford Research Center)*

General Motors president Alfred P. Sloan (on right wearing spats) with GM board member and Du Pont chairman Pierre DuPont (left). *(Courtesy of the Library of Congress)*

A Minneapolis trolley
burns in 1952
*(Courtesy of the Mankoff
Collection and the
Minnesota Street Car
Museum via John Diers)*

Newark trolleys burn in late 1930s
(above and left); an ordinary
working Newark trolley (bottom).
*(Courtesy of the Mankoff
Collection and the Minnesota
Street Car Museum via John Diers)*

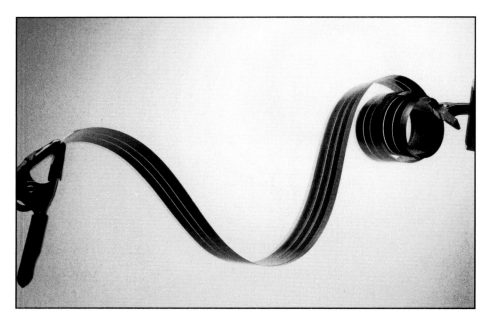

This is a strand of film with embedded Konarka nanosolar. *(Courtesy of Konarka Technologies, Inc.)*

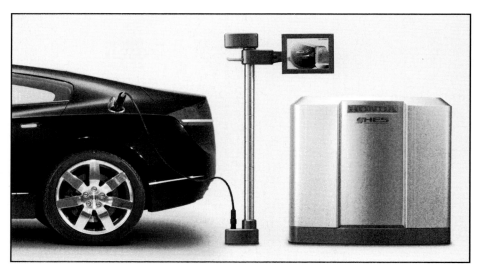

Honda Hydrogen Fuel Car, FCX, with home refueling unit, being rushed into development. *(Courtesy of the American Honda Co.)*

nation served by thousands of electrified mass transit systems to a nation reliant on the automobile for most transportation. Snell's report called GM's scheme not just a plan to eliminate trolleys but nothing less than "a drive by GM to sell cars and trucks by displacing rail and bus systems." That, Snell argued, was by implication at the root of the nation's petroleum dependence.[29]

In other words, first acquire the trolley lines, then convert them to unlikable and unprofitable bus lines, and finally make those bus lines disappear altogether, leaving only highly profitable gas-guzzling automobiles. This final assertion—the actual killing of mass transit in *any* form, electric or motorized—added an additional conspiracy not found in the prosecution's documentation. It was the "extra" conspiracy that gave GM, its defenders, and surrogates the basis to discredit Snell's otherwise exhaustive and largely correct study and to attack any who sought to learn more about this corrupt chapter.

After Snell's report was presented, GM immediately went on the counterattack, denying Snell's charges and demanding that the Senate Judiciary Committee cease circulating its own report, The automaker then created its own misleading and fact-shaded rebuttal report, entitled "The Truth About 'American Ground Transport,'" and further demanded that the Senate never permit its own report to be distributed without GM's rebuttal. The Senate agreed.[30]

In the years that followed, a small clique of urban planning scholars along with a cortege of transportation buffs and armchair hobbyists, aided by the Internet and by self-appointed conspiracy-theory debunkers, launched their own attack campaign against Snell and the very word "conspiracy." The debate was all intensified by a live-action animated film entitled *Who Framed Roger Rabbit*, which contained a fleeting atmospheric subplot about the destruction of the Los Angeles trolley system by an evil corporate schemer. The villain—the black-garbed "Judge Doom," no less—was of course inspired by the known facts about the nation's mass transit dilemma. But the silliness of the quasi-cartoon *Roger Rabbit* enabled both academics and self-appointed Internet experts to invoke the film's title as a means of denigrating Snell and acquitting GM of any conspiracy whatsoever.[31]

None of the GM urban experts would deny that King John was an inhumane monarch because of Robin Hood spoofs, or deny the crimes of the Third Reich because of the film and Broadway hit *The Producers*. But this tack has been taken against those journalists and scholars exploring the GM Conspiracy. Several academic papers on the topic even included "Roger Rabbit" in their title. One respected academic author of such a work conceded this was done as a "hook to make it more interesting." The consequence of all this has been to shout down legitimate journalistic attempts to learn the facts of GM's conduct. Just inquiring about the provable facts or court record invokes public ridicule by a corps of so-called experts. The result has been the hazing over of vital urban history.

Not a few of the circle of experts have adopted a "So what?" approach, asserting that electrified mass transit was dying anyway, so GM's action was simply clever business.[32]

The topic has become so supercharged that many of the key debaters themselves have receded from their once irrepressible defense of GM. One urban planning historian complained emotionally, "I really don't care anymore; I am not really interested in this topic. You want to know why? Because it haunts me. I constantly get calls from kooks and crackpots. I tried to get away from it and still I get the calls."[33]

More than half a century after GM's criminal conduct and conviction, the facts remain forgotten and indeed buried. In no small part the story has been forgotten because the scandal has remained shrouded in the urban legend stridently perpetuated by the small group of experts who should have investigated the deeper facts as a cautionary tale for the future. Many of the most esteemed academic experts are indeed versed in the operational history of one or more local transit systems. Speaking to a dozen of the leading and most often quoted debunkers of the GM Conspiracy is more than revealing. When contacted, the various urban history students, teachers, and other experts in the debate have confirmed they have no experience or training in corporate criminality or antitrust conspiracy. None of the debaters contacted even understands the meaning of the criminal concept of "conspiracy" that led to GM's prosecution and conviction. One of the most respected authors on the subject wrote an academic chapter on the topic and throughout mistakenly referred to the government's criminal prosecution as a "lawsuit."[34]

Most important, despite their many position papers, Internet postings, academic journal articles and university dissertations, all the experts contacted confirm that they have never examined any of the fifteen boxes of court documents in a Chicago archive; the seven hundred pages of FBI documents in a basement in High Point, North Carolina; fifty-four linear feet of National City Lines' own corporate documents in an obscure repository in Atlanta; a collection of National City Lines reports in a New York library manuscript collection; the personal papers of Judge William J. Campbell at a Chicago facility; the private archived papers of key transit principals and gangsters stored in little-known locations from Minneapolis to Los Angeles; or the original smoking-gun contracts, memorandums, and correspondence of the conspiring executives that are located in various repositories and back rooms around the country.[35]

But anyone who examines the actual documents, instead of merely guessing at the contents, would have little trouble seeing why prosecutors, judges, and congressmen all concluded that GM did engage in a transit conspiracy, and why the submerged details explain much about this nation's oil dependence.

The story begins in 1921. Post–Great War speculation suddenly came crashing down in 1921 in a short depression marked by massive unemployment, collapse of the transportation sector, deflation of all manufactured goods, and the worst year ever for the automobile industry.[36]

A *Wall Street Journal* retrospective summarizing the year told the story in its headline: 1921—DEFLATION: SPECULATIVE MARKETS COLLAPSE—INDUSTRIAL ENTERPRISES LAG—UNEMPLOYED TOTAL 6,000,000. The article explained, "The year 1921 was one of intense depression in trade with few parallels in the mercantile and financial history of the country, marking the complete collapse of the speculative postwar boom which culminated so suddenly at the close of 1920. The height of the depression was reached in the summer. . . . All manufacturing and industrial enterprises lagged, but in the iron and steel trade particularly, the depression was more pronounced. Month after month orders continued to fall off despite a series of price reductions and wage cuts. Everywhere the process of deflation ruled. . . . Unemployment reached unprecedented levels of 6,000,000 in July; wage cuts, dividend reductions and suspension were the order of the day.[37]

"The year was one of the worst for our railroads," the *Wall Street Journal* stated. "More mileage was abandoned than built, acquisition of new equipment fell to a low point. . . . Most of the year, the railroads struggled to keep out of bankruptcy."[38]

Detroit automakers were particularly hard hit. Their industry was thrown into a depression. A *Christian Science Monitor* article on March 24, 1922, was clear: MOTOR COMPANIES PASS THROUGH A SEVERE PERIOD. The article opened, "American automobile companies experienced their most trying year in 1921, but as a whole they have weathered the storm, and as a result of their drastically reducing inventories and costs of production their prospects for 1922 are much brighter. During the last three years the motor concerns have experienced a complete change in fortunes. During 1919 and 1920 they did capacity business, rolled up huge profits and distributed dividends liberally, but in 1921 they saw the other side of business—depression."[39]

No automaker was harder hit than General Motors. GM had oversupplied and saturated the automobile market. The decrease from 1920 to 1921 threw the entire conglomerate into chaos. Buick, down from 112,208 units to 80,122. Chevrolet, the major brand, halved from 134,117 units to 68,080. Pontiac, down from 34,839 units to 11,852. Total vehicle sales of 393,075 in 1920 dropped to 214,799. Adding all the lost sales revenue and unsold inventory, GM recorded a $65 million deficit for the year.[40]

In a lead front-page article on March 13, 1922, entitled GENERAL MOTORS SHOWS RESULTS OF DEFLATION, the *Wall Street Journal* declared, "The loss is staggering."[41]

GM president Alfred Sloan recalled years later the "1920–1921 crisis" laid bare the company's inability to forecast the national demand for automobiles.[42] In 1921, the market was temporarily saturated. To diversify its income streams, GM expanded into trucks and added buses.

Meanwhile, the nation's transit systems suffered a drop in ridership from 15.5 billion in 1920 to 14.5 billion in 1921. With six million unemployed, and even remaining wage earners taking home substantially reduced paychecks, commuting and pleasure riding flattened. The downturn in transit revenues came at a crucial time for transit systems. Cities and their suburbs were sprawling. Transit systems were obligated both by municipal franchise and popular mandate to provide coverage to the farthest residential and commerce zones. Metro transit needed to add lines. But not all lines were created equal. Some of the newer routes, especially those in outlying areas, generated fewer passengers and less revenue. Therefore, it was harder to justify the capital-intensive construction of electrical wires, rails, and other infrastructure to expand service. At the same time, even the profitable, well-traveled lines were beginning to show wear. Seat cushions and other interiors needed to be replaced. Car mechanisms needed repair. New equipment was needed. Modernization was overdue.[43]

A cheap alternative was needed. Gasoline-burning motor buses were inferior. They smelled and sprayed thick clouds of smoke wherever they drove. They literally changed the landscape and the lifestyle of the towns that purchased them. People called them stink wagons or stinkmobiles. Many people found them cramped and uncomfortable. Unpopular as they were, however, gasoline buses seemed to many transit operators an expedient, if not necessary, short-term cost-cutting compromise for their most ancillary service.[44]

In the short run, gasoline buses of course seemed more economical. In the early twenties, buses could be purchased quite cheaply, often for between $3,500 and $8,000, whereas streetcars could easily cost two or three times that amount. Buses could be garaged cheaply and could be deployed at once on city streets without track being laid. That said, buses were a bad capital investment because they needed to be replaced within six to eight years. Traditional streetcars could easily run for two to three decades. Trackless trolleys, which began proliferating late in the decade, generally lasted twelve years. Maintenance on buses was greater than for trolleys. Moreover, buses carried far fewer passengers per vehicle than streetcars — generally seventeen to forty-five passengers in a cramped bus, and generally sixty-five passengers in a spacious trolley. Hence, buses were initially thought of as mere ancillary vehicles.[45]

Nonetheless, during the early twenties when cash was short, metro transit companies found themselves acquiring more and more motor buses on newer and less traveled routes and as feeder lines to their existing trolley routes, elevated lines, and subways. In 1920, fewer than seventy-five buses were in use nationally for these limited purposes. Within a few years, several thousand buses were operating. However, despite the fast growth of bus use, the transit industry was determined to keep them tertiary and not use them to replace mainstay streetcars. New York transit companies were typical in their entrenched loyalty to streetcars. In 1923, nationally known transit consultant John Allen Beeler, who would later begin to favor buses, typically informed the state's Transit Commission that even though motor buses in certain respects were less expensive to operate and acquire, these vehicles could simply not replace streetcars in the five boroughs of New York. Beeler even authored an article for *Electric Railway Journal* headlined BUSES COULD NOT FILL PLACE OF STREET CARS IN NEW YORK CITY.[46]

True, operating costs for most streetcar models were generally about 45.7 cents per mile, while buses generally cost 41.5 cents per mile, explained Beeler. But because buses offered fewer seats and were known for incessant "lurching and abrupt movement," they were unacceptable to standees. Hence, when streetcar companies calculated the added benefits of standees, and the indirect costs of dismantling the infrastructure and repaving, Beeler concluded, "The cost of bus service . . . is approximately 65 per cent greater than the average cost of the street railway service."[47]

Beeler added that while 1,002 streetcars could serve Manhattan during rush periods, the same task would require 2,538 buses, and such a fleet would impose intolerable congestion on city streets.[48]

One transit official summed up the prevailing mood among transit experts in a 1924 issue of *Electric Railway Journal*: "The bus cannot replace streetcars in ordinary service. . . . Most railways find it unsuitable for regular service."[49] That would change—and soon.

Electric transport worked and its popularity was measured in billions of passenger boardings annually, but it could not keep working without funding for infrastructure upgrades and extensions. One idea proposed by Congress would create a so-called superpower zone extending from Maine to Maryland. The zone would electrically unify the 315 public utilities, 18 electric railways, and 96,000 industrial sites within the zone. The result, if implemented, would electrify nineteen thousand new miles of railway throughout the urban and rural centers of the Northeast. The federal government's proposed "superpower" zone would save local economies a half billion dollars annually within a decade and provide the modernization and extensions urban transit systems needed to cement the idea of electric transport as an economic linchpin.[50]

But General Motors had other ideas. GM believed in internal combustion as the solution to every motive question. In the face of uncertainty about future automobile sales, GM decided to branch into transit motor buses. The company was convinced it could systematically convert thousands of electric transit systems throughout the nation to oil burners.

General Motors, even in the twenties, functioned as vastly more than just a Detroit carmaking company. The megacorporation that had years earlier surpassed Ford was nothing less than a billion-dollar conglomerate of transportation-related entities that included manufacturing, sales, finance, and operational firms in the fields of automobiles, trucks, and trains. Generally, when GM wanted to add to its diversification, it acquired existing companies or combined bits and pieces to form new ones, sometimes publicly, sometimes secretly, sometimes creating a wholly owned division and sometimes controlling via a quiet interest. The corporation moved its executives around from division to division and company to company like knights on a chessboard. By this means it could defend and expand its empire at will.

So it was with GM's decision to convert American transit from clean electric to petroleum, a campaign that would involve hundreds of communities and their transit systems. That campaign began in earnest in 1925 at the doorstep of the collection of the companies associated with Yellow Cab and Yellow Truck.

Yellow Cab was founded by Austrian native John Hertz, whose family emigrated from their home in the mountains north of Budapest to Chicago in 1883 when he was only four years of age. Hertz grew up in poverty, his father supporting the household on just $15 per week. Chronically nervous, Hertz flitted from job to job on doctor's orders just to preserve his health. He worked as a police reporter for the *Chicago Daily News*, a delivery-wagon driver, and any other job he could snare. But he seemed most successful as one of the nation's earliest automobile salesmen.[51]

Hertz and a partner in 1907 began their own taxi company using trade-in vehicles. In 1915, Hertz broke off from his original partner and founded Chicago's Yellow Cab Company. Hertz painted his forty or so vehicles attention-getting bright yellow as a means of street advertising. He had read a University of Chicago study identifying that hue as the most conspicuous color any person could notice. Eventually, Yellow Cab sprouted hundreds of manufacturing and operating subsidiaries, including a car-rental business later named Hertz Rent-A-Car, and yellow cab companies across the country. But the conglomerate's most important unit was Yellow Coach Manufacturing, which built those iconic yellow taxicabs. Yellow, in fact, assembled 90 percent of all cabs in the nation.[52]

In 1923, Hertz expanded into the emerging field of buses, acquiring four square blocks in Chicago to erect a manufacturing factory. That year, Yellow Coach sold 207 buses. That was only the beginning. The next year, 1924, Yellow produced as many as six units per day. In 1924, Hertz combined a recently purchased local bus line, Chicago Motor Coach, with New York's decades-old Fifth Avenue Coach Company. Putting the two companies together in a $25 million deal, Hertz created the Omnibus Corporation. The *New York Times* headline read JOHN HERTZ INVADES NEW YORK. Fifty Avenue Coach Company officials became Omnibus officials as Hertz hired and shuffled executives from subsidiary to subsidiary. Despite his high corporate maneuvers, Hertz spurned such descriptions as "financier" or "banker," preferring to call himself an "operator." When Omnibus took over Fifth Avenue Coach Company, which had successfully been running petroleum buses for about two decades, Hertz also acquired Fifth Avenue Coach Company's bus manufacturing plants, which had been expanded since World War I. The Omnibus acquisition made Yellow not only America's largest taxi concern, but also the nation's preeminent bus manufacturer.[53]

GM took notice. GM president Sloan approached Hertz about a merger. On July 7, 1925, the deal was consummated. Hertz agreed to sell GM eight hundred thousand Yellow shares—slightly more than half of Yellow Cab Manufacturing's stock, for $16 million. That $16 million sales price included $10.5 million in capital. GM's deal was subject to a special Yellow stockholder meeting to rubber-stamp the decision. When approved, the taxi and bus company would be renamed Yellow Truck and Coach Manufacturing. With this merger, GM would acquire Yellow's massive bus-building capabilities. In turn, Hertz, who had long eyed the truck market, would have access to GM's truck assembly plants.[54]

Hertz was ecstatic, hailing the merger as "the greatest achievement in their history."[55]

For Sloan, acquiring control of Yellow was the pivotal gateway to the transit bus business. Not only did Yellow give GM bus manufacturing capability, but because Yellow owned New York's Omnibus and other transit operating companies, the merger made GM itself a transit company—not openly, but circuitously through its control of Yellow. As such, GM was able to use its influence not only to entrench itself as a supplier but to effect the conversion of electric streetcars and later trackless trolleys to petroleum-burning buses. Yellow was the key.

Sloan explained to his colleagues, "The Yellow Cab Manufacturing Company, apart from its position in the taxicab business, occupies a strong position in the bus field. . . . General Motors Corporation has recognized the importance of the bus and believes that the . . . merger with the Yellow Cab Manufacturing Company will immediately place it in a strong position in the bus business, with the opportunity of enjoying a really unique position in the future development in that field."[56]

Within a few months of the September 1925 merger ratification, the first fruits of the GM-Yellow union became apparent. On December 28, 1925, the Public Service Railway Company in Newark, New Jersey, granted Yellow the largest transit bus order in history, 333 coaches plus parts and services, all valued at $3 million. Buses were to be shipped at the rate of one hundred per month. Public Service Railway would use them as feeders and on newly purchased routes.[57] This was big—but not big enough for Sloan.

Sloan lived for bigness. Slender and natty, attired in the latest collars and ties, Sloan commonly wore spats, even to the White House. He often outdressed his former GM boss, millionaire Pierre du Pont. A strategic thinker, electrical engineer, and Massachusetts Institute of Technology graduate, Sloan was as driven by a compulsion to grow his company as he was compelled to breathe oxygen. "Deliberately to stop growing is to suffocate," Sloan wrote about his years at GM. "We do things in a big way in the United States. I have always believed in planning big, and I have always discovered after the fact that, if anything, we didn't plan big enough. I put no ceiling on progress."[58]

Now, with the massive New Jersey bus order in hand, Sloan was more than sure of himself. Just days after the New Jersey order, Sloan issued a prediction to a *Washington Post* business writer: "Our research and study of this whole transportation problem leads us to believe that the railroads and electric railways of this country will eventually be the largest users of commercial motor vehicles in the world." The sureness of this prediction stood in stark contrast to the industry belief of the day that buses possessed a limited future. Just days earlier, Lucius Storrs, managing director of the American Association of Street Railways, repeated to the *New York Times* the mantra of the transit world: "I believe that buses will become during the next few years a necessary adjunct to the street railways, but they must remain an adjunct and not compete with the electrically operated lines. . . . For this reason, street railways must control all buses operating in urban communities." Storrs's assertion came just as the nation's electrical systems boasted record passenger loads.[59]

Nonetheless, even as electric transit—subways, elevated lines, and streetcars—continued to attract between 14.5 and 15.5 billion passenger trips annually, bus usage in the twenties continued to climb. In 1922, more than 400 million passenger trips on petroleum buses were logged by the members of the American Electric Railway Association. Of course, the true national bus usage number was undoubtedly greater because many independent bus companies were not reporting members of the electric railway organization, a group seen as their natural competitor. By 1924, annual bus boardings had risen to a billion. By 1925, electric railways were operating about 4,400 buses—a 60 percent growth during the prior twelve months. By 1928, of the nation's more than 17 billion passenger trips, more than 2.5 billion were on some 90,000 buses. But the vast majority of ridership still remained on trolleys and other electric transit systems. Hence, on September 25, 1928, transit expert Beeler assured the *Wall Street Journal* that even though small cities with populations of about one hundred thousand might select the financially expedient motor bus, "The future of streetcars is better than ever." Yet, at that very time, Sloan still felt the opposite was true.[60]

"I predict a rapid increase in the use of buses by electric railways in cities large and small," promised Sloan in January 1928, "and an even greater development in the so-called interurban field, whether by rail or independent operators. I believe this new arm of transportation is destined to a future that surpasses the most optimistic dreams of the ardent enthusiasts of a few years ago."[61]

A tension was in play. Passengers by the millions in cities across America continued to use and enjoy the trolleys, elevated lines, and subways with billions of rides annually. Transit engineers and professionals foresaw a brilliant, virtually indispensable future that needed to be preserved with updating, modernization, and expansion. Meanwhile, local management and ownership fiddled with the finances and engineering reports and often allowed its service to deteriorate. Buses and their cheapness allowed most electric railway managements to stave off plowing further funds into infrastructure. Ironically, the economic realities at play were often more rooted in corrupt business practices than intelligent public policy or transportation sense.

Transit companies in some of the larger cities were municipal agencies. But in most cities and towns, the transit systems were privately owned enterprises, often controlled by the local utility, and commonly misused as personal piggy banks, slush-fund sources, or venues for stock manipulation. Known for deep-seated corruption, hidden ownership practices, and unlimited avarice, transit owners commonly eschewed spending money on new equipment and lines when they could stretch old vehicles and infrastructure yet another day and yet another year. It was not unusual to dispense false or uneven engineering and financial comparisons to sway public opinion and government action. Too often, twenty- and thirty-year-old electric vehicles and rail infrastructure were compared to brand spanking new gasoline buses. "No one expects a trolley built in 1905 to be as up-to-date as a brand-new bus," complained one streetcar passenger in a letter to the editor of the *New York Times*.[62]

Moreover, it was hard to determine the true finances and operating costs of many trolleys and other electrical lines because so many inflated charges and personal enrichment schemes were loaded into the numbers. Theft, looting, bribery, embezzlement and public deception among transportation owners and executives was legendary throughout the industry.

For example, Minneapolis's Twin City Rapid Transit was owned by a New Jersey firm that maintained secret minute books. In 1908, four years after the system's latest corporate incarnation, company officials met in Manhattan where they passed a resolution: "That two hundred and fifty thousand dollars ($250,000) of the accumulated surplus of the company be transferred to a special reserve fund to care for such extraordinary outlays as may have to be incurred for purposes other than operating expenses, such as defending attacks on the company's franchise." The company's franchise did not expire until 1923—another fifteen years. Various state and local investigations of Twin City Rapid Transit revealed a long, damning list of inexplicable money movements. In one case, $30,000 of transit company money was transferred to "miscellaneous" and in another $574,523 was written off as "incidental" or "nature of expenditures not shown."[63]

When the Pacific Electric Railway incorporated in Los Angeles, the first order of business on September 14, 1911, for majority shareholders was not investing millions of their own funds as owners, but creating a $100 million bond issue and mortgage. This indebtedness was regularly refinanced and recollateralized with massive fees to the mortgage bankers, all associates of the shareholders themselves. Those fees provided bountiful compensation to insiders. One financial underling in accounting eventually complained that such continuous high-cost financing was breaking the company at a time when it could afford it least. His objections were ignored.[64]

Yellow Taxi in Chicago, after decades of management and ownership reorganizations, created additional dozens of captive suppliers, often mere fronts, to sell itself fuel, parts, insurance, and other day-to-day necessities. In some cases, the fronts were nothing more than an office and phone. For example, at one point, the combined Yellow and Checker taxi companies were purchasing more than 12 million gallons of fuel per year through Parmalee Motor Fuel Company, which charged a halfpenny per gallon surcharge—causing a $60,000 fuel hike. Parmalee was a Yellow and Checker captive operating out of the back of a garage. At the same time, two insurance companies, Calumet Mutual and City Mutual, both at the same address, raised the taxi company's liability and collision premiums by 25 percent to $4 million annually. Both insurance companies were also captives. Through this maze of self-dealing, Yellow was able to regularly and surreptitiously inflate its operating costs to exceed the fare-hike expense thresholds in Chicago's taxi ordinance.[65]

In the years before the Fifth Avenue Coach Company was swallowed by Yellow through Omnibus, it and other independent New York transit lines were widely considered to be dens of corruption with hidden ownership. In one case, the police inspector's wife was discovered as the real owner of one small Manhattan bus line. Typical was the broadside launched by New York mayor John F. Hylan on October 28, 1922, against Fifth Avenue Coach Company when he protested, "The people of this city needed buses badly because the owners of the traction lines and their 'receivers' would not or could not provide proper service." Hylan added, "The Fifth Avenue Coach Company, which operates buses on the principal streets of the city on a ten-cent fare . . . want the bus privileges and they do not want the city or anyone else to have them."[66]

Referring to the network of corrupt businessmen who controlled or coveted Fifth Avenue Coach Company and other transit lines by their traditional derisive name, "the traction ring," Hylan's speech held back nothing. He accused the owners of Fifth Avenue Coach Company of trying to falsely justify higher fares with fake expenses while making a 50 percent profit. "The traction ring," he declared, ". . . knows that as long as I am mayor and my associates are with me . . . [the] higher-fare plan cannot go over. They think . . . they can hoodwink the people. . . . The City of New York can make a good profit on bus operation on a five-cent fare. The traction ring knows this and is anxious to grab all the bus routes that the city has established. [However], these bus routes will remain in control of the city and will not be given to the traction ring, the Fifth Avenue Coach Company, or any other subsidiary corporation."[67]

Nor were the corrupt practices limited to the transportation companies. Those in local and state government who could influence the transit owners, or be influenced by them, were often paid bribes, and not infrequently the officials required bribes. One investigation of the Twin City Transit Company found that from 1916 to 1921, $41,000 had annually been paid to E. E. "Big Ed" Smith of Minneapolis and $20,000 annually to R. T. O'Connor of St. Paul. Smith was the "unofficial" boss of the Republican machine in Minnesota. O'Connor held sway as boss of the state's Democratic machine. Both men were known as ruthless to their enemies but loyal to their friends. The list of political payments was long. In one well-publicized case, two staunch political opponents of the transit line's high $24 million valuation who changed their mind overnight mysteriously received payments of $15,000 and $2,600 from Twin City Transit Company.[68]

In New York, Fifth Avenue Coach Company and its regulators were continually excoriated by New York mayor Hyland; the "state legislature

[was] controlled by the traction ring." In Chicago, graft and corruption among and between aldermen, regulators, financiers, and transit companies was a legendary lifestyle. In the late twenties, the U.S. Senate Judiciary Committee launched an investigation of the highly publicized charges of "collusion" between Chicago railways, receivers, and Westinghouse Electric.[69]

Government corruption by and against transit companies was in fact a cliché of the Roaring Twenties. One transportation study concluded that from the turn of the century right through the twenties, the overwhelming majority of American cities were racked by either fierce legal confrontations, heated public-fare conflicts, or investigations for scandalous transit corruption. When pressed at one federal hearing, a company owner openly admitted, "We insiders are selling out just as fast as we can, and when ten years are up, you will not find your uncle Dudley or any one of us that will own a share of stock or a bond [in electrical transit]."[70]

Currents and currency drove the trolleys, elevated lines, and subways of America, each in their way. Graft and gasoline fueled the buses of America, each in their way. Round and round spun both the wheels and the coins of mass transit, each in its own way. Lubrication took on several definitions, depending upon the speaker and the friction in question. Transit crises like oil shortages could be created at will if the purpose suited either the regulated or the regulators. Equipment languished or could be rejuvenated at will if the purpose suited either the regulated or the regulators. For those who regulated, governed, invested in, or operated urban transportation, it was a mad, elbowing, backstabbing dash for the bank. But for the average citizens who depended upon electrical transportation, it was about getting from point A to point B safely and economically. Caught in the midst of this traction was the public. Mobility and mendacity in the Roaring Twenties were on a collision course. The moment of impact finally came on October 29, 1929, when the stock market crashed and the resulting Great Depression gripped the nation.

Now, money and jobs were short while breadlines were long. From October 1929, ridership tallies began to fall sharply when as many as 15 million Americans—some say a third of the nonfarm workforce—were thrown out of work. Some 85,000 businesses, once worth $4.5 billion, toppled into bankruptcy. Consumer prices crashed. Deflation racked all values and savings. Suicide and murder multiplied into an epidemic. For too many, their last moment of travel was a hopeless jump from a high window. People murdered for the price of a nickel streetcar fare or a crust of bread, take your pick.[71]

Yet some companies, such as GM, prospered and expanded. True, to-tal transit ridership from 1929 to 1933 fell by more than a third, from 17 billion to 11 billion. True, GM's American auto and truck sales dropped dramatically during this period, from nearly 1.8 million in 1929 to just a half million in 1932—the lowest level since the 1921 depression. True, during those same Depression years, streetcars rides were slashed almost in half, even as subway and elevated boardings remained constant at about two billion boardings. But by 1932, motor-bus usage—the cheap, short-term alternative—rivaled that of elevated and subways. Even as electric transit usage stagnated in thousands of cities and towns across the nation, motor-bus passenger volume increased, both numerically and proportion-ately. GM spearheaded the trend in New York, where GM buses were vo-raciously adopted by GM and Yellow's Omnibus Corporation, as well as by other neighboring transit systems.[72]

When Depression-era municipality funds dwindled too low and out-side financing shriveled, for some cities the only solution to their aging, broken electric fleets was GM and Yellow. As GM general counsel Henry Hogan recalled, the company "decided that the only way this new market for [city transit] buses could be created was for it [GM] to finance the con-version from streetcars to buses in some small cities." That in mind, on June 29, 1932, GM quietly created United Cities Motor Transit, a special holding company to finance small-city conversion from streetcars to petroleum-burning vehicles. A GM attorney explained, "To develop mo-torized transportation, our company should initiate a program of this na-ture and authorize the incorporation of a holding company with a capital of $300,000."[73]

The method: First, United Cities Motor Transit would locate a fi-nancially unstable transit system where the trolleys needed to be rescued. Second, United Cities Motor Transit would help create a new, properly fi-nanced rival company. Often GM invested directly. Third, the manage-ment of the new transportation company would quickly orchestrate the termination of electric lines in favor of total GM motor-bus operations. Fourth, GM and Yellow would liquidate their own presence, turning the local company over to others.[74]

GM's general counsel, Hogan, confirmed as much in one federal in-vestigation. "In such case," Hogan stated, GM "successfully motorized the city, turned the management over to other interests, and liquidated its investment."[75]

Systems in Kalamazoo and Saginaw, Michigan, as well as Springfield, Ohio—all in the throes of bankruptcy—were among United Cities Motor Transit's initial targets. In Kalamazoo, GM invested as little as $20,000 in the new transit company. In Saginaw, the newly formed company began with rented buses first and then moved to outright purchases. In Springfield, Ohio, GM invested just $30,000 in the new company; within a year, after ensuring conversion to buses, GM sold its ownership to local interests.[76] In each case, the streetcar system was not resuscitated, modernized, updated, or rescued by local city authorities. The money was put into oil-burning buses. The rails were pulled up, streets paved over, and trolley cars disposed of. The electric streetcar lines would simply vanish. Only the buses remained. GM's fingerprints did not.

By 1935, the American Transit Association (ATA) was clearly upset over GM's actions. Its members were being undercut and virtually eliminated by GM United Cities Motor Transit. Certainly, Depression-era transit systems were in trouble everywhere, but the ATA wanted clean electric systems updated and saved—not obliterated. A test case came in Portland, Oregon, as GM pushed hard to add that city to its list of financed conversions. A special ATA advisory committee was created to investigate. On April 30, 1935, the advisory committee's report was presented to the Executive Committee, which was moved for the first time in its history to propound a set of business ethics to condemn such manipulations. Later that year, at its September annual meeting, the ATA adopted Rule 11: "It is considered unethical for a manufacturer to furnish directly or indirectly, financial aid or technical advice, or otherwise assist in any franchise negotiation, public hearing or referendum election, which would have the effect of displacing an existing operator who is conducting or endeavoring to conduct his business." The ATA then voted a formal censure of United Cities Motor Transit.[77]

Stung by the ATA's censure, GM dissolved United Cities Motor Transit.[78] Nonetheless, Sloan would not retreat from his conversion campaign. Indeed, that campaign, which was test-driven so successfully in the small cities targeted by United Cities Motor Transit, would now go into high gear. But henceforth GM would act stealthily through a front company in a broad conspiracy. Ironically, the federal government itself created the perfect conditions for Sloan and GM to shift into high gear.

As the Depression ravaged families and businesses alike, President Franklin Roosevelt sought to restructure American society and in many ways protect the country from ruthless manipulations of big business. He called it the New Deal, a system of new laws and regulatory agencies designed to save the average man and woman from ruination and to stop the powerful from using the type of corporate manipulations that had caused so many upheavals in the past. A prime target of Congress's reforms were the corrupt community of local utilities companies, commonly owned by secretive out-of-state syndicates and holding companies that were only one face of a complex of self-dealing pyramids. This in mind, the Roosevelt administration engineered the passage of the Public Utility Holding Company Act of 1935, which sought to dismantle those pyramids and force divestiture.

Roosevelt was merciless in his condemnation of utility holding companies. The holding company, said FDR in a message to Congress, "is a corporate invention which can give a few corporate insiders unwarranted and intolerable powers over other people's money. In its destruction of local control and its substitution of absentee management, it has built up in the public utility field what has justly been called a system of private socialism which is inimical to the welfare of a free people. . . . It is time . . . to reverse that process of the concentration of power which has made most American citizens, once traditionally independent owners of their own businesses, helplessly dependent for their daily bread upon the favor of a very few, who, by devices such as holding companies, have taken for themselves unwarranted economic power."[79]

A pivotal provision of the Public Utility Holding Company Act intended to protect the public called for the immediate divestiture by all utilities of their local transit companies.[80] The intent was to insulate electrical transit from the manipulations of the unscrupulous.

Instead, a great transit power vacuum was created. This was the time for public policy on the local, state, and federal level to implement measures to preserve, modernize, and rejuvenate the clean electric systems within their midst. That did not happen. Into the vacuum stepped GM.

The linchpin of GM's operation was E. Roy Fitzgerald, president of National City Lines. Through National City Lines, Fitzgerald controlled a pyramid of allied, associated, and subsidiary transportation entities including the transit systems in scores of American cities, large and small. His rise was virtually meteoric, from relative obscurity to the absolute pinnacle of the nation's mass transit—or at least, it seemed he was at the pinnacle. Who was GM's partner in American transit? Who was this powerful chief executive of transportation?

Fitzgerald was an uneducated bus driver.

One of five brothers of rugged rural Minnesota stock, Fitzgerald dropped out of school in the seventh grade in Mankato. That was during the early years of the twentieth century when internal combustion machines were first making their entrée. As a youngster who needed to work, Fitzgerald became a common laborer in a railroad camp, helped out summers on the family farm, took odd jobs, and in 1916 became the night man in a garage in the tiny, north-Minnesota community of Eveleth. Without mechanic skills, Fitzgerald worked mainly at washing cars, pumping gas, and some office work. But it paid him twenty dollars every week. That was food on the table. In 1919, after three years of helping out, the garage allowed Fitzgerald to drive its bus on a short two-mile shuttle run for miners.[81]

In 1920, Fitzgerald and two of his brothers bought the garage's shuttle bus, plus another used bus from Wisconsin. The boys put up some savings, and the rest was financed through the local bank. The Fitzgerald brothers drove those two buses from morning till night, shuttling miners, schoolchildren, and anyone else they could coax into a ride. By 1922, the hardworking Fitzgerald boys had stretched their routes some sixty miles, using fifteen-passenger, custom-stretched Packards. By 1925, the Fitzgeralds' tiny company, Range Rapid Transit, was operating twenty-five secondhand buses. All told, the shoestring operation provided little more than living expenses, or "barely enough to get along on," as E. Roy Fitzgerald remembered. But that year, 1925, things changed. The brothers sold out to a successful nearby Minnesota bus operator, Carl Wickman, the man who later organized Greyhound bus lines. The three Fitzgeralds cleared $33,000 each from their sale to Wickman. But that was only the beginning of their association. That same year, Wickman joined Fitzgerald in establishing a new company named Royal Rapid Transit, which bought small area bus lines. By now, two other Fitzgerald brothers joined the enterprise, making a total of five Fitzgeralds available to drive buses and make their fledgling company work.[82]

In 1927, the Fitzgeralds actually consolidated their new company, Royal Rapid Transit, with Wickman's Greyhound. At about that time, Royal Rapid Transit stopped buying secondhand vehicles from various makers and began purchasing spanking new buses from GM's Yellow Coach. GM manufactured almost all of Greyhound's buses. Fitzgerald was quite fortunate. As part of the transfer of his small bus line, Fitzgerald received a significant block of Greyhound stock, which was subject to a buyback at a tidy profit a year later.[83]

Thus, from his meager beginnings as a struggling, uneducated rural bus driver and operator, Fitzgerald was suddenly able to enjoy the benefit of stock buy-ins, buyouts, and buybacks, all courtesy of Wickman and Greyhound. By this time, 1928, E. Roy Fitzgerald was no longer driving buses. He had moved from the big bus to the big boss. He also moved to the nice house and the comfortable farm estates of McHenry County, northwest of Chicago. Fitzgerald had become a man of means. Indeed, Greyhound had more in store for Fitzgerald.[84]

In 1928, Greyhound wanted more. Now Fitzgerald was to create a special financing entity called Rex Finance. "Greyhound Corporation furnished $100,000 worth of cash to help us start that company," Fitzgerald later testified. Now Rex would finance purchases of GM and Yellow buses by small intercity lines, such as the one from Chicago to Evansville, Indiana. Rex's highly affordable financing made it easy for these small companies to modernize their equipment.[85] As those intercity routes received new, easily financed buses, the updated service ably competed with older intercity trolley lines. Moreover, trolleys required expensive track and overhead wire. Buses rolled free of charge on government-built highways. Hence, route by route, motor transit enjoyed a significant competitive edge. As bus lines became more viable, Greyhound could acquire them or advantageously enter a market already solidified by competition that Greyhound itself had quietly helped create.[86] In this process, buses regularly won. Trolleys regularly lost.

Throughout, GM maintained a close working business relationship with Greyhound. In fact, so close was the relationship that a few years later, in 1931, during the Depression, General Motors simply "absorbed" $1 million of Greyhound debt. One million dollars during the Depression was equal to $12 million in twenty-first-century money.[87]

For some five years, the Fitzgeralds, Greyhound, GM, Yellow, and Rex proliferated petroleum buses to take the place of small Midwest intercity trolleys. Then in 1933 a new opportunity presented itself. George McLean, the Chicago-based GM and Yellow Coach salesman who handled Rex, met with Fitzgerald. During that meeting, McLean suggested that Rex move into urban lines. This was a big difference. It was one thing to take over long-distance routes between cities. But this was in-city transit. Rush-hour commuting, pleasure travel, minute-to-minute schedules, neighborhood service, community regulation—the issues were numerous and complex. Fitzgerald was a long-distance bus driver and hardly a savvy executive. He understood the highway. He had no understanding of the intersections and curbsides of metro transit. City transportation had just never occurred to him. Prior to that meeting with McLean, the plainspoken Fitzgerald remembered, "I never gave it any consideration."[88]

But the corporations behind Fitzgerald wanted him in urban transit.

Fitzgerald's attorney later explained the context of the times in a sworn statement: "During the period from 1920 to 1930, local transportation operations in the United States were largely streetcar operations. Motor buses were being used in some cities, and in some instances to extend the service rendered by streetcar lines. The local transportation operations of the country were owned largely by electric power companies. Beginning in about 1931, the revenues of these operations began to decline, due not only to the Depression, but also because the streetcar tracks, power transmission lines, and streetcars themselves were in general in a dilapidated condition, and in many cases the centers of population had moved away from the areas in which the streetcar tracks had been laid."

Fitzgerald's attorney made it clear that the solution could have gone either way: electric or gasoline. "The owners," the attorney confirmed, "did not have the funds necessary to extend or modernize the streetcar systems or to install motor-bus equipment due to failure to set up adequate reserves. Also, the operations being largely owned by electric power companies, the owners often had no desire to make further investments in the transportation business, which was incidental to their main business of generating and selling electric power. This was particularly true as to purchase of motor buses since that would not involve use of electric power."[89]

Here was the crossroads. After a period of years, all transit equipment needs updating, renewal, and redirection. Would new Depression-era moneys and development rejuvenate the aging trolleys that had for years been allowed to deteriorate, or would vast corporate resources be deployed to impel the abandonment of electric service in favor of gas-burning vehicles?

With Greyhound-financed Rex behind them, and wielding extraordinary GM and Yellow equipment credit terms that allowed a virtual cashless takeover, the Fitzgeralds would systematically move from community to community. The plan was not to rescue those electric systems, but convert them to oil-burning buses. In 1933, GM's McLean suggested that the local trolley line in Galesburg, Illinois, was prone and should be the first takeover. McLean made it clear that the owner, Illinois Power and Light Corporation, wanted to unload Galesburg City Lines without regard for whether it continued as an electrical system. Thus, tiny Galesburg became city one in the national urban conversion campaign that would soon spread across the American map.[90]

Fitzgerald's attorney conceded that the initial move into Galesburg and like communities made Fitzgerald's company "the first organization to embark upon a program of acquiring local transportation operations and converting them into modern, efficiently run motor-bus operations."[91]

During his later prosecution, Fitzgerald was asked in open court about the 1933 takeover of Galesburg's system: "Did you take it over?" Fitzgerald answered, "We took it over." He was asked, "Did you install new buses?" Fitzgerald answered, "Yes." What type? Small seventeen-passenger Yellow buses were purchased to replace the aging trolleys.[92]

Next, in 1934, Fitzgerald and his allies targeted Joliet City Lines just outside Chicago for a similar takeover from Illinois Power and Light. This time, the change literally occurred overnight. Again, Fitzgerald was asked in open court, "Did you take it over?" Again, Fitzgerald answered, "We took it over." He was asked, "What did you do about the streetcars?" Fitzgerald came back in simple words: "We never done anything about the streetcars. They discontinued operating the streetcars in the city one night, and we started operating modern buses, a modern bus system—the next day." What type? Larger twenty-one-passenger Yellow buses were purchased to replace the aging trolleys.[93]

East St. Louis, Illinois, was the third city. Quickly, it too was converted from a mainly streetcar system to one rolling on rubber and burning oil. Of course, Fitzgerald acting by himself lacked the resources to purchase these old trolley lines, one after another, let alone purchase the new GM buses needed and then operate these transit companies. But with financial help from his outside partners and suppliers, it all became possible. Asked in open court how he was able to afford the conversions without money, Fitzgerald plainly admitted, "We ran out of capital and was low on capital and I talked to the Firestone [tires] man." Fitzgerald explained that Firestone then extended extraordinary credit terms that permitted no payment for a year. He was then asked, "Were you buying General Motors buses on time too?" Fitzgerald responded in his unpolished grammar, "During them days all our buses were bought on time from General Motors. The Yellow Coach Acceptance Corporation—we didn't have money to pay cash for buses. We had to pay them out of revenues."[94]

Pressed for an answer during his criminal trial, Fitzgerald was asked in open court about Greyhound specifically: "Why did you want to get help from them?" Fitzgerald answered, "Because we had to have the capital." The next question hammered home the point, "You didn't have the money?" Fitzgerald confirmed, "We didn't have enough money." The next question, specifying Greyhound, asked, "They became your partners in this East St. Louis [transit] property?" The reply: "Yes."[95] Ironically, during this time, Greyhound's generosity to Fitzgerald remained constant even as the bus company struggled from its own Depression woes, barely surviving except for that beneficial assist when GM absorbed $1 million of Greyhound's debt.

After the Public Utility Holding Company Act mandating transit divestiture went into effect in 1935, a cavalcade of other small Illinois cities rapidly fell from electric operation to petroleum thanks to Fitzgerald's accelerating conversion campaign. He was guided by detailed city surveys provided by the General Motors Survey Department outlining the profitability of any given acquisition. Fitzgerald and Rex rolled through the state of Illinois like a machine. Decatur City Lines, acquisition approved November 25, 1936, and then quickly converted. Quincy City Lines, acquisition approved October 1, 1936, and then quickly converted. Champaign-Urbana City Lines, acquisition also approved October 1, 1936, and then quickly converted. Danville City Lines, acquisition approved November 25, 1936, and then quickly converted. Bloomington–Normal City Lines, acquisition approved December 2, 1936, and then quickly converted.[96]

While urban electric lines were dependent upon large outlays of capital to renovate, update, and extend their systems, Sloan and GM along with Firestone and Greyhound made it possible for Fitzgerald, a struggling, undercapitalized Minnesota bus driver and operator, to become a transportation tycoon. For Fitzgerald, being a tycoon was the good life. For the communities affected, life changed. The beloved, hop-on/hop-off trolleys simply vanished from small-town Main Streets. In their place, people were greeted by the rumble and black clouds of GM buses.

Throughout 1936, Fitzgerald's expansion continued through the Midwest. Jackson and Kalamazoo, Michigan, were next. But Sloan and GM wanted expansion beyond the Midwest. The South was eyed. The transit system in Montgomery, Alabama, was the first in a Southern city to become a Fitzgerald property. GM prepared a transportation survey, after which Fitzgerald went forward with the acquisition.[97]

At about the time of the Jackson and Kalamazoo acquisitions, it became clear that larger urban centers were next. The scope was becoming too large for Rex Finance and Fitzgerald's other closely held entities. It was decided that Fitzgerald should organize a public company so Wall Street backing could be obtained. A new entity was conceived: National City Lines. This new firm took over most of the properties acquired by Rex. National City Lines would be financed by $2.25 million in shares to continue its conversion crusade. But public financing was an expensive, time-consuming proposition, costing $350,000 in fees to the financial houses and brokers. Additionally, when National City Lines acquired the Rex Finance transit systems, it also acquired the substantial debt that those lines owed to General Motors Acceptance Corp. (GMAC), which weighed negatively against the books of the newly invented National City Lines. Moreover, some Illinois and Michigan transit line acquisitions were not yet final because Fitzgerald simply lacked the money to complete the purchases. Indeed, the whole concept of a public company with a national acquisition campaign was completely beyond Fitzgerald's simple experience.[98]

Not to worry. Once again, one of the corporate giants behind Fitzgerald stepped in. At the end of 1936, GM gave National City Lines a temporary loan of several hundred thousand dollars. "Some of it was used for [transit lines in] these cities [in Illinois and Michigan]," testified Fitzgerald during his criminal trial, adding, "$150,000 [was used] to pay back General Motors Acceptance Corporation, and some more of it to pay off the $350,000 [in financing costs]."[99]

Hence, GM was able to facilitate the creation of National City Lines as a public company by providing the cash so several key Midwest transit systems would be added to its assets, then negating its own $150,000 GMAC debt to reduce the National City Lines liabilities, thus improving the new company's apparent value. What's more, GM helped defray the cost of the Wall Street financing itself. Certainly, Fitzgerald was the president of this new company, and his name and signature graced the tops and bottoms of all the paperwork. But all this big business was beyond Fitzgerald. Behind Fitzgerald, however, and indeed hovering above him, were Sloan and GM, and others in their motor transport combine. Surely they thought no one would ever know. Surely, they thought it would all remain sub-rosa.

But years later, the truth was discovered. Thus, history records that at the turn of 1936 and in 1937, at the stealthy creation of National City Lines, the shadowy conglomerate that would soon ravage mass transit from coast to coast, the secretive efforts of GM, and other commercial giants, skidded down the well-lubricated slope of corporate misconduct. Here, at the incarnation of National City Lines, the misconduct leapt from a clandestine operation to a prosecutable conspiracy.[100]

The government said it best years later. Referring to GM and a circle of other corporate icons in plain words, on page 7 of the indictment, in section IV, labeled "THE CONSPIRACY," senior federal prosecutors and the grand jury jointly declared, "Beginning on or about January 1, 1937, the exact date being to the Grand Jury unknown, and continuing to and including the date of the return of this Indictment, the defendants, together with other persons to the Grand Jury unknown, have knowingly and continuously engaged in a wrongful and unlawful combination and conspiracy to acquire or otherwise secure control of or acquire a substantial financial interest in a substantial part of the companies which provide local transportation service in the various cities, towns and counties of the several states of the United States, and to eliminate and exclude all competition in the sale of motorbuses, petroleum products, tires and tubes to the local transportation companies owned or controlled by or in which National City Lines . . . had a substantial financial interest . . . in violation of Section 1 of the Act of Congress of July 2, 1890 . . . commonly known as the Sherman Act." The indictment was signed by the grand jury foreman and countersigned by six prosecutors plus U.S. Attorney James M. Carter.[101]

Fitzgerald fully understood that the new Public Utility Holding Company Act exerted pressure on electric companies to sell their aging systems, lines that Fitzgerald, backed by his corporate partners, would convert. He was asked during his conspiracy trial, "You knew at that time there was a so-called Public Utility Act that had been passed by Congress, didn't you?" Fitzgerald replied, "That is right." The next question: "And that affected the availability of local transit properties to be purchased by your company?" He answered, "Well, yes, because it was the law that they had to divest themselves of transportation properties in these several cities they operated in." The next question: "That resulted in a number of local transportation companies being put on the market because they were owned by the power company; is that right?" Again Fitzgerald replied, "That is right."[102]

Fitzgerald was next asked in court, "Did you go ahead and acquire the Beaumont [Texas] property that had been owned by the power company?" He replied, "We did." The next question: "Did you then operate the streetcars?" Fitzgerald replied, "No, sir; we motorized the system." He was asked, "Did you also acquire Port Arthur, Texas, about that time?" Fitzgerald replied, "We did at the same time, from the same people. We put in a bus operation . . . General Motors . . . twenty-one-passenger buses."[103]

Continuing, Fitzgerald was asked in court during his trial for conspiracy, "In 1937, did you also acquire Cedar Rapids, Iowa?" He replied, "Yes, sir. It was a streetcar system, wholly in a run-down condition. There was not any service, and they were losing money there." When asked, "Did you continue to operate the streetcars?" Fitzgerald testified, "No, sir; we motorized, got a new franchise. . . . The streetcar tracks were taken up and the streets were paved."[104]

In 1937, the West Coast was eyed. Another corporate creature was invented. This one was called Pacific City Lines. It began when an executive of an obscure entity called City Coach Corporation approached Fitzgerald asking if he would expand operations to California. The first three cities suggested for takeover were Stockton, San Jose, and Fresno. Fitzgerald testified, "I told him [the City Coach executive] . . . we didn't have any capital to expand our operations out on the West Coast. He told me that it was his opinion that he could borrow money from bankers, investment bankers, and so forth, on the West Coast, and, he said, finance a company for that purpose, and asked us if we would become interested if he could raise the capital. . . . I told him that we would be glad to do so, but his job was to get the capital." Asked who was really behind City Coach, Fitzgerald testified, "It was made up of executives of the Greyhound Corporation."[105]

But neither City Coach nor Greyhound could attract bank financing for the new California venture because the targeted transit systems in Stockton, San Jose, and Fresno maintained "no record of earnings," as Fitzgerald recalled in court, "nothing to justify the investment bankers or any companies in putting up the money, because the companies showed no earnings, no earnings in the company for a period of years, to justify any financial backing."[106]

A million dollars was needed to finance the new California subsidiary. Fitzgerald had no money, and the investment community would not join the enterprise. Where would it come from?

Once again, the corporate giants behind Fitzgerald stepped in. At the end of 1937 and the beginning of 1938, Fitzgerald contacted GM. Expanding his list of backers to another petroleum interest, Fitzgerald also called Standard Oil of California. Standard Oil and GM jointly agreed to provide most of the money for the new venture. National City Lines put up $150,000, City Coach invested $150,000. The remaining $700,000 was provided by GM and Standard Oil, with the oil giant functioning through a surrogate company. When asked in court, Fitzgerald didn't even recall the name of the Standard Oil subsidiary that invested several hundred thousand dollars. He told the court the investment was made by "Standard Oil Company of California or a subsidiary company, I don't remember which, and General Motors Corporation—Yellow Truck and Coach." As for the corporate paperwork for the new entity, that was handled by Greyhound corporate attorneys.[107]

During his conspiracy trial, after detailing the investments and assistance of GM, Standard, and Greyhound in creating an entity to take over California transit systems, Fitzgerald was asked, "Is that the origin of the Pacific City Lines?" Fitzgerald replied, "That is the origin of the Pacific City Lines." He added that although National City Lines and City Coach were minority investors, they each received 37.5 percent of the stock, that is, a total of 75 percent; whereas Standard and GM, which provided 70 percent of the capital, split the remaining 25 percent of the stock. Thus, the true economic powers behind the new company appeared to be just minority players. Percentages, however, were less important than control. In short order, Pacific City Lines acquired the Stockton, San Jose, and Fresno lines, which included both streetcars and aging motor-bus fleets. All three city systems were updated with Yellow coaches that utilized Standard Oil gasoline, lubrication, and other petroleum products.[108]

Almost from the outset, Standard was worried about its link to the enterprise, which would later cause the company to be prosecuted as a coconspirator. Shortly after agreeing to fund Pacific City Lines, representatives of Standard and National City Lines met in Chicago to discuss details. At the time, Standard was still stinging from infamous disclosures that had made headlines in the 1890s, a half century earlier, about its bid-rigging with and improper relationship to Southern Pacific railroad. Standard did not want a repetition of that debacle with Pacific City Lines.[109]

In Chicago, Standard's representative Victor Palmer made it clear that the corporation was willing to advance Fitzgerald $300,000, but only through a discreet partnership that would hide the oil company's true connection. Moreover, the investment would avoid acquiring common stock that would enable voting rights, since controlling voting rights would eventually be disclosed under federal law. In reviewing the stock holdings of GM and Standard, senior National City Lines vice president Foster Beamsley later explained, "Originally, Yellow and Standard's holdings of both classes of stock [common and preferred] were the same; however Standard later requested that due to their identity becoming known through hearings held before the California Railroad Commission at the time of the acquisition of the Southern Pacific properties, they thought it best to own no voting stock."[110] The solution: invest via a partnership called Bush and Company.

A National City Lines executive, Merrill Buffington, worried about the reliability of so large a cash investment from an uncertain partnership like Bush and Company. What was Bush and Company? Would the money ever come? On February 28, 1938, Buffington wrote to GM attorney H. C. Grossman explaining, "Mr. Palmer had proposed a partnership subscribed [for stock] in the place of Standard Oil of California. . . . [But] we have no assurance that the subscription . . . is within the partnership powers [of Bush and Company] or enforceable against the partnership assets, and we have no knowledge of what these assets are." What's more, the Bush and Company assets that could be discerned worried Buffington. Those assets appeared to be surrogate holdings committed to others and therefore, he cautioned, "would be of little protection to us." Both Buffington and Greyhound executives wanted "Standard Oil or some other corporation . . . to furnish us with satisfactory evidence that we have a binding commitment by someone with proper responsibility."[111]

On March 2, 1938, GM's Grossman reassured Buffington that Standard would not renege and was not trying to avoid financial liability for its investment promise. "I believe that I understand why Standard Oil Company is desirable of subscribing to stock through an agency other than their own company. . . . Their present arrangement is not motivated by a desire to circumvent their liability." Grossman suggested Buffington ask Standard for a written confirmation in black and white. "I see no harm in, and would consider it good business, to request reasonable assurances from Standard Oil of California."[112]

Buffington took Grossman's advice, writing a Standard Oil executive on March 5 that Bush and Company, the proposed partnership fronting for Standard, may have "ample assets. However, its articles of partnership indicate that it does not own outright property, but merely holds title to property as a nominee or agent for others. Under these circumstances, I would suggest you send us an agreement in the form of a letter to Pacific City Lines . . . backed up by proper financial responsibility."[113]

Several days later, Standard Oil's Palmer complied, furnishing the requested letter confirming that "Bush and Company is the undersigned's nominee to subscribe to stock of Pacific City Lines, Inc., and that the undersigned guarantees the payment." Palmer signed in his corporate capacity for Standard Oil. In so doing, the invention of Pacific City Lines to convert California metro transit systems was finalized.[114]

The conspiracy against mass transit was first and foremost a conspiracy to convert cities from electric to petroleum systems. Secondarily, the campaign was designed to reward the conspiring companies with a monopolistic edge over their competitors in the gasoline, tire, and bus business. True, most of the cities being affected were relatively small, such as Beaumont, Decatur, and Fresno. The smaller the city, the more vulnerable its transit line was to takeover and the easier the conversion. But as National City Lines and Pacific City Lines absorbed and converted one city transit line after another, the bounty became greater in scope. As the campaign succeeded, the monopolistic conspiracy widened. How? A small combine of automotive suppliers would fund National City Lines transit takeovers by buying preferred stock. The supplier then received exclusive anticompetitive purchase contracts from the newly acquired systems.

On May 13, 1939, Fitzgerald sent a letter to a small group of prospective supplier investors outlining the bargain. "We contemplate using the proceeds from the stock sold pursuant to these stock contracts for the expansion of our operations," wrote Fitzgerald, "through the establishment or acquisition of additional bus lines in various municipalities. We have several such projects under investigation or active negotiation at the present time. In order to be sure that we will not be delayed in establishing any such project by a lack of free capital, we have entered into a contract with Continental Illinois National Bank and Trust Company of Chicago, whereby we are given a credit of $750,000."[115] But the bank credit line was hardly enough. National City Lines needed more.

Firestone was the first to join GM and Standard in financially backing National City Lines. On May 15, 1939, Firestone executed the first of several contracts funding National City Lines acquisition and conversion activities conditional on a series of anticompetitive contracts to exclusively provide tires for the newly converted transit lines. Firestone's initial contracts called for the tire maker to provide $250,000 toward the acquisition by Pacific City Lines of the three targeted California transit lines—Fresno, Stockton, and San Jose—plus a fourth system in Canton, Ohio. The tire company purchased five thousand shares of National City Lines $50 convertible cumulative preference stocks—that is, preferred stock with the right to convert to common shares. In return, Firestone's contract stipulated, the acquired transit lines would purchase tires only from Firestone—and from no other tire maker.[116]

"National will cause said four units [transit lines about to be taken over in Fresno, Stockton, San Jose, and Canton] to execute contracts with

Firestone," Firestone's contract mandated, continuing that "all corporations and other entities which it [National City Lines] now controls or may control in the future, either directly or indirectly, shall equip and shall continue to equip all their transportation units with Firestone products to the exclusion of any products competitive thereto, except as this covenant may conflict with operating contracts now in effect." Any existing contracts for tires "in effect" were allowed to lapse without renewal or terminated outright and replaced with Firestone contracts. The words "to the exclusion of any products competitive thereto" caught the eye of prosecutors, who deemed the agreement anticompetitive and monopolistic.[117]

Quickly, competition in the purchase of tires vanished from systems controlled by National City Lines because other tire companies were simply blocked, creating local transit monopolies for Firestone. For example, for years U.S. Rubber Company had supplied bus tires on a price-competitive basis to many transit systems. But once National City Lines took over a system, U.S. Rubber was effectively precluded from the business. A Federal Bureau of Investigation agent interviewed a U.S. Rubber executive about the subject. The agent recorded the executive's complaint that Fred Nolan, president of the Baltimore Transit Co., stated, "There was nothing to prevent him [a U.S. Rubber executive] from bidding, but that it would be a waste of time." The U.S. Rubber executive protested that whenever National City Lines acquired a transit system, the U.S. Rubber "contract is terminated," adding that U.S. Rubber "has never received a request to submit a bid on a tire mileage contract with a National City Lines operation."[118]

Phillips Petroleum was next to join the conspiracy. Standard Oil of California monopolized National City Lines petroleum purchases in the West. But transit systems east of Standard's territory were available for Phillips. As in the case of Standard, there was concern about obscuring the supplier's involvement with National City Lines.

On April 18, 1939, National City Lines' outside attorney Guido Pantaleoni wrote to Phillips trying to dissuade Phillips from registering its stock to comply with federal law. Registration would reveal Phillips's ownership. "The trouble is," wrote Pantaleoni, "that I feel very strongly not only that registration would be of no assistance on this point, but also that registration might be positively damaging through being used hereafter as evidence against you on the question as to whether you had an intention to resell at the time of your purchase and, hence, should have been named as an underwriter."[119]

Pantaleoni's next sentences virtually outlined the quid pro quo at the heart of the later prosecution. "First: You are buying the stock only as part of a larger deal which gives you the oil contract. Second: Neither you or any of the other purchasers [e.g., Firestone, GM, and Standard] are in the business of distributing securities. Third: You are buying the stock at $50 a share, when the market, which is very thin, is about $38 a share. Fourth: Certain privileges of yours under the oil contract are affected by your holding or failure to hold your stock."[120]

Making clear that revealing ownership through registration could endanger the entire circle of supplier investors, Pantaleoni cautioned, "Until we get this question settled, it is impossible to push the rest of the deal through. Because everyone involved is interested in this aspect of the problem, I am taking the liberty of sending a copy of this letter to Roy Fitzgerald, to the bankers who are represented on the Board, and to Firestone."[121]

Ultimately, Phillips went along with the group, executing its contract on July 14, 1939. Once Phillips joined the combine, it became common knowledge within the oil and lubricating industry that National City Lines would shift all its eastern purchases to Phillips. This eliminated price-lowering competitive opportunities for such oil companies as Sinclair and Mid-Continent Oil.[122]

When Phillips wrote its investment and product exclusivity contracts with National City Lines, the oil company added a dynamic new dimension in Clause 6. Clause 6 required that the acquired transit systems never again use a nonpetroleum-based form of propulsion without Phillips's permission. In other words, the transit systems would not be permitted to reinstitute electric service even if called for. Fitzgerald barely understood the legalisms inherent in this contractual clause. When asked during the conspiracy trial, Fitzgerald specified his confusion over "certain other things in the contract that I am not too familiar with, that were objectionable." The next question: "Now, you are referring particularly in your last testimony, are you, Mr. Fitzgerald, to Clause 6 of Government's Exhibit 84, which reads, 'National agrees that neither it nor any of its subsidiaries or lessees or persons operating the equipment . . . shall in Phillips's territory change any present type of equipment or purchase any new type of equipment to use any fuel or method of propulsion other than gasoline without the consent of Phillips.'" Fitzgerald replied, "That is the clause I am referring to."[123]

Referring to all the supplier investment contracts, Fitzgerald was asked point-blank in open court, "These contracts, the language of these contracts wasn't your personal language was it?" Fitzgerald answered, "No." The next question pinned down Fitzgerald's level of understanding: "They were drawn up by the attorneys?" In his simplistic way, belying his status as the chief executive of a national conglomerate, Fitzgerald responded, "Attorney language, I call it."[124]

On August 1 and 2, 1939, the last two supplier contracts were finalized. As the supplier attorneys conceded to prosecutors, "In a large measure they [the contracts] formalized the relationships existing before the contracts." GM had been Fitzgerald's bus supplier for years based on verbal understandings, handshakes, and quiet quid pro quos. But now as the program broadened to include dozens of cities and operating companies under the National City Lines umbrella, GM set forth in writing exactly what it expected for its money. In exchange for a fresh investment of $500,000, GM demanded "not less than 85 percent of the dollar volume" of all bus purchases for all transit systems already wholly or partially controlled by National City Lines or Pacific City Lines. Clause 5 of GM's contract listed the transit systems National City Lines had taken over thus far: "Aurora City Lines, Aurora Elgin Bus Line, Beaumont City Lines, Beaumont–Port Arthur Bus Line, Bloomington–Normal City Lines, Canton City Lines, Cedar Rapids City Lines, Champaign-Urbana City Lines, Danville City Lines, Decatur City Lines, East St. Louis City Lines, Elgin City Lines, Joliet City Lines, Kalamazoo City Lines, Montgomery City Lines, Pontiac City Lines, Port Arthur City Lines, Portsmouth City Lines, Quincy City Lines, Rex Equipment Sales, Saginaw City Lines, Southern Limited, Terre Haute City Lines, Tulsa City Lines."[125]

Being careful not to phrase its contract with the same exclusionary language of Firestone, Standard Oil, and Phillips, GM only asked for 85 percent of the volume, not 100 percent as the others had. Moreover, moving forward, GM was willing to split sales to future transit system acquisitions with Mack Truck fifty-fifty. GM's Clause 6 specified that future subsidiaries purchase "not less than 42.5 percent of the dollar volume," or exactly half of 85 percent.[126]

One day earlier, August 2, 1939, Mack Truck concluded its own agreement with National City Lines. Like GM, Mack invested $500,000 in exchange for purchases by the future acquisitions, that is, "subsidiary corporations hereafter formed or acquired by it." Those new systems purchases would equal, per contract, "approximately 42.5 percent in dollar volume of all the new buses and equipment requirements for said subsidiary corporations of National." Hence, Mack's contract mirrored GM's as the two manufacturers split future bus business fifty-fifty.[127]

In practice, the bus exclusives often meant that along with dozens of GM and Mack vehicles in any system, there were commonly one or two lone Ford buses in operation to forfend the appearance of monopoly. Rather than mask the monopoly, the calculated tokenism only attracted the attention of prosecutors, who saw it as evidence of the combine's true intent. More often, when National took over a transit line it simply canceled all other bus sales.[128]

Typical was the case in Spokane. On July 9, 1945, bus manufacturer Twin Coach Company was sent a letter by the assistant purchasing agent of Spokane United Railways: "Under date of September 5, 1944, Spokane United Railways placed with you a conditional order for 10–32 passenger Train Coach Buses. . . . On July 7, 1945 the fiscal property and equipment of the Spokane United Railway will be transferred to Spokane Pacific City Lines, subsidiary of Pacific City Lines. . . . Now that the deal has been consummated . . . it is necessary that this order for equipment be cancelled. Will you therefore consider this letter as cancellation of the conditional order, and please acknowledge receipt so that our files will be complete."[129]

Mack always understood that it was acting in concert with partners as a member of a combine. For weeks prior to signing its contract with National, Mack officials had been circulating memos specifying exactly how much the other supplier partners—GM, Firestone, Standard, and Phillips—would invest. Later, an FBI agent would interview a senior Mack official about the company's August 2, 1939, agreement with National. The FBI agent reported, "He [the Mack official] stated there was no agreement whereby National City Lines Inc. committed itself to buy buses in return for stock purchases by Mack Trucks." Ironically, by this time, the FBI had obtained a copy of the agreement in question.[130]

From the beginning, Mack knew that even though it would be a junior partner to GM in the National City Lines enterprise, the rewards would still be substantial. While trolleys lasted two to three decades, buses needed to be replaced every six to eight years. This would be expensive for the transit lines, but profitable for Mack. A June 29, 1939, internal Mack memo to its president, E. C. Fink, made this clear: "It is estimated that National City Lines present fleet of approximately 860 buses will require replacements of at least 130 buses annually. Based on past experience in the employment of this amount of capital, it is estimated $2 million of additional gross revenue can be secured." As for trolley conversion, the Mack memo added, "If such properties require complete conversion from rails to rubber, approximately 200 additional new buses will be needed."[131]

The five major suppliers came together to act through National City Lines. In large measure, the companies did not interact separately but in close coordination, since their interests were necessarily interwoven. For example, on July 26, 1939, just before GM and Mack sealed their early-August 1939 investment and purchase contracts with National City Lines, Phillips attorney R. M. Riggins dashed off a short note to Firestone assistant treasurer R. S. Leonard, stating, "Roy Fitzgerald advised me that General Motors and Mack Truck are going in for $500,000 each on the same basis as the rest of us, in connection with purchase of equipment."[132]

Just days earlier, Fitzgerald assured Phillips officials in a letter, "In connection with the contracts hereto and executed by us today, we want to advise you that it will be our policy to discuss in advance with the proper officers of your company any proposed borrowing or investments by National City Lines."[133]

In practice, National City Lines and Pacific City Lines officials asked for their suppliers' permission before making any transit system acquisitions, knowing full well that those manufacturers controlled the purse strings. For example, in June of 1943, as he was finalizing the purchase of three properties, Pacific City Lines president J. L. Haugh wrote a letter to senior officials of Standard, GM, and Firestone: "I am continuing negotiations for the acquisition of the bus operating properties at Sacramento and Salt Lake City, and the capital stock of the California Street Cable Railroad Company. This is in accordance with our talks at your respective offices at Akron, Pontiac and San Francisco. The estimated cost of these three properties, including costs of acquisition, legal expense, and initial working funds, is as follows: Sacramento, $420,000, Salt Lake City $705,000 and California Street Cable R.R. Company $325,000. Total $1,450,000." Of this amount, Haugh stated that Pacific City Lines would contribute only $350,000 and would require "net amount of additional capital to be supplied by preferred stockholders: $1.1 million."[134]

Haugh continued to keep senior corporate officials of the combine apprised on the pending acquisitions until on June 29, 1943, he felt he could wait no longer on the Sacramento effort. "Important to close this quickly," cabled Haugh, "as their labor agreement expires tomorrow and negotiations have been held in abeyance pending our purchase." On July

1, 1943, the permission slips began arriving. For Firestone, Russell A. Firestone sent a telegram: "Agreeable conclude Sacramento transaction as stated in your telegram today." At the same time, GM's attorney Grossman wired Haugh: "Received your wire after conversation. You may conclude transaction on basis represented, H.C. Grossman, General Motors Truck."[135]

Once a city system was secured, National hardly purchased its supplies at the lowest price. For example, GM's contract included a completely contradictory and convoluted provision stating that prices would be "the lowest available"—except they would not. Clause 8 stipulated in exquisite doublespeak: "The prices at which buyer agrees to purchase . . . shall in no instance be greater than the lowest price at which such motorbus equipment is at the time being offered by manufacturer to the largest users of motorbus equipment, except, however, sales by manufacturer to the Greyhound Corporation, the Omnibus Corporation, Public Service Corporation of New Jersey, and companies subsidiary to and affiliated with them, United States Government, and all municipal bodies. It being understood and agreed that Buyer is not entitled to the same prices which these last mentioned customers receive."[136] Hence, National City Lines transit systems, despite the collective purchasing clout, did not qualify for the best discounts. The extra cost was passed on to the citizens.

National City Lines began its existence by acquiring some of the smallest city systems in the Midwest and South. When operations were expanded to small urban centers along the West Coast, the company and its partners formed and funded Pacific City Lines. When bigger cities were targeted in 1943, a third holding company was formed, named American City Lines. The same corporate combine of five automotive suppliers created this third major entity, except that Standard Oil's participation was now funneled through a subsidiary innocuously called Federal Engineering. American City Lines, directly or indirectly, acquired a controlling interest of such major urban transit systems as the ones in Los Angeles, St. Louis, and Baltimore.[137]

Prosecutors calculated that between National City Lines, Pacific City Lines, and American City Lines and their dozens of subsidiaries spread across at least forty-two cities in sixteen states, GM ultimately invested more than $3.1 million, Standard invested more than $2 million, and Phillips invested more than $1.5 million, while Firestone and Mack each invested more than $1.3 million.[138]

Prosecutors also calculated that over a decade, from 1936 to 1946,

GM enjoyed $25 million in bus sales to National City Lines, Pacific City Lines, and American City Lines systems, while Mack sold the companies approximately $3.5 million. During that same decade, Phillips annually sold the companies as much as $900,000 in petroleum products in its territory, while Standard sold as much as $700,000 annually in its western territory. Firestone annually sold all the operating companies in excess of $450,000 in tires.[139]

When National City Lines or its subsidiaries gained control over urban systems, they always moved expeditiously to convert from electrified buses and trolleys to motorized transport. GM's Survey Department would first scout the city, then turn the survey over to National City Lines. Survey in hand, the transit conglomerate would proceed with the local powers that be. Dozens of city systems were converted in this fashion. Tampa, which converted in 1946, followed the pattern. In that vein, on March 13, 1946, a National City Lines internal memorandum from C. J. Helbing to Cone T. Bass opened, "Complying with your telephone request of yesterday, March 12th, 1946, I am enclosing a GM Survey of Tampa, Florida, which was made during June of 1941, together with a map of Tampa's street car system, showing the street car routes, together with a summary of their schedules on the various routes they operate."[140]

The internal memo outlined plans for converting the various electric lines and replacing them with buses. "By a rough estimate," wrote Helbing, "I anticipate we would require approximately 75 additional buses of the 36 to 40 seating capacity type, in order to provide adequate service. Allowing approximately 10% for spares, would permit us to schedule approximately 115 coaches."[141]

In many cases, state commissions or local city councils had already voted to mandate the dismantling of the streetcars because city planners had often consciously failed to incorporate electric buses, trolleys, and light rail into their metropolitan growth. This policy amounted to a mixture of planned obsolescence and strategic neglect. In some cases, city officials were indifferent. In some cases, they were induced to vote for trolley abandonment. In St. Petersburg, Florida, for example, rumors were rife that councilmen, municipal engineers, and others had been bought off with Cadillacs to facilitate the conversion by National City Lines and GM.

On September 4, 1947, the U.S. attorney general received a letter from a Florida resident, a so-called insider, complaining, "At the present moment, this group [National City Lines and American City Lines] is making every effort to prevail upon the City Councilmen of St. Petersburg, Florida to scrap the electric railway system and the electric power plant, both owned and operated by the municipality. . . . A representative from General Motors has been 'practically sleeping with the City Councilmen' for the past six months or more, and has succeeded in biasing them against the electric railway."[142]

The insider charged that the technical assessments against the trolley were equally tainted: "The City Utilities Engineer, who might normally be expected to do what he could to defend the efficient electric railway and the power plant, has evidently been similarly influenced, as he publicly criticizes the electric railway and the power plant, and invents all manner of foundationless reasons why they should be eliminated." The insider appealed to the FBI, "St. Petersburg needs your help quickly."[143]

How did the insider believe officials were being tainted? With free Cadillacs. "The retiring City Councilmen," wrote the insider, "who vacated their offices July 1 [1947] mysteriously and simultaneously acquired a fleet of new Cadillac cars, having previously placed an order for a fleet of buses for the city. The retiring mayor also acquired one, at the same time. Can you believe that this is just a coincidence?"[144]

FBI director J. Edgar Hoover received a copy of the letter, and a full investigation was ordered.

An FBI agent interviewed the insider and recorded, "He [the insider] stated that the councilmen were being retired July 1, 1947 and being replaced by a new council, and that they rushed to pass the bill to scrap the electric transportation system and buy buses before they retired. . . . He said that the unfair practice consisted of pressure and gifts, and that the councilmen all acquired a new Cadillac just about the time they retired which to him looked suspicious." The complaining insider added that the city utilities engineer who was charged with stilting his reports "also received a new Cadillac."[145]

Checking with a City Hall source, the FBI agent on the case reported that the second individual also "stated that he is personally cognizant of the rumors which are rampant in the city concerning the alleged gifts of Cadillac cars to the members of the outgoing City Council, in return for assistance in doing away with the electrical streetcars presently operating in most sections of the city . . . in spite of the fact that the streetcars afford adequate and full transportation facilities for the city and are making money for it."[146]

The City Hall source added that "equipment including the overhead wires are to be dismantled as quickly as possible under this resolution. He indicated that buses have been used in other sections of the city [merely] to augment the streetcars and that during the first year the buses were in operation it cost the city approximately $28,000, while during that same time the streetcars yielded a net profit of over $300,000 and that during the past year, the buses have shown a net profit of $134,000, while the streetcar system furnished a net profit of $146,000. He indicated that [the] City Manager . . . is part of the plot to get rid of the streetcars in favor of buses." Repeating the familiar refrain that lines had consciously been allowed to deteriorate, the City Hall source told the FBI, "The City Manager . . . had deliberately permitted the equipment to become obsolete, so that the public would complain about the service, the poor condition of the equipment and thus bring about a demand for improved transportation. He stated that no attempts have been made to replace the obsolete equipment or to keep the present in a usable condition."[147]

The FBI agent concluded his report, "The transition of the city transportation system to motorbuses is one of the weightiest political issues presently evident in this city."[148]

Indeed, the political sensitivities of converting the electric system of Tampa had been brewing for some time and were made known to the National City Lines backers. For example, on December 1, 1944, National City Lines vice president Beamsley wrote to an official at Standard Oil to report that following conversion of Baltimore's system, American City Lines had dramatically been increasing its gasoline consumption in that city to ten million gallons. At the same time, Beamsley continued, he thought it best to not disturb existing oil and lubrication contracts in Tampa for the present. Tampa "within a reasonable length of time could be delivered," Beamsley wrote, "but for a while at least the political situation is such that present contracts should not be disturbed." That said, he reminded the official that the combine was using a front called Andover Finance Company: "Andover, as you will recollect, is owned one half by National City Lines and one half by American City Lines, we having used it to make investments in situations beyond the legal limit."[149]

In every city, large and small, people wept for their lost way of life. Certainly, automobile drivers often cheered the demise of the streetcars and electric buses that competed with them for road space. But for the millions who cherished local transit, losing their streetcars and electric buses made them feel vanquished.

The first total conversion to buses after the end of World War II was in Lincoln, Nebraska, where the final run was so nostalgic, even the fall 1945 National City Lines employee newsletter took notice: "All the way out to the end of the line, and all the way back, guest patrons pulled the stop cord. . . . The old whistles blew and blew. People gathered at curbs and on lawns and porches to wave a last farewell. Guests of the front car called out places of interest along the route even though their companions all had lived in Lincoln for many years and knew all the spots. There was an intimate sort of relationship between the folks in the cars and people along the way. . . . Kids on bedecked bicycles rode behind the sound truck. Lincoln's dogs, sensing the unusual, barked at the cars for the last time and many chased the procession for blocks."[150] Progress had come to Lincoln.

Letters to the editor of the local newspapers in city after city commonly excoriated the conversions. In Tampa, weeks after the conversion, a December 8, 1946, letter protested, "The most cruel thing ever done in Tampa was to take away the streetcars and give us these jolting buses that never take you where you want to go. I have walked the soles off two pairs of shoes since riding on them. It is too bad that the citizens have no say in what they get. The only ones who are praising this new system are those who drive cars. They are glad to have the streetcars out of their way. Signed, Ruby Seely." Another letter to the Tampa newspaper, September 19, 1947, possibly alluding to the rumors of Cadillac bribes, declared, "I respectfully suggest that our City Fathers put their fine cars in their garages and ride these buses for one week, especially during the rush hours, and maybe we poor devils would get some relief from this diabolical mess of transportation. Signed, One of the Fed Ups."[151]

In Baltimore, the city had invested several million dollars since 1940 ordering more than one hundred state-of-the-art, streamlined trolleys. The publicly owned transit line boasted that the new cars would give Baltimore "one of the largest fleets of modern rail urban transit cars in the United States." Moreover, a fifty-year ironclad contract for electricity, signed in 1922, locked in the power cost for three more decades. Paid ridership rose from 121.4 million in 1935 to 142.8 million in 1941 and reached a wartime high of 271.8 million, when gasoline was rationed. Operating income rose regularly during these years with an increase of 33 percent, from $1.5 million to $2 million during the twelve-month period from 1941 to 1942.[152]

But trolley infrastructure expansion was neglected during the protracted throes of Baltimore's city sprawl. What's more, new postwar one-way traffic patterns were inaugurated to relieve congestion. These two factors combined to frustrate the future value of electric mobility in spite of its successes. Consequently, as soon as American City Lines finished its takeover of Baltimore's transit system in 1946, conversion, not modernization, was implemented. The annual obligatory expense of the electricity contract for thirty more years was simply absorbed. Those new streetcars were sold off or contracts canceled. The tracks and wires were systematically ripped away. Citizen lawsuits seeking to stop the first seventy-seven miles of rail abandonment were unsuccessful. As routes were terminated, "mourners" would board in a "death watch," seeing their beloved vehicles ride into oblivion. Route 1 was first, on June 21, 1947, followed by Routes 17 and 29. More than fifteen years later, when the last Baltimore trolley, Number 8, made its last run, "mourners" hooted and booed when the replacement bus pulled down the street.[153]

National City Lines always kept tabs on citizen anguish over losing trolleys. A file folder in many offices marked ABANDONMENT OF THE TROLLEY was kept brimming with the latest newspaper clippings bemoaning the conversion. The threnodies and complaints in these folders chronicle the painful changes each city endured.[154]

Ironically, in 1942, a key time of expansion for National City Lines, the United States was at war with Nazi Germany. Pursuant to a presidential executive order issued just days after Pearl Harbor, the Office of Defense Transportation's Division of Local Transportation in April 1942 promulgated instructions to all private and public transit systems mandating their return to trolley. Motorized city transit was to be curtailed wherever possible.[155]

"Our present policy in the following matters is determined almost entirely by the stoppage of rubber imports and the desperate need for conserving all the rubber now in our possession," the Division of Local Transportation declared. "Waste of rubber tires under present conditions is little short of disloyalty to the national interest. . . . Transit companies and regulatory authorities should take immediate steps to obtain the fullest possible use of all operable rail lines and equipment. This will require discontinuance of bus and trolley coach services which are being provided over routes where street railway lines are or can be made operable, as well as on street railway routes now being served part of the time by buses or trolley coaches."[156]

But the five-page order received by National City Lines went counter to the plans of Sloan and GM. In many ways, Sloan did not believe the war rules applied to his company. Sloan had been tangling with the Roosevelt administration for years. In 1934, when Sloan telephoned Secretary of Labor Frances Perkins to renege on a promise made to meet with labor strikers, Perkins lashed out bitterly at the GM chief. Shocked at the reversal, Perkins shouted into the phone, "You are a scoundrel and a skunk, Mr. Sloan. You don't deserve to be counted among decent men. . . . You'll go to hell when you die. . . . Are you a grown man, Mr. Sloan? Or are you a neurotic adolescent? Which are you? If you're a grown man, stand up, and be a man for once."[157]

A flabbergasted Sloan protested, "You can't talk like that to me! You can't talk like that to me! I'm worth seventy million dollars and I made it all myself! You can't talk like that to me! I'm Alfred Sloan."[158]

Yet at that very time, Sloan and GM were being profoundly deferential to Adolf Hitler. GM became a key Nazi collaborator in the growing Hitler war machine that was publicly rearming despite international sanction. The corporation's wholly owned Opel division prospered as the number two auto manufacturer in the Third Reich. Overseeing GM's German operation was James D. Mooney, president of the General Motors Overseas Corporation. Mooney had learned early on to pump his arm diagonally, palm outstretched, in the Hitler salute. On one occasion, in 1934, Mooney practiced his "Heil, Hitler" salute in a mirror to get it just right before an important meeting with *der Führer* in Hitler's chancellery office. Ironically, that day Hitler did not return Mooney's salute, but merely shook the GM official's hand. Mooney, like others, found Hitler to be fascinated by all things automotive.[159] GM and the Hitler regime found great common ground.

Quickly, Sloan, Mooney, and GM realized that the Reich military machine was its best customer in Germany. In large measure, the Nazi army moved in GM trucks and automobiles, especially the three-ton Opel Blitz trucks. Sales to the army yielded a greater per truck profit than civilian sales—a hefty 40 percent more. So GM preferred supplying the military, which from the outset loudly declared it was preparing for war against Europe. Almost 17 percent of Blitz truck production was sold directly to the Nazi military in 1937, despite Hitler's open threats to overrun Europe. That sales figure was increased to 29 percent in 1938—totaling some six thousand Blitz trucks that year alone. The *Wehrmacht*, the German military, soon became Opel's number one customer by far. Other important customers included major industries associated with the Hitler war machine. The expansion of its German workforce from seventeen thousand in 1934 to twenty-seven thousand in 1938 also made GM one of Germany's leading employers. Unquestionably, GM's Opel became an integral facet of Hitler's Reich.[160]

In 1938, Mooney on behalf of GM received one of Hitler's highest medals, the Merit Cross of the German Eagle with Star. A year earlier, the Merit Cross of the German Eagle with Star was created for Thomas Watson, president of IBM. The award had been bestowed upon Watson in 1937 in an opulent Berlin ceremony in recognition of the information technology IBM had invented to organize the Reich's programs of racial supremacy, economic recovery, and war preparedness. The citation accompanying the medal was to "honor foreign nationals who made themselves deserving of the German Reich." The Merit Cross of the German Eagle with Star ranked second in prestige only to Hitler's German Grand Cross, reserved for German nationals.[161]

In the months leading up to the feared invasion of Poland, Sloan defended his close collaboration with the Nazi Reich. In a long April 1939 letter to an objecting stockholder, Sloan wrote, "General Motors Corporation is an international organization. It operates in practically every country in the world where motor cars are used. . . . Its export activities have been quite an outstanding achievement of its development and represent an evolution of something like twenty years of aggressive, and I believe in the main, intelligent effort. . . . The profits which the stockholders have received as a result of its overseas activities have been outstanding."[162]

Brushing off attacks for his partnership with a Nazi regime notorious for filling concentration camps and dismantling Jewish communities, its takeover of Austria and now its threats to install the Master Race across Europe, Sloan was stony and proud. He stated that GM needed to be sensitive to the Reich's social and societal desires as well. "Now I believe," he continued in his April 1939 letter to the stockholder, "that if an international business, such as General Motors, engages in the commercial activity of any country with the idea of making a profit . . . that it has an obligation to that country, both in an economic sense as well perhaps as in a social sense. It should attempt to attune itself to the general business of the community; make itself a part of the same; conduct its operations in relation to the customs. . . . I believe further, that that should be its position, even if, as is likely to happen and particularly as was the case during the past few years, the management of the Corporation might not wholly agree with many things that are done in certain of these countries. In other words, to put the proposition rather bluntly, such matters should not be considered the business of the management of General Motors."[163]

Once war broke out on September 1, 1939, the Blitz truck became an indispensable factor in the blitzkrieg launched against Poland, which ignited World War II. German troops mercilessly overran Poland in GM trucks. At the same time, GM and Standard Oil of New Jersey jointly worked with I. G. Farben to produce tetraethyl lead, eliminating ping and knock from German internal combustion machines, especially those operating on synthetic coal-derived fuels. The fuel additive became indispensable both for Blitz trucks and the JU-88 bombers that were manufactured in GM German plants once the war began. Those JU-88 bombers rained terror and devastation from above upon civilian populations.[164]

In 1940, as France and Western Europe were under invasion and brutal occupation, Mooney resisted all pressure to return the commendation, declaring he would "do nothing to make Hitler mad."[165]

In May 1941, a year and a half after World War II broke out, with millions displaced, murdered, ghettoized, or enslaved by Nazi aggression and genocide and at the height of the rape of Poland, with most of Europe occupied, as London was being blitzed, as Jews throughout Europe were being rounded up and shipped into hellish ghettos and concentration camps—all of which blared across the front pages of America's newspapers and the newsreels of movie theater screens—Sloan told his closest executives during a Detroit briefing, "I am sure we all realize that this struggle that is going on through the world is really nothing more or less than a conflict between two opposing technocracies manifesting itself to the capitalization of economic resources and products and all that sort of thing."[166]

Sloan continued in a rambling, incoherent fashion, "The materials that we use are the materials that are needed the most and the things that count the most, and the technical skills that we have, likewise, is needed the most in the things that count the most, and likewise the fact that most of the things that are needed in such prodigious quantities that it needs a type of organization that is used to doing things in a very big way in order to meet the demands that are upon us."[167] Few, if anyone, understood what he might have meant.

GM collaboration with Hitler would come back to haunt the Detroit automaker. Later, that collaboration became a pivotal factor in the examination of its record in American mass transit. A generation later, in 1974, when Bradford Snell and the special House subcommittee released its stinging report on GM and National City Lines, the first several pages of the key accusatory section dwelled exhaustively on GM's far-reaching collaboration with the Reich. Indeed, the only photographs in the Snell Report were those illustrating GM's activities on behalf of Germany. The implication was that in the thirties and forties, at a time when GM was un-

dermining American transport and urban mass transit, the bus and auto giant was doing all in its power to enhance Reich transport. Moreover, the
years-long collaboration was cited by Senator Philip A. Hart (D-Michigan)
as he introduced legislation, the Industrial Reorganization Act, designed to
break up GM and other great Detroit automakers.[168]

GM was so riled by the charges of collaboration that the first six
pages of rebuttal in its eighty-six-page reply to the House and Snell were
devoted to denying that GM "actively assisted in the Nazi war effort." The
automaker attached numerous newspaper clips showing how documentation assembled by the House and Snell had resonated with the media and
the public. GM's rebuttal termed the House documentation of its Nazi
collaboration to be nothing less than "slander," "totally misleading," and
"totally irresponsible."[169] GM claimed it never happened.

During the war years and during the immediate postwar months, local
complaints of bribery, collusion, anticompetitive actions, and restraint of
trade streamed into the Department of Justice from across the country. Finally, the federal government took notice.

October 2, 1946, Department of Justice to J. Edgar Hoover, director
of the Federal Bureau of Investigation:

"The Antitrust Division has received numerous complaints concerning the activities of National City Lines, Inc., and various associated companies in connection with the acquisition and operation of local transit
systems acquired by those companies in various cities throughout the
country. Through a series of contracts, manufacturers of buses, tires and
petroleum products have become important stockholders in the National
City Lines. Investigation of the complaints disclosed the probable existence of a systematic campaign by National City Lines, acting with its
manufacturing stockholders, to secure control over local transportation
systems in various cities. As soon as control is secured, the local transportation company is directed to buy buses, petroleum products and tires from
the manufacturing stockholders of National City Lines in accordance with
the contracts between the manufacturers and National City Lines. The
purpose of the plan is to set up an integrated scheme of control whereby
manufacturing stockholders furnish supplies of buses, tires and petroleum
products to local transportation companies on terms agreed upon by the
National City Lines and manufacturers. . . . It appears that National City
Lines and its manufacturing associates have entered into a plan to secure

control over local transportation systems in important cities of the United States. . . . One result of the plan for integrated control over local transportation has been the elimination of electric railway cars in city transportation controlled by these companies."[170]

Prosecution is a dance with only one willing partner. During late 1946 and early 1947 the dance began. Agents in blue suits fanned out across America interviewing executives, transit experts, community leaders, and local officials. Subpoenas for masses of documents were served. Documents, once seized, were delivered to the FBI labs for handwriting analysis. Memos with investigative notes were exchanged among many FBI field offices. Excuses and explanations were proffered by many executives. Phone calls were placed to many defense counsels. Reviews were undertaken by many Justice Department supervisors. Joint action was undertaken by a team of hard-nosed assistant attorneys general, with outside lawyers brought in for the unprecedented corporate strike. Tall stacks of evidence were hauled from one Justice Department conference room to another. Presentations were made to the federal grand jury.[171]

April 9, 1947, the waiting was over. True bills of indictment were handed down. Two counts of criminal conspiracy were unsealed.[172]

The United States of America v. National City Lines, Inc., American City Lines, Inc., Pacific City Lines, Inc., Firestone Tire & Rubber Company, General Motors Corporation, Phillips Petroleum Company, Mack Manufacturing Corporation, Standard Oil Company of California and its subsidiary Federal Engineering Corporation, plus National City Lines executives E. Roy Fitzgerald, and Foster G. Beamsley, as well as General Motors executive H. C. Grossman, Standard Oil executive Henry C. Judd, Firestone executives L. R. Jackson, and Phillips executives B. F. Stradley, and A. M. Hughes, all defendants.[173]

Count 1 alleged a conspiracy to control mass transit through systematic acquisition. The defendants, the indictment charged, "knowingly and continuously engaged in a wrongful and unlawful combination and conspiracy to acquire or otherwise secure control of or acquire a substantial financial interest in a substantial part of the companies which provide local transportation service in the various cities, towns and counties of the several states of the United States, and to eliminate and exclude all competition in the sale of motorbuses, petroleum products, tires and tubes to the local transportation companies owned or controlled by . . . National City Lines." The count also alleged that none of the transit systems, once taken over, "could convert or change the equipment used by them from a type using the product sold by the supplier defendant to any other type."[174]

Count 2 alleged a "conspiracy to monopolize" the bus business by creating a network of transit companies that were forbidden to "use products other than the products sold by supplier defendants." Moreover, count 2 continued, "the motor bus, petroleum, tire and tube business of defendants, National American and Pacific and their operating companies, would be allocated and divided among the supplier defendants in an artificial, arbitrary and noncompetitive manner."[175]

The prosecution made clear in its subsequent bill of particulars that the action of the defendants was in fact a long-lived and snowballing conspiracy: "The defendants National City Lines, Inc., Pacific City Lines, Inc., General Motors Corporation, Standard Oil Company of California and The Firestone Tire and Rubber Company joined the conspiracy on or about June 1, 1938. The participation in the conspiracy by the defendant General Motors Corporation prior to September, 1943 was through the Yellow Truck and Coach Manufacturing Company. The defendant Phillips Petroleum Company joined the conspiracy on or about July 11, 1939. The defendant Mack Manufacturing Corporation joined the conspiracy on or about August 1, 1939. The defendant Federal Engineering Corporation joined the conspiracy in or about October, 1943. The defendants E. Roy Fitzgerald, Foster G. Beamsley and H. C. Grossman joined the conspiracy in or about the year 1938. The defendant Henry C. Judd joined the conspiracy in or about August 1943. The defendant L. R. Jackson joined the conspiracy on or about May 15, 1939. The defendants B. F. Stradley and A. M. Hughes joined the conspiracy on or about July 11, 1939."[176]

Moreover, the government wanted all to understand that the conspiracy was not the product of a handful of colluding businessmen. The alleged collusion permeated senior management. In long columns on page after page, prosecutors listed numerous senior executives, directors and officers, and entire committees of the board of directors as coconspirators. The point: The conspiracy was broad and the corporate undertakings were not renegade transactions but deep-rooted official policy.[177]

The streetcar conspiracy trial caused a sensation throughout the country, especially in the dozens of cities listed in the indictment. Typical was the headline in the *New York Times*: TRANSIT LINE PLOT LAID TO NINE FIRMS. All the companies promptly issued denials along the lines of the one released by Standard Oil of California: "Standard unequivocally denies that they participated in any conspiracy or any other arrangement to acquire control of transportation . . . monopolize or restrain trade, or exclude competition."[178]

The defendants hired some of the best defense attorneys in the nation. The case dragged on for two years in both California and then, when the venue was changed, in Chicago. Prosecutors were up against not just one or two defense lawyers, but multiple teams of defense lawyers who filed motion after motion over the smallest question and demanded strict proof at every turn. The paperwork extended for yards. Of particular interest were long motions and debates over what instructions the judge could issue to the jury, with strict attention to the issues they could and could not consider. That argument was important. The case was universally considered one of the most complex and precedent-setting conspiracy trials in recent memory, and the first to have such issues go to a jury.[179]

The so-called "housewife jury," composed of a dozen Chicago women identified in the press as "housewives," returned their verdict. None of the women understood high finance. Not a few had relatives gainfully employed in the automotive and transportation industry. Indeed, the judge reminded the women paternalistically to sign the verdict using their own names, and not to use their husbands' names, as in "Mrs. John Smith." On March 12, 1949, they delivered their decision.[180]

Count 1: Conspiracy to secure control of transit systems. Not guilty.[181]

Count 2: Conspiracy to monopolize the transit business for their own oil, tires, and buses. Guilty as charged.[182]

Forty-two cities in sixteen states were converted, and dozens more targeted. Millions of Americans were affected. Some $9.5 million was invested. On April 1, 1949, the judge handed down his sentence: a $5,000 fine to each corporate defendant except Standard, which was fined $1,000. As for Fitzgerald and his coconspirators, they too were fined. Each was ordered to "forfeit and pay to the United States of America a fine in the amount of one dollar."[183]

The cases were appealed—even the one-dollar penalties. It went all the way to the U.S. Supreme Court, which allowed the convictions to stand. The government filed a civil action against the same circle of companies trying to stop their continued conduct. The government was unsuccessful.[184] Moreover, the penalties were never adjusted to more than one dollar per executive. At those rates, GM and its combine felt they could continue the same conduct. National City Lines continued to acquire and convert systems.

In most cities, streetcar service had been allowed to deteriorate slowly only to be replaced by motor-bus service that was allowed to deteriorate on the fast track. Once National City Lines took over, fares were hiked, routes were truncated, transfers were eliminated, and schedules reduced. These unpopular changes became a standard operating procedure, so much so, the company undertook them almost instinctively.

A March 13, 1946, internal National City Lines memo written shortly after the company took over the Tampa system was typical. "In the event we maintain a 5 cent fare in Tampa," the memo advised the Chicago head-quarters, "without transfer privileges, my thought was to terminate all routes downtown. In other words, eliminate all crosstown through service."[185]

The day motorization occurred in Tampa, a local newspaper editorial complained, "Will Tampa Transit Lines, Inc. which will have a monopoly because of the discontinuance of the street car system, furnish the service the people need and want?" Drastic reductions in service decreed from Chicago quickly answered the question. Shortly after Tampa's service was curtailed, several hundred residents filed formal petitions with City Hall to restore service. National City Lines persevered, claiming it could not run buses over unpaved streets.[186]

Mobile, Alabama, was equally unsettled by service reductions. A letter to City Hall from the area director of the War Manpower Commission, written July 9, 1945, just weeks after the war in Europe concluded, questioned whether National City Lines even intended to run a proper service. "It is my considered judgment," the federal manpower director wrote, "that a comparison of the Company's schedule runs as of, for example, July 1944 with July 1945 will reveal a reduction in service well beyond any decline in employment or reduction in local demand for service. The reduction is clearly not due to any shortage in equipment. I am reliably informed that the Company has disposed of a number of busses and now has additional busses idly parked here in Mobile. I note also that the employment of the Company has declined from 368 in March of this year to 304 on our most recent report."[187]

In Port Arthur, Texas, residents complained, "Big areas here are not served by buses—some not at all and others not satisfactorily. . . . Before we begin paying higher fares, I think we are entitled to substantially improved service."[188]

In Beaumont, Texas, the mayor himself dispatched an urgent telegram to the National City Lines regional office in East St. Louis, Illinois. "Believe that it is imperative," the mayor wired, "that something be done about bus service immediately. We average fifty complaints daily and have received five or six petitions. I frankly think the answer is more busses in service during the peak hours. Please consider this wire a personal one. Otho Plumer, Mayor City of Beaumont." Proving that National City Lines possessed the resources to do it right when pressured by officials, the Chicago headquarters immediately dispatched six modern buses, then four more, for a total of ten suddenly provided to Beaumont.[189]

Residents of the largest cities such as Los Angeles, Baltimore, and St. Louis were just as dissatisfied as their counterparts in smaller urban centers. A letter to the *Los Angeles Times* during that city's 1946 transit strike complained that National City Lines was of course making "substantial earnings" because it imposed overcrowding on its underserviced lines. "Almost every bus," wrote the upset reader, "regardless of the time of day, carries double the number of passengers it should carry." The theme was echoed in publication after publication, such as a lead October 1947 article in the *Los Angeles Herald and Express* illustrated with irked crowds trying to cram through the narrow doors of a narrow bus. The *Los Angeles Herald and Express* article bemoaned the indicted Fitzgerald clan's takeover of the Los Angeles transit system and the shrinkage of service. "In Los Angeles," the magazine declared, "the curtailment of the trolley lines into bus lines already jammed, and in a city swiftly growing, has created an uproar."[190]

In the 1950s, other factors not related to monopolistic collusion conjoined to undermine the viability of the bus companies. Running segregated buses in the apartheid South was neither cheap nor efficient. National City Lines subsidiaries in the South were expected to obey and enforce racist transit laws. Therefore, along many Southern routes National City Lines operated separate colored and white buses. This played havoc with schedules, cost, and customer satisfaction. No white or black person in a rush or in the rain wanted to see one or more buses pass him by because they were for the wrong skin color. Sometimes drivers were arrested for breaking the rules and picking up a black woman in the rain in a white bus. When buses were finally consolidated in a city, "coloreds" were required to ride in the back of the bus. Drivers were given police powers in this regard. Sometimes drivers did the arresting or called the police and signed the complaint. Occasionally, the policy resulted in blacks being beaten and removed from a bus. Segregated transit had economic consequences not only because such systems were expensive, but because black bus boycotts broke out with regularity. Boycotts were local, but their impact was felt far beyond the city limits by National City Lines.[191]

A typical November 1946 weekly report to Chicago headquarters from the Jackson, Mississippi, subsidiary explained, "Last week it was necessary for one of our operators to call the police officer for a colored passenger that refused to move back from the front of the bus so white passengers could be loaded. This colored passenger's name Elport Chess had to be taken off the bus by force by the police and it was necessary for the police officer to strike him with his club in order to subdue him. . . . This colored party was a G. I. Veteran with five years in the Pacific and was attending the colored school. . . . As a result of this negro being arrested, the colored school children at the school he attended boycotted the busses."[192]

In December 1955, a woman named Rosa Parks riding the Montgomery bus refused to move to the back. She was arrested, and this sparked a broad boycott, expensive litigation, and the modern civil rights movement. The bus had become a flash point in urban society.

After World War II, metro transit service declined in popularity for a web of reasons. New automobile sales exploded. Cities mushroomed, creating a historic nation-changing urban and suburban sprawl. Cars became the desired mode of traffic. The advent of the interstate highway system transformed automotive transportation. But the network was justified less as a transportation necessity than as a Cold War national defense measure. In fact, interstate development came under the portfolio of the secretary of defense, who helped name the road network the National System of Interstate and Defense Highways, also known as the interstates. The growth took many by surprise.[193]

In 1952, federal highway legislation authorized a meager $25 million annually for the fiscal years 1955 and 1956. Such spending was always authorized two to three years in advance. But in 1953, Dwight D. Eisenhower's incoming secretary of defense made highway construction a national priority like never before. An astonishing $350 million was spent during the next fiscal periods, from 1956 to 1957, yielding the beginnings of a state-of-the-art highway system. Additional millions in construction money were permanently locked away in a new economic creation, the highway trust fund. Moreover, these new highways would not only link cities, they would also link neighborhoods and suburbs within a metropolis.[194]

But while millions of hard-lobbied dollars were devoted to automotive transport and road building, little was done for mass transit. No money was allocated for urban systems, which stagnated as a public became more and more unwilling to ride. Just when mass transit needed it most, during the country's postwar industrial boom, the emphasis was turned to internal combustion and done so against a backdrop of fiery mass approval. The secretary of defense marshaling the great new highway expansion was Charles Wilson, who from 1941 to 1952 had served as president of GM.[195]

At his confirmation hearings, Senator Robert Hendrickson (R–New Jersey) pointedly challenged Wilson, asking whether he had a conflict of interest considering his forty thousand dollar shares of GM stock and years of loyalty to the controversial Detroit company. Bluntly asked if he could make a decision in the country's interest that was contrary to GM's interest, Wilson shot back with his famous comment, "I cannot conceive of one because for years I thought what was good for our country was good for General Motors, and vice versa. The difference did not exist. Our company is too big."[196]

New highway construction resculpted America's cities and the country's sense of mobility. The concomitant abandonment of transit financing for American cities ensured that the national love affair with the automobile came at the expense of mass transit—electric or gas-burning. Congestion, pollution, and the petropolitical consequences of moving atop a fulcrum of oil were always understood by policymakers.

Highways became the new rivers and the new railroads, and they brought democracy to every driver—white or black. One man, one vote. Soon one man, one car. The expressway and interstates divided and conquered America's cities. Where they coursed, they gave breath to towns and neighborhoods. But that breath was blackened and thickened, and the economic lungs of the country became polluted and addicted.

Nineteenth-century transit systems were rarely updated to the twentieth-century realities of metropolitan life. As the decades progressed, the beloved trolleys and electric buses were not reconfigured into dedicated tramways, trolleyways, and busways. Yet cars were given express highways to radically update their viability. Midstreet tracks made less and less sense for overcongested cities. Trolleys simply never changed with the times. Automobiles did. Urban planners and managers allowed the neglect without regard for the environmental, economic, or political consequences.

One by one, the transit systems failed—not just those controlled by National City Lines, but also the largest and the smallest independents.

None of them could compete against the sexed-up, finned-up, high-octane, go-anywhere, drink-gas-like-water automobile. Chiffon and chrome, glitz and guzzle, were transduced to an automobile culture without compare.

The combine that ran National City Lines was not civic-minded. They were profit-minded. In the fifties, National City Lines joined the national mania to move to the internal combustion machine. As the firm systematically raised fares and reduced service, its systems became less and less acceptable to the public. In 1956, fares were raised. Champaign-Urbana fares rose from 12 cents to 15 cents. Stockton's three tokens that cost 35 cents now cost 40 cents. East St. Louis's fares went from 13 cents to 15 cents. Baltimore's first zone was increased from 18 cents to 20 cents. St. Louis's weekly permit went from 75 cents to 90 cents.[197]

As ridership crumbled, National City Lines began selling off its dying systems to the cities and counties that could not exist without them. It did so at a profit. From Kalamazoo to Los Angeles, the holding company began liquidating its transit lines, pleading economic necessity but reaping millions from the sales. The company's 1957 annual report to stockholders notes, "During the year of 1957, the City of Kalamazoo leased the bus system of Kalamazoo City Lines, Inc., on terms comparable to the Jackson lease reported last year. Both leases have been operating very satisfactorily. . . . [198]

"As stated in the last annual report, the franchise of Tulsa City Lines, Inc. expired June 30, 1957, and the company is being liquidated. It is anticipated the final liquidation will give a profit to National City Lines, Inc. The garage building formerly occupied by Terre Haute City Lines, Inc., has been leased to the Highway Commissioners of Vigo County, who have an option to purchase it. Both the lease and the option are on terms very favorable to National City Lines, Inc.[199]

"Los Angeles Transit Lines sold its operating properties to Los Angeles Metropolitan Transit Authority, a municipal corporation, on March 3, 1958, and is now in process of liquidation. It is anticipated that this will bring an eventual profit to National City Lines, Inc., of at least $6,500,000 after all taxes."[200]

National City Lines profits were not channeled into mass transit for other viable cities but into truck rental firms, such as a new subsidiary called National City Truck Rental. Proceeds from system sell-offs were also used to acquire existing freight carriers such as United Motor Express and Sioux City Motor Express. After investing in trucks, National City

Lines turned next to aircraft. The company provided the paperwork needed to secure tax breaks for leased aircraft. An annual report described the aircraft business as "strictly financial transactions, that is, the company performs no service in connection with the airplanes."[201]

Hence the profits of National City Lines' urban transit companies were systematically exhaled into other petroleum-based transportation businesses, giving them new life, but leaving those original neglected municipal systems to fend for themselves. Generally taxpayers did the fending—and the moneys were always insufficient. With lines reduced and mortally underfunded, Americans often had little recourse but to turn to automobiles to get from here to there, for work or play. In the fifties, gas was cheap. New cars became an acquired birthright. The national reliance on automobiles only deepened as transit systems fell from grace—whether they were owned by National City Lines or independents.

The men of National City Lines cultivated a mentality that influenced mass transit throughout the nation. Executives of their dozens of subsidiaries were sought after by other transit companies seeking to abandon trolleys and join the modern era of urban transit. When these executives transplanted themselves, they brought their years of corporate conduct with them. After the trial and conviction, GM placed mileage between the company and the Fitzgeralds. GM no longer needed conspiratorial rings. A community of bus-thinking, trolley-abhorring transit experts and officials took root throughout the American transportation establishment.

At the top of the National City Lines operational hierarchy was B. M. (Barney) Larrick, the conglomerate's operations manager who for twenty years had been deployed by the company in city after city, where he would convert trolley lines, break unions, raise fares, and outmaneuver politicians who did not promote the National City Lines agenda. The conglomerate had brought Larrick to Los Angeles, Oakland, Pasadena, Salt Lake City, Tampa, and many other cities precisely because he was so effective at transforming transit systems.[202]

But in 1948, in the throes of the federal prosecution, Larrick left National City Lines to sell his considerable skills to any independent system that would pay his price. His modus operandi was to spend two years raising fares, converting streetcars to motor buses or expanding the existing bus fleet, and then move on to the next city. His first such stint was as president and general manager of Miami's transit lines, which had already switched to buses and under Larrick were about to undergo a bus expansion. Two years later, Larrick moved up to Buffalo to assume the post of general manager of that city's system, which had also just converted and was in the midst of a bus expansion program. National City Lines did not own either the Miami or Buffalo system, but where Larrick went, he brought the National City Lines style of doing business and a determination to place more GM buses on local streets.[203]

The Twin City Rapid Transit Company in Minneapolis–St. Paul was considered by many to be a model urban transit system. The much loved Minneapolis–St. Paul trolley system traced its heritage back to nineteenth-century horse-drawn operations. The firm was owned by some three thousand shareholder citizens nationwide, led by a circle of major stockholders who saw the enterprise as a civic duty. During the twenty-year span that preceded World War II, the directors had virtually sworn off dividends, even though the stock traded on the New York Stock Exchange for as much as $108. During the war years when trolley systems made strong profits because of gasoline rationing, the company used its excess cash to pay down more than half its $14 million debt, and to purchase a fleet of sleek, new streetcars. For some reason, probably lack of financial self-boosting, the company's stock had dwindled to just $10 a share and was therefore massively undervalued. This caught the sharp eye of New York gangland financier Charles Green, who in 1949 jumped at the chance to make a market killing. He purchased six thousand shares.[204]

But when no dividends materialized, an unhappy Green started a fierce crusade against the existing management. He wrote an incendiary letter to the three thousand other stockholders demanding the board's resignation. At the same time, Twin City Rapid Transit Company began showing the results of the national turndown in ridership—a 41 percent decline for Minneapolis–St. Paul. Therefore, shortly after Green's buy-in, the company reported a significant deficit and this only enraged Green further. He demanded service be slashed to save money and generate dividends. When the president of the transit line refused, Green snickered, "All offers are off. We'll play winner takes all."[205]

Green wanted a vicious proxy war. He was that kind of guy. Green described himself as "always ready to make a fast buck." But he needed help. He turned to the state's most notorious gangster, a thug who had been arrested and/or tried for a range of crimes from simple bootlegging and pickpocketing to murder and kidnapping. This gangster's most recent murder trial was for the 1935 machine-gunning of journalist Walter

Liggett in front of the newspaperman's wife and daughter. Green turned to Isadore Blumenfeld, aka Kid Cann.[206]

Cann, himself a minority stockholder of Twin City Rapid Transit, was also concerned about dividends. The racketeer Cann suggested they team up with a friend of his, Fred Ossanna, a two-fisted attorney for Yellow Cab Company and a local labor union. Ossanna had a knack for slush funds, kickbacks, and bribery. Ossanna and Cann would head up Green's proxy war.[207]

Green, Ossanna, and Cann met frequently at a known mob hangout, Club Carnival, to discuss tactics. They decided to commence an elaborate mail campaign to stockholders across the United States to attract enough proxies "to oust them [senior management] at the next stockholders meeting." The proxy campaign was successful. Green won out, becoming president of Twin City Rapid Transit. He advocated an immediate fare hike. The Minnesota Railroad and Warehouse Commission had just voted a penny hike to twelve cents. Not enough. Green insisted on a rise to fifteen cents and then seventeen cents.[208] Or else.

Or else what? The Minnesota Railroad and Warehouse Commission wanted to know. Green answered by immediately firing eight hundred employees, about 25 percent of the workforce, which reduced the payroll by $1.8 million. Schedules were slashed, leaving Twin Cities' citizens shivering in subzero weather on street corners waiting for a trolley. The public, newspapers, and regulators revolted. Just before Green carried out a threat to completely shut down the St. Paul half of the company, officials rushed into court and secured a temporary restraining order. The state, the community, and the riders demanded to know how a private company operating a public utility could act so contrary to the public interest.[209] The public?

"The public be damned!" Green yelled. "I intend to force a profit out of this company! If necessary, I'll auction off all the streetcars and buses and sell the rails for scrap iron!"[210] That is exactly what happened.

Despite the open conflict with the community, a stockholder effort to remove Green was unsuccessful. Green personally controlled more than 19,200 shares, and more through a block held by gangsters and friends of Kid Cann's. Through nominees and fronts, such as personal friends or family, shares were controlled by such hoodlums as Tommy Banks, the gambling and liquor king who jointly ruled the Minneapolis rackets with his chief accomplice, Kid Cann. Banks had purchased blocks of shares through his brother, his attorney, and McCarthy's Café, a restaurant Banks's wife was associated with, and also through numerous other partners and associates involved in pinball machines and casinos. Other shareholders included Kid Cann's personal doctor and childhood friends of Kid Cann's. Eventually, the stockholder's registry was brimming with mob-connected personalities, such as Phillip "Flippy" Share, previously imprisoned for the cigarette torture of a boy, the bombing of a restaurant, and kidnapping, and who was twice arrested for murder. The stockholder list even included Charles Holleran, an associate of both Banks and the infamous Jake "Greasy Thumb" Guzik, the financial brain and a collector for Al Capone.[211]

The Minnesota Railroad and Warehouse Commission concluded that Ossanna controlled 12,600 shares, Banks and associates controlled 15,800 shares, and Cann controlled 10,800 shares.[212]

"Over 25 per cent of the Twin City Rapid Transit stock is held by persons of questionable character," complained commission chairman Leonard E. Lindquist. "It is obvious that this is a strong enough faction to control management votes." The comments were in Lindquist's report to both the governor of Minnesota and the Special Senate Committee on Organized Crime in Interstate Commerce, headed up by Senator Carey Estes Kefauver (D-Tennessee). The crime commission that riveted America's attention in the early 1950s was commonly known as the Kefauver Committee.[213]

Lindquist also told the governor, "While the holdings of Mr. Ossanna, Kid Cann, Tommy Banks and associates may not constitute a numerical majority of the outstanding stock, so much of the other stock is . . . in small lots or in the hands of people living at distant points that the combined holdings of Ossanna, Kid Cann, Tommy Banks and associates are sufficient in actual practice for them to exercise effective control of this company."[214]

Green handily rebuffed the March 1950 effort to oust him as president. He was reelected and was more determined than ever to destroy the trolley system and convert to GM buses. But soon Green was deposed by Ossanna and Cann in a power play for the reins of the company. Ossanna and Cann had rallied their own proxy votes, 192,000 over Green's 73,000. Police expected violence at the March 1951 stockholder meeting that would decide the issue. Green was frisked at the door, and his revolver taken. But once inside, the parties agreed to disagree peacefully. Green just resigned.[215]

Now Ossanna was in charge. He took over from Green as president. But the campaign to destroy the trolleys was still a mantra of management. Ossanna liked everything about the bus conversion. First and foremost, the conversion would help him loot the company. Ossanna wanted a slush fund established to bribe city officials. When he was at Yellow Cab, he had created slush funds and mastered political bribery by securing kickbacks from suppliers. Now Ossanna suggested that kickbacks be used based on fuel purchases for some 350 buses. "That is the way we built up a slush fund at Yellow Taxi," said Ossanna, Green later testified.[216]

But acquiring GM modern diesel buses would take money. Ossanna approached the local banks, but with the uproar over gangster ownership and the shattered public image, the company's credit was no good. So Ossanna contacted GM executive vice president Roger Kyes about helping them finance 25 new diesels. Kyes, who would later become deputy secretary of defense under GM's Wilson, was more than receptive to Ossanna's request. Kyes sent in a team of experts and a survey team.[217]

After GM's team of experts visited Minneapolis in 1951 to survey the facts on the ground, Kyes was encouraged about Twin City Rapid Transit and its management. Despite the community revolt and the public charges of racketeer control and credit unworthiness, GM found in Ossanna and his circle of managers people that the Detroit corporation could do business with. Just a few weeks later, Ossanna was invited to Kyes's office in Detroit. Kyes was said by some to have the "personality of a pit bull." One senior executive colleague described him as a "spooky guy." But Ossanna and Kyes apparently found common ground, and Ossanna left their meeting shocked and jubilant. GM had offered the scandalized company not just 25 buses, but twenty-one times that number—525—and all on favorable credit terms.[218]

Quickly, Larrick, previously of National City Lines, was brought in by Ossanna to be general manager and oversee the conversion. More than 700 streetcars, including 141 state-of-the-art trolleys, would have to be taken out of service and replaced with the 525 buses to achieve the conversion.[219]

Many believed the conversion would take a half decade. It took only two years. Ossanna went on a rampage of conversion. First 700 trolleys were systematically idled. Then the rails, copper, and equipment were sold as scrap metal. Then real estate was disposed of. Who bought the trolley infrastructure and land? American Iron and Supply and Mid-Continent

Development and Construction, both of which were controlled by Kid Cann and another hoodlum stockholder, Harry Isaacs. For example, Kid Cann and Isaacs bought two substations for approximately $225,000, and then split a fast $57,000 profit. Another $500,000 in iron and copper was purchased by American Iron as scrap under advantageous terms for speedy resale.[220]

As for the trolleys, old and brand-new, some of them were sold to systems in Mexico City, Newark, and Cleveland, but none of that was fast enough for Ossanna and Larrick. India offered to barter jute bags, Brazil offered coffee beans, and Argentina offered beef, but the trolleys could not be sold off as quickly as Ossanna wanted.[221] But Ossanna had a schedule to keep if those 525 shiny new GM diesel buses were to roll across the streets of Minneapolis and St. Paul. Ossanna wanted every trolley gone—and he wanted them gone faster than anyone could manage.

So he decided to burn them. One by one, Ossanna's men isolated the streetcars and torched them.

```
May 14, 1952
Mr. L.G. Bakken
Gen. Supt. of Transportation
Minneapolis, Minnesota


Dear Sir:
The following cars were burned on May 14, 1952: 1272, 1279, 1280,
1282, 1281, 1277, 1278, and 1401.


Very truly yours,
H.P. Jacobson
Cc: B.M. Larrick222


Dear Sir:
The following cars were burned on May 15, 1952: 1284, and 1348. Dear
Sir: The following cars were burned on June 13, 1952: 59, 1254,
1273, 1274, 1276, 1347, 1507. Dear Sir: The following cars were
burned on August 20, 1952: 1612, 16, 1731, 1728, 4.223
```

Ossanna wanted it faster. Day after day, the skies over Minneapolis and St. Paul carried the billowing smoke.

Dear Sir:

The following cars were burned on September 12, 1952: 2028, 2003, 2013, 2008, 2024, 2030, 2017, 2005. Dear Sir: The following cars were burned on September 17, 1952: 2000, 2018, 2020, 2022, 2023, 2025, 2027, 2029.[224]

More. Faster.

Dear Sir:

The following cars were burned on September 19, 1952: 2006, 2009, 2015, 2016, 2010, 2026, 2021, 2019. Dear Sir: The following cars were burned on November 21, 1952: Car no. 4, 1230, 1247, 96, 2007, 48, 2012, 2014. Dear Sir: The following cars were burned on December 10, 1952: Car no. 47, 1136, 1408, 1534, 1655 and 1774.[225]

The pyres continued until June 1954, when the last streetcar was torched in spectacle fashion. Shunted to a side track, and from there pulled from the rails, the last streetcar in Minneapolis and St. Paul was shoved until it reposed in the dirt on a sad tilt. Flammables were poured over it and stuffed into its interior. Then that last trolley that had brought so many people so many places for so many years was gleefully ignited by Ossanna himself. The prone, burning streetcar, embodying the long crusade against electric traction, quickly exploded into sky-reaching flames. Out of every window and from the front door, the flames wrapped tightly around the vehicle and consumed it. Dressed in spats, Ossanna smiled for cameras as the immolation rose behind him.[226]

All of Minneapolis was watching when that last trolley was burned. The IRS intelligence unit had been watching since the beginning. Audits of American Iron's accounts revealed that conversion transactions constituted the majority of the company's business in 1954. Seventeen checks totaling $101,000 were deducted under the description "business expense."[227]

September 18, 1959, the grand jury returned true bills. Fred Ossanna, B. M. Larrick, Harry Isaacs, Isadore Blumenfeld aka Kid Cann, and others were indicted on conspiracy, mail fraud, and other charges arising out of the two-year bus conversion. Isadore Blumenfeld was also indicted separately on white-slavery charges for transporting a woman, Anita Carlson, from Miami Beach to Minneapolis for the "purpose of prostitution, debauchery and immoral practices."[228]

August 6, 1960, after five days of deliberation, the jury rendered their verdict. As the nine men and three women filed into the courtroom, all stared straight ahead, making no eye contact. The judge took four or five minutes to read through the many typewritten verdicts stuffed into the envelope handed him by the clerk, who passed it on from the jury foreman.[229]

Ossanna and Larrick, both guilty as charged: six counts of mail fraud, two counts of wire fraud, and three counts of interstate shipment of stolen property. Isaacs, guilty of five counts on the same charges. They were all sentenced to prison time.[230]

Except Kid Cann. Once again, he beat the rap. The jury somehow found him not guilty.[231]

For decades, questions have haunted every aspect of the GM Conspiracy. Did GM by its actions and those of its cohorts allied with National City Lines "kill mass transit" in America? The answer: absolutely not.

National City Lines acquired control of less than one hundred cities. Many of those cities, such as Tulsa, East St. Louis, and Salt Lake City, were important but limited components of the nation's overall transit picture. True, National City Lines also gained control of some of the biggest systems in America, such as those in Los Angeles, Oakland, St. Louis, Baltimore, and Philadelphia. However, the dozens of cities affected taken together still constituted less than a majority of the ridership in America.

But did GM try? The answer: yes.

During GM's conspiracy trial, National City Lines was compelled to provide a list of dozens of additional cities targeted by the conspirators. These purchase efforts had been under way, but unsuccessful as of the trial date. But the acquisition of new territories became more likely as each new city system was converted, and as an entire generation of transit officials was led to believe that internal combustion was better. Therefore the list is revealing about the ultimate aims of the combine. The list given to the court revealed that some of the most important systems in the nation were eyed for future conversion, additional consolidation, or additional investment. In several areas that were already converted, the list demonstrates the intent to wipe out the last vestiges of independent lines in those cities. The list:

In New York: Albany, Binghamton, Elmira, Schenectady, and Staten Island. In Illinois: Chicago—both its regional commuter trains and its local rapid transit lines, plus Peoria, Rock Island, Moline, and Springfield. In Massachusetts: Boston and Worcester. In Michigan: Flint and Grand Rapids. In California: Sacramento and Santa Barbara. In Florida: Miami,

Miami Beach, Pensacola, and St. Petersburg. *In Ohio:* Akron, Cincinnati, Cleveland, Columbus, Sandusky, and Youngstown.[232]

In Pennsylvania: Allentown, Oil City, Reading, Pittsburgh, Scranton, and York. *In Alabama:* Anniston and Gadsden. *In Arizona:* Phoenix and Tucson. *In Arkansas:* Hot Springs and Little Rock. *In Georgia:* Columbus, Rome, and Savannah. *In Indiana:* Indianapolis, Evansville, Muncie, Fort Wayne, and Gary. *In Iowa:* Clinton, Davenport, Waterloo, and Cedar Falls. *In Kansas:* Topeka and Wichita. *In Kentucky:* Covington, Lexington, and Louisville. *In Louisiana:* Alexandria and Baton Rouge.[233]

Plus many more in Maine, Maryland, Minnesota, Missouri, New Hampshire, North and South Carolina, Oregon, Tennessee, Texas, Utah, Virginia, Washington, West Virginia, and Wisconsin.[234]

Why did GM fail in its national designs? The answer: The company was stopped by prosecutors in 1947, but thereafter found that the motorized transit revolution GM and its cohorts had set in motion had caught fire across the nation and now burned of its own volition. By the fifties, conspiracies were no longer necessary. It was just progress.

Did GM deliberately convert electric traction systems to bus systems with the intent to then cause the demise of those companies, leaving nothing but automobiles to clog cities? The answer: No, there is not a single line of evidence in thousands of pages of documentation to suggest this. GM wanted to sell buses. But in many ways, that is what happened anyway.

The rapacious crippling and looting of mass transit by GM, its co-conspirators, and the independent owners of systems, juxtaposed with the meteoric rise of the automobile, naturally led to the systematic decline of urban transit. But it is also important to remember that GM struck mainly where city systems were weak and vulnerable, where city planners had left streetcars and electric buses out of urban progress, and where policymakers did not think twice about the harmful changes they were systematically bestowing upon the nation.

None of the comparative economic numbers can be believed because in so many instances the transit systems had been fleeced and manipulated long before GM ever arrived. Moreover, no one ever factored in the cost to the environment, the cost to human health, and above all, the reality that trolleys never needed an army or a navy to support their fuel source. Motor buses did. Buses used petroleum, which from 1928 was increasingly coming from an unstable Middle East. No one ever added in the military costs. As such, the portrayal of internal-combustion versus electric costs may be the biggest financial scandal of the twentieth century.

Ironically, during the same decades when trolleys, light rail, and electric buses were deemed to be obsolete, unworkable, and unusable in American cities, they flourished throughout the world, in all the great cities of Europe, in the congested nations of Asia, and the spread-out urban centers of Latin America. Across the globe, trolleys have been and continue to be mainstays of city living, successfully woven into the transit fabric of the twenty-first century. But not in America, which is only now returning to the decades-old concept of trolleys and electric buses.

Therefore, when GM stood in the dock to face charges of conspiracy, and when it bristled at the report of Snell and others who documented its activities, the company should not have been alone. Its crime—limited or not, economic or more—could never have occurred without the neglect and participation of policymakers and the public itself. When GM and its collaborators were indicted, when they were prosecuted, when they were convicted, and when they were reviled, public policy and the American public, singly and severally, were unindicted coconspirators, and they should coequally have shared the blame.

GM may have killed some important fraction of mass transit. But the policymakers who let it happen—they got away with murder.

CHAPTER ELEVEN

MANHATTAN NOW

A century of lies about internal combustion arising from a millennium of monopolistic misconduct in energy has wounded the world's collective health, fractured a fragile environment, and ignited a deadly petropolitical war that has become nothing less than a cataclysmic clash of cultures. Oil is the root of all this tribulation. In energy as in politics, power corrupts. Through the ages, power has indeed corrupted those who need it, those who produce it, and those who control it. Today our high-energy world teeters at the brink. The gauge is edging toward empty, and as it does, the political, environmental, medical, and economic costs continue to squeeze humanity. The crisis is not new, but more urgent.

Tragically, from the first barges of coal controlled by the Hostmen of Newcastle centuries ago, to the choking pollutants of steam locomotives, to the scandal-plagued development of the battery of the nineteenth century, to Edison and Ford's struggle to mass-produce their electric car in 1914, to the abandonment of urban mass transit, the world has cried out for sweeping solutions to correct the mistakes undertaken in the name of energy. Those mistakes have left the twenty-first century a hostage to internal combustion, which consumes some 63 percent of America's petroleum use. Yet a legacy of corporate looting, deception, manipulation, and misinformation has so successfully obscured the facts that society can't discern the true energy solutions for our petroliferous society. Many do not even comprehend the true problems that internal combustion has wrought.

No one needs a book to stay current on the health consequences of the internal combustion machine, or the alternative sources and technology to overcome it. The latest information is continuously delivered by the fast-paced media of the day, from official Web sites, television and radio, to the nation's magazines and newspapers. But all too often, the enormity of the threat to public health and the sensible alternatives are lost in the incremental coverage.

Start with health. In a word, we are killing ourselves by the mile.

Driving internal combustion machines does to the world's population what cigarette smoking does to the individual. Tailpipe emissions from diesel- and gasoline-burning vehicles contain toxic nitrogen dioxide, carbon monoxide, as well as arsenic, formaldehyde, chromium, and a poisoned well of other ingredients. This brew also contains fine particulate matter. These particles embed in the lungs of everyone who breathes the air that trucks and automobiles befoul. Smaller toxic substances—ultrafine particles or nanoparticles—can penetrate the lung's membranes and contaminate the blood. Nitrogen oxide and hydrocarbons combine with sunlight to create ozone, which irritates the lungs and eyes. The result is elevated levels of heart and blood diseases, cancers, nervous system toxicity, and impairments to fetal development resulting in low birth weight and premature deliveries. Asthma has become epidemic. One in six children in California's Central Valley carries an inhaler to school. Lung cancer has become the nation's leading form of cancer.[1]

It has been difficult to separate out exactly how many deaths are caused by engine exhaust, but the American Lung Association estimates the national death toll from particle pollution to be in the tens of thousands annually. California's Air Resources Board and the American Lung Association of California believe fine and ultrafine particulate matter from all pollution sources now kill as many Americans annually as traffic accidents and secondhand smoke. In California alone, all forms of air pollution annually cause some nine thousand premature deaths, nine thousand hospitalizations, 1.7 million cases of respiratory illness, 1.3 million school absences, and 2.8 million lost workdays, according to the state's Air Resources Board.[2] How much of that air pollution damage is attributable to exhaust pipes?

Transportation sources account for some 60 to 90 percent of all air pollution in Los Angeles County and three adjacent counties, according to estimates of California's Air Resources Board and the South Coast Air Quality Management District, which encompasses four Los Angeles–area counties. What's more, state air-quality officials acknowledge that the nation's top five ozone-polluted areas and eight of the top ten particulate-polluted counties are in California.[3]

The U.S. Environmental Protection Agency estimates that 60 percent of all carbon dioxide emissions are spewed by motor vehicles, and in some cities the number is as high as 95 percent. Nonroad vehicles employing petroleum-based engines add to the transportation sector's overall pollution profile.[4]

Internal combustion kills. Few of us realize that, as we drive to nonsmoking restaurants, everyone around us is inhaling toxic gases as deadly as that in any cigarette.

Because mass transit was fatally undermined and America's love affair with the automobile has only deepened, and because car-enabled metropolitan sprawl has become an immutable urban reality, congestion has added its own miasmic dimension. Most suburban families now operate two or three automobiles, which collectively take a dozen trips daily, annually turning odometers 31,000 miles per vehicle. Highway traffic is up 130 percent since 1973 when the oil shock first woke us from oil-induced slumber. In America, more than 80 percent of all trips are now made by automobile, which is double the European number. Europe enjoys extensive urban and intercity transit systems, which reduce auto traffic. In 1996, road congestion cost America's top seventy cities an aggregate $74 billion for 4.6 billion lost hours and 6.7 billion wasted gallons of fuel, according to the Texas Transportation Institute; a decade later, these numbers are even more dramatic.[5]

Certainly, a nation in gridlock massively wears away at productivity and heightens toxic levels, but it also creates what experts call "environmental injustice." The same amount of pollution will not affect all communities in an area equally. Those who dwell and work along the highways, commonly lower-income minority groups, suffer most because those toxic effects are concentrated most along the source—the highway itself. Moreover, during congested times, the same number of cars will spew that much more in tailpipe emissions because of idling, bumper-to-bumper traffic and the very nature of clogged rush-hour traffic. A map pinpointing cancer concentrations in an urbanized area, such as greater Los Angeles, reveals frightening veins of deadly hot spots coursing on either side of the highway.[6] The expressways themselves have become the slow killing fields of our transportation system.

Environmental damage caused by the petroleum industry and its consumers is earth-shattering, literally. Oil spills such as that of the *Exxon Valdez* inflict severe local ecological disasters where they occur. The *Exxon Valdez* spilled 10.8 million gallons into Alaska's Prince William Sound in March 1989, devastating the shore along with the area's sea life, birds, and furry animals. The *Exxon Valdez* incident is famous, but hardly the largest spill in recent years. Saddam Hussein's intentional destruction of Kuwaiti oil wells caused 24 million to 60 million gallons of crude to gush into the Persian Gulf. But the largest spill on record is from Pemex's Ixtoc I; from June 3, 1979, until it was capped forty-two weeks later, Ixtoc I dumped an estimated 151.2 million gallons of crude into the Gulf of Mexico, most of which floated toward the Texas coastline.[7]

The list of major oil spills is long and spans the globe. In fact, during the past twenty years, the world has witnessed thirty oil spills larger than the *Exxon Valdez*. During the 1990s, 346 spills occurred in excess of two thousand gallons, or about 10.6 million gallons annually—that is, an additional *Exxon Valdez* every year.[8]

What a spill can do as a huge incident, all of us do incrementally. Daily gasoline runoff from streets, driveways, and other domestic leaks pour nearly 11 million gallons—equal once again to an *Exxon Valdez* spill—into American waterways every eight months, according to the National Academy of Sciences. The damage from all these spills—from slight to very *Exxon Valdez*—lasts years longer than scientists originally thought.[9] The food chain and the world's waters are progressively being poisoned, as are the coastlines; the damage is worsening faster than nature's ability to repair itself.

What oil does to the water, it also does to the land. Coastlines suffer from oil spills with the familiar scenes of tar-coated shores, blackened and crippled birds, and hapless furry creatures unable to come clean. But the environmental destruction from routine exploration, drilling, extraction, refining, and distribution can exceed the damage of a major oil spill, according to a University of California study. Adverse ecological effects include deforestation of large tracts of wooded regions, chemical contamination of land, and concomitant harm to whole animal populations.[10]

What's more, America's oil and gas industry creates more solid and liquid waste than all other municipal, agricultural, mining, and industrial sources combined. In 1995, the American oil industry by itself spawned 146 million barrels of drilling waste and 22 million barrels of so-called associated wastes. Associated wastes include the "produced water" used in drilling operations. This water is often discharged into the American water system, yet it is at least four times saltier than ocean water and commonly contains megaconcentrations of toxins such as benzene, xylene, and ethylbenzene. Produced water can in some instances be a hundred times more radioactive than nuclear power plant effluent.[11]

What oil does to the water and land, it also does to earth's atmosphere. Every gallon of gasoline used spews twenty-four pounds of heat-trapping emissions, vastly heavier than the gasoline itself, according to the Union of Concerned Scientists. A heat-trapping blanket—causing the famous "greenhouse effect"—has enveloped the earth. America consumes about a quarter of the world's oil. Total American tailpipe emissions generate two-thirds of the carbon monoxide, a third of the nitrogen oxides, and more than 27 percent of the country's overall contribution to the greenhouse effect, which has pushed our planet into global warming.[12] Some say the damage may soon be irreversible.

Global warming is raising the seas, changing and intensifying climates, rewriting the wind patterns, and shifting plant and animal populations. Arctic and antarctic ice is suddenly melting more rapidly than anyone expected, which is raising the level of the sea. Scientists fear that key glacial structures have begun melting, thus allowing an accelerated meltdown of other ice sheets. Indeed, Antarctica is losing as much as 36 cubic miles of ice annually. Alpine and Alaskan glaciers are melting far more rapidly than anyone expected. In Alaska, some homes are now dropping through holes in the thinning permafrost. In 1996, detaching Greenland ice formations dropped water into the ocean in an amount equal to 90 times the water consumption of Los Angeles. In 2005, Greenland ice deposited water equal to 225 times the water consumption of Los Angeles. The British Antarctic Survey estimates that the sea may soon rise by five millimeters annually, or an inch every five years. Each vertical centimeter of sea level covers one horizontal meter of beach, according to the Intergovernmental Panel on Climate Change. A 50-centimeter rise in sea level would inundate 8,500 to 19,000 square kilometers of coastline and would dramatically impact such low-lying cities as Boston, Miami, and New York. Indeed, more than 75 percent of all humans live within 60 kilometers of a coast. Scientists fear an irreversible tipping point is upon us. There is no known human defense for so vast a world-changing high-water incursion.[13]

Global warming does not always mean a warmer place. It means there is more energy and moisture in the atmosphere, which in turn produces more rain, more violent storms more frequently, and sometimes a colder world for traditionally warm climes. Each 1.8 degree Fahrenheit (one degree centigrade) rise in temperature allows the atmosphere to hold 6 percent more water vapor. This causes more rainfall in some places and therefore longer drought in other places. Certainly weather cycles are always at play. But those cycles have been prodded and intensified by potent changes in the atmosphere and oceans due to global warming, according to numerous overlapping, international scientific studies. Since the hydrocarbon-rich industrialization of the late nineteenth century, the earth has warmed more than one degree Fahrenheit, and the mean temperature is still rising. Adding to the problem is a radical change in salt content in the rising ocean waters. Glaciers are composed of freshwater. As they melt, glaciers dilute the ocean's natural salinity and therefore change the density of surface water. Less saline, less dense, warmer surface water does not sink as readily, thereby disrupting the natural ocean currents that keep Europe temperate and the tropics tropical. One component of the Gulf Stream is already flowing about a third slower than it did during the early 1990s. Warmer waters in the Gulf of Mexico mean more frequent and suddenly explosive hurricanes. Hurricane Katrina was an example—the first of many predicted. The alphabet has become exhausted as hurricane season starts earlier in spring and extends longer into the fall and early winter.[14] Katrina's cousins are coming.

Wind currents have already changed. Westbound coast-to-coast flights take longer, require more fuel and sometimes refuel stops, and are therefore more costly. Flights east are shorter, propelled by mighty tailwinds from the west.[15]

Warmer weather is rewriting animal habitation and insect infestation. Mosquitoes are thriving in more places, and droughts force mosquitoes to migrate to moist realms, bringing disease with them. Malaria parasites take advantage of the warmer times to achieve full maturity more frequently. West Nile virus, discovered in 1937, is no longer an African disease. It is now found in many places in the United States from Brooklyn to Los Angeles, as well as such northern nations as Canada and the Czech Republic. Lyme disease, carried by deer ticks, has now exploded as the causal bacterium thrives farther and farther north, scientists suggest. The Centers for Disease Control report that Lyme disease incidence in the northeast, mid-Atlantic, and north-central states nearly doubled during the decade beginning in 1991. Higher temperatures and milder winters in Canada have allowed the mountain pine beetle to flourish, infesting and devouring vast tracts of timberlands in British Columbia and the Rocky Mountains. Entomologists predict milder temperatures will permit the beetle to easily move north and east, plundering whole forests along the way.[16]

Oil is fracturing our very world.

Petroleum, especially foreign oil, is also breaking us. In the wake of the 1973 Arab-Israeli Yom Kippur War, the Organization of Petroleum Exporting Countries (OPEC) retaliated against the industrial world for its connection to Israel with an "oil shock" that caused long lines and served as a wake-up call to America and the West. But in the decades since, the world has continued to sleepwalk. In 1973, just before OPEC's oil shock, the nominal average price of gasoline was about 39 cents per gallon; our nation imported some 30 percent of our petroleum. In twenty-first-century money, that 1973 price would equal about $1.71. In 2005, the price at times broke the $3 per gallon barrier; in 2006, industry watchers predicted a fast rise to $5 per gallon. Yet since 1973, imports have doubled to 60 percent of overall consumption. Transportation is the leading source of those additional import needs—more than 60 percent.[17] The pump price increases expected in the years to come are fundamentally unknown. They depend on wars, political instability, and hurricanes. Only hurricanes can reliably be predicted—and even those just days in advance.

The high cost of fuel has created unemployment and fiscal hardship. Expenses have dramatically risen for aviation fuel, truck fuel, fertilizers, and every other form of nontransportation petroleum product. The industrial world has been disrupted by oil price shocks four times in the past three decades. Each of the first three shocks has been followed by a recession in America. The latest 2005 price hikes have reduced U.S. gross domestic product by about $150 billion, or about 2 percent.[18]

The true price of every gallon of gasoline, adding in expenditures for tax subsidies and government programs, harm to health, environmental damage, and military operations to protect the supply, is almost impossible to reliably calculate. The range of estimates of what are called external costs is so dramatic as to be an exercise in fuzzy mathematics. It is like counting stars. We know they are out there but can only guess at the astronomical figure.

Some of the most quoted and informed studies conclude the true cost of gasoline to be between $5 and $15 per gallon, creating a yearly national pump-supporting expenditure of between about $231 billion and $1 trillion. The numbers defy hardening because the costs, such as military expenditures—amounting to about $6 billion per month in Iraq—require a political measuring stick to attribute them to oil. But this much is known about external costs: They are real and massive. The Defense Department allocates from $55 billion to $96.3 billion annually to safeguarding petroleum supplies, two-thirds of which are pumped from the Persian Gulf. Tax incentives and government programs supporting oil are estimated to be at least $38 billion and perhaps as much as $114.6 billion annually. America's 2005 energy legislation by itself extended $8 billion in tax incentives to oil producers despite the industry's record gargantuan profits. Social, health, and environmental programs add staggering sums, but segregating how much of those expenditures are rooted in petroleum is impossible, even though most experts agree the expenses are significant.[19]

While the true cost of a gallon of oil still eludes the analysts, most agree that it is a soaring number that shakes all understanding of pump price and distorts the true comparative dollar appeal of alternative fuels. No baker could sell a loaf of bread, no builder could sell a new home, and no automaker could sell a car if the external costs were double or even quadruple the actual selling price. Oil has escaped a financial accounting. Beyond mere cash expenditures, the human toll of death and dismemberment arising from America's necessary protective military presence in the Middle East as well as the harm done to the health of its citizens is incalculable. Family anguish is not measured in joules, but in jolts.

Meanwhile, since 2003, OPEC and its members have spent some $13.3 million on federal lobbying, about half of which comes from Saudi Arabia. Since 2003, oil companies have spent $59.4 million supporting the price of oil and our dependence on it. In 2005, one oil company alone, ExxonMobil, logged a string of stunning record quarterly profits. ExxonMobil's third-quarter results, after Hurricane Katrina had wiped out Gulf Coast facilities, yielded $9.9 billion. That was a three-month record. Fourth-quarter 2005 profits rose to $10.7 billion, again a record. ExxonMobil's profit of $1,146 per second could purchase enough gasoline for the average car to drive almost 10,300 miles. Quarterly profits for ExxonMobil alone for the rest of the century's first decade are predicted to continue to exceed the earnings of all nonoil Fortune 500 companies combined.[20]

Petroleum is not just financially suffocating, it has caused the biggest transfer of wealth in the twentieth century—more than all the invasions and repressive asset seizures of dictators and warmongers. In 2002, America spent $200,000 per minute—about $105 billion per year—on foreign oil. More than $25 billion was spent that year on Persian Gulf oil. By mid-2006, foreign oil payments had escalated to $500,000 per minute. Since that first "oil shock" of 1973, more than $1.16 trillion has been transferred from the United States to oil-producing nations. The next trillion, experts estimate, will be flash-transferred in the four years between 2006 and 2010.[21]

When British and French petro-imperialism invented the oil states in the years after World War I, local Arab potentates swept through the desert atop camels and steeds, looting travelers and protecting tribal water wells. *Forbes* magazine recently declared that in the three decades since the 1973 oil shock, ten new Saudi billionaires have been created along with whole tribes of millionaires—all from the transfer of industrial wealth to desert kingdoms and totalitarian regimes. When Western money transfers to the volatile Islamic Middle East, it often directly or indirectly finances anti-American and anti-Western causes, including agitation, religious intolerance, and terrorism.[22]

Petropolitics, petromilitarism, and petroterrorism have thrown our world into a true clash of cultures, one that the industrialized world antithetically rushed toward with zeal and abandon. Gasoline fumes can be intoxicating. Since the dawn of the twentieth century, the Middle East has been the object of Western oil imperialism. In those first twentieth-century years, Europe's capitals prepared for an inevitable world war of numbing proportions. France, England, and Russia eyed the Ottoman Empire of the Turks as the "Sick Man of Europe" and trembled with anticipation waiting for the sultan's realm to break apart and leave its oil-rich Middle East territories unprotected. To win this predicted war, Winston Churchill craved fast oil-burning naval ships to replace Britain's coal-burning fleet. Churchill understood the adage "oil don't grow in England," but he knew it was obtainable from Persia and Mesopotamia—that is, Iran and Iraq. Then, beginning in 1914, the men who ran the world achieved precisely what they feared most: an inevitable world war of numbing proportions.[23]

World War I: 8 million dead, 21 million wounded, 2 million missing in action, $180 billion spent. The Great War that many thought would be concluded within weeks dragged on mercilessly for nearly half a decade. In numbers that defy the darkest imagination, young men continually climbed out of muddy trenches to valiantly charge barbed wire, mines, and machine-gun fire. They were blown to bits, poisoned by gas clouds, and starved en masse in the irrepressible bloody conquest, loss, and bloody reconquest of mere meters of territory.[24]

The disastrous 1915 Gallipoli campaign alone killed more than a half million men from both sides. During the Battle of the Somme in 1916, about a million men died from all countries; on just the first day, there were 58,000 British casualties, a third of whom were killed. At Verdun in 1916, the dead and missing were generally estimated to be nearly a million. Russia lost more than any country: mobilizing 12 million, suffering 1.7 million fatalities, 5 million wounded, and 2.5 million missing or taken prisoner. Germany's numbers were almost as staggering.[25] The best explanation of why the nations of Europe went to war and sacrificed so many men was this: They just wanted to.

But from the madness that was World War I, the industrialized world was able to standardize on oil. Thomas Edison and Henry Ford's 1914 dream of an electric car in every barn and garage succumbed to the heartbreaking events of its demise. But even then, decades of recurring "oil famines" had placed the future on notice that oil was finite. The petroliferous Second Industrial Revolution was self-extinguishing.

Within days of World War I erupting in August 1914, the British invaded Mesopotamia to control the vast untapped petroleum that nation would yield more than a decade later when its first gusher came in. From the steps of Baghdad, the British commander in 1919 read a grandiose proclamation: "We come not as conquerors, but as liberators." But British officials on the ground did not stop military actions, even after the ceasefire, until in 1919 they had cobbled together a new nation from a key oil-producing region of eastern Turkey and three Mesopotamian provinces to create a new oil state. London renamed this territorial assemblage Iraq.[26]

Not being a member of the League of Nations, America was unable to help carve up the Persian Gulf colonies of the Ottoman Empire. Victorious Great Britain and France were primed to control all Middle East oil as spoils—that is, until American oil interests objected. The American Petroleum Institute and Standard Oil led the charge. Typical was the ominous report to Woodrow Wilson's administration submitted on May 13, 1919, by M. L. Requa, a former director of the U.S. Fuel Administration now working closely with the oil industry. Requa vigorously warned the undersecretary of state that America owned 90 percent of the automobiles in the world; it was the most rapidly industrializing nation on earth. The country was already forced to import more than 60 million barrels annually from Mexico. But Mexican exports were declining due to political conditions and were "dependent upon the whim of whatever desperado may be temporarily in the saddle in Mexico for the supply of fuel oil . . . to meet a deficit which the United States cannot supply." No matter how domestic reserves and growth were extrapolated, argued Requa, "our petroleum reserves . . . will not last over seventeen years."[27]

Requa stressed that the United States would run out of oil unless it secured equal access to Iraq. That caused the Wilson administration to launch the 1920 Open Door policy, which demanded that war victors Great Britain and France share Iraqi oil with U.S. oil companies. After years of oil imperialism that created oil states run by hand-selected sheikhs and British-ordained kings to sign on the dotted line, the famous but secretive 1928 Red Line Agreement carved up Iraq and adjacent regions into American, British, and French monopolies and spheres of interest. American, British, and French oil imperialism spread from Iraq to all of the Persian Gulf.[28]

The oil industry, since its inception on August 29, 1859, at a depth of 69.5 feet below the oily creek south of Titusville, Pennsylvania, has never been a free-market capitalistic enterprise. John D. Rockefeller built his oil empire on the legendary monopolistic fraud, deception, and anticompetitive conspiracies of Standard Oil. England built its oil empire on a governmentally controlled and propelled entity called the Anglo-Persian Oil Company, later renamed British Petroleum. France brought together an empire of independent importers under the government-controlled Compagnie Française des Pétroles, thus forming its national oil-producing arm. When America demanded to join as a Red Line partner, Washington encouraged key oil companies, seven at first—Standard Oil of New Jersey, Standard Oil of New York, Gulf Corporation, Atlantic Refining, Sinclair Oil, and two smaller firms—to create an American oil empire ultimately called the Near East Development Company. These three Western oil empires were brought together in the secret Red Line Agreement, entrenched and protected by Western military power, diplomatic prowess, economic collusion, and local avarice. Thus Mideast oil became a business acquired by government through closely or wholly controlled corporations that were completely dependent upon continuous military and diplomatic support. No other business enjoys this sponsorship, which began at the outset and continues to this day.[29]

Historically, the oil cartel established by the League of Nations and America collided with the seething Lawrence of Arabia–era demand by Arab and other Islamic populations to achieve independent, national rights, free of decadent Turkey and free of infidel Christian presence. On July 24, 1920, Arab nationalists learned that their hoped-for national rights had been snubbed by the League of Nations and its mandate system of colonies. Great Britain and France, aided by America, would gain domin-

ion over their lands and the control of a precious resource that the unin-
dustrialized people there did not need—but the modern West did. Moreover, even as the League of Nations denied national recognition to the
Arabs, it created a refuge for persecuted Jews seeking the right of return,
thus enshrining in international law the concept of a Jewish homeland in
Palestine.[30]

As a result, three intertwined evils—the infidel European Allies, the
infidel Zionists, and the black substance the West craved—now became
conflated in the Arab mind to create one great Satan. Indeed, these three
evils would galvanize the Arab consciousness for virtually the next century.
For the first time in fifteen hundred years, the Arabs stopped fighting each
other. Sunni and Shia, tribal enemies, those of the desert and those of the
city, the intellectual and the peasant, could all unite under one Islamic
banner, because 1920 was *am al-nakba*. Forevermore, 1920 would be a
black year in the collective Arabic consciousness. In Arabic, *am al-nakba*
means "the year of the catastrophe." The day, July 24, 1920, was nothing
less than the day the jihad against the West was born.[31]

Immediately, populations in Syria, Lebanon, Iraq, and elsewhere in
the extended Mideast revolted against the West and anything associated
with its oiled aspirations. During that year, pan-Arab and pan-Islamic jihad
exploded in a diverse wave of bus bombings, beheadings, arsons, brutal
atrocities against missionaries, massacres of civilians, and railroad sabotage. The unmitigated violence was subdued only superficially by massive
British aerial bombardment, an extended French and British occupation,
and Whitehall-selected Hashemite rulers imported from the Arabian
Peninsula. Certainly, these British-picked rulers cooperated with big oil.
But the despots remained unloved by the disenfranchised people they governed. Moreover, the local populations did not seek the form of government London and Paris savored, theoretical democracies that could be
counted upon to perpetuate oil supplies.[32]

With or without Hashemite kings or local strongmen, the angry,
restive populations would find no common ground with the West on their
own land. Arab and Islamic movements fervently reviled the West as infi-
dels, "the enemies of Allah," and "the sons of apes and pigs." It was oil, not
sand, that brought the West to the dunes of the Middle East. It was neither
our programs nor our politics that the local people detested; the people
had coexisted with all manner of egregious and detestable programs and
policies for centuries. It was our very presence they detested. That presence was predicated on one product: petroleum.[33]

The West stayed too long, drilled too deep, and assumed too much. In 1919, the supreme elected Arab leader, Faisal, trepidatiously warned the League of Nations that his people would not sit still without a fulfillment of national aspirations even as their oil wealth was being exported. "In the old days the area was too huge," Faisal admitted, "and in parts necessarily too thinly peopled, to communicate common ideas readily." But, Faisal explained, "The unity of the Arabs in [southwest] Asia has been made more easy of late years, since the development of railways, telegraphs, and airroads [air lanes]."[34]

Railways, telegraphs, and air lanes. Telephones, motorcars, and highways. Computers, cell phones, and Internet. Airplanes. The West is now at war with radical Islam. The industrial civilization spawned by oil is now threatened by those who possess it. Every object of modernity and technological convenience has become a weapon against the West—from the simplest cell phone that can coordinate an attack or trigger a bomb, to great 767s that can be converted into fiery missiles to destroy the tallest skyscrapers. Despite the political dangers, the social consequences, the environmental damage, and the seemingly incalculable cost both out of pocket and out of society, our addiction keeps us fixated on the substance. Like all other addictions, the addiction to oil imperils our very way of life, and indeed our survival.

No more inefficient system of energy exists than drilling for it and transporting it from the far corners of the earth and the bottom of the seas, especially when those operations are contingent on military conquest or protection. The single most fuel-inefficient undertaking on earth is arguably the heavily armed military convoy escorting oil tanker trucks in Iraq. More petroleum is undoubtedly consumed to protect the delivery than is carried in the tanker itself. Since improvised explosive devices have entered the equation, fatalities per gallon have created frightening new mileage charts.

The world is running out of oil right now. Conservation at home does nothing to reduce the wild growth in automobiles and other oil consumption in hyperindustrializing China, India, Pakistan, Russia, and elsewhere in the emerging world. The real rate of world consumption will be determined not on Main Street or Piccadilly Circus, but on the bustling new highways of New Dehli, Islamabad, Moscow, and Beijing. Bicyclers in Beijing had never seen a privately owned motor vehicle on their streets until 1984. Twenty years later, five beltways encircle Beijing as its congested sprawl copes with nearly two million automobiles. About a third of the country's new cars are purchased by just-created millionaires who prefer such guzzlers as Hummer and Rolls-Royce. China only began importing oil in 1993 but is now the world's second-largest consumer.[35]

Estimates of petroleum reserves sufficient to power an industrialized globe for the next fifteen to twenty-five years provide momentary reassurance. "Hubbert's Peak" is not a mountaintop but the acme of the oil industry's bell curve, the statistical moment of peak worldwide oil production predicted by geophysicist M. King Hubbert. But all the permutations of Hubbert's Peak do not take into account sabotage, terrorism, petropolitics, OPEC embargoes, or draconian price hikes. The main sources of oil are in the Middle East, followed by unstable Nigeria and Venezuela, both of which have been struggling with shaky oil industries plagued by kidnappings, facility invasions, and politicized manipulations. Three well-placed suicide bombers at Saudi Arabia's oil choke points, a political showdown with Iran, or a Katrina-sized hurricane destroying the refinery infrastructure that hugs the Gulf of Mexico could bring the peak tumbling down. Little or no supply cushion exists to satisfy the world's daily addiction of at least 80 million barrels of petroleum, a number that is steadily climbing with every emerging consumer in India and China. More than just transportation, the industrialized world also needs petrochemicals for the cosmetics on its cheek, the shirt on its back, the fertilizer in its fields, the drugs in its veins, and the food in its belly.[36] Producing a single 1,250 pound steer requires 283 gallons of oil.

In many ways, the world is coasting on fumes.

A September 2005 U.S. Army Corps of Engineers study on the coming energy shortage declared, "The supply of oil will remain fairly stable in the very near term, but oil prices will steadily increase as world production approaches its peak. The doubling of oil prices in the past couple of years is not an anomaly, but a picture of the future. Peak oil is at hand with low availability growth for the next 5 to 10 years." The study ominously warned, "Once worldwide petroleum production peaks, geopolitics and market economics will result in even more significant price increases and security risks. To guess where this is all going to take us would be too speculative. Oil wars are certainly not out of the question."[37]

Hence from all corners comes a desperate cry for an all-encompassing solution, some way to magically transform our society's energy reliance from oil to something else—anything else. The radiance of solar does not require an overseas army to defend the supply line or a foreign policy to manage it. The wild wind does not require an overseas army to defend the supply line or a foreign policy to manage it. Homegrown combustibles such as corn-based ethanol do not require an overseas army to defend the supply line or a foreign policy to manage them. None of the alternatives requires an army or a foreign policy. Whatever the alternative, it will require a crash program to implement it. The clarion call of a frustrated world invokes the memory of a prior all-out program to achieve a highly technological objective—two Merlinesque words that have become icons of national will.

America wants a "Manhattan Project." The world needs it.

On December 7, 1941, tightly formed squadrons of Japanese bombers dived from the sky with deadly precision to mercilessly attack the American fleet at Pearl Harbor. The next day America declared war on Japan. Three days later, Nazi Germany, honoring its Axis alliance, declared war on the United States. On December 18, 1941, now in a two-theater war, Franklin Delano Roosevelt inaugurated a national crash program to develop atomic weapons before either Japan or Germany did so. Both Axis nations had active atomic programs under way. America's secret atomic program, code-named the S-1 Project, enjoyed unlimited funding as it brought thousands of physicists, weapons specialists, and other engineers together in a network of newly constructed or suddenly invented locations around the nation. "Site X" was at Oak Ridge, Tennessee, and "Site Y" at Los Alamos, New Mexico. Four years after the S-1 Project was launched, four bombs were successfully created: a test bomb; Little Boy, which was dropped on Hiroshima; Fat Man, which was dropped on Nagasaki; and a fourth, never-used bomb.[38]

The unprecedented S-1 Project became known as the Manhattan Project. Ever since, the idea of a massively financed crash program of hyperengineering has become part of American folklore and mystique. The very term "Manhattan Project" is popular shorthand for "we can do anything—and quickly." Understandably, those concerned with shifting from oil to alternative fuels constantly beckon for a Manhattan Project to achieve that goal. Many see a Manhattan Project for energy as an almost unattainable dream. But few understand the true nature and cost of the Manhattan Project and how easy it would be to launch such a project to fulfill the twenty-first century's hope of extricating itself from petroleum.

The Manhattan Project of Roosevelt's day did not as much discover nuclear science as it codified, expanded, and applied the knowledge gained over prior years of experimentation, creating a radical, new, world-changing technology. In the same vein, a Manhattan Project for energy would codify, expand, and implement our existing knowledge of alternative power sources such as solar, wind, and ethanol. Such a project would develop more than mere theories; it would yield the working infrastructure to make green energy independence a near-term reality.

Could any nation afford the financial cost of a Manhattan Project? The true numbers are more feasible than nearly anyone imagines. Total expenditures for the original Manhattan Project were about $1.89 billion in World War II dollars, spent over four years. That sum included slightly more than $512 million for the key Gaseous Diffusion Plant and $477.6 million for the Electromagnetic Plant so indispensable to fission. Actual research and development, however, clocked in at only $69.6 million. The World War II total of $1.89 billion equals about $20 billion in 2006 dollars.[39]

By way of perspective, during World War II and the Manhattan Project years, America spent much more on other weaponry—the 1996 equivalent of $31.5 billion on ordinary bombs, mines, and grenades, $24 billion on small arms, and $64 billion on tanks.[40]

How realistic is an expenditure of $20 billion today to develop independence by means of alternative fuels? Answer: It simply requires national will and a national priority. Examples abound.

The Apollo program to land a man on the moon totaled nearly $20 billion, or about $135 billion in 2005 dollars; each of the rocket programs alone, such as the Saturn rocket, cost between $28 and $45 billion in 2005 dollars—both more than a Manhattan Project. The Hong Kong Airport, which required the frenetic creation and deconstruction of several islands, opened in 1998 at a cost of $19.9 billion. The Chunnel under the English Channel cost an estimated $15 billion in the 1990s. The Trans-Alaska Pipeline, which was rushed into construction after the first Arab oil shock in 1973, cost nearly $9 billion at the time, which equals about $45 billion in 2005 money. The Taishet-Nakhodka Pipeline, now under construction, will carry natural gas from Siberia to northwest China over a tortuous 2,581-mile course at a projected cost of between $15 and $18 billion. Another just-announced natural gas pipeline, this one from Alaska to the lower forty-eight under the aegis of ExxonMobil, BP, and ConocoPhillips, will require between $25 and $30 billion. The Trans Texas Corridor, a newly planned network of some 4,000 miles of intermodal highways spanning Texas, will cost $31.4 million per centerline mile or an estimated total of about $145.4 billion to $183.5 billion—give or take a few billion.[41]

The war in Iraq cost about $6 billion per month, or three Manhattan Project–sized enterprises annually—that is, seventeen weeks of war in Iraq costs about the same as the Manhattan Project.[42]

Since the United States dropped two atomic bombs on Japan in August 1945, the country has been willing to undertake great enterprises like the Manhattan Project regularly. The nation has not been shy about spending large sums. If energy-starved partners in Europe and Asia were included in the finances, $20 billion over four years—the Manhattan Project budget—would emerge as a rather unspectacular sum, especially if split among the top ten industrialized nations. Indeed, all industrial nations have a vested interest in sharing clean, renewable energy to wean the world off oil.

ExxonMobil alone could fund its own Manhattan Project with six months of its 2006 hyperprofit.[43]

But if the United States and possibly its partners commit to a Manhattan Project for alternative energy, what form of energy would be chosen?

All too often, the simple sense, clarity, and reliability of the available energy solutions are obscured by the many lobbyists, pressure groups, and other special interests that want to spin their pet solution to the funding forefront. Some undertakings are little more than cash-intensive boondoggles projected to run for decades with no hope for an immediate cure to the world's current precarious oil addiction. Some ventures appear to be mere public relations, tokenism by big oil or big auto as they tread technological water while the last drop of petroleum is drilled regardless of the consequences. Some seem a fanciful diversion from the shortest, smartest path to clean energy independence—like an all-out push to land a man on the moon but only after undertaking an expedition to Pluto.

Moreover, the biggest idea in energy may be the smallest solution—not great towers trailing over the horizon, but little boxes in our backyard.

Man cannot race toward an energy catholicon without stopping and looking to the heavens, for it is the sun that gave man life, and it is the sun that will sustain all future life. Even the blackest substances, such as coal, derive their dark density from the remnants of once-thriving sun-enabled lifeforms subjected to the crush of centuries. No wonder Pharaoh Akhenaton in about 1350 BC proclaimed the visible sun disk to be the first all-encompassing God—not merely the chief god among a panoply of gods,

but the sole God, the one God. The monotheistic cult of the sun disk pre-
dates quasi-monotheistic Zoroastrianism and completely monotheistic Ju-
daism. Famed archaeologist and Egyptologist H. R. Hall understandably
saluted Pharaoh Akhenaton as propounding a truly "rational" religion.[44]

But which forms of sun-imbued energy should any Manhattan Project turn to first? Experts agree that the concept of "one size fits all" is not
a viable answer. Indeed, it was such a mandate that caused our addiction
to fossil fuels as an omnisource. Diverse regional, seasonal, and even periodic solutions, approached in a variety of modalities, are envisioned as the
basis for any new network of green renewable energies. Nations and regions should call upon their strengths to power their future. Windy places
can capture wind. Sunny places can capture solar. Coastal realms and
suitable terrain can capture forms of thermal. They can do so cleanly and
inexhaustibly.

There are numerous alternative energy sources under development—
too many to be adequately addressed in a single chapter of any book. But
among the salient ones is something called clean coal. For many, the concept of clean coal is oxymoronic, like natural hairspray. But Washington is
now subsidizing a $2 billion decade-long project to develop clean coal. The
coal in question will not be shoveled and burned in boilers as it has been for
centuries, but subjected to steam and oxygen treatments in a complex
chemical combination and shift process called an integrated gasification
combined cycle. The coal will be used to create noncarbon fuels, and the
coal itself will be stripped of its harmful composition. The plan, enshrined
in the Clean Coal Power Initiative Act, is to create a working clean coal
technology by 2020 that can then be implemented in actual industrial use
over subsequent decades.[45]

Clean coal comes complete with an attractive patriotic advertising
program, a pretty logo, and a catchy name—FutureGen. But before coal
ever arrives at a cleaning location it will require traditional strip and surface
mining, petroleum-burning giant diggers, trucks, and other heavy-industry
machinery. It will need to be transported by mighty diesel-burning railroad
engines. The FutureGen project does not address that strip-mining coal is
killing whole mountain ranges, altering the landscape, and wreaking
havoc with the ecology. Coal mining is one of the most environmentally
destructive industries in existence, and a voracious consumer of petroleum
in the process. To provide the coal to be cleansed will consume vastly more
petroleum that it could ever save.[46]

What's more, just mining the coal subjects workers to one of the most hazardous forms of labor known to man in an industry with one of the worst safety records in history. In 2006 alone, a cascade of spectacular mine accidents and deaths spotlighted the historical deadliness of coal mining. After sixteen men were killed in four West Virginia tragedies during just several weeks of January 2006, West Virginia governor Joe Manchin issued an emergency order compelling all 544 mines in his state to stand down for a safety review.[47]

Dirty coal currently provides about half of America's energy needs. Worldwide, coal is utilized similarly. King Coal is expected to continue to rule for the coming decades. Projections promise that no matter how fast U.S. energy use expands, and how many alternatives come online, coal will continue to provide about half of U.S. energy needs. Other nations currently using coal have made similar predictions for their own use.[48]

Cleaning dirty coal seems a protracted diversion when it is possible to merely capture existing clean sources, such as solar, wind, and ocean power. The Coal Utilization Research Council, an industry lobby group, is not eager to discuss the sense of its place in the world's pending national petroleum emergency even as it enjoys a $2 billion decade of government-funded research. The Coal Utilization Research Council in Washington, D.C., declined to accept questions.[49]

A tenth of a Manhattan Project has already been diverted to the concept of clean coal. One or two full Manhattan Projects over the coming decades will undoubtedly be required to achieve this alchemist's dream. In a similar category is nuclear energy. Nuclear reactors, as profoundly complex as they are, as many billions as they cost, as many years for construction as they require, as potentially lethal as they can become, merely heat water to create steam to turn an electricity turbine. As such, nuclear reactors represent the most intricate, costly, complicated, and deadly water boilers since man discovered flame. Nor are clean coal and nuclear energy the only costly boondoggles being pursued. It would require a thick dedicated volume to list them all.

However, numerous promising methods of harnessing energy are being overlooked, underfunded, or developed in slow motion. Many of these methods date back decades or even centuries. Many were either proven long ago or are waiting to be resurrected and brought to fruition. Not a few share a common flaw—they are simple.

Various types of thermal energy are available. Warm water rises—a fact of simple science. As it rises, the water creates a temperature differential that can be processed by a heat exchanger. Long but simple intake pipes are needed to duct the water as it rises. Ocean thermal-energy conversion, a nineteenth-century idea, has been demonstrated throughout recent decades in Cuba, Brazil, and Hawaii. In 1984, the Department of Energy's National Renewable Energy Laboratory tested the idea and obtained an astounding 97 percent energy conversion efficiency. But ocean thermal-energy conversion development in America has been shut down.[50]

A variant of the thermal-energy principle is the Deep Lake Water Cooling project now being constructed in Toronto. Large tubes resembling great alpine horns are submerged five kilometers along Lake Ontario's natural slope. The cold water provides chill for air-conditioning, then proceeds harmlessly to the city's potable water system. The first three intake pipes now under construction will assure seventy-five thousand tons of refrigeration, enough to air-condition one hundred of Toronto's architectonic glass-and-steel skyscrapers or sixty-eight hundred homes. This thermal project subtracts that much of the city's hydrocarbon signature, which would otherwise contribute to deadly global warming even as it creates delightful office cooling.[51]

Geothermal energy—that is, tapping the earth's everlasting font of internal heat and steam to turn turbines and thereby make electricity—is a worldwide reality today. The process was conceived in 1903 in Larderello, Italy, in scenic Tuscany when the local prince began tests to drill into the hot steam pockets below, capturing the steam to turn power turbines. By 1904, the prince's small test system, looking less sophisticated than a backwoods Kentucky whiskey still, was powering lightbulbs. In 1905, the palace and residences of Larderello were electrified. By World War I, a 250-kilowatt turbine powered by subterranean steam had electrified all the chemical plants and villages of the entire Larderello region. This included the area's well-known industrial boric acid works.[52]

Today, hundreds of geothermal sites around the world are providing more than 8,000 megawatts of electricity. One megawatt is thought sufficient to power some 750 to 1,000 homes. As of 2000, Iceland generated 172 megawatts of geothermal-based electricity, which as of then satisfied about half its energy needs; it also supplied geothermal heat to 86 percent of Iceland's homes. Indonesia annually generates some 600 megawatts of geothermal. The Philippines annually generates more than 1,900 megawatts of geothermal.[53]

The United States generates more than 2,800 megawatts of geothermal, mainly in the West. In California's Lake and Sonoma counties, where some of the nation's finest wine is produced, nineteen geothermal electric plants are operated. These simple installations, many concentrated in an area known as The Geysers, each generate between about forty and seventy-two megawatts, providing about 70 percent of the residential power needs from the Golden Gate Bridge north to the Oregon border. Geothermal plants are also operated in volcano-rich Hawaii, as well as in Nevada and Utah.[54]

But global unexploited geothermal resources are vast. Experts disagree on how vast because—just as with oil—the proposition requires speculative drilling, sometimes just a few hundred feet below the surface, and sometimes several thousand below. Once erected, geothermal electric plants are remarkably reliable. Geothermal stations remain online 95 percent of the time, while nuclear plants are online only 65 percent and coal plants 75 percent of the time, according to a 2003 State of California study. In Italy, a century later, those Larderello plants are still generating electricity.[55]

The geothermal process itself is relatively simple. Experts at the Geothermal Energy Association trade group as well as the Department of Energy's National Renewable Energy Laboratory agree that geothermal is essentially "just a big pipe in the ground." If done correctly, they add, the power supply and the sunken pipe works are "permanent."[56]

Many countries in the world are dramatically increasing their pursuit and funding of geothermal energy—but not the United States, whose geothermal research and drilling has almost ground to a halt. The Geothermal Energy Association, in March 2006; complained that budget proposals under consideration would zero out the government's future support for geothermal. A survey has identified forty-six potential plant sites in Alaska, Arizona, California, Hawaii, Idaho, New Mexico, Nevada, and Utah. Together, these plants would generate an estimated 2 gigawatts of electricity, enough to power cities the size of Albuquerque, Las Vegas, Sacramento, and Seattle combined. Yet these site proposals have not been acted upon.[57]

In fact, complained the Geothermal Energy Association, a long backlog exists at the Bureau of Land Management (BLM) on applications to develop geothermal sites. How long? Geothermal Energy Association executive director Karl Gawell answered, "Twenty-five years." Gawell stated that in a Katrina-like government response, the Bureau of Land Management claims it lacks the clerical and administrative support to process the applications—and has lacked it for twenty-five years.[58]

Internal BLM summaries of outstanding applications from 1970 to 2004 include 59 applications in California, covering 97,116 acres, plus 77 in Nevada, covering 128,235 acres, and 79 in Oregon, covering 137,314 acres. The BLM's list shows 226 lease applications waiting years for action. The BLM's own March 2005 "Comprehensive Strategic Plan," marked "For Internal Use Only," clearly identifies many of the ignored applications. In Oregon, for example, application OR54587 in the Willamette National Forest, dated January 31, 1974, is still awaiting a response; application OR54517 in the Mt. Hood National Forest, dated February 25, 1974, is still awaiting a response; application OR12443 in the Mt. Hood National Forest, also dated February 25, 1974, is still awaiting a response[59]

Gawell added that one method the BLM has used to clear its backlog is to send letters to the original individual applicants, only to learn that, up to a quarter century later, they are deceased. The application is then removed without checking if it was passed to a successor individual or commercial entity. "It's true," protests Gawell, "some applicants have died waiting. The BLM's solution is to wait until people die off before acting." Gawell added that even if the applicants died waiting, site action should be taken. "If the lands have geothermal potential and are likely to be good candidates for development," he said, "they [the BLM] still should do the planning review," thereby locating the most suitable geothermal sites.[60]

When asked, a defensive BLM official blamed the backlog on the U.S. Forest Service for not producing the proper environmental impact statement. "We are waiting on the Forest Service," said the BLM spokeswoman. To the question why the BLM did not follow up with the Forest Service after decades, no answer was forthcoming. A Forest Service spokeswoman did not respond to the implications of the BLM charge or Gawell's complaint. But she confirmed that her agency was aware of the backlog and hoped to catch up within a half decade, then make their recommendations to the BLM, which would then start its own lengthy process. Only after the BLM acts can industry proceed on the site development. Thus, the Forest Service spokeswoman acknowledged, significantly expanding geothermal in America was probably decades away. "Ironically, Congress just passed a big new package of tax incentives for new geothermal plants that get on line by 2008—a very few will be developed, but for most sites, that will never happen."[61]

But for Gawell and the geothermal industry, their relatively simple contribution to overall energy independence is consciously being orphaned. "This all has a chilling effect," Gawell stated. "When an applicant sees it can take decades just to get an application process—and you can die waiting—why bother?" The BLM counters that since 2001 the agency has acted on some two hundred site applications within its backlog. The agency states that this progress is ten times faster than in prior years, but concurs that new development is still an inexorably slow process measured in many years.[62]

Natural gas is said to be a cheaper form of electrical generation by a few pennies per kilowatt.[63] But when external costs for military, health, and environmental damage are added, geothermal is less expensive than natural-gas-fired plants—which also require drilling. Moreover, geothermal does not depend upon a $25 billion pipeline crossing the continent or supertankers that require naval protection, or diplomatic intervention. Geothermal is just a pipe in the ground.

As promising as geothermal is, it is just a portion of any overall solution. Partnering in importance are wind and solar energy.

Wind energy has been used for centuries to pump farm water from the ground, mill grain, and send great ships across the ocean. The media is constantly filled with fascinating articles about elaborate wind-power endeavors. Everyone knows the familiar image of a modern, high-efficiency windmill resembling a giant propeller mounted on a tall tower. Denmark today derives 20 percent of its total energy needs from wind turbines; they are all privately owned. Germany now operates more than 16,000 wind turbines, mainly in the northlands near Denmark; the country is systematically phasing out all its nuclear reactors, and by 2010, wind will provide about 12.5 percent of Germany's total power requirements. Ireland generates about 500 megawatts, of which 25 megawatts is conveyed from offshore installations.[64]

The United States could satisfy 40 percent of its energy needs from the steady winds of North Dakota alone. North Dakota is the windiest state in the Union with a potential of 1.2 gigawatts, followed by Texas, possessing 1.1 gigawatts, and then Kansas, South Dakota, and Montana, each offering a full gigawatt of potential. Just twenty states from coast to coast possess enough windy terrain to power most of the country's needs. Indeed, when all states are included, enough wind energy blows to supply the United States' power needs three times over.[65]

Critics assail giant windmills for their appearance, especially in otherwise visually appealing land areas. The elongated blades, with even longer ones constantly in development, have killed birds and bats. Proponents argue that oil wells, power lines, nuclear reactors, and the other edifices of an energy infrastructure all disrupt the landscape and also kill their share of birds and bats. Indeed, windmill advocates argue, skyscrapers regularly kill numbers of birds.[66]

Wind technology is constantly improving, making every new generation of wind turbine that much more powerful. In the current century, Denmark replaced most of its existing 1,300 turbines, which were capable of generating 100 megawatts each, with just 300 turbines capable of 300 megawatts each. Major wind farms, with their long arrays of giant windmills, are being planted worldwide, from the desert north of Palm Springs, California, to Ireland to Germany. General Electric alone has produced some 5,000 windmills worldwide. State-of-the-art 1.8-megawatt wind machines costing about $1 million to $2 million could each power some 500 to 600 homes. Yet wind energy now provides a meager 1 percent of America's energy. Federal energy officials and even industry sources do not expect to supply as much as 6 percent of the nation's needs until 2020. At the same time, all the stops are being pulled out to approve and finance gargantuan natural gas pipelines traversing the world's most defying terrain and costing between $10 billion and $30 billion each. Wind experts estimate that for every billion dollars invested in wind energy, 2 billion kilowatt hours will be generated daily for twenty years. By comparison, that same billion spent on natural gas will purchase just about 20 billion cubic feet, or just a two-day supply of electricity.[67]

Even more promising than wind is solar. The traditional picture of solar energy is thick, glass-encased panels generating electricity through photovoltaic cells. Those panels are becoming increasingly more efficient, but they still require a decade of use before they achieve cost-effectiveness. Without government assistance, the affordability of solar energy is out of reach for most. Moreover, as important as they are, those panels are restricted to certain types of spacious surfaces or landmasses.[68]

Critics argue that panels would require a landmass of 10,000 square miles to renewably generate all of America's energy. Advocates suggest utilizing great tracts of unused American desert and prairie, as well as highway median strips, offshore sites that would function much as offshore oil-drilling platforms or wind farms do, abandoned military bases, and, most important, rooftops. "We have virtually unlimited flat rooftops in America—millions of square miles," affirms Jon Slangerup, CEO of Solar Integrated Technologies of California. He adds, "Consider millions and millions of square feet of industrial flat rooftop just in California. That untapped potential alone could generate ten gigawatts of electricity per sunlight hour—and that doesn't even count the additional rooftops of residential and governmental sites."[69]

Moreover, the latest generation of solar is not a rigid panel, but thin, flexible film just a sixteenth inch thick, completely unprotected and exposed to the elements, that can be installed atop any structure from a flat warehouse roof to a slanted military tent. Solar Integrated Technologies utilizes solar film in great rolls. The product has already been installed on numerous warehouse and school roofs in California. Each installation generally produces enough power to feed electricity back into the grid. That earns money or credit with the local utility where the law mandates that utilities pay for private electricity transmitted back into the grid.[70]

But the most astonishing development in solar energy will completely rewrite the rules of solar energy and electrical generation. Konarka of Boston is one of an elite group of companies that is developing *nanosolar*, that is, organic nanotechnology. The photovoltaic electricity will be generated not by panels big enough to hold in your hand but at the molecular level. Nanosolar materials will routinely be printed, stamped, and transparently admixed into fabrics, plastics, and wallpaper. Solar will become cheap and abundant, an intrinsic aspect of mass production like stain-resistant coatings. Nanosolar will become an innate part of the surfaces of future laptops, roofing tiles, drapes, and other objects. Straight, flat surface requirements will be a thing of solar energy's past as this seemingly magical technology works invisibly even in common devices such as cellular phones, binoculars, gutters, vests, and entire building exteriors.[71]

Konarka has already attracted some $60 million in investment as well as partnerships with such multinationals as Chevron Oil, Eastman Chemical, Siemens, and DuPont, with additional participation by such national entities as the Swiss Federal Institute of Technology and Électricité de France. Other nanosolar companies are scampering to proliferate their own product partnerships. Nanosolar is not a far-future development. True, nanosolar is years away from omnipresence. But the U.S. military is already developing applications, and major partners such as Chevron, Siemens, various textile makers, and others are planning product rollouts as early as 2010.[72]

There are many forms of nonpolluting, renewable alternative energies. Their value to the world's overall energy solution is more than just in their ability to generate electricity, which eliminates dependence on earthkilling hydrocarbons, such as natural gas and coal. Yes, clean, renewable forms of electricity such as solar, wind, and geothermal will replace the coal used to heat our homes, run our appliances, and power our factories. But equally or perhaps more important, those new renewable forms will also be used to make fuel to operate our motor vehicles.

Creating fuel requires an industrial process that requires energy. It takes energy to make fuel. No one can wave at the wind, bask in sunlight, or wade in water to harness the power needed to drive a car. These power sources require machinery to extract the energy of the sun directly or indirectly stored or transduced in such sources as fossil matter, coal, wind, photosynthesis, and of course solar itself.

When the source of the energy that creates, refines, and distributes the fuel is clean and renewable, then we have truly begun energy salvation. But which fuel is best? Numerous seemingly nonpolluting fuels are available. Among them are biodiesel, methane, and ethanol. Each comes equipped with its own high-pressure lobby group. But ethanol, made of corn, has taken the lead in national attention as an alternative to petroleum. What began as an additive functioning as a 10 and 15 percent gasoline extender has become elevated to a potential major ingredient in a gallon of gas. E85, for example, is an emerging blend of automobile fuel composed of 85 percent ethanol and only 15 percent gasoline. Dedicated E85 pumps are now being established at gas stations, mainly in the Midwest's corn-rich farm belt.[73]

At first blush, ethanol from corn appears to be a solution from America's heartland, a win-win proposition in the struggle to free the world from harmful hydrocarbons and politically embroiling fuel. But American ethanol cannot stand on its own. Ethanol actually depends upon the continued use of petroleum and by necessity increases petroleum consumption and greenhouse gases. Many experts say ethanol simply uses more petroleum than it saves. For example, a key series of studies was conducted by Tad Patzek, a University of California geoengineer, and David Pimentel, a Cornell University expert in life sciences, energy, and sustainable agriculture. Pimentel's and Patzek's studies asserted that "ethanol production using corn grain required 29 percent more fossil energy than the ethanol fuel produced" and that even proposed alternative ethanol cellulose sources other than corn, such as switchgrass, wood, and straw, "required 50 percent more fossil energy than the ethanol fuel produced." Those energy expenditures cover a range of hydrocarbon users from the diesel-burning tractors and combines on the farm to the ordinary trucks needed for transport to and from the industrial centers.[74] "In plain words,"

Pimentel explained, "it takes 1.29 gallons of petroleum or petroleum equivalents to produce one gallon of ethanol."[75]

The conclusion that ethanol drank more petroleum than it saved subjected the two researchers to a vilification campaign by ethanol industry lobbyists, according to Pimentel. "Our first such report was reviewed by twenty-six top scientists who advised the secretary of energy," he said, "and they unanimously approved it. But two members of Congress from ethanol-producing states had us investigated, our very honesty was investigated." Patzek and Pimentel say they welcomed the investigations, which they say sustained their findings. "But now I would like another investigation," Patzek insisted, "a thorough investigation of this entire affair."[76]

When asked about the Pimentel and Patzek studies, a National Ethanol Vehicle Coalition spokesperson stated that such studies were "discredited," adding, "Only uneducated people would write such a thing, or believe such a thing." A second official from the organization stated, "I concur. Such people are uneducated."[77]

Patzek denied he was uneducated, citing his coauthorship of 177 scientific papers, and five books soon to be published. His résumé includes degrees in chemical engineering and engineering physics, as well as a prior stint with Shell Development, where he worked on "enhanced oil recovery methods and evaluated the future of U.S. energy supply from tar sands, heavy oil, and coal." He added, "I have taken more courses in thermodynamics than almost anyone at Berkeley." Patzek, who has published his findings widely, says he will not back down and has more scientific peer-reviewed journal articles on the topic coming out. However, said Patzek, he must now must keep future articles a secret until after publication to avoid pressure on academic editors by ethanol interests.[78]

Pimentel also denied he was uneducated, explaining he was an Oxford University graduate and author of six hundred scientific papers and twenty-five books. "The problem is the ethanol people have a lot of money," says Pimentel, adding staunchly, "This is not about energy or science. What is driving ethanol is politics and big money. You can quote me!"[79]

A senior alternative fuels expert from a leading company within the automotive industry that has abstained from the ethanol bandwagon concurred. "Ethanol is just a scam," he said, "and I hope you have the courage to say so publicly!"[80]

Criticizing corn carries a price. Even a March 1997 study by the Government Accountability Office (GAO) documenting the adverse energy-tax effects of ethanol was viciously attacked by corn interests. After the study, Senator Charles Grassley of Iowa, in a long letter written June 6, 1997, demanded an official explanation and self-investigation by the GAO of itself. Throwing down the gauntlet, Grassley demanded answers to a series of fiery, accusatory questions. Question 2: "[Explain why] the report is most egregiously flawed by giving the appearance of being a cost-benefit analysis when it clearly is not." Question 4: "Was it your intention to deceive Congress and the public, or was this the unavoidable outcome given the narrow, specific nature of the questions you were required to answer?" Questions 5 and 6: "Why did you bury your admission on page 23 that this report should not be viewed as a cost-benefit analysis, instead of highlighting this crucial point at the beginning?" Question 9: "Why did you fail to report that the elimination of the alcohol fuels tax incentives would create additional consumer costs in the reformulated gasoline markets?" Questions 12, 13, and 14: "Did you not realize that by framing your discussion of energy impact by measuring ethanol's energy security benefit in relation to its displacement of crude oil instead of [the deadly additive] MBTE, that you would be obscuring the importance of ethanol in reducing MBTE imports?" Grassley's letter even excoriated the GAO for including the history of congressional action on behalf of ethanol. Question 16: "What purpose was served by Appendix I, Chronology of the Legislation and Events Affecting Ethanol Fuel Use?"[81]

Despite Grassley's "J'accuse," GAO officials answered point by point and reiterated their assertion about ethanol appending that the additional attendant military cost was therefore a foregone conclusion: "We concluded in our report that the alcohol fuels incentives do not significantly reduce petroleum imports. Therefore, defense expenditures and foreign assistance to protect oil supply lines from the Middle East were appropriately beyond the scope of this report."[82]

The ethanol industry itself advocates the least negative study available, this one by Argonne National Laboratory, which concludes that only three-quarters of a million BTUs of fossil fuels are required for each 1 million BTUs of ethanol delivered, or about three-quarters of a gallon of petroleum or equivalents to produce a single gallon of ethanol. But, says Pimentel, "Argonne left out many of the energy inputs, such as the energy used by farm machinery and their maintenance. They left out processing equipment. They left out the petroleum used in the production of hybrid corn."[83]

The ethanol industry trumpets the Argonne analysis because the same study also concludes that traditional gasoline production requires even more petroleum, about 1.23 million BTUs of fossil energy consumed for each million BTUs of gasoline delivered. The higher cost of producing a traditional gallon of gasoline sets forth the ecologic and economic sophistry that it takes "more gasoline to make gasoline" than to make ethanol—ethanol is therefore preferred, not because it functions as a solution, but because it is the lesser of two energy evils. Either way, these studies ipso facto demonstrate the inherent inefficiency of the whole concept of gasoline-based internal combustion. Numerous studies agree that it takes more than a gallon of petroleum to produce and deliver a gallon of gasoline. Importantly, all the key studies generally bypass the oil burned by the tanks, trucks, aircraft, and naval ships that attach to the oil industry.[84]

American ethanol by definition must work with gasoline. An oil disruption today would halt or radically reduce ethanol production, depending upon the severity of the disruption. Therefore, ethanol is not an alternative as much as an adjunct with a strong lobbying and advertising movement behind it.

Moreover, ethanol requires farmland and heavy petroleum-burning farm machinery. There is not enough farmland to produce all the ethanol the nation needs to replace gasoline. Indeed, ethanol industry proponents and experts believe ethanol comes with a built-in ceiling: only 30 percent of the nation's needs could be solved by ethanol, and even that would require an estimated two to three decades of additional farm, distillery, and distribution expansion. However, even if doable, that expansion in ethanol comes at a significant cost.[85]

The American government pays an unnecessary 51-cent-per-gallon subsidy for every gallon of ethanol, a price support achieved by a convergence of lobbying and commercial interests. This subvention is granted to the oil-company blenders as an "incentive" to blend the ethanol yielded by such giant agribusiness concerns as Cargill and ConAgra. One of those leading corn interests, Archer Daniels Midland, has been the subject of multiple criminal investigations, and in October 1996 it agreed to pay the largest criminal antitrust fine in history, $100 million, for lysine price fixing. The company's executives in Decatur, Illinois, were indicted right along with the company. Among the statements secretly videotaped by the FBI's mole was the assertion "The customer is the enemy."[86]

The new 51-cent-per-gallon subsidy comes by way of HR 4520, the American Jobs Creation Act of 2004, signed into law on October 22, 2004, by President George W. Bush. Within the Jobs Creation Act was the little-noticed Volumetric Ethanol Excise Tax Credit. The next year, 2005, $2.1 billion in tax credits were issued to oil companies to blend some four billion gallons of ethanol. These were not tax deductions, but tax credits that allow a write-off directly from the oil companies' bottom-line tax bill. In turn, the 51-cent subsidy boosted ethanol demand, which in turn raised the price of a bushel of corn for producers such as Cargill, and concomitantly inflated the cost of ethanol at the pump by as much as 30 percent. Sources in the ethanol industry readily concede this subsidy functions as "a pass-through subsidy" to corn and ethanol producers.[87]

The fast growth of ethanol is in large measure also pegged to the introduction of flex-fuel cars from General Motors and Ford. These cars, which employ a capability first achieved decades earlier by Henry Ford in the Model T, enable twenty-first-century vehicles to seamlessly operate on a combination of fuels, from traditional gasoline to ethanol-rich E85. At first appearance, the introduction of flex-fuel cars appears to be a dynamic move toward homegrown energy independence. Ford has already sold 1.6 million such flex-fuel cars and trucks and will by the end of 2006 add another 250,000 vehicles. GM is aggressively marketing E85 in various parts of the Midwest.[88] But every gallon of American ethanol consumed requires the world consume and endure more petroleum burning.

America's ethanol industry is keenly aware of its dependence upon petroleum. Its industry trade group has called for new processing plants to be partially driven by renewables and is also investigating utilizing other cellulose products, such as switchgrass. But those developments are many years away.[89]

However the 51-cent-per-gallon subsidy is here today. That has started a frantic gold rush to produce corn to sell to oil companies to blend. Those GM and Ford flex-fuel vehicles and pumps sprouting throughout the Midwest and beyond only expand the market. In 2006, 97 ethanol plants produced four billion gallons. But the industry hopes to double its output by 2012. Some 40 plants are now under construction and 150 are fast jumping from drawing board to construction. But coal is cheaper than natural gas, so ethanol will now also become a daily consumer of tons of coal. Hence, many of those new ethanol plants will be rushed into operation as cheap coal-burning facilities.[90]

For example, the Gold-Eagle Cooperative of Iowa is now burning 300 tons of coal daily—three railroad carloads—to produce 150,000 gallons of ethanol a day. Affable Gold-Eagle Cooperative general manager Brad Davis happily explained that hazardous particulate matter was greatly reduced by his refineries. "This is clean coal," he said proudly. "You can't even see the smoke coming out of the chimney." Asked if the coal was mined by traditional smoke-spewing, heavy, diesel-thirsty coal-mining equipment, then transported by diesel trains and off-loaded and processed by any number of greenhouse-inducing diesel processes, Davis answered, "I guess it is."[91]

Ironically, ethanol is achieving genuine green independence for Brazil. Brazilian ethanol comes from sugarcane, which American soil cannot grow in cheap abundance. Most important, ethanol refineries are driven not by coal or hydrocarbons but by a sugarcane by-product called bagasse. Hence, Brazilian ethanol is genuinely renewable and sustainable. Flex-fuel vehicles manufactured by Ford and GM for the Brazilian market can use ethanol that exceeds an 85 percent admixture. They can run on E100, that is, 100 percent ethanol. Zooming petroleum prices in 2006 pushed Brazilian ethanol into profitability and has already ended the country's importation of foreign oil. Indeed, Brazil has been exporting millions of gallons of ethanol to the United States. Today, more than 28 percent of all Brazilian vehicles operate on either 100 percent sugarcane ethanol or a substantial ethanol mix. Brazil owes its success story to more than two decades of ethanol production heavily subsidized by the government, Manhattan Project–style, plus an intelligent choice of sugarcane as a feedstock, and the ability to drive the industry by burning alternative bagasse. Today, Brazilian ethanol stands on its own, almost free of subsidy, as a free-market fuel—homegrown and almost pollution free.[92]

Brazilian sugarcane ethanol packs eight times the energy of a gallon of corn ethanol. Yet the American importation of Brazilian ethanol is profoundly obstructed by a 54-cent-per-gallon special tax designed to keep this energy solution out of the country in favor of petroleum-dependent corn ethanol. Indeed, even American investment in Brazilian sugarcane ethanol has been limited by Washington-imposed restrictions.[93]

Whether American ethanol becomes a hot new gasoline displacer or just continues as a popular extender, the process will already have received nearly a fifth of a Manhattan Project. The balance of a Manhattan Project should be paid by 2010. When that occurs, society will not be much closer to decreasing oil imports or petroleum-based pollution.

Then what is the answer for an industrialized world thirsting for energy, panicking that its petropolitical supply may at any moment be fatally ligated by terrorist attack, by governmental blackmail, or by a world so warmed that its hurricanes are now vastly more powerful and unstoppably more frequent? Does the answer lie in great new infrastructures, massive new pipelines, or monumental arrays? Many say the real answer lies in the water in our glass, the palms of our hands, and a small box in our backyard.

Once more, it is the inestimable power of the sun and its fundamental universe force that commands, a force as prodigious as a great star and yet as infinitesimal as a molecule. Of all the elements of the known universe cataloged by the periodic table, this one leads them all. It is number one, the first, the most elemental, the beginning of all life and for many its salvation as well.

It is hydrogen.

CHAPTER TWELVE

HYDROGEN SOLUTION

In the beginning, all was dark and formless.[1]

But suddenly, within an infinitesimal fraction of a second, a span so inestimable that it defies imagination, a time slice quantified by awed experts as 10^{-43}, or "a one, preceded by forty-two zeros and a decimal point," an event inadequately if not raptly described as lasting vastly less than a "trillionth of a trillionth of a trillionth" of a second—during this incomprehensible primordial moment, the mysterious preexisting quintessence of the universe exploded, inflating into the newly created dimensions of space and time. That was the beginning of things, the Big Bang, and it was very long ago, so long ago that when man humbly looks to the heavens and sees the distant stars above or even beholds the palm of his hand, he perceives a reality 13.7 billion years in the making.[2]

Hydrogen was the first of the universe's elements to form after the Big Bang created all things. It is the most abundant atom in all of existence—about 98 percent of all matter. For longer than water will flow, longer than our sun will burn, and longer than any number of other life-sustaining attributes shall exist, there will be hydrogen—a power so mighty it can become the fiery furnace of the greatest bomb, and yet be the cool current of a nurturing river. Hydrogen is nature's inner soul.

Simple yet potent, hydrogen is the most basic ingredient, just one proton controlling a single electron through a magical bond that even Edison admitted he could not fathom. When a sole electron is freed of its proton, an electrical current is generated that can power the smallest keychain flashlight and the mightiest vehicle. Hydrogen drives buses on the cosmopolitan streets of Europe, propels great submarines beneath the sea for Germany, Greece, and South Korea, and powered man's first flight to the moon. Today, hydrogen also fuels common passenger automobiles that fundamentally operate like any other—except for their clean, renewable fuel source.[3]

Hydrogen is the endgame, the final objective in man's multimillennial quest to become energy independent without perishing in the process—that is, without dying either slowly as a result of poisonous side effects, or suddenly because of deadly military action. Hydrogen, when used as ordinary fuel, is gentle to the environment and nontoxic. In most instances, hydrogen produces little more than harmless water vapor as a byproduct.[4] Nothing is cleaner.

Many in the world recognize that hydrogen is the answer to a planet cracking and choking under the rule of petroleum. That is why the United States, Iceland, and some two dozen other countries have each adopted or are creating a "Hydrogen Roadmap" to total energy independence. The list includes not only the key industrialized nations, such as Japan, Germany, and Canada, but also emerging industrial powerhouses such as China and India, who have realized that their mushrooming energy appetites cannot sensibly be satisfied by oil much longer.[5]

Iceland leads the European Union in aggressively converting to a so-called hydrogen economy, which will soon run its fisheries, automobiles, and ocean vessels on hydrogen greenly extracted from water by power provided by the country's network of geothermal plants. With a national population of less than 300,000, and more than 180,000 private cars, Iceland enjoys the world's highest per capita auto ownership. Iceland's government has mandated that all cars convert to hydrogen fuel in the coming years. Hydrogen buses with a 125-mile range, manufactured by Mercedes-Benz, have been rolling through the streets of Reykjavik since 2003 and regularly fuel up at one of the world's first commercial hydrogen filling stations. Iceland intends to convert its entire 2,500-ship fishing fleet to hydrogen fuel by 2015. This far northern nation's Hydrogen Roadmap is supported by the European Union, which has contributed $3.1 million to the campaign's initial automotive efforts.[6]

America has also adopted its own Hydrogen Roadmap. Hydrogen has been an alternative-energy focus in the United States for years. In 1989, the National Hydrogen Association (NHA) was founded by ten commercial and scientific hydrogen pioneers who believed hydrogen could cleanly power our transportation needs, heat our homes, run our appliances, and offer a global exit strategy from oil. On April 2, 2002, the NHA and the Department of Energy convened a strategic hydrogen workshop that in November 2002 produced the Department of Energy's fifty-page "National Hydrogen Energy Roadmap." In his January 28, 2003, State of the Union address, President George W. Bush launched the country's first formal hydrogen-fuel initiative, which sought $228 million to develop the technology. The idea was to slowly make fuel cells competitive with gasoline vehicles by 2015. The Department of Energy's road map, published just two months earlier, stated, "Probably the only time most consumers in the United States think about fuel . . . is when fuel prices rise to $2 per gallon of gasoline."[7]

In 2005, gasoline broke $3 per gallon.[8]

Throughout the Department of Energy's program literature, hydrogen is hailed as "the fuel of the future," and even then only as a partial energy solution attainable after decades of incremental development. The government's projected dates for substantially switching to a hydrogen economy coincide conveniently with the best projections for the end of abundant oil, that is, between 2025 and 2045.[9] In other words, hydrogen is not scheduled to go into high gear until oil is close to depleting. Abrupt stoppages outside normal supply and demand, such as terrorism, petropolitical blackmail, or natural disaster have not been calculated into the government's timetable. Nor has the disruption by terrorism or natural disaster of the world's overtaxed refinery capacity been calculated into the timetable; such a disruption would stop gasoline flowing whether or not crude is available, just as a rifle without bullets cannot function as a firearm. The basis for America's visionary "decades-long" approach is rooted in the *futuristic* notion of hydrogen. Unfortunately, the very act of praising, hailing, and envisioning hydrogen as a "futuristic" technology only delays its rapid return and implementation. In truth, hydrogen is a 240-year-old story waiting to be revived.

In 1766, English physicist Henry Cavendish first identified hydrogen gas as a distinct substance. Among the first internal-combustion-engine attempts, albeit unsuccessful, was one in 1807 by François Isaac de Rivaz that was designed to burn hydrogen gas and oxygen. Several years later, an illuminating gas composed of 50 percent hydrogen began appearing atop streetlamp posts throughout England. The gas was so widely used to light up English streets and to cook with, it became known as town gas, so named because virtually every town in England used it before the lightbulb. The nineteenth-century hydrogen that England ubiquitously used was not the clean and green gas power advocated today. Town gas, derived from coal, was notoriously sooty and smelly. During the nineteenth century, town gas, also known as manufactured gas, continued proliferating throughout the world. It was widely used in the United States from the early 1800s, and such countries as New Zealand and Slovakia adopted it in the 1860s. Town gas remained a central power source in England, the United States, and elsewhere until well into the twentieth century. Today, many parts of China and neighboring Asian countries still use town gas.[10]

In 1839, a rudimentary hydrogen fuel cell, producing electrical current from hydrogen and oxygen in the presence of an electrolyte, was invented by Welsh physicist Sir William Grove. The Grove Fuel Cell Symposium now held annually in London to review the most advanced technology in the field is named for him.[11]

Hydrogen gas provided lighter-than-air lift to the famous zeppelin *Hindenburg*, which exploded over Lakehurst, New Jersey, in 1937. Although hydrogen was originally blamed for the explosion, later investigation revealed it was the flammable outer coating of the *Hindenburg*'s skin that first ignited—not the gas. The hydrogen explosion was secondary.[12]

The Nazis, bereft of good supplies of gasoline, extensively used hydrogen-treated coal to create synthetic fuel. In the last years of the Third Reich, Germany built about one thousand motor vehicles powered by hydrogenated coal synfuels. Hydrogen was not the fuel, but was the gas required to industrially create the fuel. The process was extremely dirty and toxic, characteristics the Nazis gladly tolerated in exchange for the war benefits. By the September 1, 1939, invasion of Poland, more than 92 percent of Germany's aviation fuel and most of its land-vehicle fuel—1.46 million metric tons annually—was synthesized by the coal-hydrogen process. Hitler's fuel was mainly produced by fourteen massive hydrogenation plants jointly established by I. G. Farben and Standard Oil of New Jersey. Standard Oil collaborated with the Nazi regime extensively throughout the Hitler years.[13]

During the war, America tried to emulate the Nazi success. But Standard Oil refused to provide the U.S. military with the same desperately needed technology the company had bestowed upon the Nazis. In 1943, West Virginia congressman Jennings Randolph led a campaign to catch up to the Reich in spite of Standard Oil. How? By resurrecting the experimental hydrogenated-coal synthetic-fuel program begun by the Bureau of Mines two decades earlier near Pittsburgh during an earlier oil shortage. In November 1943, to dramatize the viability of synfuels, Randolph even flew to Washington, D.C., from West Virginia in a private airplane powered by coal-based synfuels.[14]

Shortly thereafter, on April 5, 1944, Congress passed the Synthetic Liquid Fuels Act, authorizing $30 million for a five-year effort to "create synthetic liquid fuels from coal, oil shales, agricultural and forestry products, and other substances, in order to aid the prosecution of the war, to conserve and increase the oil resources of the Nation, and for other purposes." Again, hydrogen was not the fuel but the gas required to industrially create the fuel. After the June 6, 1944, Normandy invasion, George S. Patton's Third Army sped across Europe so quickly that he outdistanced Allied supply lines. To continue moving forward, Patton's armored units drained captured German vehicle tanks of their coal-derived fuel and completed his drive into Germany—ironically on Hitler's own coal-based synthetic fuel. Patton and Germany demonstrated that airplanes and the heaviest military vehicles, as well as the lightest personal cars, could be propelled by hydrogenated synfuels.[15]

But after the war, the value of America's promising synfuels program was criticized and politically undermined by the oil industry. Big Oil's scientific studies—disputed science for sure—showed the program to be "vastly too expensive." In 1953, the Senate Appropriations Committee convened and immediately killed funding for all synfuels programs. A former member of the House, Estes Kefauver, the crusading senator who later chaired Congress's famous investigation of organized crime, blamed oil industry pressure for the sudden demise of the synfuels program.[16]

However, hydrogen as a main fuel source was still considered viable by scientists. Arguably the first hydrogen-and-oxygen-fueled vehicle was an Allis-Chalmers tractor created in about 1958, as a demonstration project. Agricultural vehicles, with their generally low mileage requirements and heavy-strength uses are perfect candidates for hydrogen, electric, or other clean alternative fuels. But Allis-Chalmers ignored the tractor—a revolution in farm-equipment fuel did not occur.[17]

Hydrogen fuel powered the Apollo mission to the moon in the sixties and during the early seventies continued to boost mighty Saturn rockets into space. During those same two decades, battery and fuel-cell pioneer Karl Kordesch created the real foundations for the hydrogen vehicle revolution. The Austrian-born scientist was spirited out of Europe in 1953 by Operation Paperclip, the secret postwar program to recruit German scientists and technicians, including many propulsion experts. Kordesch was brought to Newark aboard a U.S. Navy vessel and then transferred to Fort Monmouth in New Jersey, where he worked on a variety of fuel cells and battery innovations for America. In 1967, Kordesch was part of a large team that helped convert a heavy GM Handivan into an Electrovan by installing a hydrogen-oxygen fuel cell that generated 160 kilowatts, enough to easily operate the 7,500-pound vehicle up and down hills. GM ignored the Electrovan—a revolution in van fuel did not occur.[18]

Three years later in 1970, Kordesch lashed six gas cylinders to the roof of his four-passenger Austin A-40 and installed a fuel cell in the trunk, thus creating the world's first hydrogen automobile that actually operated day-in, day-out. Kordesch drove that Austin A-40 as his personal car with a regular state license plate on public roads for thousands of miles during a three-year period, enjoying a 180-mile range. As of the summer of 2006, the vehicle is parked in Kordesch's garage in Ohio, still in operating condition and ready to roll again if revived with fresh fuel cells. Kordesch's breakthrough was ignored by the big automakers—a revolution in passenger cars did not occur.[19]

But in 1973, the Arab-imposed oil shock shook many alternative-fuel advocates into reconsidering hydrogen as a fuel for automobiles. But progress was slow because Big Oil and the Big Automakers preferred to wait out the oil crisis as long as possible. Nonetheless, over the next three decades, the impetus for hydrogen expanded. The National Hydrogen Association came together in 1989 to press for energy independence based on the most abundant element in the universe. Finally, in 1991, Mazda created the first working hydrogen car from a major automaker, albeit a Japanese firm. During the nineties, Mazda assembled several other working hydrogen vehicles. But Mazda's beginning was not advanced—a revolution did not occur.[20]

Finally, in the twenty-first century, America committed to standardizing on hydrogen as an energy source—a process declared so "futuristic" that it could only be seriously started within the coming several decades, and this along the tortuous, slow-speed routes of the Hydrogen Roadmap. But despite the pretty logos, interactive government Web sites, and grandiose announcements, the federal road map to a "hydrogen future" is in truth a mere resurrection of a "hydrogen past"—a past in search of a Manhattan Project to help it solve a present on the oil brink.

Hydrogen has been an energy source and industrial workhorse for more than two centuries. But the long-neglected issues of hydrogen have deepened into an onionskin of interlocking technical and manufacturing challenges. True, those challenges are easily oversimplified and reduced to catchy slogans. But they are not easily solved piecemeal in a real world.

"Hydrogen immediacy" for vehicles requires concerted, thoughtful planning and effort. Four key issues dominate: (1) creating the hydrogen that must then be converted to fuel; (2) using that hydrogen sensibly in a vehicle; (3) mass-producing the hydrogen vehicles; and (4) constructing the infrastructure to refuel the vehicles.

First: creating the fuel. To operate trucks and automobiles, hydrogen must be converted into fuel. True, hydrogen can be found abundantly in water, but it can also be found in coal, natural gas, and other substances. Separating out the hydrogen, or cracking it from the original matter, requires energy.

Three of the most discussed methods of creating ready hydrogen involve extracting it from water, natural gas, or coal. Electrolysis decomposes water—H_2O—into its components, which are oxygen and hydrogen; many argue that this process is inherently the cleanest and the most desirable. Natural gas, or methane gas, requires a reforming process, accomplished by employing high temperatures to separate the natural gas or methane molecule—CH_4—into its components, carbon and hydrogen; but that process releases carbon that unites with oxygen to form carbon dioxide, a climate-altering greenhouse gas. Coal is the least attractive option, requiring high-heat gasification, which for the foreseeable future remains an intrinsically dirty process, dependent upon a supply chain that exudes deadly by-products; it will take decades to perfect coal as a clean alternative from mine to manufacturer. However, electrolyzing water and reforming natural gas are well-entrenched, proven technologies that can broadly be implemented today.[21]

But either electrolyzing water or reforming natural gas requires electricity to power those machines. It always takes energy to make fuel. Where that electricity comes from and how that electricity is generated determines how cheap or costly it is to create the clean, renewable hydrogen fuel. Many believe electricity comes from a socket. It of course comes from a central generating utility feeding power into the grid. This is why hairdryers blow, newspaper presses print, and computer hard drives whir. Because the total chain must be considered when evaluating oil, coal, gas, or any other energy use, the source of the original electricity driving the production of hydrogen leads to what some in the field glibly call "black hydrogen" and "green hydrogen."

Black hydrogen production is, or can be, powered by the electricity generated today by traditional polluting energy sources, such as ordinary coal-fired central electrical utilities. More than half the nation's electrical power is still generated by coal, and much of the remainder is produced by greenhouse-gas-releasing natural gas or other environmentally harmful methods.[22]

Green hydrogen is produced by electricity generated by such clean and renewable sources as wind, solar, thermal, hydro, and other methods. These well-established green sources are now enjoying a rapid resurgence. Leapfrogging progress is constantly being announced in the daily media. Costs and barriers continuously come down and efficiency continuously goes up.[23]

An August 2005 study by the U.S. Department of Energy's National Renewable Energy Laboratory "verified that there are abundant solar and wind energy resources to meet hydrogen transportation fuel for the entire country." Indeed, more than eight times our gasoline demand can be supplied by green hydrogen. "The gasoline consumption of the United States as a whole," the National Renewable Energy Laboratory study asserted, "was 128 billion gallons of gasoline in 2000. The potential for hydrogen production from PV [photovoltaic] and wind for the entire country is 1,110 billion kilograms of hydrogen. As a kilogram of hydrogen is roughly equivalent to a gallon of gasoline in energy content, 8.6 times the year 2000 gasoline consumption in the United States can be met using hydrogen produced from PV and wind."[24]

The calculation that more than eight times America's gasoline consumption could be supplied by domestic green solar-produced and wind-produced hydrogen was based on excluding all national-forest land and other protected or sensitive zones. About 60 percent of a kilogram of hydrogen cost is based on electricity expense—for capital for new equipment and actual generation. As renewable green electricity systems come online, that cost will dramatically flatten and could actually approach $1.60 per kilogram of hydrogen, this using 2004 technology and applying a cheap kilowatt supply.[25]

How can green kilowatt costs be dramatically lowered? Local and state government ownership and control of green electricity generation facilities—which will come online only after taxpayer investment—could be a key factor in massively reducing electrical cost and increasing hydrogen production. Cities and states already own and control their own waterworks, sewage treatment, garbage pickup, airports, highways, transit systems, and ports. Historically, utility and transit systems in many cases became public property only after abandonment or economic misconduct by the original private companies. In many communities, electrical utilities are already community-owned cooperatives.

Petropolitical independence from oil is hastened by black hydrogen even as the environmental damage continues. So those who want to solve the economic and political hazards of the world's oil addiction first and foremost encourage hydrogen in any hue—black or green. Black hydrogen, as of summer 2006, is abundantly available and can be processed through our normal electrical grid as a temporary "bridge technology" until windmills, solar, thermal, and like methods are deployed to provide the industrial-strength electricity needed to furnish green hydrogen. Hydrogen pioneer Kordesch stresses, "Everyone argues there is plenty of hydrogen everywhere, but the nagging question is still how you get it into the pipe."[26] Whether powered by black or green sources, the "how" of creating hydrogen will affect cost for the foreseeable future, and that formula will change faster than any book can project.

Whether powered by renewable electricity or traditional hydrocarbons such as coal or natural gas, hydrogen must be extracted from something else in nature. Extracting it from natural gas is cheaper, many argue, because methane is easier to break into its components of carbon and hydrogen; that process, as of summer 2006, requires less electricity. Getting hydrogen from water requires much more electricity, as of summer 2006, so even though the water that contains hydrogen seems fundamentally free or inexpensive as it is in most industrialized regions, the additional electrical wattage increases the end cost. But all costs are dramatically changing almost daily. Even while this paragraph was being typed in summer 2006, General Electric announced a prototype machine to electrolyze water and extract the hydrogen for less than half the cost prevailing the day before. The new machine will do the job for about $3 per kilogram—down from $8 per kilogram. That new cost is about the same as the equivalent process needed to produce gasoline. GE cut its electrolyzer cost by more than half by using plastics and reducing other capital costs.[27]

Once hydrogen is supplied, it leads to the second question: How will this gas be used by automobiles and trucks? Answer: either of two ways. *Hydrogen internal combustion engines*, called H-ICEs, burn hydrogen instead of gasoline; the car remains fundamentally the same, but a different fuel—hydrogen—is ignited in the cylinder. Better but more complicated is the *hydrogen fuel cell* vehicle, which replaces the traditional motor with a complex device that converts the innate power of hydrogen into the electrical energy needed to make the vehicle move.[28]

H-ICEs are relatively easy to make. Small modifications are made in the engine and fueling intake, and two or three steel gas cylinders are installed to supply hydrogen gas rather than traditional gasoline. H-ICEs have the advantage of starting in extremely cold weather. These hydrogen vehicles can be put into production immediately with no waiting. Ford has sold a small fleet of eight hotel-style H-ICE airport shuttle buses in Florida under a subsidized program. But the shuttle buses constitute a mere token project driven by taxpayer subsidy. As of summer 2006, Ford has not made plans for its so-called Model U passenger H-ICE vehicle, a concept car the company unveiled at a 2003 auto show. Ford sources stated it may be a decade before its Model U or anything like it is available to the public. Instead, company sources stated, Ford is concentrating on coal-intensive, petroleum-dependent ethanol cars, the flex-fuel vehicles. Asked why the company was helping to build an infrastructure and ramping up for problematic ethanol instead of implementing hydrogen internal combustion vehicles to use existing hydrogen supplies, a spokesman replied, "That is a good question. I don't have an answer."[29]

General Motors is even more committed to ethanol than Ford. GM, which declined to accept questions on the subject, is helping erect a network of Midwest ethanol outlets as it ramps up production for large fuel-inefficient SUVs that can flexibly run on either traditional petroleum or an ethanol blend.[30] Both Ford and General Motors are constantly reevaluating their plans as they see foreign competitors racing toward the hydrogen launchpad. But the two financially devastated Detroit giants are so frantically busy salvaging their past at dusk, they cannot spare a moment to cope with the coming sunrise of a hydrogen future.

Many will not wait for Ford or GM to produce H-ICEs—the right now alternative. The California Highway Patrol retrofitted one of its own cars to burn hydrogen instead of gasoline as a test, and the vehicle is achieving perfect performance in real-world operation. Small companies are springing up around the country to do the same. Hence, scores of garage-tinkered H-ICEs are rolling onto American streets, fueled by industrial hydrogen sources. But these conversions, which require the vehicle-by-vehicle installation of heavy steel hydrogen tanks, are simply too costly at low volumes and too scattered to amount to anything more than symbolism and popular energy defiance.[31] In many ways, they are cries for help.

Better than the H-ICE but far more complex is the fuel cell, which typically works by bringing the hydrogen in contact with two electrodes coated on one side with a thin catalyst layer. That thin catalyst layer divides the hydrogen into protons and electrons. Those "freed electrons" are the power that makes the automobile engine work and eventually turns the wheels. Hundreds of demonstration hydrogen cars and trucks are in operation around the world, scores of them in America as of 2006. Buses running in Amsterdam, Barcelona, London, Madrid, Oakland, Reykjavik, and other cities have already served more than four million passengers. Germany has deployed four stealthy hydrogen submarines, with more being ordered by Greece, Italy, and South Korea.[32]

All hydrogen vehicles face one stumbling block: storage. Hydrogen is light and hard to handle. Pound per pound, hydrogen packs nearly three times the energy of gasoline — 120 megajoules per kilogram for hydrogen against 44 megajoules per kilogram of gasoline. But on a volume basis, the numbers are inverted. Light and expansive hydrogen yields only 3 megajoules per liter at 5,000 pounds per square inch or 8 megajoules per liter as a liquid, even as gasoline delivers 32 megajoules per liter. Hence it takes a greater volume of hydrogen to deliver the same range and power as gasoline. Hydrogen must be compressed to deliver portable energy. More important, while gasoline can be stored in a cheap and compact gas tank, compressed hydrogen requires heavy steel cylinders, which add weight and a great deal of cost. Experts, such as Kordesch, say that a typical tank's weight is composed of 2 percent hydrogen and 98 percent heavy steel. Volume production of hydrogen cars can bring the cost down, but the cylinder still adds a great deal of weight and expense.[33]

Storage problems can be solved. Among the most discussed is cryogenics, that is, cooling the hydrogen down to a frigid liquid at -453 degrees Fahrenheit. That makes the hydrogen portable as a liquid. But the volatile liquid hydrogen actually boils furiously at room temperature and requires sophisticated and expensive controls to maintain its cold and then carefully convert it to gas. BMW, however, has tackled the problem and plans by 2009 to roll out a limited-production Series 7 hydrogen car that uses advanced cryogenic fuel tanks that will give its automobiles great range. The carmaker would help proliferate liquid-hydrogen-dispensing pumps at ordinary gas stations.[34]

Another solution, says Kordesch, is to distribute fuel in the form of ordinary ammonia, which is among the most common chemicals on earth. Everyone has come into contact with ammonia, the household product commonly found in kitchen and toilet cleansers, and universally sold. Ammonia is 75 percent hydrogen and 25 percent nitrogen. Kordesch states that ammonia could be stored in any hydrogen car in a "very cheap, simple plastic fuel container" and processed through an onboard automotive catalytic cracker to "crack" the molecule, releasing the hydrogen to a fuel cell. In its "uncracked state," the fluid is safe enough to be classified as nonflammable by the U.S. Department of Transportation. Yet, ammonia powered the X-15 rocket plane, says Kordesch, who worked on the U.S. space program. It is potent. Demonstration ammonia-based fuel cells have already been assembled in Graz, Austria. China sells more ammonia than gasoline. America produces some twenty million tons annually. It can easily be distributed at any filling station, propane-dispensing outlet, or grocery store. The main problem is that in the event of a leak, the process releases one of the most malodorous of smells—that fertilizer reek would have to be chemically neutralized to be tolerable to consumers.[35]

Other solutions talk of injecting hydrogen into exotic chemical compounds that act as carriers and are then filled into containers big and small made of advanced materials that can fuel everything from a cell phone to a semitruck. One of the most intriguing suggestions is embedding hydrogen into nanocarbon, that is, fibers woven from microscopic tubular structures a billionth of a meter in diameter. Nanocarbon is up to one hundred times stronger than steel—yet one-sixth its weight. Experts at thirty universities and U.S. Department of Energy laboratories are now devising new methods of storing hydrogen. Storage issues are now front and center, but they will soon be solved—perhaps quite basically at first, and certainly they will vastly improve with time.[36]

The final challenge is one of infrastructure. Where do drivers fuel up their hydrogen automobiles? Except for a few heavily government-subsidized demonstration pumps, there are no hydrogen stations—no infrastructure. American automakers who go slow on hydrogen loudly justify their phlegmatic approach with a ready-made answer: "We cannot make cars that cannot be refueled." These companies claim that hydrogen is just not being distributed the way gasoline is, that is, in pipelines, railroad cars, and large tanker trucks. GM, typical of go-slow automakers, claims infrastructure will be in place by 2020. The hydrogen movement calls this the "chicken-egg" debate, meaning which comes first, the stations with hydrogen to dispense or the cars to use them? No cars can be built without stations, no stations without cars. Many oil companies are preparing to jump into the hydrogen distribution business—but not until future decades and even then only incrementally as oil runs critically short. Until then, the oil companies assert, progress on energy independence can only inch along.[37]

To counter a sluggish industry response, California governor Arnold Schwarzenegger has become a hydrogen warrior and a real-life alternative-energy hero by committing his state to developing a "Hydrogen Highway." Others have followed, including Florida and British Columbia. Schwarzenegger's vision, which has become a cause célèbre for environmentalist and hydrogen advocates, mandates the establishment of some two-hundred commercial hydrogen filling stations, one every twenty miles along the freeways of California, and all within easy reach of every motorist. Schwarzenegger's target date for completion is 2010.[38]

"The goal of the California Hydrogen Highway Network initiative," Schwarzenegger declared, "is to support and catalyze a rapid transition to a clean, hydrogen transportation economy in California, thereby reducing our dependence on foreign oil, and protecting our citizens from health harms related to vehicle emissions. We have an opportunity to deal with these problems by investing in California's ability to innovate our way to a clean hydrogen future, thus bringing jobs, investment, and continued economic prosperity to California. We have an opportunity to prove to the world that a thriving environment and economy can coexist."[39]

Schwarzenegger's vision requires an estimated investment of as much as $200 million and years of industrial effort almost from scratch.[40] However, the flamboyant governor and his allies in hydrogen advocacy are finding the effort an uphill battle precisely because of the chicken-egg argument that mandates inch-by-inch progress. However, the infrastructure argument is false, just the latest daily dose of a century of lies, and a pretext for hydrogen delay.

Hydrogen is the most abundant matter in the universe and is also massively distributed throughout the world and in the United States. More than 9 million tons of hydrogen are annually manufactured and distributed in the United States alone; each year, bulk hydrogen is distributed by some 10,000 shipments by rail, truck, and existing pipelines to more than 300 destinations. Among the major industrial companies supplying bulk hydrogen worldwide by the millions of tons are Air Liquide, which operates 130 subsidiaries in 65 countries; Air Products, which maintains 100 miles of hydrogen pipeline in America and distributes 190,000 kilograms of hydrogen daily to more than 20 American customers, including leading oil refineries, which depend upon it to make cleaner gasoline; BOC Group, which operates hydrogen plants world-wide; Linde, which works extensively in America and Europe; and Prax-air, which maintains seven hydrogen pipelines worldwide, including a 310-mile hydrogen pipeline system along the U.S. Gulf Coast, which as of summer 2006 delivers 700 million cubic feet daily to more than 50 chemical plants, steel factories, metallurgical facilities, and oil refineries. Two Praxair plants completed in 2004 by themselves produce some 200 million cubic feet of hydrogen daily. The company also ships liquid hydrogen daily. Praxair sales for all gases, including hydrogen, exceed $7.6 billion annually.[41]

Linde has partnered with BMW to produce the cryogenic hydrogen fuel tank due out before 2010. Air Products and Praxair are both active in the National Hydrogen Association and the movement to create a hydrogen vehicle. At a March 2006 hydrogen conference in Long Beach, California, representatives of both Praxair and Air Products publicly scoffed at notions that the hydrogen highway was awaiting a supply network for hydrogen. "We have enough hydrogen right now to fuel more than a million hydrogen cars—and many more if we try," said one Praxair senior manager. Praxair and Air Products officials agreed that the initial hydrogen highway already exists along their hundreds of miles of pipelines and along their active distribution routes. The first consumer hydrogen stations, executives say, would not need to be grandiose multimillion-dollar government-subsidized enterprises; they could be simple, low-cost stations adjacent to their pipelines and depots that would resemble any neighborhood gas station. From this initial highway along hundreds of arterial miles, growth could proceed in all directions, innervating the country with hydrogen access.[42]

Portable electrolysis and reforming units, many just slightly larger than a man with new models constantly becoming more compact, are available to create hydrogen fuel anywhere, anytime. They can be planted in the middle of the Mojave Desert or at a downtown Boston gas station, where they can convert water or other carriers such as common ammonia into hydrogen fuel. Intelligent Energy's Hestia hydrogen generator can produce pure hydrogen within one hour of a cold start-up, can be stacked to create large-scale operations, and can run on a range of alternative fuels including ammonia. Those compact hydrogen-fuel-producing facilities can be connected to Intelligent Energy's electricity-generating hydrogen fuel cells. Militaries throughout the world are looking at remote hydrogen production and electricity generation because they must ensure fuel supplies.[43]

In fact, the hydrogen highway is so ready to be opened to traffic that it already runs right into the sea. In 2004, the world's first oceangoing, self-contained, renewably powered hydrogen-production platform sailed into action. Germany's *Hydrogen Challenger* produces bulk hydrogen at sea using unlimited wind power to create its electricity. The *Hydrogen Challenger* literally maneuvers into the wind to achieve optimal power. Generally, the ship anchors off the windswept Niedersachsen coast. Its two deck-mounted, vertical-axis wind rotors and integrated generators subject water to electrolysis until the *Challenger* fills its belly with energy-rich hydrogen — 1,194 cubic meters at a time. The ship then sails to any coastal transmission point or factory to dispense its load, or even to another hydrogen-powered vessel to refuel it just as petroleum fuel ships do now for oil and colliers did for the British navy in the early twentieth century.[44]

In other words, the initial hydrogen highway already exists but is merely awaiting some on-ramps.

A telling exchange on the so-called absence of an infrastructure occurred with a Ford spokesman. Asked why the company was not proceeding on hydrogen cars, the spokesman repeated the well-worn explanation: "Because there is no hydrogen out there for anyone to refuel their car," adding, "Where are the stations?" Asked whether Ford was not establishing from scratch a farm-belt-based ethanol infrastructure, helping to create stations or a pump network, this in timed tandem with ever-mounting flex-fuel car production, the spokesman answered, "Yes." The spokesman was asked if it could be done for ethanol given the fuel's adverse ecological effects, why could it not be done for climate-friendly hydrogen, especially in regions such as the Gulf Coast where hydrogen is voluminously distributed by pipeline. Ford's spokesman paused, then replied, "That is a very good question. To be honest, there is no answer."[45]

The twentieth century has proved that good technology is impervious to a chicken-egg debate, which is in fact a canard. Roads required automobiles and automobiles required roads; they were built across the country until they connected every place with every other place. Lightbulbs required electricity and electricity companies needed lightbulb customers. Gasoline buyers required gas stations and gas stations required gasoline buyers; they were built. Leaded gasoline was phased out and unleaded gasoline was phased in; slender fuel apertures were installed in cars and station pumps converted to thin nozzles within a matter of years. Cellular phone users required towers and towers required users; they were built at an amazing rate, outpacing all prior network expansion. Then in the late nineties, cellular systems switched from analog to digital; towers sprouted first along the interstates from Washington to Baltimore and within a few years became omnipresent. DVDs required users with players and users required DVDs to play; the new format was adopted so quickly that VHS tapes became virtually obsolete within a matter of a few years.

Even now, Big Corn and Detroit carmakers are establishing a new network to produce and distribute petroleum-based ethanol, which requires ethanol-burning flex-fuel cars, which are being rolled off assembly lines at great speed.

But in spite of false futures and delayed futures, false pasts and recurring pasts, the long-postponed hydrogen revolution is under way. Petropolitical independence, a U-turn from ecocide and the restoral of the freedom and productivity that energy in general and automobiles in particular promised is all at hand. Deliverance will not come from Ford. It will not come from Chevrolet, Buick, Pontiac, or any other division of General Motors. It will come first, fastest, and most reliably from one company: American Honda.

The Honda solution will rewrite everything the public knows about automobile travel. No more gasoline. No more gas stations.

Honda, as of summer 2006, is at the tip of the hydrogen spear with its smooth-driving Hydrogen FCX. The Honda FCX drives exactly like any other car, stem to steering wheel, providing the automotive excellence and performance that Honda customers have learned to love—but this vehicle runs on clean hydrogen fuel. Honda is developing the fuel cell engine on its own dime, almost devoid of government subsidies. The company's FCX fleet, as of summer of 2006, is composed of more than thirty vehicles, each handmade in Japan at about $1 million per copy. These vehicles are leased for daily use by municipalities in both warm and cold climes in Japan, California, Nevada, and New York. In summer 2005, a California family was chosen to drive the first regular consumer FCX. Jon and Sandy Spallino of Redondo Beach, California, are paying for a two-year lease with their own money and driving under normal conditions. The 2006 FCX has all the appearances of a Spartan economy car.[46]

But production of a sleek, stunning, and compelling next-generation FCX was accelerated to commence before 2010. Jammed with advanced biometrics that recognize the driver as he or she approaches the door and adjusts the seat, steering wheel, dash icons, and pedals; outfitted with a new hydrogen absorption material that carries enough hydrogen for a 350-range; styled with enough rich verve to appeal to any enthusiast, the coming Honda FCX is not designed to be a stripped-down green alternative but literally the next-generation, must-drive, hot and handsome vehicle.[47]

More than a car, the Honda FCX comes with its own home-based hydrogen energy station that obsoletes gas stations and gasoline—and even cuts the tether to utility bills. About the size of a common home air-conditioning unit, the Honda Home Energy Station will be driven by natural gas, not electricity, and will create enough hydrogen daily to fill one or more FCX vehicles and heat and power an individual home. Honda's Home Energy Station is no pipe dream. Plug Power, an upstate–New York fuel-cell maker with more than six hundred installations worldwide, supplied Honda home power stations for several years before March 16, 2006, when they jointly announced the smallest model yet and most ambitious phase of their partnership—the FCX program. Honda's Home Energy Station will soon be configured to run on solar, either from panels or perhaps from nanosolar materials embedded in its sleek case or other nearby home surfaces. An estimated twenty square yards of nanosolar wrapped around a pole or a building surface could independently power Honda's Home Energy Station. A Plug Power source confirmed that the company's home station can be mass produced for the price of an air conditioner, opening the way to scalable untethered energy. Honda controls the license on Plug Power's home station technology.[48]

Beyond nanosolar is bacterial hydrogen. Scientists at Berlin's Technical University, Penn State, and elsewhere have been able to extract hydrogen from wastewater, biomass, and even dung using a variety of common algae. The algae receive a tiny electrical jolt, as little as a quarter volt, one-tenth the power needed for normal electrolysis. They produce bacteria that extract the hydrogen, which is then fed to a fuel cell. Right now, the amount of hydrogen power is still small. Craig Venter, the scientist behind the Human Genome Project, has created a new business venture called Synthetic Genomics expressly to create new microorganisms that will abundantly create hydrogen. Joining him is a dream team of research leaders and scientists, including Aristides Patrinos, former director of the Department of Energy's Office of Biological and Environmental Research; Hamilton Smith, an expert in DNA manipulation, who won the 1978 Nobel Prize for his work on restriction enzymes, a fundamental tool in recombinant DNA technology and techniques; and Juan Enriquez, founding director of Harvard Business School's Life Sciences Project. If Synthetic Genomics and numerous other scientific projects are successful, energy will be extracted from refuse and wastewater, which itself will then be cleansed.[49]

Plug Power and Honda are embarking upon what the energy industry calls distributed generation, that is, decentralized energy, energy detached from a central generating utility such as a coal-fired or nuclear plant. Decentralization has occurred in much technology and has in many ways defined the advanced nature of any society. Telephones migrated from switchboards to home land lines to tiny cellular phones. Dramatic productions went from central theaters to movie houses to home television, and now the biggest Hollywood blockbuster can be viewed on laptops or even mobile phones. Computers evolved from room-sized devices to mainframes, and within less than two decades evolved almost beyond imagination to personal computers and then to handheld cheap personal digital assistants or PDAs. The earliest nineteenth-century battery itself was an effort to go wireless. Air-conditioning is generated remotely, not centrally.

There is little sense in digging a hole thousands of miles away to be empowered by petroleum to run down to the market for a gallon of milk, or digging a hole hundreds of miles away to be empowered by coal or natural gas to turn on the lights. A nagging question arises: Why are we driving to the 7-Eleven via Saudi Arabia? Distributed generation of energy is a phenomenon long delayed. Distributed generation is the be-all and end-all of energy. But the idea is not modern. Thomas Edison advocated the same idea in 1912 — home energy stations for every home and farm — and he even built his own working mansion based on the self-generated power.

Honda's new FCX system finally gives the gift of total individual energy self-sufficiency, independent from the violent winds of Mideast petropolitics, the battering winds of Gulf hurricanes, or the escalating winds of monopolistic energy costs. It is the culminating intersection of centuries of energy history. FCX and many emulators who will follow will not cause wars — they will avoid them. Honda's approach is to supply not a grumbling alternative but a glittering success story that will succeed on its own inbred merits of design and functionality, as well as its absolute necessity as an answer to the petropolitical, human health, and ecocidal crises arising out of a century of internal combustion.

In its fast-tracked campaign, Honda rejected coal- and oil-based ethanol, as did many foreign carmakers who examined the prospect. Foreign carmakers without a vested interest in gas-guzzling SUVs or 51-cent-per-gallon subsidies quickly realized that ethanol was just substituting one oil-based system for another. Ethanol, they concluded, was just what it asserts it is: a gasoline additive or extender. Creating an ethanol diversion would only drag out the rule of King Oil and delay the day of true distributed-energy independence.[50]

Honda also rejected the notion of the standard battery-powered or grid-charged electrical car that is the dream of many alternative-fuel advocates who want off oil today and not tomorrow. Toyota's Prius electric-gasoline hybrid is so hotly in demand that green-motivated motorists pay thousands above sticker price just to drive one. The Prius smartly generates its electricity from the generator in tandem with braking. But it is in fact a petroleum car with better mileage by virtue of its reliance on electrical systems. A rebellious movement of Prius evangelists now modify their Prius vehicles as plug-ins, trying to get them closer to the Holy Grail of a purely electrical car. Toyota, however, bristles at those who tinker with their Priuses and assures that a purely electrical car is not even being considered.[51]

Electric cars were subverted a century ago when internal combustion overtook the roads. In the seventies, after the first Arab oil shock, electric cars were reintroduced by GM, Honda, and other major carmakers. But those highly successful cars were all systematically destroyed as GM, Honda, and other car companies invoked their lease rights, repossessed the beloved vehicles from their fiercely loyal drivers, and then sent the cars to metal crushers. The inexplicable campaign of repossession and destruction of electric cars by their makers has spawned an entire movement of protesters who curse the day they were forced to give up their leased electric cars.[52]

But in fact, the new Honda FCX is the first of a new generation of twenty-first-century electric cars. The FCX is driven by electrons, not internal combustion. But those electrons are not created by a heavy industrial battery dating back to the nineteenth century, they are created by a hydrogen fuel cell like the one that boosted a man to the moon. The untethered electricity that powers the FCX and its adjacent household does not require coal, and one day will not even utilize natural gas, which pumps about two-thirds the level of greenhouse gases released by petroleum.

Honda is not alone in pursuing hydrogen cars. Most major automakers—both here and abroad—are dabbling in the field. GM and Ford have both built demonstration hydrogen cars heavily subsidized by Department of Energy grants. But it is the foreign carmakers, essentially disqualified from taxpayer moneys, that have done the most to race to the hydrogen highway on-ramp. At the March 2006 National Hydrogen Association annual conference in Long Beach, the automakers strutted their best efforts. This writer test-drove many of them in ordinary Long Beach city traffic and then along that city's famous Grand Prix track. The taxpayer-subsidized Ford vehicle certainly proved the technology moved but to many lacked finesse. The taxpayer-subsidized GM passenger car combined a confusing mix of supposedly modern dash controls but rendered a noticeably unsmooth, almost jolting ride. GM also previewed a taxpayer-subsidized heavy-duty pickup truck, developed for the military, which was as loud and shaky as a World War I–era Model T. The Mercedes-Benz vehicle was cramped and noisy inside because of the engine. The Audi offered an excellent ride and almost rocketlike acceleration that would make it desirable to any car enthusiast. All these vehicles were years away from production, and most seemed not ready for prime time.[53]

But the Honda FCX offered every comfort and quality of a regular Honda, drove seamlessly, smoothly, and handled like the best vehicles the company makes. Except for the decal on the side, there was no way to know the car was powered by a hydrogen-fuel-cell stack. It was a machine that anyone would desire and never detect a compromise.[54]

Steve Ellis, manager of fuel-cell marketing for American Honda, discussed the engineering accomplishment and the company's vision. Seated in a quiet corner of an emptied section of the Long Beach convention hall, Ellis looked up and recalled that day on September 11, 2001: "As soon as I saw those two airplanes fly into the World Trade Center, I knew we had to get busy."[55] But his answer is not a half measure, a diversion, or a compromise product. Ellis and Honda want to deliver a car that will not only solve the energy problem, but will also be a product to be proud of and one that will make real money, justifying the substantial investment Honda is making.

BMW is chasing Honda at high speed. Its Series 7 promises to deliver a BMW-quality vehicle based on cryogenics and liquid hydrogen, expected to go into production not long after the FCX goes into production, about 2009 or 2010. However, BMW's path does not, as of summer 2006, include the distributed generation or home fueling that Honda is scheduled to deliver.[56]

Toyota is quieter about its hydrogen plans but has actively been engaged in hydrogen development since the late eighties. The company inaugurated fuel-cell research in the early nineties and by 1996 constructed a demonstration car with a hydrogen-absorbing alloy tank. The next year, the company developed a system that extracted hydrogen from methane via an on-board reformer. In March 2001 in Tokyo, Toyota unveiled its advanced FCHV-3. Toyota has been adding functionality every year and has expanded into hydrogen-powered city buses. "Honda leads for now," a Toyota source stated. "For now. But one day soon, we will lead." The company official blasted Department of Energy subsidies to develop demonstration hydrogen cars that were limited to "American companies," and therefore excluded Toyota, Honda, and BMW. "All the foreign car companies have been excluded," he protested.[57]

Ironically, the American companies will not be leading the parade onto the hydrogen highway. That will be Honda, which will have to look over its shoulder continuously as it is chased by BMW, Audi, Toyota, and other foreign carmakers. When any of the companies roll out their production models in 2009 or 2010, those cars will not be available at showrooms, but to select commercial and governmental customers, such as municipalities, the military, or major corporate or government fleet owners. It will be another year or two for the production volume to bring the costs down to consumer levels.

Anticipating the years-long rollout, Honda already has in place a bridge technology that uses compressed natural gas. Honda's CNG car, which has been available since 2005, operates on the same natural gas commonly supplied to kitchens and backyard grills. The heavy CNG tanks take up most of the trunk, leaving only enough space for a few briefcases. That makes the CNG a personal city car or a fleet car. But it delivers the first measure of petropolitical independence because it uses no gasoline. Moreover, Honda's CNG, like the FCX, comes with its own home filling station. The CNG home-fueling device, called Phill, is purchased either directly from Honda in some states, or elsewhere from the fueling-machine manufacturer. It can be installed as easily as a gas grill.[58]

Honda's CNG and its slender home-fueling machine were to be rolled out with great fanfare in April 2005 because it represented a revolutionary option to oil-based automobiles and tethering to gas stations. But on the day the breakthrough was to be announced, a confused young Georgia woman, Jennifer Wilbanks, disappeared en route to her wedding. At first, authorities thought Wilbanks was kidnapped. Soon it emerged that Wilbanks was a just an overstressed woman who had cracked under wedding jitters and simply run away. In a nonstop media circus, television, radio, and many newspapers focused on what became known as "the runaway bride." Every other news development seemed to pale by comparison. Hence, Honda's breakthrough could not break through to the American public. Nonetheless, the CNG, which employs a Honda Civic body, drives with as much pep and versatility as any other Honda Civic. Any individual or fleet searching for an immediate solution to gasoline can purchase one.[59]

Compressed natural gas, which enjoys the industry-inspired moniker "clean natural gas," is actually not clean. True it is less hazardous to health than oil and coal in many key aspects. But according to the natural gas industry's own figures, its hydrocarbon-based product is still a significant source of greenhouse gases and a contributor to global warming. True, natural gas's mercury and sulfur dioxide emissions are nil compared to oil and coal. But natural gas releases almost 10 percent as much particulate pollution as oil combustion, and about a fifth as much nitrous oxide as oil or coal. At the same time, natural gas actually releases more carbon monoxide than oil burning, and 117,000 pounds of carbon dioxide per billion Btu of energy, compared to 164,000 for oil and 208,000 for coal. Hence, driving Honda's CNG or riding as a passenger in one of the growing fleet of CNG city buses emblazoned with "clean natural gas," and rolling through American cities does significantly advance petropolitical independence and reduces emissions harmful to health. But using natural gas only slows the slide toward climate change. Natural gas remains a major source of global warming.[60]

A hierarchy of threats and crises confronts a world under the rule of petroliferous internal combustion. The disastrous effects of global warming may already be irreversible, or there may still be time to halt the process. That is being debated by experts and pundits. But the disastrous effects of another Hurricane Katrina or a choking terrorist attack on the oil infrastructure, or petropolitical blackmail from countries such as Iran or a new regime in Saudi Arabia, may be upon the world in the twinkling of an eye. During such a disruption, oil could quickly become scarce or unaffordable. The Strategic Oil Reserve, which maintains a ninety-day emergency supply of crude, still requires refineries to turn the petroleum into oil and lubricating products. If extreme weather, industrial accident, or terror disables America's fragile refining ability, the dramatic effects could spring to life within hours. During the brief refinery disruptions of Hurricane Katrina in 2005, gasoline prices at the pump skyrocketed at some gas stations, as often as three times in a day for the very same oil reposing in their tanks.[61] These near-term threats impart towering immediacy to breaking free of the oil addiction, and all the alternatives within reach are advocated by those who sense the danger.

In the absence of a government-launched Manhattan Project, the public must turn first not to the White House or the statehouse, but to the largest fleet owners in the country. Those fleets can impact the automobile market and the internal combustion threat with the ink on a purchase order. For-hire carriers in 2004 operated 675,000 trucks; the top ten include such companies as UPS, Federal Express, and Yellow Roadway. UPS alone deploys some eighty thousand brown trucks daily as it makes thirteen million deliveries every twenty-four hours. Only about a thousand of UPS's massive fleet ran on CNG as of summer 2006. Within Federal Express's 70,000-vehicle fleet, the company operates 30,000 medium-duty trucks, of which less than a hundred are hybrid diesel, as of summer 2006.[62]

Some six million additional vehicles are owned by private commercial fleets such as Sysco, Wal-Mart, Halliburton, and Frito-Lay. Wal-Mart alone operates 3,300 trucks that in 2005 drove 455 million miles to make nine hundred thousand deliveries. Verizon operated 70,000 trucks and cars in 2004. Waste Management operated about 28,000 vehicles in 2004. Krispy Kreme doughnuts operated 750 vehicles in 2004. City, state, and federal agencies, as well as universities, comprise just a fraction of America's 38,000 private fleets.[63]

Fleets—governmental, commercial, and private—have a compelling purchasing power no automaker can ignore. If fleet managers issued a hierarchy of purchasing that mandated hydrogen cars first, fully electric cars second, and CNG cars third, the race would be on among all truck and heavy-duty vehicle manufacturers from GM to Mercedes to be the first to fill those orders. Volume purchasing will multiply and accelerate the technology, bring down costs, and migrate it swiftly from commercial fleets to average consumer.

Therefore, the public and environmentally conscious companies can choose to ship green, shop green, drink green, and even communicate green. For example, in choosing an overnight shipper, will it be Federal Express or UPS? In buying soda, will it be Coke or Pepsi? Corporate policies, such as nondiscrimination, labor fairness, environmental damage, and other conduct are already determining factors for many in choosing where to place their business. Therefore, there is more power in one petition to UPS and Federal Express than to all members of Congress combined.

Ironically, the federal government itself maintains America's single largest fleet by far—some 600,000 vehicles. Environmental groups have consistently sued the federal government to compel it to follow its own alternative-fuel guidelines. The Energy Policy Act, passed after the first Gulf War, mandates all federal agencies to reduce oil dependence by ensuring that some 75 percent of new vehicle purchases use alternative fuels. The law has been totally ignored. A steady cascade of court rulings has rejected government requests for delays. Government purchases alone could spur the rapid adoption of any category of alternative-fuel vehicle—hydrogen or otherwise.[64]

Governments and regimes since the time of the pharaohs, since the days of medieval England, since the advent of the Industrial Age, since the rise of the battery, since the demise of the electric car, since the triumph of petroleum, have declined to exercise a public policy that exercises sane stewardship over energy and those who control it.

Distributed generation can be more than passing power from central control to individuals to run mere hairdryers and televisions. Power can also flow to individuals determined to run their world and their lives in such a way that will preserve their lives and their world, preserve their way of life and their prosperity. Internal combustion has slowly been burning through the human, economic, and environmental resources of civilization. But the fuel is finite.

Many believe the notion that man inherits the earth. Not so, he only holds it as a precious legacy for succeeding generations. That inheritance must not be squandered or reduced to rubble because of the war, industrial epidemic, or ecocidal damage arising from the intoxicating but toxic fumes of internal combustion.

NOTES

Chapter 1: The Plan Against Oil

1. "Edison Sees His Vast Plant Burn," *New York Times*, December 10, 1914, 1, 3. Letter, W. G. Bee to Henry Ford, December 10, 1914, Benson Ford Research Center, Acc 1630 4-4-5.
2. "Edison Sees His Vast Plant Burn," 1, 3. Letter, Bee to Ford, December 10, 1914.
3. "Edison Sees His Vast Plant Burn," 1. "Mrs. Edison Saved Husband's Records," *New York Times*, December 11, 1914, 9. Letter, Bee to Ford, December 10, 1914.
4. Letter, W. G. Bee to E. G. Liebold, December 17, 1914, Benson Ford Research Center, Acc 1630 4-5.
5. Ibid.
6. "Newspaper Specials," *Wall Street Journal*, December 12, 1914, 2. "Edison Never Flinches at $7,000,000 Fire," *Boston Globe*, December 10, 1914, 1–2. Matthew Josephson, *Edison: A Biography* (New York: McGraw-Hill, 1959), 429.
7. "Edison Sees His Vast Plant Burn," 1. " 'Wizard' Edison Loses $7,000,000 by Flames That Sweep His Plant," *Atlanta Constitution*, December 10, 1914, 1.
8. Generally see chapter 8.
9. Ibid.
10. Generally see chapters 5 and 6.
11. Generally see chapters 7 and 8.
12. Generally see chapter 7.
13. Ibid.
14. Gijs Mom, *The Electric Vehicle* (Baltimore, MD: Johns Hopkins University Press, 2004), 82–83.
15. Morris A. Hall, "The Fuel Question and Kerosene Carburetors," *Horseless Age* 30, no. 12 (September 18, 1912): 445. Henry T. Sullivan, "Henry Ford's New Scheme," *Boston Globe*, January 18, 1914, 48.
16. Hall, "Fuel Question," 445. Also see "Hopes to Expand Fuel Range," *New York Times*, February 16, 1913, 86.
17. "Hopes to Expand Fuel Range," 86.
18. Generally see Craig Colten, "A Historical Perspective on Industrial Wastes and Groundwater Contamination," *Geographical Review* 81, no. 2 (April 1991): 215–28.
19. "Sewer Explosion Terrifies a Block," *New York Times*, November 9, 1913, 3.

20.   "Convention of Electric Vehicle Association of America," *Horseless Age* 30, no. 16 (October 16, 1912): 597. "Electric Vehicle Association Discusses Cheap Electrics," *Horseless Age* 32, no. 14 (October 1, 1913): 549. Ford R. Bryan, *Friends, Families & Forays: Scenes From the Life and Times of Henry Ford* (Dearborn, MI: Ford Books, 2002), 155–56.

21.   Bryan, *Friends, Families*, 156.

22.   "Edison's Latest Marvel—the Electric Country House," *New York Times*, September 15, 1912, SM9.

23.   Ibid.

24.   Letter, Thomas Edison to W. C. Anderson, November 20, 1911, Benson Ford Research Center, Acc 1630 Box 2, Folder 2-22. Letter, Thomas Edison to W. C. Anderson, November 30, 1911, Benson Ford Research Center, Acc 1630 Box 2, Folder 2-23. Bryan, *Friends, Families*, 155.

25.   Letter, Thomas Edison to Henry Ford, October 29, 1912, Benson Ford Research Center, Acc 1630 Box 2, Folder 2-28.

26.   Letter, Thomas Edison to Harry, undated. Bryan, *Friends, Families*, 154–55. "Ford Discusses Radical Scheme," newspaper clipping, Henry Ford Archive, Vertical File—Electric Cars.

27.   "Ford Discusses Radical Scheme."

28.   Ibid. "Ford Plans New Auto," *Washington Post*, January 12, 1914, 9.

29.   "Ford Plans New Auto," 9.

Chapter 2: Power Struggle

1.   Alan W. Cramb, *A Short History of Metals* (Department of Materials Science & Engineering, Carnegie Mellon University), 2. See "Documenta Prehistorica XXIX: Neolithic Studies 9, Abstracts," http://www.ff.uni-lj.edu. See Theodore A. Wertime, "The Furnace versus the Goat: The Pyrotechnic Industries and Mediterranean Deforestation in Antiquity," *Journal of Field Archaeology* 10, no. 4 (Winter 1983): 445–50. See T. A. Rickard, "The Primitive Smelting of Iron," *American Journal of Archaeology* 43, no. 1 (January–March 1939): 85–88. Also see Peter R. Schmidt and D. H. Avery, "More Evidence for an Advanced Prehistoric Iron Technology in Africa," *Journal of Field Archaeology* 10, no. 4 (Winter 1983): 421–34.

2.   Cramb, *Short History*, 1–5. See Wertime, "Furnace versus Goat," 446–47, 450. See Rickard, "Primitive Smelting," 87, 100. See J. R. McNeill, "Woods and Warfare in World History," *Environmental History* 9, no. 3 (July 2004), 2. Also see generally V. Biringocchio, *Pirotechnia*, trans. C. S. Smith (New York: Dover, 1942). Also see generally T. Wertime and S. Wertime, eds., *Early Pyrotechnology: The Evolution of the Fire Using Industries* (Washington, DC: Smithsonian, 1982). Also see generally W. H. Gourdin and W. D. Kingery, "The Beginnings of Pyrotechnology: Neolithic and Egyptian Lime Plasters," *Journal of Field Archaeology* 2, no. 1/2 (1975). Also see Henri Limet, *La Travail du metal au pays de Sumer au temps de la IIIme Dynastie d'Ur* (Paris: Bibliothèque de la Faculté de Philosophie et Lettres de l'Université de Liège, 1960), as cited by Wertime, "Furnace versus Goat."

3.   Cramb, *Short History*, 1–3. See Wertime, "Furnace versus Goat," 445–48, 450, 452, and generally. See McNeill, "Woods and Warfare," 2. Also see Ellen Churchill Semple, "Climatic and Geographic Influences on Ancient Mediterranean Forests and the Lumber Trade," *Annals of the Association of American Geographers* 9 (1919): 17, 21. Also see gener-

ally J. Donald Hughes, "How the Ancients Viewed Deforestation," *Journal of Field Archaeology* 10, no. 4 (Winter 1983).

4. Cramb, *Short History*, 2. See Wertime, "Furnace versus Goat," 449. Also see Semple, "Climatic and Geographic Influences," 13–40. See http://www.biologydaily.com/biology/History_of_Cyprus. See McNeill, "Woods and Warfare," 2, 3.

5. A. Bernard Knapp, Vasiliki Kassianidou, and Michael Donnelly, "Copper Smelting in Late Bronze Age Cyprus: The Excavations at Politiko Phorades," *Near Eastern Archaeology* 64, no. 4 (December 2001): 204, 206.

6. http://nefertiti.iwebland.com/alasiya.htm. See Knapp, Kassianidou, and Donnelly, "Copper Smelting," 204.

7. http://nefertiti.iwebland.com/alasiya.htm. See Knapp, Kassianidou, and Donnelly, "Copper Smelting," 204. See McNeill, "Woods and Warfare," 2.

8. See Semple, "Climatic and Geographic Influences," 17, 19–20. Also see McNeill, "Woods and Warfare," 6–7, 8, 14. See Robert Biddulph, "Cyprus," *Proceedings of the Royal Geographical Society and Monthly Record of Geography*, n.s., 11, no. 12 (December 1889): 710.

9. Biddulph, "Cyprus," 709–10; McNeill, "Woods and Warfare," 2; http://www.geocities.com. See J. V. Thirgood, *Man and the Mediterranean Forest* (London: Academic Press, 1981), as cited by McNeill, "Woods and Warfare," 2. See Semple, "Climatic and Geographic Influences," 17, 19, 39–40. See Wertime, "Furnace versus Goat," 448. Also see Alessandra Nibbi, *Ancient Egypt and Some Eastern Neighbors* (Park Ridge, NJ: Noyes Press, 1981).

10. McNeill, "Woods and Warfare," 2–8. Wertime, "Furnace versus Goat," 448, 450–52. Semple, "Climatic and Geographic Influences," 31. H. A. Koster and H. A. Forbes, "The Commons and the Market: Ecological Effects on Communal Land Tenure and Market Integration of Local Resources in the Mediterranean" (unpublished paper presented 1978 at this symposium), as cited by Wertime, "Furnace versus Goat." See Ian Shaw, *Egyptian Warfare and Weapons* (Princes Risborough, UK: Shire Publications, 1991), 31–44, as cited by McNeill, "Woods and Warfare." See Anthony Snodgrass, *Arms and Armour of the Greeks* (Ithaca, NY: Cornell University Press, 1967), as cited by McNeill. Also see Leonard U. Salkield, "The Roman and Pre-Roman Slags at Rio Tinto, Spain," in *Early Pyrotechnology*, ed. Wertime and Wertime, as cited by Wertime, footnote 39. Also see Russell Meiggs, *Trees and Timber in the Ancient Mediterranean World* (Oxford: Clarendon Press, 1982), as cited by McNeill. See generally Wertime. See Semple, 19, 21. See McNeill, 12. See Koster and Forbes, 450.

11. McNeill, "Woods and Warfare," 9–12, 14. See Semple, "Climatic and Geographic Influences," 16, 21. McNeill, 9, 10, 14. Semple, 16–17.

12. I. G. Simmons, *An Environmental History of Britain: From 10,000 Years Ago to the Present* (Edinburgh: Edinburgh University Press, 2001), 94. See http://www.domesdaybook.co.uk. Also see http://www.fordham.edu/halsall/source/domesday1.html. See Dorothy Whitelock, ed. and trans., *The Anglo-Saxon Chronicle 1086–1087* (New Brunswick, NJ: Rutgers University Press, 1961); http://www.maxwell.syr.edu; http://www.royal.gov.uk. See http://www.yale.edu/lawweb. Also see Ernest F. Henderson, *Select Historical Documents of the Middle Ages* (London: George Bell, 1896).

13. Charles R. Young, "English Royal Forests under the Angevin Kings," *Journal of British Studies* 12, no. 1 (November 1972): 1–14. Elizabeth Cox Wright, "Common Law in the

Thirteenth Century English Royal Forest," *Speculum* 3, no. 2 (April 1928): 166, 168. See Charles Petit-Dutaillis and Georges Lefebvre, *Studies and Notes Supplementary to Stubbs' Constitutional History* (Manchester, 1930), 166, as cited by Young, "English Royal Forests." Petit-Dutaillis and Lefebvre, 166. Assize of Woodstock and Forest Assize of 1198 in *Pipe Roll 31 Hen. 2*, 123, 148. (P.R.O.). See Charles R. Young, "The Forest Eyre in England During the Thirteenth Century," *American Journal of Legal History* 18, no. 4 (October 1974): 321–31. See G. J. Turner, ed., *Select Pleas of the Forest* (Selden Society) (London: B. Quaritch, 1901): 63–64. See Jude James, interview with the author, August 9, 2005. See Petit-Dutaillis and Lefebvre, *Studies*, as cited by Young, "English Royal Forests." See William H. Te Brake, "Air Pollution and Fuel Crises in Preindustrial London, 1250–1650," *Technology and Culture* 16, no. 3 (July 1975): 350.

14.　James A. Galloway, Derek Keene, and Margaret Murphy, "Fuelling the City: Production and Distribution of Firewood and Fuel in London's Region, 1290–1400," *Economic History Review*, n.s., 49, no. 3 (August 1996): 456. Young, "English Royal Forests," 12, 13. Wright, "Common Law," 166. Margaret L. Bazeley, "The Extent of the English Forest in the Thirteenth Century," *Transactions of the Royal Historical Society*, 4th ser., 4 (1921): 140–72, as cited by Young, "English Royal Forests," 12. Also see James, interview.

15.　Richard fitz Nigel, *Dialogus de Scaccario* (Dialogue of the Exchequer) (c.1178), ed. and trans. Charles Johnson (London 1950), 60, as cited by Young, "English Royal Forests," 8. Young, 14. See Assize of Woodstock and Forest Assize of 1198, as cited by Young, "English Royal Forests," 12. Bazeley, "Forest of Dean," 169. *Pipe Roll 5 John*, 160–61; *Pipe Roll 10 John*, 202–5; *Rotuli Litterarum Patentium* 1, 27a, 29b, 78b, 106a, as cited by Young, "English Royal Forests," 9. See *Pipe Rolls Hen. 2* (scattered references), as cited by Young, "English Royal Forests," 10. See James H. Ramsay, *The Angevin Empire* (London, 1903), 194–95, as cited by Young, "English Royal Forests," 11. See Forest Proceedings, Treasury of the Receipt, 5 (P.R.O.), as cited by Young, "Forest Eyre," 325. See *Rotuli Litterarum Patentium* 1, 31b, as cited by Young, "English Royal Forests," 10–11. See fitz Nigel, *Dialogus*, 56–59, as cited by Young, "English Royal Forests," 11. See Forest Proceedings, Treasury of the Receipt, 235; *Pipe Roll 14 Hen. 2*, 44 (P.R.O.), as cited by Young, "English Royal Forests," 11.

16.　Wright, "Common Law," 168. Young, "Forest Eyre," 321, 327–28. Robert Grosseteste, *Epistolae*, ed. H. R. Luard (Rolls Series), 353, as cited by Young. See Young, "English Royal Forests," 5–6. See Wright, 168.

17.　Young, "English Royal Forests," 11–14. Forest Proceedings, Treasury of the Receipt 251, m.2; 76, m.9; 79, m.6; as cited by Young, "Forest Eyre," 326. Young, "Forest Eyre," 321–22, 326. Roger of Howden, *Chronica* (1198), ed. William Stubbs (Rolls Series) (London, 1950), 4:60, as cited by Young, "Forest Eyre," 321. See Assize of Woodstock and Forest Assize of 1198. Also see *Pipe Roll 27 Hen. 2*, 23; *Pipe Roll 30 Hen. 2*, 60, 144; *Pipe Roll 8 John*, 16; *Rotuli Litterarum Patentium* 1, 3b, as cited by Young, "English Royal Forests," 9. Also see James, interview.

18.　*Laws of William I. Laws of Henry I*, ed. L. J. Downer (Oxford: Clarendon Press, 1972), 145. Benedict of Peterborough, *The Chronicle of the Reigns of Henry II and Richard I*, ed. William Stubbs (Rolls Series) (London, 1867), 2: 74, as cited by Young, "English Royal Forests," 6. Benedict, *Chronicle*, 2:157, as cited by Young, 5. Benedict, *Chronicle*, 1:92–94, 99, 105, as cited by Young, 5–6. Ralph of Diceto, *Ymagines Historiarum* (Historical Works), ed. William Stubbs (Rolls Series) (London, 1876), as cited by Young, 6. Forest Proceedings, Treasury of the Receipt, 251, m. 2; 76, m. 9; 79, m. 6. (P.R.O.), as cited by Young, "Forest Eyre," 326. Young, "English Royal Forests," 1–8, 13. Fitz Nigel, *Dialogus*, 59–60, as cited by Young, "English Royal Forests." Wright, "Common Law," 167–68. See F. H. M. Parker, *The Forest Laws and the Death of William Rufus*, E.H.R. 27 (1912), 38, as cited by Young, "English Royal Forests," 2. Te Brake, "Air Pollution," 350. See Turner, *Select Pleas*, 1, 3–4, 6–7, as cited by Young, "English Royal Forests." Also see James, interview. See generally, Young, "Forest Eyre."

19. Galloway, Keene, and Murphy, "Fuelling the City," 447–48, 450, 451, 454, 457–58. G. Hammersley, "The Charcoal Iron Industry and Its Fuel 1540–1750," *Economic History Review*, n.s., 26, no. 4 (1973): 593–613. H. R. Schubert, *History of the British Iron and Steel Industry* (London: Routledge & Kegan Paul, 1957), 112–13. See generally Hammersley.

20. Young, "English Royal Forests," 4. Galloway, Keene, and Murphy, "Fuelling the City," 451–52. *Pipe Roll 2 Rich. I*, 145, and *Pipe Roll 4 Rich. I*, 214, as cited by Young. See http://www.hants.org.uk/newforest/history/history2.html.

21. Galloway, Keene, and Murphy, "Fuelling the City," 451–52. Te Brake, "Air Pollution," 345.

22. Magna Carta, http://www.bl.uk/treasures/magnacarta/translation.html, sections 47–48. http://www.bl.uk/treasures/magnacarta/basics.html.

23. *Charter of the Forest* (Henry III), http://www.constitution.org/sech/sech_045.htm. William Stubbs, *Select Charters and Other Illustrations of English Constitutional History* (Oxford: Clarendon Press, 1921), 344. Te Brake, "Air Pollution," 346. *Close Rolls, 1247–51*, 17, as cited by Young, "Forest Eyre," 327. Turner, *Select Pleas*, 136–37, as cited by Young, 324. Also see *Pipe Roll 2 Rich. I*, 145 and *Pipe Roll 4 Rich. I*, 214, as cited by Young, "English Royal Forests," 4. Young, "Forest Eyre," 324, 327.

24. Schubert, *British Iron and Steel Industry*, 111–15. Galloway, Keene, and Murphy, "Fuelling the City," 447, 456. Te Brake, "Air Pollution," 343, 351. Also see Simmons, *Environmental History of Great Britain*, 94–95.

25. Schubert, *British Iron and Steel Industry*, 114–15. http://www.hants.org.uk/newforest/history /history2.html. Also see Nicholas Flower, "The Management History and Structure of Unenclosed Woods in the New Forest, Hampshire," *Journal of Biogeography* 7, no. 4 (December 1980): 311–28. Also see http://www.coppice.org.uk/index.html. Also see Colin R. Tubbs, *The New Forest: An Ecological History* (Newton Abbott, UK: David & Charles, 1968). See James, interview. Simmons, *Environmental History of Great Britain*, 94–95.

26. http://www.boldoutlaw.com/realrob/realrob2.html. http://www.lib.rochester.edu/camelot/ rh/rhhome.htm.

27. http://smtc.uwyo.edu/coal/swamp/coalification.asp. Derek Keene, "Feeding Medieval European Cities, 600–1500," http://www.history.ac.uk/eseminars/sem24.html, 4. http://www.out ofoblivion.org.uk/coal.asp. See http://www.peatresources.com/. See "Hundreds of Thousands of People Affected by Smoke Haze from Fires in Peat Swamp Forests," http://www.cifor.cgiar.org/fire-project/fire_up/intro.htm.

28. Te Brake, "Air Pollution," 341–44, and generally.

29. L. Dudley Stamp, "Britain's Coal Crisis," *Geographical Review* 38, no. 2 (April 1948): 179. http://www.thenortheast.fsnet.co.uk/page49.htm. http://www.seaham.i12.com/sos/sea coal.html. Schubert, *British Iron and Steel Industry*, 44, 114. Te Brake, "Air Pollution," 343–44.

30. Galloway, Keene, and Murphy, "Fuelling the City," 449, 451–53, 456, 468. Te Brake, "Air Pollution," 343. See Adam Smith, *An Inquiry into the Nature and Causes of the Wealth of Nations*, ed. Edwin Cannan (New York: Modern Library, 1937), 165.

31. http://www.nationmaster.com/encyclopedia/Bishop-of-Durham. http://www.thisisthenorth east.co.uk/the_north_east/history/coal/1100_1500/. http://www.thenortheast.fsnet.co.uk.

32. http://www.thenortheast.fsnet.co.uk/CoalMiningandRailways.htm. http://www.thisisthe northeast.co.uk/the_north_east/history/coal/1100_1500/.

33. *Extracts from the Records of the Company of Hostmen of Newcastle-upon-Tyne* (Durham, UK: Andrews, 1901), xxvii–xxxii. John U. Nef, *The Rise of the British Coal Industry* (London: Cass, 1932), 1:19–21, 78–80, 102–3.
   http://www.thenortheast.fsnet.co.uk/CoalMiningandRailways.htm.

34. Nef, *British Coal Industry*, 1:281. *Company of Hostmen*, xix. See George Muncaster, "Coal Mining in County Durham (Part 5)," http://www.durham-miner.org.uk/miner/projects.nsf/. http://www.thenortheast.fsnet.co.uk/page49.htm.

35. Muncaster, "Coal Mining."

36. Marvin Rosen, *Consolidating Capitalist Rule: Parliament and Capital, 1688–1722* (1999), http://www.afn.org/~afn31294/marvin/chapter10.txt. Turner, "Keelmen of Newcastle," 543, 545. http://www.thenortheast.fsnet.co.uk/CoalMiningandRailways.htm. Muncaster, "Coal Mining." Nef, *British Coal Industry*, 1:401, 405.

37. Neal Shipley, "Thomas Sutton: Moneylender," *Business History Review 50*, no. 4 (Winter 1976), 458. Nef, *British Coal Industry*, 1:150–51.

38. Shipley, "Thomas Sutton," 458–59.

39. Rosen, *Consolidating Capitalist Rule*.

40. Hammersley, "Charcoal Iron Industry," 607–8. Muncaster, "Coal Mining." http://www.hants.gov.uk/newforest/history/history2.html.

41. William Page, *The Victoria History of the County of Durham* (London: Constable, 1905), as cited by Durham Mining Museum, "Mining History," http://www.dmm.org.uk/history/vhced2.htm.

42. *Company of Hostmen*, xxxii–xxxiii. Rosen, *Consolidating Capitalist Rule*. Muncaster, "Coal Mining."

43. Durham Mining Museum, "Mining History." Hammersley, "Charcoal Iron Industry," 593–95. Rosen, *Consolidating Capitalist Rule*. Raymond Turner, "English Coal Industry in the Seventeenth and Eighteenth Centuries," *American Historical Review 27*, no. 1 (October 1921): 2n12.

44. Rosen, *Consolidating Capitalist Rule*. Turner, "English Coal Industry," 2n12.

45. Turner, "English Coal Industry," 3.

46. Rosen, *Consolidating Capitalist Rule*.

47. Turner, "English Coal Industry," 8.

48. Ibid., 3, 5. "House of Commons Journal, 8 June 1643," *Journal of the House of Commons 3* (1643–44) (1802): 120–21, http://www.british-history.ac.uk. Rosen, *Consolidating Capitalist Rule*. Nef, *British Coal Industry*, 1:25, 196, 197, 198; 2:69. See Conrad Russell, *The Crisis of Parliaments: English History 1509–1660* (Oxford: Oxford University Press, 1990), 355.

49. Raymond Turner, "English Coal Industry," 5. Rosen, *Consolidating Capitalist Rule*. Nef, *British Coal Industry*, 2:69.

50. Rosen, *Consolidating Capitalist Rule*. *Company of Hostmen*, xxxiv.

51. Rosen, *Consolidating Capitalist Rule.*

52. Turner, "English Coal Industry," 9–12.

53. Rosen, *Consolidating Capitalist Rule,* n. 17. Turner, "English Coal Industry," 20–21, n. 130.

54. Turner, "English Coal Industry," 13. Turner, "Keelmen of Newcastle," 543–44.

55. Te Brake, "Air Pollution," 339.

56. Ibid., 340.

57. Ibid., 337–38.

58. Ibid., 338.

59. Richard Schallenburg, *Bottled Energy* (Philadelphia: American Philosophical Society, 1981), 5–7.

Chapter 3: Metals and Monopolies

1. Luigi Galvani, *Commentary on the Effects of Electricity on Muscular Motion* (Norwalk, CT: Burndy Library, 1953), 47. I. Bernard Cohen, introduction to Galvani, *Commentary,* 35. "Luigi Galvani," *Catholic Encyclopedia,* http://www.newadvent.org/cathen/06371c.htm.

2. Cohen, introduction to Galvani, *Commentary,* 20, 23, 28, 33, 38, and generally.

3. Paul R. Heyl, "What Is Electricity?" *Scientific Monthly* 41, no. 1 (July 1935):38. Cohen, introduction to Galvani, *Commentary,* 48n4. See generally http://chem.ch.huji.ac.il/~eugeniik/history/gilbert.html and http://chem.ch.huji.ac.il/~eugeniik/instruments/archaic/leyden_jars.htm.

4. Cohen, introduction to Galvani, *Commentary,* 20, 33. http://chem.ch.huji.ac.il/~eugeniik/instruments/archaic/leyden_jars.htm.

5. Cohen, introduction to Galvan, *Commentary,* 33. I. Bernard Cohen, "The Two Hundredth Anniversary of Benjamin Franklin's Two Lightning Experiments and the Introduction of the Lightning Rod," *Proceedings of the American Philosophical Society* 96, no. 3 (June 20, 1952): 331–36.

6. Cohen, introduction to Galvani, *Commentary,* 25. Galvani, *Commentary,* 45–47. Generally see Matthew Yatman, *Animal Electricity; or, Observations on the Origin and Identity of the Electric and Galvanic Fluids, Etc.,* 2nd ed. (London: 1805).

7. Galvani, *Commentary,* 45–47.

8. Ibid., 47.

9. Ibid., 47–48.

10. Cohen, introduction to Galvani, *Commentary,* 10.

11. Ibid., 20.

12. Galvani, *Commentary,* 59.

13. Cohen, introduction to Galvani, *Commentary,* 20–21, 30, 32–33.

14. Ibid., 32–33.

15. Ernest Yeager, "Fuel Cells," *Science* 134, no. 3486 (October 20, 1961): 1178. Richard Schallenberg, *Bottled Energy* (Philadelphia: American Philosophical Society, 1981), 20–21. See George W. Heise and N. Corey Calhoon, eds., *The Primary Battery* (New York: John Wiley, 1971), 1:35, as cited by Schallenberg.

16. Richard B. Du Boff, "Business Demand and the Development of the Telegraph in the United States, 1844–1860," *Business History Review* 54, no. 4 (Winter 1980): 461. Frank G. Halstead, "The Genesis and Speed of the Telegraph Codes," *Proceedings of the American Philosophical Society* 93, no. 5 (November 30, 1949): 448. See

http://www.personal.psu.edu/users/e/m/emr150/group.html. See http://inventors.about.com/library/inventors/bltelegraph.htm.

17. Du Boff, "Business Demand," 461.

18. Ernest Rubin, "The Demography of Immigration to the United States," *Annals of the American Academy of Political and Social Science* 367 (September 1966): 16–17. Abbott Payson Usher, Chester W. Wright, John Ise, A. Berglund, Vanderveer Custis, Harry W. Laidler, and Francis Tyson, "The Rise of Monopoly in the United States," *American Economic Review* 23, no. 1 (March 1933): 2–3. See Glenn D. Bradley, *The Story of the Santa Fe* (Boston: Gorham Press, 1920), 44–49, 107–38. See Elizabeth Black, interview with the author, December 7, 2005. See generally Edwin Black, *War Against the Weak* (New York: Four Walls Eight Windows, 2003), 21–22. See generally Edwin Black, *Banking on Baghdad* (Hoboken, NJ: John Wiley, 2004), 95–99.

19. Schallenberg, *Bottled Energy*, 24–29.

20. Thomas Gray, "The Development of Electrical Science," *Science*, n.s., 7, no. 169 (March 25, 1898): 402, 405.

21. Jill Jonnes, *Empires of Light* (New York: Random House, 2003), 47, 55.

22. Edwin Black, *IBM and the Holocaust* (New York: Crown Publishers, 2001), 24.

23. Usher et al., "Rise of Monopoly," 1–11. Richard T. Ely, "The Nature and Significance of Monopolies and Trusts," *International Journal of Ethics* 10, no. 3 (April 1900): 273–88. Arthur P. Dudden, "Men Against Monopoly," *Journal of the History of Ideas* 18, no. 4 (October 1957): 587–93.

24. Usher et al., "Rise of Monopoly," 4. Keith Poole, "The Sherman Anti-Trust Act," http://voteview.com/antitrst.htm.

25. Poole, "Sherman Anti-Trust Act." See John D. Archbold to John D. Rockefeller, July 6, 1886, Rockefeller Family Archives, RG 1, box 51, fol. 378, Sleepy Hollow, New York. See Noel H. Pugach, "Standard Oil and Petroleum Development in Early Republican China," *Business History Review* 45 (1971): 452–53. See R. W. Ferrier, *The History of the British Petroleum Company* (Cambridge, UK: Cambridge University Press, 1982), 1:1, 259–60, 548. Generally see Ida Tarbell, *The History of the Standard Oil Company*, vols. 1 and 2 (New York: McClure, Phillips, & Co., 1904), http://www.history.rochester.edu/fuels/tarbell/MAIN.HTM. Also generally see Black, *Banking on Baghdad*, 104–5.

26. David C. Cloud, *Monopolies and the People* (Muscatine, IA: Allen Broomhall, 1873), http://name.umdl.umich.edu/ABZ0161.0001.001, 9. Dudden, "Men Against Monopoly," 588, 590.

27. Henry Demarest Lloyd, "The Lords of Industry," *North American Review* 331 (June 1884), http://www.fordham.edu/halsall/mod/1884hdlloyd.html.

28. Ibid.

Chapter 4: Stench and Scandal

1. Clay McShane and Joel A. Tarr, "The Centrality of the Horse in the Nineteenth-Century American City," in *The Making of Urban America*, ed. Raymond A. Mohl (Wilmington, DE: Scholarly Resources, 1997), 112, 117–18, 121–22. McShane and Tarr, "The Decline of the Urban Horse in American Cities," *Journal of Transport History* 24, no. 2 (September 2003): 184–85. Steve Jacobs, "Entomological Notes: House Flies,"

http://www.ento.psu.edu/extension/factsheets/houseflies.htm. Stanhope Bayne-Jones, MD, *The Evolution of Preventative Medicine in the United States Army, 1607–1939* (Washington, DC: U.S. Government Printing Office, 1968), chap. 7, http://history.amedd.army.mil/booksdocs/misc/evprev/ch7.htm.

2.   U.S. Bureau of the Census, Interior Department, *Remarks upon the Statistics of Agriculture, Ninth Census* (1870), 697, 699–701. U.S. Bureau of the Census, Department of Commerce and Labor, *Agriculture Part 1, Farms, Livestock, and Animal Products, Twelfth Census V* (1990), clxxxvii, http://www2.census.gov/prod2/decennial/documents/33398096v5ch2.pdf. McShane and Tarr, "Centrality of the Horse," 106, 108, 110.

3.   McShane and Tarr, "Centrality of the Horse," 111–12. See U.S. Bureau of the Census, *Report on the Transportation Business in the United States, Eleventh Census* 18, pt. 1 (Washington, DC: Government Printing Office, 1895), 682, 684, 714–20, as cited by McShane and Tarr.

4.   McShane and Tarr, "Centrality of the Horse," 108, 112–14. Tarr, "A Note on the Horse as Urban Power Source," *Journal of Urban History* 25, no. 3 (March 1999): 435.

5.   McShane and Tarr, "Centrality of the Horse," 105–6, 125. See *Nation* 383 (October 31, 1872): 277–78, as cited by McShane and Tarr.

6.   McShane and Tarr, "Centrality of the Horse," 106, 120–21. http://www1.agric.gov.ab.ca/$department/deptdocs.nsf/all/hrs3186. http://horsecare.stablemade.com/articles2/water2.htm.

7.   McShane and Tarr, "Centrality of the Horse," 121. Jacobs, "Entomological Notes."

8.   McShane and Tarr, "Centrality of the Horse," 121–22. "The Age of Noise," *Horseless Age* 1, no. 4 (February 1896): 5.

9.   McShane and Tarr, "Centrality of the Horse," 122. McShane and Tarr, "Decline of the Urban Horse," 179. Joel A. Tarr, interview with the author, August 24, 2005. See "Through Broadway," *Atlantic Monthly* 18 (December 1866): 717, as cited by McShane and Tarr. See George E. Waring Jr., comp., *Report on the Social Statistics of Cities*, pt. 2, *The New England and the Middle States* (Washington, DC: Government Printing Office, 1887), 591, as cited by McShane and Tarr. See "Clean Streets and Motor Traffic," *Literary Digest* 49 (September 5, 1914): 413, as cited by McShane and Tarr.

10.   Christine Meisner Rosen, "Businessmen Against Pollution in Late Nineteenth Century Chicago," *Business History Review* 69 (Autumn 1995): 351–54. Charles A. Benjamin, "The Science of Smoke Prevention," *Science*, n.s., 19, no. 482 (March 25, 1904): 488.

11.   F. H. Bowman, "Improvements in the Storage of Electricity," *Science* 22, no. 562 (November 10, 1893): 258.

12.   "Storage of Electricity," *Electrician* 8 (April 15, 1882): 358. Richard Schallenberg, *Bottled Energy: Electrical Engineering and the Evolution of Chemical Energy Storage* (Philadelphia: American Philosophical Society, 1981), 51–52. Thomas Parke Hughes, "British Electrical Industry Lag: 1882–1888," *Technology and Culture* 3, no. 1 (Winter 1962): 27.

13.   "Storage of Electricity," 358. Schallenberg, *Bottled Energy*, 51. Thomas Edison, letter to *Science*, reprinted in *New York Times*, May 28, 1881, 5. "On M. C. Faure's Secondary Battery," *Science* 2, no. 51 (June 18, 1881): 291. "The Discussion on Storage-Batteries before the Electrical Conference in Philadelphia," *Science* 4, supp. to no. 89 (October 7, 1884): 383.

14.   "Discussion on Storage-Batteries," 383. Schallenberg, *Bottled Energy*, 59–60. William Thomson, "Electric Storage of Dynamical Energy," *Electrician* 7 (June 11, 1881): 57.

Thomson, "On the Sources of Energy Available to Man for the Production of Mechanical Effect," *Science* 2, no. 67 (October 8, 1881): 477–78. S. Wyman Rolph, *"Exide": The Development of an Engineering Idea—a Brief History of The Electric Storage Battery Company* (New York: Newcomen Society in North America, 1951), 10.

15.   "Philippart's Last Failure," *New York Times*, November 8, 1879, 1. "Notes from France," *New York Times*, March 26, 1875, 8.

16.   "Notes from France," 8.

17.   "The French Crédit Mobilier," *New York Times*, July 4, 1875, 8. "M. Philippart's Career," *New York Times*, November 23, 1879, 2. "The Philippart Collapse on the Paris Exchange," *New York Times*, May 21, 1875, 6.

18.   "Philippart's Last Failure," 1.

19.   Ibid. "A Bold Bank Wrecker," *Washington Post*, November 8, 1879, 1. "Financial Journals from the Past," *Newsletter from the EABH*, February 2002, 23.

20.   "Philippart's Mishaps," *Chicago Daily Tribune*, August 1, 1880, 11.

21.   Schallenberg, *Bottled Energy*, 55–56, 59–60. Hughes, "British Electrical Industry Lag," 27–28. "Electrical Storage Batteries," *New York Times*, May 24, 1882, 7. See William Thomson, letter to the editor, *Times* (London), June 9, 1881, as cited by Schallenberg. See also Thomson, "Electric Storage," 57.

22.   Robert P. Merges and Richard R. Nelson, "On the Complex Economics of Patent Scope," *Columbia Law Review* 90, no. 4 (May 1990): 887–88. "City and Suburban News," *New York Times*, March 19, 1890, 3. See http://library.case.edu/ksl/speccoll/brush/brushservi.html. Generally see Edwin Black, *War Against the Weak: Eugenics and America's Campaign to Create a Master Race* (New York: Four Walls Eight Windows, 2003), and author's files: "Charles Brush Foundation and Eugenics."

23.   "Historical Weather Events, 1850–1899," htpp://homepage.ntlworld.com/booty.weather/climate/1850_1899.htm.

24.   "Storage of Electricity," 358. Schallenberg, *Bottled Energy*, 63. "The Successes and Tragic End of a Genius," *Scientific American* 50, no. 5 (August 2, 1884): 64.

25.   "Successes and Tragic End," 64. Schallenberg, *Bottled Energy*, 63–64. "The Sellon and Volckmar Secondary Battery," *Electrician* 8 (April 8, 1882): 343.

26.   "The Faure Electric Accumulator Company," *Electrician* 8 (March 4, 1882): 243. Schallenberg, *Bottled Energy*, 64. See also http://www.acmi.net.au/AIC/AYRTON_BIO.html.

27.   Schallenberg, *Bottled Energy*, 64.

28.   "Sellon and Volckmar Battery," 342–43. Schallenberg, *Bottled Energy*, 64–65. Hughes, "British Electrical Industry Lag," 29. "Successes and Tragic End," 64. "Storage of Electricity," 358.

29.   Hughes, "British Electrical Industry Lag," 29, 34.

30.   Schallenberg, *Bottled Energy*, 65. "Storage of Electricity," 358.

31.   "Secondary Batteries," *Electrician* 8 (April 29, 1882): 393.

32.   Schallenberg, *Bottled Energy*, 65. "The Sellon and Faure Battery," *Electrician* 9 (May 20, 1882): 1. "Railway and Other Companies," *Times* (London), April 17, 1884, 11.

33.   Schallenberg, *Bottled Energy*, 65–66. "Sellon and Faure Battery," 1.

34.   Schallenberg, *Bottled Energy*, 67. "Railway and Other Companies," *Times* (London), May 27, 1882, 13. *Times* (London), November 7, 1882, 11.

35.   Schallenberg, *Bottled Energy*, 66. "The Cost of Motive Power from Electrical Accumula-

tors," *Scientific American* 50, no. 1 (January 5, 1884): 6. "The Electric Tramcar in Paris," *Electrician* 11 (September 15, 1883): 412.

36. "Belgium Brussels April 12," *Times* (London), April 13, 1883, 5. "Belgium Brussels May 7," *Times* (London), May 8, 1883, 5. "Railway and Other Companies," *Times* (London), May 31, 1883, 11. "M. Philippart," *Electrician* 11 (May 26, 1883): 25.

37. "Railway and Other Companies," *Times* (London), May 31, 1883, 11. "Faure Electric Accumulator Company (Limited)," *Electrician* 11 (June 2, 1883): 71.

38. "Railway and Other Companies," *Times* (London), June 28, 1883, 11. "The Faure Electric Accumulator Company (Limited)," *Electrician* 11 (June 30, 1883): 167–68.

39. "Railway and Other Companies," *Times* (London), April 17, 1884, 11.

40. "Discussion on Storage-Batteries," 383. "Successes and Tragic End," 64.

41. "Discussion on Storage-Batteries," 383. "Ernest Volckmar," *Electrician* 13 (July 26, 1884): 258. "Successes and Tragic End," 64.

Chapter 5: Batteries and Bicycles

1. Randy Houk, "Railroad History: Important Milestones in English and American Railway Development," Pacific Southwest Railway Museum, http://www.sdrm.org.

2. "Electric Storage Batteries: A Successful Experiment on Board the Steam-Ship Labrador," *New York Times*, May 13, 1882, 8. "The Electric Storage Battery: The Brush Company Claims Priority of Invention Over M. Faure," *New York Times*, May 17, 1882, 8. S. Wyman Rolph, *"Exide," the Development of an Engineering Idea; A Brief History of the Electric Storage Battery Company* (New York: Newcomen Society in North America, 1951), 9, 11. Neil Baldwin, *Edison: Inventing the Century* (Chicago: University of Chicago Press, 1995, 2001), 137. "Electricity Instead of Gas," *New York Tribune*, September 5, 1882, as cited by Baldwin, *Edison*, 137. "Philadelphia Gas Works: Agency History," Agency Information, Philadelphia Information Locator Service, http://www.phila.gov.

3. Rolph, *"Exide,"* 9, 11.

4. Ibid., 11.

5. Thomas Parke Hughes, "British Electrical Industry Lag: 1882–1888," *Technology and Culture* 3 (Winter 1962): 34. Rolph, *"Exide,"* 11.

6. "The Storage Battery," *Electrician* 10 (February 17, 1883): 329–31.

7. "Supplement: The Discussion on Storage-Batteries before the Electrical Conference in Philadelphia," *Science* 4 (October 17, 1884): 383.

8. Rolph, *"Exide,"* 12.

9. *Transactions of the American Electrochemical Society* 3 (1903): 159–60.

10. *Edison Bulletin #18*, May 31, 1883, 9–10. *Electrician* 18 (December 24, 1886): 151. *Electrician* 12 (January 5, 1884): 182. See also *Edison Bulletin #16*, February 2, 1883, 31.

11. "Electric Storage Battery," 8.

12. "Supplement: The Discussion on Storage-Batteries," 388–89, 391. See Schallenberg, *Bottled Energy*, 214–15.

13. Schallenberg, *Bottled Energy*, 83. David A. Kirsch, *The Electric Vehicle and the Burden of History* (New Brunswick, NJ: Rutgers University Press, 2000), 34.

14. "Hero's Engine," Rockets in Ancient Times, Timeline of Rocket History, http://history.msfc.nasa.gov. Robert H. Thurston, *A History of the Growth of the Steam-Engine* (New York: D. Appleton and Company, 1878), chap. 1. "Models Showing Develop-

ment in the Steam Engine," *Christian Science Monitor*, April 19, 1915. "Steam Ball," Science Shop, http://www.science-shop.de/artikel/713544.

15. Ernest H. Wakefield, *History of the Electric Automobile: Battery-Only Powered Cars* (Warrendale, PA: Society of Automotive Engineers, 1994), 39. "Cugnot, First Automobolist," *Washington Post*, August 18, 1910, 6. "Anecdotes of the Steam Engine No. VII," *New York State Mechanic*, April 23, 1842, 169. Cornelius Mulvihill, "They Motored Here in the Oxcart Age," Cave box 1–20, Detroit Public Library NAHC.

16. Carl W. Condit, "The Pioneer Stage of Railroad Electrification," *Transactions of the American Philosophical Society*, n.s. 67 (1977): 4. Clark C. Spence, "Early Uses of Electricity in American Agriculture," *Technology and Culture* 3 (Spring 1962): 2–3. Robert C. Post, "The Page Locomotive: Federal Sponsorship of Invention in Mid-19th-Century America," *Technology and Culture* 13 (April 1972): 143. David Cardwell, "Science and Technology: The Work of James Prescott Joule," *Technology and Culture* 17 (October 1976): 677, 678. "An Electric Carriage," *Scientific American*, March 23, 1895, 177. "Jeantaud's Electric Carriage," *Scientific American*, April 6, 1895. Gijs Mom, *Electric Vehicle: Technology and Expectations in the Automobile Age* (Baltimore: Johns Hopkins University Press, 2004), 17.

17. Bill Dunn, "Internal Combustion Engine," *Times* (London), April 5, 2002. Edwin Black, *Banking on Baghdad* (Hoboken, NJ: John Wiley & Sons, 2004), 97. See Lynwood Bryant, "The Origin of the Four-Stroke Cycle," *Technology and Culture* 8, no. 2 (April 1967): 178–98.

18. "Americans Pay Tribute to German Car Pioneer," *Washington Post*, February 23, 1930, A6. James J. Flink, *The Automobile Age* (Cambridge, MA: MIT Press, 1998), 11, 12. Dunn, "Internal Combustion Engine." See "Patent No. 37,435 Was a Winner," *New York Times*, January 29, 1961, S11.

19. C. E. Corrigan, "Condition of the Horseless Carriage Industry," *Western Electrician*, January 1, 1989, 9, as cited by Kirsch, *Electric Vehicle*, 29.

20. Richard H. Schallenberg, "The Anomalous Storage Battery: An American Lag in Early Electrical Engineering," *Technology and Culture* 22 (October 1981): 749–50. "A Perfect Storage Battery," *Washington Post*, October 10, 1894. Andrew C. Irvine, "The Promotion and First 22 Years History of a Corporation in Electrical Manufacturing" (master's thesis, Temple University, 1954), 21. Rolph, *"Exide,"* 10, 12, 14, 15.

21. Irvine, "Promotion," 27–28, 37–38. Herman L. Collins, *Philadelphia Inquirer*, May 16, 1927, 27, as cited by Irvine, 28. Hiram Percy Maxim, *Horseless Carriage Days* (New York: Harper & Brothers, 1937), 58.

22. Irvine, "Promotion," 39, 40.

23. Schallenberg, *Bottled Energy*, 123–24.

24. Rolph, *"Exide,"* 14–15.

25. Irvine, "Promotion," 44.

26. Rolph, *"Exide,"* 14. Irvine, "Promotion," 47.

27. Irvine, "Promotion," 50–51. See Rolph, *"Exide,"* 15.

28. Irvine, "Promotion," 49, 50, 51.

29. Ibid., 52, 53.

30. Ibid., 53. Rolph, *"Exide,"* 15. Mom, *Electric Vehicle*, 92.

31. "Morris and Salom's Electric Wagons, the 'Electrobat,'" *Horseless Age* 1 (November 1895):

47. Rolph, *"Exide,"* 18. Mom, *Electric Vehicle*, 26. Schallenberg, *Bottled Energy*, 255–56. See "Some American Motor Carriages," *Scientific American*, February 15, 1896, 105–6.

32. Schallenberg, *Bottled Energy*, 256, 257. See "The First American Electric Carriage," *Horseless Age* 3 (December 1898): 18. See "The Growth of the Automobile Industry in America," *Outing Magazine*, November 1907, 210.

33. "Morris and Salom's Electric Wagons." Mom, *Electric Vehicle*, 181, 182, 183. See "To Test Electric Motors," *New York Times*, June 4, 1893, 8. See "Storage Car Tested," *Chicago Daily*, November 23, 1893, 3. See "Successful Storage Battery," *Chicago Daily Tribune*, January 3, 1893, 14.

34. "Supplement: The Discussion on Storage-Batteries," 390.

35. Schallenberg, *Bottled Energy*, 257.

36. "The Chicago Motocycle Race," *Scientific American*, December 7, 1895, 357. "Horses Not in It," *Atlanta Constitution*, November 3, 1895, 17. See "The Horseless Carriage Races," *Scientific American*, August 10, 1895, 82–83. See "The Horseless Carriage," *New York Times*, April 19, 1895, 28. Schallenberg, *Bottled Energy*, 257. Flink, *Automobile Age*, 23. Mom, *Electric Vehicle*, 25. Kirsch, *Electric Vehicle*, 34.

37. "Endurance Tour's Steady Progress," *New York Times*, May 1, 1910, XX5. Rolph, *"Exide,"* 18. Maxim, *Horseless Carriage Days*, 53. Flink, *Automobile Age*, 23. Kirsch, *Electric Vehicle*, 34. "Details and Dimensions of Motor Vehicles," table, *Horseless Age*, February 1896, 11.

38. "An Electric Hansom," *Scientific American*, March 13, 1897, 166. "Electric Storage," *Wall Street Journal*, December 6, 1895, 1. Schallenberg, *Bottled Energy*, 258. Mom, *Electric Vehicle*, 25.

39. "Morris & Salom's Prospectus," *Horseless Age* 1, no. 3 (January 1896): 24. "Prospectus of the Electric Carriage & Wagon Company," *Horseless Age* 1, no. 8 (June 1896): 26. "New Vehicles of the Electric Carriage and Wagon Company," *Horseless Age* 1, no. 11 (September 1896): 18. "To Popularize the Electric Vehicle," *Horseless Age* 1, no. 7 (May 1896): 22. See "An Electric Hansom," 165–66.

40. "The Chicago Motocycle Race." "The Barrows Electric Vehicle," *Horseless Age* 1, no. 1 (November 1895): 22. "The Arnold Electric Carriage," *Horseless Age* 1, no. 1 (November 1895): 23. "The Sturges Electric Motocycle," *Horseless Age* 1, no. 1 (November 1895): 24. "Dey System of Propelling Street Cars and Wagons," *Horseless Age* 1, no. 1 (November 1895): 25. "Columbia Perambulator Co.'s Electric Wagon," *Horseless Age* 1, no. 1 (November 1895): 28. "The Perry Lewis Electric Wagon," *Horseless Age* 1, no. 1 (November 1895): 29. "The Baker and Elberg Wagon," *Horseless Age* 1, no. 1 (November 1895): 32. "Professor Elihu Thomson Experimenting," *Horseless Age* 1, no. 1 (November 1895): 32. "The Holtzer Electric Wagon," *Horseless Age* 1, no. 1 (November 1895): 37–38. "The Riker Electric Trap," *Horseless Age* 1, no. 1 (August 1896): 18. "Progress on the Dey Electric Carriage," letter Harry E. Dey to editor, *Horseless Age* 1, 10 (August 1896): 22. See "How Edison Will Make Automobiles the Poor Man's Vehicle," *Chicago Daily Tribune*, June 15, 1902, 37. See "Growth of Electric Cars," *New York Times*, March 17, 1912, C12. See Wakefield, *History of the Electric Automobile*, 68, picture from the Collections of Henry Ford Museum and Greenfield Village, P.B. 32967.

41. Hermann Cuntz to Henry Cave, October 13, 1941, Cave box 9, folder 16, Detroit Public Library NAHC. "Salutatory," *Horseless Age* 1, no. 1 (November 1895): 2. "Foreign Notes," *Horseless Age* 2, no. 1 (November 1896): 27.

42. "No More Red Flags," *Horseless Age* 2, no. 1 (November 1896): 22. "Foreign Notes," 27. Mom, *Electric Vehicle*, 36. Flink, *Automobile Age*, 21.

43. "Mr. Salom on 'Automobile Vehicles,'" *Horseless Age* 1, no. 6 (April 1896): 4, 5.

44. Ibid., 5.

45. Charles E. Duryea, "Bogies," *Horseless Age* 1, no. 10 (August 1896): 3.

46. Ibid.

47. Ibid.

48. Ibid.

49. "The 'Noise' Question," *Horseless Age* 2, no. 2 (December 1896): 1.

50. "The Oil Famine Bugaboo," *Horseless Age* 2, no. 3 (January 1897): 1. Black, *Banking on Baghdad*, 97–98.

51. "The Oil Famine Bugaboo."

52. "New Vehicles of the Electric Carriage and Wagon Company," *Horseless Age* 1, no. 11 (September 1896): 18. "An Electric Hansom," *Scientific American*, March 13, 1897, 165. "A Horseless Brougham," *Scientific American*, August 7, 1897, 85. "To Run Electric Cabs," *New York Times*, March 7, 1897, 10.

53. "To Run Electric Cabs." "Electric Carriages for New York," *Wall Street Journal*, November 23, 1896, 1. Kirsch, *Electric Vehicle*, 56. Mom, *Electric Vehicle*, 28, 65, 69, 85. See "Electric Vehicle Company," advertisement, *New York Times*, January 12, 1898, 8. See Schallenberg, *Bottled Energy*, 250.

54. Kirsch, *Electric Vehicle*, 38–39, 50–51. Speed is various in various sources. Wakefield, *History of Electric Automobile*, 51–54. Mom, *Electric Vehicle*, 81–83.

55. "Electric Vehicles Then and Now," *IEEE Monitor* 53, no. 3 (March 2005): 9–10. Mom, *Electric Vehicle*, 79, 81. Wakefield, *History of Electric Automobile*, 51. "New Vehicles of the Electric Carriage and Wagon Company," *Horseless Age* 1, no. 11 (September 1896): 18. "Morris and Salom's Prospectus." Kirsch, *Electric Vehicle*, 176.

56. "Electric Vehicles," *Electrical World* 30, no. 7 (August 14, 1897): 182.

57. Ibid.

58. Wakefield, *History of Electric Vehicle*, 53. "Electric Vehicle Company," advertisement, *New York Times*, January 12, 1898, 8. Schallenberg, *Bottled Energy*, 259–60. Irvine, "Promotion," 56. Mom, *Electric Vehicle*, 82.

59. "Electric Storage," *Wall Street Journal*, September 8, 1897, 2.

60. "Electric Vehicle Company," *New York Times*, September 28, 1897, 5. Wakefield, *History of Electric Vehicle*, 53. *Horseless Age* 2, no. 11 (September 1897): 2. "Electric Vehicle Company," advertisement, *New York Times*, January 9, 1898, A9. John B. Rae, "The Electric Vehicle Company: A Monopoly That Missed," *Business History Review* 29, no. 4 (December 1955): 299–300. See Gary McCue, "Isaac L. Rice," http://www.geocities.com/gwmccue/People/Rice.html?20058.

61. Kirsch, *Electric Vehicle*, 41, 58. Schallenberg, *Bottled Energy*, 260. Rae, "Electric Vehicle Company," 299–300. "Isaac L. Rice." "Electric Vehicle Company," advertisement, *New York Times*, January 9, 1898, A9. Irvine, "Promotion," 56. "Electric Carriages," *Wall Street Journal*, September 29, 1897, 1.

62. "Blizzard in Boston," *Washington Post*, February 2, 1898, 1. "Cost of the Storm," *Boston Globe*, February 2, 1898, 1. "Terrific in Lawrence," *Boston Globe*, February 2, 1898, 9. "Work of the Big Storm," *New York Times*, February 2, 1898, 1. "New York Snow-Bound,"

Los Angeles Times, February 2, 1898, 2. "Fury of the Storm," *Chicago Daily Tribune*, February 2, 1898, 1. "Snow a Foot Deep on Western Land," *Atlanta Constitution*, January 26, 1898, 2. "Wisconsin Has a Blizzard," *Atlanta Constitution*, January 24, 1898, 2. "Blizzard Sweeping Through Colorado," *Washington Post*, January 21, 1898, 1. "Blizzard at Buffalo," *New York Times*, January 3, 1898, 1.

63. "A New Year's Blizzard," *New York Times*, January 2, 1898, 1. "Severe Storm Up the State," *New York Times*, January 1, 1898, 1. "Blizzard in Pittsburgh," *New York Times*, January 1, 1898, 1. "Snow and Blizzards," *Washington Post*, January 24, 1898, 1. "Work of Wind and Tide," *Boston Globe*, January 24, 1898, 1. "Blizzard in Wisconsin," *New York Times*, January 24, 1898, 1. "Storms and Floods," *Chicago Daily Tribune*, January 24, 1898, 3. "Horses Killed by Live Wires," *Chicago Daily Tribune*, January 23, 1898, 3.

64. "Storm King Reigns," *Chicago Tribune*, January 23, 1898, 1. "Work of Wind and Tide." "Death and Destruction," *Boston Globe*, February 2, 1898, 1. "Bad Weather," *Los Angeles Times*, January 24, 1898, 1. "Milwaukee in a Blizzard," *Boston Globe*, February 21, 1898, 10.

65. "Work of the Big Storm." "Gotham in the Storm's Grip," *Chicago Tribune*, February 2, 1898, 2. "Under a White Robe," *Chicago Tribune*, February 1, 1898, 1. "Blizzard Feared in New York," *Washington Post*, February 1, 1898, 9. "New York Snow-Bound."

66. Wakefield, *History of Electric Vehicle*, 53. "Progress of the Electric Vehicle Co.," *Horseless Age* 3, no. 10 (January 1899): 13. "The Winter of Our Content," *Horseless Age* 3, no. 9 (December 1898): 6. "Snow and Mud Pictures," *Horseless Age* 3, no. 9 (December 1898): 14–15. Kirsch, *Electric Vehicle*, 48.

67. "Progress of the Electric Vehicle Co." "Snow and Mud Pictures." Kirsch, *Electric Vehicle*, 48.

68. "More Electric Cabs for New York," *Horseless Age* 3, no. 11 (February, 1899): 13. Wakefield, *History of Electric Vehicle*, 53.

69. Mark D. Hirsch, *William C. Whitney: Modern Warwick* (New York: Dodd, Mead & Company, 1948), 1–2, 17, 223–24.

70. Ibid., 224–25, 600.

71. Ibid., 440.

72. Mom, *Electric Vehicle*, 86. Schallenberg, *Bottled Energy*, 260. Hirsch, *Whitney*, 556–57. Herman F. Cuntz, "Pope Mfg Co. — Columbia Automobile Co. and The Electric Vehicle Company" (unpublished manuscript, June 1947, Cave box 8, folder 8, 2, Detroit Public Library NAHC).

73. Mom, *Electric Vehicle*, 86. Schallenberg, *Bottled Energy*, 260. Hirsch, *Whitney*, 556–57. Cuntz, "Pope Mfg Co.," 2.

74. Mom, *Electric Vehicle*, 86. Schallenberg, *Bottled Energy*, 260. Hirsch, *Whitney*, 556–57. Cuntz, "Pope Mfg Co.," 2.

75. *Horseless Age* 4, no. 2 (April 12, 1899): 11. Hirsch, *Whitney*, 557. Schallenberg, *Bottled Energy*, 263.

76. Cuntz, "Pope Mfg Co.," 2. Schallenberg, *Bottled Energy*, 264–65.

77. Schallenberg, *Bottled Energy*, 263–64. William Greenleaf, "The Selden Patent Suit" (PhD diss., Columbia University, 1955), 119. Irvine, "Promotion," 61. "Electric Vehicles Then and Now," 10. Kirsch, *Electric Vehicle*, 176. Cuntz, "Pope Mfg Co.," 3.

78. "French Jottings," *Autocar*, May 6, 1899, 371–73. Mom, *Electric Vehicle*, 48.

79. Bob Mionske, "Legally Speaking with Bob Mionske: The Monopoly Machine, Part 1," February 5, 2005, http://www.velonews.com/news/fea/7550.0.html.

80. Stephen B. Goddard, *Colonel Albert Pope and His American Dream Machines: The Life and Times of a Bicycle Tycoon Turned Automotive Pioneer* (Jefferson, NC: McFarland, 2000), 73–74. O. A. van Nierop, A. C. M. Blankendaal, and C. J. Overbeeke, "The Evolution of the Bicycle: A Dynamic Systems Approach," *Journal of Design History* 10, no. 3 (1997): 259–61.

81. Greenleaf, "Selden Patent Suit," 124–25. Goddard, *Colonel Albert Pope*, 238–40. Mom, *Electric Vehicle*, 26.

82. Greenleaf, "Selden Patent Suit," 125–26. Goddard, *Colonel Albert Pope*, 238–40.

83. Greenleaf, "Selden Patent Suit," 136.

84. Bruce Epperson, "Failed Colossus: Albert A. Pope, the Bicycle and the Dawn of the American Auto Industry" (unpublished manuscript, 2006), 69–71.

85. Ibid., 70–71.

86. Ibid., 75, 78, 80–81.

87. Ibid., 82–84.

88. Ibid., 106. Goddard, *Colonel Albert Pope*, 78, 79, 81–82.

89. Maxim, *Horseless Carriage Days*, xiii. "Maxim Gun," http://www.spartacus.schoolnet.co.uk/FWWmaximgun.htm. John H. Lienhard, "No. 694: Hiram Maxim," http://www.uh.edu/engines/epi694.htm.

90. Greenleaf, "Selden Patent Suit," 132. Kirsch, *Electric Vehicle*, 36–37. Maxim, *Horseless Carriage Days*, 52–53. Cuntz, "Pope Mfg Co.," 1.

91. Epperson, "Failed Colossus," 288. Goddard, *Colonel Albert Pope*, 119. Cuntz, "Pope Mfg Co.," 2.

92. Mom, *Electric Vehicle*, 29. Cuntz, "Pope Mfg Co.," 2–3. "More Electric Cabs for New York," *Horseless Age* 3, no. 11 (February 1899): 13.

93. Hirsch, *Whitney*, 557. Cuntz, "Pope Mfg Co.," 3. Goddard, *Colonel Albert Pope*, 153.

94. Hirsch, *Whitney*, 557. Cuntz, "Pope Mfg Co.," 3. Maxim, *Horseless Carriage Days*, 165.

95. Hirsch, *Whitney*, 557. Cuntz, "Pope Mfg Co.," 3–4. Goddard, *Colonel Albert Pope*, 153. Maxim, *Horseless Carriage Days*, 165.

96. Hirsch, *Whitney*, 557. Cuntz, "Pope Mfg Co.," 3–4. Goddard, *Colonel Albert Pope*, 153.

97. Hirsch, *Whitney*, 557. Cuntz, "Pope Mfg Co.," 4–5. Goddard, *Colonel Albert Pope*, 153.

Chapter 6: The Selden Strategy

1. "Annual Statement of the Electric Vehicle Company," *Horseless Age* 4, no. 26 (September 27, 1899): 8. William Greenleaf, *Monopoly on Wheels: Henry Ford and the Selden Automobile Patent* (Detroit: Wayne State University Press, 1961), 66. Gijs Mom, *The Electric Vehicle: Technology and Expectations in the Automobile Age* (Baltimore: Johns Hopkins University Press, 2004), 86–87.

2. "Annual Statement of the Electric Vehicle Company," 8. "Minor Mention," *Horseless Age* 4, no. 26 (September 17, 1899): 12. "$25,000,000 Electric Vehicle Company Incorporated," *Horseless Age* 3, no. 12 (March 1899): 7. "Pennsylvania to Have Electric Cabs," *Horseless Age* 3, no. 12 (March 1899): 8. William Greenleaf, "The Selden Patent Suit" (PhD diss., Columbia University, 1955), 145–47. Mom, *Electric Vehicle*, 29–30, 87. David A. Kirsch, *The Electric Vehicle and the Burden of History* (New Brunswick, NJ: Rutgers University Press, 2000), 56. Richard Schallenberg, *Bottled Energy: Electrical Engineering and*

the Evolution of Chemical Energy Storage (Philadelphia: American Philosophical Society, 1981), 263.

3. H. F. Cuntz, "Story of the Selden Case and Hartford," Cave box 9, folder 2, Correspondence, September 12, 1940, 2, Detroit Public Library NAHC. See H. F. Cuntz to Mrs. Wendell Patro, November 23, 1948, "Proudly We Acclaim," Cave box 1, folder 19, 2, Detroit Public Library NAHC. See H. F. Cuntz to Mr. A. F. Scheaf, May 8, 1947, "Pope History," Cave box 3, folder 15, Detroit Public Library NAHC. Mom, *Electric Vehicle*, 28, 32. Stephen B. Goddard, *Colonel Albert Pope and His American Dream Machines* (Jefferson, NC: McFarland, 2000), 151. Michael Brian Schiffer, *Taking Charge: The Electric Automobile in America* (Washington, DC: Smithsonian Institution Press, 1994), 50, 79, 84.

4. See H. F. Cuntz to Mr. Henry Cave, September 9, 1940, Cave box 9, folder 1, Detroit Public Library NAHC.

5. Cuntz, "Story of the Selden Case and Hartford," 3–4. See H. F. Cuntz to Mr. Henry Cave.

6. Cuntz, "Story of the Selden Case and Hartford," 7.

7. Cuntz, "Pope Manufacturing Company—Columbia Automobile Company and The Electric Vehicle Company," 5–6. Goddard, *Colonel Albert Pope*, 153. Mark D. Hirsch, *William C. Whitney* (New York: Dodd, Mead, 1948), 557. Cuntz, "Story of the Selden Case and Hartford," 7.

8. Cuntz, "Story of the Selden Case and Hartford," 7.

9. Blake McKelvey, *Rochester: The Flower City, 1855–1890* (Cambridge, MA: Harvard University Press, 1949), 246. See Carl W. Witman, "George Baldwin Selden," in *Dictionary of American Biography* (New York: 1926), 16:567–68; *National Cyclopedia of American Biography* (New York: 1893), 20:222–23; Raymond H. Arnot, "Rochester; Background of Its History," *Publications of the Rochester Historical Society, Publication Fund Series* 1 (1922): 99–100; McKelvey, *Rochester*, 152, 157, 158, as cited by Greenleaf, "Selden Patent Suit," 13–17. Greenleaf, "Selden Patent Suit," 13–17.

10. See undated notebook entry (early 1877), *Selden Case Record*, VIII, 3560; notebook entries, October 24, 25, 1877, *Selden Case Record*, 3563, 3565, as cited by Greenleaf, "Selden Patent Suit," 46–47. Greenleaf, "Selden Patent Suit," 46–47.

11. "Otto's New Gas Engine," *Van Nostrand's Eclectic Engineering Magazine* 18 (January 1878): 66–68. Lynwood Bryant, "The Origin of the Four-Stroke Cycle," *Technology and Culture* 8, no. 2 (April 1967): 178–98. Rudolph Slaby, "Father of the Gas Engine," *Automobile Magazine* 5 (December 1903): 1090–94. See *Selden Case Record*, 3, 649–54 (Frank H. Clement, December 1, 2, 1905), 709–710, 741 (William Gomm, December 15, 18, 1905), 1173–77 (George B. Selden, May 7, 1906); *Selden Case Record*, 616 (William Gleason, November 28, 1905); *Selden Case Record*, 584 (James A. Peoples, November 27, 1905), 686–87 (James Fitt, December 14, 1905), 774–75 (William M. Rebasz, December 20, 1905); *Selden Case Record*, 708, 710–711, 721 (William Gomm, December 15, 16, 19, 1905); *Selden Case Record*, 1250–51 (George B. Selden, May 22, 1906); *Selden Case Record*, 4, 1741, 1861 (Dugald Clerk, August 7, 17, 1906); *Selden Case Record*, Frederick P. Fish et al., Appellate Brief, 45, as cited by Greenleaf, "Selden Patent Suit," 10–11, 41, 48–51. Greenleaf, "Selden Patent Suit," 10–11, 30–33, 41, 48–51.

12. See *Selden Case Record*, 3, 649–54 (Frank H. Clement, December 1, 2, 1905), 709–710, 741 (William Gomm, December 15, 18, 1905), 1173–77 (George B. Selden, May 7, 1906);

Selden Case Record, 616 (William Gleason, November 28, 1905); *Selden Case Record,* 584 (James A. Peoples, November 27, 1905), 686–87 (James Fitt, December 14, 1905), 774–75 (William M. Rebasz, December 20, 1905); *Selden Case Record,* 708, 710–711, 721 (William Gomm, December 15, 16, 19, 1905); *Selden Case Record,* 1250–51 (George B. Selden, May 22, 1906); *Selden Case Record,* 4, 1741, 1861 (Dugald Clerk, August 7, 17, 1906); *Selden Case Record,* Frederick P. Fish et al., Appellate Brief, 45. See *Selden Case Record,* 3, 772, 777–79 (William M. Rebasz, December 20, 1905); *Selden Case Record,* 717–18, 727, 757, 759–760 (William Gomm, December 15, 16, 19, 1905), 1178–79, 1192–93 (George B. Selden, May 8, 9, 1906), as cited by Greenleaf, "Selden Patent Suit," 49–53. Greenleaf, "Selden Patent Suit," 49–53.

13. See *Selden Case Record,* 649–51 (Frank H. Clement, December 1, 1905); 8, 3577, Selden to M. T. E. Chandler, December 20, 1877. *Selden Case Record,* 772, 777–79 (William M. Rebasz, December 20, 1905); *Selden Case Record,* 717–18, 727, 757, 759–60 (William Gomm, December 15, 16, 19, 1905), 1178–79, 1192–93 (George B. Selden, May 8, 9, 1906) as cited by Greenleaf, "Selden Patent Suit," 48, 51–52. Greenleaf, "Selden Patent Suit," 48, 51–52.

14. J. Harold Byers, "The Selden Case," *Journal of the Patent Office Society* 22, no. 10 (October 1940), Cave box 8, folder 28, 726–27, Detroit Public Library NAHC. Greenleaf, "Selden Patent Suit," 84–85. See *Selden Case Record,* XIV, 4427–38, as cited by Greenleaf, "Selden Patent Suit," 84–85.

15. Byers, "Selden Case." Greenleaf, "Selden Patent Suit," 92–95.

16. F. R. Williams, "A Dissertation on the Selden Patent," *Automobile* 17 (November 14, 1907): 734. See *Selden Case Record,* R. A. Parker, Trial Brief, 463. *Selden Case Record,* 6, 3180 (George B. Selden, August 13, 1908), as cited by Greenleaf, "Selden Patent Suit," 93, 95–98. Greenleaf, "Selden Patent Suit," 93, 95–98.

17. Greenleaf, "Selden Patent Suit," 89.

18. See *Annual Report of the Commissioner of Patents for the Year 1897* (Washington: 1898), 9; *Annual Report of the Commissioner of Patents for the Year 1887* (Washington: 1888), 3; *Annual Report of the Commissioner of Patents for the Year 1895,* 13, 14, as cited by Greenleaf, "Selden Patent Suit," 85–86, 91. Greenleaf, "Selden Patent Suit," 85–86, 91.

19. Greenleaf, "Selden Patent Suit," 95.

20. Ibid., 94. See *Selden Case Record,* 14, 4427–38, as cited by Greenleaf, "Selden Patent Suit," 94.

21. "The Investor's Opportunity," *Horseless Age* 2, no. 12 (October 1897): 1. "Broad Claims on a Hydro-Carbon Road Engine," *Horseless Age* 2, no. 2 (December 1896): 16–17.

22. Cuntz, "Story of the Selden Case and Hartford," 9–10.

23. Ibid., 11–12. See *Selden Case Record,* 2, 435–50; *Selden Case Record,* 1, 37–38 (Hayden Eames, June 27, 1904), as cited by Greenleaf, "Selden Patent Suit," 142–43. Greenleaf, "Selden Patent Suit," 142–43.

24. "Motor Vehicles in the Stock Market," *Engineering News* 42 (November 2, 1899): 289. "Scramble for Patent Control," *Motor Age* 1 (September 12, 1899): 13. See *Cycle and Automobile Trade Journal* 12 (May 1, 1908): 24; *Motor Age* 1 (November 7, 1899): 178, as cited by Greenleaf, "Selden Patent Suit," 111, 114–15. Greenleaf, "Selden Patent Suit," 111, 114–15.

25. *Automobile Magazine* 1 (March 1900): 641. See *Cycle and Automobile Trade Journal* 12

(May 1, 1908): 24, as cited by Greenleaf, "Selden Patent Suit," 110–11. Greenleaf, "Selden Patent Suit," 110–11.

26. "000,000,000,000," *Horseless Age* 5, no. 7 (November 15, 1899): 5–6.

27. "Lead Cab Literature," *Horseless Age* 7, no. 4 (October 24, 1900): 9. "Annual Statement of the Electric Vehicle Company," *Horseless Age* 4, no. 26 (September 27, 1899): 7–8. Greenleaf, "Selden Patent Suit," 149.

28. "Lead Cab Financiering," *Horseless Age* 5, no. 17 (January 24, 1900): 11.

29. "Loans of State Trust Company," *New York Times*, January 14, 1900, 1. "Lead Cab Financiering," *Horseless Age* 5, no. 17 (January 24, 1900): 11.

30. *Horseless Age* 5, no. 17 (January 24, 1900): 10. "Lead Cab Financiering," 11.

31. "Lead Cab Finale," *Horseless Age* 5, no. 12 (December 2, 1899): 8. "Lead Cab Financiering," 11. John B. Rae, "The Electric Vehicle Company: A Monopoly That Missed," *Business History Review* 29, no. 4 (December 1955): 303. See "A British View of Accumulators and Electric Vehicles," *Electrical Review* (New York), December 20, 1899, 393; "Lead Cab Finale," 8; "A short history of the electric taxi-cab," *Electric Vehicles* (U.S.), July 1916, 2, as cited by Mom, *Electric Vehicle*, 90–91.

32. "Lead Cab Scandals," *Horseless Age* 8, no. 24 (September 11, 1901): 491. Greenleaf, "Selden Patent Suit," 149, 153. Greenleaf, *Monopoly on Wheels*, 73–74. Kirsch, *Electric Vehicle*, 62.

33. "The Trust," *Horseless Age* 5, no. 20 (February 14, 1900): 9.

34. Cuntz, "Story of the Selden Case and Hartford," 14.

35. "Big Patent Suit Threatened," *Motor Age* 2 (June 14, 1900): 417–25.

36. Greenleaf, "Selden Patent Suit," 158.

37. "About the Selden Patent," *Motor Age* 2 (June 21, 1900): 449–52, as cited by Greenleaf, "Selden Patent Suit," 158–59. Greenleaf, "Selden Patent Suit," 158–59.

38. See *Selden Case Record*, 14, 4625; *Motor World* 6 (August 6, 1903): 695; *Motor Review* 5, n.s. (November 7, 1901), 41; *Automobile and Motor Review* 7 (October 18, 1902): 28–29; *Cycle and Automobile Trade Journal* 8 (March 1, 1904): 68–79, as cited by Greenleaf, "Selden Patent Suit," 160–62. Greenleaf, "Selden Patent Suit," 160–62.

39. *Horseless Age* 6, no. 15 (July 11, 1900): 9. See *Motor Age* 2 (July 19, 1900): 636–37, as cited by Greenleaf, "Selden Patent Suit," 162–63. Greenleaf, "Selden Patent Suit," 162–63.

40. "The Selden Patent Case," *Horseless Age* 7, no. 8 (November 21, 1900): 20. "A Prominent Patent Lawyer's Opinion," *Horseless Age* 7, no. 8 (November 21, 1900): 21. "The Selden Patent Case," *Horseless Age* 7, no. 9 (November 28, 1900): 13. Greenleaf, "Selden Patent Suit," 163–64.

41. "Defendants File Answer in the Selden Patent Suit," *Horseless Age* 7, no. 23 (March 6, 1901): 16–17. "Present Status of Automobile Patent Litigation," *Horseless Age* 10, no. 13 (September 24, 1902): 327. See *Selden Case Record*, 10, 1372–84; *Selden Case Record*, 10, 1405, 1407; *Motor Age* 3 (April 2, 1903): 10, as cited by Greenleaf, "Selden Patent Suit," 170. Greenleaf, "Selden Patent Suit," 170.

42. "Present Status of Automobile Patent Litigation," *Horseless Age* 10, no. 13 (September 24, 1902): 327. See *Selden Case Record*, 10, 1405, 1407; *Motor Age* 3 (April 2, 1903): 10; Herman F. Cuntz, Memorandum, August 15, 1954; *Selden Case Record*, 14, 4625, as cited by Greenleaf, "Selden Patent Suit," 171–72. Greenleaf, "Selden Patent Suit," 171–72.

43. *Selden Case Record*, 3, 1113–15 (Thomas Henderson, March 21, 1906), as cited by Greenleaf, "Selden Patent Suit," 172. Greenleaf, "Selden Patent Suit," 172.

44. Cuntz, "Story of the Selden Case and Hartford," 22–23. See *Selden Case Record*, 3, 1113–15 (Thomas Henderson, March 21, 1906); *Selden Case Record*, 9, 171–72 (Charles E. Duryea, September 15, 1904), as cited by Greenleaf, "Selden Patent Suit," 172–73. Greenleaf, "Selden Patent Suit," 172–73.

45. "Lead Cab Service Discontinued?" *Horseless Age* 7, no. 23 (March 6, 1901): 19. "Illinois Lead Cab Company in Liquidation," *Horseless Age* 7, no. 24 (March 13, 1901): 14. Mom, *Electric Vehicle*, 91.

46. "Lead Cab Funerals," *Horseless Age* 8, no. 1 (April 3, 1901): 1. "Illinois Electric Vehicle Transportation Company," *Electrical Review* (New York), March 16, 1901, 354, as cited by Mom, *Electric Vehicle*, 91. Greenleaf, *Monopoly on Wheels*, 73.

47. "Lead Cab Nemesis," *Horseless Age* 8, no. 2 (April 10, 1901): 25.

48. See *Motor Review* 5, n.s. (December 19, 1901): 2. *Commercial and Financial Chronicle*, March–September 1901, 72–73, as cited by Greenleaf, *Monopoly on Wheels*, 73. Greenleaf, *Monopoly on Wheels*, 73.

49. "Lead Cab Scandals," 489. "Lead Cab Finale," *Horseless Age* 8, no. 28 (October 9, 1901): 577. "Lead Cab Trust Sued Again," *Horseless Age* 8, no. 28 (October 9, 1901): 582. Greenleaf, *Monopoly on Wheels*, 73–74.

50. "Minor Mention," *Horseless Age* 11, no. 28 (March 4, 1903): 334. "As Some Men View It," *Motor Vehicle Review* 3, n.s. (September 6, 1900): 2–3. "A Four Hundred Dollar Automobile," *Motor Vehicle Review* 4, n.s. (March 21, 1901): 4. "A Remarkable Variety of Spare Parts," *Motor Vehicle Review* 1 (December 26, 1899): 9–11. "Passing of the Quickly Assembled Car," *Automobile* 16, no. 13 (March 28, 1907): 564. "Mainly about Man and Motors," *Automobile Magazine* 5 (April 1903): 412–13. "Motor's Historical Table of the American Motor Car Industry," *Motor* 11 (March 1909): 36–42. "The Deposit System," *Horseless Age* 18 (October 10, 1906): 436. "Judgement Applied to Business," *Motor Vehicle Review*, May 23, 1901, 3–4. "Economy in Manufacturing," *Cycle and Automobile Trade Journal* 8 (December 1, 1903): 21–22. See *New York Tribune*, August 5, 1917; John K. Barnes, "The Romance of Our Automobile Makers," *World's Work* 41 (April 1921): 561–64; Lawrence H. Seltzer, *A Financial History of the American Automobile Industry* (Houghton, Mifflin, Boston and New York: 1928), 22, 155; *Detroit Evening News*, October 8, 1902; *Detroit Journal*, May 26, 1903; John K. Barnes, "The Men Who Created 'Cooperative Competition,'" *World's Work* 42 (May 1921): 60–61; Benjamin Briscoe, "The Inside Story of General Motors," *Detroit Saturday Night* 15 (January 22, 1921), Section Two, 7; *Motor Age* 2 (March 15, 1900): 3; David T. Wells, "The Growth of the Automobile Industry in America," *Outing* 51 (November 1907): 213; *New York Times*, n.d., extracted in *Motor World* 4 (July 17, 1902): 462; *Motor World* 6 (June 18, 1903): 443; *Motor Age* 4 (April, 25, 1901): n.p.; *Detroit Free Press*, July 13, 1902. "Minor Mention," *Horseless Age* 10 (July–December 1902); 11 (January–June, 1903); Ralph C. Epstein, *The Automobile Industry: Its Commercial and Economic Development* (Arno Press Chicago and New York: 1928), 163–64, 229n; Herman F. Cuntz, "Circulation of Money Due to Automobiling," *New York Herald*, February 7, 1909, as cited by Greenleaf, "Selden Patent Suit," 175–82. Greenleaf, "Selden Patent Suit," 175–82.

51.   See "Motor's Historical Table," 36–42; Epstein, *Automobile Industry*, 163–64, 229n; Cuntz,
        "Circulation of Money," as cited by Greenleaf, "Selden Patent Suit," 181–82. Greenleaf,
        "Selden Patent Suit," 181–82.

52.   "Mainly about Men and Motors," *Automobile Magazine* 4 (September 1902): 781.

53.   Charles Clifton, "Cooperation and Its Results: How It Saved the Automobile Industry at a
        Critical Stage," *Automobile Topics* 40 (December 18, 1915): 461. See Joy to Packard, Janu-
        ary 4, 1903, Joy Papers; Joy to Day, January 5, 1903, Joy Papers; Joy to Packard, January 8,
        1903, Joy Papers, Joy to Day, January 8, February 9, 1903, Joy Papers; *Selden Case Record*,
        3, 944–46 (Elihu H. Cutler, February 21, 1906), as cited by Greenleaf, "Selden Patent
        Suit," 195–99. Greenleaf, "Selden Patent Suit," 195–99.

54.   See Henry B. Joy to S. T. Davis Jr., February 21, 1903, Joy Papers; F. L. Smith, "Motoring
        Down a Quarter Century," *Detroit Saturday Night* 22 (October 20, 1928): 3; George H.
        Day to Joy, February 25, 1903, Joy Papers; Joy to Edward Rector, February 28, 1903, Joy Pa-
        pers; Joy to S. T. Davis Jr., February 28, 1903, Joy Papers; Joy to J. W. Packard, March 2,
        1903, Joy Papers, as cited by Greenleaf, "Selden Patent Suit," 200–02. Greenleaf, "Selden
        Patent Suit," 200–202.

55.   See *Automobile Magazine* 5 (January 1903): 89–90, as cited by Greenleaf, "Selden Patent
        Suit," 199. Greenleaf, "Selden Patent Suit," 199.

56.   See F. L. Smith, "Motoring Down a Quarter Century," Parker Papers, 3, as cited by Green-
        leaf, "Selden Patent Suit," 203. Greenleaf, "Selden Patent Suit," 203.

57.   "Nine Years Agreement on Selden Patent," *Motor World* 6 (April 2, 1903): 18. "M. J. Bud-
        long," *Motor Age* 3 (February 12, 1903): 7. See Smith, "Motoring Down a Quarter Cen-
        tury," 3; *Motor World* (April 16, 1903): 99; "Mainly about Men and Motors," *Automobile
        Magazine* 5 (November 1903): 1025–27; *Motor Age* 5 (February 1, 1904): n.p., as cited by
        Greenleaf, "Selden Patent Suit," 203–5. Greenleaf, "Selden Patent Suit," 203–5.

58.   Greenleaf, *Monopoly on Wheels*, 69. See section 4 of "License Agreement" and
        "Articles of Agreement of Association of Licensed Automobile Manufacturers," *Selden
        Case Record*, 14, 4643–53; *Selden Case Record*, 9, 688 (George H. Day, January 17, 1905);
        W. J. Morgan, "Selden Patent War Nears End," *New York Globe and Commercial Adver-
        tiser*, December 24, 1910. *Selden Case Record*, 6, 2871–74 (George B. Selden, July 6,
        1908), as cited by Greenleaf, "Selden Patent Suit," 205–7. Greenleaf, "Selden Patent Suit,"
        205–7.

59.   See Joy to Winton Motor Carriage Company, March 9, 1903, Joy Papers; Joy to Packard,
        March 11, 1903, Joy Papers; *Selden Case Record*, 10, 1409, 1410–11; *Selden Case Record*,
        9, 682–87 (George W. Mills Jr., January 17, 1905), 707–8 (Robert N. Kenyon, January 18,
        1905). *Selden Case Record*, R. A. Parker and W. Benton Crisp, Trial Brief, 351–65; *Selden
        Case Record*, R. A. Parker, Trial Brief, 9–18, as cited by Greenleaf, "Selden Patent Suit,"
        208–10. Greenleaf, "Selden Patent Suit," 208–10.

60.   See *Selden Case Record*, 3, 907–9 (Milton J. Budlong, February 16, 1906); opening clause
        and Article 13, "Articles of Agreement," *Selden Case Record*, 14, 4646, 4650; *Horseless Age*
        11 (April 1, 1903): 426; *Horseless Age* 11 (April 29, 1903), 519; *Selden Case Record*, 14,
        4519, as cited by Greenleaf, "Selden Patent Suit," 222. Greenleaf, "Selden Patent Suit," 222.

61.   See Herman F. Cuntz, Memoranda, August 10, 19, 1954, as cited by Greenleaf, "Selden
        Patent Suit," 216. Greenleaf, "Selden Patent Suit," 216.

62. "Selden Patent Matters," *Horseless Age* 11, no. 25 (June 24, 1903): 746. "Day Explains Policy of A.L.A.M.," *Motor Age* 4, no. 6 (August 6, 1903): 10. See "Automobile Topics Trade Talk No. 1," *Selden Case Record*, 14, 4515–19, as cited by Greenleaf, "Selden Patent Suit," 216–17, 220. Greenleaf, "Selden Patent Suit," 216–17, 220.

63. "Co-operative Benefits," *Motor World* 7 (December 24, 1903): 456. See U.S. Bureau of the Census, Bulletin 66, *Automobiles and Bicycles and Tricycles*, 12; *New York Tribune*, August 5, 1917; John K. Barnes, "The Romance of Our Automobile Makers," *World's Work* 41 (April, 1921): 561–64, as cited by Greenleaf, "Selden Patent Suit," 174–76, 218. Greenleaf, "Selden Patent Suit," 174–76, 218.

64. "Canada Gets Bulk of Our Exports," *Automobile* 27 (July 25, 1912): 165. Epstein, *Automobile Industry*, 76. "Cars for All the People," *Motor Age* 6 (September 29, 1904): 4. See *Selden Case Record*, 3, 931–32 (Milton J. Budlong, February 19, 1906), as cited by Greenleaf, "Selden Patent Suit," 228–30. Greenleaf, "Selden Patent Suit," 228–30.

65. See *Motor Age* 3, no. 8 (February 19, 1903): 18.

66. "Decisive Action Taken at Meeting of the Licensed Association," *Automobile* 9 (August 29, 1903): 219. "Mainly about Men and Motors," *Automobile Magazine* 5 (October 1903): 943–45. See Fred A. Shannon, *The Farmer's Last Frontier* Farrar & Rinehart (New York and Toronto: 1945), 302–3, as cited by Greenleaf, "Selden Patent Suit," 225–26, 261–62. Greenleaf, "Selden Patent Suit," 225–26, 261–62.

67. "Automobilists and Licensed Makes," *Automobile Topics* 6 August 1, 1903): 1083. Greenleaf, "Selden Patent Suit," 226.

68. See Elihu H. Cutler to editor, "From Members of the Association," *Cycle and Automobile Trade Journal* 8 (September 29, 1903), as cited by Greenleaf, "Selden Patent Suit," 224. Greenleaf, "Selden Patent Suit," 224.

Chapter 7: Defiance

1. See David Lewis, *The Public Image of Henry Ford* (Detroit: Wayne State University Press, 1976), 143; Keith Sward, *The Legend of Henry Ford* (Toronto: Rinehart, 1948), 160; *Chicago Tribune*, March 8, 1923; *Detroit News*, December 31, 1931; David L. Lewis, "Henry Ford's Anti-Semitism and Its Repercussions," *Michigan Jewish History* 24, no. 1 (January 1984): 5–6; *New York Times*, July 31, 1938; *Detroit News*, July 31, 1938; A. Scott Berg, *Lindbergh* (New York: Putnam, 1998), 375, as cited by Albert Lee, *Henry Ford and the Jews* (New York: Stein and Day, 1980), 45–46, 283–85. "Ford, at 75, Looks to 'Going Ahead'; Huge Parties Given Him in Detroit," *New York Times*, July 31, 1938, 1; *Detroit Free Press*, July 31, 1938, 1; Accession 285, box 2149, Fritz Hailer, Benson Ford Research Center, as cited by Max Wallace, *The American Axis* (New York: St. Martin's Press, 2003), 145–46. James E. Pool and Suzanne Pool, *Who Financed Hitler* (New York: Dial Press, 1978), 90–91; "'Heinrich' Ford Idol of Bavaria Fascisti Chief," *Chicago Tribune*, March 8, 1923, 2; Morton Rosenstock, *Louis Marshall, Defender of Jewish Rights* (Detroit: Wayne State, 1965), 128–41, as cited by Edwin Black, *The Transfer Agreement* (Washington, D.C.: Dialog Press, 1999), 27.

2. Direct testimony, Henry Ford, United States Circuit Court, Southern District of New York, No. 8566, No. 8579, No. 8638, vol. 1, VBG 75-4194, 33 Q, 46–47. Henry Ford in collaboration with Samuel Crowther, *My Life and Work*, (Garden City, 1923), 28–30, 35–36. William A. Simonds, *Henry Ford: His Life—His Work—His Genius* (Los Angeles, Califor-

nia: F. Clymer, 1943), 61. See *Official Gazette of the United States Patent Office* 12 (Washington, DC; 1878), 277–78; New England Cotton Manufacturers' Association, *Proceedings of the Seventeenth Annual Meeting* (Boston: 1992), 46; Accession 42, box 1, Marvin Buckberry Records, Benson Ford Research Center; Selden Case Record, 9, 47, testimony of August 9, 1904; *Detroit Journal*, June 6, 1896; Fair Lane Papers, Box 79; *Detroit Journal*, November 30, 1901, as cited by Allan Nevins, *Ford: The Times, the Man, the Company* (New York: Scribner, 1954), 83, 90–91, 112–13. See *Detroit Saturday Night* 1 (July 27, 1907): 7; *Detroit Free Press*, August 19, 1899, as cited by William Greenleaf, "The Selden Patent Suit" (PhD diss., Columbia University, 1955), 234.

3. Direct testimony, Henry Ford, United States Circuit Court, 47. See Ford, *My Life and Work*, 36; Oliver E. Barthel, *Reminiscences*, Benson Ford Archives, Oral History Section, as cited by Nevins, *Ford*, 212–13, 221–22.

4. See U.S. Board of Tax Appeals, *Estate of John F. Dodge et al. v. Commissioner of Internal Revenue*, Transcript of Hearings held at Detroit and Washington, D.C., January 11–February 25, 1927, 1277–79 (John W. Anderson, January 21, 1927); *Dodge v. Ford Motor Co.*, 204 Michigan Records and Briefs (January Term 1919), 96 (Henry Ford, November 14, 1916); John W. Anderson to Wendell A. Anderson, June 4, 1903, Accession 23, box 8, Benson Ford Research Center; Nevins, *Ford*, chaps. 9–11; Ford-Malcomson Agreement, August 20, 1902, Accession 140, box 1, Benson Ford Research Center, as cited by Greenleaf, "Selden Patent Suit," 234–36.

5. See U.S. Board of Tax Appeals, *Dodge v. Commissioner of Internal Revenue*, 1277–79 (John W. Anderson, January 21, 1927); *Dodge v. Ford Motor Co.*, 96 (Henry Ford, November 14, 1916), as cited by Greenleaf, "Selden Patent Suit," 234–36.

6. Greenleaf, "Selden Patent Suit," 117. Ernest H. Wakefield, *History of the Electric Automobile: Battery-Only Powered Cars* (Warrendale, PA: Society of Automotive Engineers, 1994), 128–29.

7. "Weight of One Gallon (U.S.) of Water, Gasoline, and Ethanol," http://www.santacruzpl.org/readyref/files/g-l/gasoline.shtml.

8. *Motor Age* 3 (June 25, 1903): 11. See James Couzens, "What I Learned about Business from Ford," *System* 40 (September 1921): 264, 360–61, as cited by Greenleaf, *Monopoly on Wheels*, 110.

9. See Report in Additional Tax Case MSS., Accession 96, Benson Ford Research Center, as cited by Nevins, *Ford*, 237–38. See Ford-Malcomson Agreement, August 20, 1902, Accession 140, box 1, Benson Ford Research Center, Ford-Malcomson-Dodge Agreement, February 28, 1903, as cited by Greenleaf, "Selden Patent Suit," 235.

10. See Barthel & Barthel to Henry Ford, November 14, 1900, exhibit item, Fair Lane Papers, Ford Archives, as cited by Greenleaf, "Selden Patent Suit," 237–38.

11. See Herman F. Cuntz to Charles B. King, August 11, 1936, King Papers; Cuntz, Memorandum, August 10, 1954; Herman F. Cuntz, "Hartford the Birthplace of Automobile Industry," *Hartford Times*, September 18, 1947; *Dodge v. Commissioner of Internal Revenue*, Transcript of Hearings, 1281–83 (John W. Anderson, January 21, 1927) as cited by Greenleaf, "The Selden Patent Suit." 238–41.

12. See *Dodge v. Commissioner of Internal Revenue*, 1281–83 (John W. Anderson, January 21, 1987), as cited by Greenleaf, "Selden Patent Suit," 240–41.

13. Ibid., 240.

14. Ibid., 240–41. Harry Barnard, *Independent Man: The Life of Senator James Couzens* (New York: Scribner, 1958), 54.

15. See Herman F. Cuntz, Memorandum, August 10, 1954, as cited by Greenleaf, "Selden Patent Suit," 241.

16. See F. L. Smith, "Motoring Down a Quarter Century," *Detroit Saturday Night* 22 (October 27, 1928): Section Two, 2. T.N.E.C. Hearings, Part 2: *Patents*, 268; W. J. Cameron, *A Series of Talks Given on The Ford Sunday Evening Hour . . . 1934–1935* (Dearborn, MI: 1935), 51, as cited by Greenleaf, "Selden Patent Suit," 241.

17. See Smith, "Motoring Down a Quarter Century," Section Two, 2, as cited by Greenleaf, "Selden Patent Suit," 248–49.

18. Theodore F. MacManus and Norman Beasley, *Men, Money and Motors* (New York and London: *Harper & Brothers*, 1929), 56. Barnard, *Independent Man*, 55.

19. MacManus and Beasley, *Men, Money and Motors*, 56.

20. See "Trade Talk—No. 1," *Selden Case Record*, 14, 4515–19, as cited by Greenleaf, "Selden Patent Suit," 262.

21. See Barnard, *Independent Man*, 54. "Trade Talk—No. 1," 14, 4515–19, as cited by Greenleaf, "Selden Patent Suit," 262.

22. See Nevins, *Ford*, illustration between pages 320–21.

23. *Motor Age* 4 (September 3, 1903), 14. See Checkbook, Ford Motor Company, Accession 103, Benson Ford Research Center; Couzens, "What I Learned"; Minute Books, Ford Motor Company, September 17–18, 1903; *Dodge v. Commissioner of Internal Revenue*, 1283–84 (John W. Anderson, January 21, 1927); *Horseless Age* 12 (September 2, 1903): 233–34; *Motor Age* 4 (October 15, 1903): 26, as cited by Greenleaf, "Selden Patent Suit," 242n105, 267–68, 275. Nevins, *Ford*. Report in Additional Tax MSS., Accession 96, Benson Ford Research Center.

24. *Horseless Age* 13 (January 6, 1904): 1. See *Motor World* 6 (August 27, 1903): 807; *Motor World* 7 (March 24, 1904): 1103, as cited by Greenleaf, "Selden Patent Suit," 257, 274.

25. Greenleaf, "Selden Patent Suit," 256.

26. See "Henry Ford at Bay," *Forum* 62 (August 1919): 241, as cited by Greenleaf, "Selden Patent Suit," 253.

27. See *Detroit Journal*, October 24, 1903, as cited by Greenleaf, "Selden Patent Suit," 285.

28. *Automobile Topics* 6 (August 1, 1903): 1082–83.

29. *Horseless Age* 12, no. 9 (August 26, 1903): 209. *Horseless Age* 12, no. 18 (October 28, 1903): 445.

30. See *Motor World* 6 (August 27, 1903): 811, as cited by Greenleaf, "Selden Patent Suit," 257.

31. Greenleaf, "Selden Patent Suit," 266–67.

32. See J. Couzens to Mr. J. W. Anderson (Detroit, MI, October 1, 1903), as cited by Nevins, *Ford*, 256–57. Barnard, *Independent Man*, 57.

33. Greenleaf, "Selden Patent Suit," 265.

34. See *New York World*, September 10, 1903, as cited by Greenleaf, "Selden Patent Suit," 265–66.

35. *Automobile* 9 (November 21, 1903): 550.

36. "Ford on the Selden Association," *Cycle and Automobile Trade Journal* 8 (October 1, 1903): 17 ff. James Couzens to editor, October 27, 1903, *Cycle and Automobile Trade Journal* 8 (December 1, 1903): 19. "No Compromise Sought by Ford," *Motor Age* 4 (October 1,

1903): 13–14. "An Opposition View of the Selden Patent and the Licensed Association," *Horseless Age* 12 (October 7, 1903): 378–79.

37. James Couzens to editor, October 27, 1903.

38. Ibid.

39. Ibid.

40. Ibid.

41. Ibid.

42. Ibid.

43. See *Motor World* 7 (December 17, 1903): 411, as cited by Greenleaf, "Selden Patent Suit," 278–79.

44. United States Circuit Court, Southern District of New York, in Equity No. 8566, *Electric Vehicle Company and George B. Selden v. A. Duerr & Company and Ford Motor Company* (February 28, 1910), Accession 295, box 1, vol. 18, 2–3, Benson Ford Research Center. United States Circuit Court, Southern District of New York, In Equity No. 8579, *Electric Vehicle Company and George B. Selden v. The O.J. Gude Company*, Accession 295, box 2, 3, Benson Ford Research Center. United States Circuit Court, Southern District of New York, In Equity No. 8638, *Electric Vehicle Company and George B. Selden v. John Wanamaker et al.*, VBG 75-4194, Benson Ford Research Center. United States Circuit Court, Southern District of New York, In Equity No. 8638, *Electric Vehicle Company and George B. Selden v. C.A. Duerr & Company and Ford Motor Company, O.J. Gude Company, and John Wanamaker et al.*, Brief on Behalf of the Defendants, Accession 295, box 2 Crisp's Briefs, 4, Benson Ford Research Center. Greenleaf, "Selden Patent Suit," 284. Greenleaf, *Monopoly on Wheels*, 127.

45. Greenleaf, "Selden Patent Suit," 298–99.

46. Direct Testimony, Henry Ford, United States Circuit Court, Southern District of New York No. 8566, No. 8579; No. 8638, vol. 1, VBG 75-4194, Q. 118–21, 30-1. Direct Testimony, Mr. Thomas J. Duffy Sr., United States Circuit Court, Southern District of New York No. 8566, No. 8579, No. 8638, Accession 1704, box 3, folder 3-1, Benson Ford Research Center. Direct Testimony, Mr. Thompson, United States Circuit Court, Southern District of New York No. 8566, No. 8579, No. 8638, Accession 1704, box 3, folder 3-1, Benson Ford Research Center. Direct Testimony, Frank Wright, United States Circuit Court, Southern District of New York No. 8566, No. 8579, No. 8638, Accession 1704, box 3, folder 3-1, Benson Ford Research Center.

47. Direct Testimony, Henry Ford, United States Circuit Court, Southern District of New York No. 8566, No. 8579, No. 8638, vol. 1, Accession 295, box 4, vol. 6, 2862–66, Benson Ford Research Center. See Oldfield Report, H.R. Committee on Patents, Report No. 1161, August 1912, in L. H. Baekeland, "The Incongruities of American Patent Litigation," *Scientific American Supplement* 74 (November 23, 1912): 322–23; Fairplay, "Opposes the 'Licensed Manufacturers Association,'" *Horseless Age* 11 (April 1, 1903): 431; John Trowbridge, "The Imperiled Dignity of Science and the Law," *Atlantic Monthly* 78 (October 1896): 494; J. Frank Duryea, *Data Relative to the Development of America's First Gasoline Automobile* (n.p., n.d.), King Papers as cited by Greenleaf, "Selden Patent Suit," 291–95, 298–300. See undated letter to H. M. Campbell, R. A. Parker Papers, Automotive History Collection, Detroit Public Library, as cited by Nevins, *Ford*, 440.

48. "Minor Mention," *Horseless Age* 5, no. 15 (January 10, 1900): 12. "Minor Mention," *Horse-*

less Age 5, no. 19 (February 7, 1900): 15. "Minor Mention," *Horseless Age* 6, no. 2 (April 11, 1900): 24. "Minor Mention," *Horseless Age* 6, no. 3 (April 18, 1900): 21. "Minor Mention," *Horseless Age* 6, no. 4 (April 25, 1900): 26. "Minor Mention," *Horseless Age* 6, no. 16 (July 18, 1900): 23. "Lead Cab Activity in Boston," *Horseless Age* 5, no. 17 (January 24, 1900): 13. "Minor Mention," *Horseless Age* 6, no. 22 (August 29, 1900): 25. "Minor Mention," *Horseless Age* 7, no. 3 (October 17, 1900): 15. "Minor Mention," *Horseless Age* 9, no. 10 (March 5, 1902): 306. "Exhibits at the Automobile Club's Show," *Horseless Age* 7, no. 6 (November 7, 1900): 34. "Next Year's Output," *Horseless Age* 12, no. 24 (December 9, 1903): 591. Ralph C. Epstein, *The Automobile Industry* (New York: Arno Press, 1972), 76. *Automobile* 27 (July 25, 1912): 165.

49.   "Boston–New York Tour in an Electric Car," *Horseless Age* 12, no. 18 (October 28, 1903): 457. "Woods Electric Tonneau," *Horseless Age* 12, no. 1 (July 1, 1903): 13. "From a User of Electric Vehicles," *Horseless Age* 12, no. 21 (November 18, 1903): 532. "Trials of Electric Cars," *Horseless Age* 12, no. 22 (November 25, 1903): 544. "Synnestvedt Electric Vehicles," *Horseless Age* 12, no. 26 (December 23, 1903): 653–54.

50.   Electric Vehicle Company, Special Bulletin No. 4, June 1, 1901, Accession 1750, box 7, folder 7-2, Benson Ford Research Center. Electric Vehicle Company, Special Bulletin No. 5, June 1, 1901, Accession 1750, box 7, folder 7-2, Benson Ford Research Center. "Boston–New York Tour," 457. "Recent Advances in Methods of Charging Electric Vehicles," *Horseless Age* 11, no. 23 (June 10, 1903): 671–72. "The Fuel Question," *Horseless Age* 9, no. 22 (May 28, 1902): 627.

51.   Paul H. Giddens, *The Birth of the Oil Industry* (New York: Macmillan, 1938): 14, 58–59, 83, 86, 87, 100–113, 114. Ida M. Tarbell, *The History of the Standard Oil Company*, vol. 1 (Gloucester, MA: Peter Smith, 1963), 10, 12, 30–33, 43–44; photo, "The Drake Oil Well in 1859—the First Oil Well," 10f. "Table of Yearly and Monthly Average Price of Refined," Tarbell, vol. 2, 384–85, 395. See Samuel Rezneck, "Energy: Coal and Oil in the American Economy," *Journal of Economic History* 7, supp. (1947): 63, 64; William Culp Darrah, *Pithole: The Vanished City* (Gettysburg, PA: William C. Darrah, 1972), 2–3. See H. D. Lloyd, "Story of a Great Monopoly," *Atlantic Monthly* 47 (March 1881): 317–34. "Yearly Production of Crude Petroleum of the Principal Oil Producing Countries Since 1900," ca. January 1918: PRO CAB21/119; Gilbert Holland Montague, "The Rise and Supremacy of the Standard Oil Company," *Quarterly Journal of Economics* 16 (1902), 267, 265–292, as cited by Black, *Banking on Baghdad*, 96–99.

52.   "The Fuel Question," *Horseless Age* 9, no. 22 (May 28, 1902): 627. "Spindletop–Gladys City Boomtown Museum Walking Tour," http://www.spindletop.org/timeline/index.html. "Spindletop" http://sln.fi.edu/fellows/fellow2/jan99/spindletop.html.

53.   "From a User of Electric Vehicles," 532.

54.   See National Transportation Committee, *The American Transportation Problem* (Washington, DC: Brookings Institution, 1933), 526–29; John McCarty, *Highway Financing by the Toll System* (Berkeley: University of California, 1951); National Council on Public Works Improvement, *Fragile Foundations: A Report on America's Public Works* (Washington, DC: Government Printing Office, 1988), 33; Federal Highway Administration, *America on the Move: The Story of the Federal-Aid Highway Program* (Washington, DC: September 1984), as cited by Owen D. Gutfreund, *20th Century Sprawl* (New York: Oxford University Press, 2004), 8–10.

55. See American Automobile Association, *Why Federal Aid in Roads* (1916) (Colorado State Archives); William Richter, *Transportation in America* (ABC-CLIO, 1995), 5, 169, 571, as cited by Gutfreund, *Sprawl*, 13–14.

56. "Horseless Carriages," *Electrical World* 29 (April 10, 1897): 468. "The Electrical Motor Carriage," *Electrical World* 29 (May 15, 1897): 608.

57. "Electromobile Accumulators," *Electrical Review* 34 (June 21, 1899): 390, as cited by David A. Kirsch, *The Electric Vehicle and the Burden of History* (New Brunswick, NJ: Rutgers University Press, 2000), 198.

58. "Electromobile," *Electrical Review* 37 (September 26, 1900): 301, as cited by Kirsch, *Electric Vehicle*, 198.

59. Arthur Huey to F. C. Armstrong, June 21, 1901, FA Armstrong papers, Henry Ford Archive, Folder 2. "Public Electric Vehicle Service," *Electrical Review* 38 (May 11, 1901): 571.

60. "Proudly We Acclaim," Henry Cave to Mrs. Wendell Patro, November 23, 1948, 3, Cave box 1, folder 19, Detroit Public Library NAHC. Electric Vehicle Company Bulletin No. 47, August 15, 1901, Accession 1750, box 7, folder 7-3, Benson Ford Research Center. Electric Vehicle Company Bulletin No. 46, August 9, 1901, Accession 1750, box 7, folder 7-3, Benson Ford Research Center. Henry Cave, "Observations of an Engineer on the Early Development of the Automobile," typed draft undated, Cave box 2, folder 7. "A Common-Sense Evaluation of the Work of the Licensed Association of Automobile Manufacturers, Mr. George H. Day of Hartford, and His Assistants," 2, Cave box 9, folder 18. "The Story of the Selden Patent Model," typed draft 1948, Henry Cave, 3, Cave box 8, folder 34. "Former Chief Inspector of HSP Retires from Consultant's Duties," *Hamilton Standard Blade*, September 21, 1944, Cave box 3, folder 9.

61. Bruce Epperson, *Failed Colossus: Albert A. Pope, the Bicycle and the Dawn of the American Auto Industry* (forthcoming, 2006), chap. 6A, version 1.1, 1–2, 6–7. Phil Patton, *Open Road: A Celebration of the American Highway* (Simon & Schuster, 1986), 56. George Chatburn, *Highways and Highway Transportation* (New York: Crowell, 1923), 128–42; See "Errors in School Books," *Manufacturer and Builder* 25, no. 2 (February 1893): 1893; Philip P. Mason, "The League of American Wheelmen and the Good-Roads Movement, 1880–1905" (PhD diss., University of Michigan, 1957); Charles E. Pratt, "The L.A.W. and Legal Rights," *Outing* 7 (January 1886): 454–56; Ross D. Petty, "The Impact of the Sport of Bicycle Riding on Safety Law," *American Business Law Journal* 35, no. 2 (Winter 1998): 185–224; Gregory C. Lisa, "Bicyclists and Bureaucrats: The League of American Wheelmen and Public Choice Theory Applied," *Georgetown Law Review* 84 (1995): 373–98; Mason, "League of American Wheelmen," 46; *Wheel and Cycling Trade Review* 8 (December 1891): 525, as cited by Bruce Epperson, *Failed Colossus*, chap. 6A, version 1.1, 1–2, 6–7. Stephen B. Goddard, *Colonel Albert Pope*, 117. See National Transportation Committee, *American Transportation Problem*, 526–29; McCarty, *Highway Financing*; National Council on Public Works Improvement, *Fragile Foundations*, 33; Federal Highway Administration, *America on the Move*; Lisa, "Bicyclists and Bureaucrats," 385, 394; James Flink, *The Automobile Age* (Cambridge: MIT Press, 1998), 4–5; Howard Preston, *Dirt Roads to Dixie: Accessibility and Modernization in the South, 1885–1935* (Knoxville: University of Tennessee Press, 1991), 171; American Public Works Association, *History of Public Works in the United States, 1776–1976*, ed. Ellis Armstrong (Kansas City: American Public Works Association, 1976), 72, as cited by Gutfreund, *Sprawl*, 8–10.

62. Chatburn, *Highways and Highway Transportation*, 128–42. Lisa. "Bicyclists and Bureaucrats," 385, 394; Flink, *Automobile Age*, 4–5; Patton, *Open Road*, 56; Preston, *Dirt Roads to Dixie*, 171; American Public Works Association, *History of Public Works*, 72, as cited by Gutfreund, *Sprawl*, 10.

63. Epperson, *Failed Colossus*, chap. 6A, version 1.1, 22–23. Bruce Seely, *Building the American Highway System: Engineers as Policy Makers* (Philadelphia: Temple University Press, 1987), 15–36. See Lisa, "Bicyclists and Bureaucrats," 375–93; Chatburn, *Highways and Highway Transportation*, 128–142, as cited by Gutfreund, *Sprawl*, 12–13.

64. American Automobile Association, *Why Federal Aid in Roads*; Richter, *Transportation in America*, 5, 169, 571, as cited by Gutfreund, *Sprawl*, 14–15.

65. J. Allen Davis, *The Friend to All Motorists: The Story of the Automobile Club of Southern California Through 65 Years, 1900–1965* (Los Angeles: Anderson, Ritchie & Simon, 1967), 32–33. See American Automobile Association, *Why Federal Aid in Roads*; Richter, *Transportation in America*, 571, as cited by Gutfreund, *Sprawl*, 13–14.

66. Author's communication with Ford Motor Company, models sold per year 1903–12. "From a User of Electric Vehicles," 532. Barnard, *Independent Man*, 57. See Couzens, "What I Learned," 263, as cited by Barnard, *Independent Man*, 57. See R. McAllister Lloyd, "The Influence of the Pioneer Spirit on Electric Vehicle Progress," *Central Station* 14 (December 1914): 180; Schiffer, Butts, and Grimm, *Taking Charge*, "A Dark Age Descends," 91–102, as cited by Kirsch, *Electric Vehicle*, 88.

67. "San Francisco Disaster," *Wall Street Journal*, April 19, 1906, 7. "Over 500 Dead, $200,000,000 Lost in San Francisco Earthquake," *New York Times*, April 19, 1906, 1. "San Francisco Badly Wrecked," *Boston Globe*, April 19, 1906, 8. "Quake: 1906 San Francisco Quake," photograph, http://quake.wr.usgs.gov/info/1906/images/sfo6.city.html.

68. "San Francisco Disaster," 7. "Over 500 Dead." "San Francisco Badly Wrecked." "San Francisco City Hall after the 1906 Earthquake," photograph, and "Photograph by Arnold Genthe shows Sacramento Street and approaching fire" (both from Steinbrugge Collection of the UC Berkeley Earthquake Engineering Research Center), http://quake.wr.usgs.gov/info/1906/.

69. "The Epic of the Dynamited Metropolis," *Los Angeles Times*, April 21, 1906, 1–3.

70. "Over 500 Dead."

71. "A Week's Losses in Values," *New York Times*, April 30, 1906, 6.

72. Kerry A. Odell and Marc D. Weidenmier, "Real Shock, Monetary Aftershock: The 1906 San Francisco Earthquake and the Panic of 1907," *Journal of Economic History* 64, no. 4 (December 2004): 1002–6. See Nathan Balke and Robert J. Gordon, "Historical Data," *The American Business Cycle: Continuity and Change*, ed. Robert J. Gordon (Chicago: University of Chicago Press, 1986), 802; Christina D. Romer, "The Prewar Business Cycle Reconsidered: New Estimates of Gross National Product, 1869–1908," *Journal of Business Economy* 97 no. 1 (1989) 22; *Commercial and Financial Chronicle*, April 28, 1906, 959; *Economist*, October 19, 1907, 1771; Gordon Thomas and Max Morgan Witts, *The San Francisco Earthquake* (New York: Stein and Day, 1971), 271; J. Eugene Haas, Robert W. Kates, and Martyn Bowden, eds. *Reconstruction Following Disaster*, Cambridge, MA: The MIT Press, 1977, 6; Kenneth A. Froot, *The Financing of Catastrophe Risk*, Chicago: The University of Chicago Press, 1999; *Economist*, October 20, 1906, 1694; O. M. Sprague, *His-*

tory of Crises under the National Banking System, Washington, DC: National Monetary Commission, 1910; R. S. Sayers, *Bank of England 1891–1944,* Cambridge: Cambridge University Press, 1976; Clapham, *Bank of England,* Vol. 2. Cambridge: Cambridge University Press, 1944; Charles E. Goodhart, *The New York Money Market and the Finance of Trade,* Cambridge, MA: Harvard University Press, 1969; Charles Kindleberger, *Manias, Panics, and Crashes: A History of Financial Crises,* New York: Basic Books, 1978; Michael D. Bordo and Antu Murshid, "Are Financial Crises Becoming More Contagious? What is the Historical Evidence on Contagion?" In International Financial Contagion, edited by Stijin Classens and Kristin J. Forbes, 367–403. London: Kluwer, 2001; as cited by Odell and Weidenmier, "Real Shock, Monetary Aftershock."

73. "Week's Losses in Values"; "California Insurance Man Quits in Protest," *New York Times,* May 28, 1906, 4. "San Francisco Badly Wrecked." "Over 500 Dead." "Insurance Rates to be Raised 25%," *Chicago Daily Tribune,* May 3, 1906, 1.

74. "Williamsburgh City Fire," *Wall Street Journal,* June 27, 1906, 8. "Insurance Rates to be Raised 25%." "California Insurance Man Quits." See Kindleberger, *Manias;* Sayers, *Bank of England; Economist,* May 5, 1906, 767, as cited by Odell and Weidenmier, "Real Shock, Monetary Aftershock," 1005, 1010.

75. *Financial Times* (London), July 6, 1906, as cited by Odell and Weidenmier, "Real Shock, Monetary Aftershock," 1002.

76. "Insurance Rates to be Raised 25%."

77. "San Francisco Badly Wrecked." "$15,000,000 Sent by Shaw," *Washington Post,* April 24, 1906, 2.

78. "Crash Crash Crash," *Boston Post,* October 18, 1907, http://www.bos.frb/about/pubs/panico fl.pdf, 2–7.

79. See *Nieuws van den Dag,* January 24, 1910 (GAA-Coll. Hartkamp, sheet 374/374A), as cited by Mom, *Electric Vehicle,* 129. See Richard W. Meade, "Influence of Standardization on Taxicab Operation," *Horseless Age* 26 (July 27, 1910): 119–20; memorandum from chief engineer G. A. Green to Richard W. Meade, February 21, 1912, box 15, folder "New York Transportation company," Meade Papers, as cited by Kirsch, *Electric Vehicle,* 78–79.

80. Association of Licensed Automobile Manufacturers Report and Accounts Six Months Ended December 31st, 1909, February 7th, 1910, Accession 1704, box 1, folder 1–5, 1–2, Benson Ford Research Center.

81. Author's communication, models per year 1903–12. Nevins, *Ford,* 326–28. See Directors' Minutes, September 7, 1906, as cited by Nevins, *Ford,* 328.

82. Author's communication, models per year 1903–12. Nevins, *Ford,* 396. See Records, Secretary's Office, Ford Motor Company, as cited by Nevins, *Ford,* 410. "Ford Model T," http://en.wikipedia.org/wiki/Model_T, 3–4. Tin Lizzie pictures, http://www.virdelldrilling.com/tinlizzie.htm. Kingsford charcoal, http://www.kingsford.com/about/index.htm.

83. Nevins, *Ford,* 420, 423–24. See Judge Hough's opinion, Selden Patent Case Record, 172 Fed. Rep. 923 (1909); September 16, 1909, Fair Lane Papers, box 142, Ford Archives; *Detroit Journal,* September 16, 1909, as cited by Nevins, *Ford,* 420, 423–24.

84. Association of Licensed Automobile Manufacturers Report and Accounts Six Months Ended December 31st, 1909, February 7th, 1910, Gunn, Richards & Co., Accession 1704,

box 1, folder 1-5, 1–4, Schedule 1, pp. 3, 9, and Exhibit "A," Benson Ford Research Center. See *Detroit Journal*, September 16, 1909; *Detroit News*, October 19, 1909; *Detroit Journal*, January 5, 1910, as cited by Nevins, *Ford*, 424, 426.

85. Nevins, *Ford*, 428.

86. See *Ford Times* 3 (June 1, 1910): back cover, as cited by Nevins, *Ford*, 431.

87. Author's communication, models per year 1903–12. See *Detroit Journal*, June 4, 1910, as cited by Nevins, *Ford*, 431.

88. Coudert's brief, Docket 4058, 10, Transcript of Record for the Appellate Court; Noyes opinion 184 Fed. Rep. 894 (1911), as cited by Nevins, *Ford*, 432, 434. Nevins, *Ford*, 628n48. See *Automobile*, January 12, 1911, as cited by J. Harold Byers, "The Selden Case," *Journal of the Patent Office Society* 22, no. 10 (October 1940): 735, Cave Collection, box 8, folder 28, Detroit Public Library NAHC.

89. Author's communication, models per year 1903–12. See *Detroit Saturday Night* 5 (January 20, 1912): 41, as cited by Nevins, *Ford*, 440–41.

Chapter 8: 1914—the End of the Beginning

1. E. G. Liebold, Reminiscences, vol. 17, Accession 65, Benson Ford Research Center. See W. J. Cameron, *Reminiscences*; William A. Simonds, *Henry Ford, His Life—His Work—His Genius* (Indianapolis: 1943), 17–18. "Henry Ford and Thomas Edison—a Friendship of Giants," http://info.detnews.com/history/story/index.cfm?id=105&category=people.

2. Henry Ford in collaboration with Samuel Crowther, *My Life and Work* (Garden City: 1923), as cited by Nevins, no. 167. "Henry Ford and Thomas Edison."

3. Ford R. Bryan, *Friends, Families & Forays: Scenes from the Life and Times of Henry Ford* (Dearborn, MI: Ford Books, 2002), 154. "Electrifying the Family Car," news clipping; cover photo, IEEE *Student Journal* (May 1967), Vertical File, Electric Cars, Benson Ford Research Center. "Thomas Edison's Latest Ambition," *Los Angeles Times*, June 15, 1902, A16. "Structural Details of the Edison Storage Battery," *Scientific American* 88, no. 6 (February 7, 1903): 92. Theodore Waters, "Many Electrical Problems Now Solved by Edison's Discovery," *Atlanta Constitution*, August 25, 1901, A10. "Edison's New Storage Battery," *Los Angeles Times*, June 6, 1901, 8. "Some Interesting Facts About the Edison Storage Battery," *Scientific American* 90, no. 19 (May 7, 1904): 358. See "Edison Solves Battery Secret," *Chicago Daily Tribune*, May 23, 1901, 5.

4. Thomas Edison to Marks, April 7, 1891, Accession 1630, box 2, folder 2-8, Benson Ford Research Center. "That Revolutionary Storage Battery," *Horseless Age* 8, no. 3 (April 17, 1901): 60. "Some Interesting Facts." "Edison Solves Battery Secret." "Edison's New Storage Battery."

5. "Some Interesting Facts." "New Edison Enterprises," *Wall Street Journal*, November 5, 1901, 3. "Thomas Edison's Latest Ambition." "Many Electrical Problems Now Solved by Edison's Discovery," *Atlanta Constitution*, August 25, 1901, A10. *The Edison Storage Battery Company, Orange, New Jersey*, Accession 1750, box 7, folder 7-1, Benson Ford Research Center. Paul Israel, *Edison: A Life of Invention* (New York: John Wiley & Sons, 2000), 413–14.

6. "Thomas A. Edison to Take a Two Years' Rest," *Atlanta Constitution*, February 15, 1903, C6.

7. Ibid.

8.   Ibid.

9.   Ibid.

10. *Edison Storage Battery Company.* Thomas A. Edison, "The Storage Battery and the Motor Car," *North American Review*, 1902, 1–4; "Tests of the Edison Battery," *Electrician* 51 (October 2, 1930), as cited by Israel, *Edison*, 415–16.

11. "The New Edison Storage Battery Is Now Ready," 8, Vertical File, Electric Cars, Benson Ford Research Center. Draft of Thomas A. Edison to Sigmund Bergmann, November 29, 1904, DF, as cited by Israel, *Edison*, 416–17.

12. "The New Edison Storage Battery Is Now Ready," 9. "Industrial Progress," *Los Angeles Times*, February 6, 1910, V19. Edison Storage Battery Company, Inspectors Report, Week Ending July 8, 1905, Edison National Historic Site. "Manufacturing storage batteries, 1915," photo, http://americanhistory.si.edu/edison/ed_d15.htm.

13. C. E. Nestor to Harry F. Miller, September 12, 1901, ESBC 2-10, Edison National Historic Site. "Passing of Trolley," *Los Angeles Times*, February 26, 1910, 11. "The New Edison Storage Battery Is Now Ready," 43–45. Anderson Carriage Co. to Thomas A. Edison, October 10, 1911, EGF 1911, 1, Autograph & Photo Request, Edison National Historic Site. "Electric Delivery Wagons," *Carriage & Wagon Builder*, November 25, 1911, 1–3, EGF 1911, Batt. Storage Delivery Wagons, Edison National Historic Site. "IEEEVM: The Electric Car and Hybrid Vehicles," photo, Thomas Edison at his West Orange, New Jersey, lab, circa 1910, with a battery-powered electric car (courtesy: National Park Service, Edison National Historic Site, http://www.ieee-virtual-museum.org/collection/event.php?id=3456880&lid=1).

14. "Edison Solves Battery Secret." Horace G. Burt to Thomas A. Edison, ESBC 2-1, Edison National Historic Site.

15. "The Fuel Question and Kerosene Carburetors," *Horseless Age* 30, no. 12 (September 18, 1912): 445.

16. Bryan, *Friends, Families & Forays*, 154.

17. A. I. Clymer to Thomas A. Edison, February 11, 1911, ESDC 2-1, Edison National Historic Site. "The 'Chloride Accumulator,'" Exide Technologies, Our History 2, http://www.exideworld.com/.

18. Bee to Edison, February 4, 1911, ESBC 2-1, Edison National Historic Site.

19. Ibid.

20. A. I. Clymer to H. F. Miller, January 17, 1912, ESBC 2-1, Edison National Historic Site. Anderson to Thomas A. Edison, January 15, 1912, EGF 1912 Battery Storage Electric Vehicle, Edison National Historic Site.

21. Thomas A. Edison to A. I. Clymer, April 27, 1911, EGF 1911, 1, Battery Storage General, Edison National Historic Site. "Sales—Edison Primary Battery," March 1, 1907 to February 28, 1908, ESBC, Edison National Historic Site.

22. "Uses for Edison Battery," October 11, 1911, EGF 1911, 1, Battery Storage General, Edison National Historic Site.

23. "Industrial Progress." Bryan, *Friends, Families & Forays*, 155.

24. Thomas A. Edison to Anderson, November 20, 1911; and November 30, 1911, Accession 1630, box 2, folders 2-22 and 2-23, Benson Ford Research Center.

25. Thomas A. Edison to Anderson, November 30, 1911, Accession 1630, box 2, folder 2-23, Benson Ford Research Center.

26. Hutch to Thomas A. Edison, May 9, 1912, EGF 1912, Battery Storage Delivery Wagon, General, Edison National Historic Site. Western Union Day Letter, Thomas A. Edison to J. J. Jenkins, October 1912, Edison National Historic Site. Thomas A. Edison to Barrett, April 18, 1912, 1–3, Edison National Historic Site. "Lansden Test," April 3, 1912, Edison National Historic Site. "List B, Credits Due the Lansden Company as of December 31, 1912," and "List C, Balance of Accounts Receivable Uncollected as of December 31, 1912," circa January 1912, Edison National Historic Site. "The Elms," 1–2, EGF 1914 Battery Storage Electric Vehicle, Edison National Historic Site. Charles Arthur Carlisle to Thomas A. Edison, April 11, 1913, Edison National Historic Site, A22.

27. Anderson to Thomas A. Edison, January 15, 1912.

28. Ibid.

29. Ibid.

30. Ibid.

31. Ibid.

32. Anderson to Thomas A. Edison, August 31, 1912, EGF 1912, Battery Storage Electric Vehicle, Edison National Historic Site.

33. Ibid. "Some Recent Developments in the Lead Battery for Electric Vehicles," *Horseless Age—Electric Vehicle Section* 30, no. 20 (November 13, 1912): 749. "The New Edison Storage Battery—Warning!" unprovenanced advertisement circa 1912, Edison National Historic Site.

34. "The New Edison Storage Battery—Warning!"

35. "Edison's Latest Marvel—the Electric Country House," *New York Times*, September 15, 1912.

36. Ibid.

37. Ibid.

38. Ibid.

39. Ibid.

40. Ibid. Woods to Thomas A. Edison, October 14, 1911, EGF 1911, Battery Storage Windmills, Edison National Historic Site. Edward G. Hobler to Thomas A. Edison, October 16, 1911, 1–2; Charles J. Jager to Thomas A. Edison, October 17, 1911; and L. Leach to Thomas A. Edison, November 8, 1911, EGF 1911, Battery Storage Windmills, Edison National Historic Site.

41. Woods to Thomas A. Edison. Edward G. Hobler to Thomas A. Edison. Charles J. Jager to Thomas A. Edison. Leach to Thomas A. Edison.

42. Handwritten note, Thomas A. Edison to A. I. Clymer, December 19, 1912, ESBC 2-1, Edison National Historic Site.

43. Thomas A. Edison to Henry Ford, October 29, 1912, Accession 1630, box 2, folder 2-28, Benson Ford Research Center.

44. Ibid.

45. Handwritten note, Thomas A. Edison to A. I. Clymer. Bryan, *Friends, Families & Forays*, 154–55.

46. Handwritten note, Thomas A. Edison to A. I. Clymer.

47. Ibid.

48. Hartford Agreement, Draft #8, November 22, 1912, 1–2, and 2 with note; and Hartford Agreement, Draft #6, 1912, 1–7, ESBC, Edison National Historic Site.

49. Ibid.
50. Hartford Agreement, Draft #6, 1912, 1–7.
51. Hartford Agreement, Draft #8, November 22, 1912, 1–2, and 2 with note.
52. "Fuel Question and Kerosene Carburetors."
53. Ibid. "Last Week's Exports," *New York Times*, August 14, 1912, 11.
54. "Club Joins in Gasoline War," *Horseless Age* 30, no. 14 (October 2, 1912): 491.
55. "Hopes to Expand Fuel Range Widely," *New York Times*, February 16, 1913, 86.
56. Generally see Craig Colten, "A Historical Perspective on Industrial Wastes and Groundwater Contamination," *Geographical Review* 81, no. 2 (April 1991): 215–28.
57. "Sewer Explosion Terrifies a Block," *New York Times*, November 9, 1913, 3. "Proposed Solutions of Gasoline Problem," *Horseless Age* 31, no. 6 (February 5, 1913): 301.
58. "Convention of Electric Vehicle Association of America," *Horseless Age* 30, no. 16 (October 16, 1912): 597. Bryan, *Friends, Families & Forays*, 156.
59. "Electric Vehicles Displayed at Chicago," *Horseless Age* 31, no. 7 (February 12, 1913): 338.
60. Liebold, Reminiscences, 10:808–11. Bryan, *Friends, Families & Forays*, 156.
61. Western Union telegram, E. G. Liebold to W. G. Bee, January 3, 1913, Accession 1630, box 4, folder 4-1, Benson Ford Research Center.
62. Hill to Meadowcroft, March 17, 1913, EGF, Battery Storage, Electric Vehicles, Edison National Historic Site. Hill to Meadowcroft, April 4, 1913, 1–3, V14, Edison National Historic Site.
63. Bryan, *Friends, Families & Forays*, 154. T. A. Boyd, *Professional Amateur: The Biography of Charles Franklin Kettering* (New York: Dutton, 1957) 60, 68, 70–71. "Exide in Peace and War," Exide Technologies—Our History 3, http://www.exideworld.com.
64. M. R. Hutchison to Thomas A. Edison, May 15, 1913, 1–2, Edison National Historic Site.
65. Thomas A. Edison to W. E. Anderson, May 20, 1913, Accession 1630, box 2, folder 2-3, Benson Ford Research Center. Liebold, Reminiscences, 10:809. Handwritten note, Thomas A. Edison to A. I. Clymer, May 28, 1913, Edison National Historic Site.
66. "The Edison Electric Garage, Boston, Massachusetts," *Horseless Age* 31, no. 19 (May 7, 1913): 841.
67. W. G. Bee to Thomas A. Edison, September 18, 1913, WGB-1-5357, Edison National Historic Site.
68. Bryan, *Friends, Families & Forays*, 157–58.
69. Telegram, W. G. Bee to E. G. Liebold; and telegram, E. G. Liebold to W. G. Bee, Accession 1630, box 4, folder 4-1, Benson Ford Research Center.
70. "Ford Discusses Radical Scheme," newspaper clipping (January 9, 1914); "Ford's Son Will Also Run Profit Sharing Shop," *New York American*, newspaper clipping (January 9, 1914); "Ford, Workmen's Good Angel, Here," newspaper clipping (January 9, 1914); "Cheap Electric by Edison-Ford," newspaper clipping (January 14, 1914), Vertical File, Electric Cars, Benson Ford Research Center.
71. "Ford Discusses Radical Scheme." "Ford's Son Will Also Run." "Ford Plans New Auto," *Washington Post*, January 12, 1914, 9.
72. "Branches and Dealers," dealer disclaimer, January 9, 1914, Vertical File, Electric Cars, Benson Ford Research Center. "Five New Cars Appear on the Market," *Automobile*, January 22, 1914, 283.
73. "Ford Plans New Auto."

74. Ibid.

75. R. M. Searle to W. H. Meadowcroft, January 12, 1914; and Jas. M. Reilly to Henry Miller, January 13, 1914, EGF 1914 Storage Battery, Edison National Historic Site. M. R. Hutchison to Thomas A. Edison, March 9, 1914, Edison National Historic Site. Letter, Baker Electric Sales Agency to Thomas A. Edison, January 14, 1914, EGF 1914 Baker, Edison National Historic Site. M. B. Church to Thomas A. Edison, January 15, 1914; and M. B. Church to Henry Ford, January 16, 1914, EGF 1914 Church Balance, Edison National Historic Site.

76. J. Campbell to W. H. Meadowcroft, February 25, 1914; and F. W. Smith to Thomas A. Edison, January 21, 1914, EGF 1914 Battery Storage Electric Vehicle, Edison National Historic Site. David A. Kirsch, *The Electric Vehicle and the Burden of History* (New Brunswick, NJ: Rutgers University Press, 2000), 100–101.

77. Thomas A. Edison to Smith, January 21, 1914; and handwritten note, Thomas A. Edison to Smith, January 21, 1914, EGF 1914 Battery Storage Electric Vehicle, Edison National Historic Site.

78. Bee to Liebold, January 22, 1914, Accession 1630, 4-2, Benson Ford Research Center.

79. "Edison Battery with Gray & Davis Ford Starter," *Horseless Age* (February 18, 1914): 295. "Gray & Davis Activities," *Horseless Age*, no. 14 (April 1914). "Gray & Davis, Inc.," *Horseless Age* 32, no. 27 (December 31, 1913): 1102. "Record Sales for Gray & Davis in 1914," *Horseless Age* 35, no. 11 (March 17, 1915). "Gray & Davis System for Fords," *Horseless Age* (February 11, 1914): 237. "Starters and Generators in Factory De Luxe," *Automobile* 30, no. 9 (February 26, 1914): 489–95. Alexander Churchward Patents, http://www.churchward.com. Churchward patents, http://www.churchward.com/cw/jack/jack/acpatents.htm.

80. Electric supply request form, February 20, 1914, Vertical File, Electric Cars, Benson Ford Research Center. Bryan, *Friends, Families, & Forays*, 157, photo.

81. Liebold to Bee, February 23, 1914; April 3, 1914; and May 5, 1914, Accession 1630, box 4, folder 4-8, Benson Ford Research Center.

82. "Henry Ford and Thos. A. Edison Buy the Detroit Electric," *Saturday Evening Post*, March 28, 1914, Vertical File, Electric Cars, Benson Ford Research Center.

83. "Baker Brings Out Electric Roadster" and "Tiffany Becomes Flanders Electric Again," *Automobile*, March 26, 1914, 696, 710.

84. R. H. Beach to Edison Storage Battery Company, March 17, 1914. "Passing of Trolley," *Los Angeles Times*, February 26, 1910, 11. Handwritten note by Thomas A. Edison on letter, Berg Storage Battery Car Co. to Thomas A. Edison, June 26, 1913, Battery Storage Edison Storage Company, Edison National Historic Site.

85. R. H. Beach to Thomas A. Edison, March 25, 1914, EGF 1914 Storage Battery Electric Street Car, Edison National Historic Site.

86. "Report of tests of various batteries on starting Ford car," Accession 1630, 4-3, Benson Ford Research Center. Bryan, *Friends, Families & Forays*, 158–59. "Henry Ford Goes to See the Start," *New York Times*, January 12, 1914, 6. W. G. Bee to Henry Ford, April 20, 1914, Accession 1630, 4-3, Benson Ford Research Center.

87. "Report of tests of various batteries."

88. Ibid.

89. Ibid.

90. Ibid.

91. Ibid.

92. Liebold, Reminiscences, 10: 810–11.

93. Ibid., 10:811.

94. W. G. Bee to E. G. Liebold, April 2, 1914, Accession 1630, 4-3, Benson Ford Research Center.

95. W. G. Bee to E. G. Liebold, April 8, 1914, Accession 1630, 4-3, Benson Ford Research Center.

96. E. G. Liebold to W. G. Bee, April 10, 1914; and April 14, 1914, Accession 1630, 4-3, Benson Ford Research Center.

97. W. G. Bee to E. G. Liebold, April 14, 1914, Accession 1630, 4-3, Benson Ford Research Center.

98. W. G. Bee to E. G. Liebold, April 23, 1914; and E. G. Liebold to W. G. Bee, April 16, 1914, Accession 1630, 4-3, Benson Ford Research Center.

99. Bee to Liebold, April 16, 1914. Accession 1630, 4-3, Benson Ford Research Center.

100. Bee to Ford, April 20, 1914. Accession 1630, 4-3, Benson Ford Research Center.

101. E. G. Liebold to W. G. Bee, April 23, 1914, Accession 1630, 4-3, Benson Ford Research Center.

102. Ibid.

103. Ibid.

104. Report, J. Chesler to Meadowcroft, May 14, 1914. Edison National Historic Site.

105. R. H. Beach to T. J. Moncke, May 27, 1914, EGF 1914 Storage Batt. Electric Street Car, Edison National Historic Site.

106. List, Bee to Thomas A. Edison, July 2, 1914; and list, Bee to Thomas A. Edison, June 4, 1914, EGF 1914 Battery Storage Electric Vehicle, Edison National Historic Site.

107. "Edison Electric Motor Future Family Carriage," *Wall Street Journal*, May 27, 1914, 8.

108. Ibid.

109. "Ford to Buy Site for Electric Car Plant," *Automobile*, May 7, 1914, 983.

110. Bryan, *Friends, Families & Forays*, 160.

111. "Report on Ford Electric Car Experiment," June 11, 1914, EGF 1914 Battery Storage Electric Vehicle, Edison National Historic Site.

112. Bryan, *Friends, Families & Forays*, 160.

113. "Report No. 5, Ford-Edison Electric Lighting System From June 11th to July 1st, 1914," Accession 1630, box 4, folder 4-4, Benson Ford Research Center.

114. Ibid.

115. "Dr. Steinmetz's Picture," *Automobile* 30, no. 2 (June 11, 1914): 1230, 1241–43. "Charles Proteus Steinmetz," C. P. Steinmetz, www.becklaser.de/hbeng/steinmetz.html.

116. Bee to Liebold, June 16, 1914, Accession 1630, box 4, folder 4-4, Benson Ford Research Center.

117. Hutchinson to Thomas A. Edison, July 17, 1914, Edison National Historic Site.

118. Bee to Liebold, July 17, 1914, Accession 1630, box 4, folder 4-4, Benson Ford Research Center.

119. Liebold to Bee, July 21, 1914, Accession 1630, box 4, folder 4-4, Benson Ford Research Center.

120. Ibid.

121. Ibid.

122. Bee to Liebold, July 23, 1914, Accession 1630, box 4, folder 4-4, Benson Ford Research Center.

123. Ibid.

124. Ibid.

125. Ibid.

126. Ibid.

127. Ibid.

128. Ibid.

129. Liebold to Bee, July 25, 1914, Accession 1630, box 4, folder 4-4, Benson Ford Research Center.

130. Ibid.

131. Ibid.

132. Bee to Liebold, July 27, 1914, Accession 1630, box 4, folder 4-4, Benson Ford Research Center.

133. Gray to Liebold, July 28, 1914, Accession 1630, box 4, folder 4-4, Benson Ford Research Center.

134. Bee to Liebold, September 29, 1914, Accession 1630, 4-5, Benson Ford Research Center.

135. "Record Attendance at Electric Convention," *Horseless Age* 34, no. 18 (October 28, 1914): 643.

136. See Edwin Black, *Banking on Baghdad* (Hoboken, NJ: Wiley, 2004), 88–89, 114–15, 133–35, 173.

137. "Memoir of Count Franz von Harrach," ca. June 1914, Primary Documents, First World War Online, Michael Duffy, ed., www.firstworldwar.com. Jevtic, "Assassination."

138. Handwritten note of Thomas A. Edison on letter, Thomas A. Edison to B. F. Miller, October 9, 1914, EGF 1914 Storage Battery Lamp, Edison National Historic Site. "Edison Still Working on Storage Batteries," *Horseless Age* 34, no. 19 (November 4, 1914). "Gray & Davis Ford System," *Automobile*, November 19, 1914, 941.

139. "Edison Still Working on Storage Batteries."

140. "Edison Sees His Vast Plant Burn," *New York Times*, December 10, 1914, 1.

141. Thomas A. Edison to Henry Ford, December 10, 1914; telegram, Charles Edison to Henry Ford, December 9, 1914; telegram, Bee to Henry Ford, December 9, 1914, Accession 1630, box 4, folder 4-5, Benson Ford Research Center. "Edison Sees His Vast Plant Burn." "Mrs. Edison Saved Husband's Records," *New York Times*, December 11, 1914, 9.

142. Bee to Liebold, December 17, 1914; Bee to Henry Ford, December 10, 1914; Henry Ford to Bee, December 26, 1914, Accession 1630, box 4, folder 4-5, Benson Ford Research Center.

143. "Concrete Buildings Defy $2,000,000 Edison Blaze," *Chicago Daily Tribune*, December 11, 1914, 1. Telegram, Bee to Henry Ford, December 10, 1914, Accession 1630, box 4, folder 4-5, Benson Ford Research Center. "Edison Sees His Vast Plant Burn." "'Wizard' Edison Loses $7,000,000 by Flames That Sweep His Plant," *Atlanta Constitution*, December 10, 1914, 1.

144. "Edison Never Flinches at $7,000,000 Fire," *Boston Daily Globe*, December 10, 1914, 1. "Edison Sees His Vast Plant Burn." "'Wizard' Edison Loses $7,000,000."

145. Liebold, *Reminiscences*, 10:810. See Harry Bennett FBI file, Freedom of Information Act, 443n62, 443n70, 443nn71–73, 443n76, as cited by Max Wallace, *The American Axis: Henry Ford, Charles Lindbergh, and the Rise of the Third Reich* (New York: St. Martin's Press, 2003), 315–18. See Liebold, *Reminiscences*, 468; Stephen Eric Bronner, *A Rumor About the Jews: Reflections on Antisemitism and the Protocols of the Elders of Zion* (New York: St. Martin's Press, 2000), 5, 121; Hannah Arendt, *The Origins of Totalitarianism* (New York: Harcourt Brace, 1979), pt. I, "Antisemitism," 7, 333, as cited by Neil Baldwin, *Henry Ford and the Jews: The Mass Production of Hate*, 142. See Keith Sward, *The Legend of Henry Ford* (Toronto: Rinehart & Co., 1948), 137, 147; Ford Archives, Black's Reminiscences, as cited by Albert Lee, *Henry Ford and the Jews* (New York: Stein and Day, 1980), 20–21. *Chapters in American Jewish History*, chap. 85, "Henry Ford Invents a Jewish Conspiracy," http://www.ajhs.org/publications/Chapters/index.cfm. Also see the Harry Bennett FBI file, FOIA. Also see Edwin Black, *The Transfer Agreement* (Washington, DC: Dialog Press, 1984), 20–32.

Chapter 9: Derailed

1. Thomas H. Ploss, *The Nation Pays Again: The Demise of the Milwaukee Road, 1928–1986* (Chicago: privately printed, 1991), 48, 89.
2. "The Olympian," brochure, Milwaukee Road Archive, Milwaukee Public Library.
3. Ibid.
4. Ibid.
5. "Engineers See End of Steam Railways," *New York Times*, April 30, 1916, 23. Jeffrey W. Schramm, interview with the author, 2006. Carl W. Condit, "The Pioneer Stage of Railroad Electrification," *Transactions of the American Philosophical Society* 67, p. 7 (1977). Noel T. Holley, *The Milwaukee Electrics* (Hicksville, NY: NJ International, 1987), 45, 66. "The Milwaukee Road Electrification," Milwaukee Road electrification, www.scn.org/cedar_butte/milw-elec.html. Rodney A. Clark, "The Milwaukee Electrification: A Proud Era Passes," special supplement, *Milwaukee Road Magazine*, July–August, 1973, 8. "The end of the Milwaukee electrification," www.northeast.railfan.net/classic/MILWdata5.html, 7.
6. Simon Ville, "Total Factor Productivity in the English Shipping Industry: The North-East Coal Trade, 1700–1850," *Economic History Review* n.s. 39, no. 3 (August 1986): 362. See Frederick C. Garnst, "The Context and Significance of America's First Railroad, on Boston's Beacon Hill," *Technology and Culture* 33, no. 1 (January 1992): 66–100.
7. See Garnst, "America's First Railroad," 66–100. See "Art at a Railway Club," *New York Times*, April 14, 1898, 9. See also "Heraldry of the Rail," *New York Times*, February 16, 1897, 2.
8. See Frank G. Carpenter, "Russia on the Pacific," *Los Angeles Times*, February 24, 1895, 17. See "The Grand Pacific Trans-Siberian," *New York Times*, September 26, 1891, 4. Edwin Black, *Banking on Baghdad* (Hoboken, NJ: Wiley, 2004), 118–19. William L. Ochsenwald, "The Financing of the Hijaz Railroad," *Die Welt des Islams* n.s. 14, no. 1/4 (1973): 129–49.
9. David Stradling and Joel Tarr, "Environmental Activism, Locomotive Smoke, and the Corporate Response: The Case of the Pennsylvania Railroad and Chicago Smoke Control," *Business History Review* 73 (Winter 1999): 679–80. Liston E. Leyendecker, Christine A.

Bradley, and Duane A. Smith, *The Rise of the Silver Queen: Georgetown, Colorado 1859–1896* (Boulder: University of Colorado Press, 2005), 234.

10. W. F. Pollock, "Smoke Prevention," *American Architect and Building News* 9 (March 26, 1881): 151.

11. Ibid.

12. "The Abolition of London Fog," *Saturday Review*, reprinted in *American Architect and Building News* 10 (October 8, 1881): 174.

13. "Getting Rid of Smoke," *New York Times*, August 3, 1882, 2. "Smoke Abatement," *Chicago Tribune*, September 19, 1884, 11. "Smoke Abatement in Montreal," *American Architect and Building News* 11 no. 327 (April 1, 1882): 145. Stradling and Tarr, "Environmental Activism," 680. Angela Gugliotta, "Class, Gender, and Coal Smoke: Gender Ideology and Environmental Injustice in Pittsburgh, 1868–1914," *Environmental History*, April 2000, http://www.looksmartsurfing.com/p/articles/mi_qa3854/is_200004/ai_n8880668.

14. "England Has the Smoke Nuisance," *Chicago Tribune*, August 3, 1890, 6. "The Smoke Nuisance Is Doomed," *Chicago Tribune*, December 3, 1890, 2. Stradling and Tarr, "Environmental Activism," 677, 679–80, 683–84.

15. "Smoke Nuisance Is Doomed."

16. Stradling and Tarr, "Environmental Activism," 680, 682, 685. "Dr. Werner Von Siemens," *Scientific American* 64, no. 2 (January 14, 1893): 21.

17. "Smoke Abatement Pays," *New York Times*, February 1, 1914, XX4. Stradling and Tarr, "Environmental Activism," 682, 696.

18. "A Smoke Bureau," *New York Times*, August 15, 1913, 6. "World Cities War on Smoke Evil," *Chicago Daily Tribune*, March 22, 1914, A1. "Finds Cancer Bred Where Coal Is Fuel," *New York Times*, October 12, 1913, C3. "Connects Burning of Coal with Increase of Cancer," *Chicago Daily Tribune*, October 10, 1913, 9. "Smoke Abatement Pays." "For Immigration Station in Boston," *Boston Daily Globe*, October 10, 1913, 13.

19. "Terminal Board Ready to Insist I.C. Electrify," *Chicago Daily Tribune*, October 27, 1916, 5. "Western Railroad Managers Still Practicing Economy," *Wall Street Journal*, January 19, 1912, 7. "Women's Fight Against the Smoke Nuisance," *New York Times*, March 30, 1913, X9. "Experts Report on Smoke Cure," *Chicago Daily Tribune*, January 9, 1914, 7. "Great Northern's Tunnel," *Wall Street Journal*, July 12, 1927, 11. "Biography of Werner von Siemens," www.siemens.com.br.

20. Matthew Josephson, *Edison* (New York: McGraw Hill, 1959), 238–40, 242–43.

21. Michael C. Duffy, *Electric Railways, 1880–1990* (Bodmin, Cornwall, UK: MPG Books, 2003), 38. Stradling and Tarr, "Environmental Activism," 689, 690. "Electric Motors for Railroads," *Chicago Daily Tribune*, September 26, 1893, 13. "Run by Electricity," *Washington Post*, July 8, 1895, 7. See "Penn R.R. Extends Electric Service to Potomac Yard," *Washington Post*, June 20, 1935, 23.

22. Brian Solomon, *GE Locomotives: 110 Years of General Electric Motive Power* (St. Paul, MN: MBI, 2003), 16–17.

23. Stradling and Tarr, "Environmental Activism," 690.

24. Ibid., 690, 700.

25. Ibid., 696.

26. August Derleth, *The Milwaukee Road: Its First Hundred Years* (Iowa City: University of Iowa Press, 2002), 265.

27.   Ibid., 142–43, 153, 195.

28.   Ibid., 265. Max Lowenthal, *The Investor Pays* (New York: Knopf, 1933), 5.

29.   Derleth, *Milwaukee Road*, 171.

30.   Ibid., 172.

31.   Ibid., 171–72.

32.   Ibid., 188–89.

33.   Ibid., 167, 188–89.

34.   Ibid., 171, 188–89.

35.   Ibid., 170, 172–73, 198. Lowenthal, *Investor Pays*, 18.

36.   Lowenthal, *Investor Pays*, 18.

37.   Ibid., 21–22. Ploss, *Nation Pays Again*, 47.

38.   Derleth, *Milwaukee Road*, 171, 188–90. Lowenthal, *Investor Pays*, 20–22.

39.   Derleth, *Milwaukee Road*, 189–90. Lowenthal, *Investor Pays*, 22.

40.   Derleth, *Milwaukee Road*, 189–90.

41.   Ibid., 190. "Making History," *Milwaukee Railway System Employees' Magazine* 3, no. 10 (January 1916).

42.   "Making History," 7.

43.   Ibid., 8.

44.   "The Milwaukee Electrification: A Proud Era Passes," *Milwaukee Road Magazine*, special supplement, July–August 1973, 9.

45.   Derleth, *Milwaukee Road*, 190–91. "Milwaukee Electrification," 1, 4, 5.

46.   "Milwaukee Electrification," 1, 5. "St. Paul Electrifies Its Mountain Divisions," *Wall Street Journal*, October 22, 1915, 7.

47.   Todd Jones, "Milwaukee Road in the 70's: What really happened?" www.trainweb.org/milwaukee/article.html, 7. Michael Sol, Informational Post (August 1, 2005), http://gardenrailways.com/community/forum/topic.asp?page=12&TOPIC_ID=22066.

48.   Lowenthal, *Investor Pays*, 26–27, 177–78, 183, 189.

49.   Derleth, *Milwaukee Road*, 200, 202–4, 208.

50.   Ibid., 207.

51.   Ibid., 206–7.

52.   Lowenthal, *Investor Pays*, 38.

53.   Ibid.

54.   Ibid., 38–39.

55.   Ibid., 35–37, 39, 41. Derleth, *Milwaukee Road*, 206–7.

56.   Lowenthal, *Investor Pays*, 64.

57.   Ibid., 6, 7, 8. Derleth, *Milwaukee Road*, 210.

58.   Lowenthal, *Investor Pays*, 67.

59.   Ibid., 67–68.

60.   Ibid., 111–14, 116, 118–19, 141–43. Derleth, *Milwaukee Road*, 212, 213.

61.   Lowenthal, *Investor Pays*, 33.

62.   Ibid., 13.

63.   Ibid., 256.

64.   Ploss, *Nation Pays Again*, 17.

65.   "General Motors Plans to Build Diesel Engines," *Christian Science Monitor*, February 14, 1935, 11. See Holley, *Milwaukee Electrics*, 45, 216.

66.   "Zephyr Trains Run 5 Million Miles Since '34," *Chicago Daily Tribune*, June 20, 1938, 19. Pacific Southwest Railway Museum Association, "Important Milestones in English and American Railway Development," www.sdrm.org/history/timeline/index.html.

67.   Holley, *Milwaukee Electrics*, 45.

68.   Ibid., 45, 48. See Holley, *Milwaukee Electrics*, 66. Solomon, *GE Locomotives*, 34, 39.

69.   Holley, *Milwaukee Electrics*, 46, 48.

70.   Ibid. Solomon, *GE Locomotives*, 34–35.

71.   Holley, *Milwaukee Electrics*, 46, 49, 54.

72.   T. A. Boyd, *Professional Amateur: The Biography of Charles Franklin Kettering* (New York: Dutton, 1957). See "Efficiency Raised in Gasoline Engine," *New York Times*, May 28, 1947, 50.

73.   Holley, *Milwaukee Electrics*, 45, 55, 57, 119, 200, 202.

74.   Northwest Rail Improvement Committee, "The Abandonment of Electric Operation by the Chicago, Milwaukee, St. Paul and Pacific Railroad Company," (typescript, Northwest Rail Improvement Committee, Everett, WA, 1975), 1–3.

75.   Ibid., 5.

76.   Ibid., 4–5.

77.   Ibid., 5.

78.   Ibid., 6.

79.   Milwaukee Road News Bureau, Press Release, February 20, 1973, Milwaukee Road Collection, Milwaukee Public Library.

80.   Ibid.

81.   Ibid.

82.   Jones, "Milwaukee Road in the 70's." Ploss, *Nation Pays Again*, 154, 155.

Chapter 10: The GM Conspiracy

1.   Herbert Lefkovitz, "State Is Shocked at Liggett Murder," *New York Times*, December 15, 1935, E11. Wayne Thomas, "Slain Editor's Widow to See Suspect Today," *Chicago Daily Tribune*, December 11, 1935, 1, 17. Author's interview with Marda Liggett Woodbury, February 9, 2006. Peg Meier, "Assassination of an Editor," *Star Tribune* (Minneapolis), June 12, 1988, 1E.

2.   Gordon Schendel, "How Mobsters Grabbed a City's Transit Line," clipping from *Collier's*, September 29, 1951, 182. See "Editor Liggett's Assault Story Denied to Police," *Chicago Daily Tribune*, October 27, 1935, 20. See press clipping "Jury Indicts Kid Cann on White Slave Charges," *Minneapolis Star*, September 19, 1959.

3.   Thomas, "Slain Editor's Widow," 17. "Editor Is Slain in Minneapolis by Gangsters," *Chicago Daily Tribune*, September 7, 1934, 1. See Arthur Evans, "Liggett Death Turns Light on Political Crime," *Chicago Daily Tribune*, December 12, 1935, 6.

4.   Author's interview with Woodbury. Marda Liggett Woodbury, *Stopping the Presses: The Murder of Walter Liggett* (Minneapolis: University of Minnesota Press, 1998), xv–xvi.

5.   Meier, "Assassination of an Editor." Author's interview with Woodbury.

6.   Ibid.

7.   "Second Witness Names Suspect Liggett Killer," *Chicago Daily Tribune*, December 17, 1935, 17. "Burglar Tries to Get Liggett Murder Files," *Washington Post*, December 20,

1935, 3. "Political Group Blamed for Vice in Minneapolis," *Washington Post*, February 8, 1936, 4. See generally Woodbury, *Stopping the Presses*, 177–96.

8. Samuel E. Moffett, "The War on the Locomotive," *McClure's* 20, no. 5 (March 1903), 4–15. See "Excursionists Like Trolleys," *Los Angeles Times*, September 19, 1937, 10.

9. Moffett, "The War," 5. See Moffett, "The War." "Excursionists Like Trolleys."

10. Moffett, "The War," 5.

11. Ibid., 5, 13. "Excursionists Like Trolleys." See "Triumphant Trolley's Great Work," *Los Angeles Times*, May 24, 1907, 113. "Trolley Cites Auto as Killer," *Los Angeles Times*, June 25, 1930, 4.

12. Moffett, "The War," 5.

13. Ibid., 9–10.

14. Ibid., 10.

15. Ibid., 8–9.

16. Ibid., 7–8, 14.

17. Ibid., 13. "Excursionists Like Trolleys." See Irving Brecher and Fred F. Finklehoffe, *Meet Me in St. Louis* (movie), Vincente Minnelli, dir. (Santa Monica: MGM, 1944).

18. "Holland's Letter: Astonishing Growth of Electric Street Railway System in the Past Twenty-five Years," *Wall Street Journal*, January 30, 1911, 1–2. "Triumphant Trolley's Great Work."

19. American Transit Association, "Transit Industry of the United States—Total Passengers Carried, 1907–1962," report, July 12, 1963. "Favor No-Track Trolley," *New York Times*, May 7, 1921, 12. See "Packard Puts Out Trackless Trolley," *Los Angeles Times*, August 28, 1921, vii.

20. "Transit Industry of the United States." Author's interviews with Clay McShane, Al Mankoff, Van Wilkins, and sources at the American Public Transit Association, 2006.

21. "Excursionists Like Trolleys." See Owen Gutfreund, *20th Century Sprawl* (New York: Oxford University Press, 2004), 71.

22. "Excursionists Like Trolleys."

23. Allan Nevins with Frank Ernest Hill, *Ford* (New York: Scribner, 1954), 1:107.

24. "Trolleys Haul 16 Billion," December 4, 1925, 12. "Transit Industry of the United States."

25. "General Motors Made Gratifying Earnings Report," *Wall Street Journal*, July 22, 1922, 1. "Memorandum for the Director, FBI, Washington, D.C. re: National City Lines, et al.," October 2, 1946. Indictment, *USA v. National City Lines, et al.*, Criminal Action No. 19270, April 9, 1947, District Court of the United States, Southern District of California, Central Division.

26. "National City Lines Guilty in Trust Case," *New York Times*, March 13, 1949, 79. Verdict, *USA v. National City Lines, et al.*, No. 47CR524, USA, Northern District of Illinois, Eastern Division.

27. Bradford C. Snell, "American Ground Transport: A Proposal for Restructing the Automobile, Truck, Bus, and Rail Industries," report to the Subcommittee on Antitrust and Monopoly of the Committee of the Judiciary, U.S. Senate, February 26, 1974, 1–3. Author's interviews with Bradford Snell, February 2006,.

28. Snell, "American Ground Transport," 1–3. Author's interviews with Snell.

29. Ibid.

30. General Motors Corporation, "The Truth About 'American Ground Transport': A Reply by

General Motors," report to the Subcommittee on Antitrust and Monopoly of the Committee of the Judiciary, U.S. Senate, April 1974, 1–4.

31. See Jeffrey Price and Peter S. Seaman, *Who Framed Roger Rabbit* (movie), Robert Zemeckis, dir. (Universal City, CA: Amblin Entertainment, 1998). See Google search on "Roger Rabbit GM Conspiracy."

32. Author's enterprise and interviews with historians, critics, and experts on the topic of trolleys, Snell, and GM.

33. Author's interview with Trolley Expert B, February 2006.

34. Author's enterprise and interviews with numerous historians, critics, and experts on the topic of trolleys, Snell, and GM.

35. Ibid.

36. "Chronology of Fifty Years in U.S. Business and Finance," *Wall Street Journal*, June 27, 1932, 51.

37. Ibid.

38. Ibid.

39. "Motor Companies Pass Through a Severe Period," *Christian Science Monitor*, March 24, 1922, 11.

40. Alfred P. Sloan Jr., *My Years with General Motors* (New York: Doubleday & Company, 1964), 446–47. "General Motors Made Gratifying Earnings Report." See "General Motors Reports Deficit of $38,680,770," *Wall Street Journal*, March 6, 1922, 1.

41. "General Motors Shows Results of Deflation," *Wall Street Journal*, March 13, 1922, 1.

42. Sloan, *My Years*, 125–27.

43. "Transit Industry of the United States." "Chronology of Fifty Years."

44. Author's interviews with Al Mankoff, February–March 2006. Author's interview with Van Wilkins, February 16, 2006. See *Glendale Star* (California), August 26, 1937, as cited by David J. St. Clair, *The Motorization of American Cities* (New York: Praeger, 1986), 177n1.

45. Author's interview with Wilkens. St. Clair, *Motorization* (table, "Motor Bus Versus Trolley Coach, Economic Analysis") 53, 184–85. See "Brooklyn Bus Case in Court Tomorrow," *New York Times*, January 11, 1920, 25. See "Says Bus System Will Win," *Wall Street Journal*, December 10, 1921, 2. See "Street Railway Men Dispute Bus Cost Figures," *Wall Street Journal*, March 23, 1923, 13. *USA v. National City Lines, et al.*, No. 47CR524, 3.

46. "New High Record in Motor Output," *New York Times*, May 6, 1923, E14. "Record Year for Motor Bus Use," *New York Times*, November 8, 1925, XX12. John A. Beeler, "Buses Could Not Fill Place of Street Cars in New York City," *Electric Railway Journal* 61, no. 2, 37–38 (see table, "Comparative Bus Operating Costs"). See St. Clair, *Motorization*, 8–9. See *USA v. National City Lines, et al.*, No. 47CR524, 2. See "Suggests Merger of Interurbans," *New York Times*, June 14, 1925, E10. See "Street Railway Transportation," *Wall Street Journal*, September 26, 1928, 9. See "The Beeler Report," *Washington Post*, August 9, 1934, 8.

47. Beeler, "Buses Could Not Fill Place of Street Cars," 37, 38.

48. Ibid., 37.

49. John Diers, "Did a Conspiracy Really Kill the Streetcar?," *Trains* 66, no. 1 (January 2006): 59. See "Railroad Business," *Washington Post*, March 22, 1926, 6. See table, "Streetcar and Motor Bus Route Miles," St. Clair, *Motorization*, 8.

50. "$510,000,000 Saving in Power Planned," *New York Times*, December 7, 1921, 19.

51. Silas Bent, "Once Immigrant Boy, Buys 5th Av. Buses," *New York Times,* July 6, 1924, XX4.

52. Author's enterprise. See "Five New Busses a Day to Be Put in Service Here," *Chicago Daily Tribune,* January 18, 1923, 5. Bent, "Once Immigrant Boy."

53. See NYC Metropolitan Transit Authority, "Early NYC Bus History," *A Century of Buses in New York City,* www.mta.nyc.ny.us/nyct/bus/centennial/page6.htm. "Five New Busses a Day." Bent, "Once Immigrant Boy."

54. "General Motors Acquires Yellow Cab Co.," *Wall Street Journal,* July 8, 1925, 12. "Yellow Cab Co. Now in General Motors," *New York Times,* July 8, 1925, 21.

55. "Yellow Cab Co. Now In General Motors."

56. Ibid. See "General Motors," *Wall Street Journal,* January 7, 1926, 18.

57. "East Orders $3,000,000 of Yellow Busses," *Chicago Daily Tribune,* December 28, 1925, 28.

58. Sloan, *My Years,* xxii. See photo, Sloan and Pierre du Pont, David Farber, *Sloan Rules: Alfred P. Sloan and the Triumph of General Motors* (Chicago: University of Chicago Press, 2002), 125ff.

59. "Trolleys Haul 16 Billion." S. S. Fontaine, "Congress Is Now Worrying Sponsors of Some Stocks," *Washington Post,* January 7, 1926, 16. "Electric Roads Uniformly Prosperous, Say Traffic Men," *Christian Science Monitor,* October 2, 1925, 1. See "Street Car Traffic Shows Small Drop," *New York Times,* June 29, 1930, 33. See "Trolley 'Czar' Visitor in City," *Los Angeles Times,* July 31, 1925, A1.

60. "Transit Industry of the United States." "New Motors Record Predicted by Sloan," *Wall Street Journal,* January 13, 1928, 16. "Street Railway Transportation," *Wall Street Journal,* September 26, 1928, 9. See John A. Beeler, "Coach and Bus Operation in New York," *Electric Railway Journal,* August 9, 1924, 195–98. "Street Car Group Widens Its Scope," *New York Times,* October 30, 1932, F2.

61. "New Motors Record Predicted by Sloan." "Says Bus System Will Win." Martin Wachs, "U.S. Transit Policy: In Need of Reform," *Science,* n.s. 244, no. 4912 (June 30, 1989): 1545.

62. Robert L. Banks, "New Buses Disliked," letter to the editor, *New York Times,* February 9, 1935, 14.

63. M. H. Hedges, "Who Corrupts Our Politics?" *Nation* 115, no. 2976 (July 19, 1922): 66–68.

64. Pacific Electric Railway Company Minute Books, vols. 1–3, 212, 1–8, Huntington Archive. See "Confidential Memorandum," LA Railway box 2, Huntington Archive. See Memorandum, Richard Sachse to George J. Kuhrts, June 5, 1928, LA Railway box 2, 5. See author's notes.

65. Edwin Black, "The Checker Connection," *Chicago Independent* (later *Chicago Monthly*), April 1975, 12–15.

66. "Hylan Raps Shearn on City Bus Inquiry," *New York Times,* October 28, 1922, 14.

67. Ibid. See "City Had to Supply New Bus Service," *New York Times,* September 23, 1919, 17.

68. Hedges, "Who Corrupts Our Politics?" 67. See "Twin City Rapid Transit Franchise for Referendum," *Wall Street Journal,* August 1, 1919, 6.

69. "Hylan Raps Shearn On City Bus Inquiry." "Senate Quiz on Transit Case Here Is Asked," *Chicago Daily Tribune,* June 13, 1929, 1. See Paul Barrett, "Chicago's Public Transportation Policy, 1900–1940s," *Illinois History Teacher* 8, no. 1 (2001): 25–38. See "City Joins Chicago Higher Fare Fight," *New York Times,* November 7, 1921, 2.

70. Glenn Yago, *The Decline of Transit: Urban Transportation in German and U.S. Cities,*

1900–1970 (Cambridge, U.K.: Cambridge University Press, 1984), 53–57. Federal Electrical Railways Commission (Washington: Government Printing Office, 1920), 1058, as cited by Yago, *Decline of Transit*, 53.

71.   See Eleanor Roosevelt National Historic Site, "The Great Depression," www.nps.gov/elro/glossary/great-depression.htm.

72.   "Transit Industry of the United States." Sloan, *My Years*, 446–47.

73.   Hogan, "Statement of the Facts from the Court Records Regarding General Motors in the National City Lines Cases," Hearings Before the Subcommittee on Antitrust & Monopoly of the Senate Committee on the Judiciary, on A Study of the Antitrust Laws—General Motors, 84th Cong., 1st sess, at 3920 (Washington: Government Printing Office, 1955), as cited by Snell, "American Ground Transport," 30.

74.   *United States v. General Motors, Pretrial Findings of Fact*, Civil Action No. 15816 (E.D. Mich.) (January 14, 1958), 26, as cited by Snell, "American Ground Transport," 30. *A Study in the Antitrust Laws*, 3920, as cited by Snell, "American Ground Transport," 30.

75.   *A Study in the Antitrust Laws*, 3920, as cited by Snell, "American Ground Transport," 30.

76.   General Motors, "Truth About 'American Ground Transport,'" 56–58.

77.   *Proceedings of the American Transit Associations and Its Affiliated Associations 1935* (New York: American Transit Association, 1935), 34, 76–77. St. Clair, *Motorization*, 58.

78.   Snell, "American Ground Transport," 30.

79.   Roosevelt, Franklin D., "Message From the President of the United States Transmitting a Report of the National Power Committee with Respect to the Treatment of Holding Companies," 74th Cong., 1st sess., *Report of the National Power Policy Committee* (Washington: Government Printing Office, 1935), as cited by Charlie Higley, "Disastrous Deregulation," *Public Citizen*, December 2000, 6–7.

80.   Public Utility Holding Company Act of 1935: Opinion of the Supreme Court of the United States in the Case of *Electric Bond and Share Company v. Securities and Exchange Commission*, 75th Cong., 3d sess., Senate Document No. 160 (Washington: US Government Printing Office, 1938), 1–10. *The Changing Structure of the Electric Power Industry 2000: An Update*, "Chapter 4: The Federal Statutory Background of the Electric Power Industry," www.eia.doe.gov. See *Implications of a New PUHCA for the Electric Industry and Regulators* (Columbus, OH: The National Regulatory Research Institute, 1992), 1–13.

81.   *United States vs. National City Lines et al.*, 47CR524, Transcript of Proceedings, testimony of E. Roy Fitzgerald, 429–31.

82.   Ibid., 430–36, 439.

83.   Ibid., 439–40.

84.   Ibid., 440–41.

85.   Ibid., 441, 452.

86.   See author's interview with Gene Nicolelli, director of Greyhound Museum, Hibbing, MN, February 20, 2006.

87.   Greyhound Historical Timeline, http://www.greyhound.com/company/media/history_text.shtml, see 1931. Author's enterprise. See author's interview with Gene Nicolelli.

88.   *US vs. NCL*, testimony of E. Roy Fitzgerald, 442–43.

89.   "Offers of Proof by Certain Defendants," *United States vs. National City Lines et al.*, Dis-

trict Court of the United States for the Northern District of Illinois Eastern Division, Criminal Action No. 47CR524, 2–3.

90.   *US vs. NCL*, testimony of E. Roy Fitzgerald, 442–46.
91.   "Offers of Proof by Certain Defendants," 3.
92.   *US vs. NCL*, testimony of E. Roy Fitzgerald, 444.
93.   Ibid., 446.
94.   Ibid., 449, 452.
95.   Ibid., 452.
96.   "Offers of Proof by Certain Defendants," 4–5. Order of Illinois Commerce Commission upon the applications of Chicago & Joliet Transportation Company, Joliet City Lines et al., Docket No. 23155, July 27, 1934; Order of Illinois Commerce Commission upon the applications of East St. Louis Railway Company, East St. Louis Electric Railway, and East St. Louis City Lines, Docket No. 23811, October 31, 1935; Order of Illinois Commerce Commission upon the applications of Illinois Power & Light Corporation and Decatur City Lines, Docket No. 25147, November 25, 1936; Order of Illinois Commerce Commission upon the applications of Illinois Power & Light Corporation and Quincy City Lines, Docket No. 24888, October 1, 1936; Order of Illinois Commerce Commission upon the applications of Illinois Power & Light Corporation and Champaign-Urbana City Lines, Docket No. 24890, October 1, 1936; Order of Illinois Commerce Commission upon the applications of Illinois Power & Light Corporation and Bloomington-Normal City Lines, Docket No. 24889, December 2, 1936; Order of Illinois Commerce Commission upon the applications of Illinois Power & Light Corporation and Danville City Lines, Docket No. 24891, November, 25, 1936, as cited by "Offers of Proof by Certain Defendants," 5. *US vs. NCL*, testimony of E. Roy Fitzgerald, 474–76.
97.   *US vs. NCL*, testimony of E. Roy Fitzgerald, 453–57.
98.   Ibid., 454–63. "National City Lines," *Wall Street Journal*, October 20, 1936, 11.
99.   *US vs. NCL*, testimony of E. Roy Fitzgerald, 463.
100. Indictment, *USA v. National City Lines et al.*, Criminal Action No. 19270, April 9, 1947, District Court of the United States, Southern District of California, Central Division, 7 subsection 4.
101. Indictment, *USA v. NCL et al.*, 7–8.
102. *US vs. NCL*, testimony of E. Roy Fitzgerald, 466.
103. Ibid., 466–67.
104. Ibid., 467.
105. Ibid., 469–71.
106. Ibid., 469.
107. Ibid., 470. "A Pot of Gold at Rainbow's End: Story of 5 Fitzgeralds, Masters of L.A. Transit, as Told by U.S. Records," *L.A. Herald and Express*, October 22, 1947, n.p.
108. *US vs. NCL*, testimony of E. Roy Fitzgerald, 470–71.
109. "Southern Pacific and Standard Oil," *Chicago Tribune*, December 31, 1892, 12. "Serious Charges," *Los Angeles Times*, December 31, 1892, 2. Letter, Foster Beamsley to Mack International Truck Co., November 7, 1939, FBI Files 60-3275 FOIA.
110. Letter, Beamsley to Mack International. *US vs. NCL*, Colloquy, 79.
111. *US vs. NCL*, Colloquy, 79.

112. Ibid., 80–81.

113. Ibid., 81.

114. Ibid.

115. *US vs. NCL*, testimony of E. Roy Fitzgerald, 496.

116. Contract between Firestone Tire and Rubber Company and National City Lines, Inc., May 15, 1939, FBI Files 60-3275 FOIA. *US vs. NCL*, testimony of E. Roy Fitzgerald, 496–97.

117. Contract between Firestone and National City Lines.

118. Report, interview with source at U.S. Rubber Company, August 13, 1948, 3, FBI Files 60-3275-90 FOIA.

119. Letter, Guido Pantaleoni Jr. to Russell Riggins, April 18, 1939, 2, FBI Files 60-3275 FOIA. *US vs. NCL*, testimony of E. Roy Fitzgerald, 497.

120. Letter, Pantaleoni to Riggins, 3–4.

121. Ibid., 6.

122. *US vs. NCL*, testimony of E. Roy Fitzgerald, 497. Report, interview with source at Mid-Continent Petroleum Company, January 28, 1947, FBI Files 60-3275-20 FOIA. Report, interview with source at Sinclair Refining Company, March 11, 1947, FBI Files 60-3275-29 FOIA.

123. *US vs. NCL*, testimony of E. Roy Fitzgerald, 497–98.

124. Ibid., 500–501.

125. *US vs. NCL*, Government's Exhibit No. 90, 1331–35. Trial Memorandum of Defendants, *USA v. National City Lines, Inc. et al.*, 14. Indictment, *USA v. NCL et al.*, 10–11.

126. *US vs. NCL*, Government's Exhibit No. 90, 1330–35. Indictment, *USA v. NCL et al.*, 10–11.

127. *US vs. NCL*, Colloquy, 93–97. Contract between National City Lines Inc. and Mack Manufacturing Corporation, August 1, 1939, 2, FBI Files 60-3275-157 FOIA.

128. Letter, John L. Wilson to E. Roy Fitzgerald, October 2, 1945, Georgia State University Special Collections, NCL 496—Coaches, General '45. Joint report of Special Agents [censored], April 5, 1947, 3, 6, FBI Files CV File No. 60-133, 60-3275-38 FOIA Report, interview with source at Twin Coach Company, July 25, 1947, FBI Files 60-3275-55 FOIA.

129. Joint report of Special Agents [censored], 18–20.

130. *US vs. NCL*, Colloquy, 93. Report, sworn statement of Mack Truck employee, December 28, 1948, FBI Files 60-3225-139 FOIA.

131. Report, interview with people's counsel in suit filed to block conversion from streetcars to buses in Baltimore, October 4, 1948, FBI Files 60-3275-103, FOIA. *US vs. NCL*, Colloquy, 94–5.

132. *US vs. NCL*, Colloquy, 96.

133. Ibid., 95–96.

134. *US vs. NCL*, Government's Exhibit No. 111, 176.

135. Ibid., Government's Exhibit No. 114–17, 178–79.

136. Ibid., Government's Exhibit No. 90, 1336.

137. Indictment, *USA v. NCL et al.*, 2, 11–12.

138. Ibid., 5, 10.

139. Ibid., 6–7. Report, Pacific City Lines, Inc., Purchases of Petroleum Products, October 4, 1948, FBI Files 60-3275-104 FOIA.

140. C. J. Helbing to Cone T. Bass, Inter-Company Correspondence, March 13, 1946, NCL-SOS Abandonment of Streetcars, Tampa 46, Georgia University Special Collections.

141. Ibid.

142. Letter to Attorney General Tom C. Clark, September 4, 1947, enclosed in office memorandum to J. Edgar Hoover, September 24, 1947, FBI Files 60-3275-67 FOIA.

143. Ibid.

144. Ibid.

145. Federal Bureau of Investigation, memorandum, "National City Lines, Inc. Et. Al.," October 30, 1947, FBI Files 60-3275-69 FOIA.

146. Ibid.

147. Ibid.

148. Ibid.

149. Letter, Foster O. Beamsley to Standard Oil Company of New Jersey, December 1, 1944, FBI Files 60-3275-62 FOIA.

150. "Trolley's Bow to Buses," *National City Liner*, October-November 1945, 7.

151. Newspaper clipping, "Call for Street Cars," *Tampa Morning Tribune*, December 8, 1946. Newspaper clipping, "Letters to the Editor," *Tampa Daily Times*, September 19, 1947.

152. "Baltimore Transit to Buy Cars, Buses," *Christian Science Monitor*, July 3, 1940, 17. Report, interview with people's counsel. See Abel Wolman et al., *Report to the Mayor of Baltimore by the Committee on Mass Transportation* (Baltimore: December 1955), 6, as cited by Aaron Michael Glazer, "Fade to Gas: The Conversion of Baltimore's Mass Transit System from Streetcars to Diesel-Powered Buses," *Maryland Historical Magazine* 97, No. 3 (Fall 2002): 340.

153. Report, interview with people's counsel. "Court Asked to Save Baltimore Trolleys," *Washington Post*, December 11, 1947, B2. "June 22, 1947: A Streetcar Named History," *Sun*, June 22, 1947, www.citipaper.com/news/story.asp?id=3639. "88-Year Era of Trolleys Bows Out in Baltimore," *Washington Post*, November 5, 1963, B4. See "Improved Traffic Conditions Are Not Around the Corner," *Baltimore Sun*, October 11, 1946, as cited by Glazer, "Fade to Gas," 348.

154. See folder "Abandonment of the Trolley," National City Lines collection, Georgia State University.

155. Directive, Office of Defense Transportation, April 17, 1942, GSU-NCL-B492 Transportation, General.

156. Ibid.

157. Farber, *Sloan Rules*, 205.

158. Ibid.

159. Charles Wertenbaker, "The World and Jim Mooney," *Saturday Evening Post*, October 30, 1937, 23. "James D. Mooney Discusses Automotive Industry with Hitler," *General Motors World*, June 1934, 1–3; Mooney, "Diary of Mr. Mooney's Visit to London and Berlin: March 27 to April 6, 1939," 6, 1–14, Mooney Papers, Georgetown University Library; Memorandum, September 16, 1936, by R. A. Fleischer, OPR 019343.

160. See Keppler to Fleischer, January 3, 1935, OPR 019046. Fleischer to Keppler, January 14, 1935, OPR 019040. R. K. Evans to J. D. Mooney, January 18, 1935, GM 001064-8. Paetsch

to Colonel Thomas, February 27, 1935 (Abschrift), OPR 019014. Paetsch to Fleischer (Abschrift), February 26, 1935, OPR 019015f. O. C. Mueller's circular memorandum of March 21, 1936, OPR 017802. A. Bangert to H. Grewenig, August 13, 1937, OPR 017729. Grewenig to Fleischer, September 17, 1937, OPR 042133); and "Gesamt-Produktion des Werkes Brandenburg der Adam Opel A.G. 1936–1940," OPR 016934ff.

161.   "General Motors Man Wins German Award," *New York Times*, August 11, 1938, 10. "Thomas J. Watson Is Decorated by Hitler for Work in Bettering Economic Relations," *New York Times*, July 2, 1937, 8. Black, *IBM and the Holocaust*, 134, 137.

162.   Farber, *Sloan Rules*, 222.

163.   Ibid.

164.   Gabriel Kolko, "American Business and Germany, 1930–1941," *Western Political Quarterly* 15, no. 4 (December 1962): 724–25, and generally.

165.   Michael Dobbs, "Ford and GM Scrutinized for Alleged Nazi Collaboration," *Washington Post*, November 30, 1998, A1.

166.   Farber, *Sloan Rules*, 227. Alfred P. Sloan Jr., Minutes of Meeting held at the D.A.C., May 21, 1941, 2, Kettering University Archives 87-11.4-18, Alumni Collection of Industrial History, GMI, Flint, Michigan.

167.   Ibid.

168.   Snell, "American Ground Transport," 1–3, 16–22. General Motors, "Truth About 'American Ground Transport,' " 1–4.

169.   "Truth About 'American Ground Transport,' " 5–10.

170.   Memorandum for the Director, Federal Bureau of Investigation, Re: National City Lines, Inc., et al., Washington, D.C., October 2, 1946, 3, 5–6.

171.   Federal Bureau of Investigation, numerous complaints, "National City Lines, Inc. Et. Al.," October 2, 1946, FBI Files 60-3275-1 FOIA. Federal Bureau of Investigation, report Superior Motor Coach and Body Company, "National City Lines, Inc. Et. Al.," October 30, 1947, FBI Files 60-3275-69 FOIA Joint report of Special Agents [censored]. Report of FBI Laboratory, signature analysis of NCL documents, September 22, 1948, FBI Files 60-3275-94 FOIA. Contract between Firestone and National City Lines. See generally author's copies of FBI FOIA documents.

172.   Indictment, *USA v. NCL et al.*, 1–21.

173.   Ibid., 1. "Transit Line Plot Laid to Nine Firms," *New York Times*, April 11, 1947, 38.

174.   Indictment, *USA v. NCL et al.*, 7–10.

175.   Ibid., 14–19.

176.   Criminal Action No. 47CR524—Bill of Particulars, *USA v. NCL et al.*, February 18, 1948, 1–4.

177.   Ibid., 1–10.

178.   "Transit Line Plot Laid to Nine Firms."

179.   Criminal Action No. 19270—Motion of Defendants National City Lines, Inc., American City Lines, Inc., Pacific City Lines, Inc., E. Roy Fitzgerald and Foster G. Beamsley for Bill of Particulars, May 12, 1947. Criminal Action No. 19270—Motion of Defendants Firestone Tire & Rubber Company and L. R. Jackson for Bill of Particulars, May 12, 1947. Criminal Action No. 19270—Motion of Defendants General Motors Corporation and H. C. Grossman, for a Bill of Particulars and Points and Authorities in Support Thereof, May 12, 1947. Criminal Action No. 19270-W—Motion for a Bill of Particulars by Defen-

dants, Standard Oil Company of California, Federal Engineering Corporation and Henry C. Judd (Under Rule 7 [f]), May 12, 1947. U.S. Supreme Court, *USA v. NCL et al.*, June 21, 1948, 1.

180. Charge to the Jury, *USA v. NCL et al.*, March 9, 1949, 22–23. "National City Lines Guilty in Trust Case," *New York Times*, March 13, 1949, 79.

181. Verdict, *USA v. NCL et al.*, April 1, 1949, 1.

182. Ibid.

183. Ibid. 2.

184. United States Court of Appeals Seventh Circuit, *USA v. NCL et al.*, January 3, 1951, 1. U.S. Supreme Court, *USA v. NCL et al.*, June 21, 1948, 1.

185. Helbing to Bass.

186. "First Order of Business for Bus Lines Is Service," *Tampa Daily Times*, August 1946.

187. Letter, Commissioner Robin C. Herndon to Burton R. Morley, July 9, 1945.

188. "To the Port Arthur City Lines," *Port Arthur News*, November 22, 1947, NCL-518, Beaumont Regional, 1947.

189. Western Union telegram, Otho Plumer, Mayor, City of Beaumont, to F. N. Hill, East St. Louis City Lines, Inc., December 1, 1947. Letter, F. Norman Hill to Mr. R. S. Moore, December 9, 1947, NCL-518, Beaumont Regional 1947, 1–2. "Five More New Buses to Arrive in Beaumont Soon," *Beaumont Enterprise*, April 26, 1947.

190. "The Streetcar Strike," *Los Angeles Times*, May 20, 1946, A4. Photo, "A Pot of Gold at Rainbow's End," *Los Angeles Herald & Express*, October 22, 1947. "Story of 5 Fitzgeralds, Masters of L.A. Transit, as Told by U.S. Records," *Los Angeles Herald & Express*, October 22, 1947.

191. See generally Georgia State University Special Collections, NCL Transportation General Mobile, 1945; also, Transportation Superintendent Jackson, 1946, and author's files on National City Lines segregation.

192. Weekly Report, R. J. Cortright to F. N. Hill, November 23–30, 1946.

193. Review: "Divided Highways: Building the Interstate Highways, Transforming American Life," *Journal of American History* 87, No. 1 (June 2000): 297. Program Administration: Dwight D. Eisenhower National System of Interstate and Defense Highways, Federal Highway Administration, www.fhwa.dot.gov/programadmin/interstate.html, 1–9.

194. Program Administration, 1.

195. "The Ordeal of Engine Charlie: How one of our most enlightened business leaders became the symbol of corporate ruthlessness," *American Heritage Magazine* 46, no. 1 (February/March 1995).

196. Ibid.

197. 1956 NCL Annual Report, 5, NYPL-SIBL XLF 456 National City Lines AR 1956.

198. 1957 NCL Annual Report, 6, NYPL-SIBL XLF 456 National City Lines AR 1957.

199. Ibid., 6–7.

200. Ibid., 7.

201. Ibid., 1959 NCL Annual Report, 2–3, NYPL-SIBL XLF 456 National City Lines AR 1959.

202. "Mayor Makes New Appeal in Deadlocked Transit Strike," *Los Angeles Times*, May 12, 1946, 1. "Thumbnail Sketches of TCRT Trial Defendants," *Minneapolis Star*, August 6, 1960, B1.

203. "Thumbnail Sketches," B1.

204. "How Mobsters Grabbed a City's Transit Line," Gordon Schendel, *Collier's*, September 29, 1951, 181, 184.

205. Ibid., 184.

206. Ibid., 181–84.

207. Ibid., 184.

208. Ibid.

209. Ibid., 185.

210. Ibid.

211. Ibid., 185–86.

212. Ibid., 186.

213. Ibid.

214. Ibid.

215. Ibid., 185, 187.

216. Ibid., 186–87.

217. Stephen A. Kieffer, *Transit and the Twins*, (Minneapolis: Twin City Rapid Transit Co., 1958), 46.

218. Ibid., David C. Smith, "GM's Jack Smith Set to Cap 42-Year Career—General Motors's Chairman," *Ward's Auto World*, July 1, 2002.

219. Kieffer, *Transit and the Twins*, 46–47.

220. Ibid. "Ossanna, Kid Cann Indicted in Sales of Streetcar Scrap," *Minneapolis Star*, September 18, 1959, 1.

221. Kieffer, *Transit and the Twins*, 46–47.

222. Letter, H. P. Jacobson to L. G. Bakken, May 14, 1952. #222: Miscellaneous Records, Twin City Rapid Transit Company Documents, Minnesota State Archives Library, Minnesota Historical Society.

223. Ibid., May 15 and June 13, 1952.

224. Ibid., September 15, November 21, and December 10, 1952.

225. Ibid., September 19, 1952.

226. Diers, "Did a Conspiracy Really Kill the Streetcar?" 63. Picture, "A Streetcar Tamed by Fire," aye verily, http://ayeverily.com/k-streetcar.html.

227. "Ossanna, 4 Others Guilty in TCRT Fraud; Cann Acquitted," *Minneapolis Star*, August 6, 1960. "Ossanna, Kid Cann Indicted," 1. "Jury Indicts Kid Cann on White Slave Charges," 1.

228. "Ossanna, Kid Cann Indicted," 1. "Jury Indicts Kid Cann on White Slave Charges," 1.

229. "Ossanna, 4 Others Guilty in TCRT Fraud."

230. Ibid. "Did a Conspiracy Really Kill the Streetcar?" 62.

231. "Ossanna, 4 Others Guilty in TCRT Fraud."

232. *US vs. NCL*, Colloquy, 105–7, 109–10.

233. Ibid., 105–8, 110.

234. Ibid., 105–7, 108–11.

Chapter 11: Manhattan Now

1. "Governor Arnold Schwarzenegger's California Hydrogen Highway Network Action Plan," Governor's Office, 2004. "The Particle Pollution Report: Current Understanding of Air Quality and Emissions through 2003," United States Environmental Protection Agency, December 2004, 2–3, 7, 9. "Technology Transfer Network National Air Toxics Assessment:

Acetaldehyde," United States Environmental Protection Agency, 2002,
http://www.epa.gov/ttn/atw/nata/pollinf2.html. "Health Effects of Diesel Exhaust," California Environmental Protection Agency's Office of Environmental Health Hazard Assessment and the American Lung Association, August 2000. "What Toxic Air Pollutants Are
Produced by Petroleum-Based Fuels and Combustion Engines?" Energy Independence
Now, circa 2002, 1. "How Do Tobacco Smoke and Car Exhaust Compare?" Energy Independence Now, circa 2002, 1. Map, "Petroleum Infrastructure and Related Pollution," Energy Independence Now, 2002, http://www.energyindependencenow.org. "What Are the
Defects and Harms of Internal Combustion Engines?" Energy Independence Now, circa
2002, 1–2. "Last Gasp," *Fresno Bee*, December 15, 2002. Joan Flores, "On the Move
Against Asthma," *Children's Advocate*, September–October 2003, http://www.4children.org.
Author's interview with Janice Nolen of ALA, March 2006. Presentation, "SCAQMD Hydrogen Program: NHA Annual Hydrogen Conference," Cynthia Verdugo-Peralta, March
13, 2006, www.aqmd.gov, 1–25. Author's interview with Cynthia Verdugo-Peralta,
SCAQMD. Author's interview with Jerry Martin, CARB, March 2006.

2. "Health Effects of Particulate Matter and Ozone Pollution, January 2004," California Environmental Protection Agency Air Resources Board. Author's interviews with Janice Nolen,
March 16 and April 7, 2006. "What Are the Health Harms Associated with Petroleum-
Based Fuels and Combustion By-Products?" Energy Independence Now, circa 2002. Author's interview with Verdugo-Peralta. Author's interview with Martin.

3. "SCAQMD Hydrogen Program." "Multiple Air Toxics Exposure Study in the South Coast
Air Basin (MATES-II)," chap. 4, SCAQMD, March 2000. "Governor Arnold Schwarzenegger's California Hydrogen Highway." "Health Effects of Particulate Matter and Ozone Pollution." "What Are the Health Harms Associated?" Author's interview with Nolen. Author's
interview with Verdugo-Peralta.

4. "Air Trends: Carbon Monoxide," U.S. EPA, http://www.epa.gov/airtrends/carbon.html.

5. David Hosansky, "Traffic Congestion," *CQ Researcher* 9, no. 32 (August 27, 1999): 731–47.

6. "SCAQMD Hydrogen Program." Author's notes.

7. "Excerpt from the Alaska Oil Spill Commission Report on the 1989 *Exxon Valdez* Oil Spill,"
http://www.evostc.state.ak.us/History/excerpt.htm. "History Detail" (Ixtoc I), http://spills.inci
dentnews.gov/incidentnews/FMPro?-db=history&-format=history_detail.htm&-
lay=history&RecID=32915&-find. "What's the Story on Oil Spills?" NOAA's National
Ocean Service, Office of Response and Restoration, http://response.restoration.noaa.gov/.

8. D. O'Rourke and S. Connolly, "Just Oil? The Distribution of Environmental and Social
Impacts of Oil Production and Consumption," *Annual Review of Environment and Resources* 28 (2003): 599, 616.

9. Andrew C. Revkin, "Offshore Oil Pollution Comes Mostly as Runoff, Study Says," *New York
Times*, May 24, 2002. Press statement, "New Study Uncovers Long Term, Unanticipated
Damage from Oil Spills," Natural Resources Defense Council, December 18, 2003. "Clean-
ing Up the Oceans: A Global Ethical Challenge," Markkula Center for Applied Ethics, 2003.

10. O'Rourke and Connolly, "Just Oil," 594.

11. Ibid., 594–95.

12. "Questions and Answers on Fuel Economy,"
http://www.ucsusa.org/clean_vehicles/fuel_economy/questions-and-answers-on-fuel-
economy.html. "This Week in Petroleum," June 2, 2005, U.S. Energy Information

Administration, http://tonto.eia.doe.gov/oog/info/twip/twiparch/050601/twipprint.html. http://yosemite.epa.gov/oar/globalwarming.nsf/content/ResourceCenterPublications GHGEmissionsUSEmissionsInventory2005.html, plus their interview, March 17, and communications. U.S. Environmental Protection Agency, "Greenhouse Gas Emissions from the U.S. Transportation Section: 1990–2003," http://epa.gov/otaq/climate/420r06003summary.htm.

13. Stacy Archfield, "Hazards of Sea Level Rise: An Introduction," http://cfa-www.harvard.edu/space_geodesy/SEALEVEL/. See generally Elizabeth Kolbert, *Field Notes From a Catastrophe* (New York: Bloomsbury Publishers, 2006). Michael D. Lemonick, "Has the Meltdown Begun?" *Time*, February 27, 2006, 59.

14. Andrew Haines, Anthony J. McMichael, and Paul R. Epstein, "Environment and Health: 2. Global Climate Change and Health," *Canadian Medical Association*, September 19, 2000, 729. "Has the Meltdown Begun?" 59.

15. David Louie, "Faster Jetstream Costly for Airlines," KABC-TV, Los Angeles, February 27, 2006. Author's personal observation. Also see pilot discussion, forums, "The Wings of the Web," http://www.airliners.net/discussions/general_aviation/read.main/.

16. Nicholas Bakalar, "Warming Will Lead to Major Disease Outbreaks, Experts Warn," *National Geographic News*, December 2, 2005, 1–2.

17. Rick VanderKnyff, "33 States Top $3 a Gallon," CNBC, September 7, 2005. "U.S. Author Forecasts $5 Gas by Next Year," United Press International, August 17, 2005. Energy Information Administration, "United States—Oil," http://www.eia.doe.gov/cabs/USA/Oil.html. "Petroleum Products," http://www.eia.doe.gov/neic/infosheets/petroleumproducts.htm.

18. David L. Greene, "Cost of Oil Dependence: A 2000 Update," prepared by the Oak Ridge National Laboratory for the U.S. Department of Energy, December 2000, 1.

19. Justin Blum, "Senate Overwhelmingly Passes Energy Bill," *Washington Post*, June 29, 2005. Erica Swisher, "The Real Cost of Oil," *Ethanol Today*, August 2005, 22, 44. CTA International Center for Technology Assessment, "Gasoline Cost Externalities: Security and Protection Services," January 25, 2005. David Gerard and Lester Lave, "CAFE Increases: Missing the Elephant in the Living Room," *AEI-Brookings Joint Center for Regulatory Studies*, June 2004, 1. Anthony H. Cordesman, "Outside View: The Costs of the Iraq War," *Washington Times*, December 14, 2004. Senator Richard Lugar, "Energy Security: Cause for Cooperation or Competition?" Brookings Institution 90th Leadership Forum Series, March 13, 2006, proceedings (Washington, DC: Miller Reporting Co., 2006). http://www.washingtonpost.com/wp-dyn/content/article/2005/06/28/AR2005062800398 .html.

20. Chris Isidore, "ExxonMobile Sets Profit Record," CNNMoney.com, January 30, 2006, http://money.cnn.com/2006/01/30/news/companies/exxon_earns. Justin Blum, "ExxonMobil Profit Soars 75%," *Washington Post*, October 28, 2005. Kevin Bogardus, "K Street Lobbyists Carry Water for OPEC," http://www.publicintegrity.org/oil/report.aspx?aid=380.

21. "Cost of Oil Dependence." National Resources Defense Council, "Safe, Strong, and Secure: Reducing America's Oil Dependence," http://www.nrdc.org/air/transportation/aoilpolicy2.asp. Nathan Vardi, "Sins of the Father?" *Forbes*, March 18, 2002, www.forbes.com/global/2002/0318/047_2.html. Swisher, "Real Cost of Oil," 45.

22. Vardi, "Sins of the Father?"

23. Edwin Black, *Banking on Baghdad* (Hoboken, NJ: John Wiley & Sons, 2004), 95–228.

24. Generally see Black, *Banking on Baghdad*, 169. "Casualty Record of Belligerents," *New York*

Times, January 19, 1919, 39. "Military Casualties of World War One," July 2003, First World War Online, Michael Duffy, ed., www.firstworldwar.com. BBC News, "The War to End All Wars," news.bbc.co.uk. "Timeline: 1914–1918—Casualty Figures," *Trenches on the Web: An Internet History of the Great War,* The Great War Society, eds., www.worldwar1.com. See "The Cost of War," *Washington Post,* November 27, 1916, 4. See "Primary Documents: D. F. Houston on U.S. War Readiness, 1917," February 2004, First World War Online.

25. Generally see Black, *Banking on Baghdad,* 169. "The Battle of the Somme, 1916," August 2001, First World War Online. "The Battle of Verdun, 1916," First World War Online. "The Gallipoli Front—an Overview," August 2002, First World War Online. BBC History, "Daily Mirror Headlines, Published 31 July 1916," January 2002, www.bbc.co.uk. "At Verdun," *New York Times,* May 3, 1916, 12. See "Allied Efforts on the Somme Called 'Gallipoli on the Continent,'" *Washington Post,* December 10, 1916, 5. See "How the Battle was Won," *New York Times,* December 17, 1916, 2. "Timeline: 1914–1918—Casualty Figures." "Military Casualties of World War One."

26. See Black, *Banking on Baghdad,* 169–228.

27. Letter, M. L. Requa to Alvey Adlee, May 13, 1920, NA RG59 800.6363/112.

28. Ibid.

29. See Black, *Banking on Baghdad,* 261–292. Generally see Black, *Banking on Baghdad.*

30. See Black, *Banking on Baghdad,* 240–46.

31. George Antonius, *The Arab Awakening: The Story of the Arab National Movement* (New York: Putnam, 1946; Reprint, New York: Capricorn Books, 1965), 312.

32. See Black, *Banking on Baghdad,* 229–292.

33. Ibid.

34. Ibid., 246.

35. Eileen T. Westervelt and Donald F. Fournier, "Energy Trends and Implications for U.S. Army Installations," U.S. Army Engineer Research and Development Center, September 2005, http://www.erdc.usace.army.mil. "The End of Cheap Oil," *National Geographic,* June 2004, 89, 94–95. "China 'Feeds' Automobiles with Corn," *People's Daily Online,* December 7, 2001, http://english.people.com.cn/200112/06/eng200112_86104.shtml.

36. "Hubbert's Peak, the Peak," http://www.princeton.edu/hubbert/the-peak.html. "CIA—The World Fact Book—Rank Order—Oil—Consumption," http://www.cia.gov/cia/publications/factbook/rankorder/2174rank.html. "End of Cheap Oil," 89, 98–99.

37. Eileen T. Westervelt and Donald T. Fournier, "Energy Trends and Implications for U.S. Army Installations," report for the U.S. Army Corps of Engineers, http://www.peakoil.net/Articles2005/Westervelt_EnergyTrends_TN.pdf.

38. "The Costs of the Manhattan Project," Brookings Institution, http://www.brookings.edu/FP/PROJECTS/NUCWCOST/MANHATTAN.htm. Carrey Sublette, "Nuclear Weapons Frequently Asked Questions: Section 10.0 Chronology for the Origin of Atomic Weapons," May 15, 1997, http://www.nuclearweaponarchive.org/Nwfaq/Nfaq10.html.

39. "Costs of the Manhattan Project."

40. Ibid.

41. National Air and Space Administration "Project Apollo: A Retrospective Analysis," http://history.nasa.gov/Apollomon/Apollo.html. "Crossroads of the Americas: Trans Texas Corridor Plan," CorridorWatch.org—Challenging the Wisdom of the Trans-Texas Co., www.corridor

watch.org. Brad Foss, "Update 1: Experts: Alaska Pipeline Won't Solve Woes," *Forbes*, March 18, 2006. "Pipeline Facts," Pipeline Facts, www.alyeska-pipe.com. Jack Lyne, "Priciest Pipeline Ever," Priciest Pipeline Ever—Site Selection Online, www.siteselection.com/ssinsider/snapshot/sf050117.htm. "Cost Estimates," NAPCO—Hong Kong Airport Core Programme, www.info.gov.hk/napco/cost.html. Genome, http://www.genome.gov/11006929.

42.   Anthony H. Cordesman, "Outside View: The Costs of the Iraq War," *Washington Times*, December 15, 2004.

43.   Justin Blum, "Exxon Mobil Profit Soars 75%," *Washington Post*, October 28, 2005: D01. Chris Isidore, "Exxon Mobil Sets Profit Record," CNNMoney.com, January 30, 2006, http://money.cnn.com/2006/01/30/news/companies/exxon_carns/.

44.   Harry Reginald Hall, *Ancient History of the Near East* (London: Methuen, 1963), 300.

45.   See author's March 2006 interview with Office of Coal and Power National Energy Technology Laboratory, DOE.

46.   Ibid.

47.   "Owners Agree to Shut W. Va. Mines," CBS News, February 2, 2006, http://www.cbsnews.com/stories/2006. Anna Sale, "West Virginia Coal Mining Halted After More Deaths," NPR, March 20, 2006, www.npr.org.

48.   See author's March 2006 interview with Office of Coal and Power.

49.   See author's notes on several attempts to call Ben Yamagata, Clean Coal Initiative, March 15–17, 2006.

50.   "Ocean Thermal Energy Conversion," U.S. Department of Energy: Energy Efficiency and Renewable Energy, March 20, 2006, www.eere.energy.gov.

51.   Press release, "Toronto Hydro and Enwave to Provide Downtown Toronto with NEW Electricity Supply," February 3, 2006. "Deep Lake Water Cooling: Chilled Water for Cooling Toronto's Buildings," Enwave Energy Corporation. "Deep Lake Water Cooling: Chilled Water for Cooling Toronto's Buildings," March 20, 2006, www.enwave.com.

52.   "Italy: Electricity Generation," International Geothermal Association, iga.igg.cnr.it. Raffaele Cataldi, UGI Vice President, "Birth and First Steps of the Geothermoelectric Industry, and Its Centenary," www.geothermie.de.

53.   "Iceland: Electricity Generation," International Geothermal Association, http://iga.igg.cnr.it. "About Geothermal Electricity," Geothermal Technologies Program: Geothermal Electricity, www.nrel.gov. Press release, Geothermal Energy Association, "U.S. Geothermal Power Poised to Double, New Survey Shows," March 15, 2006. See author's notes on interview with Karl Gawell, IGA. "Installed Generating Capacity," International Geothermal Association, http://iga.igg.cnr.it.

54.   Alex Sifford and R. Gordon Bloomenquist, "Geothermal Electric Power Production in the United States: A Survey and Update for 1995–1999," *Proceedings World Geothermal Congress 2000*, 441–45, 450.

55.   "California's Geothermal Energy: Present and Future Strategies," Public Interest Energy Research: California Energy Commission, October 8, 2003.

56.   See author's interviews with NERL and GEA.

57.   See author's interview with Karl Gawell, March 20, 2006. GEA, "U.S. Geothermal Power Poised to Double."

58.   See author's interview with Gawell.

59.   Ibid. GEA, "U.S. Geothermal Power Poised to Double."

60. See author's interview with Gawell.

61. See author's interview with Boddington, Gawell, and Valetkevitch, March 21, 2006.

62. Ibid.

63. See author's interview with the Natural Gas Supply Association.

64. "Germany Split over Green Energy," BBC News International Version, February 25, 2005, http://news.bbc.co.uk. "Wind Energy in Ireland," Irish Wind Energy Association Online, http://www.iwea.com/windenergy/index.html.

65. "Wind Energy Fact Sheet," American Wind Energy Association, http://www.awea.org.

66. Report, "Wind and Wildlife: Learning from the Past, Changing for the Future," American Wind Energy Association, 2003.

67. "Wind Energy Fact Sheet." Report, "Wind Power Today," American Wind Energy Association. Danish Wind Industry Association, http://www.windpower.org/en/stats/capacityDK.htm. "Wind Energy at GE," GE Energy, http://www.gepower.com/businesses/ge_wind_energy/en/index.html. Meredith MacKensie, "Wind Energy Grows Through On Site Turbines," UPI, March 13, 2006. Author enterprise.

68. "Solar Panels," Worldwatts, http://worldwatts.com/panels.html.

69. Author's communication with Jon Slangerup, Solar Integrated Technologies, March 2006.

70. "BIPV Solar Electric Roofing for Sustainable Buildings," http://www.solarintegrated.com/bipv.htm. See author's communication with Slangerup.

71. "Konarka Products," http://www.konarka.com/products/. "Nanosolar—Products," http://www.nanosolar.com/products.htm. Press release, Konarka Technologies Inc., "Smart Fabrics 2006 Conference Features Konarka's Chief Marketing Officer Daniel McGahn as Industry Speaker," March 7, 2006.

72. "Smart Fabrics." Author's interview with Daniel McGahn, April 2006. Author's interview with Jon Slangerup.

73. "GM Partners with Verasun and Shell for E85 Push in Chicago," Green Car Congress, http://www.greencarcongress.com/2006/02/gm_partners_wit.html.

74. David Pimentel and Tad W. Patzek, "Ethanol Production Using Corn, Switchgrass, and Wood; Biodiesel Production Using Soybean and Sunflower," *Natural Resources Research* 14, no. 1 (March 2005). David Pimentel, "Energy and Dollar Costs of Ethanol Production with Corn," M. King Hubbert Center for Petroleum Supply Studies, April 1998. Author's interviews with David Pimentel and Tad W. Patzek, March 2006.

75. Pimentel and Patzek, "Ethanol Production Using Corn, Switchgrass, and Wood." Author's interviews with Pimentel and Patzek.

76. See author's interviews with Pimentel and Patzek.

77. See author's interview with National Ethanol Vehicle Coalition.

78. See author's interviews with Pimentel and Patzek.

79. Ibid. See curriculum vitae, David Pimentel. See curriculum vitae, Tad W. Patzek.

80. See author's interview with automotive alternative-fuel source.

81. Letter, Linda D. Willis, Director, Tax Policy and Administrative Issues, U.S. GAO to the Honorable Charles E. Grassley, Chairman, Subcommittee on Administrative Oversight and the Courts, June 23, 1997, GAO Files (with enclosure).

82. Ibid.

83. Report, "Argonne National Laboratory Ethanol Study: Key Points," Office of Energy Efficiency and Renewable Energy, U.S. Department of Energy, March 28, 2005, 1-3.

84.   Ibid.

85.   Author's interview with National Ethanol Vehicle Association March–April, 2006.

86.   Press release, "Acher Daniels Midland Co. to Plead Guilty and Pay $100 Million for Role
       in Two International Price-Fixing Conspiracies," U.S. Department of Justice, October 15,
       1996. "Federal Regulations: VEETC," Renewable Fuels Association, http://www.ethanolrfa.
       org/policy/regulations/federal/veetc/. See Mark Whitacre as quoted in "My Life as a Corpo-
       rate Mole for the FBI," *Fortune*, September 4, 1995, 55.

87.   "Federal Regulations: VEETC." See H.R. 4520, 2004,
       http://www.ethanolrfa.org/objects/pdf/PublicPolicy/Regulations/HR4520.pdf.

88.   Press release, "Ford F-250 Super Chief Concept: A Bold, American Flex Fuel Pickup That
       Delivers Tomorrow's Fuel Today," Ford Motor Company, January 6, 2006. "GM—Only
       GM," http://www.gm.com/company/onlygm/energy_flexfuel.html. See author's interview
       with representative of Ford.

89.   Mark Clayton, "Carbon Cloud over a Green Fuel," *Christian Science Monitor*, March 23,
       2006, http://www.csmonitor.com/2006/0323/p01s01-sten.html.

90.   Ibid. Author's interview with Brad Davis, Gold-Eagle Cooperative, March 2006.

91.   Clayton, "Carbon Cloud over a Green Fuel." Author's interview with Davis.

92.   See generally presentation, Emilio Lebre La Rovere, "The Brazilian Ethanol Program: Bio-
       fuels for Transport," International Conference for Renewable Energies, Bonn, Germany,
       June 2004; La Rovere, "The Challenge of Limiting Greenhouse Gas Emissions Through
       Activities Implemented Jointly in Developing Countries: A Brazilian Perspective," Ernest
       Orlando Lawrence Berkeley National Laboratory, November 1998; La Rovere, "Climate
       Change and Sustainable Development Strategies: A Brazilian Perspective," OECD, 2002.

93.   Larry Rohter, "With Big Boost from Sugar Cane, Brazil Is Satisfying Its Fuel Needs," *New
       York Times*, April 10, 2006, A1.

Chapter 12: Hydrogen Solution

1.   See Genesis 1:1–5, *New International Version Study Bible* (Grand Rapids, MI: Zondervan,
       1995). See Paul Shestople, "Big Bang Cosmology Primer," January 27, 1998, http://
       cosmology.berkeley.edu/Education/IUP/Big_Bang_Primer.html.

2.   See "Fermilab—Press Pass—Photo Gallery—Graphics and Illustrations,"
       http://www.final.gov/pub/presspass/vismedia/gallery/graphics.html. Shestople, "Big Bang
       Cosmology Primer." Dennis Overbye, "Astronomers Find the Earliest Signs Yet of a Violent
       Baby Universe," *New York Times*, March 17, 2006.

3.   Aloysius I. Reisz, "earthrise," www.memagazine.org/. "World's First Fuel Cell–Propelled
       Submarine Starts Sea Trials," *Howaldtswerke Deutsche-Werft* News Archive, April 7, 2003.
       "Ballard Secures US$8.3 million Contract for Fuel Cell Bus Field Service: 27 Ballard Pow-
       ered Mercedes-Benz Citaro Fuel Cell Buses on the Road in Europe for an Additional Year,"
       news release, March 2, 2006. Alton Parrish, "Germany Launches Submarine Fuel Cell Era
       with 'U31,'" *Fuel Cell Today*, May 20, 2002, www.fuelcelltoday.com/.

4.   International Partnership for the Hydrogen Economy, "Fuel Cells: A Hydrogen Enabling
       Technology," January 18–20, 2006.

5.   "National Hydrogen Energy Roadmap," based on the results of the National Hydrogen En-
       ergy Roadmap Workshop, Washington, DC, April 2–3, 2002. Steven Chalk, "U.S. Hydro-
       gen Program" (5th Implementation—Liaison Committee Meeting, Shanghai, China,

January 18–20, 2006). See author's enterprise. International Partnership for the Hydrogen Economy, "A Vision of the Hydrogen Economy."

6. Asgeir Sigfusson, "Iceland: Pioneering the Hydrogen Economy," *Foreign Service Journal*, December 2003, 62–63. "Hydrogen-Filling Station Opens . . . in Iceland," *USA Today*, April 25, 2003. "Vision of the Hydrogen Economy."

7. "National Hydrogen Energy Roadmap," 19. "Background on the Hydrogen Fuel Initiative," www.hydrogen.gov/. "National Hydrogen Association," http://www.hydrogenassociation.org/about/. See Patrick Serfass, interview with the author, April 2006.

8. Chris Isadore, "$3 gas—is it here to stay?" CNN.com, September 8, 2005, http://money.cnn.com/2005/09/07/news/economy/three_dollar_gas/index.htm.

9. "The President's Hydrogen Fuel Initiative," www.hydrogen.gov.

10. Bill Dunn, "Internal Combustion Engine," *Times Online*, April 5, 2005. "Natural Gas History in New Zealand," Natural Gas History—New Zealand—Pure Energy, www.pure energy.co.nz/gas_info/history.php. "Gas Industry Museum," Slovensky Plynarensky Priemysel, www.spp.sk/. Hydrogen Now! "A Brief History of Hydrogen," http://hydrogennow.org/. The Bellona Foundation, "5.2 Town Gas," Report 6:2002, www.bellona.no/. "History and Chronology of Manufactured Gas," www.hatheway.net/01_history.htm. "Prospects for a Hydrogen Economy," *postnote*, Parliamentary Office of Science and Technology, October 2002, No. 186.

11. Ninth Grove Fuel Cell Symposium, http://www.grovefuelcell.com/. "History and Chronology of Manufactured Gas."

12. "Brief History of Hydrogen."

13. Arnold Krammer, "Fueling the Third Reich," *Technology and Culture* 19, no. 3 (July 1978): 400–403. Raymond G. Stokes, "The Oil Industry in Nazi Germany, 1936–1945," *Business History Review* 59, no. 2 (Summer 1985): 268.

14. Krammer, "Fueling the Third Reich," 401. U.S. Department of Energy, "The Early Days of Coal Research," http://fossil.energy.gov/aboutus/history/syntheticfuels_history.html.

15. "Early Days of Coal Research."

16. Ibid.

17. Pat Grimes and Karl Kordesch, interviews with the author, April 2006. General Hydrogen, "Brief History of Vehicle Fuel Cells," http://www.generalhydrogen.com/tech_fuelcells.shtml.

18. See Grimes and Kordesch interviews. "Saturn V: America's Moon Rocket," http://www.nasm.si.edu/exhibitions/gal114/SpaceRace/sec300/sec384.htm. "Karl Kordesch," http://chem.ch.huji.ac.il/~eugeniik/history/kordesch.html. Danny Hakim, "An Electrovan, Not an Edsel," *New York Times*, November 17, 2002, http://www.nytimes.com/.

19. Grimes and Kordesch interviews. "Karl Kordesch."

20. Mazda, "Mazda Delivers First Rotary Hydrogen Vehicles to Corporate Customer Fleets," press release, circa 2004.

21. Hank Wedaa, interview with the author.

22. Author's interviews at National Hydrogen Association Conference, Long Beach, CA, March 2006.

23. Ibid. J. I. Levine, M. K. Mann, R. Margolis, and A. Milbrandt, "An Analysis of Hydrogen Production from Renewable Electricity Sources," National Renewable Energy

Laboratory/ISES 2005 (conference paper, Solar World Congress, Orlando, FL, August 6–12, 2005), http://www.nrel.gov/docs/fy05osti/37612.pdf.

24. "Analysis of Hydrogen Production from Renewable Electricity Sources," 3.

25. Ibid., 5.

26. Author's interviews at National Hydrogen Association Conference. Kordesch interview.

27. David Talbot, "Cheap Hydrogen Fuel," *Technology Review*, March 9, 2006. Author's interviews at National Hydrogen Association Conference.

28. Hydrogen Now! "Frequently Asked Questions," http://www.hydrogennow.org/Facts/FAQs.htm. "Brief History of Vehicle Fuel Cells." Ballard Power Systems, "Fuel Cell Technology: How the Technology Works," http://www. ballard.com/be_informed/fuel_cell_technology/how_the_technology_works.

29. "Ford Moves Forward with Hydrogen Engine Research," press release. Author's interview with Ford source. Gene Johnson, H2 Nation, interview with the author. Hydrogen Now! "Frequently Asked Questions." "2003 North American International Auto Show: Ford Model U," January 5, 2003, www.edmunds.com.

30. General Motors, "General Motors Announces Collaboration with Abengoa Bioenergy and Kroger Stores to Help More Texans Power Their GM FlexFuel Vehicles with E85," press release, March 30, 2006. IHS Automotive Standards, "GM, Chevron, Pacific Ethanol Plan E85 Project in California," January 5, 2006, http://auto.ihs.com/.

31. "Hydrogen Proponents See 2020 as Showtime," MSNBC, March 17, 2006, http://www.msnbc.msn.com/id/11875890. See H2Nation, http://www.h2nation.com/.

32. "London Buses—Fuel Cell Buses," http://www.tfl.gov.uk/buses/fuel-cell-buses.asp. "Fuel Cell Bus Club," http://www.fuel-cell-bus-club.com/. "AC Transit," http://www.actransit.org/. Parrish, "Germany Launches Submarine Fuel Cell Era." Robin Young, Ballard, interview with the author, March 2006.

33. National Academy of Engineering, Board on Energy and Environmental Systems, *The Hydrogen Economy: Opportunities, Costs, Barriers, and R&D Needs* (Washington, DC: National Academies Press, 2004), 38. Johnson and Kordesch interviews. "Hydrogen Proponents see 2020 as Showtime."

34. "BMW World—BMW 750hL," http://www.bmwworld.com/models/750hl.htm. "Praxair, a Supplier of Hydrogen, Liquid or Gas," http://www.praxair.com/. Kordesch interview. Author's interview with source at BMW.

35. Kordesch interview. K. Kordesch, G. Faleschini, V. Hacker et al., "Alkaline Fuel Cell–Hybrid Systems with NH3 Cracker as H2-Producer" (report, Fuel Cell Seminar 2005, Palm Springs, November 2005). "X-15 Hypersonic Research Program," NASA Dryden Fact Sheets, http://www.nassa.gov/centers/dryden/news/Fact Sheets/. Johnny Armstrong, "Expanding the X-15 Envelope to Mach 6.7," http://www.edwards.af.mil/history/.

36. "National Hydrogen Energy Roadmap," 17. "Remarks Prepared for Energy Secretary Spencer Abraham, April 21, 2004," U.S. Department of Energy, http://www.energy. gov/news/1791.htm. Anthony J. Lachawiec, Gongshin Qi, and Ralph T. Yang, "Hydrogen Storage in Graphite Nanofibers and the Spillover Mechanism" (presentation, University of Michigan, Department of Chemical Engineering, May 20–24, 2005).

37. Author's notes from National Hydrogen Association Conference, Long Beach, CA. Author's enterprise. Wedaa interview. Author's interview with Praxair, April 2006.

38.	Governor's Office, *Governor Arnold Schwarzenegger's California Hydrogen Highway Network Action Plan*, 2004.

39.	Ibid.

40.	Ibid.

41.	National Academy of Engineering, *The Hydrogen Economy: Opportunities, Costs, Barriers, and R&D Needs*, (Washington, DC, National Academies Press, 2004): 38. "OCEES Hydrogen." Hydrogen & Fuel Cell Investor, "Bulk Hydrogen," www.h2fc.com/industry/infra/bulkH2.shtml. See author's interview with Praxair. "Praxair Expands Hydrogen Pipeline Capacity," May 2, 2002, www.praxair.com.

42.	See author's interview with Praxair. Also see author's enterprise.

43.	Intelligent Energy, "Hestia hydrogen generator," http://www.intelligent-energy.com/index_article.asp?SecID=12&secondlevel=809 and http://www.intelligent-energy.com/images/uploads/scalable_hydrogen_generator_usa_format.pdf.

44.	"Hydrogen-Producing Ship Will Use Wind," *Energy Bulletin*, Europe Intelligence Wire, October 4, 2004, www.energybulletin.net/3111.html. *Hydrogen Challenger*: The World's First Hydrogen-Production Ship, www.kdserv.net/.

45.	See author's interview with Ford sources.

46.	Honda Worldwide, "Honda to Begin Producing Next Generation FCX Hydrogen Fuel Cell Vehicle," January 8, 2006, http://world.honda.com/. See author's enterprise.

47.	Honda to Begin Producing Next Generation FCX." See author's enterprise.

48.	"Honda to Begin Producing Next Generation FCX." See author's enterprise. Daniel McGahn of Konarka, interview with the author, April 2006.

49.	J. Craig Venter Institute, "IBEA Receives $3 Million Dept. of Energy Grant for Synthetic Genome Development," press release. Synthetic Genomics corporate information, www.syntheticgenomics.com/corporate.htm. Michael S. Rosenwald, "J. Craig Venter's Next Little Thing: Tackling the World's Energy Problems," *Washington Post*, February 27, 2006. "Hydrogen Production by Means of an Artificial Bacterial Algal Symbiosis (Project ArBAS)," www.bionik.tu-berlin.de/institut/xs2solar. Lucy Sheriff, "Scientists Push Bacteria to Quadruple Hydrogen Production: Amazing What a Zap of Electricity Will Do," *Register*, April 26, 2005. Jessica Gorman, "Biological Production of Hydrogen Fuel," *Science News*, October 12, 2002. "A Three-Step Microbial Hydrogen-Producing System: First Results," http://www.bionik.tu-berlin.de/institut/PosterBiohydrogen2002.pdf.

50.	See author's enterprise. See author's interviews with foreign auto makers.

51.	See author's interview with Toyota. "CalCars: The California Cars Initiative—100+ MPG Hybrids," www.calcars.org/. "Plug-in Prius Now Offered in UK," 4Car News from Channel 4, www.channel4.com/. Matthew Shechmeister, "Making a Plug for Hybrids," *Wired News*, July 11, 2005.

52.	All-day, all-night vigil to save the last EV1 from the crusher, http://www.ev1.org/vigil5.htm. The Campaign to Save Electric Cars, www.dontcrush.com/.

53.	See author's notes, National Hydrogen Association Conference, March 2006.

54.	Ibid.

55.	Ibid. Steve Ellis, interview with the author, March 2006.

56.	See author's enterprise. "BMW 750hL—the Ultimate Clean Machine," www.bmwworld.com/. "BMW Hydrogen Cars," www.bmwworld.com/hydrogen/. "BMW

Hydrogen Racer H2R: BMW Sets Speed Records with Specially Designed Hydrogen Race-car!" www.bmwworld.com/.

57.   See author's interview with Toyota. Ellen Chrismer, "Toyota Delivers First Fuel-Cell Car to UC Davis," *Dateline UC Davis*, December 6, 2002. "Toyota Jointly Develops Fuel-Cell Hybrid Bus, the FCHV-BUS1," www.toyota.com.

58.   Honda, "All-New Natural Gas–Powered 2006 Civic GX to Be Introduced to NY Consumers," press release, April 13, 2006.

59.   Ibid.

60.   Environmental Protection Agency, "Global Warming: Climate," http://yosemite.epa.gov/oar/globalwarming.nsf/content/index.html. "Natural Gas and the Environment," www.naturalgas.org/.

61.   U.S. Department of Energy, "Strategic Petroleum Reserve—Quick Facts and Frequently Asked Questions," www.fe.doe.gov/. Tom Johnson, "N.J. Sues Gas Stations Over Rapid Price Hikes: Two Dozen Face Charges of Gouging During Katrina," *Star-Ledger*, September 27, 2005.

62.   Kevin Chandler, Kevin Walkowicz, and Nigel Clark, "United Parcel Service (UPS) CNG Truck Fleet: Final Results," DOE/NREL Truck Evaluation Project, August 2002. Max Donath, Dan Murray, and Jeff Short, "Homeland Security and the Trucking Industry" (report, Intelligent Transportation System Institute, Center for Transportation Studies, July 2005), 1, 3. FedEx Corporation Facts, Fedex, www.fedex.com/.

63.   "Homeland Security and the Trucking Industry," 1, 3. "The Wal-Mart Nobody Knows," Wal-Mart 1998 Annual Shareholder Report, www.walmartstores.com/. "Fleet Owner 500: America's Top Private Fleets," *Fleet Owner*, March 8, 2004. Anthony Schoettle, "Fedex Ready to Test Hybrid Delivery Vehicles," *Farm to Table*, July 14, 2003.

64.   "Court Rejects Attempt to Delay Alt-Fuel Vehicles Purchase Plan for Federal and Private Fleets," *Government Fleet*, April 4, 2006. See directory, Federal Fleet Policy Council (FED-FLEET), circa 2004.

SOURCES

Archives

Original papers and documents were accessed at several dozen archival repositories, record collections, and unprocessed files in the United States. Most of the
repositories utilized are listed below, but space precludes a complete roster.

United States

Automobile Club of Southern California Archives   Los Angeles, CA

Benson Ford Research Center, The Henry Ford   Dearborn, MI
     E. G. Liebold Reminiscences (Accession #65)
     Eugene J. Farkas Reminiscences (Accession #65)
     Henry Ford Office Papers (Accession #62)
     Selden, Ford Legal Records (Accession #295)
     Selden Patent Suit Papers (Accession #1704)
     Thomas Edison Papers (Accession #1630)

DeGolyer Library, Southern Methodist University   Dallas, TX
     Chicago, Milwaukee, St. Paul & Pacific Railroad Papers
     Denver and Interurban Electric Folders
     Everett Lee DeGolyer Collection
     Great Northern Railway (Great Britain) Documents
     Illinois Power Company Documents
     Joliet and Southern Traction Company Collection
     Mexican Railway Company, Ltd. Reports
     Ministerio da Viacoa e Obras Públicas Portfolios
     Oklahoma Short Line Electric Letters
     Pacific Electric Papers

Railroad Modeling Newsletters
Sprague Electric Railway and Motor Company Letters

Detroit Public Library   Detroit, MI
    Burton Historical Collection
      Rapid Transit Commission Papers
    Municipal Reference Library
    National Automotive History Collection
      Henry Cave Collection

Edison National Historic Site   West Orange, NJ
    Edison General File (EGF)
    Edison Storage Battery Company (ESB)

Huntington Library and Archives   Pasadena, CA
    Fletcher Bowron Collection
    John Anson Ford Collection
    Kenneth Hahn Collection
    Los Angeles Railway Corporation Collection
    Pacific Electric Railway Minute Books

Kettering University   Flint, MI
    Richard P. Scharchburg Archives
      Charles Kettering Collection

Milwaukee Public Library   Milwaukee, WI
    Milwaukee Road Archives

Minnesota Historical Society   St. Paul, MN
    Minnesota State Archives Library
      Twin City Rapid Transit Company Documents

New Jersey Historical Society   Newark, NJ
    William F. D. Crane Collection

Philadelphia City Archives   Philadelphia, PA
    Philadelphia Gas Works

U.S. Department of Justice   Washington, DC
    Federal Bureau of Investigation

U.S. National Archives and Records Administration   College Park, MD

United Kingdom

British Library (BL), Oriental and India Office Collections   London
    Military (L/MIL)
    Political and Secret (L/PS)

British Motor Industry Heritage Trust   Coventry

BP Archives   Coventry
    Anglo-Iranian Oil Company (AIOC) Files
    Anglo-Persian Oil Company (APOC) Files
    British Petroleum Company (BP) Files
    Iraq Petroleum Company (IPC) Files
    Turkish Petroleum Company (TPC) Files

Modern Records Centre, Warwick University   Coventry

Public Record Office (PRO)   London
    Admiralty (ADM)
    Air Ministry (AIR)
    Board of Trade (BT)
    Cabinet Office (CAB)
    Colonial Office (CO)
    Foreign Office (FO)
    GCHQ (HW)
    German Foreign Ministry (GFM)
    Ministry of Fuel and Power (POWE)
    Prime Minister's Office (PREM)
    Treasury (T)
    War Office (WO)

Libraries

Libraries are crucial to research because many possess unique collections of small-circulation books and pamphlets. In addition, many libraries maintain manuscript collections of original papers or organizational files. Most of the libraries we accessed are listed below, but space precludes a complete roster.

United States

Alvin Sherman Library, Nova Southeastern University   Fort Lauderdale, FL
Burndy Library, Massachusetts Institute of Technology   Cambridge, MA
Central Library, University of Texas   Arlington, TX
Columbia University Library, Columbia University   New York, NY

Columbus Metropolitan Library	Columbus, OH
DeGolyer Library, Southern Methodist University	Dallas, TX
Detroit Public Library	Detroit, MI
Emerson Library, Webster University	St. Louis, MO
Fenwick Library, George Mason University	Fairfax, VA
Fondren Science Library, Southern Methodist University	Dallas, TX
Gelman Library, George Washington University	Washington, DC
Goleman Library, San Joaquin Delta College	Stockton, CA
Harold B. Lee Library, Brigham Young University	Provo, UT
Harold Washington Library Center, Chicago Public Library	Chicago, IL
Helen A. Ganser Library, Millersville University	Millersville, PA
Hoover Institution on War, Revolution and Peace	Stanford, CA
Huntington Library and Archives	Pasadena, CA
John W. Barriger III National Railroad Library, University of Missouri	St. Louis, MO
Johnson Center Library, George Mason University	Fairfax, VA
Klau Library, Hebrew Union College	Cincinnati, OH
Lamont (Microform Library), Harvard University	Cambridge, MA
Lauinger Memorial Library, Georgetown University	Washington, DC
Libraries of the University of Wisconsin–Madison	Madison, WI
Library of Congress	Washington, DC
Library, Fontbonne University	St. Louis, MO
Library, Gallaudet University	Washington, DC
Library, Tarrant County Community College, Northeast	Hurst, TX
Library, University of California–Santa Cruz	Santa Cruz, CA
Mary Couts Burnett Library, Texas Christian University	Fort Worth, TX
Merrill Learning Center, Gallaudet University	Washington, DC
Milwaukee Public Library	Milwaukee, WI
Monterey County Public Library	Monterey, CA
Monterey Institute of International Studies Library	Monterey, CA
Montgomery County Public Libraries	Rockville, MD
Mullen Library, Catholic University of America	Washington, DC
National Museum of American History Library	Washington, DC
New York Public Library, Main Branch	New York, NY
New York Public Library, Science, Industry and Business	New York, NY
Olin Library, Washington University of St. Louis	St. Louis, MO
Perkins Library, Duke University	Durham, NC
Pius XII Memorial Library	St. Louis, MO
Research Park Library, University of North Texas	Denton, TX

Reuther Library, Wayne State University	Detroit, MI
St. Louis City Library	St. Louis, MO
St. Louis County Library	St. Louis, MO
Washington Research Library Consortium	Upper Marlboro, MD
Willis Library, University of North Texas	Denton, TX

United Kingdom

British Library	London
Camden Library, Holborn Branch	London
Camden Library, Swiss Cottage Branch	London
Charing Cross Library, Westminster	London
Library of Motoring	Beaulieu
University of Warwick Library	Coventry
Wiener Library	London

France

Bibliothèque Municipale Paul Eluard	Achères

Selective Secondary Sources

Literally hundreds of books and journal articles were consulted, from personal memoirs to scholarly works, on a range of topics. It would be impossible to list them all. However, a few hundred of the salient volumes are itemized below in this selective list.

Unpublished Manuscripts — Selective List

Cuntz, Herman G. "Pope Mfg Co. — Columbia Automobile Co. and The Electric Vehicle Company." June 1947. Detroit Public Library NAHC, Cave box 8, folder 8.

Greenleaf, William. "The Selden Patent Suit." Ph.D. diss., Columbia University, 1955.

Irvine, Andrew C. "The Promotion and First 22 Years History of a Corporation in Electrical Manufacturing." Master's thesis, Temple University, 1954.

Lipson, David. "GM, NCL, and the Motor Bus: The Motor Bus' Role in the Decline of Mass Transit in the U.S." Honors diss., Harvard University, 1987.

Mason, Philip P. "The League of American Wheelmen and the Good-Roads Movement, 1880–1905," Ph.D.diss., University of Michigan, 1957.

Taylor, Brian Deane. "When Finance Leads Planning: The Influence of Public Finance on Transportation Planning and Policy in California." Ph.D. diss., University of California–Los Angeles, 1992.

Northwest Rail Improvement Committee. "The Abandonment of Electric Operation by the Chicago, Milwaukee, St. Paul and Pacific Railroad Company." (Report by the Northwest Rail Improvement Committee, 1975.)

Books—Selective List

Ágoston, Gábor, *Guns for the Sultan: Technology, Industry, and Military Power in the Ottoman Empire*. New York: Cambridge University Press, 2004.

Anderson, Curtis D., and Judy Anderson. *Electric and Hybrid Cars: A History*. Jefferson, NC: McFarland, 2005.

Antonius, George. *The Arab Awakening: The Story of the Arab National Movement*. New York: Putnam, 1946; Reprint, New York: Capricorn Books, 1965.

Ashworth, William. *The History of the British Coal Industry*. Vol. 5, *The Nationalized Industry*. New York: Oxford University Press, 1986.

Automobile Quarterly Magazine. *General Motors: The First 75 Years of Transportation Products*. Princeton, NJ: Automobile Quarterly, 1983.

Baldwin, Neil. *Edison: Inventing the Century*. Chicago: University of Chicago Press, 2001.

———. *Henry Ford and the Jews: The Mass Production of Hate*. New York: Public Affairs, 2001.

Barnard, Harry. *Independent Man: The Life of Senator James Couzens*. New York: Scribner, 1958.

Benson, John, Robert G. Neville, Charles H. Thompson, and Great Britain National Coal Board. *Bibliography of the British Coal Industry: Secondary Literature, Parliamentary and Departmental Papers, Mineral Maps and Plans, and a Guide to Source*. New York: Oxford University Press, 1982.

Berger, Michael L. *The Automobile in American History and Culture: A Reference Guide*. Westport, CT: Greenwood, 2001.

Black, Edwin. *Banking on Baghdad: Inside Iraq's 7,000-Year History of War, Profit, and Conflict*. Hoboken, NJ: Wiley, 2004.

———. *IBM and the Holocaust: The Strategic Alliance Between Nazi Germany and America's Most Powerful Corporation.* New York: Crown, 2001.

———. *The Transfer Agreement: The Dramatic Story of the Pact Between the Third Reich and Jewish Palestine.* Washington, DC: Dialog Press, 1999. Reprint, New York: Carroll & Graf, 2001.

———. *War Against the Weak: Eugenics and America's Campaign to Create a Master Race.* New York: Four Walls Eight Windows, 2003.

Bonsall, Thomas E. *Disaster in Dearborn: The Story of the Edsel.* Stanford, CA: Stanford General Books, 2002.

Bottles, Scott L. *Los Angeles and the Automobile.* Berkeley and Los Angeles, CA: University of California Press, 1987.

Boyd, T. A. *Professional Amateur: The Biography of Charles Franklin Kettering.* New York: Dutton, 1957.

Bradley, Glenn D. *The Story of the Santa Fe.* Boston: Gorham Press, 1920.

Brain, Insley J., Jr. *The Milwaukee Road Electrification.* San Mateo, CA: Bay Area Electric Railroad Association and the Western Railroader, 1961.

Bryan, Ford R. *Friends, Families & Forays: Scenes from the Life and Times of Henry Ford.* Dearborn, MI: Ford Books, 2002.

Bryan, George S. *Edison: The Man and His Works.* New York: Knopf, 1926.

Church, Roy. *The History of the British Coal Industry.* Vol. 3, *Victorian Pre-eminence.* New York: Oxford University Press, 1986.

Clark, Ronald. *Edison: The Man Who Made the Future.* New York: Putnam, 1977.

Collins, Teresa, and Lisa Gitelman. *Thomas Edison and Modern America.* New York: Bedford/St. Martin's, 2002.

Cray, Ed. *Chrome Colossus: General Motors and Its Times.* New York: McGraw-Hill, 1980.

Darley, Julian. *High Noon for Natural Gas: The New Energy Crisis.* White River Junction, VT: Chelsea Green, 2004.

Darrah, William Culp. *Pithole: The Vanished City.* Gettysburg, PA: William C. Darrah, 1972.

Davis, J. Allen. *The Friend to All Motorists: The Story of the Automobile Club of Southern California through 65 Years, 1900–1965*. Los Angeles: Anderson, Ritchie & Simon, 1967.

Dendy, F. W., ed. *Extracts from the Records of the Company of Hostmen of Newcastle-upon-Tyne*. Durham, UK: Andrews & Co., 1901.

Derleth, August. *The Milwaukee Road: Its First Hundred Years*. Iowa City: University of Iowa Press, 2002.

Dintenfass, Michael. *Managing Industrial Decline: The British Coal Industry Between the Wars*. Historical Perspectives on Business Enterprise Series. Columbus: Ohio State University Press, 1992.

Douglass, Paul F. *Six Upon the World: Towards an American Culture for an Industrial Age*. Boston: Little, Brown, 1954.

Duany, Andres, Elizabeth Plater-Zyberk, and Jeff Speck. *Suburban Nation: The Rise of Sprawl*. New York: North Point Press, 2000.

Duffy, Michael C. *Electric Railways 1880–1990*. Bodmin, Cornwall, UK: MPG Books, 2003.

Dyer, Frank L., and Thomas C. Martin. *Edison: His Life and Inventions*. New York: Harper, 1929.

Edinger, Raphael, and Sanjay Kaul. *Sustainable Mobility: Renewable Energies for Powering Fuel Cell Vehicles*. Westport, CT: Praeger, 2003.

Edison, Thomas A. *Address Delivered at the Presentation of Achievement Medal Bestowed by the Congress of the United States*. New York: Columbia University Archives, 1928.

———. *America Marches Forward with Edison*. West Orange, NJ: Thomas Alva Edison Foundation, 1936.

———. *The Papers of Thomas A. Edison*. Edited by R. Jenkins. Baltimore: Johns Hopkins University Press, 1989.

———. *Storage Battery Transportation*. West Orange, NJ: Edison Storage Battery Company, 1931.

Ehsani, Mehrdad, Yimin Gao, Sebastien E. Gay, and Ali Emadi, eds. *Modern Electric, Hybrid Electric, and Fuel Cell Vehicles: Fundamentals, Theory, and Design*. Boca Raton, FL: CRC Press, 2005.

Farber, David. *Sloan Rules*. Chicago: University of Chicago Press, 2002.

Fayola, Toyin, and Ann Genova. *The Politics of the Global Oil Industry: An Introduction*. Westport, CT: Praeger, 2005.

Fine, Sidney. *Sit-Down: The General Motors Strike of 1936–1937*. Ann Arbor: University of Michigan Press, 1969.

fitz Nigel, Richard. *Dialogus de Scaccario* (Dialogue of the Exchequer). Edited and translated by Charles Johnson. New York: Oxford University Press, 1983.

Flink, James J. *America Adopts the Automobile, 1895–1910*. Cambridge, MA: MIT Press, 1970.

— — —. *The Automobile Age*. Cambridge, MA: MIT Press, 1998.

Flinn, Michael W. *The History of the British Coal Industry*. Vol. 2, *The Industrial Revolution*. New York: Oxford University Press, 1984.

Ford, Henry. *Edison As I Know Him*. New York: Cosmopolitan, 1930.

Ford, Henry in collaboration with Samuel Crowther. *My Life and Work*. Garden City, New York: Garden City Publishing Co., 1922.

Freeland, Robert F. *The Struggle for Control of the Modern Corporation: Organizational Change at General Motors, 1924–1970*. New York: Cambridge University Press, 2001.

Galvani, Luigi. *Commentary on the Effects of Electricity on Muscular Motion*. Translated by Margaret Glover Foley. Norwood, CT: Burndy Library, 1953.

General Accounting Office. *Electric Vehicles: Likely Consequences of U.S. and Other Nations' Programs and Policies: Report to The Chairman, Committee on Science, Space, and Technology, House of Representatives*. Washington, DC: General Accounting Office, 1994.

Giddens, Paul H. *The Birth of the Oil Industry*. New York: Macmillan, 1938.

Goddard, Stephen B. *Colonel Albert Pope and His American Dream Machines: The Life and Times of a Bicycle Tycoon Turned Automotive Pioneer*. Jefferson, NC: McFarland, 2000.

Goodstein, David L. *Out of Gas: The End of the Age of Oil*. New York: Norton, 2005.

Greenleaf, William. *Monopoly on Wheels: Henry Ford and the Selden Automobile Patent*. Detroit: Wayne State University Press, 1961.

Gunnell, John. *GMAC: The First Hundred Years*. Iola, WI: Krause Publications, 2002.

Gutfreund, Owen. *20th Century Sprawl: Highways and the Reshaping of the American Landscape*. New York: Oxford University Press, 2004.

Hall, H. R. *Ancient History of the Near East*. London: Methuen, 1963.

Hatcher, John. *The History of the British Coal Industry*. Vol. 1, *Before 1700: Towards the Age of Coal*. New York: Oxford University Press, 1993.

Heinberg, Richard. *The Party's Over: Oil, War and the Fate of Industrial Societies*. Gabriola, BC: New Society Publishers, 2003.

——. *Powerdown: Options and Actions for a Post-carbon World*. Gabriola, BC: New Society Publishers, 2004.

Hirsch, Mark D. *William C. Whitney: Modern Warwick*. New York: Dodd, Mead, 1948.

Holley, Noel T. *The Milwaukee Electrics*. Hicksville, NY: NJ International, 1987.

Husain, Iqbal. *Electric and Hybrid Vehicles: Design Fundamentals*. Boca Raton, FL: CRC Press, 2003.

Israel, Paul. *Edison: A Life of Invention*. New York: Wiley, 2000.

Jacobs, Jane. *The Death and Life of Great American Cities*. New York: Vintage Books, 1963.

——. *The Economy of Cities*. New York: Random House, 1969.

Jakle, John A., and Keith A. Sculle. *The Gas Station in America*. Baltimore: Johns Hopkins University Press, 1994.

Jones, David W. *Urban Transit Policy: An Economic and Political History*. Englewood Cliffs, NJ: Prentice-Hall, 1985.

Jones, Francis. *The Life Story of Thomas Alva Edison*. New York: Grosset & Dunlap, 1931.

——. *Thomas Alva Edison: Sixty Years of an Inventor's Life*. New York: T. Y. Crowell, 1908.

Jonnes, Jill. *Empires of Light: Tesla, Westinghouse and the Race to Electrify the World*. New York: Random House, 2003.

Josephson, Matthew H. *Edison: A Biography*. New York: McGraw-Hill, 1959.

Kashin, Seymour, and Harre Demoro. *An American Original: The PCC Car.* Glendale, CA: Interurban Press, 1986.

Kennelley, Arthur. *Biographical Memoir of Thomas Alva Edison.* Washington, DC: National Academy of Sciences, 1933.

Kieffer, Stephen A. *Transit and the Twins.* Minneapolis: Twin City Rapid Transit Co., 1958.

Kirsch, David A. *The Electric Vehicle and the Burden of History.* New Brunswick, NJ: Rutgers University Press, 2000.

Klare, Michael T. *Blood and Oil: The Dangers and Consequences of America's Growing Petroleum Dependency.* New York: Metropolitan Books/Holt, 2004.

Kolbert, Elizabeth. *Field Notes from a Catastrophe.* New York: Bloomsbury, 2006.

Krieger, Joel. *Undermining Capitalism: State Ownership and the Dialectic of Control in the British Coal Industry.* Princeton, NJ: Princeton University Press, 1984.

Larminie, James, and John Lowry. *Electric Vehicle Technology Explained.* Hoboken, NJ: Wiley, 2003.

Lee, Albert. *Henry Ford and the Jews.* New York: Stein and Day, 1980.

Lewis, David. *The Public Image of Henry Ford.* Detroit: Wayne State University Press, 1976.

Leyendecker, Liston E., Christine A. Bradley, and Duane A. Smith. *The Rise of the Silver Queen: Georgetown, Colorado, 1859–1896.* Boulder: University of Colorado Press, 2005.

Lowenthal, Max. *The Investor Pays.* New York: Knopf, 1933.

Luecke, John C. *Dreams, Disaster, and Demise: The Milwaukee Road in Minnesota.* Eagan, MN: Grenadier Publications, 1988.

Lynch, Brendan. *Triumph of the Red Devil: The Irish Gordon Bennett Cup Race, 1903.* Dublin: Portobello Publications, 2002.

MacKenzie, James J. *The Keys to the Car: Electric and Hydrogen Vehicles for the 21st Century.* Baltimore: World Resources Institute, 1994.

Madsen, Axel. *The Deal Maker.* New York: Wiley, 1999.

Maxim, Hiram P. *Horseless Carriage Days.* New York: Harper, 1937.

May, George S., ed. *Encyclopedia of American Business, History, and Biography.* Vol. 1, *Automobile Industry, 1896–1920.* New York: Facts on File, 1990.

Maynard, Micheline. *The End of Detroit*. New York: Random House, 2003.

McCarty, John. *Highway Financing by the Toll System*. Berkeley: University of California, 1951.

McKelvey, Blake. *Rochester, The Flower City, 1855–1890*. Cambridge, MA: Harvard University Press, 1949.

McKillop, Andrew, and Sheila Newman, eds. *The Final Energy Crisis*. Ann Arbor, MI: Pluto, 2005.

Meadowcroft, William. *Edison and His Storage Battery*. West Orange, NJ: Thomas A. Edison, Inc., 1935.

Melosi, Martin. *Thomas A. Edison and the Modernization of America*. Edited by O. Handlin. Glenview, IL: Little Brown Higher Education, 1990.

Millard, A. J. *Edison and the Business of Innovation*. Baltimore: Johns Hopkins University Press, 1990.

Mohl, Raymond A., ed. *The Making of Urban America*. Wilmington, DE: Scholarly Resources, 1997.

Mom, Gijs. *The Electric Vehicle: Technology and Expectations in the Automobile Age*. Baltimore: Johns Hopkins University Press, 2004.

Montgomery, Robert. *The 1903 Irish Gordon Bennett: The Race That Saved Motor Sport*. London: Bookmarque Publishing, 1999.

National Academy of Engineering, Board on Energy and Environmental Systems. *The Hydrogen Economy: Opportunities, Costs, Barriers, and R&D Needs*. Washington, DC: National Academies Press, 2004.

National Council on Public Works Improvement. *Fragile Foundations: A Report on America's Public Works*. Washington, DC: Government Printing Office, 1988.

National Research Council, Standing Committee to Review the Research Program of the Partnership for a New Generation of Vehicles; Board on Energy and Environmental Systems, Division on Engineering and Physical Sciences, Transportation Research Board. *Review of the Research Program of the Partnership for a New Generation of Vehicles: Seventh Report*. Washington, DC: National Academies Press, 2001.

National Transportation Committee. *The American Transportation Problem*. Washington, DC: Brookings Institution, 1933.

Nef, John U. *The Rise of the British Coal Industry*. London: Cass, 1966.

Nerney, Mary Childs. *Thomas A. Edison: A Modern Olympian*. New York: Smith and Haas, 1934.

Neuman, Andrzej Marcin. *Economic Organization of the British Coal Industry*. London: Routledge, 1934.

Nevins, Allan. *Ford: The Times, the Man, the Company*. New York: Scribner, 1954.

New International Version Exhaustive Concordance. Grand Rapids, MI: Zondervan, 1990.

New International Version Study Bible. Grand Rapids, MI: Zondervan, 1995.

Office of Technology Assessment. *Increased Automobile Fuel Efficiency and Synthetic Fuels: Alternatives for Reducing Oil Imports*. Washington, DC: Office of Technology Assessment, 1982.

Ploss, Thomas H. *The Nation Pays Again: The Demise of the Milwaukee Road, 1928–1986*. Chicago: privately printed, 1991.

——. *Supplemental Memoirs to "The Nation Pays Again."* Antioch, IL: Our Publishing Co., 1998.

Poremba, David Lee. *Detroit 1860–1899*. Charleston, SC: Arcadia Publishing, 1998.

Pursell, Carroll, ed. *Technology in America: A History of Individuals and Ideas*. Cambridge, MA: MIT Press, 1981.

Roberts, Paul. *The End of Oil: On the Edge of a Perilous New World*. Boston: Houghton Mifflin, 2004.

Rolph, Samuel Wyman. *"Exide," the Development of an Engineering Idea; A Brief History of the Electric Storage Battery Company*. New York: Newcomen Society in North America, 1951.

Rosenstock, Morton. *Louis Marshall, Defender of Jewish Rights*. Detroit: Wayne State University Press, 1965.

Rutledge, Ian. *Addicted to Oil: America's Relentless Drive for Energy Security*. London: I. B. Tauris, 2005.

Sarnoff, David. *The Indispensable Man*. Edited by G. Probst. New York: Shorewood, 1962.

Saunders, Richard, Jr. *Main Lines: Rebirth of the North American Railroads, 1970–2002.* DeKalb: Northern Illinois University Press, 2003.

———. *Merging Lines: American Railroads 1900–1970.* DeKalb: Northern Illinois University Press, 2001.

Schallenberg, Richard. *Bottled Energy: Electrical Engineering and the Evolution of Chemical Energy Storage.* Philadelphia: American Philosophical Society, 1981.

Schiffer, Michael B., Tamara C. Butts, and Kimberly K. Grimm. *Taking Charge: The Electric Automobile in America.* Washington, DC: Smithsonian Institution Press, 1994.

Schubert, H. R. *History of the British Iron and Steel Industry from c. 450 B.C. to A.D. 1775.* London: Routledge & Kegan Paul, 1957.

Schwantes, Carlos A. *Going Places: Transportation Redefines the Twentieth-Century West.* Bloomington: Indiana University Press, 2003.

Shnayerson, Michael. *The Car That Could: The Inside Story of GM's Revolutionary Electric Vehicle.* New York: Random House, 1996.

Sieferle, Rolf Peter. *The Subterranean Forest: Energy Systems and the Industrial Revolution.* Cambridge, UK: White Horse Press, 2001.

Simmons, I. G. *An Environmental History of Britain: From 10,000 Years Ago to the Present.* Edinburgh: Edinburgh University Press, 2001.

Simmons, Matthew R. *Twilight in the Desert: The Coming Saudi Oil Shock and the World Economy.* Hoboken, NJ: Wiley, 2005.

Simonds, William A. *Henry Ford, His Life—His Work—His Genius.* Los Angeles, California: Floyd Clymer, 1943.

Sloan, Alfred P., Jr. *My Years with General Motors.* Edited by John Mcdonald with Catherine Stevens. Garden City, NY: Doubleday, 1964.

Smil, Vaclav. *Energy in World History.* Boulder, CO: Westview Press, 1994.

Snell, Bradford. *American Ground Transport: A Proposal for Restructuring the Automobile, Truck, Bus, and Rail Industries.* Washington, DC: U.S. Government Printing Office, 1974.

Solomon, Brian. *GE Locomotives: 110 Years of General Electric Motive Power.* St. Paul, MN: MBI, 2003.

Sprague, Harriet. *Frank J. Sprague and the Edison Myth.* New York: William Frederick Press, 1947.

Standiford, Les. *Meet You in Hell: Andrew Carnegie, Henry Clay Frick, and the Bitter Partnership That Transformed America.* New York: Crown, 2005.

St. Clair, David J. *The Motorization of American Cities.* New York: Praeger, 1986.

Steinheimer, Richard. *The Electric Way Across the Mountains: Stories of the Milwaukee Road Electrification.* Tiburon, CA: Carbarn Press, 1980.

Supple, Barry. *The History of the British Coal Industry.* Vol. 4, *The Political Economy of Decline.* New York: Oxford University Press, 1987.

Sward, Keith. *The Legend of Henry Ford.* Toronto: Rinehart & Co., 1948.

Sweezy, Paul Marlor. *Monopoly and Competition in the English Coal Trade: 1550–1850.* Westport, CT: Greenwood Press, 1972.

Tarbell, Ida M. *The History of the Standard Oil Company.* Vol. 1. Gloucester, MA: Peter Smith, 1963.

Tate, Alfred. *Edison's Open Door: The Life Story of Thomas A. Edison, a Great Individualist.* New York: Dutton, 1938.

Thomas, G. Scott. *United States of Suburbia.* Amherst, NY: Prometheus Books, 1998.

Turner, Henry A. *General Motors and the Nazis.* New Haven, CT: Yale University Press, 2005.

Wachhorst, Wyn. *Thomas Alva Edison: An American Myth.* Cambridge, MA: MIT Press, 1981.

Wakefield, Ernest H. *History of the Electric Automobile: Battery-Only Powered Cars.* Warrendale, PA: Society of Automotive Engineers, 1994.

———. *History of the Electric Automobile: Hybrid Electric Vehicles.* Warrendale, PA: Society of Automotive Engineers, 1994.

Wallace, Max. *The American Axis: Henry Ford, Charles Lindbergh, and the Rise of the Third Reich.* New York: St. Martin's, 2003.

Wood, John C., and Michael C. Wood, eds. *Alfred P. Sloan: Critical Evaluations in Business and Management.* 2 vols. London: Routledge, 2003.

Woodbury, Marda Liggett. *Stopping the Presses: The Murder of Walter Liggett*. Minneapolis: University of Minnesota Press, 1998.

Wren, Daniel A., and Ronald G. Greenwood. *Management Innovators: The People and Ideas That Have Shaped Modern Business*. New York: Oxford University Press, 1998.

Wright, J. Patrick. *On a Clear Day You Can See General Motors: John Z. De Lorean's Look Inside the Automotive Giant*. Grosse Pointe, MI: Wright Enterprises, 1979.

Yago, Glenn. *The Decline of Transit: Urban Transportation in German and U.S. Cities, 1900–1970*. Cambridge, U.K.: Cambridge University Press, 1984.

Yates, Brock. *The Decline and Fall of the American Automobile Industry*. New York: Empire Books, 1983.

Yatman, Matthew. *Animal Electricity; or, Observations on the Origin and Identity of the Electric and Galvanic Fluids, Etc.*, 2nd ed. London, 1805.

Forthcoming Books

Epperson, Bruce. *Failed Colossus: Albert A. Pope, the Bicycle, and the Dawn of the American Auto Industry*. 2006.

Electronic Books

Bayne-Jones, Stanhope, MD. *The Evolution of Preventative Medicine in the United States Army, 1607–1939*. Washington, DC: U.S. Government Printing Office, 1968. http://history.amedd.army.mil/booksdocs/misc/evprev/default.htm.

Rosen, Marvin. *Consolidating Capitalist Rule: Parliament and Capital 1688–1722* (1999), http://www.afn.org/~afn31294/marvin/chapter10.txt.

Transcripts, Recordings, and Oral Histories

Edison, Charles (speaker). "Reminiscences of Charles Edison: Oral History, 1953." New York: Columbia University Board of Trustees, 1953, 1975.

Edison, Thomas A. (speaker). "Address Delivered at the Presentation of Achievement Medal Bestowed by the Congress of the United States." New York: Columbia University Archives.

Farkas, Eugene J. Reminiscences (Accession #65). Benson Ford Research Center, The Henry Ford, Dearborn, MI.

Liebold, E. G. Reminiscences (Accession #65). Benson Ford Research Center, The Henry Ford, Dearborn, MI.

Journals and Periodicals

American Architect and Building News
American Economic Review
American Journal of Archaeology
American Journal of Legal History
American Speech
Annals of the American Academy of Political and Social Science
Annals of the Association of American Geographers
Annual Review of Energy and the Environment
Annual Review of Environment and Resources
The Autocar
The Automobile
Automobile and Motor Review
Automobile Quarterly
Business History Review
Columbia Law Review
CQ Researcher
Economic History Review
Edison Bulletin
Electric Railway Journal
Electrical World
The Electrician
Environmental History
Geographical Review
Horseless Age
IEEE Monitor
In Transition
International Journal of Ethics
Journal of American History
Journal of Biogeography
Journal of British Studies
Journal of Design History
Journal of Economic History
Journal of Field Archaeology

Journal of the History of Ideas
Journal of the House of Lords
Journal of the Patent Office Society
Journal of Transport History
Journal of Urban History
Motor Coach Age
Natural Resources Research
Near Eastern Archaeology
New Electric Railway Journal
The New York State Mechanic
North American Review
Oxford Economic Papers
Proceedings of the American Philosophical Society
Proceedings of the American Transit Association and Its Affiliated Associations
Proceedings of the Royal Geographical Society and Monthly Record of Geography
Proceedings of the World Geothermal Congress 2000
Science
Scientific American
Scientific Monthly
Speculum
Technology & Culture
Technology Forecasting and Social Change
Transactions of the American Electrochemical Society
Transactions of the American Philosophical Society
Transactions of the Royal Historical Society
Die Welt des Islams
Western Political Quarterly

Newspapers, Magazines, Wire Services, and Other Media

ABC News
Atlanta Constitution
American Heritage Magazine
Baltimore Sun
Boston Globe
British Broadcasting Corporation (BBC)
Cable News Network (CNN)
CBS News
Chicago Independent
Chicago Tribune

Christian Science Monitor
Collier's
Ethanol Today
General Motors World
Government Fleet
The Guardian
Irish Times
Los Angeles Herald and Express
Los Angeles Times (LAT)
Milwaukee Railway System Employees' Magazine
Milwaukee Road Magazine
Minneapolis Star Tribune
The Nation
National City Liner
National Geographic News
National Public Radio (NPR)
New York Times (NYT)
New York Tribune
Philadelphia Inquirer
Public Broadcasting System (PBS)
Saturday Evening Post
Tampa Daily Times
Time
Times (London)
Trains
Wall Street Journal (WSJ)
Washington Post (WP)
Washington Times

Court Records
Columbia Motor Car Company and George B. Seldon v. C.A. Duerr & Company and Ford Motor Company et al., 184 F. 893 (2d Cir. 1911).

United States v. National City Lines, et al. 186 F.2d 562 (7th Cir. January 3, 1951).

Electronic Sources
Electronic and digital sources were extensively used. Modern research cannot be efficiently undertaken without the use of Internet search engines as well as institutional databases. However, while Internet research is essential to historical

investigation, the caveat remains that the Web is proudly unreliable, including some Web sites operated by respected academic entities. At the same time, I found certain official organizational and governmental sites important, as were a limited number of private research sites. Hence, while I consulted and searched through hundreds, perhaps thousands of Web sites, only a precious few of the most reliable are listed below. On the other hand, the digital databases of documents and publications that I used were pivotal to my work.

Digital Archives
Atlanta Constitution Historical Digital Archive
Boston Globe Historical Digital Archive
British History Online
Chicago Tribune Historical Digital Archive
Christian Science Monitor Historical Digital Archive
Foreign Relations of the United States, Electronic Facsimile
Los Angeles Times Historical Digital Archive
New York Times Historical Digital Archive
Times (London) Digital Archive
Wall Street Journal Historical Digital Archive
Washington Post Historical Digital Archive

Digital Databases
JSTOR, The Scholarly Journal Archive
Lexis-Nexis
ProQuest
Questia
WorldCat

Web Sites
Avalon Law Project, Yale University Law School, www.yale.edu/lawweb/avalon
Electric Railway Historical Association of Southern California, www.erha.org/
Energy Independence Now, www.energyindependencenow.org/
National Museum of American History Library, www.sil.si.edu/libraries/nmah

INDEX